THE
JEWS OF
BOHEMIA
AND
MORAVIA

THE JEWS OF BOHEMIA AND MORAVIA

FACING THE HOLOCAUST

LIVIA ROTHKIRCHEN

Published by the

UNIVERSITY OF NEBRASKA PRESS, *Lincoln,*

and YAD VASHEM, *Jerusalem*

Library of Congress
Cataloging-in-Publication Data
Rothkirchen, Livia.
The Jews of Bohemia and Moravia : facing the
Holocaust / Livia Rothkirchen.
p. cm. — (The comprehensive history of the
Holocaust)
Includes bibliographical references and index.
ISBN-13: 978-0-8032-3952-4 (cloth : alk. paper)
ISBN-10: 0-8032-3952-1 (cloth : alk. paper)
1. Jews—Czechoslovakia—History—20th
century. 2. Jews—Czech Republic—Bohemia—
History—20th century. 3. Jews—Czech
Republic—Moravia—History—20th century.
4. Holocaust, Jewish (1939–1945)—
Czechoslovakia. 5. Holocaust, Jewish (1939–
1945)—Czech republic—Bohemia. 6.
Holocaust, Jewish (1939–1945)—Czech
republic—Moravia. 7. Czechoslovakia—Ethnic
relations. 8. Bohemia (Czech republic)—Ethnic
relations. 9. Moravia (Czech Republic)—Ethnic
relations. 10. Czechoslovakia—History—1938–
1945. I. Title. II. Series.
DS135.C95.R68 2005
940.53′18′09437—dc22   2005009414

The publication of this series was

made possible by the generous gift of the

Ike and Roz Friedman Family Foundation,

in loving memory of

Ike Friedman and Janis Friedman Yale

and all those who perished in the Holocaust.

All of the Hardships that Befell Us

The order of the world fell apart . . .
the bloody corpses of babies, men young and old,
boys and virgins, were wildly hipped together . . .
Now . . . Father of us all, it is time to proclaim
that killings must come to an end! Say it now
that not a single one will be added
to the terrible number of victims any more!
Long enough were they killed and choked to death
to the world's derision, long enough!

From the Elegy of the renowned Prague rabbi and poet
Avigdor Isaac ben Kara on the victims of the 1389 Easter Massacre

Contents

Preface *xi*

Acknowledgments *xv*

Prologue: Prague and Jerusalem: Spiritual Ties between
Czechs and Jews *1*

1 The Historical Setting *8*

2 Years of Challenge and Growth: The Jewish Minority in Czechoslovakia
(1918–38) *26*

3 The Aftermath of Munich: The Crisis of the Intellectuals *63*

4 Under German Occupation (1939–45) *98*

5 The Protectorate Governments and the "Final Solution" *138*

6 The Czechoslovak Government-in-Exile in London: Attitudes and
Reactions to the Jewish Plight *160*

7 Jews in the Czech Home Resistance *187*

8 The "Righteous" and the Brave: Compassion and Solidarity with the
Persecuted *216*

9 Gateway to Death: The Unique Character of Ghetto Terezín
(Theresienstadt) *233*

10 The Spiritual Legacy of the Terezín Inmates *265*

Epilogue: Between 1945 and the Velvet Revolution of 1989 *284*

Conclusions *297*

Abbreviations *309*

Notes *311*

Bibliography *391*

Index *421*

Preface

For several decades now I have been pursuing extensive research on Nazi policy in East-Central Europe, perusing the mammoth accumulation of records, documentation, and literature: the degradation of humanity and the machinery of genocide. I came to realize that Germany's system of ruling in conquered Europe varied from country to country, as did the persecution of Jews. This meant ultimately that the toll of Jewish lives was by and large determined by the nature and extent of German control, by the Führer's postwar global aims, and in a certain measure by the attitude of the local population.

I sensed a definite need to approach this subject with a panoramic view and in a broader context, delving into earlier history such as the Czech-German conflict.

Two issues that seem diametrically opposed are examined in detail: the traditional sources of empathy and solidarity of the host nation with the Jewish community, and Czech anti-Semitism in the recent past. Ivan Klíma, the noted Czech-Jewish writer, has commented on the latter issue: "If we speak of the magnificent surge of Jewish culture that Prague witnessed more than anywhere else, we must recognize also that there has never been a long period here without some sort of anti-Semitism." I presumed that this two-pronged enquiry might serve my exploration, broadening intellectual horizons and providing new insights for the scope of this study.

One of the cardinal questions requiring elucidation is why even in this enclave, known as the most democratic country "east of the Rhine" and perceived as markedly philo-Semitic, the losses suffered by the Jewish population were numerically so high. Josef Korbel in his standard *Twentieth-Century Czechoslovakia* made this significant point concerning the victims of the "Final Solution" in the so-called Protectorate of Bohemia and Moravia: "The grim reality remains that in the Czech lands, in the former Republic of T. G. Masaryk who had fought anti-Semitism throughout his long life, the results were the same as all over Hitler's Europe."

Korbel's statement encapsulates several interconnected questions historians have thus far avoided formulating. I shall venture to ask the following: Was the interwar republic's approach toward the Jewish entity outright positive? To what degree did Nazi ideology influence Czechs? Did the long tradition of Jewish presence in this enclave and the Jews' unique role in economy and culture affect Czech society's attitudes during the Nazi occupation? Did the notions of hatred toward the common enemy and of parallel destinies link Czechs and Jews? I presume that despite all the methodological problems involved and the lack of standardized contemporary surveys or polls, certain conclusions may still be drawn.

During the four decades of the Communist regime's isolationism and provincialism, Czech historiography of the twentieth century in general and the sphere of Jewish studies in particular suffered a long hiatus. Summarizing matters in "Czech Historiography at a Turning Point" in 1992, Jan Křen pointed out: "A typical example of "this nationalism of ignorance' was the history of the Jews, without whom many periods in the history of the Czech lands can hardly be imagined. In historiography too . . . virtually nothing was done in this sphere of historical studies over the past two decades."

One of the problems I encountered was the choice of material and references in light of the enormous amount of documentation made accessible in Czechoslovakia after 1989, following the collapse of Communism. I would like to think that the new documentary sources and the various seminal conferences I attended in the years 1990–2001 in Prague, Ostrava, and Terezín have opened up new vistas, augmenting the scope of my research.

The study relies heavily on World War II primary documentary sources held in Czech archives, on government publications, and on holdings in German, British, American, Swiss, and Israeli archives. In addition, I have employed reminiscences and diaries, survivors' testimonies, and private correspondence smuggled out to the free world during the war.

The core of the book, namely the chapters dealing with the period of the Holocaust and its antecedents, is based largely on a variety of archival sources and memoir literature. In the prologue, the historical setting, and the epilogue I have to a greater extent had recourse to secondary literature—the findings of other historians—presenting these with my own emphases and interpretations.

The prologue presents a survey of the centuries-old spiritual ties between Czechs and Jews, the main features of which were a common bond to the Old Testament and future-oriented beliefs in the restoration of statehood. This unique affinity culminated in modern times in Masaryk's role as an "apostle of truth" during the Hilsner affair; his impact on Prague's leading Zionists; the struggle for Czechoslovakia's independence; and the recognition of the Jews as a national minority.

An overview of the history of the Jews in Bohemia and Moravia is given in chapter 1. It shows development from an autonomous, strictly isolated, and close-knit religious community into a pluralistic, liberal-minded society. The process of Jewish assimilation, both German and subsequently Czech, yielded to the transformation of Jewry at the *fin de siècle* and the rise of the Czech-Jewish movement and of Jewish nationalism (Zionism).

In chapter 2 the part played by the Jewish minority in the Parliament of the first Czechoslovak Republic (1918–38) is viewed against the background of the multinational structure of the overall population, the vital role of the Jews in the economy, and their participation in all spheres of public and cultural life. With Hitler's ascent to power in Germany in 1933 came the massive impact of Nazi propaganda upon rightist groups, the escalation of anti-Semitism, and Sudeten German irredentism and its effects.

The 1938 September crisis is the focus of chapter 3. The refugee problem and the faltering of a stratum of Czech writers, journalists, and professionals meant a dilemma for the Jewish community leadership. "Aryanization" of the Czech Writer's Club, the tragic consequences of the Munich *Diktat*, and the dismemberment of Czechoslovakia would follow.

Chapter 4 surveys the isolation of the Jewish entity in the Protectorate of Bohemia and Moravia; the "Nisko campaign"; and the actions of the Council of Jewish Religious Communities (JRC) during the so-called pacification period in 1939–41. Along with the reeducation, professional training, and emigration campaign came confiscation of Jewish property, Aryanization, forced labor, and the onerous and humiliating tasks imposed by the Nazi authorities upon the "Council of Jewish Elders" in the deportation campaign (1941–43).

The retardation policy of the Czech Protectorate government under General Alois Eliáš is described in chapter 5, as are the introduction of the Nuremberg Laws by *Reichsprotektor* Constantin von Neurath and the issue of the "privileged Jews." With the arrival of Reinhard Heydrich as the new acting Reichsprotektor (September 27, 1941) came the arrest of Premier Eliáš, the state of civil emergency, wiping out of the resistance cells, and wholesale deportation of Jews. Completing the picture are Heydrich's assassination (May 27, 1942), the Jewish culprits of the *heydrichiáda*, the servility of the second Czech collaborationist government, and the nazification and reeducation of Czech youth.

Chapter 6 views matters farther afield—the policy of the London-based Government-in-Exile; recruitment of Jewish volunteers in Palestine in the fall of 1939; and Jewish participation in the Czechoslovak units abroad. The discussion covers attitudes and responses to the plight of the Czech population in general and that of the Jews in particular as well as President Beneš's policy and his ties with the Home Resistance (1939–45).

The resistance groups engaged on the home front are profiled in chapter 7. Jewish individuals and groups participated in various acts of defiance and resistance—intelligence, sabotage, and a clandestine press. Also delineated are the strategy of the Moscow-based Czechoslovak leadership and their influence upon the Communist resistance cells and the shaping of government policy in the postwar years.

Chapter 8 deals with the reaction of the local population to the persecution of the Jews. Among the responses were Czech writers' assistance to their Jewish friends and solidarity and compassion from gentile individuals and groups reaching out to Jews by arranging their safe passage abroad or providing them with shelter or false papers. Individuals caught by the Nazis for sheltering Jews faced a cruel fate.

The dual tasks of Ghetto Terezín are unraveled in chapter 9: decimation was the crux, but it was also designed for propaganda and alibi—to camouflage the Nazi annihilation policy. Central to its effect were the stance of the Jewish "Self-Government," the wartime collaboration of the International Committee of the Red Cross with Nazi authorities, and the "inspection visits" of the ICRC delegation in Terezín in 1944–45.

The unique manifestation of defiance and courage by inmates of the ghetto of Terezín, especially the cultural elite of writers, poets, musicians, artists, and educators, are explored in chapter 10. Care was devoted to cultural activities and the education of children and youth. Artists and musicians on the threshold of death exercised their creativity in songs, music, satirical opera, and an "open university" in the struggle to boost morale and preserve the sanity and lives of the doomed population.

The epilogue surveys the postwar years. Renewal of community began for the "saved remnant" but was affected by mass emigration to Israel and the decline of communal life under the Communist regime. The manifestations of Prague Spring, the "Normalization" period, and the 1989 November Revolution and its aftermath bring the story to the present.

Acknowledgments

When I embarked on this project the Iron Curtain still hung over Eastern Europe, and contacts with colleagues and friends in Czechoslovakia were limited and strained. There was no access at all to documentation held in the state archives and other institutions.

Consequently, it was only in the eighties that I began to focus on the fate of the Jews of Bohemia and Moravia, realizing that research on Czech Jewry was lagging behind. This led to numerous visits abroad to locate archives and institutions that held documentation on prewar Europe and World War II.

I was gratified to find the documents relating to the Czechoslovak Government-in-Exile in the Public Record Office in London. Eventually, it was this topic that formed the kernel of my research in the years to come. I thus continued visiting major institutions and archives: the British Museum's British Library and the Wiener Library (London), the Institut für Ost-Europa (München), the U.S. National Archives (Washington DC), the Joint Distribution Committee Archives (New York), and the Hoover Institution for War and Peace (Stanford, California).

The year of the "Velvet Revolution," 1989, marked a turning point in my academic undertakings with free access to all the important sources held in the various archives in Prague, Terezín, and elsewhere. A period of fruitful cooperation and personal contacts with colleagues in Czechoslovakia began. Conferences, meetings, and exchange of ideas, along with access to major depositories, gave a new impulse to my research.

It gives me pleasure to express my gratitude to readers, colleagues, and all those friends who have helped me over the years. My thanks are due to Prof. Yoav Gelber, former head of the project at the Yad Vashem Research Institute, who initially guided this enterprise. I am greatly indebted to Edna Ben-Dov, my first reader and editor, for her devoted work, stimulating observations, and friendly attitude. To Jana Veselá I am grateful for help in correcting the text. Special thanks are due to Jill Berinson for her assistance and patience in helping to compile the bibliography. I also want to express my thanks to the staff of the Yad Vashem archives and library for their readiness to attend to my requirements.

To those who accepted the invitation of the publishers to act as critics of my lengthy manuscript, I owe special thanks and gratitude. I sincerely appreciate their insight on several key issues in the text and their detailed comments and useful proposals, which I gratefully accepted. I am sure they will note the improvements.

And I owe special thanks to my friend and colleague Petr Brod, BBC bureau chief in Prague, who since the inception of the project has steadily provided information on new publications relating to my field of inquiry. To him and his wife I am also indebted for their warm hospitality whenever I visit Prague.

Throughout all these years my beloved nephew Yoel Minz and nieces Rina Vizer and Tamar Barkan-Lederer and their spouses and children have provided me with spiritual help and comfort. Last but not least I would like to express my thanks to the Yad Vashem Editorial Board and especially Dr. Bella Gutterman, head of the Publication Department, for her untiring help in bringing this work to press.

I see the overall task of the volume as providing both the student and the general reader with a survey from the earliest history of the Jews of Bohemia and Moravia up to the modern era: the birth of the Czechoslovak Republic (1918–38) and the crucial post-Munich period (1938–39). The core of the work deals with the tragic situation of the Jewish entity in the Protectorate during the dark, harrowing years of the Holocaust—the mass deportations, the dumb suffering, and at the same time the heroic stance and mutual help and resistance on the threshold of death in the ghetto of Terezín.

It is my hope that the effort will broaden perception and stimulate scholarly research into the unique contribution and achievements of Czech Jewry in commerce and industry as well as in the various fields of cultural endeavor.

Prologue

Prague and Jerusalem
Spiritual Ties between Czechs and Jews

It is the ancient Jewish quarter in the heart of the city of Prague that most authentically bears witness to the checkered history of the centuries-old Czech-Jewish coexistence.[1] The echoes of bygone times still reverberate in Josefov, the former Josefstadt, known also as the first district. Countless monuments, synagogues, and the ancient Jewish cemetery with "the multitude of quaint tombs" keep firing the imagination of poetic souls.[2]

No wonder that from time immemorial Prague has inspired poets, artists, mystics, and travelers. A most imaginative saga attaches to the founding of the neo-Gothic Altneuschul, the Old-New Synagogue, the construction of which was completed in 1270.[3] Legend has it that its cornerstone was formed from the ruins of the Second Temple brought to Prague by exiles under solemn oath, as the Hebrew term *al-tnai* (on condition) implies: once the Temple of Jerusalem is restored, these stones will be returned. It was this unique message of continuity that inspired Theodor Herzl in 1899 to name his utopian novel *Altneuland* (Old new land).[4]

Two sculptures created by Czech artists and located in the heart of the Old City symbolize spiritual values and universal greatness. The statue of Moses the Lawgiver, carved by František Bílek in 1937, stands in the tiny romantic park in the vicinity of the Altneuschul.[5] Not far away, in front of the New Town Hall, one encounters Ladislav Šaloun's striking sculpture of the mysterious High Rabbi Judah ben Bezalel (Liwa) Loew—the Maharal (c. 1525–1609). The artist portrayed the venerated sage in his death, as described by the poet Jaroslav Vrchlický.[6]

There is a distinct symmetry between Czech and Jewish renascence unparalleled between other nations, augmented by the unique role played throughout history by both Prague and Jerusalem as citadels of national struggle and fulfillment.[7] The genesis of spiritual rapprochement is exemplified as early as the eleventh to thirteenth centuries in Slavic-Bohemian glosses of Talmudic scholars' manuscripts, described as "the earliest traces of written Czech."[8] Three hymns have come down from Hussite days preserved in the so-called *Jistebnický kancionál*.[9] One of these hymns—"Povstaň, povstaň" (reminiscent of the famous "Arise, arise, Jerusalem, great city!")—originated in Prague in 1420, evoking the prophet Isaiah's "Awake, awake; put on thy strength O Zion" (52:1).

One should also bear in mind that the translation of the six-part *Kralice Bible*, a labor of love accomplished in the years 1579–94 by the later followers of Hussitism, the Unity of Bohemian Brethren, was carried out in Moravia in secret because of continuing persecution. More recent studies indicate that the Maharal, while officiating in 1553–73 as chief rabbi of Moravia and head of the famous Yeshiva of Mikulov, located close to Ivančice—as of 1558 the cultural center of the Bohemian Brethren—maintained steady contact with Czech humanists and read the Calvinist writings (in Hebrew translation). The theologian J. B. Čapek refers to "traits of mutual influences" in their works.[10] It may thus be surmised that the treatises of the "Great Rabbi of Prague," especially those dealing with universal aspects—"ideas of nationhood," "the dilemma of exile"— as well as educational and pedagogical theories might have generated reciprocal influences.[11]

In the wake of the 1947 discovery of the Qumran Scrolls shedding new light on the "Dead Sea Sect," Stanislav Segert discussed the fifteenth-century *Unitas Fratrum* in a profound study.[12] He pointed to the striking analogies in the sacred songs of the Essenes and the hymns of the Bohemian Brethren: the very same passages that once inspired the Maccabees rallied the Hussite "Warriors of God" (*Boží bojovníci*).[13] It transpires that the return from the Babylonian exile inspired the Bible-loving Czechs more than any other people.

The Brethren can be credited with the publication of four renditions of Josephus's *Wars of the Jews*, in Czech, in the second half of the sixteenth century. However, while expressing deeply felt sympathy for the Jews' cause, they warned their own people to cling together, citing the internal discord leading to the disastrous fate that befell the Jews.[14] The Scriptures were eventually embraced by the spiritual leaders of the Czech reformation, whose hallmark was a new and just social order. As of the sixteenth century the Bible became a *centrum securitatis*—a source of hope and of freedom of conscience, of yearning for the rebirth of the nation and deliverance from the Habsburg yoke.

Jan Amos (Comenius) Komenský's (1592–1670) profound attachment to the Bible and his use of the Old Testament in presenting his pansophistic ideas are widely known. Of special significance is his unique "Bequest of the Dying Mother, the Unity of Brethren," conveying to future generations his belief in redemption.[15] His apt use of the metaphor "heirloom" brings to mind Heinrich Heine's famous "portable homeland."

One should also realize that the Restoration of Judah in the fifth to sixth century BCE fired the imagination of many a nation, as the American archeologist William F. Albright noted: "At no other time in world history, so far as is known, has a people been destroyed, and then come back after a lapse of time and reestablished itself."[16]

In effect, this motif gained new impetus with the efflorescence of modern Czech literature in the first half of the nineteenth century, coinciding with the national revival in Bohemia.[17] The work of Karel Hynek Mácha (1810–36), the greatest Czech romantic poet, which bears a strong resemblance to Byron's *Hebrew Melodies*, is considered to be a milestone in the development of Czech lyrical poetry. The imagery of the Bohemian forests in his love song "Máj" evokes the "Song of Songs."[18]

Antonín Dvořák, too, turned to the book of Psalms in attempting to overcome his profound sorrow—"the darkness and thunderclouds"—over the approaching death of his father. Far off in another land, and longing for his home, he sought solace in the Book of Books: no wonder his own liturgical "Biblical Songs," opus 99, are considered to be the most beautiful of his liturgical works.

In more recent Czech literature four major figures, three of whom were of partly Jewish origin, made a lasting contribution to the popularization of the Bible: Julius Zeyer (1841–1901), Jaroslav Vrchlický (pseudonym of Emil Frída, 1853–1912), and Ivan Olbracht (pseudonym of Kamil Zeman, 1882–1952).[19] Jaroslav Seifert (1901–86), the 1984 Nobel Prize laureate, related to the Bible on the basis of his personal outlook and approach to Judaism as a whole.[20] He often turned to Jewish motifs, recreating in his poems the image of Rabbi Loew and the Golem as well as the ancient Jewish cemetery. His attitude to Jewish historic relics is projected in one of his poignant essays on Prague, lamenting the disappearance of the Gothic Jewish town. In 1958 he also enriched Czech literature with *Píseň Písní*, a modern but classical translation from the original Hebrew of Song of Solomon.[21]

It appears that Czech affinities and attraction to Judaism continued unabated through the centuries. However, as is well known, influence flows both ways. Mention of the issue of reciprocity is thus unavoidable. One has to recall that although Jewish historiography had had a glorious beginning, it also suffered from a protracted hiatus. According to Bernard Lewis, despite the abundance of significant intellectual events it became stagnated and fragmentary, thin and sparse: "Virtually it came to an end some time after the return from Babylon and did not resume until comparatively modern times."[22]

It was only in the nineteenth century that the interconnection between Jewish history and what is called general history commenced anew. In the Bohemian lands the movement of national awakening, heralding the Czech renascence, acted as an incentive. The unique example of its harbingers (Jungmann, Kolár, Šafařík, and Palacký), who succeeded in reviving the native language, ancient Czech history, and literature, struck a responsive chord among the members of the Bar Kochba Association of Jewish Students in Prague. They realized that the time was ripe to revitalize the Zionist movement by launching cultural enterprises, to "breathe life" into Jewish national conscience.

The model of the Czech Reformation highlighting moral values also had a profound impact upon members of the Bar Kochba Association. As the philosopher Felix Weltsch put it: "National independence was not a goal in itself but the means to a higher end—improving the lot of mankind."[23] This trend was further enhanced by the spiritual conception of Ahad Ha'am, which left an indelible mark on a whole generation of intellectuals.[24]

Masaryk, "the apostle, who taught equality in all things," drew upon the Bible for both philosophical and religious conceptions. His public stance in defense of Leopold Hilsner in the infamous 1899–1900 "blood libel" trial, his courage and rectitude in speaking out for justice, made of him a true hero in the eyes of civilized nations and especially of Jewry throughout the world. As his contemporary Josef Penížek observed, "they constituted an army upon which Masaryk was able to rely."[25] Only twenty years later, when embarking on his campaign for the establishment of Czechoslovakia, did Masaryk become aware of his popularity abroad. The ovation accorded to him on the occasion of his visit to the United States was overwhelming. He kept referring explicitly to the aid of his countrymen, recalling especially the political support and devotion of Congressman Adolf J. Sabath and of Judge Louis D. Brandeis, both of whom originated from Bohemia.[26]

In his conversations with Czech-Jewish intellectuals Masaryk would often remark: "Without Judaism and the Old Testament you cannot understand the bases of European thought and feeling."[27] What he valued most about Jews was their creed, the way they adhered—more than any other people—to the faith of their fathers. This "ingrained perseverance and patience of the Jews," Masaryk realized, could serve as a paradigm for the Czech nation.

On the whole Masaryk perceived Zionism as the regeneration of Judaism—

"a drop of oil of the prophets." Even though he considered its political fulfill-ment as purely utopian for the time being, he set out to translate his conception into realistic terms. Ahad Ha'am's thesis led him to define the difference be-tween assimilation and dissimilation in terms of an ethical struggle distinguish-ing between right and wrong. First and foremost it brought him to condemn assimilation strongly: "That which is most holy within the nation is its moral character. The Czech [who] becomes a German [does it] only out of ulterior motives . . . he is without character . . . A person who possesses character will not be unfaithful to his nation under any circumstances."[28]

Masaryk, as is well known, disliked any manifestation of hyper-nationalism. He could not fathom those Czech Jews who, forgetful of their Jewishness, "upheld their Czechness."[29] Even though some of his close associates came from Czech-Jewish circles he never abandoned this stance and in fact often found himself in a quandary when choosing to side with Jewish national aspirations.

It was therefore symbolic that with the rebirth of the independence of Czechoslovakia in 1918, the newly elected president T. G. Masaryk, delivering his first message to the nation, cited Komenský's prophetic lines from his "Bequest," thus bridging the gap of three hundred years of political vacuum in the history of his people.[30]

For their part, the Jewish leadership learned much from Masaryk's relentless campaign abroad and his efforts for self-determination. His arduous "small work" (*drobná práce*) served as an example for the Jewish / Zionist struggle for independence. Thus, during his historic visit in Palestine in 1927 President Masaryk was greeted as a hero and a prophet by the Yishuv in general and by his countrymen, many of whom were members of kibbutzim, in particular. This admiration was briefly expressed in Vladimir Jabotinsky's tribute on the occa-sion of Masaryk's eightieth birthday: "He has proved that dreams based on right come true . . . what a lesson that man!"[31]

Czech-Jewish symbiosis reached its apex during the interwar period (1918–38): along with the president a range of Czech intellectuals related to Jewish nationalism in their writings and public activities, giving their full support to Zionist aspirations. Many of these were greatly influenced by Martin Buber's famous *Three Addresses* (1909, 1911). The most eminent prewar intellectual, F. X. Šalda, in his essay "The Greek and the Hebrew Genius," highlights the core of Jewish thinking and its primary concerns for spiritual values.[32] Citing Buber's lecture on the topic of nation-building, Šalda underscores the Jewish genius in creating a superior collective, united by a spiritual mission, a concept he was ready to adopt as his own.

Since most of Kafka's biographers have overemphasized Kafka's German cultural orientation, it seems appropriate to pay more attention to the Czech point of view. The first scholar to bring into focus Kafka's belonging to Prague ("genius loci") was Pavel Eisner in his pioneering study *Franz Kafka in Prague*.[33]

In fact it was František Kautman who in an eloquent presentation raised the argument of Kafka's allegiance to Prague (*pražantsví*) at the 1963 Liblice conference, with these remarks: "Kafka's native land is Bohemia (Čechy), notwithstanding the fact that he was not a Czech and that he wrote in German . . . The particular location of the Old City of Prague, the traces of the demolished ghetto, the narrow tortuous streets, the gloomy churches and synagogues, the dusty offices, taverns below ground level, the quays of [the River] Vltava and the baroque gardens . . . all these together formed the atmosphere of Kafka's tortured visions."[34] By coining the phrase "Der jüdischer Schriftsteller deutscher Zunge," Max Brod himself inadvertently contributed in his writings to this theory of Kafka's allegiance to Prague.[35]

The idea of affinity emerges poignantly from Dr. Gustav Sicher's solemn address delivered at the Altneuschul on June 29, 1947, on the occasion of the festive ceremony of his reinstatement as chief rabbi in the Czech lands.[36] His discourse, rich in biblical texts, imbued with profound grief and human warmth, evokes the emotional aura and timeless appeal of the two cherished cities: Prague and Jerusalem.[37]

> When the summons to take up the office of Chief Rabbi of Prague reached me, I felt as if Isaiah's vision had come alive: "I have blotted out . . . thy transgression . . . I have redeemed thee.' (Isaiah 44, 22) . . .
>
> Returning to Prague after the crucial period when human dignity was utterly trampled, recalling the prewar Jewish community, one feels ashamed to be a man, and seeing what has become of it, how can one not cry? . . .
>
> And lo! When I walk through the streets of liberated Prague—where, thank God, the merry crowds of people throng again, passing by the walls of buildings in which my acquaintances and friends used to live, I sense as if here too there are "Wailing Walls" upon which echoes the lament of Israel on the ruins of the ancient Temple: Woe over the House, my children where have you gone: priests, sages, teachers, where are you?
>
> . . . And to this Lord of the House of Israel, who is the Lord of the fate of all of us, I turn with the prayer of Moses, the God-fearing man, for the Jewish and for the Czech people: Rejoice us the same way as we were humiliated in the days of affliction.

The traditional spiritual ties between Czechs and Jews suffered a long hiatus during the era of Nazi persecution and Communist tyranny. The November

1989 revolution opened up new vistas for future interaction. On the occasion of his historic visit to Israel in May 1990, President Václav Havel emphasized how Jews and Czechs revered the written word and those works that have kept their language and traditions alive. Thus both nations were especially indebted to the Book of Books, seeking in it a source of strength and solace. "We were both small nations whose existence could never be taken for granted. An unceasing fight for survival, a feeling that our existence was always being called into question, was projected into the cultural and behavioral patterns of both our nations."[38]

This assertion on the common traits in Czech and Jewish traditional values adds a new dimension to our understanding: placing the issue of Czech-Jewish relations on the doorstep of our own generation, the particular aspects of which the present research aims to explore.

I

The Historical Setting

Throughout the centuries early Jewish settlement in the Bohemian Crownlands has intrigued many a scholar trying to determine the precise date of its beginning. The crux of the ongoing discussion appears to be the presence of Jews in the city of Prague.[1] Legend has it that "they had dwelt unmolested in that city from time immemorial. No one knew when they had first settled there; but tradition said it was in times when Bohemia was yet heathen." Even today views differ widely, and in fact historiography to all intents and purposes avails itself both of records and of ancient chronicles and legends as points of departure.[2]

Owing to its geopolitical situation, laying astride important trade routes, Prague acted from the beginning as crossroads connecting East and West. First reference reaches back to the early tenth century, to the so-called Raffelstatten Toll Ordinances (903–906), which regulated relations between the Great Moravian and Carolingian empires, and which note the Jewish slave-traders in this enclave.[3] The second important record is the description of the noble Spanish Jew Ibrahim Ibn Yaqub, who in his travelogue from the year 965 presents Prague as a highly prosperous center of trade where among merchant caravans, converging from near and far, Jewish traders barter their goods and wares.[4]

The relatively favorable conditions were disrupted at the time of the First Crusade in 1096. Many of the Jews were massacred, their property looted; others were forced to convert.[5]

In the thirteenth and fourteenth centuries economic conditions encouraged the growth of Jewish settlements. As elsewhere, the Jews engaged in trading, money lending, agriculture, and manufacturing, rendering them useful to the monarchs. Their function as *servi camerae regiae* (servants of the royal chamber) afforded them status and protection. Historians describing the relationship between the monarch and his Jewish subjects likened their usefulness to that of bees, whose personal safety had to be guaranteed for the benefit of the royal treasury.[6]

As in other European countries, in Bohemia and Moravia life became harsh and insecure with the burgeoning of social and religious unrest, while the flourishing of Judaism coincided with general progress and well-being.[7]

In the late fourteenth and fifteenth centuries the power struggle among the monarchs, the nobility, and the towns for the right to control the Jews and to collect their taxes led to the repeal of protection. This in turn resulted in holding for ransom; massacres under various pretexts, such as allegations of blasphemy and desecration, culminated in the onslaught upon the Jews of the Prague Ghetto at Easter of 1389—hundreds were murdered in the streets, the great cemetery was devastated, and the tombstones destroyed.[8]

The changes in the social structure of the Jews introduced by the Hussites created more tolerant conditions: "they had to give up money-lending and mingled with the rest of the town people, working as artisans, shopkeepers. On the other hand they were freed of the humiliating signs which they were earlier forced to wear and also later, pilloried as impure by the Christian society."[9]

The ceaseless influx of learned immigrants from neighboring Germany, Poland, the Balkans, Spain, and Portugal enhanced the cosmopolitan nature of the community. In the Middle Ages Prague was the seat of famous rabbis and talmudic scholars, renowned for their high standards of learning.

The rule of Maximilian (1564–76) and of Rudolph II (1576–1612)—"the Golden Era of Czech history"—is associated with Mordechai Maisl (1528–1601), the burgomaster of the old Jewish town in Prague, and Jacob Bassevi of Treuenberg, in charge of the output of Bohemian silver mines, the first Jew in Bohemia to be elevated to the nobility.[10] It was during this period that the monumental Jewish Town Hall and the nearby synagogues were erected.

The towering figure known as the Maharal lived in the Jewish community of Prague for over three decades. Both his interpretations of halakhic (ritual) rules and his treatises on worldly affairs, pedagogical theories, and ethics left an indelible mark on Jewish life in the Czech lands as well as on Judaism in general.[11] Between the years 1553 and 1573 he officiated as *Landesrabiner*—chief rabbi of Moravia—and headed the famous Nikolsburg (Mikulov) Yeshiva.

Bohemia existed as an independent kingdom until the late Middle Ages, when it became affiliated with the Holy Roman Empire. From 1526 it constituted part of the hereditary Habsburg dominion, and after the Battle of the White Mountain (1620) Bohemia lost its independence. The execution of the Czech noblemen in the Old Town Square in Prague and the ensuing Counter-Reformation unleashed a wave of persecution. All non-Catholic religions except for Judaism were declared illegal. Protestant priests were ordered to leave the country. Czech lands and fortunes were confiscated, the Czech language was proscribed, the Czech faith condemned; bibles and books were burned and individuals were put to death. Habsburg absolutism was imposed and the ensuing seventeenth and eighteenth centuries became engraved in Czech historical consciousness as the time of darkness (*Temno*).[12]

The Peace of Westphalia (1648), "the seventeenth-century Munich," as the historian Otakar Odložilík put it, transformed Bohemia and Moravia into a mere administrative appendage of the Habsburg Empire.[13] The native Czech language, being overwhelmingly replaced by German, fell into decay, bringing general intellectual life to a standstill. It was this situation that triggered the gradual Germanization process of Bohemian Jews, to evolve later into a firm attachment to German education and culture.

By the end of the seventeenth century almost half of Bohemian Jewry (around ten thousand persons) lived in Prague.[14] The rest, the so-called *Landes-judenschaft* of twenty-five to thirty thousand, were scattered throughout the countryside and townlets as traders under the protection of local nobility. Their main function was to sell the surplus produce of the domains, such as wool, hides, down, and cheese, and to supply the nobles' households with articles of luxury.

In Moravia the Jewish population at the time is estimated to have been around 25,500, for the most part acting as merchants and tradesmen. After they had been expelled from the royal cities (Jihlava, Brno, Olomouc, Znojmo, Neustadt, and Uherské Hradiště) they settled in villages and small towns under the protection of feudal lords on whose estates they performed various functions. Some of the Jews became military purveyors, attaining status and respectability. A large section engaged in crafts as artisans and tailors and as cloth and wool merchants, laying the foundations of the textile and clothing industry.

At the end of the century Prague was widely known to be the best established and most thriving site of Jewish residence; the population of the Jewish Town amounted to 11,500. John Toland (1670–1722), one of the radical followers of the Enlightenment in Britain, who visited the European continent prior to issuing his protest pleading for the naturalization of the Jews in Britain and Ireland (1714), made special mention of this. He reviewed the situation of the Jews in the major European cities, demonstrating how valuable their presence was, and he referred to Prague as the greatest of all.[15]

The government census of 1724 indicated that the Jews of Bohemia were scattered among eight hundred localities, six hundred of which were small villages in which only a handful of Jews lived. At the same time Moravian Jewry was distributed among fifty-two communities of "medium" size.[16]

The accession to the throne of Charles VI was marked by the Familiants'

Law (Familiantengesetz) in 1727, which limited the number of Jewish families in Bohemia to 8,541 and in Moravia to 5,106; only one son from any household was permitted to marry and establish a family. Maria Theresa's forty years of absolute rule (1740–80) were marked by steady adherence to the policy of curtailments in mobility and family life as well as heavy taxation of the Jewish population. For alleged espionage activities during the Prussian War, the Jews were ordered in 1744 to leave Prague with no delay; four years later, following diplomatic intervention, the empress rescinded the law and the Jews were allowed to return.[17]

The second half of the eighteenth century witnessed a Messianic upheaval among Jews in Bohemia and Moravia: Sabbateian Frankism spread among sections of the populace. Joseph II's accession to the throne in 1780 ushered in a new era of wide-ranging changes and reforms engendering the process of modernization within the Jewish communities. His ultimate goal was to bring about administrative unification in his various domains—making German the lingua franca of the whole empire. One outcome of the new reforms was the suspension of Jewish judicial autonomy. The emperor's new policy encompassed in the 1782 Edict of Tolerance (Toleranzpatent) aimed at the gradual abolition of existing limitations.[18] His policy set out utilizing the Jews' potential to the benefit of the state economy.

At the same time a systematic process of Germanization compelled the Jews to adopt family names and to establish secular schools, with the German language as the medium of teaching. They were to cease using Hebrew and Yiddish in business transactions, to be replaced by German for their records.

The Haskalah (the Jewish Enlightenment movement) reached Prague at the turn of the century. It may be assumed that in addition to the Mendelssohnian trend, contemporaneous cultural yearnings were influenced by Herderian nationalism, namely by Josef Dobrovský (1753–1829), the harbinger of the Czech Awakening. With the spread of Haskalah throughout Bohemia, enlightenment evolved into a vehicle paving the way for assimilation and integration into society at large.[19]

The Mendelssohnian trend put German alongside Hebrew as a language of religious life, thus bringing German into the synagogues, the communal institutions, and the rabbinates and granting it a dominant role in everyday usage. The transition from the vernacular Judeo-German of everyday life to a language spoken by many millions of people the world over had some real advantages and was regarded by many as the gateway to the "great wide world." At this period Czech scholars also availed themselves of the German language. František Palacký, founder of modern Czech historiography, first published his seminal history of the Czech people in Bohemia and Moravia in German (1836). And so did T. G. Masaryk at a later date. It has been recorded that in the 1830s "it was quite exceptional to hear better-clad people conversing in Czech in the streets of Prague."[20]

After the Josephinian emancipation, during the reign of Leopold II and Francis I, a regression set in, followed by a dramatic change in the year 1848, viewed as "the spring of the nations." In Bohemia and Moravia the most important innovation was the law of free movement (*Freizügigkeitsgesetz*) of 1849, which allowed Jews to leave the narrow confines of the ghetto and to scatter throughout the country. It also opened up new vistas of thinking, opportunities for individuals, and not least a radical break with tradition.

Within a relatively short time, following the law of free movement, Prague became the center of German-Jewish culture and a hub of developing trade and industry. Of special importance was the entry of Jews into the cotton industry in Prague and other localities (by 1835, of the 117 cotton-processing establishments, fifteen of the largest were owned by Jews).[21]

A large number of Jews settled in predominantly German northern Bohemia (called Sudetenland by the Nazis) and integrated relatively smoothly into various occupational fields. In the Czech countryside, however, the newcomers were greeted with distrust, the peasants viewing them as Germans, exploiters, and villains.[22] It took long years to win over the confidence of the overwhelmingly suspicious and bigoted local inhabitants. In contrast to their co-religionists in the big cities who had become assimilated, the village Jews, for the most part peddlers, remained devoted to Judaism.

One of the immediate consequences of the large-scale population movement was a radical change in the Jews' social structure. Their advance in the fields of industry and commerce elicited growing rivalry and ill-feeling accompanied by occasional riots and strikes against Jewish manufacturers. According to Alfred Meissner, a staunch liberal and socialist of the era, the Jews' inroads into society created a "sort of medieval Jew-hatred," which in practice meant larger or smaller daily burglaries of innocent inhabitants of the Jewish quarter in Prague and elsewhere.[23]

The year 1848 became a political landmark in the life of the ethnic groups of Bohemia, the beginning of conflicts and hostility between Germans and Czechs that had long been smoldering beneath the surface. Nevertheless, the genesis of spiritual and national awakening of the Czechs had already begun, gaining momentum during the ensuing revolutionary period of brewing national strife.

It was at this juncture that a window of opportunity for a Czech-Jewish dialogue opened up. The harbingers of this new approach were two literati:

Václav Bolemír Nebeský and his Jewish friend, the physician-poet Siegfried Kapper.[24] Both men believed in the possibility of a true symbiosis between the Czechs and the Jews. Nebeský claimed that old-established Jews could be viewed as Czechs by nationality and Jewish by faith.[25]

Prompted by the desire for a rapprochement with the Czech nation, a group of "Young Bohemian" poets published a series of poems, some drawing a parallel between the plight of the Czech people longing for redemption and the fate of unredeemed Palestine and the people of Israel. The foremost representatives were Moritz Hartmann and Siegfried Kapper.[26] Hartmann was the first to conjure up the vision of the Czech national defeat at the White Mountain in the "Böhmische Elegien." Kapper began his literary activities by translating folk songs, publishing *Slavische Melodien* (1844), followed in 1846 by his poetical work *České listy* (Czech leaves), the first literary composition written by a Jew in Czech. Moreover, while expressing a heartfelt allegiance to the homeland, he at the same time nurtured a warm and genuine attitude toward Judaism.[27]

His "intrusion into the sanctuary of Czech literature" was, however, greeted with devastating criticism by Karel Havlíček Borovský, the most prominent journalist of his time, who represented the Czech national bourgeoisie. In a series of articles he reviewed Kapper's poems, exploring the question of interrelationship between "Czechs and Jews" and their historical implications. Havlíček, however, on national grounds, categorically rejected Kapper's ideas of friendly interaction, consequently blocking the way for all those Jews who desired cultural assimilation with the Czech nation. Although Havlíček's criticism contained phrases of unmitigated anti-Semitism, Guido Kisch viewed his interpretation in a positive vein, stressing that "Havlíček was far ahead of his time": in his evocative associations of Jewish past and glory he spoke of Judaism in terms of the nascent modern Jewish nationalism.[28]

Notwithstanding the massive opposition to the integration of Jews in social and public life, the process of equal opportunity begun in 1848 and with it the constant interaction with the surrounding non-Jewish population was well under way. While the descendants of the prominent Jeiteles and Landau families associated with the Enlightenment period were passing on, acculturation and assimilation were steadily gaining a foothold within Jewish society. Moses Israel Landau (1788–1852), the grandson of Prague's noted chief rabbi Ezekiel Landau, although still officiating as a rabbi in Prague, was already a fully emancipated "free-thinker."[29] Although entirely self-taught, he became a translator and wrote poetry.

In 1849 Landau was the first Jew to be elected a representative on the Board of Prague Magistrates, and as of 1850 he became a town councilor. His public and social activities may be considered a milestone in the transformation of Jewry on the road toward acculturation and assimilation. Dr. Wolfgang Wessely (1801–70) was the first Jew to receive a doctorate in law as well as a Ph.D., in Vienna and at Charles University.[30] As of 1846 he gave lectures on the Hebrew language and rabbinical literature at Prague University, and in 1861 he became a full professor, a position he retained until his death (1870).

The historic compromise (*Ausgleich*) in 1867 resulted in the dualistic state of Austria-Hungary; in the Czech territories a new momentum for the national struggle began. Overwhelmed by an awakening nationalist consciousness, the Czechs viewed the Jews with rancor, blaming them for being instruments of Germanization, whereas German circles, influenced by the then proliferating ideas, considered the Jews aliens. Under the impact of the new racist doctrine the German university in Prague was a hotbed of anti-Judaism. August Rohling, who served as professor of theology at Prague University, published in 1871 his *Der Talmudjude*, a compilation of quotations in which he defended the veracity of accusations of ritual murder leveled against the Jews in the Middle Ages; this volume gained popularity among wide strata of the learned population and clerics.[31]

In the years 1870–71 two Catholic political associations were formed in the Czech lands: one for Bohemia and one for Moravia. Simultaneously a Catholic press alliance (Katolický spolek tiskový), was founded in Prague, which initiated a massive outpouring of popular anti-Jewish diatribes and pamphlets.[32] The late sixties witnessed an additional innovation: religious services in the Czech language paving the way to a closer link with the surrounding native population.[33]

The struggle for political liberty and growing national consciousness together with booming industrial and commercial activities produced a wealthy Czech middle class, competing for positions with their German counterparts. The growth of a new intelligentsia fostered the establishment of several national institutions, which in turn nurtured the genesis of a literary and artistic renaissance. The pivotal event in the revival of the Czech nation was the division of the Charles Ferdinand Prague University into separate German and Czech institutions in 1882.[34]

Other major landmarks were the founding of the first Czech political newspaper, *Národní listy* (1861); expansion of the gymnastic association Sokol (1862); establishment of the first major Czech bank, Živnostenská Banka (1868), and the Czech Academy of Science, Literature and Arts (1880); culminating in the opening of the National Theater in Prague (the edifice was built by private subscription in 1881). The regeneration and rebuilding of the Czech entity was under way.

With the persistent growth of the Czech nationalist movement, Jewish academic youth perceived the urgent necessity of changing their orientation. In 1876 they established Spolek českých akademiků-židů (sČaŽ, Society of Czech-Jewish academics) and began openly supporting the aspirations of Czech progressive circles.[35] Among the active members who were later to play a dominant role in Czech-Jewish interaction we find Adolf Stránský, Leopold Katz, Jakub Scharf, Augustín Stein, Josef Žalud, Karel Fischer, Bohumil Bondy, and Alois Zucker. One of the tangible outcomes of their efforts in public life was a successful campaign among the Jews of the Josefov district when in 1881 Dr. Tomáš Černý was elected the first Czech mayor of the city of Prague.

The Czech-Jewish movement was to serve several aims: it encouraged study of the Czech language and established in Prague a society for the promotion of worship in Czech and Hebrew (Or-Tomid—"Eternal light"), advocating the publication of some of the Hebrew prayerbooks in Czech translation.[36] Among its major publications was the annual *Kalendář česko-židovský*, launched in 5642 (1881–82).[37] For the first four years it appeared under the editorship of Augustín Stein, with articles on Jewish life, history, and culture openly supporting Czech national aspirations.

Thanks to the endeavors of the second editor, Karel Fischer, numerous first-rate Czech writers (J. Arbes, A. Heyduk, H. Jelínek, A. Jirásek, Fr. Kvapil, J. S. Machar, G. Preissová, L. Stroupežnický, F. X. Šalda, Z. Winter, and others) became contributors to the annual, enhancing its prestige in the eyes of the Jewish and non-Jewish readership alike.[38]

In 1883, at the height of growing Czech nationalism, the Neues Deutsches Theater (New German theater) came into being. Although the German nobility of the city were the founding members of the Theaterverein (theatrical society), the Jews of Prague also played a major role in its creation.[39] The first director of the theater was a Jew, Angelo Neumann, a former opera singer. Moreover, the overwhelming majority of the audience consisted of Jews who were regularly attending the gala performances of the Königliches Landestheater, opened a decade earlier. Jewish social and cultural life in the capital centered mostly around these two theatrical institutions. Jews also constituted a solid element in the Lese und Redehalle deutscher Studenten (Reading and lecture hall of German students) as well as in the German casino.[40]

The end of the nineteenth century saw the birth of several assimilationist organizations, the most important of which was the National Union of Czech Jews (Národní jednota českožidovská) founded in 1893, headed by Jakub Scharf, Bohumil Bondy, Alois Zucker, Mořic Baštýř, and Julius Reitler.[41] One year later (1894) the bimonthly magazine *Českožidovské listy* made its appearance. A sec-

ond journal with a similar ideological basis, *Rozvoj* (Development), began publication in Pardubice ten years later in 1904, under the editorship of the physician and humanitarian Dr. Viktor Vohryzek. (The two merged in 1907; the new
publication continued to appear as a weekly under the name *Rozvoj* until March
1939, with a short suspension.) Vigorous efforts were made to inculcate Czech
education among the Jews of the rural areas.

On the whole the Czech-Jewish movement made its mark only upon a thin
stratum of the more liberal, urban Gentile society. The majority, especially the
village populace, deeply imbued as it was with prejudices and superstitions,
remained hostile in outlook.

Between the years 1894 and 1896 sixty-four Catholic clubs were founded in
Bohemia and Moravia.[42] Many of these published weeklies and gazettes, spreading their views among party followers. Behind the hectic political activism
against the "destructive blaze" was the Christian socialists' antagonism toward
lawyers and physicians—both spheres considered Jewish domains, labeled as
foreign elements whose aim was "to destroy the Christian social order" in order
to rule over all nations.

It is not without interest that almost at the same time the *Protocols of the
Elders of Zion* and other forgeries were published elsewhere. An event of special
importance was the First Congress of the Czech Slavonic Working People at
Litomyšl (September 8, 1894), attended by several clerics who were authors of
notorious anti-Jewish pamphlets. The speakers described the invasion of society
"by liberal and atheistic bacteria," be they Freemasons or Jews.[43]

Two years later, in 1896, an international congress against Freemasonry took
place in Trento, with the blessing of Pope Leo XIII and with the participation of
prominent church dignitaries. The Bohemian daily *Čech* carried detailed accounts of the meeting. Robert Neuschl, professor of theology in Brno, wrote in
his "Christian Sociology" that "Jewish talmudism begot freemasonry that begot
liberalism . . . which in turn begot social democracy."[44] His arguments were
obviously influenced by Rohling's *Talmud Jude*, which had gone into several
Czech translations. There is no doubt that anti-Semitic ideas spread by other
popular authors, such as Karl Lueger and Edouard Drummond, exerted great
influence upon the Bohemian clerics. Their use of these incitements, especially
in the pre-election campaigns, referring to the "Jews' rule over the entire industrial sector, trade, and press" was echoed in an essay by Rudolf Vrba entitled
"National Self-protection."[45] He suggested the adoption of measures (set out in
sixteen paragraphs) to protect the Czech people from material and moral ruin.
Among others things he proposed compulsory marking of all Jewish businesses
and newspapers; removal of Jews from public office; and cancelation of voting

rights. He recommended a special order forbidding any change in their names.[46] This and other ideas were later used in various campaigns aimed at boycotts of Jewish enterprises.

Under the influence of a constant outpouring of virulent anti-Semitic literature—pseudoreligious pamphlets "For the people" (*Pro lid*)—distributed by Catholic preachers, ill feeling mounted.[47] It was under these circumstances that rumors of various blood libels spread throughout the country, occasionally reaching the law courts.

With the upsurge of nationalism the growing political pressure soon focused on economy and business: in 1892 a countrywide campaign was launched against German and Jewish merchants and shopkeepers under the slogan of "each to his own" (*Svůj k svému*); rioting and looting occurred in towns and villages such as Kladno and Kutná Hora.[48] Further disturbances occurred in the wake of the 1897 Badeni language ordinances (issued in order to ensure Czech-German linguistic equality for employees of the courts and administration). Two years later, following the revocation of the Badeni ordinances aimed at pacifying German nationalist elements, new disturbances instigated by Czech nationalists directed against Germans and Jews broke out in many localities both in Bohemia and Moravia.

It was in this atmosphere that the infamous blood libel trial of Leopold Hilsner took place, rocking the entire society.[49] Masaryk's courageous stance, and his two pamphlets tearing to shreds the argument of ritual murder and demanding a retrial to demonstrate that the forensic evidence was inadequate, turned the whole affair into a *cause célèbre*. Masaryk confided that he was prompted by a sense of humanity, based on his conviction that "belief in ritual murder casts disgrace on the Czech people."[50] What disturbed him most was the effect of anti-Semitism on the highest circles of the intellectual class and the fact that "university professors here and elsewhere had succumbed to blood libel."

The turmoil in 1897 and subsequently in 1899 generated a popular outpouring of anti-Semitism. The anti-Jewish slogans, the attacks of the National Liberals (in their mouthpiece *Národní listy*), and the betrayal of the so-called *Mladočeši* (Národní strana svobodomyslná)—regarded as natural allies—left the younger wing of the Czech-Jewish camp bewildered. The leading spokesmen, Vohryzek, Lederer, and Klineberger, felt it imperative to redefine their goals and drastically revise their manifesto in order to carry on with their task.

In 1900 Dr. Viktor Vohryzek issued a call for cooperation on behalf of the National Union of Czech Jews entitled "Letters to Czech Jews," signed by thirty leaders, setting forth the Czech-Jewish relationship on new grounds and arguing that neither recent developments nor patterns of cultural allegiance could account for anti-Semitic outbursts.[51] He described anti-Semitism as a moral flaw, and as such, he claimed, it was ultimately a Czech and not a Jewish problem.

Lederer also tried to offer a remedy. In his treatise *Žid v dnešní společnosti* (The Jew in contemporary society, 1902), presenting a substantive defense against the charges leveled against the Jews, he advocated a new ethical approach based on traditional Judaism to match Masaryk's ideas with regard to cultural transformation.[52] It is worth noting Vohryzek's admission in the first issue of *Rozvoj* in 1904 that as far as their program was concerned, "the intellectual fund has not sufficed" in coping with the difficult task of promoting integration into Czech society.[53]

Masaryk for his part is known to have challenged one of the basic tenets of the Czech-Jewish movement by urging its leaders to spell out precisely to what extent they envisaged their assimilation would progress. His own views were clear. Although he genuinely believed in cultural assimilation, he had strong doubts with regard to national assimilation. He clarified his stance thus: "Of course the Jews can become culturally Czech, but there still remains a difference: that of separate origins, of race—which of course cannot be exactly established—of religion and tradition."[54]

Masaryk never retreated from his original position and continued to view the Jews "as a distinct element within a nation." In one of his encounters with Lev Vohryzek in 1908 he made a pointed remark about the initial Czech-Jewish movement.[55] Masaryk stressed that Vohryzek's view, putting Jewish nationality on a par with religion, appealed to him much more.

The last year of the turbulent decade, 1900, heralded the "national turnabout" of the Jews in Prague. While in 1890 about two-thirds of Bohemian Jewry and three-quarters of the Jews of Prague declared their language of daily use to be German, ten years later more than 54 percent of both Bohemian and Prague Jews proclaimed Czech as their everyday language.[56] The breakup of the traditional system of German-Jewish primary education, the radicalization of Czech national politics, the anti-Semitic outbursts that began in 1892 and swept the country in 1897 and 1899, and finally the political pressure exerted by Czech Jews in an effort to challenge the predominance of German in various spheres of Jewish community life—all these forces combined to produce the surprising census results, which signaled the beginning of a new trend toward the "Czechization" of Bohemian Jewry.

One of the signs of this change was the removal of bilingual or German-only store signs, to be replaced by signs in Czech.[57] The changing of the names of the shopkeepers themselves, rendering them Czech or Czech-sounding, would wait another two decades.

The Jews of Moravia were more conservative and observant in religious practice than those in Bohemia. They also differed from their co-religionists in the use of language: in 1900, 77 percent declared German as their mother tongue, 16 percent Czech, and 7 percent other languages.[58]

At the turn of the century in Prague and Brno, the two major centers of Jewish population, a large Jewish textile industry developed. Numerous well-established Jewish families (Bondy, Teller, von Hahn) reached important positions in industry and the economy—in textile, leather, chemical, and dye businesses—attaining a high-water mark of prosperity some decades later.[59]

The Jews' advancement was impeded at higher levels in the various branches of the national economy, where they were not able to attain positions. In banks, financial institutions, insurance companies, or other Czech financial concerns and factories, Jewish investors often faced the sullen barrier of anti-Semitism. Most instructive on this point is a series of articles by Dr. Alois Zucker.[60] He informed the Czech public about the liberal approach toward Jewish entrepreneurs prevailing in Hungary, where recent arrivals from other parts of the monarchy often benefited the national economy.[61] A case in point were several Hungarian Jewish magnates, members of the Upper House, who had originally hailed from Bohemia and Moravia and subsequently made sensational careers in Hungary proper.

There were, of course, several exceptions. The most remarkable was Bohumil Bondy (1832–1907), scion of the patrician Bondy family, whose father Lazar Gottlieb Bondy was the founder of the old Prague L.G.B. iron firm. Bohumil Bondy, industrialist and patron of the arts, was a member of the Prague Town Council (1864–69).[62] In 1877 he became president of the Prague Chamber of Commerce and was highly regarded by both the Czech nation and the imperial court. His son Leon continued in his footsteps, becoming president of the chamber of commerce in 1902, to hold this position for many years.[63] Bohumil Bondy's interest in and general financial support for cultural enterprises led him in 1906 to the publication of the two-volume documentation project *The History of the Jews in Bohemia, Moravia and Silesia 906–1620*. He also initiated the establishment of the Museum of Arts and Crafts (Umělecko-průmyslové Muzeum) in Prague.

Another prosperous stratum developed in the rural areas. These were Jewish landowners and leaseholders who were among the first to utilize various technological innovations and agricultural machinery for modern crop cultivation. A prime example of these prosperous farmers was Alexander Brandeis (1848–

98), known as "a friend and patron in the generation of the National Theater," who was himself an enthusiastic connoisseur of the arts.[64] His estate served as a retreat and venue for many figures of the Czech cultural scene and for artists including Mikuláš Aleš, Josef Václav Myslbek, Václav Brožík, František Ženíšek, Chitussi, Mauder, and many others.

IN SEARCH OF IDENTITY

The traditionalist Orthodox way of life gave way in the second half of the nineteenth century to modernization and innovation, a shortened liturgy, and use of the organ and a mixed choir at services. Henceforth the rabbis, cantors, and sextons of the Orthodox synagogues also wore clerical robes. Still, the only one of the twenty congregations in Prague to adopt the characteristic features of Reform worship was the liberal Altschul synagogue, on Dušní Street. This synagogue became widely known for its association with two Czech musicians, the brothers Johan Nepomuk and František Škroup.[65]

The vast majority of the urban Jewish population grew indifferent to religion and their links with the community became feeble. In Prague there remained only a few families who were faithful to tradition. František Langer referred to them in his recollections as "the remnant of the religious aristocracy." Max Brod, Felix Weltsch, Hans Kohn, Robert Weltsch, Hugo Bergmann, and other contemporaries reminiscing about this period touched in a similar vein upon this total ignorance of normative Judaism. Kafka, in a letter to his father, spoke of the prevailing religious void: "the insignificant scrap of Judaism" he himself possessed, which in the course of time "all dribbled away."[66]

The Jews nevertheless retained a feeling of deep reverence for their past, cherishing their ancient synagogues, historical monuments, cemeteries, and organized community framework known for its social and charitable activities. Those who emigrated carried with them this amalgam of tradition: in the United States, "Bohemian" synagogues and congregations are known to have observed the customary rituals of the home country.

Under the impact of assimilation and urbanization, Jewish society underwent a radical transformation, losing its cohesive structure, the rabbinate ceasing to dominate the mainstream of communal life. Although the officiating rabbis of Prague, such as Alexander Kisch (1886–1917); Nathan Ehrenfeld (1890–1912) and Heinrich (Hayyim) Brody (1912–30), were university-educated and liberal men, their influence upon their flock and public life nevertheless diminished distinctly. The once religious community of Bohemia evolved into a pluralistic society of liberals and socialists, nihilists and atheists, assimilationists and Zionists. The marked internal mobility caused further havoc in Jewish communal life already plagued by alienation from Judaism and the new phenomenon of mixed marriages (in 1881, 0.15 percent; in 1910 reaching 1.75 percent).[67]

Torn between the deeply hostile camps, a small section of Jews sought a solution in Theodor Herzl's political aspirations and later in Ahad Ha'Am's cultural Zionism. A proclamation issued in 1894 by the nationalist students' organization Maccabi in Prague claimed that "the Jews are neither German nor Slavs, they are a nation in their own right."[68] Moravian students were the first to organize a Zionist student club, Veritas, in Brno in 1894 under the guidance of Berthold Feiwel, which in turn led to the founding of Zionist organizations throughout the Moravian communities.

Reflecting on the identity dilemma of Czech Jews in an article titled "The Hunt in Bohemia," Herzl himself mused: "In Prague they are reproached that they are not Czech, in Žatec (Saaz) and in Cheb (Eger) for being Germans. Poor Jews, where should they stand? Some tried to be Czechs; these were assaulted by the Germans. Others wanted to be Germans, and then both the Czechs and the Germans attacked them. What a situation! One can lose one's mind."[69]

As of 1899 with the establishment of the Bar Kochba Association of Jewish University Students in Prague, the influence of two thinkers, Ahad Ha'Am and especially Martin Buber, grew steadily. Noteworthy are Masaryk's influence and his contacts with the founding members of the association. Under the leadership of Hugo Bergmann (1903–8), Bar Kochba became a focus for disseminating Jewish cultural values.

In Prague the first Zionist association was formed in 1900 under the name of Jüdischer Volksverein. Among the founders were Moritz Löwy, Professor Jakob Wertheimer, Filip Lebenhart, Rabbi Aladar Deutsch, and Anton Glaser. In 1901 the women organized a group of their own, Der Jüdischer Frauenverein. The first chair of this group was Sophie Roubitschek, educator and principal of a Jewish boarding school in Prague.[70]

In 1907, after the new edition of *Rozvoj* appeared, the Bar Kochba Association created a new platform for promoting ideas and discussions by launching the Prague Zionist weekly *Selbstwehr* (Self-defense). It was to portray the social, economic, and cultural activities of the community and challenge the attacks both of German and Czech assimilationists.[71]

Caught as they were in the throes of the Czech-German nationality controversy, Prague Zionists sought a way out, determined to steer clear of both sides. Dr. Leo Herrmann, a young Socialist who was elected leader of Bar Kochba in 1908, took a new initiative.[72] With a view to igniting self-awareness he invited the Berlin-based Jewish philosopher Martin Buber to address the student body on the social history of Jews.[73]

Buber's three lectures "On Judaism," "Judaism and Mankind," and "The Renewal of Judaism" (January 1909 and April and December 1910) offered hope and justification as a new challenge and provided a genuine service to the intellectuals of Prague, cut off as they were by time and place from the well-springs of national Jewish culture. Buber's presentations resulted in the publication of *Drei Reden über das Judentum* (Three addresses on Judaism) in 1911, bringing home to his audiences the significance of Jewish heritage and Hebrew language.[74] In due course Czech Zionists became bearers of what was described as the *Prager Richtung im Zionismus* (the Prague orientation of Zionism).[75]

It is noteworthy that in 1909 a Czech-oriented branch of the Bar Kochba Association was formed in Prague under the name Theodor Herzl (Spolek židovských akademiků Theodor Herzl), the founding members of which were to play a considerable role in public and cultural activities.[76] One of the tenets of the society was "to make the values of Zionism available to Jews whose daily language is Czech, without adopting at the same time German cultural traits."

Hugo Herrmann's declaration "The Czech-Jewish Question" spelled out the new line adopted on the Czech-German conflict: "We Jews are Jews as a nation (*der Nation nach*) and do not seek to assimilate with anyone." At the same time he pledged commitment to participate "as reliable, true allies" in the struggle of the Czech nation.[77] Herrmann's unequivocal assertion acknowledged "the influence of our [Czech] environment." One is aware that these were not merely empty words. It is apparent that already in 1911, before the dawn of Czech nationhood, Prague Zionist leaders were cognizant of the immense impact exerted upon them by the burgeoning national upsurge of the Bohemian capital.

What is singularly remarkable was Buber's impact on a whole range of foremost Czech intellectuals, including F. X. Šalda, František Krejčí, Arne Novák, J. S. Machar, and J. J. Svátek.[78] The basic tenets of Zionism appealed to them, and they came to view the Jewish entity as a distinct ethnic group and spoke out in favor of Jewish nationalism.[79] Thus, for instance, the poet J. S. Machar, when answering a questionnaire distributed by the editor of *Rozvoj* as to whether Jews could be considered a nationality, replied that he found himself in a ridiculous situation: "I persistently write Jews (Židé) with a capital Ž to prove that they are a nation while they themselves use a small ž to imply that they are not to be considered as such."[80]

The philosopher František Krejčí spelled out his views in 1909 in an article entitled "Assimilation and Zionism from the Ethical Point of View," arguing that the prime element of Czech nationality was the Czech language whereas

Judaism was faith tightly interwoven with national identity, a phenomenon unique among the nations.[81]

The last decades preceding World War I, dubbed "Kafkas böses Böhmen," were marked by the mounting Czech-German national conflict, tension stirring every aspect of social and economic life.[82] These years of "nervous splendor," as Harry Zohn put it from a different angle, produced the unique group Der Prager Kreis (the Prague Circle). Several members of this group are of special interest in our context because of their role as bridge builders, promoting and translating the works of Czech authors and poets into German.

A particular common denominator positively affected the older generation of Jewish writers (Czech Jews, German Jews, and national Jews as well): their receptiveness to all the resources existing within the empire—German, Czech, Austrian, and Jewish. This situation lent their writing a broad cosmopolitan outlook and a quality of exaltation bordering on transcendental metaphysical contemplation. An illustrious example is Franz Kafka, the symbolic figure of this era. Other leading members of the Prague Circle were Max Brod, Franz Werfel, Egon Erwin Kisch, Oskar Baum, Hugo Salus, Johannes Urzidil, and Kamil Hoffmann. They partook of a triple world of contrasts and rivalry.[83]

Kafka, like others, was conscious of the fact that they were not fully accepted by either German or Czech society. In Pavel Eisner's interpretation the triple dimension of Jewish existence in Prague is embodied in Kafka's *The Trial*: his protagonist Josef K. is (symbolically) arrested by a German (Rabensteiner), a Czech (Kullich), and a Jew (Kaminer). He stands for the "guiltless guilt" that imbues the Jew in the modern world, although there is no evidence that he himself is a Jew.[84]

In his essay "A Chapter of Czech-German Co-Existence" Eisner added a new dimension to this complex issue, claiming that almost everything created in "German Prague" by the last generation of Jewish artists and men of letters revealed a measure of "positiveness vis-à-vis Czech culture." He regarded this development as a kind of "biological process," the Jews thereby ridding themselves of the depressing ghetto atmosphere. Moreover, Eisner saw in the German-speaking intellectuals of Prague the initial intermediaries between Czechs and Germans, bridging the spiritual gap between them. It was through their translation of Czech literature into German (and to a lesser degree vice versa) that the Germans were made aware of the creative potential and spiritual values inherent in the Czech nation. Siegfried Kapper, Viktor Vohryzek, Hugo Salus, Friedrich Adler, Otto Pick, Rudolf Fuchs, Kamil Hoffmann, and Max Brod became the foremost cultural intermediaries, translating the best works produced by Czech authors.[85] The most telling example of the "positive" approach is the translation by Rudolf Fuchs of the "Silesian Songs" written by Petr Bezruč in 1916. The book appeared in the midst of World War I when the Czech nation was engulfed in a struggle for self-determination. The poetry of the rebellious Bezruč was a national and social outcry of miners against the owners' exploitation; a protest against the Polonizing and Germanizing of the regions of Ostrava and Teschen by the Austrian aristocracy and some Jewish overlords (Rothschilds, Guttmans). Both the translator and Franz Werfel, who wrote an emotional introduction, gave voice to their utmost empathy with the Czech cause, notwithstanding the anti-Semitic overtones that prevailed throughout this book of verses.[86]

On the eve of World War I a second generation of educated professionals and writers emerged within the ranks of the Czech-Jewish movement who from their early childhood identified with the native national culture and who felt totally devoted to the Czech cause. The foremost representatives of this period—Jindřich Kohn, Otakar Guth, and Viktor Teytz—left an indelible mark on the movement: Kohn as the leading philosopher, whose credo embraced the universal mission of Judaism, and Guth and Teytz as editors of *Rozvoj* and *Kalendář česko-židovský*. They were still cognizant of their Jewish roots and within the historical context spoke of their "distinctiveness." They contended that they would never call themselves "the descendants of the Hussites" but could fully identify with Czech history in their own lifetime.[87]

With the outbreak of war the issue of loyalty surfaced to give rise to psychological stress: old ethnic resentments took new forms, gaining in intensity. On the whole the Jewish entity, caught between the Russophile nationalist sentiment of the Czech people and German-Austrian patriotism, tended to side with the latter, especially the German-speaking Jews who embarked on a vociferous campaign for the war effort, thus drawing down upon themselves harsh criticism. Before leaving for abroad Masaryk exhorted "the more reasonable" Jewish leaders "to curb the zealous patriotism" of their co-religionists lest it provoke anti-Semitic outbursts.[88]

The war brought to a standstill the activities of the major Czech-Jewish organizations, most of the youngsters enlisting in the army. The situation was similar in the Zionist camp, where the various organizations engaged in social work, launching relief campaigns for those in need. The streams of refugees fleeing from Galicia and the Carpathians brought the misery of Eastern Jewry to the threshold of the Bohemian and Moravian communities. The last year of the war signaled the impending changes following the Wilsonian declaration on national self-determination for the peoples of Austria-Hungary. To the Czech Jews it meant the fulfillment of their aspirations.

The struggle for Czechoslovak independence inspired not only Zionist leaders abroad, who maintained close contact with exiled Czech leaders, but also leading figures in Prague. The latter, emboldened by the Czech example, made the first move to consolidate Jewish nationalism within the context of the Czechoslovak state in the making. During their meetings with members of the Czech national leadership toward the end of 1917 and in 1918, the Zionist representatives led by Dr. Ludvík Singer reassured the Czech leaders of their forthcoming support and of their intention to constitute a loyal body in the nascent Czech state, linguistic and cultural affiliation notwithstanding.[89] In keeping with this line in April of 1918 a new Czech-language paper was launched— *Židovské zprávy* (Jewish news), edited by Dr. Ludvík Singer—to keep the readership abreast of current activities and policies.[90]

Many of the key figures of the Bar Kochba student association left for Palestine before the end of World War I or in the first years following the establishment of the Czechoslovak Republic.[91] Their departure as well as the withdrawal of Martin Buber from active political life brought about the decline of the Bar Kochba Association. Henceforth the Czech-oriented sister society, the Theodor Herzl group, gained strength in all spheres of public life.[92] Some of its foremost members were mainly active as editors and writers.

In his perceptive study *The Making of Czech Jewry*, Kieval convincingly illustrates the two poles that arose within post-emancipatory Jewry in the wake of the Czech-German national conflict: two trends of self-affirmation and search for identity striving toward different objectives.

2

Years of Challenge and Growth
The Jewish Minority in Czechoslovakia (1918–38)

A national state or a state of nations? This question touches the core and the essence of the First Republic and its fate and as such lends itself to various interpretations. The Czechs constituted but half the population of the new state; however, together with the Slovaks, they made up the decisive majority, the *raison d'être* of the "Czechoslovak nation," which in a broader context was embraced by the "Czechoslovak Jews" as well.[1]

Aside from Czechs and Slovaks, the new democratic Czechoslovakia established on October 28, 1918, in the wake of the collapse of the multinational Austro-Hungarian monarchy included a number of other ethnic groups: Germans, Hungarians, Ruthenes, Jews, Poles, and Gypsies. It was the thirteenth largest state in Europe, with an area of 54,244 square miles, incorporating the provinces of Bohemia, Moravia, part of Silesia, Slovakia, and Subcarpathian Ruthenia.[2]

According to the Declaration of Independence issued by President Masaryk on October 18, 1918, in Washington, the new state was to "guarantee complete freedom of conscience, religion and science, literature and art, speech and press, and the right of assembly and petition. The Church shall be separated from the State . . . The rights of the minorities shall be safeguarded by proportional representation. National minorities shall enjoy equal rights. The Government shall be parliamentary in form and shall recognize the principles of initiative and referendum."[3]

The main feature of future foreign policy of the Czechoslovak state was outlined by the president in his first message (December 22, 1918) to the members of the Prague National Assembly: "The Republic will be a barrier against the German plan of conquest toward the East," and for this purpose a confederation of the small states extending from the Baltic to the Adriatic should be created.[4]

On the very day the republic was proclaimed the representatives of the newly created Jewish National Council (Národní rada židovská), led by its chairman Dr. Ludvík Singer and vice-chairmen Dr. Max Brod and Karel Fischl, appeared before the Czech National Committee (Národní výbor).[5] They submitted a memorandum the gist of which was a claim for recognition of a Jewish nationality with minority rights as well as for state recognition of the religious community

The demand for minority rights was taken up at the Paris Peace Conference by the Comité des délégations juives, augmented by the Prague representatives—Ludvík Singer, Hugo Bergmann, and Norbert Adler. In the course of discussions with the Jewish National Council in Paris, Foreign Minister Eduard Beneš clearly rejected including "any specific clause pertaining to the protection of the Jews," his opposition stemming from the conviction that such a clause would hint at some mistrust on the part of the Allied Powers.[6] (Talking with Nahum Sokolow, Beneš even claimed that signing the Jewish articles of the Polish treaty would constitute a "yellow badge"—a stigma that Czechoslovakia would not deserve.) His second argument, perhaps carrying even more weight, implied that inclusion of Jewish minority rights would imply taking sides with one party, namely Zionism, versus assimilationism. Notwithstanding his overt sympathies, even Masaryk could not publicly approve such a motion. (Such an act would have antagonized the Czech-Jewish movement already aggravated over the achievement of national Jews functioning as political representatives.)

Although uneasy about the chauvinistic euphoria, the Jewish public at large viewed the new development favorably, pinning its hopes on President Masaryk's uprightness and moral rectitude.[7] But the transition period after the overthrow of the old Austrian regime loosed evil temper and hypernationalistic ill feeling. Anti-Semitic demonstrations and looting took place in Prague and some other localities, occasionally accompanied by bodily attacks.[8] The most severe assault occurred in the Moravian Holešov; the riots in December 1918 were initiated by members of an army unit from Kroměříž, who together with the local mob looted and destroyed Jewish homes and institutions.[9] Among the victims were Hugo Gratzer (aged forty-three) and Heiman Grünbaum (twenty-one); ironically enough, both were assaulted on their return from the front. Police curfew and a special unit brought in from Brno finally put an end to the three-day pogrom.

This was not the last of the rioting. May 1919 saw demonstrations against high prices and profiteering, and Jewish shops and businesses were looted again in greater Prague. After a year of respite more severe disturbances occurred on November 16, 1920: mobs attacked the ancient Jewish Town Hall, which was temporarily sheltering Galician refugees. The mobs destroyed furniture and paintings and vandalized part of the community archives. The rioting became so violent that the American consul in Prague ordered that the American flag be hoisted over the Town Hall in order to protect the community premises.[10] An alarmed Franz Kafka, witnessing the disturbances from the window of his apartment, recorded some of the appalling scenes.[11]

The declaration of minority rights, the so-called treaty of St. Germain-en-Laye of September 10, 1919, was signed by the forcign minister of the Czecho-slovak Republic, Dr. Edvard Beneš. The minority clauses were subsequently embodied in article 128 of the Constitution of the Republic of February 29, 1920, stipulating equality for all national, religious, and language minorities within the republic.[12] The preamble expressly stated that the Jews, before all authorities and at all times, could declare their national identity and be recognized as such. This principle was subsequently embodied in the census regulations, on the basis of which the Jews were free to declare themselves as belonging to the Jewish nationality irrespective of their mother tongue. The Czechoslovak Government regarded this act as a means for decreasing the numbers of Germans and Hungarians in the country, for a portion of the Jewish population had claimed these nationalities during the Austro-Hungarian era.

In an effort to bring the Jews professing Jewish nationality under one umbrella organization and thereby strengthen their political status, a conference was called in Prague in January 1919 at which the Jewish Party of Czechoslovakia was established as an instrument for electoral activities.[13] Though Zionist influence was prevalent in the Jewish National Council established in 1918, there were also liberal groups led by Alois Hilf and Salomon Hugo Lieben, who identified with and supported the council's more general policy. The Czech assimilationists openly contested the council's legitimacy in representing the entire Jewish population of Czechoslovakia.

At the same time, however, alarmed by the growing anti-Semitic campaign in the press, the Czech-Jewish movement issued a proclamation in its newly established daily *Tribuna*, under the editorship of Ferdinand Peroutka, declaring their unwavering loyalty to the republic.[14] The main aim of the daily was to help build the nation and the state. Numerous articles in the first issues, some penned by the editor himself, dealt in depth with the phenomenon of anti-Semitism, responding to continuous attacks in the various right-wing newspapers.

Among external events, it was first and foremost the Russian Revolution that in the immediate postwar period exerted its impact on the newly formed Czechoslovakia, where a segment of the leadership and political parties shifted to the left. This trend was also apparent within the Zionist factions, where the so-called left center youth groups were on the move. The impact of the Balfour Declaration (1917) and the incorporation of national minority rights in the peace treaties and in the Czechoslovak Constitution afforded the Zionist leadership an official basis for a long-range national Jewish policy that viewed its fulfillment in Eretz Israel.

It is noteworthy that the Jewish leaders of Bohemia and Moravia took up the struggle for nationality rights and led the election campaign for the Jewish Party, although the bulk of the voters came from the eastern parts of the republic, mainly from Subcarpathian Ruthenia.[15] At the same time the Jewish Party faced vociferous opposition from the ultra-Orthodox section and the Hasidic *rebbes* of these areas, who viewed Zionism as "heresy and atheism."

In 1921 the Jews of the republic numbered 354,000 out of the population of 13,613,172. Of these, 180,855 claimed Jewish nationality (in Bohemia 11,251 out of 79,777 and in Moravia-Silesia 19,016 out of 45,306). It should also be mentioned that many Jews listed Czech, German, or Magyar as their mother tongue or nationality.[16]

As of the first elections the Jewish minority took an active part in political life: its representatives sat on the town councils and on the district and provincial councils. Paradoxically, despite the fact that religion per se was losing ground, those adhering to religion still outnumbered the sector adhering to Jewish nationality, as was clearly indicated by the census returns of 1921 and 1930. This pattern began to change in the late thirties under the impact of National Socialism in Germany and the rise of anti-Semitism.

Within the new republic the Jews of the historic crownlands of Slovakia and of Subcarpathian Ruthenia (former provinces of Hungary) came to live within the same political framework. The Jewish communities of the eastern regions, the majority of whom remained Orthodox, differed significantly from their co-religionists, the assimilated Jews of Bohemia and Moravia, in their way of life, level of education, and economic and cultural standards.[17]

One of the immediate issues affecting the communities was a new influx of several thousand Jewish refugees from Bukovina and Galicia, hundreds of whom reached Prague during and immediately after the war. A great part of these newcomers settled in Moravian localities, namely in Moravská Ostrava. The conspicuous presence of Yiddish-speaking *Ostjuden* with beards and side-locks, wearing shabby garments and black hats, caused embarrassment, especially in Prague and other Czech-assimilated environments.[18] At the same time their poverty, lack of education, and poor physical condition placed a burden upon the community, whose reduced resources also had to provide for this new stratum of proletariat. The cultural gap between native and immigrant Jews gave rise in this country, as in Germany, to intracommunal tensions. Nevertheless integration in Czechoslovakia was much smoother. A group of Prague Jews volunteered their services to care for the newcomers' welfare and spiritual needs. Upon the initiative of Dr. Alfred Engel a school for young refugee girls was set up, instructing them in commerce and agriculture.[19] Some of the noted intellectuals such as Dr. Max Brod gave language instruction and literature courses in an effort to help with immigrant integration into the new surroundings. It is noteworthy that in the course of time this nationally conscious element stemming from Bukovina and Galicia became the solid base of the Zionist party, especially in Moravia.

Although a Zionist tradition had existed in prewar Bohemia and Moravia, it never became a mass movement. It did, however, put out roots, which came to develop during the late thirties. Initial activities began early. After the end of the war Zionist local centers were set up in the various provinces: the Prague office acted as central headquarters. After the Second Zionist Territorial Conference in Brno in 1921, the seat of the Czechoslovak Zionist Executive was transferred from Prague to Moravská Ostrava.[20] The midway position of this city enabled the executive to maintain close contact with the two eastern provinces of the republic. Dr. Josef Rufeisen served as chair of the executive until 1938 when he was succeeded by Dr. Paul März, while Dr. Franz Kahn acted as secretary of the executive throughout the whole period of the First Republic.

One of the main characteristics of Czechoslovakia's constitutional life was the large number of political parties, reflecting the plethora of sociocultural backgrounds and religions, finding expression through proportional representation.[21] The constitution provided for 300 deputies and 150 senators in the Parliament of Prague. It can, however, be safely established that apart from a period in the late twenties, of the twenty-three parties it was five Czechoslovak parties that constituted the backbone of coalition governments. The most prominent were the Czechoslovak Social Democratic Workers' Party (the largest force in the National Assembly), Czech Socialist Party (in 1926 renamed Czechoslovak Nationalist Socialist Party), Czechoslovak Populist Party, Czechoslovak National Democratic Party (after 1935 renamed the National Union), and the Agrarian Party. Of the minor Czechoslovak parties, many of which were short-lived, the most important was the Tradesmen's Party (Živnostenská strana), representing small businessmen and tradesmen, which cooperated closely with the Agrarians and which managed by manipulation to draw votes from Jewish religious circles in the eastern provinces. In addition there were a number of minority parties that also drew Jewish votes: German, Hungarian, and Polish parties and the Communist Party of Czechoslovakia.

One of the core issues in newly established multinational Czechoslovakia was the language problem, which affected internal policy in the spheres of education, culture, electoral criteria, and religious communal affairs. The Language Law regulating the relationship between the state and the minorities was passed on February 29, 1920. It established first and foremost that Czech and Slovak were to serve as official languages on an equal basis.[22] As far as the use of minority languages was concerned, the law stipulated that these could be used officially in agencies of local self-government only within a jurisdiction where a census of the members of such a language group numbered at least one-fifth of the population.[23]

According to the constitution, the terms *national* and *nation* were not employed in the sense of the French term *nationalité*, which denotes both citizenship and ethnic grouping. The term *national* primarily implied membership in a language group. However, membership in a linguistic minority did not always coincide with membership in a national minority. The Jews could be recognized as a national minority as long as they regarded themselves as a nationality in their own right, even if they did not use a language of their own in their daily transactions. Although they did not constitute a linguistic minority, there were no restrictions on the use of Yiddish and Hebrew in business correspondence or in account books, publishing, or other fields of intellectual activity.

Time and again the language problem became a bone of contention in the political and public life of the republic, and complaints were addressed by the German and Hungarian minorities to various bodies such as the local judicial authorities and, primarily, the League of Nations.

Ultimately it was this principle of the Language Law that became a stumbling block in electoral rules, making it difficult for minorities to return candidates to Parliament. Due to dispersion of its members over various localities the Jewish Party (as well as other minority groups) suffered several defeats in the initial electoral campaigns. It was only in 1929, following a vote agreement with the Polish minority, that two representatives of the Jewish Party were elected to the Prague Parliament: Dr. Ludvík Singer (succeeded after his death in July 1931 by Dr. Angelo Goldstein) and Dr. Julius Reisz.

Reviewing his party's efforts to enter the national political arena, Singer recalled on January 6, 1931, at the Zionist Convention in Moravská Ostrava, that it was thanks to the electoral district of Ostrava that the Jewish Party finally won in the election campaign. "We were defeated four times: we were double-crossed four times to make sure that no Jew would be able to enter the legislative chamber as a representative of the Jewish people. You know that prior to the last parliamentary elections we joined forces with the Polish minority and emerged victorious in the voting. But be it said to the credit of the Poles that they were the only ones who were not afraid to link their names with ours."[24]

It is noteworthy that the chairman of the party, Dr. Emil Margulies, as well as a number of other members, opposed this agreement, insisting that the Jewish Party stand for election alone and under its own name.[25] When outvoted the chairman resigned from his position and was replaced by Eng. Arnošt (Ernst) Frischer, who subsequently headed the party for many years.[26] The Jewish Party numbered Zionist as well as nonaffiliated members and cooperated mainly with the Poalei-Zion Workers' Party and the religious Mizrachi Party up to the last days before the Munich crisis of 1938.

During the next elections in 1935, after an arrangement with the Czech Social Democrats, Dr. Angelo Goldstein and Dr. Chayim Kugel came to represent the Jewish Party in the Prague Parliament.[27] The most crucial issues on their agenda were improvement of the economic situation; efforts to alleviate the hardships of the pauperized Jewish population in the eastern provinces; legalization of the congregations; official recognition of the Hebrew school system in Subcarpathian Ruthenia; and protests against the bureaucratic attitude of the local authorities in the handling of the question of "stateless" persons—a relic of the former Austro-Hungarian regime. During the 1930s the Jewish Party representatives spoke out against the campaign waged by Nazi agitators within the republic, challenging the rabid local nationalists and anti-Semites.[28]

With the emergence of the republic the Czech-Jewish movement, representing the assimilated and for the most part religiously indifferent segment, widened the scope of its activities.[29] It was initially a small but forceful group: in 1924 it had two thousand organized members hailing mainly from the Czech rural areas. In Moravia their number was minute. Its membership consisted primarily of the cultural elite of Bohemia, journalists and professionals and several leading authors and thinkers.

The most outstanding leaders of the movement were Dr. Edvard Lederer (Leda), its political theorist, and Dr. Jindřich Kohn, foremost thinker and interpreter of universal assimilationism.[30] Kohn believed in the special mission of the Jews among the nations and interpreted the concept of the "chosen people" in his own way: because of their acute sensitivity to prejudice and persecution, the Jews were ordained by destiny to be the guardians of human civilization for the benefit of mankind.

Moving farther and farther away from the ideals of the founders, the extreme assimilationists gradually embarked on a new course regarding assimilation as an end in itself: complete amalgamation into the Czech nation. The Prague community served for decades as the central arena for the overzealous members among the assimilationists to air their criticism and attacks against the Zionists: *Rozvoj* versus *Židovské zprávy*. Blaming their adversaries for "Germanization" and for "underrating the importance of the Czech language," the Czech Jews very often asked the authorities to interfere, on occasion generating acrimonious clashes.

Aside from the press, a wide range of booklets and pamphlets published by the rival parties reflects their continuous strife. Thus, for instance, in the late twenties the student organization of the Czech-Jewish movement, in an effort to expand its membership in Moravia (and in Slovakia) distributed a questionnaire among public personalities delineating the goals of their program: "The aim of our movement is to ensure that Jews living in a Czech environment, who not from their own volition and sometimes even against their own will abandoned elements of their independent Jewish nationality, merge with their Czech surroundings and thus do not constitute a foreign and hostile element therein."[31]

Among the questions listed, the two paraphrased here can be singled out for their pertinent content. No. 4 says the main obstacle to the Czech-Jewish movement is the indifference of the public to its aims, or even to anti-Semitism: what is your opinion? And no. 5 says another obstacle is posed by so-called Zionism. This was a movement that originated in Vienna, founded by Dr. Herzl and Dr. Nordau, which asserts that Jews both in our country and in the West constitute a genuine independent Jewish nationality . . . have you any comments as far as the question of Zionism in our country is concerned, and if you follow the politics of the minority struggle in our country, what is your opinion?

To accentuate cultural ascendancy Czech Jews listed the most prominent individuals, both in the past and those still active within their ranks (Kapper, Zucker, Scharf, Vohryzek, Klineberger, Bohumil Bondy, and Žalud) as well as important writers (Otokar Fischer, František Langer, and Josef Kodíček); this list also included Richard Weiner. It was the use of the name of Weiner—who actually opposed the Czech-Jewish movement—that spurred František Friedmann, representing the Jewish Party on the Prague Municipality, to take issue with the questionnaire.[32] In a pamphlet entitled "Ethics or Opportunism" Friedmann availed himself of Weiner's own article openly refuting the aims of the Czech-Jewish movement, to say: "They do not grasp that their work is counterproductive" and that their aspirations to bring about "a complete assimilation with the Czech nation are futile." It is noteworthy that Richard Weiner made the following scathing remark about the alienation process of Czech Jews—"they bore their Czechness with joy and their Jewishness as a bitter drop in it."[33]

Numerically the Orthodox constituted the weakest group within Czech Jewry. After World War I, following the influx of Orthodox Jews from neighboring Poland, their ranks in some of the provincial Moravian communities were reinforced.[34] While there was a vibrant Jewish religious life including social and educational activities in most of the Moravian communities, religious life in Bohemia, in contrast, centered on communal institutions. There were, however, a few old, established families who played an important role in public and social life, among them the Liebens. Dr. Salomon Hugo Lieben was a leading scholar of Jewish history and founder of the Jewish Museum in Prague (1906). His cousin, also named Dr. Salomon Lieben, was a well-known Prague physician who played a key role in community affairs, participating in the Jewish National Council and representing Orthodox Jews on the board of the Prague community and in other social and welfare organizations. Karel Čapek modeled his protagonist Dr. Gallen, the idealist and man of conviction in the anti-Nazi play *The White Plague*, on Lieben's exemplary figure.[35]

THE STATUS OF THE JEWISH COMMUNITY

Owing to historical developments the legal status of the Jewish religious communities of Czechoslovakia was governed by two separate codes: Bohemia, Moravia, and Silesia (the hereditary lands of the Bohemian Crown under Habsburg rule, henceforth referred to as the historic lands) had taken over the old Austrian code of 1890, while Slovakia and Subcarpathian Ruthenia carried on according to the rules of legislation enacted by Hungary in 1870. Thus the administrative structure in the historic lands remained basically unchanged; the right to levy taxes and collect fees was maintained. The main function of the community was "to provide for the religious needs and support the institutions needed for the purpose."[36]

After 1918 there were three federations of communities representing: (1) Greater Prague, České Budějovice and Plzeň; (2) the Czech speaking communities; and (3) the German-speaking communities. For some years the situation remained complicated due to language problems that prevented the creation of one unified association for all Bohemia. It was only in 1926 that together with the Federation of Communities in Moravia and Silesia a joint Supreme Council of the Federations of Jewish Religious Communities in Bohemia, Moravia, and Silesia (Nejvyšší rada svazu náboženských obcí židovských v Čechách, na Moravě a ve Slezsku) was established.[37] It was first headed by Dr. Augustin Stein of the Czech-Jewish movement and later (1931) by Dr. Joseph Popper, followed by Dr. Maxim Reiner (1934).

One of the shortcomings of the Supreme Council stemmed from the fact that the provincial delegates on its governing bodies functioned according to the rules and interests of their parties, often paralyzing the council's workings.

Although the study of Jewish history, literature, and religion was steadily losing ground, the Supreme Council could claim some notable achievements: it was instrumental in establishing the Jewish Museum in the ancient community of Mikulov, in sponsoring publications on the history of some of the communities, in translating the Pentateuch into Czech (by Rabbis Dr. Isidor Hirsch and Dr. Gustav Sicher), and in establishing at Charles University of Prague a chair for Semitic philology, including modern Hebrew, headed by Dr. Rudolf Růžička.[38]

The resolution adopted in 1928 by the Supreme Council viewed the enormous cultural undertaking of translating into Czech the paramount treasure of the Jewish people as a felicitous gift to mark the tenth anniversary of the establishment of the republic. The hope was expressed that "a revival of the Five Books of Moses in the Czech language will not remain without influence on mutual relations of the Czech nation and Jewry."

However one of its major demands, namely for a legally recognized "unified association" for all Jewish congregants in Bohemia, Moravia, and Silesia, and facilities for providing the congregations with rabbis and religious instructors, failed utterly. How crucial this issue was can be understood from the report of the Supreme Council in 1934, which revealed that nearly half of the congregations in Moravia and Silesia were without rabbis. In the rural congregations of Bohemia the situation was even worse. The 1935 report included the following passage on the state of religious education: "It is almost impossible for individual congregations to provide adequate religious instruction for their young people, due to the lack of qualified and devoted instructors, huge gaps in textbook coverage, lack of uniformity among curricula and schedules, indifference on the part of parents, and blunt interference by the government, particularly with respect to the number of teaching hours to be devoted to this subject . . . The training of teachers of religion, particularly in the secondary schools, cannot be organized without the establishment of a seminary for rabbis and teachers of religion."[39]

The effort to bring about the establishment of a rabbinical seminary dragged on until 1937. Finally, when permission was given by the authorities and funds were procured for its maintenance, the political situation—the Munich crisis—forestalled the opening of this institution.[40]

The Supplement to the Law of the Organization of the Jewish Religious Community came up for final debate in Parliament on January 21, 1937, and was presented by Deputy Dr. Angelo Goldstein with an in-depth survey of the situation of the Jews in the historic lands and of the community's organizational structure.[41] The report analyzed Jewish population mobility over the previous half century, showing a steady and rapid decrease in Bohemia's Jewish population of almost 40 percent within the preceding forty years; the proportion of Jews in the total population had diminished even more rapidly—from 1.66 to 1 percent.

An important role in the life of the community was played by the B'nai B'rith Lodge and several other fraternal orders with spiritual, moral, and philanthropic objectives, which had functioned since the last quarter of the nineteenth century.[42] After the founding of the republic these became active in community and public life as well. The most significant period was the last chapter under the chairmanship of Dr. Joseph Popper, who officiated for twenty-nine years. For some time he also served, along with a number of distinguished associates, as president of the Supreme Council of the Federations of Jewish Religious Communities. The social projects of B'nai B'rith included aid to homes for the aged, a school for the mentally retarded, public soup kitchens, centers for students, hostels for apprentices, and orphanages.

The outstanding accomplishment of the Prague lodges was the founding in 1928 of the Society for the History of the Jews in the Czechoslovak Republic, under the guidance of Professor Samuel Steinherz of Charles University. Within a single decade (1929–38) nine volumes of the yearbook *Jahrbuch der Gesellschaft für die Geschichte der Juden in der Čechoslovakischen Republik* were published under Steinherz's editorship.[43] The yearbook is of lasting scholarly value and importance. Among its contributors were Josef Bergl, Berthold Bretholz, Oskar Donath, Tobias Jakobovits, Salomon Hugo Lieben, Jaroslav Prokes, Käthe Spiegel, Ruth Kestenberg, and Guido Kisch. These authors succeeded in arousing keen interest in the Jewish past, and in their wake new and popular journals came into being, such as *Zeitschrift für Geschichte der Juden in der Tschechoslowakei* edited by Hugo Gold (Brno) and *Alt-Prager Almanach* edited by Paul Nettl (Prague).[44]

Whether their everyday language was German or Czech, the Jews were convinced liberals, and some of them regarded themselves as Czechs or Germans of the "Mosaic faith." The separation of church and state in the newly created republic, the legalization of civil marriage, and the free choice of religious denomination all worked to the detriment of the Jewish religious establishment. Another factor that facilitated acculturation and amalgamation into the Czech people was the profound change occurring in large segments of the Czech population, many of whom joined the newly formed "Czechoslovak Church" or simply claimed no affiliation to any religion whatsoever (*bez vyznání*). Some of the secularized Jews did the same, and it was for this reason, as well as due to their very low birth rate, that the Jewish population in the historic lands decreased; by 1930 there were 76,301 Jews in Bohemia and 41,250 in Moravia and Silesia.[45]

The number of congregations in Bohemia fell at this period to 150. Another phenomenon marking the First Republic was the growing number of mixed marriages—one of the highest proportions existing in interwar Europe. In 1927 this rose to 24.3 percent and in 1933 it reached 30.73 percent (22.1 percent involved male and 25.25 percent female partners).[46] Further inroads were made by conversion. Between January 1, 1938, and July 1, 1938, in Prague alone, 314 Jews converted to Christianity, while a total of 1,130 resigned their membership in the Jewish community.[47]

ECONOMY, OCCUPATIONS, AND THE CULTURAL ELITE

Throughout the existence of the First Republic, Czechoslovak society was primarily oriented toward industry and agriculture. The greatest share of the former empire's industrial wealth, ranging between 70 and 80 percent—heavy, light, and consumer goods industries—was inherited by Czechoslovakia and was mostly located in the Sudeten German border areas of the country.

The economic activities of the Jews in the Czech lands conformed to the typical Western pattern. In agriculture, one of the most important economic sectors for the non-Jewish population, their proportion was minimal. A significant number of Jews were employed in public service and the professions: 14.8 percent in Bohemia and 14.6 percent in Moravia. About 60 percent of the economically active Jews of Bohemia and Moravia engaged in business, finance, and communications. In Bohemia 22.6 percent engaged in industry and crafts, while in Moravia the figure was 28.5 percent.[48] Of the total capital investment in Czechoslovak industry, 30–40 percent was made by Jews.[49] Firms like Petschek and Weinmann were developing mining in northern Bohemia, while the Gutmann family was associated with the steel industry in Moravská Ostrava. Foreign trade and export industries—textiles, wood and paper, insurance, and private banking—were pioneered by Jews. It was estimated that four-fifths of the glass exporters were Jews.

Later on, the concentration of capital in the national banks, agrarian reform, the development of agricultural and consumers' cooperatives, and the preference given to enterprises set up by Czech Legion veterans tended to limit the extent and importance of Jewish economic activity. The slump of 1929–30 affected many Jewish businessmen, and the number of Jews in industry and commerce declined.

In demographic distribution the Jews of the Czech lands, highly urbanized and grouped mainly in the capital cities, nonetheless constituted only an insignificant percentage within the general population.[50] In Bohemia nearly 50 percent of all Jews (35,463) lived in Prague, with over 25 percent (11,103) residing in the capital city of Brno and 6,865 in Moravská Ostrava, where their number rose steadily following population shifts from the eastern provinces of the republic. These patterns reflect the general socioeconomic situation and had important implications for all aspects of Jewish life in the region.

Remarkable changes occurred in the field of education in general and in that of higher education in particular. A large proportion of Jewish youngsters attended universities and technical colleges. They were joined by many students from neighboring countries who flocked to the Czechoslovak universities and high schools due to the *numerus clausus* in their native countries (Poland, Hungary). For the most part they enrolled in the German University in view of their greater fluency in German. The survey of students for the winter semester of 1929–30 reveals a student body of 30,955 at the various institutions, of whom 2,516 claimed Jewish nationality.[51] Their number was five times greater than their proportion within the population of Czechoslovakia (excluding those Jews who claimed Czech or German nationality). In the 1932–33 school year there were altogether 3,133 Jewish students in Prague, of whom 1,499 studied at Czech institutions, 1,569 at German institutions, and 62 attended other institutions of higher learning. The last statistical survey available for the school year 1935–36 indicates that 11.9 percent of all university students were Jews. According to the report of the Jewish Council for Vocations (Židovská poradna pro volbu povolání), established by the Prague community in 1936, 18 percent of all university students in Czechoslovakia were Jews, while their proportion in the overall population was only 2.5 percent.[52]

Notwithstanding the resentment and often biased approach of certain conservative elements, Jewish academics were appointed professors at the Czech and German universities of Prague and other academic institutions; they made careers in all walks of life and reached high positions in political life, trade unions, and public institutions.[53] There were four ministers of Jewish origin in the various governments of the republic.[54] Among the individuals attaining leading positions in political parties were Adolf Stránský (National Democrat), Alfred Meissner and Lev Winter (Czechoslovak Social Democrats), and Ludwig Czech and Siegfried Taub (German Social Democrats). Stránský, Meissner, Czech, and Winter served as ministers in the various government coalitions. All of them held distinguished positions aside from their public careers.

Dr. Adolf Stránský (1860–1932), who had been a member of the Austrian Parliament for many years, was the man who took over the administration of the province of Moravia from the last Habsburg *Statthalter*.[55] He became Czechoslovakia's first minister of commerce. In November 1918 and from 1920 until his death, he represented the National Democrats as a member of the Senate. Aside from his political appointments he exerted great influence as the founder and proprietor of the Brno *Lidové noviny*. The paper was taken over by his son Jaroslav Stránský (1884–1973), professor of penal law at Masaryk University in Brno. During the war he acted as minister of justice in Beneš's Government-in-Exile and in 1945-48 as deputy premier, minister of justice, and minister of education.

A foremost political figure in the Czechoslovak Social Democratic Party was the lawyer Dr. Alfred Meissner (1871–1952), who had already served as a member of the Revolutionary National Assembly (1918–20) and was one of the main authors of the country's democratic constitution of 1920.[56] He was regularly reelected to Parliament and was a member until 1939. He also served as minister of justice and was instrumental in modernizing and humanizing many aspects of the legal system. In 1934 he took over the Ministry of Social Welfare for one year.

Dr. Ludwig Czech (1870–1942), a Brno attorney, had been the leading representative of the German Socialist movement in Moravia since the beginning of the century.[57] After 1918 he was among the founders of the German Social Democrats in Bohemia, Moravia, and Silesia; in 1919 he was elected chairman and in 1920 leader of the party. He held this office for eighteen years. In 1929 Dr. Czech took over the Ministry of Social Welfare, later the Ministry of Public Works, and subsequently the Ministry of Health. Throughout these years he kept striving for understanding between Czechs and Germans. He perished in 1942 in Terezín.

Particularly prominent were the three brothers of the Winter family. Dr. Lev Winter (1876–1935) served as the country's first minister of social welfare after World War I, from 1918 to 1920.[58] A member of Parliament until his death, he gained recognition through acting as party spokesman at international conferences and for his personal contribution in shaping the social policy of the country. His younger brother Dr. Gustav Winter (1889-1943), a brilliant journalist, served in Paris as Social Democratic Party representative on the Executive Committee of the Labor and Socialist International.[59] He authored many books and was a leading expert on France. (His last book dealt with the French

Collapse of 1940.) Arnošt Winter, youngest of the three and a high-ranking railway official, was also a member of the Czechoslovak Senate from 1935 to 1939 and specialized in questions of foreign policy.[60]

Another member of the Senate for the whole span of the republic was Dr. Zikmund Witt, an attorney from Moravská Ostrava. Robert Klein represented the Czechoslovak Trade Union Movement in the International Federation as secretary of the union's white collar workers and was a member of Parliament between 1920 and 1939, exerting considerable influence in issues of labor legislation.[61]

One of the most remarkable careers was that of Julius Firt (1897-1979), a notable Czech publisher, an intimate friend of the Čapek brothers and other prominent writers, and a member of the literary "Friday Circle."[62] An important role in journalism was played by several experts on the national economy, columnists and analysts such as Josef Münzer-Penížek (1858–1932), an editor, writer, and columnist highly respected for his commentaries in the daily *Národní listy*. Another well-known economist was Gustav Stern of the Prague daily *Tribuna*, who published two leading weeklies, *Economic Archives* and *Der Neue Weg*, as well as the *Osteuropäischer Volkswirt*.

One realizes that a great number of outstanding literati, whether writing in Czech or German, made their living as journalists for leading daily newspapers and periodicals. Their talent and quality of work contributed greatly to the high standard of the Czech and German press in the First Republic, each in his own category.

Richard Weiner (1884–1937), throughout his career the Paris correspondent of *Lidové noviny*, revealed rare sensitivity in his poetry and prose "full of hidden irony and ambiguity" and bearing considerable resemblance to Proust and Franz Kafka. Only recently has his work been given more deserving appraisal.[63]

Karel Poláček (1892–1944), the humorist, was associated with *Tribuna* and *Lidové noviny*; for many years he served as court reporter and also contributed to various magazines. His Jewish heroes set against the backdrop of provincial cities were "real characters." Poláček wielded his wry humor to ridicule poor taste and hypocrisy. Some of his best novels were reprinted in numerous editions and made into motion pictures.

Egon Erwin Kisch (1885–1948), a scion of the established Prague Kisch family, was known as "the Raging Reporter" after the title of his successful book; he worked for the *Prager Tagblatt* and *Bohemia*. He engaged in political criticism as a Communist and social reformer, putting his literary talents at the service of society. Kisch's reportage and books were translated into many languages: his travelogues on America, China, and Mexico and his unique stories on the underworld of his native city Prague brought him international fame.

Max Brod (1884–1968), novelist, composer, dramatist, and philosopher, worked for many years for the *Prager Tagblatt* as music and theater critic. Throughout his life he acted as a cultural intermediary, doing his utmost to assist others and promote new talents, helping several of his countrymen (Janáček, Hašek, and Weinberger) to attain international fame. Brod was the first to recognize Hašek's stature as a humorist and predicted that he would someday be viewed "on a level with Cervantes and Rabelais."[64] Above all he gained world acclaim by saving the manuscripts of his intimate friend Franz Kafka for posterity.

Ernst Rychnowský (1879–1934) worked for the *Prager Tagblatt* first as music critic and later as diplomatic correspondent. He was an expert on Czech music, publishing a biography of Smetana (in German), and he authored several studies on T. G. Masaryk, editing the jubilee volume *Masaryk and the Jews* on the occasion of the president's eightieth birthday.

Alfred Fuchs (1892–1941), whose literary career reflects his personal transformation, started out as a Zionist journalist and a devout Jew, later joined the Czech assimilationist movement, and ultimately embraced Catholicism. He was chairman of the Kapper Society, frequently contributing to *Rozvoj*. As of 1921 he worked on the praesidium of the Ministerial Council in the press section, editing *Revue quotidienne de la Presse Tchechoslovaque* and later also the *Prager Abendblatt*. Much of his literary work is devoted to the Church, papal politics, encyclical letters, Christian saints, and biographical novels. At the same time he engaged in the study and translation of biblical texts, psalms, liturgy, and poetry. He perished in the concentration camp of Dachau in 1941.

MAJOR CZECH–JEWISH LITERARY FIGURES

Already in the early twenties German-Jewish culture in the Czech lands was on the wane, signaling the end of a historical process. The Czech-Jewish-oriented writers were, at the same time, gaining ascendancy along with a nucleus of the first generation of Jewish literati who, imbued with national aspirations, rallied around the Zionist *Selbstwehr*, *Židovské zprávy*, and other newspapers.[65]

The pattern of relationships between Czechs and Jews changed considerably; having achieved statehood, the Czech cultural elite came to view the Jewish entity with more sensitive perception, tending to mutual cooperation and understanding. An illustrative example is the honest evaluation by Arne Novák, the leading literary historian of Charles University. In his *Concise History of Czech Literature* Novák claims that even before Siegfried Kapper entered the Czech literature scene, several German-Jewish writers of Prague (Uffe Horn, Mauritz Hartmann, Alfred Meissner, and Georg Karl Herloszsohn) had made a solid contribution to its development. As a predilection, they chose themes from the Reformation period, the glorious figures of Hus and Žižka. Thus, it was through their novel approach in writing, permeated with liberal and democratic spirit, Novák stresses, that the idea of the Czech national movement became widely known to the outside world.

A great contribution in exploring Czech-Jewish ties in modern times was made by Oskar Donath in his standard monograph *Jews and Judaism in Nineteenth- and Twentieth-Century Czech Literature*. Coming to grips with the negative attitudes and anti-Jewish sentiments projected in the past by the overwhelming majority of Czech writers on both the national and social levels, Donath opened up new vistas of criticism in evaluating the role of Jewish writers in modern Czech literature. Many years later it was Pavel Eisner (1889–1958) who devoted his erudition to assessing the contribution of Jewish literati, writing in both German and Czech, to the development of Czech literature.

Notwithstanding their small number (only 1 percent of the total population of Bohemia and Moravia), Jews can claim an unprecedented role in art, music, theater, and the sciences during the interwar years in addition to their roles in literature and journalism. In the gallery of leading figures of Masaryk's Republic, Otokar Fischer (1883–1938), František Langer (1888–1965) and Egon Hostovský (1908–73) take pride of place. The most important among them was doubtless Fischer—poet, playwright, translator, theater critic, professor of German literature at Charles University, and director of the Drama Division of the National Theater.[66]

Fischer, a true adherent of the Czech-Jewish movement and striving for complete amalgamation, assimilated to the point of being baptized. Nevertheless, throughout his lifetime he had felt tortured over "not fully belonging" and not being able to disassociate himself from his ethnic roots. Finally in his fortieth year Fischer came to terms with his origin, mainly under the impact of the literary legacy of his "spiritual brother," Heinrich Heine (his two-volume monograph on Heine was published in 1922–24).[67] Fischer's distress over not being fully accepted by the Czechs and the estrangement from his own nation are expressed in his poem "To the Roots": "I am one of them, and yet less and more. I am chosen and both old and young. Only a newcomer, a guest, a half-breed. So different from those whose song I sing. A renegade from those whose blood I have, am cursed but happy too."[68]

A month before his death on March 12, 1938, Otokar Fischer's last collection of literary-historical essays made its appearance in a volume entitled *Slovo a svět*

(The word and the world), in which he included a chapter on "Jews and Literature" relating to his Jewish past, to the "Promised Land," and to perennial Jewish values. It seems that in the crucial days of European twilight he sought solace in his ancient heritage.[69] However, the predominant component of his ego, he claimed, remained his Czechness, emanating from his profound affection for his mother tongue—the Czech language. Fischer was posthumously granted the supreme accolade: his enormous merits in enriching Czech cultural life through his theoretical works, literary criticism, and studies of German classics (Goethe, Kleist, and Nietzsche, to name the most important) are widely acclaimed to this day.[70]

Pavel Eisner, eulogizing "The Guest Otokar Fischer" upon his untimely death, analyzed Fischer's search for identity and his alienation complex, expressing certain reservations about his oversensitivity and the fact that he considered himself *exsul patria*—a guest and stranger—in the last years of his life. Eisner concluded his obituary with the following assessment: "There never lived amongst the Czechs a Jew who gave his host nation as much as this guest has given."[71]

While Fischer's fame spread primarily within academic circles, František Langer's popularity rested on wider strata of readership, encompassing the very young. Langer was a playwright, novelist, and physician who served with the Czech Legions during World War I and held the rank of general as head of the Army Medical Corps during World War II. He had acted for many years as president of the Czechoslovak P.E.N. club, an international literary club of prominent playwrights, poets, essayists, and novelists; in 1947 the title of "National Artist" was bestowed upon him.

Next to Karel Čapek, Langer was the only writer widely known outside his country in his own time. His best plays—"Outskirts" (1925), "Grand Hotel Nevada" (1927), and "The Camel through the Needle's Eye" (1929), translated into many languages and produced in Max Reinhardt's stage versions—were internationally acclaimed. As a leading figure of the Masaryk Friday Circle (*Pátečníci*), he was deeply influenced by the president-philosopher's humanistic ideas.[72]

Langer was regarded as the most acculturated man of letters of the republic, viewing his Jewish origin as his sole link with Judaism. At the age of eighteen he made his literary debut with the play "St. Wenceslas." His later writing is equally devoid of Jewish themes with the exception of a single character in his "Philatelistic Series"—pan Popper—a beggar (*Schnorrer*), an eternal misfit and loser. Langer's outlook would not have been considered exceptional in the prevailing climate had not his younger brother Jiří (Mordechai) Langer, author of the now famous *The Nine Gates to Chassidic Mysteries*, adopted a diametrically opposed life path.[73] Jiří, a product of the same half-assimilated Czech-Jewish family, "lukewarm in the practice of religion," joined the Hasidic movement in his early youth, becoming a devout Orthodox Jew.

In his foreword to the English edition of *The Nine Gates*, published in the United States in 1961, František Langer dwells on his ancestral heritage. The great master of words recounts how each generation of his forebears dropped some of the symbolic rituals of the Jewish creed, gradually merging with Czech urban society. The phenomenon of his brother's joining the Hasidic movement on the eve of World War I, journeying "two, or even five centuries back in time," came as a shock to his circle.[74] Jiří adopted the (Galician) Belz Hasidic attire, gait, and customs, which made him a laughingstock in the streets of enlightened Prague, greatly embarrassing the whole family with whom he lived under one roof. (After the Nazis occupied Czechoslovakia Jiří Langer fled to Palestine and died in Tel Aviv in 1943.)[75]

One should realize that František Langer wrote these reminiscences after the traumatic years of the Second World War, the Holocaust, and the political changes that took place in Czechoslovakia (the Communist takeover in 1948 and the notorious Slánský trials in 1952), while his son was languishing in a Communist prison. All these events *ipso facto* radically changed his outlook.[76] He gave vent to his inner grief at the martyrdom of Hasidic settlements, barbarously wiped out by Hitler's cohorts. Langer died a year later, in 1965.[77]

Egon Hostovský (1908–73) is perhaps the most typical representative of Czech-Jewish writers of this generation: "the poet of the young." He was considered to be one of the most translated Czech authors and was published in twenty languages. Early on Hostovský joined the Czech intellectual avant-garde, befriending writers and poets, among them Záviš Kalandra, Ivan Olbracht, and František Halas.[78] He was one of the regulars convening at Café Arco, the popular meeting place of Jewish writers. At eighteen he published his first book, *Zavřené dveře* (The closed door, 1926), followed almost annually by some new work.[79]

In the early thirties Hostovský became a member of the Kapper Society and for a number of years edited *Kalendář česko-židovský* (the Czech-Jewish calendar). For some time he came under the spell of Hasidic motifs, legends, and folklore and was closely associated with Jiří Langer.[80] In 1937 he joined the staff of the Czechoslovak Ministry of Foreign Affairs and later served as a diplomat in Belgium, France, and Portugal. (Up until the end of the Second World War he worked on the staff of the consulate in New York.)

The tragic days of the Munich crisis and the demoralization that ensued left deep scars on his soul. The phenomenon of the pariah gained wider scope as he himself became an émigré: the fate of the Jew projecting on the fate of humanity. His most famous books are *Letters from Exile* (1942), *The Hideout* (1943), *Room Wanted* (1946), *Missing* (1948), *Midnight Patient* (1951), made into a film in Hollywood, and *The Plot* (1961).[81] The Communist coup in 1948 found Hostovský as chargé d'affaires in Oslo. A year later he resigned from his post and until his death lived in exile in the United States. In his last novel *Three Nights* (1964) he reflected upon his past, analyzing the bleak atmosphere of the fifties.

The lives and deaths of the two most admired and outstanding Czech-Jewish poets, Hanuš Bonn (1913–41) and Jiří Orten (1919–41) perpetuate most symbolically the end of an era and the tragic fate of Czech Jewry.[82]

THE IMPACT OF FASCISM AND NAZI IDEOLOGIES

It is generally held that Czech fascism was weak, "lacking roots and *raison d'être*," and that anti-Jewish sentiments in public life were on the whole marginal.[83] This indeed holds true in comparison with the neighboring East European countries (Poland, Rumania, and Hungary), with their massive nationalist movements and vociferous fascist and anti-Semitic political groups. The general atmosphere in Czechoslovakia was outwardly liberal and calm; several anti-Semitic outbursts nonetheless occurred in the twenties at the Prague German University, incited by *völkisch* nationalist students, as did other incidents, like the plastering of signs on Jewish shops, organized by extreme rightist elements.

The first organized anti-Jewish disturbances occurred as early as 1922 when Professor Samuel Steinherz was elected rector of the German University of Prague.[84] This protest "against the judaizing (*Verjudung*) of the German University" was frustrated by the Czechoslovak minister of education, Rudolf Bechyně, a Czech Social Democrat who gave his full support to the new rector. Steinherz resigned at the end of his term of office. From then on he devoted his life to research regarding Bohemian Jewry.

Two years later an announcement by the University Senate on June 23, 1924, designed to limit the rights of Jewish students and to reduce their number, provoked reactions of protest.[85] The Central Federation of Jewish University Students and its affiliated fraternities presented a memorandum to the Senate and to the Students' Council of the German University of Prague, protesting against the ruling by which "only students who profess German nationality will have the right to vote and to be elected to membership."[86] German students exploited every opportunity to demonstrate against a Jewish presence at the universities.

In Bohemia and Moravia, fascism was associated with the former chief of staff General Rudolf Gajda, whose National Fascist Community (*Národní obec fašistická*) based on the Italian model was constituted as a political party in 1927.[87] Although it drew but a small membership of chauvinist elements, their activities were often in the public eye. (Gajda was later tried, sentenced, and imprisoned for libeling a minor functionary and was expelled from Parliament; so was another politician of the extreme right, Jiří Stříbrný, a former government minister, who was indicted on a charge of corruption.)

In retrospect it can be established that as of the late twenties there was a constant stream of abusive literature as well as articles in the daily press. A whole range of books and pamphlets appeared during 1926–27 deriding Jewish traditions and rituals, obviously inspired by fascist ideology. The most clearly provocative example was the rhymed anti-Jewish pamphlet of Karel Relink, which appeared in 1927.[88]

The various Jewish institutions including the Czech-Jewish movement were kept busy protesting against the dissemination of this literature. Thus, for instance, the distribution of a book entitled *Židovstvo* (Jewry, authored by F. L. Eisner) was banned upon the decision of the district authorities of České Budějovice in the wake of Jewish intervention.[89] Right-wing journalists of diverse hues exploited every possible occasion to slander the Jewish entity, focusing mainly on the Jewry of Subcarpathian Ruthenia, spreading tales about their poisoning the local populace by means of alcoholism. The Czechoslovak Red Cross, which actively participated in the welfare program in that area, joined in the campaign of defamation.[90]

In the thirties Nazi propaganda orchestrated from Berlin was reinforced: in 1931 disturbances took place at the Bratislava Komenský University and the German University of Prague, instigated by *volksdeutsche* students. At the same time, similar riots occurred in Budapest and Vienna. Refugees reaching Czechoslovakia from Nazi Germany were met with open protests by rightist circles.[91] Events such as the signing of the Czechoslovak-Soviet treaty of mutual assistance (May 2, 1935), the promulgation of the Nuremberg Laws in Germany, and the victory of the Sudeten German Party were accompanied by a host of anti-Jewish pamphlets published in Czech and German and widely distributed throughout the country. In the rightist papers agitation began against what was termed "Judeo-Bolshevism."

The continuing anti-Semitic campaign was challenged by some of the foremost spokesmen of the Czech intelligentsia and liberal journalists, who viewed the increase of Nazi propaganda with growing concern. F. X. Šalda saw the writing on the wall as early as 1935.[92] As a professor of the history of modern literature and a literary critic—a pupil of Ruskin, Taine, Hennequin, and

Croce—he was the first to pay close attention to the social function of literature and art and to the issue of nationality. His sense of justice and human compassion is projected in a short story entitled "Blazes" (*Požáry*), which sounds a prophetic note.[93] Against the background of World War I and raging famine, he portrays the frantic mob in its desperation seeking a scapegoat. The choice falls upon the Jews of the village. To slake their lust the crowd hurls a wretched Jewish child into the flames. Šalda was among the first to reach out a hand to the anti-Nazi refugees arriving in Czechoslovakia in 1933.[94]

CZECHOSLOVAK TIES WITH THE YISHUV IN PALESTINE

In spite of anti-Semitic overtones in the rightist press and in literature, the late twenties also witnessed positive trends in the life of the Jewish entity in Czechoslovakia. Several Jewish public institutions were set up and the year 1926 marked the beginning of closer relations with the Yishuv in Mandatory Palestine, following the opening of the Czechoslovak Consulate in Jerusalem. The first consul, lawyer Vladimír Frič, arrived in January 1926 to take up his post, paving the way for mutual commercial contacts with Palestine, which in due course developed into a thriving exchange of goods (citrus and grapes against cotton, glass, textiles, and iron).[95]

Cultural ties with Palestine were reinforced with the introduction of modern Hebrew and literature courses at Charles University of Prague, instructed by Professor Rudolf Růžička, which also included readings from Bialik and Tchernichovsky.[96] On the occasion of the twentieth anniversary of *Selbstwehr* František Krejčí, a professor of philosophy known for his staunch support of ethical Zionism, wrote about the significance of Zionism as purifying Jewry from a non-nationalism that only demoralizes private and public life.[97] The inauguration of the Hebrew University in Jerusalem was widely celebrated throughout the country. Speaking at the Brno synagogue on that occasion Arne Novák, a professor of literature and a leading Czech intellectual, traced a parallel between the Czech Revival movement and the striving Jewish national movement.[98] Referring to the impact made on him by Martin Buber and Max Brod, Novák underlined his conviction that faith and nationality, closely interwoven, were the greatest asset a nation may possess.

Funds were raised for a *beit ha'am* (cultural center) to be opened in Prague to house students' dining halls and meeting and reading rooms for the Maccabi and Tchelet Lavan movements.[99] Even before the Oriental Club was established in Prague (1932) many Czech intellectuals, educators, and scholars traveled to Palestine and reported their impressions in the press.

For the first time a stream of tourists (including Dr. Th. Bartošek, Counselor J. F. Beneš, Bohuslav Milič, and V. Mussik) arrived in Palestine, not only visiting the holy places but taking an interest in the new Jewish colonies and the building of the Yishuv.[100] One of the most impressive descriptions was written by geologist J. Petrbok, who visited Palestine three times during 1925–26.[101] In 1925 he even spent an extended period at Kibbutz Beit Alpha, whence he launched geological excursions. Although his main interest lay in palaeological and archaeological finds, in his travelogue *Trampem od Nilu až k Jordánu* he wrote of the colonies in the Jezreel Valley, of the continuous struggle of the settlers, and of feuding between the Jewish colonists and the Arab intruders from the surrounding villages. He described various types of colonies (*Kvutza*, *Gdud Ha'Avoda*), highlighting the care of the children and the modern teaching methods; "Zionist Palestine is a paradise for children."[102]

President Masaryk also lent the weight of his own personal prestige to the Zionist endeavor in 1927; accompanied by his daughter Alice Masaryková, he paid a visit to the Yishuv of Palestine, the first statesman to do so. His visit was closely followed by the local press and commented upon in great detail. The Zionist press saluted this event jubilantly, expressing the hope that Masaryk would see for himself that he was giving moral support to a worthy and hopeful cause: "He will see Jewish agricultural settlement and the Jewish laborers and on the streets and in the schools he will hear the sound of the revived Hebrew language and he will encounter the new Jewish generation."[103]

The Czech press also reported daily on T. G. Masaryk's visits to various points, singling out Beit Alpha and Sarid, established by the first Czechoslovak immigrants.[104] Special significance was given to his arrival in Jerusalem on Friday morning, April 8, where he was greeted by Colonial Secretary Sir Mark Sykes and Mayor Ragheb Bey Nashashibi.[105] On Sunday afternoon, Chief Rabbi Kook held a reception in his honor at the Churva Synagogue, and later that evening he was hosted by Rabbi Sonnenschein and the Slovak-Jewish colony in Jerusalem, numbering around three thousand, half of whom resided in Mea Shearim.

Jews greeted Masaryk throughout the country with posters saying "We welcome you to our country with feelings of love and reverence." The president, while observing with admiration how much had been achieved, revealed his highly realistic approach. How thoroughly Masaryk grasped the problems facing the Yishuv is evident from the questions he posed to his hosts during a visit to Beit Alpha.

Time and again Masaryk asked about the statistics of the birth and death rates of children, the increase in the Jewish population, and contrasted it with that of the Arabs . . . Masaryk looked on the entire idea [of a national home] with favor. He understood what it would mean to world Jewry to have a strong Jewish nation in Palestine, if it were constructed upon sound economic grounds and upon the principles of work and productivity . . . At the same time he realized the difficulties that lay in the construction of a Jewish community, especially the political aspect of living together with the Arabs, whose nationalism grows stronger daily in Palestine and the neighboring countries.[106]

Masaryk granted a special interview on his trip to Palestine to the correspondent of the *Prager Tagblatt*, in which he envisaged difficulties of a demographic nature, expressing his fear that the Jews "will hardly ever achieve a majority in numbers in the land. It will be almost impossible to surpass the numerical growth of the Arabs."[107]

In retrospect it can be asserted that Czechoslovakia's concessions to Jewish nationalism were unprecedented. The influence and personality of the president-philosopher T. G. Masaryk had enormous impact on the outlook of the younger generation and on the development of a new relationship between Czechs and Jews. Both Masaryk's and Beneš's interest in Jewish nationalism and Jewish cultural renewal were more persuasive than the Czech-Jewish assimilationist trend. One of the outward signs of this approach was Czechoslovakia's hosting some of the most important Zionist Congresses: in 1921 and 1923 in Karlovy Vary and 1933 in Prague. In fact the Czech-Jewish movement, in total contrast to its own line, was faced with the paradox of an independent Czechoslovakia supporting separate Jewish national development.

From the late twenties rapprochement between Czechs and Jews, especially among the elite, was on the rise. The integration of Jews into Czech society went hand in hand with acculturation, especially in higher intellectual circles. Jewish writers, artists, and musicians as individuals were fully accepted on ideological or artistic grounds. This close professional interaction generated social contacts resulting in intermarriage, which rose to the highest proportion existing in Europe.

Some years later George Kennan made the following astute remark on this phenomenon of Czech-Jewish relationships: "The Czech claim that they have had no difficulty with the Jews because they have been able to hold their own with them in a commercial, professional, and social way. The Czech intelligentsia, and the wealthy land-owning society, furthermore are very extensively bound up with Jewish society through intermarriage. It is constantly being reported with respect to nearly everyone of the present leaders that he has Jewish blood or is related to Jews."[108]

Nevertheless Czech anti-Semitism, albeit lacking the pronounced racial element prevalent in the surrounding countries, in effect still existed, primarily in the socioeconomic realm. It surfaced variably, provoked suddenly by some unexpected event but then eagerly taken up by the rightist press.

In 1931 F. X. Šalda, outraged both by a court ruling exonerating Corporal Horák—charged with the murder of a Jewish family in Slovakia during the turbulent period of the takeover (1918)—and by the repercussions that appeared in the press, made this profound observation about Czech anti-Semitism: "A strange phenomenon—we do not have in our country a political party, be it ever so small, having anti-Semitism, racial hatred or antagonism as part of its platform. This is often referred to as our great political advantage over other countries. Our republic is regarded in Central Europe as outspokenly philo-Semitic. There must thus exist in the depths of the soul of our people a kind of hatred toward Jews, which bursts out at the opportune moment and casts its shadow over the issue as clearly as two and two are four. What terrifies me most is its latent nature gnawing at the very roots of the national character."[109]

THE ADVENT OF NAZISM

Hitler's rise to power in Germany in January 1933 had far-reaching repercussions in Czechoslovakia, first among the German minority but also among the Slovak autonomists and the Ruthenian and Hungarian nationalists in the eastern provinces. The most burning issue became that of the Sudeten German nationals who, exposed to the German propaganda machine, turned to irredentism. The 3 million Germans (23.32 percent of the population), the largest *Volksdeutsche* community in any non-German state, imbued with racist and nationalist intensity, were from the onset indignant over their status as a minority in the republic. However, it should be borne in mind that in the parliamentary elections of 1920, 1925, and 1929 the moderate German parties, the "activists," were ready to collaborate within the framework of the republic.[110]

Czechoslovakia was the only country on the continent of Europe in which a national minority was represented in the government. As of 1926 Franz Spina, leader of the German Agrarians, and Robert Mayr-Harting, leader of the Christian Socialists, served as ministers (of public works and of justice). In 1929 Ludwig Czech, a Social Democrat, became the chief of the Ministry of Social Welfare. An aspect of national policy that was criticized was the fact that Germans, Hungarians, and Poles were not represented in the civil service according to their numerical strength in the country.

It should be also remembered that the Jewish intellectuals representing the

German Socialist movement included the elite of progressive-minded personalities excelling in all walks of life, men of the caliber of Ludwig Czech, Siegfried Taub, Dr. Ludwig Spiegel, and others.[111]

Fascism appealed to certain Slovak circles and Ruthenians as well. The extreme autonomous group, especially, looked admiringly upon the "dynamic" totalitarian regimes, dissatisfied as they were over the question of Slovak autonomy (implied in the Czecho–Slovak Agreement of Pittsburgh, May 30, 1918) and the friction existing between themselves and the centralist Czechoslovak government. Throughout the years Slovak centralists and autonomists engaged in ardent polemics over the issue of "one nation or two," often with the aid of elaborate historical and philosophical arguments concerning the spelling of Czechoslovakia with a hyphen or without; the autonomists, stressing Slovak distinctiveness, favored the hyphenated version. Encouraged by events in Germany, on August 13, 1933, Andrej Hlinka, head of the Slovak People's Party, and his populist followers turned the celebration of the eleven hundredth anniversary of the first Christian church at Pribina-Nitra into a wild antigovernment demonstration.[112] This and other nationalist manifestations were accompanied by anti-Semitic overtones in the Slovak press.

Under the impact of Hitler's ascent to power the great majority of the Jews who had culturally and politically supported the German parties shifted their loyalties to the Czechoslovak government. This change became clearly evident in the editorial policies of Prague's two chief German-language newspapers, *Prager Tagblatt* and *Bohemia*, which began openly criticizing events in Germany.[113]

The radical transformation in Germany's policy posed serious problems for the German minister in Prague, Dr. Walter Koch, who firmly supported Sudeten German activists cooperating with the Czechoslovak authorities, among whom were Jewish parliamentarians for whom he had the highest regard. It is most instructive to read Koch's report sent from Prague in May 1933 in response to Berlin's enquiry about the Czechs' attitude toward the Jews:

> There is no discrimination against Jews in Czechoslovakia, either in civil service careers or in the sphere of society, economy, or anywhere else, not even in sports. Such steps would be contrary to the tendencies of President Masaryk, who has always acted as an outspoken friend of Jewry . . . who counted and still counts . . . Jews . . . among his best friends. Jews in Czechoslovakia are not only professors at Czech and German universities but in many cases high state officials . . . headmasters or teachers at grammar schools, etc. The most important Czech club, the Společenský klub, accepts Jewish members without hesitation; Jews are likewise recognized as equals in

sport clubs. In view of these facts it does not seem possible to me, when refuting attacks on measures taken in Germany, to point out similar occurrences in the field of racial policy in Czechoslovakia.[114]

The guiding principles of government policy firmly anchored in the constitution were reflected in Foreign Minister Dr. Beneš's statement of June 1933 in connection with Hitler's anti-Jewish policy: "There is no Jewish question in Czechoslovakia . . . I do not intend to betray the basis of my whole thinking and convictions to a transitional constellation. It is my belief that in Czechoslovakia all nationalities must be fully recognized and protected. No one, and naturally no Jew, declaring himself a member of the German nation—and I underline that—could in our country be persecuted because of this, as long as his allegiance to our state remains beyond doubt."[115]

The upheaval in Germany coincided with the Great Depression; unemployment was rife in the German-inhabited, highly industrialized regions of Czechoslovakia.[116] This factor no doubt helped irredentist pro-Nazi sentiments to surface among the rightist elements in the country.

With the formation of the Sudeten German Party (SDP) Konrad Henlein, until 1933 an obscure Turnverband gymnastics teacher, appeared on the scene. The activities of the newly founded party and the agitation of the right-wing press generated anti-Semitic overtones and tension. At the end of November 1934, extreme Czech nationalist students at Charles University staged noisy demonstrations in Prague, demanding that the law passed in 1920 over the transfer of the ancient insignia held by the German University be enforced and handed over to the Czech University.[117] (Since the days when Prague University had been divided into Czech and German institutions, the insignia had been held by the German University.) The rightists tried to exploit this gathering, channeling it into demonstrations against Masaryk and the leftist parties; German students too joined in, outraged by the rumor of the transfer of the insignia. Each party voiced its own slogans, and the streets echoed: "Germans out of the government!" "Out with the emigrants!" "Out with the Jews!"

Commenting on the riots in the capital, which caused considerable alarm among the public, Karel Čapek ironically remarked: "It would seem that our republic indeed has a spiritual and ideological affinity with the Third Reich, or as if Lueger's legacy from anti-Semitic Vienna is about to be revived . . . A peculiar type of Czech anti-Semitism."[118] He viewed the chauvinistic outbursts of Czech fascist groups as an effort to revive the anti-Semitism of the nineties: "Smashing of windows in Prague to the tune of patriotic songs" seemed a return to narrow-mindedness, to the times of "national provincialism."[119]

In Prague a Jewish Committee for Aid to Refugees from Germany was established in 1934, headed by Dr. Joseph Popper, chairman of the Supreme Council of the Communities and president of the Grand Lodge of the Czechoslovak B'nai B'rith. Among the members of the committee's Executive Board were two valiant women: Marie Schmolka, a noted social worker, and Hanna Steiner, president of the Women's International Zionist Organization (WIZO) in the historic lands.[120] This organization was to play a crucial role in the lives of many Jewish refugees from Germany, Austria, and the Sudetenland. The committee saw as its first objective to procure housing for the refugees and to ensure their sustenance: courses in modern Hebrew were launched for refugees for this purpose.

In March 1935 Dr. Angelo Goldstein addressed the Parliament's Constitutional Committee on the Law Regarding the Residence of Aliens, referring to the plight of the Jewish refugees from Hitler's Germany who were entering Czechoslovakia in ever-increasing numbers—"victims of our times" whose economic insecurity reduced them to despair: many of them upon their enforced return to Germany were taken to concentration camps.[121] He asked the government and the minister of the interior that law-abiding fugitives should be permitted to petition the authorities for residence permits without being subjected to trouble and difficulties and that they be granted right of residence in accordance with the new law. Minister of Interior Josef Černý gave assurances that the authorities would be duly considerate toward those aliens whose political conduct was "irreproachable."

There were also several nonsectarian committees that dealt with refugee problems: the Social Democratic Relief Committee, the Communists' Central Association to Aid Refugees, and the Czech intellectuals' Šalda Committee.[122] The scope and activities of the Jewish aid committee were by far the broadest. As the situation of the Jews of Central Europe deteriorated, Marie Schmolka's manifold functions expanded. The American Joint Distribution Committee (JDC) entrusted her with tasks; the Jewish Colonization Association (ICA) recognized her as the representative of Czech relief work; and HICEM, a composite of the Hebrew Emigration Aid Society (HIAS), ICA, and Emig[ration]-direct, appointed her director of its Prague office. Upon the suggestion of the Czechoslovak Government all these relief committees merged to form a National Coordinating Committee. In July 1936 Marie Schmolka was nominated as its head, to represent Czechoslovakia at a conference of member states at the League of Nations convened by Sir Neil Malcolm. A memorandum submitted on behalf of the Coordinating Committee described the situation of the refugees as well as the regulations concerning residence permits.[123]

The lion's share of the funds for refugee aid in Czechoslovakia came from wealthy individuals and public figures, from religious and relief organizations in England, and from the Quakers in the United States. The Freemasons and even the "Red Help" in Moscow regularly sent donations. Generous sums were donated by President T. G. Masaryk and his successor Eduard Beneš.[124]

People in the first wave of fugitives from Germany fleeing on racial and political grounds were received with open arms both by the authorities and by the population. Because of its geopolitical situation Czechoslovakia became in the thirties host and haven to refugees of all categories who fled from Nazi Germany. Many of these were intellectuals, writers, journalists, and artists who became active in the anti-Nazi campaign. A great part of the Jewish refugees were professionals (lawyers, physicians, etc.), artisans, and businessmen. However, because of the economic situation and unemployment, they were barred from working, which circumstance gradually made their life unbearable.

Due to the constant agitation of the rightist elements (the Agrarians, the Sudeten German Party, and the Nationalist parties) in the daily press as well as the political pressure exerted from Berlin in the years 1935–36, a marked change occurred in the attitude of the authorities: the border police tightened control and created difficulties for fugitives at the frontier checkpoints. Upon the initiative of the Agrarian Party a law was enacted in 1935 curtailing the rights of the fugitives, limiting their sojourn in the country and cutting the allowances accorded to them. Some of the fugitives who were not able to gain entry to other countries were made to return to Germany. Those who stayed behind had to subsist on the meager support given to them on a monthly basis.

A memorandum compiled by the National Coordinating Committee and submitted to the high commissioner for refugees contained statistical information on the situation of the fugitives. Aside from the economic difficulties the Jewish community had to face additional problems: among the emigrants there were sick people and others suffering from undernourishment and depression. The Coordinating Committee was instrumental in transferring thirty-six hundred refugees to other countries.[125]

A report by the Social Institute of the Jewish Religious Congregations of Prague for the years 1936–37 reveals the catastrophic situation of the emigrants and the helplessness of the Jewish organizations in coping with the problem.[126]

The influx of German-speaking refugees prompted representatives of the Czech-Jewish movement to call a meeting of the Prague Jewish organizations to discuss the issue of how to counteract "Germanization" (*němčení*), which was viewed with disdain and which provoked criticism on the part of the Czech population.[127] It was decided to advise the Jewish communities to instruct the rabbis and burial societies that priority be given to the language of the state in sermons and ceremonies. In Prague, Plzeň, České Budějovice, Brno, and Moravská Ostrava fifteen thousand circulars were distributed instructing Jews to this effect.

FACING GERMAN PROPAGANDA AND MILITANCY

The new spirit prevalent in the Reich triggered anti-Semitic outbursts at the medical school of the German University of Prague. In response, two interpellations were made in Parliament on behalf of the Social Democratic Party (Václav Jáša and Eng. Jaromír Nečas) and the Jewish Party (Dr. Angelo Goldstein).[128] One cited the tragic case of Dr. Gach of the Surgical Clinic, whose suicide evoked wide comment in the press; he was both a socialist and of Jewish origin, and for eight and a half years he had been a candidate for appointment, working without a salary. The second cited the opposition of the German University against the nomination of Prof. Dr. Hans Kelsen, an internationally recognized expert in law. There were also grievances of other kinds: it transpired that a whole array of teachers and assistants in the medical school were suspected of anti-state activities. Professor Karl Titz of the philosophy department gave vent to his racial views, making blatantly anti-Semitic remarks.[129]

In response to the promulgation of the infamous Nuremberg Laws in Germany on September 10, 1935, the Jewish Party issued a special proclamation warning that "the provocation of anti-Semitic tendencies threatens to undermine the power of resistance of the countries that are within the reach of this expansionist thirst for power."[130] The proclamation also called upon the Jews to rally around the timeless moral values of Judaism. A protest against the disenfranchisement and defamation of Jews in the German Reich was dispatched to the Assembly of the League of Nations.

The Supreme Council of the Federation of Jewish Religious Communities at its session on September 22, 1935, passed the following resolution in response to the enacting of the Nuremberg Laws in Nazi Germany: "In the name of humanity we call upon the governments of all civilized nations, and as Czechoslovak citizens upon the government and nation of Czechoslovakia, to extend a helping hand to the victims of the German regime within the framework of the League of Nations."[131]

Some interesting observations touching upon the enactment of the Nuremberg Laws are to be found in the recollections of Dr. Nahum Goldmann.

During a meeting at the Hotel Beau Rivage in Geneva the Czechoslovak foreign minister, Dr. Eduard Beneš, was disturbed about the events and reproachfully demanded to know "why the Jews did not react on a grand scale." He thought an international Jewish Congress declaring an "all-out war on the National Socialist Regime" should have been invoked. Dr. Beneš further predicted with profound insight and understanding that "Hitler's example will be contagious and encourage all the anti-Semites throughout the world."[132]

The deteriorating economic situation of large strata of the Jewish population caused much concern. One of the reasons was the ruin of small business and trade as a result of the massive growth of the National Association of Cooperative Stores. The convention of the Jewish Party adopted a resolution dealing with the steadily declining situation of the Jewish population.[133] In order to promote normalization of the economic structure of the community it was decided to set up vocational guidance offices and to seek the support of government institutions for the projected reorientation drive.

The year 1935 constituted a watershed in Czechoslovakia's political life. The victory of Henlein's Sudeten German Party and the election results—15.2 percent of the total vote and 66 percent of the German vote in Czechoslovakia (which meant forty-four seats in the Chamber of Deputies)—reflected the rise of influence and prestige of Nazism within the German ethnic group.[134] The growing menace of Hitler's revisionist policy cast a deep shadow over the future of the state. On November 5 President Masaryk, whose health had deteriorated, decided to retire. He left office on December 14. On December 18, 1935, Beneš succeeded him as president, supported by the Slovak populists, Dr. Milan Hodža became prime minister, and distinguished Czech historian Dr. Karel Krofta became the foreign minister.[135]

The debut of the new president was made in the most difficult and intimidating of circumstances. Beneš realized that the country must be militarily prepared for the gravest emergencies: he ordered the building of fortifications and a thorough rearmament of the Czechoslovak army.

The militancy of Germany and the persistent irredentism of Hungary on the eastern flank affected both foreign and domestic policies in Czechoslovakia. Already in 1920 Beneš had signed the agreement known as the "Little Entente"—a common defense pact of the states threatened by Hungarian irredentism—which in the course of time developed into a league for the defense of the postwar status of Central Europe. The signatories were Czechoslovakia, Yugoslavia, and Rumania. However, the cornerstone of the Czechoslovak system of alliances was a mutual assistance and friendship treaty signed with France in 1924, which was supplemented in May 1935 by a similar treaty with the USSR.[136] The signing of the Czechoslovak-Soviet treaty of mutual assistance (appended to the Franco-Soviet treaty of May 2) augured a change in approach.

It is noteworthy to add that while until 1935 the Communist Party in Czechoslovakia had led a hostile campaign against the "bourgeois" republic, after the signing of the treaty it adopted a stance of fervent Czechoslovak patriotism. Identifying with the anti-fascist forces, the Communists exploited every sign of social unrest for loud demonstrations. The radical right-wing press and clerical circles, mainly in Slovakia, reacted with a spate of articles. In Bratislava there were also demonstrations in the streets during which slogans such as "Judeo-Bolshevism," "Down with Marxism!" and "Jews Out!" were frequently voiced.[137]

During the crucial years Czechoslovak Jewry rallied around the republic more closely than ever before. One of the manifest forms of material support was their readiness to subscribe to the Defense Loan launched in June 1936. The Executive Board of the Jewish Party issued a call to all Jews to subscribe and to participate in the Defense Training Program (*kursy brannosti*) set up in most of the cities. The Supreme Council's subscription of 100,000 Czech crowns was followed by the congregations throughout the country; Jewish institutions and individuals contributed many millions.[138]

A special issue in the press the world over was that of the Olympic Games. In view of Nazi Germany's policy, the possibility was raised of transferring the games to another country. As early as September 18, 1935, the General Secretariat of the Jewish Party appealed to the Prague Sokol organization urging the representatives of Czech sport to take a stand on this issue.[139] The standpoint of the Jews of the country was clear, the appeal said: "Under no circumstances should Jewish sportsmen participate in the Olympic Games in a country that, guided by racial theories, is perpetrating atrocious crimes, first and foremost against the Jewish nation."[140]

The late thirties can be characterized by increased propaganda subsidized by Germany and more vocal agitation of the SDP for autonomy. Henlein's February 23, 1936, speech in Prague, the *Kultur-Rede*, concentrated on "un-German" professors and the greater liberty accorded to the "un-German" newspapers appearing in German.[141] His allusions were well understood. It was obvious that the *Prager Tagblatt* and the other democratic newspapers challenging Nazi Germany were a thorn in the side of the SDP. So were the "un-German" professors. In October 1936 hostile demonstrations again occurred at the German University on the occasion of the inaugural lecture of Professor Kelsen, "tainted both with genuine liberalism and Jewish descent," whose appointment had long been delayed on racial grounds.[142]

Already in 1936, although mainly in ominous 1937, a massive outpouring of Goebbels's propaganda flooded the press and the radio, backed by Polish and Hungarian anti-Czech agitation. Large quantities of anti-Semitic booklets and brochures appeared in book stores and shop windows—literature that for years had been put aside as dubious. Bugs were sneaking out of their holes. In his memoirs Julius Firt commented in the same vein on the morbid symptoms of those days.[143]

A new series of anti-Semitic pamphlets was issued by Jaroslav Slavata entitled Tracts of Young Czechoslovakia (Traktáty mladého Československa).[144] The series included Jan Neruda's famous *Pro strach židů* (For fear of the Jews), originally published in 1869. Neruda castigated the Jews for siding with the Germans and called for emancipation "from the Jews." With appropriate racist comments this publication sold six printings within two years (1935–37).

Slavata's own contribution *Židé a my* (The Jews and ourselves), published in 1937, had a new approach to offer, arguing that the so-called Czech-Jew was a "double renegade: from Judaism to Germandom and from Germandom to Czechdom." Anti-Semitism, according to Slavata, can exist only on a racial basis; it has no meaning otherwise. Other brochures in this series dealt with H. S. Chamberlain's racial theories and with "The Jews in the opinion of great men of all times" (*Židé v názorech mužů všech dob*). Emil Zak discussed the "Jewish question" (*Židovská otázka*) in the light of Catholic dogma in a special tract, stressing the idea that the Jews are the "yeast" of decay in society.

In response to this avalanche of Reich-subsidized propaganda, the Jewish organizations made strenuous efforts to counteract the massive agitation.[145] The League against Anti-Semitism (established in 1933 as a branch of the Paris-based "League International contre l'Antisemitism, LICA) did likewise: meetings, rallies, and lectures were initiated to disseminate information about Judaism and Zionism in order to rehabilitate the Jewish image.[146] The league issued ten thousand brochures entitled *Židé mezi námi* (Jews among us: A talk in our times) written by Pastor Bohumil Vančura. Another publication, *Před zraky národů* (Before the eyes of the nations), told the story of the Slovak-Jewish journalist Stefan Lux, who shot himself at the League of Nations on July 3, 1936, to alert the conscience of the world to the threat of Nazism.

The Czech-Jewish movement for its part launched a campaign to challenge anti-Semitic attacks and to create a better understanding of Judaism. The initiative came from the younger generation, including writers like Hanuš Bonn, Jiří Orten, Egon Hostovský, Zdeněk Thon, and Ervin Neumann. They organized series of lectures and read essays at the Kapper club: "The members of this student organization were concerned with the study of Judaism and not with its liquidation. Their monthly magazine, which first appeared in 1934, engaged in more debates with *Rozvoj*, the official organ of the Czech-Jewish movement, than with the Zionists."[147]

The movement decided to publish in Czech an anthology of works by Yiddish writers and to make available to Czech readers Čeněk Zíbrt's work on the origin and the influence of the Passover Haggadah (*Ohlas obřadních písní velikonočních Haggadah*) and the posthumous edition of Jindřich Kohn's two-volume *Asimilace a věky* (Assimilation and the ages). Steps were taken to augment the movement's activities by coopting prominent figures in Jewish life who could give the general public some knowledge of recent history: a special circle of friends of Czechoslovak legionnaires of Jewish origin was created, headed by Dr. Otakar Guth. Under its aegis a brochure was issued entitled *František Winternitz, Český žid-legionář*, recalling the bravery of this Czech-Jewish volunteer legionnaire during World War I.[148] This publication was distributed to 250 secondary schools with a request to make it available to teachers, pupils, and other readers using the libraries.

From the pen of the erudite Ervin Neumann a study on the contribution of the Jewish spirit in world culture (*Židovský duch ve světové kultuře*) presented the philosophic credo of Jindřich Kohn, designated as Czechdom, humanity, and universalism. Of special note was Jiří Langer's work based on primary Hebrew sources—a popular booklet about the Talmud and its origins, incorporating samples of ancient Jewish wisdom and injunctions and permeated by profound humanistic ideas with allusions to the brutality inherent in Nazi theories.[149] Langer also translated into Czech a selection of old Hebrew poetry—*Písně odsouzených* (Songs of the rejected), giving prominence to the celebrated elegy by Avigdor Kara on the Prague Ghetto massacre (1389)—and published Kara's now famous Hasidic legends, *Devět bran*.

The Zionist Federation of Czechoslovakia published a number of books in an effort to inform the Czech public about the national aims and activity of the Jews: Hans Lichtwitz's history of the Zionist movement (*Dějiny cionistického hnutí*, translated from the German with an introduction by Viktor Fischl; Chaim Weizmann's *Právo na domovinu* (The right to a homeland); and the report placed in 1936 before the Peel Commission in Jerusalem.[150]

The last full year of what was popularly known as Masaryk's republic, 1937, witnessed a number of gracious gestures: František Bílek's statue of Moses was solemnly installed in ancient Prague; a street in the city was named in honor of Justice Louis D. Brandeis of Boston, a Zionist leader of Bohemian extraction; and Professor Louis Eisenmann of the Sorbonne was awarded an honorary doctorate by the Philosophy Faculty of Charles University. Both men were honored in acknowledgement of their invaluable service to the Czech cause during World War I, paving the way for the foundation of the republic.[151]

On March 12, 1937, Prime Minister Milan Hodža received deputies Dr. Goldstein and Dr. Kugel, and Eng. Otto Zucker (deputy chair of the Jewish Party), who set forth the cultural, economic, and social claims of the Jewish minority. The prime minister assured them that all the regulations enacted by the government under the declaration on minority questions of February 18, 1937, applied automatically to the Jewish minority as well.[152]

The year was marked by the death of T. G. Masaryk and a number of major public figures of the older generation (F. Kramář, F. X. Šalda) who had stood by the cradle of the newly established state. It was also the year in which Hitler finally decided to exploit the "grievances" of the Sudeten Germans to dismember the republic and to set into practice his *Drang nach Osten* policy.

The first signal of foreboding, the Austrian *Anschluss* on March 13, 1938, came like a thunderbolt. It would transpire that the scenario for the next move had already been set by the Führer. Today we know that as the Wehrmacht was nearing Vienna, a small unmarked airplane flew from Bavaria over the Czechoslovak border dropping clouds of leaflets conveying greetings from Hitler: "Sagen Sie in Prag, Hitler lasst Sie grüssen."[153] Then came the proud and successful May mobilization, a kind of respite for some further months.

The crisis came to a head in midsummer 1938, when Czechoslovakia was both eroded from within by its "unruly" minorities and threatened from the outside by the Third Reich. Nazi "whisper propaganda," economic boycott, pressure, coercion, social ostracism, and organized violence and rowdyism were rife: the most active elements in organizing physical assaults were the Henleinist stormtroopers in the Sudeten area. The main targets of these excesses were Jews, but Czechs and democratically minded Germans also came in for their share. Members of the SDP party frequently posted themselves outside non-Henleinist shops, whether Jewish or Czech, warning customers not to enter. Jewish shops were plastered with signs reading: "Don't buy from the Jews!"[154] In Cheb (Eger) and Rychnovec (Rumburg) Jewish shops had to close down in the wake of the boycott. (It is not without interest to note that Eger had been a citadel of Georg Schönerer's pan-German movement in imperial days.)

While clouds were gathering over the republic in August 1938, the world press concerned itself with Lord Walter Runciman's mission, dispatched by Neville Chamberlain to Prague to arbitrate between Czechoslovakia and Germany over Konrad Henlein's claims, which became known as the Karlsbad Eight Point Program. The outcome of these nefarious dealings summed up in the Runciman Report of September 28 (later issued as a government White

Paper) ended with the urgent call that "self-determination be given to the Sudeten population at once" so that "these frontier districts should at once be transferred from Czechoslovakia to Germany."[155]

It transpires that the team of British experts accompanying Runciman acquired during its stay in Prague a substantial body of reports, statistics, and political analyses, some of these stemming from positive-minded elements of the Sudeten area (the German Social Democrats, Christian Socialists, and Small Traders' parties). The latter reports, clearly divorcing themselves from Henlein's aggressive demand, clearly indicated that Sudeten grievances could be redressed within the historical frontiers of the Czechoslovak state through sound economic policy, building of new industries in the distressed areas, and cooperation with the Czechs. Some of these documents contained descriptions about the merciless and brutal terrorism of their own countrymen, forcing them to join the SDP. However, this body of reports and analyses was not taken into account.

The statistical material assembled by the members of the mission also provides evidence that Czechoslovakia fulfilled its obligations to the German minority as "the most enlightened and generous of any regime in Europe." Within this collection there is a memorandum of the Supreme Council of the Federation of Jewish Communities in Bohemia discussing the situation of the Jews in the Sudeten area, claiming that several thousand Jewish inhabitants living in the German districts were exposed to the undisguised terrorism of the Henleinists, facing the threat of imminent "destruction" should the SDP gain any form of autonomy or self-administration.[156]

Encouraged by the concessions extracted from the Czechs by the Runciman Mission, the Führer demanded in his speech on September 12, 1938, that "the oppression of the Sudeten Germans be ended and replaced by the right of self-determination." This was a signal for Henlein and his agents to break off negotiations with the government and flee to Germany. Once safely in Germany Henlein reiterated Hitler's proclamation, demanding the return of the Sudetenland to Germany. Now assaults against the state were approaching open warfare. At certain localities in the Sudeten area the demonstrations reached such a pitch that all the windows of Czech and Jewish shops were broken. There were cases when Henleinists fired on gendarmerie patrols. It was also recorded that President Beneš was hanged in effigy on the police station door.

According to the statement of the official Czechoslovak Press Bureau (ČTK), by September 14 twenty-three persons had been killed and seventy-five wounded. After martial law was declared in sixteen districts order was restored to the Sudetenland, but this was no more than the calm before the storm. In this pathetic situation whoever could possibly do so tried to escape to the interior of Czechoslovakia.[157]

The disintegration of the republic was under way: in his speech in the Sportpalast in Berlin on September 26, Hitler demanded self-determination not only for the Sudeten Germans but also for the other nationalities, namely for the Slovaks. It seems that at this point his plan to use Slovak separatism for the dismantling of Czechoslovakia had matured fully.

3

The Aftermath
of Munich
The Crisis of the
Intellectuals

The agony of that "once admired model democracy of Central Europe" in the fall of 1938 and after the Munich *Diktat* has been a cardinal theme in postwar historiography.[1] It has provoked widespread dispute and controversy.[2] The accumulated corpus of memoir literature by some of the *dramatis personae* sheds new light on these crucial years.[3]

Since its establishment in October 1918 the Czechoslovak Republic had been plagued by acute nationality and minority problems resulting from the ethnic diversity of its population. Its Achilles' heel was the large and truculent German minority (3 million, 23.32 percent of the population), who had lived for centuries along the interior of Bohemia, enjoying privileged status as the dominant national entity. At the end of the First World War, with the dissolution of the Habsburg monarchy, the Böhmer (called Sudeten Germans since the twenties) found themselves a minority overnight, along with other ethnic groups, in the new Czechoslovakia.

With the advent of Nazism their national aspirations for territorial autonomy mounted to militancy. Henlein's Sudeten Deutsche Partei subsidized by Germany became more aggressive after the 1935 elections, when it polled 1.2 million votes (33 percent of the total German votes), greatly outnumbering the "activists"—moderate German parties—prepared to cooperate with the government.[4]

German propaganda and local irredentism increased in the ensuing years, when Hitler resolved to expand eastward to "liberate" more than 10 million Germans living in two of the states adjoining Germany—Austria and Czechoslovakia. To achieve his aim of destroying Czechoslovakia he set out to exploit the complaints of "suppression" voiced by the Sudeten Germans. His main objective was, of course, military: elimination of Czechoslovakia's potential as a rear base for operations in the West and as a Russian air base.

The dark years 1937 and 1938 became landmarks of death and bereavement, tragic days of national calamity. Like "a torrent, tearing away boulders that seemed to be so firmly entrenched," one by one the guardians of the republic fell, champions of human rights and universal values were lost.[5] On September 14 T. G. Masaryk, the founding father of the first Czechoslovak Republic, passed away. A few months earlier, another great intellect on the Czech cultural scene had died—the writer and critic F. X. Šalda, whose seminal imprint on the cultural life of the interwar period was nationwide.

Otokar Fischer, poet and dramatist and the most eminent Jewish cultural figure in prewar literature, died on the night of March 12, 1938, of a heart attack brought on by the impact of the Austrian *Anschluss*.[6] The most symbolic death, at the age of forty-eight and attributed to pneumonia, was that of Karel Čapek, author of the play RUR and of the famous anti-Nazi *The White Plague*. It was generally believed that grief and agony over the Munich disaster put an end to his life.[7]

Everything seemed to fall apart. France, led by the Daladier government, adopted a defeatist policy: the treaty signed in 1924 stipulating that France come to Czechoslovakia's assistance in the event of German aggression was not honored. Great Britain, although not bound by any treaty, had played a dominant role in the adoption of this fatal course, lending full support to the French Cabinet's position. A pact of mutual assistance signed between Czechoslovakia and the Soviet Union in 1935 made Soviet participation operative only if France also fulfilled her obligation. The Czechoslovak army, numbering 1.5 million men—thirty-two divisions—equipped with the most modern weapons, with mountain fortifications to meet any emergency, was paralyzed.

The Sudeten Germans kept upping their demands while Berlin fanned the flames. Paris and London, in an effort to bring "peace in our time," decided to appease Hitler. On September 21, at 2:30 a.m., an ultimatum was handed to President Beneš.[8] The French envoy delivering his government's message wept; the British envoy remained impassive and looked down at the floor.[9] The next day the Czech government gave in. Only two parties had consistently opposed capitulation, the National Democrats (National Unity Party) on the right and the Communist Party on the left.[10] The others had wavered or been prepared to give in.

In Prague, Parliament was not called into session. A mere handful of public figures was urging an active stand in defense of the republic. It is noteworthy that aside from Chief of Staff General Ludvík Krejčí and a few generals, the only people calling for resistance were the leadership of the semi-illegal organization known as "We Remain Faithful" (properly the PVVZ, discussed later).[11] The spokesmen for a special ten-member Committee for Defense of the Republic, which included Dr. Ladislav Rašín, Klement Gottwald, and Dr. Jaroslav Stránský, were received by the president but could not convince him to withdraw the government's submission to the Franco-British ultimatum.[12]

The rest is only too well known. The Munich Agreement was reached among the Big Four. The Soviet Union was not invited to attend, nor were the Czechs allowed to be present at the meeting. A memorandum signed at 2:00 a.m. on September 30 essentially accepted Hitler's ultimatum: the Sudetenland was to be evacuated in five stages beginning on October 1, and the operation was to be completed within ten days. The new frontiers cut deeply into the body of the Czech lands.

The 1938 Munich crisis—with Hitler's anti-Czech tirades, the Sudeten problem, the Runciman Mission, and the abdication of President Beneš— ultimately led to the creation of the second Czecho-Slovak Republic. The events are now all headings in standard history textbooks, recounting how an indifferent world stood by in silence to watch this ancient citadel of Central Europe "drifting into the German sphere of power."[13] There were only a few signs of protest: the three open letters, entitled "An Appeal to the World"— addressed to Roosevelt, Chamberlain, and Daladier—dispatched to five hundred of the most prominent statesmen, editors, writers, and artists in the free world.[14] The appeal, pleading for action on behalf of the German emigrants who found asylum in Czechoslovakia and whose existence "hangs in the balance," reminded the statesmen of their responsibility "before history and before God."[15]

On September 1, 1938, the Czech nobility addressed to President Beneš a declaration of loyalty, speaking out for democratic principles and the integrity of the country's boundaries.[16] Messages of encouragement were also sent to Prague from World Jewish Congress headquarters, offering active help for the besieged republic.[17] And last, there was the famous letter of the German theologian Karl Barth addressed to Professor Hromádka on September 19, condemning the consent of the Western powers to "the insane demands" of Germany.[18] These affirmations of support were, however, voices in the wilderness.

There were, of course, many poignant reactions by noted individuals. A telling example is that of Franz Werfel, who after his escape from Nazi Austria lived temporarily in France. It was there that news of the Munich Dictate reached him. He immediately contacted the Czecho-Slovak Consulate in Marseilles offering his services to the government to help in whatever way he could.[19] He also wrote a series of articles on the annexation of the Sudeten territories for the Paris and London-based exile newspapers, expressing his solidarity with the Czech people and in defense of Czechoslovak statehood. Werfel saw the Munich Agreement as "the culmination of horror and humiliation," threatening the future destiny of Europe.[20]

The public became more and more sharply divided. Even the manifesto of the writers, addressed to leading statesmen and the Czech public, became a controversial issue among the various ideological factions. As early as May 15, 1938, the first manifesto, *Věrni zůstaneme* (We remain faithful), signed by 308 leading cultural and scientific figures, pledged to fight for the defense of the republic. This was how the organization known as the Petition Committee (Petiční výbor "Věrni zůstaneme," PVVZ) came into being. It was headed by Professor Bedřich Bělohlávek and his deputy Dr. Josef Fischer.[21]

By the beginning of September that year, when the struggle over the defense of the republic entered a decisive stage, PVVZ had more than a million signatures on its manifesto. On September 21, 1938, the Petition Committee issued an appeal: *Pryč s kapitulanty! Pryč s vnitřními nepřáteli!* (Down with the defeatists! Down with the internal enemies [of the republic]!). They refused to surrender, even after the Munich Dictate was made public. A new appeal, directed toward world public opinion, was sent to the League of Nations, to governments, and to outstanding cultural and public figures in France, Great Britain, and the United States.[22] The final version issued by the Association of Czech Writers appealing to *K svědomí světa* (the conscience of the world) was signed by twenty-nine noted Czech and Slovak writers, including F. Halas, J. Hora, J. Kopta, J. Kvapil, F. Langer, M. Majerová, B. Mathesius, V. Nezval, I. Olbracht, J. Seifert, the brothers J. and K. Čapek, M. Pujmanová, A. M. Tilschová, V. Vančura, P. Jílemnický, E. B. Lukáč, and L. Novomeský. The first to express support and sympathy were Berthold Brecht and Anna Seghers, followed by H. G. Wells; the French Association of Writers enclosed a check for ten thousand francs to be used for the defense of the republic. The reaction of Soviet writers came on October 6, a week after the Munich Dictate, when *Pravda* in Moscow printed a message of support from the Soviet writers.

The bleak atmosphere of those crucial months unfolds in its many facets in a series of gripping articles by Milena Jesenská, who appeared as a beacon on the turbulent Czech scene, "a light in the darkness."[23] She described with great poignancy the plight of the refugees and the assault on the nation as a whole: "How our nerves cracked in this epoch."[24] Jesenská, later known as "Kafka's Milena," who until the late thirties had had a reputation as an eccentric—escapades, drugs, and adventurous love affairs—became a political journalist.[25]

She took up the most sensitive issues plaguing her nation and became the voice for human rights and for the persecuted. She had previously served as a correspondent and later had written the fashion and domestic affairs column for the Czech-Jewish liberal *Tribuna*. After a prolonged stay in Vienna, and then in Germany, she returned to Prague and in 1937 joined the staff of the liberal-democratic weekly *Přítomnost* (Present) under the editorship of Ferdinand Peroutka.

It is worth noting that this journal had come into being in 1924 through the joint commitment of T. G. Masaryk and Peroutka; the president himself laid the financial foundation by personally donating 500,000 Czech crowns [26] From the very outset it had a tremendous impact on political and cultural events in the republic as the leading intellectual magazine. Jesenská's attitudes were based on her innate sensitivity to human suffering, her compassion, and her cosmopolitan views. Through her first husband, Ernst Polák, Jesenská began her long association with "Arco, Arconauten," which became known as the Prager Kreis, or Prague Circle. Through Polák, she also developed friendly connections with Brod, Kisch, and Kraus and began her unique and intimate friendship with Franz Kafka. Jesenská's command of German was total; as a translator of Kafka's work into Czech she had an essential grasp of his images, symbols, and human concern and was deeply conscious of his genius. Peroutka must have realized that the serious monthly, a factual publication, would gain from her human touch.

Jesenska's early articles drawn from everyday life, psychological inquiries and the like, soon turned to weighty issues, exploring the various aspects of the refugee problem. An avid concern for the underdog and her reporter's instinct led her to present closely observed human stories. Already in the twenties, Kafka had written of Milena's "penetrating eye" and of her power to "look beyond." She wanted to know people's feelings, individual details about their lives, and their idiosyncrasies. In 1937, embarking on her new commitment, she was the most eminently suited professional in her field. Most of her articles dealt with the lives of the German fugitives who reached the borders of the republic, their sad plight, and the generous assistance given to them by the local populace.

Disappointment over the stand taken by the Western Allies—"the betrayal of France and the singularly obtuse policy of Chamberlain"—left a deep scar on the soul of the Czech public. Otakar Vočadlo, professor of Anglo-American literature, in his open letter "Finis Bohemia" published on October 15, 1938 in the *New Statesman and Nation*, expressed the bitterness and frustration of all those who viewed England and its cultural heritage as their ideal: they were "deserted by their friends and harassed by the jackals of the German lion."[27] He also predicted that Munich was not to be the end of German expansion. Hitler was a "voracious beast" whose appetite was insatiable and the more he ate, the stronger he grew.[28] Doreen Warriner, a former assistant lecturer in economics at University College, London, worked in Prague during the winter of 1938 as representative of the British Committee for the Refugees in Czechoslovakia. With the help of some dedicated volunteers she enabled many individuals to make a last-minute escape. In her reminiscences she commented with great empathy on the resentment of the Czechs toward the Western Allies. "At this time the Czechs were embittered against the various organizations that had come out from England to help them . . . In the crisis of betrayal they drew closer together and went to ground, seeing that internationalism had failed them . . . Charity and sympathy from England was more than they could bear."[29]

Indeed articles and editorials in the Czech press related with unmitigated reproach to the "wholesale abandonment" by their allies, dismissing any gesture or aid offered. Jesenská too dealt with this issue with scorn and disdain: "In France and England funds are raised to assist the democratic German refugees," but no one of our generation could feel grateful for this act.[30] She points a relentless finger at their betrayal: "You stood by the cradle of our newly established state and after twenty years of independence now you yourselves have become its ill-advised Fates."[31]

In an aide-mémoire addressed to the secretary of state, the American minister in Prague Wilbur J. Carr, who it seems identified fully with Czechoslovakia, dealt emphatically with moral obligations engendered by the catastrophe visited upon the republic, an entity "in part the creation of the United States of America, upon whose form of government the Czechoslovaks were proud to model their own . . . and attempted to preserve in Central Europe an independent state devoted to the principles of liberty for which the United States stands."[32]

The government capitulated, but there was no revolt; only spontaneous processions heading through the streets of Prague to the castle. The silent columns demonstrating against the dictate of Munich conveyed the helplessness, desolation, and abandonment the people felt. Shortly after Munich the prevailing sense of despair found expression in "A Prayer for Tonight" by Karel Čapek: "O Lord Creator . . . to Thee we need not describe what misfortune has befallen us or how our heads are bowed . . . we do pray that Thou will inspire each of us with the spirit of faith and hope; that Thou will let none of us yield to despair . . . We need internal strength."[33]

In those grim days tales of a flying monster (*perák*) auguring misfortune and calamity circulated throughout the country. A prophecy gained currency telling of an impending war in which the rivers would be swollen with blood. The country would undergo immense suffering and only late, in the darkest hour, would the Knight of the Mountain (alluding to the famous Blaník legend), led by St. Wenceslas riding on a white horse, deliver the country and restore its freedom.

Material losses deriving from Munich in effect lamed Czechoslovakia both economically and strategically.[34] The country lost three-tenths of its territory, one-third of its population, and four tenths of the national income (including 66 percent of the coal and 80 percent of the lignite reserves, 80 percent of textile production, and 70 percent of iron and steel as well as of electric power capacity). Its main railroad lines were severed. From a military point of view the diminished state was at the mercy of Germany; at one point the German frontier was a bare twenty-five miles distant.

The speedy German occupation of the Sudetenland was intended to prevent the Czechs from constructing a new defense line, to "deprive us of every safeguard for our national existence."[35] Poet Ilse Weber's letter to a friend abroad conveys the genuine grief felt by many.[36]

> Witkowitz, October 10, 1938
> Dear Lilian,
> Your letter only took four days [to reach me], which is wonderful if one considers that mail from [the rest of] Moravia now takes six days. I have been longing so for news from you!
> First! [Mährisch] Ostrau has remained Czech! But the Polish and the German borders are now only minutes away from here. The new borders totally disregard all human rights, which is outrageous! Ostrau is totally isolated from the rest of the world. Since yesterday, when Schönbrunn [Svinov] was occupied, it has been without milk and electricity. The radio station is also in German hands.
> Lilian, what we have suffered during the last few weeks is hard to describe. It is mental torture without parallel. We all love peace, because we know what war means, especially for us near the borders.
> The mobilization of the men into the army [prior to the occupation of Witkowitz by the Germans], was followed very seriously and willingly by the population. Those who stayed home volunteered for air-raid duty and the women for the Red Cross or, like me, donated blood.
> We hoped for help from our allies. It was clear that our small country

could not stand up [alone] against mighty Germany. Our nerves were near breaking point. Especially as the German radio propaganda had whipped up the feelings [of the local Germans] no end. In spite of it, not a single German was harassed [although] the Sudeten-Germans spread shocking stories . . . against the Jews.

Then the wireless receivers were confiscated, which had the advantage of our no longer being disturbed by conflicting reports. In front of our windows, they dug shelters and the children played in them. All the people with means left. We stayed, but in what circumstances? Especially when we began to doubt that our "friends" would ever help us.

There was a blackout every evening and there we sat from six o'clock in the dark, without a radio, mostly without candles, which were sold out at once, feverish and filled with a terrible fear.

The suitcases of the children, who were ready to be evacuated with their schools, stood ready packed. Each child had been given a locket with our picture in it. They were mischievous and carefree as always and we were rather short-tempered with them.

And then, at the last minute, came the Four-Power Conference. We were still hoping for a favorable result but the [simple] people knew at once: "They are going to sell us!" One could hear in the streets. But they have not just sold us, they have sold us out! Never before have souls been sold out so dastardly! Hitler wanted "his" Germans. Good! But why did England allow him to take so many hundreds of thousands of Czechs and Jews?

Lilian! Totally Czech regions have fallen to Germany, where not even one person speaks German. [And] the Germans, living in those undivided parts don't even consider moving to Germany. Why should they? They have their nice property [here], their well-paid jobs, which they want to keep.

They were a perfect tool in Hitler's hands; they have undermined the Republic by fostering artificial hate between the Germans and the Czechs. But they are going to stay here, because freedom in Germany [proper] does not seem [so] desirable for everyone.

Yes, after the prey fell, the vultures came and pounced on the carcasses. Poland has taken away huge assets from us; the wonderful foundries of Trzynietz and all those collieries, which were our lifeblood. And again the same injustice: Czech towns and villages were given away.

My maid comes home with red eyes—she has just read that as of tomorrow she will be Polish . . . The girl from downstairs comforts her: "Dear God, you are only [becoming] Polish! But I [now] belong to Germany and in our village—Polanka—not one soul speaks German!" Wilma has become

Polish as have my relatives in Oderberg, but they are not as unhappy as they would have been had they become Germans.

Why did they not think about the Jews there, in Munich? Did Chamberlain not realize the danger in store for the Jews when he sold us out to the Germans? What will all the poor people do, who have suddenly joined the many other "bothersome refugees"? How can Chamberlain, cursed by all those hundreds of thousands whose home he has taken away, still live in peace?

Our home here has been destroyed! Anti-Semitism here is growing fearfully. The local people say: "It is all the fault of the Jews. The Jews have sold us out!" Where is the logic [in that]? But hate does not require logic!

I kiss you,

Ilse

Worse even than the material loss was the psychological one. The public's confidence in the international system and treaties and its own democratic leaders was shattered. The humiliating acquiescence to Munich after less than twenty years of national sovereignty was devastating in its impact upon all the creative and democratic forces in the country. "The man who stood by at the birth of the Republic, President Beneš, the loyal follower of T. G. Masaryk, was forced to leave the country as a *conditio sine qua non* set by Hitler."[37]

The way was paved for extreme political tendencies and vociferous propaganda campaigns, poisonous press columns, anonymous letters, and German whisper propaganda, continually announcing new dates for "The Day" of Hitler's arrival. The viability of the post-Munich state was doubtful, and the feeling of uncertainty was all-pervading. Hitler soon made it clear that Germany could not tolerate in the heart of the Reich the "abscess" of an independent though attenuated Czech state.[38] The elite's morale was shaken. Nazi propaganda, obviously streamed by agencies and local fascist groups that surfaced from their semi-illegality, pervaded the press and the radio.

One of the symptoms accompanying the new political climate was the removal of the portraits and busts of the two presidents, Masaryk and Beneš, from schools and public places, to storage rooms. All the Czechoslovak legations abroad were ordered to destroy the official portraits. In London where T. G. Masaryk's son served as minister, the embarrassed staff could not bring themselves to do this. To save the situation Jan Masaryk gently took down the picture of his revered father.[39]

Jew baiting became a cardinal issue. Czech journalism sank to its lowest ebb; it was like "a tree that had lost all its leaves except one or two at the top," wrote

Jesenská. Years later, Marie Pujmanová, one of the foremost writers of the Czech nation, stated about this period: "I daresay that never before had it been so bleak in Bohemia as during the Second Republic. A man would devour his fellow man out of sheer despair and for the simple fact that we had been abandoned by each and all. It was as if the nation's spine had been broken; there was a callous moral atmosphere. One soiled one's own nest. An infectious pestilence seemed to reign."[40]

In the wake of criticism from Berlin the daily *Národní osvobození*, organ of the legionnaires of the First World War, was forced to cease publication; the Municipal Council of Prague was dissolved and Petr Zenkl, a staunch supporter of the former regime, was removed from office. From now on Germany was not to be slandered in the press, and for the first time, on January 30, 1939, the anniversary of Hitler's coming to power, the swastika was hoisted on a number of buildings in Prague.

Also in January 1939, during his second visit to Berlin, Foreign Minister František Chvalkovský was asked to cede to the Reich part of the gold reserves of his country. As a result of the negotiations between the Reichsbank and the Czechoslovak National Bank (February 26–March 4) the Czechoslovak bank transferred 465.8 million crowns in gold, and 15.2 million in foreign exchange.[41] The clouds were gathering.

CZECHOSLOVAKIA—HAVEN AND HOST TO REFUGEES

The boundary between Germany and Czechoslovakia was eleven hundred miles long and crossing could be effected with ease, especially in the region of the Bavarian forest or the Krkonoše mountains. Many people made their escape from Germany in 1933 by these routes. Prague, the outpost of democracy of the thirties, served as haven and host for thousands of Jewish and non-Jewish refugees who fled Nazism.[42] The bilingual world of the Czech capital with its exhilarating mixture of cultures—Czech, German, and Jewish—gave the preponderantly intellectual and political-minded refugees a sense of safety and spiritual affinity. Czech, Jewish, and leftist Sudeten German circles vied for their company and opened the pages of the press to them; they wrote for the leading dailies *České slovo* and *Lidové noviny* and the weekly *Přítomnost*, the Zionist *Selbstwehr*, the *Jewish Review*, and other periodicals. The Petcheks, Weinmanns, and other Jewish families extended help to them, and as already noted, several refugee committees (Socialist, Communist, and the most active of all, the Jewish Relief Committee) sprang up to offer all the assistance they could. The cream of the cultural elite active in the antifascist movement and on behalf of the refugees included František X. Šalda, Professor Zdeněk Nejedlý, Otokar Fischer, Vladislav Vančura, Ivan Olbracht, Karel Čapek, Egon Erwin Kisch, Franz Carl Weisskopf, Dr. Rudolf Rábl, and Dr. Ivan Sekanina.[43]

The refugees arrived in Czechoslovakia in three waves; the first were the political refugees—workers, editors, writers, trade unionists, and youngsters from the German socialist movements, who crossed the borders on foot after Hitler's rise to power. Somewhat later came the Jewish emigrants and individuals whose situation had become precarious as a result of mixed marriages. After this group came the so-called economic emigrants—for the most part Jewish businessmen and entrepreneurs (*Wirtschaftsemigranten*). In the third wave came individuals who had spent time in jail or a concentration camp and were anxious to leave for abroad. The Czechs provided them with a bona fide residence and accommodation for the waiting period.

Czechoslovakia became the European country most actively engaged in an anti-Nazi campaign; a great number of German intellectuals, writers, journalists, and actors assembled in Prague.[44] They produced books, papers, brochures, and comic magazines, which were then smuggled over the borders to Nazi Germany. And so it happened that in the Café Continental, once the meeting place of Kafka and his friends, German refugees converged. Among the frequent guests were the Mann brothers, Thomas and Heinrich, Anna Seghers and Willy Schlamm, and also Berthold Brecht, who called there whenever he visited Prague.

At the outset the authorities adopted a highly favorable attitude toward the refugees in general and toward some of the prominent intellectuals in particular. The most enthusiastic welcome was accorded to Thomas and Heinrich Mann.[45] Upon the initiative of both Masaryk and Beneš the brothers Mann were awarded Czech citizenship in 1936. The pledges of allegiance were sworn at the consulates in Zürich and Marseilles; the ceremonies were widely publicized in the world press. This, of course, was not the only instance. Already in December 1933 Čapek had persuaded Masaryk to agree to confer citizenship on Jacob Wassermann; this gesture, however, did not materialize because of the author's untimely death. Between 1935 and 1937, Czechoslovak citizenship was granted to 891 rank-and-file German émigrés.[46]

There was nevertheless some fierce opposition voiced against the refugees, and occasionally members of the German Communist Party and other left-wing elements encountered open hostility. The Czech fascist leaders (Gajda and Stříbrný) as well as the right wing of the Agrarian Party, headed by Beran, and even the Nationalists (Kramář), Christian Socialists, and Henlein party led a campaign of systematic agitation against them, claiming that their presence in the republic marred bilateral relations between the two countries. Arguments were raised on economic grounds and steps were demanded to protect local labor in the light of growing unemployment and financial depression. In 1935, at the instigation of the Agrarian Party, two laws were enacted by Parliament.[47] The first related to registration of residence and the second to permits of sojourn for foreigners, both with a view to protecting the country against the entry of undesirable elements. The American consul general in Prague, Orme Wilson, in his report of April 18, 1935, ascribed the government's moves to the "difficult problems arising from the propaganda issuing from Germany."[48] In order to eliminate anti-Nazi activities Germany applied threats, intimidation, and other methods. The Gestapo sent spies into Prague and other parts of the republic, and Nazi agents infiltrated the country, threatening the lives of prominent political refugees. Some of these were kidnapped and others, including Professor Theodor Lessing[49] and engineer Rudolf Formis,[50] were murdered by Nazi agents.

Upon Beneš's initiative 1.75 million crowns from the funds of the Foreign Ministry and the president's chancellery were allocated between 1933 and 1937 to exile institutions, press, and theaters run by emigrants (600,000 crowns for the support of emigrants and 700,000 crowns for the press).[51]

The entry by German troops on March 6, 1936, into the demilitarized zone in the Rhineland radically altered the balance of power in Central Europe. The failure of France and Great Britain to take action against the violation of the Versailles and Locarno treaties was fully grasped in Czechoslovakia and, of course, in Germany as well. To President Beneš it sounded the first alarm as to the extent to which he could rely on his Western allies, whereas to the German politicians it suggested new options in the political arena well worth taking up.[52] It was Dr. Albrecht Haushofer who led off: in a memorandum of April 1936, he set out the "Political Possibilities in the Southeast," which he personally discussed with Joachim von Ribbentrop.[53] His next move was to assay Beneš's response to secret negotiations on a nonaggression plan with Germany; to this end Haushofer approached the Czech minister to Berlin, Dr. Vojtěch Mastný, on October 18, 1936. It is worth noting that Haushofer and Count Trautmannsdorf, who accompanied him to Prague, conferred in mid-November 1936 with Beneš (upon his express wish) and with Foreign Minister Dr. Kamil Krofta, discussing Germany's political demands, which meant in essence international discrediting and isolation of Czechoslovakia from her allies and an explicit demand imposing restraint on the activities of the refugees.[54] How anxious Beneš was to reach an agreement with Nazi Germany we can learn from the concessions he offered on this issue. Haushofer's notes about their parley in

Prague contain this statement: "Beyond desiring a press agreement, he [Krofta] promised that if a general understanding were reached the Czech Government would tolerate no activities against the German state by the émigrés, meaning primarily the German Social Democratic Party whose headquarters were still in Prague at this time."[55]

In the final analysis it transpires, however, that Czechoslovakia was not prepared to sacrifice her ties with the League of Nations and her allies in favor of the Führer's offer of a "nonaggression pact" and becoming a vassal of Germany.

How serious Hitler was about reaching an agreement with Czechoslovakia is evident from instructions he issued to Haushofer, asking him "to drag out the negotiations." Obviously the Führer had already made up his mind with regard to his policy vis-à-vis Czechoslovakia. At the now famous conference of November 5, 1937, Hitler informed his close associates gathered in the Reichschancellery that in his war strategy the first objective would be "to overthrow Czechoslovakia and Austria simultaneously in order to remove the threat to our flank in any possible operation against the west."[56]

The secret negotiations were instrumental in one sphere—curbing the freedom of the refugees. Apart from strengthening police control on the borders, the Czech authorities decided to restrict refugee presence to certain designated areas of Bohemia.[57] In practical terms this meant that they had to move and again adjust themselves to new surroundings.

On account of this abandonment of the German émigrés the state was criticized and questioned in several articles in *Přítomnost* in a series titled "Is the Policy of the Government Right?" Peroutka himself pointedly tackled this issue on May 8, 1938, predicting that "the reputation of the State will suffer thereby." The most eloquent support of German émigrés was voiced by Karel Čapek on April 27, 1938, projecting the significance that this issue would bear on postwar developments after the fall of Nazism.[58] It is symptomatic that in July 1938 the administrative procedure of according citizenship to Lion Feuchtwanger and Arnold Zweig was suspended, lest Berlin be irritated by this act.[59]

In one of her articles Jesenská related the case of a certain Josef B. (a new version of alienation, reminiscent of Kafka's Josef K.): "One day J. B. was ordered to leave the locality in which he had had the bonus of seventy-two meals already allotted to him, and had to move to the Jihlava district designated by the police authorities. All the protests staged by the local citizens were to no avail . . . Imagine yourself as a refugee, for the second time driven away from the meager mouthful, making his way, kilometer by kilometer on foot, in order to reach the locality he does not know, which he has never seen before and where he would be again a stranger to all."[60]

Reduction in the aid to the refugees was another action that followed from this change of policy. In 1934 the allowance per day came to 6.50 Czech crowns (Kč); in 1937 it was reduced to 4.30 Kč. Some localities paid even less. In Brno the local committee provided only 2.60 Kč This support was, as was sarcastically noted, "too much to die on and too little to sustain oneself even at a very low level."[61]

Thus, during 1936–37, when military circles launched a campaign to build new relations with the Sudeten Germans and especially with the so-called activists, it was also supported by Czech writers. As part of this move Milena Jesenská—a staunch believer in new terms of coexistence—was dispatched by Peroutka to the Sudeten area to examine the situation and the mood of the population, its readiness for a rapprochement.[62] When touring the Sudeten area in 1937, Jesenská sensed widespread hatred, boycotting, organized anxiety, and fear—gulfs yawning between the various sections of the populace. She especially noted the plight of and discrimination against the Jews of the area, reporting on this in a paragraph headed "Jews, Murder by Rumor, Whispering Campaign." "Although only a few Jews (mostly business people, professionals) live in this region, the local people shun them, making their situation unbearable, through gossip, lies, slander and trumped-up charges. In the shops they are served only reluctantly. They hardly dare to leave their houses," wrote Jesenská with compassion.[63]

The *sauve qui peut* attitude that set in after the Anschluss created new turmoil in neighboring Czechoslovakia: all roads from Austria to the frontier were jammed with fleeing taxicabs and private cars. Stormtroopers, half uniformed, robbed train passengers quite openly, relieving them of their money, jewelry, watches, and furs. Being well acquainted with the Austrian scene Jesenská described conditions there, the virulent anti-Semitism prevalent among wide sections of the population, the violence on the streets of Vienna, and asked bluntly: "Why cannot the voice of the workers of this country be heard?"[64]

The hundreds of thousands of fugitives from Austria did not find an open door in Czechoslovakia. To limit the number of refugees police regulations became more stringent. The rigidity of the order not to grant entry to Austrian refugees or to political activists in danger of their life evoked massive criticism. Subsequently the stiff regulations were modified and exceptional assistance and shelter were granted to individuals in life-endangering situations.[65]

Actually it was the nomination of General Syrový that signaled the oncoming havoc all over the country. "The month of September led to the placing of the country on a complete war footing, characterized by the establishment of what was a military dictatorship . . . General Syrový found himself faced with the task of not only preserving order and discipline throughout a period of indescribable difficulty, but also remaking the constitution and of setting up a wholly new civil regime to which power could be turned over."[66]

Following the Munich Agreement of September 30, 1938—the hasty evacuation of territory with all its attendant features of chaos, misery, and panic—a new process began: the cession of territories to Poland as well as to Hungary (in keeping with the Vienna Award of November 2, 1938). The new influx of refugees and the return of masses of Czech military, administrative, and teaching personnel from these regions created increasing unemployment and housing shortages.

The plight of the Jewish population, and especially of the Jewish refugees, grew worse. The Jewish issue in all its severity was taken up in most of the articles written by Jesenská during this period: in autumn 1938, at a time when Jew baiting, gutter demagogy, and petty chauvinism became blatant features in the Czech press, she wrote about their plight in *Přítomnost*.[67] In one of her earlier articles she had reported on the international conference that took place on June 21 in Frankfurt under the cosponsorship of l'Association Internationale pour la Protection de l'Enfance.[68] This conference under the aegis of Joseph Goebbels was intended to demonstrate the concern of the German regime for the children of that country. Jesenská cited the speech of Colonel Locker-Lampson (a British Conservative MP), who had cabled Hitler asking why he constantly attacked the helpless and weak minorities rather than those who were more of a match. Had Germany revealed the way she treated Jewish children? How they were barred from school or were forced to occupy special benches? How they were excluded from high schools and universities, prohibited from visiting public baths and sports grounds, recreation centers?[69]

The massive influx of Jews, Czechs, and democratic anti-Nazi Sudeten refugees after the Munich Agreement created an internal problem in the diminished state. The government, turning to London and Paris, sought financial aid, which was granted in the form of a £10 million loan on condition that a large proportion of this be used to finance the emigration of Germans and Jews from Czechoslovakia.[70] The British representative in the loan negotiations was Robert J. Stopford of the Treasury, who had been a member of the Runciman Mission and was deeply sympathetic on the Jewish issue as well as on the fate of the anti-Nazi refugees. From the proceedings of the negotiations preserved at the National Bank in Prague it transpires that the proposal for the loan came about through the initiative of the London-based Rothschild and Nathan banks.[71]

The city of Prague, flooded by refugees from the ceded territories, was described in late summer 1938 by Karel Poláček as "a mix of population the world has not yet seen."[72] This "disaster" was more than Poláček could tolerate. His only wish was to find reprieve from the nerve-wracking (*rumrejch*) chaos; he did so by occasionally running off to the countryside. Jesenská too portrayed in gloomy colors the newly arrived fugitives in Prague: "Homeless people have been trailing for years from one border to the other, without means, without work; we are all aware of them, we are all horrified to watch the heart-rending sight. Today they are here in the center of 'gossamer' Prague; among us . . . the sadness of people who have abandoned their homes, so to speak, relinquished the four walls, their own bed, the cooking stove, a few pots, the meager security a person acquires within a few square meters of privacy."[73]

The Czech population, grieving over the political calamity and the harsh realities of the new situation, could no longer tolerate the physical presence of the fugitives. The question tormenting the authorities was the high rate of unemployment, and the lack of opportunities to provide work for the officials, teachers, professionals, and others who had returned from the ceded territories.

Jesenská's tone radically changed after the country was flooded with Czech returnees. The crippled country could not extend help to refugees from other states. This was, she wrote, "beyond our power": "It is not our fault that they have had to put up with such bad experiences. As long as our home stood firm, we were hospitable and kindhearted. Now all we can do is to wish them a new and good life, somewhere far away."[74]

Jesenská deemed that they would have to leave.[75] Marie Schmolka, the dedicated president of the National Coordinating Committee for Refugees in Czechoslovakia, voiced the same opinion. At the meeting of the League of Nations convening in Paris in December 1938 to aid the Austrian and German refugees, presided over by Sir Herbert Emerson, Schmolka declared bluntly: "After the Munich Agreement Czecho-Slovakia cannot offer asylum any more."[76] More extended asylum would endanger the host country and could eventually jeopardize relations between Czecho-Slovakia and the Reich.

As of October 1, 1938 (the day after the signing of the Munich Agreement) there were at least 5,000 refugees from Germany and Austria in Czechoslovakia. After the detachment of the Sudetenland a cable dispatched on November 23, 1938, from the American Legation in Prague refers to 91,632 registered refugees from the Sudetenland; of these approximately 6,700 were Jews.[77] The number of unregistered refugees was estimated at between 10,000 and 15,000.

Altogether some 17,000 Jews from the Sudetenland (out of the 27,073 Jews of the 1930 census) had moved into the interior of Czechoslovakia.[78] Most of the refugees found shelter in Prague, Brno, Moravská Ostrava, and Olomouc, but some landed in smaller places, where shortages of food and housing were attributed to the newcomers and created further grounds for anti-Semitic propaganda. The government, beset as it was with various problems, feared the creation of new enclaves of an unduly large German minority within its new frontiers.

The option "choice of residence" set forth in the Munich Agreement was not honored by the authorities. Notwithstanding representations made to General Syrový by High Commissioner Sir Neill Malcolm and by General Faucher of the French military mission in Prague, newly arrived Jewish fugitives from German-occupied areas were expelled. In the hasty implementation of expulsion orders many families were broken up. The whole problem had arisen so suddenly that no organization was prepared to take charge of these refugees: the police registered them and gave them forty-eight hours to return to their original homes. Some were caught at railroad stations and turned back then and there. The tribulations of these unfortunates were recorded in reports and cables sent by Wilbur J. Carr: "The suicide toll among refugees mounts, but it is impossible to convey the figures as the Czech radio station has stopped mentioning these cases unless the dead are prominent citizens, such as the editor of the *Prager Tagblatt* [Thomas Rudi]."[79]

In response to the plight of the refugees, the Lord Mayor's Fund was set up in London. A campaign launched by the London *News Chronicle* raised £20,000 to help resettle refugee families. The committee in charge of this campaign was headed by the former British minister in Prague, Sir Ronald Maclay.[80] Its members included representatives of the Czechoslovak Red Cross and of the Czechoslovak Government; Wenzel Jaksch, the leader of the Sudeten German Social Democrats, who represented the German Aid Committee (to assist anti-Nazi refugees from the Sudetenland); and Marie Schmolka, who spoke for the Jewish refugees.

After the German forces marched into the Sudetenland, expulsion of Czechs and Jews from that region took place daily. Human beings were hunted down like animals. The German authorities drove groups of refugees from the Sudetenland to the Czech frontier; some of these people managed to pass into Czech territory illegally and proceed to Prague or Brno, but others, both Jews and gentile anti-Nazis, were turned back by Czech border guards. Since they could not reenter the German-occupied territory they had left, they remained stranded in no-man's-land. On October 12, 1938, Carr sent this message to the secretary of state in Washington: "Blanket order of expulsion within forty-eight hours of refugees from Czechoslovakia back to German occupied areas has been upheld this morning. Neill Malcolm, High Commissioner for Refugees of the

League of Nations, and General Faucher late of the French Military Mission, pleaded with General Syrový to cancel this order for at least two weeks, giving the League and the Evian Committee and private refugee charities an opportunity to save these refugees. This request was flatly and finally refused."[81]

The relief organizations were no longer able to cope with the situation. Marie Schmolka worked tirelessly, visiting the border areas where refugees were concentrated, gathering evidence with a view to mobilizing public opinion, and sending appeals and reports to foreign ambassadors in Prague and to Jewish social and philanthropic agencies in other countries. Her apartment in one of the ancient buildings of old Prague, with its arched ceilings and recesses (Max Brod was to describe it as "a dark, mighty castle whence battling ghosts were sent out to the world") became the heart of the rescue campaign.[82] It was upon Schmolka's suggestion that Milena Jesenská traveled to the Slovak-Hungarian border and wrote the moving report "In No-Man's-Land" for *Přítomnost* on the plight of the refugees.[83]

In the Sudeten area the police began to arrest political opponents and Jews immediately after the celebrations of the annexation were over. At the end of October and the beginning of November the Gestapo could claim to have arrested 1,157 "opponents" just in the two cities of Karlovy Vary and Cheb: 971 Communists, social democrats, and antifascists. *Kristallnacht* of November 9–10 was marked by savage pogroms and the burning of synagogues in Cheb, Mariánské Lázně, Františkovy Lázně, Falknov, Kinšperk, Hroznětín, Most, Liberec, Jablonec, and Nisou.[84] Firemen stood near the synagogues, watching closely lest the fire spread to neighboring buildings. Records reveal how jubilant, rowdy crowds chanting Nazi slogans were chasing naked Jews along the streets in several localities. On the morrow the remaining Jews in the Sudeten area (the majority had fled before the territories were ceded to the Reich) were rounded up and concentrated in the camps of Olšovy Vraty.[85]

The chaotic conditions in truncated Czecho-Slovakia made it clear that everything had to be done to transfer the refugees to other countries. The National Coordinating Committee assumed a major role in the rescue operations. Although cooperation with the Communists had met with many difficulties, a proposal was made to request Soviet Russia to accept those refugees stranded in Czechoslovakia, France, Belgium, etc., who were members of the Communist Party and were in dire peril. Upon the request of Kurt Grossmann, executive secretary of the National Coordinating Committee, the High Commissioner Sir Neill Malcolm inquired officially on November 2, 1938, whether Russia would accept such refugees.[86] The answer addressed to Sir Neill, signed by Ivan Majsky, the Soviet ambassador in London, noted: "You explained to me that about nine-tenths of these refugees are Jews, and that their economic existence in the aforementioned countries is extremely precarious . . . You suggested that the Soviet government should allow the entry into the USSR of a certain number of refugees, and especially those belonging to two groups: a) highly qualified specialists such as engineers, doctors, architects, agriculturists, and b) people who by virtue of their previous experience are most suited for working on the land and in farming."[87]

In his reply the Soviet ambassador asserted that his government was "prepared in principle to allow the entry into USSR of a certain number of refugees of the above-mentioned type, but each case *will be considered individually on its own merits*" (italics mine).[88]

In a decree of November 8, 1938, the Czecho-Slovak Government took steps to prevent Jewish refugees from the Sudeten areas from establishing themselves in Bohemia in commerce or in the liberal professions. The decree further provided for a review of all permits and licenses issued subsequent to March 1, 1938. At the end of November the situation became so precarious that the Czecho-Slovak authorities demanded "a solution of the refugee problem" within eleven days, by the beginning of December 1938.[89] However, since entry visas were not available for prospective emigrants, their plight continued unabated. Visas for Great Britain were being granted on an individual basis only.

In December 1938 negotiations took place between the Czech, British, and French governments for further financial assistance, the result of which was that the amount rose to a total of £16,000 (half of which was an outright gift, the other half a loan).[90] To compensate the refugees for the fate that befell them as a consequence of the Munich Agreement, £4,000 were to serve for their relief and resettlement. One of the by-products of this proviso was the "Czech transfer"—an agreement signed on January 13, 1939, between the Czecho-Slovak Ministry of Finance and the Jewish Agency for Palestine, which provided for the emigration of twenty-five hundred Czechoslovak Jews and the transfer of £500,000 via the Bank of England to the British Mandatory Government of Palestine.[91] Most of the individuals involved in this enterprise were Zionist-oriented public figures, including leaders of the Jewish Party.

It is estimated that between September 1938 and May 1939, a total of seven thousand fugitives arrived in Great Britain either directly from Czecho-Slovakia or via Poland. Among these were some active members of various political parties, journalists, intellectuals, members of liberal professions, and former high officials of the government. A few hundred fugitives left for France or the northern European countries, and a considerable number emigrated to the United States, South America, and various Central American countries.[92] In addition there were several rescue enterprises involving children and young girls hired for household work.

Most active in the rescue campaign for children was Nicholas Winton, a young stockbroker. His office in Prague, established some months before the Germans marched in, was taking care of compiling a list of children. At the same time a search was conducted throughout England to find sponsors and foster parents for them and thus to assure their entry. As a result 664 children reached the shores of England in safety.[93]

INTERNAL DISCORD: 1938–1939

After twenty years of constructive struggle and development the position of the Jews in Czechoslovakia approached a new and precarious phase. Of the 356,830 persons of Jewish religion living in Czechoslovakia, according to the 1930 census, only one third resided in the historic lands: 76,300 (1.07 percent of the general population) in Bohemia and 41,300 (1.16 percent) in Moravia and Silesia. The other two thirds resided in Slovakia and Subcarpathian Ruthenia.

In 1930, 46.4 percent of Jews in Bohemia and 17.6 percent in Moravia were Czech-speaking; of these, however, only a thin stratum was organized within the Czech-Jewish movement. The Zionist camp had the support of 20.3 percent (national Jews) in Bohemia and 51.7 percent in Moravia. German-speaking Jews constituted around 30 percent; the majority of those who had claimed German nationality in the 1930 census drifted conceptually to the national Zionist stream after 1933.[94]

This trend is well illustrated in a Jewish publication touching upon the question of the use of the German language, specially as far as the education of the youth was concerned: "We have to reject [adhering] to German nationality despite the fact that we were its biggest propagators. We speak this language only because it became for us . . . a universal medium of understanding, because it brought us nearer to our great writers, scientists, and to us Jews ourselves; for the youth, however, the study of this language has lost sense."[95]

The official community organizations continued to concentrate on social and philanthropic activities according to tradition. The influx of refugees and their plight, as well as the aggravated situation of certain strata of the local Jewish population, placed additional demands on them. The fact that there was no overall umbrella organization of Jewish congregations of Bohemia and Moravia to meet the challenges of the time—even Greater Prague had seven separate congregations—created a difficult problem in a period when rapid decisions and united efforts were needed.[96]

In the second half of 1938 the Jews were faced with the challenge of mustering their forces under completely new and disagreeable circumstances. In view of political developments, many Jewish public figures foresaw the disintegration of the Jewish Party and the passing of leadership to the Zionist organization of Czechoslovakia. The new objective became the emigration of as many Jews as possible; and to facilitate this, vocational reorientation-retraining for manual labor and language courses were set up.

On September 30, 1938, in response to the Munich Diktat, the Jewish Party and the Executive Committee of the Central Zionist Federation jointly issued a proclamation solemnly reiterating their "vow of unchanging love and loyalty" to the state.[97] Ironically enough the next day President Beneš appointed a cabinet of experts under General Jan Syrový, which within the short-lived Second Republic evolved into a kind of military dictatorship liquidating all vestiges of democracy.[98]

With the elimination of the Zionist press, the Jewish Community Bulletin in Prague (*Věstník židovské obce náboženské v Praze*) gained eminence.[99] It became the ever-shifting mirror image of the insecurity, fear, and demoralization, and the "liquidation psychosis," that engulfed the Jewish population. This community organ, hitherto known for its balanced and restrained character, radically changed its tone after the Munich events. Its front pages now carried psalms invoking divine help, grace, and mercy. One of the symptoms of this desperate situation was an increase in the number of resignations from membership in the official Jewish community.[100] Thus, while in the years 1930–37 an average of seventy-three individuals resigned their membership annually, in 1938, within a single year, 709 Jews, many of whom embraced Christianity, left the community.[101]

The leading article of the November 9, 1938, issue was entitled "Refugees."[102] Its author Dr. Emil Kafka, president of the Jewish Congregation of Prague, gave vent to the feelings of alienation elicited by the exclusion of the Jewish population from the mainstream of life.[103] He reiterated his appeal to the refugees from the Sudeten territory to refrain from using German in public and "in their own interest" not to fill the cafés and restaurants: "Better stay at home and visit with each other," and thus avoid irritating the Czechs.[104] He took a critical stance toward a certain stratum of the Czech population, the so-called "intelligentsia," for their anti-Jewish agitation.[105] Dr. Kafka wrote: "The Czech nation, following the great injustice inflicted upon it, has every right to rise in anger and voice its indignation against those who damage the national character of the state and of its capital city. This sensitivity can be condoned so long as it is prompted by purely national considerations. However, it is inexcusable when this wrath is directed against the Jews in general with the goal of subjecting them to unjust humiliation, accusation, abuse and slander. Against this, I must raise my voice, for Jewry does not deserve this."[106]

As a result of the apprehension arising in the Jewish community, the U.S. Consulate General's office was inundated with visa seekers.[107] During the two weeks ending November 19, more than fifty-three hundred persons, the vast majority of whom were Jews, were received at that office, with roughly 95 percent registering for visas. The situation was echoed in the December 20 issue of the community weekly: the editorial "Suffering and Insecurity," quoting Psalm 13: "How long, O Lord, will thou forget me, forever? How long . . ."

Under the impact of the political climate, the defeatism that had set in, and the chauvinistic attitude of Czech compatriots, some noted Jewish personalities put an end to their own lives. A slight but significant stratum of Jewish intellectuals, deeply entrenched in Czech society and culture, rejected abandonment of their native country, choosing a kind of self-imposed confinement, an "internal exile."

The escalation of anti-Semitism in Germany and its reverberations within Czech society of the late thirties brought the ultra-assimilationists within the Czech-Jewish movement, who strove for complete amalgamation with the Czech nation, to a critical juncture. In the face of the growing racist gutter propaganda, the basic tenets of their credo, grounded in the ideas of liberalism, became null and void. They had in fact drifted far from the ideals of the founding fathers of this movement and were now stranded. Factional differences arose, and the most extreme among the members sought radical solutions, cowering before the authorities and rejecting anything emanating from their adversaries, the national-Zionist Jews. A true picture of this development, which peaked during the period of the Second Republic, can be found in the 1938–39 issues of *Rozvoj*.

A heated debate was provoked by "Something about the Czech Nation and the Jews," an article from the pen of Ferdinand Peroutka, the leading liberal journalist.[108] His highly critical comments related to the "unwanted" Jewish refugees from Rumania seeking asylum in Czechoslovakia. The rightist press responded to this issue with numerous venomous articles: the Agrarian *Venkov* even recommended learning from the Goga Government, especially insofar as the ousting of Jews from the economy was concerned.[109]

The gist of Peroutka's article was a warning to the Jews not to increase their numerical presence in the country—that is, not to campaign for their Rumanian co-religionists. In his view, Czech-Jewish coexistence rested on a kind of "silent accord"—an unwritten law—the most important aspect of which was their "inconspicuous" ratio: a reasonable percentage of Jews in the public and economic life of Czechoslovakia. He admitted that there was quite a lot of "oral" anti-Semitism proliferating, but given the prevailing conditions, things were still under control. However, should this balance be upset there could be a dangerous change for the worse.

Peroutka's assessment of Czech-Jewish relations descended like a bolt of lightning upon the Jewish public at a time when anti-Semitism was gaining in vehemence.[110] It also coincided with controversy within the Jewish community: discussion on a new constitution for a unified umbrella organization, a matter that had dragged on for several years in the Parliament of Prague. The subject of dispute between the two camps was the scope of activities to be pursued by the Jewish communities: the national Jews—the Zionists—advocated a broad educational and national-cultural network, as opposed to the existing limited sphere of activities consisting of synagogue and charitable affairs, which was backed by the Czech-Jewish movement.

Peroutka's article triggered a wave of sharp reactions in the Czech press.[111] His warning with regard to an "inconspicuous" presence reverberated within Czech-Jewish circles as well; for some time they had been alarmed over the continuing "internal migration" of Jews from the eastern provinces of the republic, namely from Slovakia and Subcarpathian Ruthenia.[112] As a "remedy" the Czech Jews immediately produced a scheme meant to serve several objectives—first and foremost, to expose their Zionist adversaries. In the manner of the Soviet experiment in Birobidjan, they proposed setting up an autonomous settlement in part of Subcarpathian Ruthenia, densely populated by Jews and "blessed by virgin soil," suitable for internal colonization.[113] This could solve the social problem caused by Jewish migration from the east toward the west and could also satisfy the aspirations (!) of those Jews of Bohemia and Moravia who claimed Jewish nationality and who dedicated their efforts and resources to the development of pioneering settlements in a remote "foreign country" (*Yishuvim* in Palestine). The only shortcoming of this project seemed to be that it could eventually encourage other ethnic groups to demand autonomy.[114] It is interesting to note that less than a year earlier Karel Sidor, deputy of the Slovak People's Party, proposed in the Prague Parliament the transfer of Jews from Slovakia to Birobijan, arguing that they were "for the most part Communists."

There were, of course, reactions of another sort to Peroutka's provocative piece. The Jewish press made a special, almost unanimous effort to prove the decline of the Jewish population in the historic lands. Lucian Benda, one of the leading members of the Czech-Jewish movement, was commissioned to undertake research on this topic; his findings were presented in statistical tables showing the demographic decline of the Jewish population and a decrease in their number in the economy and business.[115] The editor of the Communist *Rudé právo*, Jan Krejčí (writing under the pseudonym Ludvík Klecanda), published the brochure *Židovská otázka* (The Jewish question), analyzing the topic from a balanced perspective.

Beset by fears over the mounting problems created by the refugees and the growing hostility of the population, *Rozvoj* in its October 21, 1938, issue condescendingly expressed approval of the campaign of the Czech cities and the press, lending its full support for a Czech national state thus: "It is not desirable that emigrants, of any religious persuasion, should settle in our cities and thus endanger not only their national character but also the very existence of the Czech people."

Furthermore, in response to the stringent resolution passed by the *Sokol* organization, the leaders of the Czech-Jewish movement convened on November 3, 1938, for a "friendly supper" with journalists in the club of the National Café in Prague. Aside from the representatives of the press—Dr. Minařík (*Národní listy*), Beran (*Národní střed*), Voska (*Právo lidu*), and Arnold (*Telegraf*)—the police counsel Dr. Antonín Jakubec participated in the meeting and drafted a report on it.[116] The topic of discussion was "the timely problem of the Jewish question." Dr. Otto Stross, the chairman of the movement, opened the meeting and Dr. Müller, the secretary general, led the discussion. The latter rejected the accusation that "the Jews were to be blamed for the historic disaster." The journalists used various arguments to urge the leadership of the Czech-Jewish movement (1) to request the government to partake in the agenda of "the solution of the Jewish question," and (2) "to draw a demarcation line between themselves and the other Jews" (i.e., German Jews and Zionists). From the press conference held by the Czech-Jewish movement on November 4, 1938, we learn that the latter proposal had been meekly accepted and thus made public: Jews "of other categories" (as implied in the 1930 census)—that is, those who claimed other than Czech nationality (including Jewish nationality)— should be considered foreign elements and leave the country.

Those responsible for this statement believed in their innocence that it might help to overcome the difficulties and pave the way for their "fuller integration" into what was left of Czecho-Slovakia. Very soon, however, ensuing events revealed how erroneous and self-deluding was their rationale.

With regard to the issue of participating in "the solution of the Jewish question" the situation evolved as follows: at the beginning of January 1939 the

Supreme Council of the Jewish Religious Communities submitted to the government and the Presidium of Parliament in Prague a memorandum touching upon the most essential issues: vocational retraining, the refugee problem, and emigration overseas.[117] They also demanded that religious freedom and the equality of rights (*iura quaesita*) of Jews be safeguarded and that their economic suppression should not be condoned. The memorandum ended with a statement to the effect that the Jewish problem in Czecho-Slovakia could be materially eased by vocational reorientation, along with the gradual emigration of those who desired to leave the country for "economic reasons." Surprisingly, however, although Zionists, Czech Jews, and the Orthodox jointly agreed about the contents of the memorandum, it was not the only paper submitted to the authorities. The Czech Jews decided to address their own observations to President Hácha, enumerating their special merits (stressing the noted literati and artists within their ranks), offering as a first remedy to get rid of the refugees as well as to promote emigration. Their move triggered the Zionists (Poalei Zion and the Revisionists separately) to present their own comments. As a result the government authorities received four memoranda altogether on the issue of "solving the Jewish problem." Needless to say, these "constructive proposals" formulated with so much effort in the memoranda went unheeded by the Beran government.

THE EVE OF NAZI OCCUPATION—
ELIMINATION OF JEWISH "INFLUENCE"

Until the crucial days of Munich, anti-Jewish propaganda was directed mainly by Hermann von Gregory, press attaché of the German Legation in Prague, in concert with the Ministry of Propaganda (*Reichspropagandaamt*) in Berlin and the Sudeten German Party headquarters. Employing different permutations according to the needs of the day, their main goal was the masses, the man in the street.[118] After the autumn of 1938 it was Berlin's political pressure that was brought to bear on the Czecho-Slovak Government with regard to anti-Jewish policy. The Foreign Ministry under von Ribbentrop's direction now assumed an important role in a subversive propaganda drive aimed at undermining morale. The fact that Julius Streicher devoted an entire issue of his hate sheet *Der Stürmer* to the Jews of Czecho-Slovakia was an ominous portent. Jewish intellectuals—politicians, writers, artists, and journalists—were now the main target.

Two weeks after the Munich Agreement, on October 13, 1938, Foreign Minister František Chvalkovský conferred with von Ribbentrop in Berlin.[119] In his summary of his country's development over the preceding twenty years he admitted to the "fallacious" policy of the former regime of Masaryk and Beneš and concurred with the German view on the "poisonous influence" on public opinion of Jews holding key positions. Chvalkovský undertook to eliminate this fault forthwith, first and foremost in his own ministry, obviously alluding to Dr. Oscar Butter (the Czech-Jewish legionnaire closely associated with Beneš and the "Mafia" during World War I), who served as head of the Foreign Ministry bureau.

The report Carr sent from Prague to the secretary of state on November 25, 1938, notes "numerous indications" that restrictive measures against Jews are to be expected in the near future. The new Czech United National Party was considering proceeding immediately to solve the "emigration problem." Some of the younger members of this party had already called publicly for "radical anti-Semitic legislation and extensive expulsion of Jews from the country on the ground that a place must be found for the young Czech generation within the reduced state."[120]

Nevertheless, the draining of Jewish capital and Czecho-Slovakia's increasing difficulties with her export trade were still instrumental in maintaining a moderate attitude in official circles. Occasionally sober views were voiced in the Prague Parliament as well. Thus in a courageous speech on December 14, 1938, the Conservative deputy Dr. Ladislav Rašín (son of the former minister of finance Alois Rašín) praised the prime minister for not succumbing to "gutter" propaganda.[121] He also warned that the result of anti-Jewish excesses would only be that markets would be closed to Czechoslovakia's exports, the promotion of which was the chief task of the government. He alluded to the boycott of Czech products in the United States of America and the warnings issued by the Jewish organizations.[122] Rašín therefore advocated, for economic reasons, legal security for Jewish concerns and for the Jews themselves.

Western observers agreed that the Czechs were in an untenable situation. Both Newton, the British minister and De Lacroix, the French minister to Prague, briefed their governments on the primacy assigned to the Jewish issue by German leaders during their parleys with Czech politicians.[123] This was also evident to the Soviet ambassador Alexandrovskij, who declared in his parting address at the Černín Palace on January 24, 1939, that "the solution of the Jewish question will be an indicator of how far Czecho-Slovakia would go in her efforts to reach an agreement with Germany."[124]

It was in this connection that on December 6, prior to the renewal of the loan negotiations, Viscount Halifax instructed Newton to demand from the Czech authorities a situation report with regard to the anti-Semitic measures and the position of the Sudeten refugees. He also recommended that the French minister should be involved in a similar undertaking.[125]

Foreign Minister Chvalkovský kept repeating to the British representatives that "it was not the intention of the Government to discriminate against the Jews." In fact, they wished to restrain the ongoing anti-Semitic agitation, and with this object in mind a general statement of the government's posture would be issued on December 13. At the same time, when conferring in Berlin with von Ribbentrop, Chvalkovský promised "to eliminate Jewish influence without delay." The Czechs indeed found themselves in an impossible situation, as the British minister reported to London: "between two fires being urged by the Germans to destroy the Jews, and by ourselves to protect them."[126]

It also became apparent that officials noted for their anti-German sentiments were being ousted from public life and influence. Thus while in some spheres of life reason and restraint maintained the upper hand, chauvinism and opportunism were surfacing in the fields of culture and professional activities under cover of nationalism and patriotic feelings.

Skirmishing had already begun in some localities in 1937. In Moravská Ostrava, Fascist groups managed to force the local management of the National Theater to replace conductor Jiří (Georg) Singer, the "Jew," and have Jaroslav Vogel, the director of the Opera, conduct the performance.[127]

Actor Hugo Haas, born in Brno in 1901, was the brother of the composer Pavel Haas.[128] Hugo recalled his part in Čapek's RUR as Consul Busman—a Jew—staged in 1938 at the Stavovské divadlo. One day, before the performance began, he was handed a letter from the management:

> Quiet descended . . . none of the actors jested or quipped their usual anecdotes . . . It became quiet, silent as a grave. I opened the letter and read . . . since I have attested to my Jewish origin in my papers the management of the theater is obliged to suspend my contract, effective immediately. And then there was a note that in the next performance I was to be replaced by someone else. I felt as if a bottomless pit had opened up in front of me. The surrounding quiet indicated that my colleagues knew. As I stood in the semidarkness behind the curtain, awaiting my entry onto the stage—slowly and softly—I was approached by Regisseur Karel Dostál, who fell on my neck and whispered in a husky voice: "Haas—forgive us . . . I am so ashamed—I beg you—forgive us." Never shall I forget that moment and often—very often—I heard that kind voice ringing in my ears: "Haas, forgive us."[129]

Ironically on his way home Haas still saw posters advertising the play: he himself, "Consul Busman," was walking in the street while the play was in progress on the stage. Hugo Haas ends his recollection by noting how two years later while acting in *RUR* on Broadway as Alquist every evening, his sad exit from the theater in Prague came back to his mind.[130]

Already during the Munich crisis personal attacks by their colleagues on Jewish actors, musicians, and writers became the vogue. They spread like a plague. In his memoirs Hanuš Thein, the famous baritone and a favorite of the Czech theater, relates a grim episode.[131] In October 1938 Thein directed a new production of "The Bartered Bride" at the National Theater in Prague. An anonymous letter published in the Agrarian *Venkov* incited the musicians to boycott him because of his Jewish origin. The next day, before the general rehearsal, one of the fascist members of the orchestra requested his fellow musicians to refuse to play under the baton of Václav Talich, who was cooperating with Thein and the painter Vincenc Beneš on the performance. The response of Talich (against whom charges of collaboration were leveled after the war) was firm and dignified: he lectured the musicians about the commendable work of Hanuš's father, Dr. Thein, physician at Pardubice, and then about Hanuš and his unique contribution to Czech culture. It was the director of the National Theater who gave in: frightened by the agitators, he ordered that Thein's name be deleted from the posters and programs.[132] Thein was forbidden to take curtain calls. And all this happened in October 1938 prior to the Nazi occupation.

The association of Czech writers set an additional example of ignominy, demonstrating new depths of self-abasement. The chairman of the writers' social club (*Společenský klub*), Dr. Karel Schieszel, who had headed the political section of the chancellery under Presidents Masaryk and Beneš, notified the Jewish writers that their membership had been canceled.[133] When the ailing Čapek learned on his sickbed of this move on the part of his close associates, he was outraged.[134] "If only I could get well," he lamented, "I would show you . . ." He wanted to know what prompted the Czech writers to take this step, and when he heard that their intention was "to forestall the Germans," he reacted vehemently: "Let the Germans do it! We do not have to help them along on this insane and criminal matter." Upon the demand of some of the members, the club's chairman had to withdraw his hasty decision. Reminiscing about this episode, humorist Karel Poláček recalled that when some days later he ran into Schieszel in Prague, the latter placatingly extended his hand. Poláček reacted in his own sarcastic way: "Henceforth I shall talk to you but will not shake hands with you."[135]

Some of the decent people were paralyzed and withdrew into private grief and anonymity. It is an enigmatic but established fact that few of the cultural elite had the courage to raise their voices in protest against discrimination or even actual attacks against their Jewish compatriots. Among the few who spoke out publicly was Professor J. L. Hromádka, head of the Comenius Theological Faculty at the University of Prague.[136] Others were the parliamentary deputy Dr. Ladislav Rašín, Milena Jesenská, and Josef Bohuslav Focrster, president of the Czech Academy of Science and Art.[137] On December 19, when the insults and slander leveled against Jewish intellectuals climaxed in the press, Foerster came out boldly against anti-Semitic agitation in the magazine *Rythmus*. He defended Jewish patrons of the arts and stressed their massive contribution to Czech culture, asking: "Are we to exclude men like Gustav Mahler and others from our cultural life solely on racial principles? No, in our country this cannot and must not happen: anti-Semitic baiting leads ultimately to the destruction of cultural heritage and the ruin of God's houses of prayer."[138]

Hromádka refers in his statement about "Christians and Jews" to the difficult and sad situation of the Jews and the helplessness and frustration of those Czechs who sympathized with them: "We cannot even cry out the way we would like to. Only one thing can we do and that we do with utmost pleasure, silently press the hands of our friends of Jewish origin, assuring them of our undiminishing and even our growing and deepening sympathy."[139]

There were frequent reports in the Jewish press about incidents of provocation and harassment by various official organs. In January 1939 public officials were calling on Jewish families upon the "order" of higher authorities, inquiring about their nationality and the language spoken at home and even showing interest in their libraries.[140] Several families received questionnaires mailed by the authorities, requesting identification of their religion, nationality, and race.

The (second) encounter between Hitler and Minister Chvalkovský, on January 21, 1939, gave new impetus to the anti-Jewish campaign. Jewish influence in the press, theater, and public offices "make the situation intolerable," proclaimed the Führer.[141] He also indicated that a solution of this problem could help to clarify bilateral relations. Beneš's policy was in fact "the work of the Jews and freemasons," he claimed.

After Chvalkovský's return to Prague a new line of policy was adopted: "to free the nation from the vestiges of Benešism."[142] Most instructive in this regard is the comprehensive report sent by the legation in Prague to the United States secretary of state, headed "The Jewish Problem in the New Czechoslovakia," detailing the changes taking place in the country.[143] Among other things it disclosed that Jewish physicians were being asked to leave their posts at public hospitals and that leading Czech athletic clubs were dropping their Jewish members. About forty-five Jewish professors in the German section of Charles

University were pensioned off. The same principle was applied in German schools throughout the country. "Purges" had also taken place in the German theatrical establishments and the German-language newspapers. Among those purged from Masaryk University in Brno was Jaroslav Stránský, professor of penal law, son of Dr. Adolf Stránský. In January 1939 a special communication sent by the minister of education, Dr. Jan Kapras (himself a professor of law), requested that Jaroslav Stránský's lectures be terminated because of his Jewish origin.[144]

The new decrees issued by the government on February 1, 1939, calling for the reconsideration of citizenship of certain classes of Czechoslovak nationals and providing for the deportation of aliens, were directed mainly against the Jews. This fact is stressed in the American consul Carr's report sent from Prague to the secretary of state on February 2, 1939. Listing the various categories (naturalized, domiciled, divorcees, and adopted children), the report notes: "Such persons are obliged to report to the provincial authorities no later than April 30, 1939. Persons residing abroad are to report in the district of last residence prior to moving abroad . . . Refugees will be obliged to leave Czechoslovakia upon request within a period of from 1 to 6 months . . . *The decrees will not apply to persons identified as Czechs, Slovaks or Ruthenians*" (italics mine).[145]

The American Consulate's report also refers to the local Germans constantly agitating against Jews, insisting that radical measures be adopted to curb their activities.[146] In this connection the Sudeten German deputy Ernst Kundt gave an interview for the Berlin *12 Uhrblatt* (quoted in the Prague *Národní politika* on February 4, 1939). Reiterating the Führer's statements about the elimination of Jewish influence in the theater, press, and public offices, Kundt emphasized that this could pave the way for better understanding and "help clarify the problem still pending between Germany and Czechoslovakia."[147]

Even at this stage moderate Czech circles were mindful that no radical action should be taken against Jews and, in particular, that the rights of the long-established Czech-Jews should be safeguarded.[148] This was a point accentuated by some of the "decent" journalists, who took up "differentiation" as a criterion: drawing a line between long-established assimilated Jews and the "others." Thus, for instance, the Association of Catholics (Sdružení katolického lidu) advised the Party of National Union (Strana národní jednoty) to adopt three criteria for membership, guided by "national and Christian ethics."[149]

It seems that Peroutka and some other public figures sincerely believed that a change in policy toward the Jews could pave the way for a *modus vivendi* with the Germans. With an eye to a new rapprochement he published "Czechs, Germans and Jews" on February 22, 1939, as his contribution to the impending Czech-

German dialogue on the Jewish issue.[150] He compared German with Czech anti-Semitism, ascribing the situation that had developed in Germany to "historical mistakes" on the part of German Jews: their wealth, the inflation, the "oriental" influx (Eastern Jews—*Ostjuden*), and most of all their overpowering presence on the German cultural scene, contrasting markedly with the "inconspicuous" ratio of Jews in Czech cultural life.[151]

Commenting on the German Jews' writing, he described it as "sensational," turbid, and resembling "a pond in which unknown substances were floating." Peroutka's wording—he obviously borrowed his coarse similes and modes of argumentation from the Nazi vocabulary—was staggering. In addition he made venomous remarks on how anti-Semitism was gaining ground in America and elsewhere, presaging evil for the future. Peroutka leveled most severe charges against the "Germanizing" Jews of his country: "had it not been for them, the Munich conference would not have cut off so much of our territory," he argued. However, he defended the "thin layer" of Czech-Jews who fully identified with the aspirations of the nation and called for a different approach toward them. When reprimanded by some of his "Czech and German-Jewish readers," Peroutka stoutly defended his review and blamed the censor for some of the "misplaced" statements. He also insisted that he had not intended "to add fuel to the blaze." On the contrary, he had meant to ease the situation of the long-established Czech-Jews.

His leitmotif, "adjustment in concert with the existing circumstances," Peroutka derived from Havlíček's political conception. Prompted by this realistic, pragmatic approach, he insisted on direct negotiations with the Sudeten German Party in January 1938 and also participated in official discussions held with the German ambassador in Prague. However, after Munich, his main objective was to safeguard the Czech nation and thus to avoid turning "the tragedy of the state into a tragedy of the nation." His stance earned him Jan Stránský's scathing remark: "howling with the wolves."[152]

During its brief lifespan the Czecho-Slovak Parliament passed two laws that were commonly viewed as directed primarily against the Jews: two decrees of January 27, 1939, one calling for a review of the naturalization proceedings by which certain individuals had obtained Czechoslovak citizenship after 1918, and the other for the deportation of certain aliens.[153] As already noted, these individuals were required to register with the provincial authorities no later than April 30, 1939. The purpose of the decrees was obviously to expel the refugees from Germany and Austria, with perhaps an additional category of German-speaking Jews, against whom strong resentment existed among the Czech populace.

The laws enacted in Parliament reflected the unmistakably deteriorating situation. Thus on March 12, 1939, three days before the occupation, the nationalist *Národní listy* came out with an unambiguous proposition on the matter of Jewish property: "In view of the international situation and in order to preserve the national character and material existence of future generations, the Jewish question is to be solved in the banks, industrial concerns, public institutions and corporations thus guaranteeing the national and 'Aryan' element an opportunity commensurate with its numerical proportion and sovereignty."[154]

THE ECLIPSE OF DEMOCRACY

In 1927 the French-Jewish philosopher Julien Benda, in his *La trahison des clercs*, discussing the role in society of the intellectuals ("clercs") of France and Germany, issued a pessimistic warning of a Dark Age "far more barbarous than the first."[155] Among other things he castigated the acquiescence and complicity of the intellectual caste and their failure to reject German nationalist doctrines outright, thus facilitating the Germans' "impending triumph." The impact of this seminal work was overwhelming, especially when later events vindicated Benda's pessimistic view. Some of the foremost representatives of the Czech cultural scene related poignantly to this issue. Among the first to comment on the book and Benda's visit to Prague shortly after its publication was F. X. Šalda. Although he expressed some objections to Benda's ideas, he stressed the value of the thesis, warning against the spread of racial bestiality and the impending catastrophe. Later, in 1933, Šalda wrote the passionate proclamation "Fascism and Culture" in response to the first wave of brutal persecution of German democrats by the Nazi regime. "To all of us whose life depends on spirituality and creativity in quest and cultivation of truth, it is imperative to be on guard and to defend ourselves."[156]

After the "auto-da-fé," one year later, Čapek commented on the German spiritual tragedy in a series of articles viewing the betrayal and the failure of the intellectuals and their complicity as a cardinal motif in the victory of Nazism.[157]

During the Second Republic the press, public, and institutions deviated dramatically from the ideas on which the foundations of "that model democracy of Central Europe" rested. The want of public courage to speak out, to raise voices against discrimination, was undoubtedly a symptom of the moral decline of Czech society. The change in attitude toward the Jews became the hallmark of this radical transformation.

This notion invites reflection and speculation. Much has been written on the Czech national traits, the centuries-old habit of "bending the spine," the best moments and spiritual achievements as well as extreme defeatism in times of crisis and adversity.[158] What is indeed staggering is the "collective acquiescence" and the plain truth that ulterior motives and opportunism were the driving force behind it. One cannot ascribe it to any ideological affinity: the Czech elite, unlike their German counterparts, did not come under the spell of the *Kulturmission* of the Germanic race or the vision of the "thousand-year Reich."

Nevertheless, the Nazis managed to manipulate a wide spectrum in mindless willingness to comply with any and all demands in public affairs and vis-à-vis the Jews. The nadir to which this behavior sank on the national level was the abysmal ignominy of the management of the National Theater in Prague, who did not dare lower its flag to halfmast to mark the death of Karel Čapek.[159] The Pantheon "did not have the coal" to heat the assembly hall and could thus not conduct an official funeral for the great humanist, symbol of the First Republic of T. G. Masaryk.

Darkness flooded the vaulted sky over the ancient city of Prague: it was only after the occupation by the German army, toward the end of 1939, that the "winds of change" set in, restoring a certain degree of mental health, resilience, and unity of outlook.[160] Passivity on the part of the army, police, and wide circles of the public accompanied the loss of independence: lack of courage and an overwhelming nonmilitancy are the predominant attributes marking the crucial period of before and after Munich; there was no sign of any effort to resist.[161]

Many years later some prominent writers reminiscing about this period claimed that apart from the political apathy that gripped a great majority of the people, they themselves had another crucial problem to deal with: how to write. Being politically and ideologically disoriented, they found themselves in a blind alley. Egon Hostovský voiced the frustration that many felt: "There was someone to fight against, but nothing to fight for."[162] Jaroslav Jelínek, a social democratic journalist, described the dilemma confronting them: "The press of all streams became helpless . . . How to write, how to lead the readers and the nation?"[163] And again it was the indomitable Milena Jesenská who found a way to wrestle overtly with this question. In several of her defiant articles she incorporated hints to her readers on how to read between the lines and interpret her references and allusions to events of the past. Her appeal: "Why do you not speak out, young people?" was a grievous *j'accuse*, exposing the indifference of the new generation.[164]

After Peroutka's arrest in March 1939 she replaced him as de facto editor of *Přítomnost*, and she continued to write her encouraging pieces about the Czech identity, as in "Česká maminka" (The Czech mom), and the innate Czech spirit, as in her evocative "O umění zůstat stát" (The art of remaining erect).[165] The latter essay was written as a prayer for continued existence: a song about the Czech home, the land and the countryside, the unique wording of the national anthem, "Kde domov můj" (Where is my home?): "a land of hills and hillocks, fields and leas, silver birches, weeping willows and broad-crowned lime trees; a land of fragrant boundaries between fields and tranquil little streams. The land where we are at home."[166]

From the perspective of half a century later, the faltering of the cultural elite—journalists, writers, students who had long played such a dominant role in the national liberation struggle (the Hussite movement, the nineteenth-century revival, and the First World War movement of independence)—adds a disturbing dimension to this phenomenon.

The radical transformation of wide segments of Czech society under the impact of Nazi propaganda and the consequences of the Munich *Diktat* caused a steady wave of alienation and open hostility toward Jews in general and German-speaking Jews in particular. This attitude generated within Jewish circles an overall feeling of disillusionment and frustration, bordering occasionally upon panic. The agitation conveyed through the press and radio, the proclamations of intellectuals, were symptoms hacking at the edifices of democracy built up during two decades. The social relations and national goals to which Jews had considered themselves party by profound conviction crumbled and collapsed around them. This sudden *volte-face* had, of course, immediate and long-term repercussions. With hindsight we could say that, paradoxically, it produced a positive result as well—as far as emigration and rescue of the Jewish population of this enclave is concerned. It is estimated that during 1938–39 around twenty-seven thousand individuals managed to leave Bohemia and Moravia and thus escape the "Final Solution."[167]

The haunting memories of Munich had other consequences too. Students of postwar history claim that one of the reasons why so many Jewish intellectuals joined the Communist Party after 1945 was that it seemed to them to be the only force opposed to Nazism, promising "to build a humanist society without racial or national discrimination."[168] In 1948 almost 50 percent of the intelligentsia of the country joined the Communist Party, acting in large part out of disappointment over the "bourgeois" democracy that faltered during the Munich crisis. It is, however, gratifying that the same generation of intellectuals who actively contributed to the Communist coup d'état in 1948 became twenty years later part of the reform movement and influenced "Prague Spring."[169]

In the long run postwar historians tend to view President Beneš's decision to choose the physical survival of his nation as both politically erroneous and, morally, immeasurably harmful. But given the international situation in September 1938, Beneš doubted the Czechoslovak Army's ability to resist alone; he considered "an isolated war at this time" to be "national suicide."[170] One may assume that as commander in chief of the armed forces Beneš was aware of the difficulties in mobilizing an army made up of at least 25 percent Sudeten Germans and Hungarians, whose loyalty was more than dubious, as well as Slovaks and Ruthenians, whose "unruly" nationalist leaders were openly courting Nazi Germany.[171]

Beneš could not envisage that a memo compiled by Hitler's senior generals on September 26, 1938 (published in France in November 1938), would reveal the despondent morale of the German population and various deficiencies in German armaments.[172] It described divergences between the political and military leadership of the Reich and noted (in the appendix) that "even if fighting without allies [the Czechoslovak Army] could hold out for three months." That opinion was confirmed by Generals Halder and Keitel at the Nuremberg Trials.[173]

Students of Czech history struggle continually with this issue.[174] Thus, for instance, Milan Hauner points out: "It's too easy to blame one man after the events had gone wrong."[175] He poses the intriguing question: "Why was Beneš allowed in the first place to concentrate so much power in his hands?" Another expert, Radomír Luža, claims that "the threat of a Polish attack presented the main reason for the acceptance of the Munich ultimatum by Czechoslovakia's military leaders."[176] There is, however, a general consensus that Beneš, the pragmatic politician, discounted the psychological factor: the impact of the government's surrender on his own people. This issue keeps engaging the Czech society. More recently the philosopher Jan Patočka gave vent to a severe critique of President Beneš, claiming that he utterly failed by giving in to Nazi demands.[177]

In the political context Munich is still a simmering issue at the very heart of the international scene; it projects the dilemma of small states with minorities whose loyalties belong to their own nations "across the border" and who thus constitute a constant threat to their host country.

The consequences of the Munich Agreement were fatal. Less than six months later "rump Czecho-Slovakia" was dismembered. On March 14, the Parliament in Bratislava proclaimed Slovakia's independence. One day later the remaining territory of Subcarpathian Ruthenia was annexed to Hungary. The same day the Wehrmacht entered Prague.

Under German Occupation
(1939–45)

Ever since the late thirties Hitler's tirades against Czechoslovakia had continued unabated. However, unlike in many other countries, in this enclave his threats signaling the day of reckoning were listened to with the closest of attention. *Mein Kampf*, Hitler's writ spelling out his expansionist policy (the so-called *Lebensraumprogramm*) had been available since 1936 both in German and in an abridged Czech version (*Můj boj*) and was widely read.[1] Czechoslovakia being in close geographic proximity—bordered on two sides by Nazi Germany—and harassed from inside by a fifth column, the country's vulnerability peaked in the autumn of 1938.[2] Nevertheless, the sudden occupation by the Wehrmacht on March 15, 1939, not six months after the Munich Dictate, took the population by surprise.

On March 16 Hitler himself came to Prague. Eager to be the first to reach Hradčany Castle, he raced with his entourage and ss guards "through the night at breakneck speed over icy roads, passing the advancing columns on the way."[3] His wish came true: posing triumphantly at the alcove window used by the presidents of Czechoslovakia on state occasions, he could look down over a defeated Prague. While staying at the castle he signed the decree incorporating the Czech historic lands into the Reich under the euphemistic designation the Reich Protectorate of Bohemia and Moravia.

The French-Tunisian agreement (1881) provided to a certain extent the structure for the occupied territory's administration. Czechs became citizens of the Protectorate, whereas all citizens of German nationality were granted citizenship of the German Reich. The Sudeten German Party merged with the NSDAP.

Germany took charge of defense and foreign relations, the communications system, customs, and currency matters. However, internal administration was left in the hands of the Czech authorities. Formalities were preserved. Emil Hácha was permitted to retain the title of president; he himself, however, and the cabinet ministers he nominated, were responsible to the *Reichsprotektor*, Baron Konstantin von Neurath, appointed on March 18, 1939.[4] Karl Hermann Frank, one of the leaders of the former Sudeten German Party, was appointed state secretary of the Protectorate. All other key positions were filled by Reich officials. Although the Beran government was not immediately dismissed, all vestiges of Czech quasi-sovereignty were de facto abolished. The parliament was replaced by a fifty-member "Committee of National Solidarity" (*Národní souručenství*), appointed by the president.[5] As a symbolic act, at Hitler's direct order the original Golden Bull of Charles IV of 1356, laying down the rights of the kingdom of Bohemia in relation to the Holy Roman Empire, was taken from the regional archives to be sent to Nuremberg.

This new national humiliation ushered in another dark period for the Czech nation. Neither President Hácha's declaration signed at the Reich chancellery on March 15, 1939, "placing the fate of the nation in full confidence into the hands of the Führer," nor his acquiescent speech the day after the invasion, viewing the republic as "a short episode in our national history," could have offered much solace to the Czechs.[6]

The German occupation of Bohemia and Moravia brought about an instant change in the life of the Jewish populace. All relief organizations had been forcibly disbanded. Together with the occupying forces the Gestapo marched in and immediately launched a wave of mass arrests under the code name Aktion Gitter (Operation bars). The first to be arrested were émigrés from Germany, politicians of the *ancien régime*, known public figures, and, of course, Jews.

Wilbur Carr's report to the secretary of state on March 19, 1939, refers to these widespread arrests done "in the usual Nazi manner" and proposes supportive action:

> The Jewish population is terrified; as are Social democrats and also those closely associated with the former regime. Consequently if action can be taken it should be done speedily. While the British Legation seems to be hopeful of obtaining exit permits for most of its refugee cases I am personally doubtful whether Germany would be receptive to requests for the departure of political refugees and Jews but it would seem to be the humane duty of our Government to support some kind of international action to this end even though doubts may be entertained as to the outcome.[7]

It appears that appeals on behalf of several hundred of these unfortunate people had already reached his majesty's government earlier. Consequently, the British minister at Prague was given urgent instructions "to give all assistance possible to facilitate the departure of all those for whom provision to enter the

United Kingdom had been given or promised." The ambassador at Berlin was also given instructions in this vein. It seems Lord Halifax believed a warning that "the detention of people who merely on racial or religious grounds desired to emigrate would create still greater prejudice against Germany" could be effective.[8]

The roundups were carried out by the Czech gendarmerie, which apparently had prepared its own lists well in advance; these were readily handed over to the Gestapo (in Přerov on April 4, 1939; in Olomouc on May 6, 1939).[9] A thousand persons were arrested during the first week of the German occupation; before long 4,639 were behind bars. Among those arrested were known champions of the Jewish public Marie Schmolka and Hanna Steiner, who were taken to the Pankrác prison.[10] Most of these early prisoners were subsequently released, except for the German-Jewish refugees, who were sent to concentration camps.

On April 27 Hácha reorganized his cabinet, appointing as the new prime minister General Alois Eliáš, who had once been a prominent figure in the Beneš administration. From the outset, Eliáš considered it his task to work for the survival of the Czech people at a minimum sacrifice of Czech lives.

While the country was under military administration—until April 15—the Germans seemed to be pursuing an ambiguous policy. Although they disseminated anti-Semitic propaganda using the media (radio lectures, leaflets), they did not openly engage in anti-Jewish activities, leaving this task to the Czech fascists. One of the first anti-Semitic papers appearing in Prague in 1939 exhorted the public to "Read the Czech Stürmer." In fact, NSDAP members in the Protectorate were under orders from party headquarters in Munich to abstain from fraternizing with Czech fascists and from molesting Jews, for fear of public unrest.[11]

Chauvinism and narrow-mindedness became more perceptible and vociferous; profound demoralization and cynicism gained the upper hand among the Czech populace. The relationship between the Czechs and the Jews in what was now the Reich Protectorate of Bohemia and Moravia reached its lowest point. In the name of Hitler's New Order, radical Jew baiters voiced their desire to free the country from the vestiges of "Benešism, Bolshevism, and freemasonry," all of which were associated in their minds with a liberal attitude toward the Jews.

The campaign against the two former presidents included publication of *The Hilsner Affair and TGM* by Jan Rys-Rozsévač, leader of the movement Vlajka (the flag).[12] The work was dedicated to August Rohling, and its main purpose was to revive old superstitions of blood libel and to incite the Czech population against the Jews. Additional measures set afoot were the demolishing of statues of Masaryk and Beneš (the iron to be used for armaments) and the launching of a steady press campaign. An article published in September 1939 designated Masaryk as "the moving force behind the process of decomposition of the Czech nation." Some of these fascist agitators went so far as to demand the exhumation of Masaryk's body at Lány. Beneš himself was described as the "hireling of the Jews."[13]

Anti-Jewish excesses began at an early stage. The synagogue in Vsetín was burned down on the day the Germans arrived; in Jihlava (Iglau) the synagogue was torched on March 30, as were the synagogues of Ostrava and Kynšperk.[14] The conduct of the local administration was often instrumental in restraining the instigators. Some synagogues were salvaged owing to the vigilance of the local population. In Klatovy, for instance, Mayor František Bíček asked to be relieved of his position, claiming that he could no longer be responsible for the maintenance of order in the town.[15]

One of the American consul's reports, sent to Washington on June 22, 1939, refers to "Bomb Explosion in Jewish Café": "On Saturday, June 17, a time bomb exploded in the Riva restaurant in Prague, a restaurant frequented chiefly by Jewish persons, 39 people are reported to have been injured . . . The bomb is believed to have been placed in the restaurant by one of the Czech fascist groups."[16]

It seems that the first attempt to destroy the Altneuschul in Prague was made as early as March 20, 1939. Miraculously the wind put out the flames.[17] The second abortive attack occurred several months later during the Shavuot holiday, when a bomb thrown from a neighboring building exploded, causing no harm. From that time on, the Jewish Religious Congregation of Prague (JRC; Židovská náboženská obec or ŽNO in Czech) employed a security guard who for several months was in charge of guarding Jewish historic sites and monuments.

The Altneuschul also witnessed incidents of humiliation and desecration early on. The first "razzia" occurred in 1939 during the New Year services. The SS and Gestapo men conducted a roundup, seizing several Jews and taking them into custody. Eichmann himself paid an "official" visit to the synagogue on October 15, 1939. It transpires that the Nazi authorities were considering how to utilize this famous historical edifice for propaganda purposes. On August 10, 1940, Dr. František Weidmann, head of the JRC, and Franz Fischof, custodian of the synagogue, were summoned to the headquarters of SS *Sturmbahnführer* Hans Günther for questioning. He proposed making a film about Jewish rituals, showing the interiors of the synagogue and all its religious appurtenances with the participation of the robed cantor surrounded by one hundred congregants (extras) "bearded, sidelocked and wearing prayer shawls."[18] For some reason this film on the "peaceful life of the Prague community" was never shown or distributed.[19]

While entry to the public parks and grounds was prohibited by order, Jews were free to use the local burial grounds, and many did so for "recreational" purposes and in their search for solace. Particularly favored was the ancient Jewish cemetery with its many famous rabbinic graves visited by Jewish pilgrims across the centuries. One presumes Günther's order on February 2, 1943, that the keys to the cemetery gate be immediately handed over to the *Zentralamt*, was intended to deny the Jews the last site of spiritual comfort.[20] (Scraps of paper addressed to the Maharal, praying for speedy redemption, were found after the war in the cracks in his tombstone.)

Jews suffered particularly harsh treatment in localities with large German populations.[21] In some places such as Roudnice and Klatovy, Jews were forbidden to use sidewalks and were forced to walk in the middle of the street. Under the pretext of reprisal for the alleged April 24 taunting by Jews of thirty German soldiers on a trolley car in Pilsen (Plzeň), 150 "Marxists" and 150 Jews were rounded up in cafés and their homes. Among those arrested were Mayor Pik of Pilsen, several members of Beneš's party, and Jewish doctors and lawyers. During the spring of 1939 several pogroms took place at Příbram, and the synagogue at Dobříš was damaged. Between May 19 and 28, fascist groups organized violent demonstrations; Jews in Brno were dragged out of cafés and attacked in the streets.[22] The first victim, brutally tortured during the assault on Café Esplanade on August 15, 1939, was Dr. Pavel Drexler, a well-established Jewish physician.[23] The autopsy naturally attributed death to other causes. To prevent public outcry his funeral took place under police escort.[24]

The fascists clamored for enforcement of the Nuremberg racial laws and for creation of a Czech secret police, to be called the "Czestapo."[25] In Moravia, rightist circles were even stronger, backed by the National Socialist Czech Workers Party and the Agrarian Party: in Brno, Olomouc, and Uherský Brod a number of synagogues were burned down without any interference. On May 25 and 26, fascists staged an anti-Semitic demonstration in the streets of Prague but were ignored by the public.[26] *Arijský boj* (The Aryan struggle), a bulletin issued by Vlajka—the most extreme among the fascist organizations in the Protectorate of Bohemia and Moravia, with a membership of about thirteen thousand—called for the ghettoization of the Jews. A special section of storm troops, the so-called Svatopluk guards organized on the model of SA and SS, specialized in assaults on Jews in Pilsen, Příbram, and Dobříš and in arousing terror.[27]

Opportunism and compliance reigned in large circles of the Czech civil service, as among the leading personnel of industry, transport, the police, and the government army. This situation allowed the Germans to economize in their own civil services, keeping their numbers low. Instead they concentrated on the special services of the ss, police, the notorious Gestapo, and the security sevices.[28]

The first sectors of the Czech population to yield to Nazi anti-Semitic propaganda were the merchants, followed by the bar and medical associations. Additional groups, prompted by their own ulterior motives, appealed to the Committee of National Solidarity and to the Czech government to oust the Jews from economic and public life.

Meanwhile, anti-Semitic agitation continued. At a meeting of the "National Aryan Cultural Union" (*Národní arijská kulturní jednota*) at Pardubiçe on July 29, 1939, the speaker, one František Drázda, advocated the complete exclusion of Jews and "Jewish freemasons" from national life, going so far as to suggest extermination as a means toward that end.[29]

The first month following the occupation served the Germans for setting the scene for a long-range policy: efforts were made to achieve "trust" and cooperation with the new Czech administration and the people at large. At the same time the Gestapo and its subsidiary organizations built up their machinery of control (movement restrictions, roundups, etc.) for dealing, among other things, with the process of destruction of the Jews. To replace the Secret Police station, located as of December 1938 in Dietrichova Street, in May 1939 new headquarters were established in the heart of the city. A huge and imposing building was taken over—the former Bredovská Street mansion of the Jewish banker Julius Petschek (built by architect M. Spielmann).[30] It was equipped with modern technical facilities such as tube mail, a printing press, photo laboratories, workshops, garages, and telephone centers. This is where the notorious "Security Police" (*Geheime Staatspolizei-Staatspolizeistelle Prag*) were based, interrogating the members of the various resistance groups in lengthy hearings and torture sessions. In the course of time four additional buildings were confiscated in which the Criminal Police (*Kriminal polezei*, or Kripo) were housed. Additional police stations operated in Pankrác and on Karlovo Square. Prague headquarters alone employed eight hundred to a thousand individuals, some of them women, carefully selected for "confidential" tasks. One of the routine activities of the Secret Police was to record the prevailing mood of the population. Besides the Security and Criminal Police forces another notorious institution came into being on July 15, 1939, which was to witness endless inhuman cruelties.[31] This was the so-called Zentralstelle für jüdische Auswanderung (Central office for Jewish emigration), an outpost of the Reichssicherheitshauptamt (RSHA, the main office of Reich security). Located in the Prague-Střešovice district in the villa of Mark Rosenthal and ostensibly headed by the chief of the Security

Police, Walter Stahlecker, the Zentralstelle was actually led by Sturmbahn-führer Günther, Eichmann's deputy.[32] As of August 20, 1942, it was known as the Central Office for the Solution of the Jewish Problem in Bohemia and Moravia.

One of the main targets of Nazi policy was to uproot Czech society both physically and spiritually while at the same time ridding the territory of Bohemia and Moravia of its cultured stratum. To this effect a secret memorandum proposed encouraging emigration of the Czech elite, considered "the irreconcilable enemy of Germany," to distant lands.[33] German emissaries were to be enlisted to search out suitable employment abroad and thus induce Czech university professors, leading economists, and political figures to leave. The memorandum quotes the case of the departure of the Petschek family, whose eleven villas and other estates created "some precious breathing space" which surely would be an asset for the "reinforcement of Germandom."

Many of the historical statues, sculptures, and other works of art were destroyed or removed and plaques, street signs, and announcements were replaced by bilingual signs: German first, followed by Czech. While the statue of the Maharal had been screened by boarding and thus salvaged for posterity, the sculpture of Moses was saved by caring citizens. Statues of Ernest Denis and Woodrow Wilson were torn down. An *Ämtliches deutsches Ortsbuch* (Official guide to localities) was issued by the Reichsprotektor, listing places by their former German names.[34] Localities in the region of Prague, for instance, were given as follows: Hloubětín—Tiefenbach, Černý Vůl—Schwarzochs, Panenské Břežany—Jungfern Breschau, Odolená Voda—Odolenwasser, Řepy—Rüben, Přemyšleni—Premischl, Líbeznice—Rotkirchen (sic).

From the very outset the Protectorate had to liquidate all vestiges of the liberal economic and social policy by means of directives, of which ample use was made. On July 5, the Protectorate Government was forced to issue a decree placing the German language on a par with the Czech language. Its aim was to abandon "the old atmosphere of national prestige," announced the *Berliner Wochenblatt* on August 23, 1939. This act was in accord with the policy toward the ultimate objective, Germanization, spelled out by Hitler himself in the early thirties in a conversation with Hermann Rauschning as *Technik der Entvölkerung* (technique of denationalization).[35]

State Secretary Frank's "Memorandum on the Czech Problem," submitted to Hitler on August 28, 1940, delineates the workings and aims of the highest Nazi echelons with regard to the Czech administrative apparatus, the ultimate goal of which should be the elimination of the autonomy of the Protectorate. However, for lack of trained civil servants the corps of Czech officials who "functioned well" should by and large be retained. Frank proposed to "fill the important key positions in the higher ranks of administration" with the body of well-trained German officials in order to lead and govern and "to direct matters with a German fist."[36]

The incorporation of Bohemia and Moravia meant harnessing gigantic concerns such as the Škoda munitions works for German military armament. Moreover, the weight of the whole Czech economy with its important coal, iron ore, and timber and its skilled manpower amplified that of the Reich in its military objectives. In addition to the valuables seized in Prague such as gold and foreign currency, on instructions from the Czech National Bank a deposit of 800,000 ounces of gold was transferred in the summer of 1939 to Berlin.[37] Of greater significance were the takeover of around 200,000 technical plans and patents and the growing expansion of overall German economic potential vis-à-vis the world market.

A dispatch sent from the U.S. Consulate General in Prague describes the economic chaos.[38] It notes long trains loaded with clothing, lubricants, and other materials moving directly from Czech warehouses into the Reich. Prevailing opinion holds that by the seizure of Czechoslovakia "Germany gained approximately one year on England in the armament race." The dispatch notes the transfer to Germany of all Czechoslovak National Bank funds and the total control imposed by the German authorities, the lack of coordination in the administrative system, and the absence of incentive on the Czech side; the exodus of many important Jewish industrialists is also reported. At this point the dispatch writer already sees fit to comment on the signs of "revenge" and "reprisal" on the part of the German administration and, particularly, on corruption in business and the tendency of the Germans "to feather their own nests." The missive also predicts the "descending of a horde of individuals from Germany to strip the country bare of all purchasable goods."[39]

CONFISCATION OF JEWISH PROPERTY

One of the main objectives of Nazi policy was to secure control over all Jewish property (17 billion Kč.). It has been estimated that before World War II, approximately one third of all industrial and banking capital in Czechoslovakia had been in Jewish hands.[40]

The largest metallurgical combine in the country, the Vítkovice Iron Works in the Moravská Ostrava district, was controlled by the Viennese branch of the Rothschild family.[41] The most important coalfield in the Ostrava-Karvinná area was initially developed by the Gutmann family. A number of mines in Kladno were also owned by Jews. The Petschek family owned a banking house in Prague and coal mines in northern Bohemia, in Most (Brüx), Falknov (now Sokolov), and Duchcov (Dux). The Weinmann family of Ústí nad Labem (Aussig) also owned coal mines in northern Bohemia. Jews were prominent in the timber industry and trade, the glass industry, hat making, hosiery manufacture, textiles, and other branches of industry. The Germans gained control of the assets of these Jewish families through "voluntary" and forced negotiations, employing blackmail and threats.[42]

As a rule they negotiated only with the largest industrial companies because many of them had connections with West European countries (the Rothschilds had managed to convert the Vítkovice Iron Works into a British enterprise as early as February 1937). The bulk of the acquired assets were incorporated into the Hermann Göring Werke, greatly enhancing the German war potential. A noteworthy case was that of the Böhmische Escompte Bank (Bohemian discount bank, BEBCA) in Prague, which was taken over by the Dresdner Bank in February 1939, a month before the German occupation.[43] The bank subsequently became the main instrument for the Aryanization of large Jewish capital holdings. Its three directors, Dr. Feilchenfeld, Dr. Löb, and Dr. Kantor were killed by the Nazis.

After the occupation of Czechoslovakia negotiations with Jewish owners of business and manufacturing concerns were suspended. From that point the Germans disregarded obligations, and the former agreements were never honored. Some members of the wealthy families were able to migrate and establish themselves overseas. While the industrial magnates and bankers took steps to safeguard their property through connections with West European countries, smaller entrepreneurs made efforts to circumvent the imminent threat through local contacts. Thus, for instance, in May 1938 Rudolf Werfel, owner of the Werfel and Böhm glove factory and father of Franz Werfel, empowered his long-standing employee Erich Fürth, a German national, to register the factory in his own name.[44] A year later Werfel tried to arrange for the transfer of all his shares in the company but to no avail.

Excesses occurred even earlier, before the occupation: local fascists in České Budějovice put their own commissars in charge of banks and Jewish enterprises. On March 17, 1939, at Benátky nad Jizerou a German police detachment took over the industrial concern producing carborundum and electrolit, dismissing at once all twenty-six Jewish workers, including the administration.[45] Most illustrative of Nazi confiscation policy was a secret guideline, dated as early as March 15, 1939: "The Meaning and Aim of the Establishment of Trusteeship

(*Treuhandstelle*), in View of the Confiscation of Jewish Property." It asserted unequivocally that the sequestrated Jewish assets would become public property: "Jüdisches Vermögen wird Volksgut."[46]

Nevertheless, for several weeks following the occupation the Czech authorities and the public at large were lulled into a false sense of security that decisions as to the measures to be taken would be in their own hands. Thus all shades of fascist ranks began to pressure the Czech Government and the National Solidarity to adopt a radical program for the elimination of Jews.[47] In addition, the large numbers of unemployed Czech officials and army personnel who had lost their positions through the ceding of territories saw in the Aryanization process an opportunity for gaining a livelihood. This notion was implied in Premier Eliáš's assertion of May 13, 1939: "A solution will be found for the Jewish problem to correspond to the interests of public life and to the demands of an unhampered economic development of the Protectorate."[48]

During the first meeting of the Beran government on March 17, 1939, a set of decrees was passed with regard to the exclusion of Jews from public life.[49] Three days later the order issued by the German Military Authority forbade the appointment of administrators in Jewish enterprises which either wholly or partially belonged to Jewish proprietors. "All matters of Aryanization were to be conducted by the Office of the Reichsprotektor."[50]

Applications of individuals and interventions by members of the Committee of National Solidarity on behalf of certain candidates flooded the authorities. On April 14, 1939, it was reported that even before the official directives were issued concerning the appointment of trustees (*Treuhänder*) and enforced managers (*Zwangsverwalter*), Lieutenant Colonel Hamšík asked that his request to be named trustee for the firm O. Ziegler, manufacturers of raincoats in Prague, be granted special consideration.[51] This was not the only case of a former military officer eager to acquire Jewish property. A report of the Trustee Surveillance Committee of the Prague *Oberlandrat*, dated June 26, 1940, quotes the records of the Ministry of Health and Social Welfare (October 12, 1939), according to which approximately four hundred former officers of the Czechoslovak army applied for trusteeships. Of these only nine applicants were appointed as trustees, eight in vinegar factories and one in a liquor depot.[52]

After the publication of the Reichsprotektor's comprehensive decree (June 21, 1939) it became clear that the law concerning "Jewish enterprises" was drawn up so as to encompass Czech property as widely as possible, including everything linked in any way with Jewish participation. This "dual act" in effect served as an eye-opener to the Czechs, disclosing that the primary aim of the decree was the strengthening of the German ethnic presence in the Protectorate.[53] The value of confiscated Jewish property was carefully accounted for in the various German agencies and reported to the Reichsbank.[54]

The segregation of the Jewish population proceeded quickly. Through the *Landräte*—the German administrative bodies set up in all the regions and districts of Bohemia—and through the Gestapo the Germans quickly acquired control over local Czech administration in the provinces. (By the fall of 1941, around 10,000 Germans were supervising a work force of 400,000 public service employees.)[55] Jews were required to register all their property and business enterprises with the Landräte, which in turn were authorized to appoint a Treuhänder and then to decide whether to Aryanize this or that enterprise or to liquidate it outright. When the deportations began, these agencies were most instrumental at every level in clearing the provinces of their Jewish population.

Jews were ordered to register and subsequently (April 30, 1940) to sell all gold, platinum, silver, precious stones, and pearls in their possession to a special public purchasing agency, HADEGA, and to deposit all their stocks, bonds, and securities at a foreign currency bank.[56]

Apart from local German inhabitants who gained considerably from the Aryanization process, about half a million Germans who had moved from the Reich to the Protectorate, of whom approximately 120,000 lived in Prague in houses and apartments vacated by their Jewish owners, netted fat profits from taking over Jewish factories and firms.[57] Thus, for instance, a report prepared for the Prague *Oberlandrat* (June 26, 1940) states that of a total of 1,205 trustees appointed in the area, 1,109 were Germans and 96—a mere 7.9 percent—were Czechs, illustrating the overwhelming German takeover.[58]

The huge quantity of confiscated valuables was immediately transferred to the empty coffers of the Reich treasury. A former employee of the Prague Gestapo has related how sometime in 1942 and 1943 she herself had seen two shipments, each consisting of twenty-five large containers holding the gold, silver, and other precious metals extorted from the Jews, being dispatched to Berlin, probably on the order of the RSHA.[59]

The daily report of the Security Police surveying the disparity between the Czech press in the Protectorate and the mood prevailing among the Czech populace had this to say: "The Czechs are not at all selective in seeking allies against the Germans . . . Also the Jew is a welcome partner for the Czech. The Czechs are convinced that international Jewry will do its utmost in order to support by all available means those who today oppose Germany, and hope for the downfall of Germany."[60]

In some cities people expressed their sympathies by shopping at Jewish firms and boycotting those owned by the Germans. In the city of Pilsen, during a performance of Elmer Rice's *Street Scene*, the audience burst into applause at the actor's words: "At long last the Jews are human beings too."[61] The Nazis employed every possible means of intimidation to bring about the isolation of the Jews. Czech gentiles caught during police raids at Jewish homes or at the community offices were taken to Gestapo headquarters for interrogation.[62] While German nationals, even those who were known as liberals, were more cautious about associating with Jews, some Czechs continued to visit their Jewish friends, mostly during the evening hours, trying to render them small services and to save them the harassments of everyday life.

The poet Ilse Weber, who lived in the industrial city of Vítkovice, known for its mixed German and Czech as well as Polish and Jewish population, wrote to her sister-in-law Zofia-Zosha ("Schusch") Mareni in Jerusalem on May 6, 1939, commenting sadly on the sudden change in the attitude of her neighbors and friends:

> Oskar has probably told you that we have always lived with all people, regardless of nationality, in peace and good friendship. . . . I loved the people just as much, and always had excuses for their occasional, visible shortcomings and now?—I shall tell you what happened to me, for example, one market day. I live quite close to the market and the way to it is not long. First I met Mrs. Röhrer (Oskar can provide the necessary comments). She was a close friend of my sister's and we liked each other very much. At first she greeted me with: "Good Morning!" but immediately afterward, she smiled mockingly and added: "Heil Hitler!" A few steps further. I met Mrs. Hocke. Oskar does not know her. She is the wife of a laborer, who had once come to me when she was in great trouble. She worked in my house . . . Suddenly she stares into the air. Then I meet Mrs. Rozehnal . . . she passes with a stony face and does not know us any more. Other German friends look at the ground. Only a very few still greet me warmly and—to tell you the truth—such are still around.[63]

At the height of summer following the escalation of the German-Polish conflict, the border area of Moravia-Silesia was subjected to special torment: Jews were arrested on various pretexts.

On the night of August 31, 1939, Reinhard Heydrich shammed an attack against the German radio transmitter at Gleiwitz, employing a crude stratagem: the "assailants," actually concentration camp detainees dressed in Polish uniforms who were simply "mown down," were left scattered in the field to be viewed by the German and neutral press.[64] The Germans, of course, did this to incriminate the Poles for starting the war. Many years later the *Informations-bulletin* of the Prague community provided additional data on this episode drawn from the testimony of one of the "assailants" who managed to escape.[65] According to this information many Jewish detainees taken hostage by the Gestapo in Bohemia and Moravia in the so-called Operation Albrecht I were driven across the Moravian-Polish border area on the eve of the war and were never heard of again.

Altogether about two thousand hostages were taken in the Albrecht I roundup, among them numerous prominent Jews from all walks of life as well as several rabbis from the Czech countryside. The following were listed by name: František Parkus (Nymburk), Filip Polák (Benešov), Bláma and Frischmann, Rabbi Dr. Hoch (Pilsen), and Rabbi Dr. Arnold Grünfeld (Jihlava), all of whom perished in concentration camps.[66]

The situation of the Jewish Religious Congregations radically changed following the issuance on June 21, 1939, of the Reischsprotektor's decree concerning Jewish property. As of July 10, the JRC became subordinate to the Zentralstelle. One of the decrees legally codified the definition of "Jews" and "persons of mixed (part-Jewish) blood," adopting the Nuremberg Laws of September 15, 1935. Thus all persons considered Jews were registered, and their ration books were stamped "J." From now on they were permitted only limited amounts of rations and clothing. They were banned from parks, cinemas, theaters, museums, and libraries and were not allowed to leave their lodgings after 8:00 p.m.; only by written permit of the Gestapo were Jews allowed to use rail transport (the back platform of the last car) and other means of communication.

Having been excluded from public and economic life, Jews were obliged to accept the work allocated to them by the Labor Exchange. They were assigned to road work, as farm laborers, as foresters, and to various other labors.

OCCUPATION OF POLAND AND THE FIRST DEPORTATION CAMPAIGN

The onset of war on September 1, 1939, engendered a more optimistic mood among the Czechs, who now hoped for a speedy defeat of the Germans. Curiously enough while members of the Vlajka enlisted as volunteers in the Wehrmacht, the general populace was amassing food products.

The Jews of the Protectorate of Bohemia and Moravia were the first to be hit by Eichmann's devilish dejudaization campaign of the annexed Polish territories launched in mid-September 1939. The Jews of the Ostrava and Frýdek-Místek districts were ordered by Eichmann and Günther to register with the JRC and simultaneously to apply for admission to a so-called *Umschulungslager* (vocational retraining camp). On October 17, 1939, all the assembled men were to leave for an unknown destination with a limited quantity of personal belongings.[67]

In the event two transports of Jewish workers (aged seventeen to fifty-five), organized by Eichmann, left Moravská Ostrava on October 18 and 27, 1939. They headed to the so-called Jewish reservation (*Judenreservat*), an area in the barren district around Lublin, in the General Government (Nazi-occupied Poland). The first transport included 901 men, the second 391 men. Originally the second transport was meant to have included women aged seventeen to fifty-five, but this plan did not materialize. The Gestapo recorded that when the JRC announced this regulation a general flight began among the Jews of Ostrava as news spread of horrors in the fate of the first dispatch of men.

According to the name-list compiled by the Gestapo in Ostrava, the two transports numbered altogether 1,292 men. The first group left Moravská Ostrava in sealed railroad cars, arriving at Nisko in German-occupied Poland on October 19. They were soon followed by a second batch, sent to a barren site southwest of Rozwadow, devoid of any accommodation for the new arrivals. Without proper materials or tools they were ordered to build living quarters. From the summary of a secret report dispatched by the Home Resistance to the Czech National Committee representatives in London on October 27, 1939, evidently compiled by Salo Krämer, the head of the Jewish community, we gain firsthand information about the ordeal of this enforced emigration "experiment."[68] (It is not without interest that via the Swiss Embassy in Berlin, similar information secretly reached Dr. Marcel Junod, the special delegate of the International Committee of the Red Cross in Geneva, who undertook some special inquiries on the issue.)

> The Jews are held completely in the clutches of the Gestapo. The *Dienststelle* of the Central Office supervises the Jewish Religious Community . . . The Chairman and the Secretary are responsible personally for every order conferred on them. These are communicated to them [solely] orally to give the impression of emanating from Czech sources . . . 18.10 . . . Of the 1,500 men, 1,000 were taken to Poland for forced labor. At Bohumín [on the border], the train was stopped and everything they had was taken away from them. The Jew Krämer [head of the community] was tortured because he informed Prague about the whole affair.[69]

Two leading members of the JRC of Prague, Jacob Edelstein and Richard Israel Friedmann (the latter had originally come from Vienna), were attached to the Nisko transport to "supervise the resettlement" of the deportees. Upon their return to Prague, Edelstein and Friedmann briefed the leaders of the community.[70] To both men this encounter with the initial Nazi sham served as a warning of utmost significance: they realized what was in store for the Jews. After consultations with members of the JRC they resolved to remonstrate openly against further shipments. They informed the authorities that "no threat of punishment could prevail upon them to lend a hand to this kind of emigration: even if the Zionist Federation were to be dissolved and its leaders sent to Dachau, they would have no part in this horror."[71]

A month later while staying in Trieste to organize the emigration of the Jews from the Protectorate (with Nazi permission), Edelstein dispatched a letter (on December 12, 1939) to Eliahu Dobkin of the Jewish Agency in Jerusalem, auguring ominous developments. He urged immediate help, expressing his fear that "if assistance would not soon be forthcoming" there would be massive deportation in due course. "All efforts should be made to forestall this danger."[72]

He also informed the representatives of the Jewish Agency in Geneva, Dr. Fritz Ullmann and Chaim Barlas, of his experiences at Nisko. It was on the basis of Edelstein's evidence about Nisko, which Chaim Barlas took to London, that Louis Namier published his uniquely important article on the "Jewish reservat" in Lublinland; it ran anonymously ("from a correspondent") in the *Times* on Saturday, December 16, 1939, under the title "The Nazi Plan: A Stony Road to Extermination."

Describing the overall Nazi scheme, Namier articulated the fact that the Jewish community was forced to "cooperate" in this gruesome transaction. So far transports from Vienna, Mährisch Ostrau, Teschen, and Katowice in Silesia were known to have reached the reservat, he stressed. The first purpose was to make room and loot areas "singled out for systematic Germanization." The greatest danger threatened the Czech Protectorate and the western provinces of Poland. Namier asserted: "It is clear that the scheme envisages a place for *gradual extermination*, and not what the Germans would describe as Lebensraum and that the maximum deportation program comprises all the Jews now under German occupation" (italics mine).[73]

In order not to involve persons by name, Namier referred to "evacuees" who managed to escape (by way of Russia) as his source of information: "Early in October the Jewish community in Mährisch Ostrau was ordered to compile a register of all male Jews between the ages of 17 and 55 . . . and to parade on October 17, at 8 a.m., at the Ostrau riding school. Each man was ordered to take a knapsack, a suitcase, food for three days, and a maximum of 300 marks . . . About 1,000 men were taken in buses to the railway station. As that goulish cortège proceeded through the streets of Mährisch Ostrau non-Jewish Czechs, and even some German women, were seen crying bitterly."[74]

Several passages of Namier's account clearly resemble the text of Edelstein's report "on the Nazi inferno," read at the Zionist convention at Geneva in February 1940 and reproduced in full in the diary of Moshe (Shertok) Sharett, who at that time acted as head of the Jewish Agency's political department: "Edelstein's lecture was shocking—both in what he said and what was left unsaid . . . A calamity which befell them recently is the demand of the man in charge of the Jews [Eichmann][75] that the Zionists send a mission to the U.S. to convince the Jewish leaders there to send envoys to Germany to negotiate with the Nazis on the "solving" of Jewish matters in the Reich . . . the real intention is to exploit this type of mission for propaganda purposes and thus create an additional barrier against America's entering the war."[76]

The Nisko campaign was suspended by the Germans in mid-April 1940. Those still in the camp were allowed to return to their hometowns. Others who were lucky enough to escape during the forced march under gunfire toward the Russian border, organized by the ss, were held in Soviet prisons after crossing the River San. (It is estimated that around three hundred of them enlisted in the Czechoslovak units formed in the Soviet Union in 1942.)[77]

THE IMPACT OF THE OUTBREAK OF THE WAR

President Beneš broadcast the first stirring appeal from his exile in London on September 19, calling upon the Czech nation to resist the oppressor: "Throughout the whole country," he said, "from the last village up to Prague, in every workshop, in every enterprise, continue to carry on the struggle."[78]

Indeed, the various home resistance groups managed to organize a number of defiant acts.[79] On September 30 (the first anniversary of the Munich Agreement) the workers of the capital refrained from using public transport: masses of people crammed into vehicles put at their disposal, others made their way on foot to their places of work, complacently watching the street trams run empty in the city. The German press insinuated that the protest in Prague was staged against the Jews using public transport.

Czechs were celebrating the beginning of a new period of resilience, wrote the London *Times*. On St. Wenceslas Day, crowds gathered around Prague's magnificent statue of the warrior prince, decorated with floral tributes by anonymous donors. The well-informed reporter also noticed that at the traditional mass sung in the Cathedral and attended by members of the government, that verse in the "St. Wenceslas Chorale" which refers to the nation's hope of resurrection was omitted.[80]

The autumn campaign culminated in demonstrations to mark the twentieth anniversary of the founding of the republic. From now on "whisper propaganda" and distribution of leaflets became widespread. Audiences gathering on various festive occasions in concert halls and theaters began to react spontaneously to meaningful words and music. The performance of Smetana's opera *Libuše* with its moving finale glorifying the "Undying Nation" was seen as a kind of collective prayer—"a mythic ritual." (In the course of time, the Germans banned this opera as well as others evoking national sentiments.)[81]

Religious pilgrimages too were exploited for outbursts of Czech patriotism. A climax was reached with mass demonstrations on Czechoslovak Independence Day, October 28, 1939. Following this came the November 17 upheaval, which ended tragically with several victims. In retaliation, over a thousand students were sent to concentration camps, and all Czech universities and institutions of higher learning were closed.[82] These developments produced a certain change in the feelings of many Czechs toward their Jewish fellow citizens, manifested by sympathetic gestures both in public and in private contacts.

Various Czech resistance groups in Prague used every opportunity to transmit messages to neutral countries through visitors, informing them of enforced German regulations and restrictions. On November 23, 1939, on leaving the Prague Town Hall a group of Dutch, Swiss, and Scandinavian journalists found fliers in English in their coat pockets. One paragraph stated that the solution of the Jewish problem was being carried out by the Germans and not by the Czech authorities. It stressed that the Aryanization of Jewish firms and industrial enterprises was merely a means to prevent the transfer of Jewish property into Czech hands with a view to Germanizing the Czech areas.[83] By this time, all semblance of leniency toward the Jews had been cast off; ordinance followed ordinance limiting their freedom of movement. Jews were denied certain food rations, sugar, and tobacco as well as articles of clothing.

The first anniversary of the occupation of Prague by the Wehrmacht was marked by troops marching across the city. According to the American consul's observation "the line of parade was almost empty of pedestrians," except at Wenceslas Square, where the watching crowd was composed exclusively of Prague Germans. The Czechs preferred the banks of the Vltava to watch the flood, which was exceptionally high that year. The same report offers observations about the change in the general mood following the massive arrests among former Czech officers and members of the Czech intelligentsia: "After Munich the Czechs were disillusioned and more resentful against England and France than against their traditional enemy, Germany. Many felt that their only salvation lay in closer relation with Berlin. This sentiment, however, was soon overcome by the activities of the Gestapo."[84] This was set forth bluntly in State Secretary Frank's "Memorandum on the Czech Problem."[85]

Soon life became unbearable for Jews, especially for young people accustomed to moving around freely but now barred from entering public places, parks, movie theaters, and sports grounds. The sensitive young poet Jiří (Ohrenstein) Orten spoke for all in describing the feelings of a pariah. He noted in his diary an incident with rowdies in a Prague tavern, when he was "caught" drinking with a non-Jewish acquaintance. He overheard his name being loudly pronounced by jeering youngsters, rowdies from a neighboring table. Terrified, he left immediately, realizing that his life was at stake: "I took my coat and left at once. I still heard those cowards shouting out my name for the last time from the back of the room. Then I found myself outside, on the freezing street, trembling with fatigue. Oh God, where have I sinned?"[86]

In the same vein Orten quotes the lamentation of Jeremiah in his own interpretation: "With what kind of wormwood has the Lord filled the hearts of those who keep denouncing us?" Orten's preoccupation with the Old Testament and the Prophets of Israel is clearly apparent in his entries during this final chapter of his life. This harrowing experience never left him. Several indications can be found in ensuing entries, and one day he sat down to list at random the prohibitions he remembered by heart. He even left some blank space for ensuing restrictions, which he came to experience only a few days before his untimely death. Although heartbroken, the sensitive and gifted young poet found some solace in his writing and the newly discovered attachment to his mother, which brought him a sense of comfort in this chapter of his life.[87]

On his twenty-second birthday, August 30, 1941, he was run over by a German vehicle on the Rašín embankment in Prague, dying in agony two days later. There are speculations as to whether his death was an act of suicide, as some of his biographers suggest.[88] It might have been his own personal protest against the tyranny and persecution. If so, Orten's suicide was not the only case of disenchantment in those days of turmoil, when human relations suffered such disruption and erosion. His older brother, Ornest, wrote after the war: "In those critical moments he could not deem that he would be able to leave behind the girl he loved, his homeland and his native language. He felt that he had to experience his lot, to be able to express it himself."[89]

His funeral was the last gathering of admirers and sympathizers, of numerous older and younger writers, led by the poet František Halas, Orten's mentor and friend. His uncle, the poet Josef Rosenzweig-Moir, and his younger brother Zdeněk, then in a Prague Jewish orphanage, were also present. (His brother Ota had by then emigrated to London.) Thanks to a thoughtful Czech attorney who promptly sent off a counterfeit warrant to Orten's mother, Berta Ohrensteinová (neé Rosenzweig) in Kutná Hora, she too could be present at her son's funeral in the Strašnice cemetery.[90] Jiří Orten's demise was symbolic, occurring on the eve of the mass deportation of Czech Jews that began in mid-October 1941.

PRAGUE'S JEWISH LEADERSHIP FACING NAZI COERCION

Prior to the Nazi seizure, there existed 136 Jewish communities in the Czech lands, numbering a total of 118,310 persons, of whom by 1940 more than 27,000 managed to emigrate abroad, escaping the fate of their co-religionists. Under a decree enacted by the Reichsprotektor on March 5, 1940, the JRC of Prague was given jurisdiction over all congregations in the Protectorate as well as over all individual Jews, including 12,680 Jews of "non-Mosaic" faith (i.e., nonpractising Jews or converts to Christianity), known as "B-Juden."[91]

The German occupation and the ensuing events broke down existing barriers and differences prevailing among the various factions of Jewry. An unwritten truce came about between the two major sectors, Czech Jews and Zionists, guided by one common aim: to save what still could be salvaged, ideological differences were overcome and replaced by mutual trust and responsibility.[92] As everywhere in occupied Europe, Jewish leadership had to function in the most precarious circumstances.

At the outset, the JRC of Prague was led by two members of the assimilationist Czech-Jewish movement, Dr. Emil Kafka as chairman and František Weidmann as secretary. After Kafka's departure for London, Weidmann was appointed chairman by the Zentralstelle and Jacob Edelstein, the noted Zionist leader and director of the Palestine Office in Prague, was appointed deputy chairman. He was assisted by Eng. Otto Zucker, who for some years had served as JRC chairman in Brno, by Dr. Franz Kahn, secretary of the Zionist Organization, and others.[93]

The initial stage of the JRC and the circumstances of its rapid growth have been described by Erich Kraus, a former member of the community leadership; as of April 1943 he acted as deputy to the last *Judenältester* (Jewish elder): "When the organization was built up in 1939 . . . community work was hardly held to be attractive. In 1939 people were primarily engaged in pursuit of self-preservation and consolidation of their own affairs, eventually with emigration . . . In order to cope with the speedily mounting tasks arising out of the emigration issue [fostered by the authorities] the organization grew larger and was joined by a number of dedicated people, Zionists and their followers as well as the activists of the Czech-Jewish Kapper Club."[94]

The first agreement reached among the Prague communities was to join forces. On April 17, 1939, the chairmen of the seven religious congregations in Prague agreed to operate in concert.[95] The next day a meeting was held in the ancient Jewish Town Hall with the participation of twenty delegates representing eleven provincial localities, who had specially arrived to discuss the pressing circumstances. Their reports were alarming: "Wherever the German population is large, the situation is grave."[96] The newly imposed regulations such as movement restriction and deprivation of livelihood demanded an immediate reaction on behalf of the community.

With the German occupation the JRC's activities were divided into three main spheres: welfare activities, service to be rendered to the Zentralstelle, and liquidation of Jewish assets. As in other countries, the community apparatus was reorganized to cope with the newly created functions.

A phenomenon unparalleled elsewhere was the active participation of the intelligentsia in public relations activities of the JRC, especially in the first stage of its establishment. This situation stemmed from the fact of their being the first to be ousted from their positions, and thus ready and willing to offer their skills and talents to boost the morale of the besieged community. It is a quirk of fate that the elite of Czech Jewry in its prime, once designated as the cream of European society, became before its ultimate destruction the chroniclers of the community's decline.

The emigration department with a staff of about ninety individuals was headed by the well-known poet Dr. Hanuš Bonn.[97] It is also noteworthy that some of the leading figures of the JRC, such as Marie Schmolka, Hanna Steiner, Jacob Edelstein, František Friedmann, and Emil Kafka were permitted to travel to foreign countries even after the war had started. Apart from fund-raising they were to conduct negotiations with relief organizations such as HICEM, ORT, and the American Joint Distribution Committee (JDC) to locate target countries for emigration.[98] Eichmann and his associates tried to exploit these trips for their own propaganda purposes. The emissaries' families, however, were detained in Prague as hostages to ensure the travelers' return. With the consent of the authorities Hanna Steiner also undertook a trip to Berlin and Hamburg to negotiate with shipping companies and consulates of neutral countries. In Germany she conferred with the consuls of Santo Domingo, Venezuela, and Ecuador as well as with the representatives of the JDC.

As emigration became the central issue, the education department launched a large-scale vocational reorientation program; courses in agriculture, hand-icrafts, industrial arts, hotel management, and foreign languages were offered for prospective émigrés. The effort invested in these activities has been well documented in graphs, statistical tables, charts, and maps prepared by a skilled team of Jewish artists engaged in the technical department.[99] These annual reports display the various stages of liquidation of the community, such as changes in the work force, population decline, and property transfer.

As of November 24, 1939, the new format of the bilingual community weekly *Jüdisches Nachrichtenblatt / Židovské listy* made its appearance.[100] Although cen-sored by the Gestapo, it was for a certain period regarded as the only "free" newspaper available in Prague.[101] (Jews were not permitted to subscribe to or purchase other newspapers.) It was edited by Dr. Oscar Singer with a number of prominent journalists and public figures contributing regularly: the composer Karel Reiner, the poets Hanuš Bonn and Jiří Orten, former *Berliner Börsen-zeitung* editor Emil Faktor, cartoonist Fritz Taussig (Fritta), and others; Singer would later be the foremost chronicler of the Łodý ghetto.[102]

The first issue, in November, announced that emigration, social assistance, and youth care were to be the most essential tasks: "Our youth is our future . . . We have to bring them up so that even under the hardest living conditions we can steadily and courageously fulfill our mission: to preserve our nation."

It also carried František Weidmann's urgent call for large-scale emigration, warning: "This is not the time for empty phrases and talk." The editorial "Vom Sinn der jüdischen Opfer" (The meaning of Jewish sacrifice) implies that al-ready at this date (December 29, 1939), the Jewish leadership was well aware of the impending threat to their very lives: "From the gravity of the Jewish situa-tion stems the particular significance of Jewish sacrifice. As the shipwrecked in a lifeboat pass around their last water bottle and then cast their belongings over-board to save their lives from the sinking ship, Jews in our times must offer their own personal sacrifice. This act means not only obeying the command to love your fellow man but is primarily prompted by the sober *instinct of self-preservation*" (italics mine).

Aside from informing the readers of the anti-Jewish laws and regulations enacted in the Protectorate, the main objective of the weekly was promoting emigration—advertising vocational training and foreign language courses, sup-plying data about prospective countries, and presenting life in Palestine by means of colorful descriptions of kibbutz life.[103] Some of the editorials ap-pealed for calm and discipline, urging affluent Jews to help their less fortunate brethren; others indulged in soul-searching, recalling the glories of bygone days, or sounded somber warnings "to avoid any action that might endanger all Jews."[104] The community weekly also carried some boldly phrased messages interspersed between the lines of the editorials and the short historical vignettes called "Little Chronicles" (*Malá kronika*), authored by the historian Jaroslav Polák-Rokycana.

Rokycana used his small column to recall events from ancient Jewish history in Bohemia to encourage his readership at the time when anti-Jewish legislation was the only substantial "reading" material in the weekly.[105] Two vignettes present allegories on the Prague Jewish clock and the ancient Czech Haggadah. The allegory of the sixteenth century Jewish clock tower drives home the need to study Hebrew and to return to Eretz Israel:

> The tower of the Old Town Hall facing the Altneuschul treasures two precious clocks: one has Roman numerals moving clockwise, and the other has Hebrew letters and moves in the reverse direction. The movement of these two clocks symbolizes at this crucial time two opposing directions: the hands of the Roman clock moving forward signify the Jews' wandering from their homeland on the Jordan River to the banks of the Vltava, and the city of Princess Libuše. The Hebrew clock, in contrast, indicates the path of return. There was a time when the Jews lived by the Roman clock, but today the bells sound an alarm . . . Look up at the clock tower and make haste in learning Hebrew. The hands of the Jewish clock show [us] the way of return.[106]

Although emigration at this point was no longer feasible in view of the change in German policy, Rokycana centers his second vignette around the Passover holiday and the story of the Exodus as presented in the oldest of Czech Haggadahs, that of 1748. Legend has it that the latter work was authored by Karel Jugl, chaplain of St. Stephen's Church, who learned Hebrew and acquired the title of *Morenu* (our teacher). The Haggadah has an illustrated frontispiece engraved by Master Hollar, portraying five Jews standing erect around a table set with a Seder plate and a paschal lamb:

> With your loins girded, your shoes on your feet, "and your staff in your hand; and you shall eat it in haste: it is the Lord's Passover." (The caption in small Hebrew letters is drawn from Exodus 12:11.)
>
> It was throughout the last centuries, in times of peace and prosperity, that our *"Ma nishtana halaila haze . . ."* had been written. The heads of the households generally chose to sit, lolling back on soft cushions with a sense of comfort and security. Ironically it is Chaplain Jugl of St. Stephen, a Christian with a distinguished Jewish title, who had to remind us of the long-

forgotten ritual: Jews, the time has come again: stand up, gird your loins, with shoes on your feet and staff in your hand—ready for departure. This is the command of the day.[107]

The outbreak of the war put an end to free emigration from the Protectorate and made it difficult, if not virtually impossible, for individuals to leave. Nevertheless, the Zentralstelle ordered all wealthy Jews to submit an emigration file (*Auswanderungsmappe*) indicating "Shanghai" or some other place as "destination," although it was obvious that the land and sea routes were closed. All this was in order to impose staggering taxes on the potential emigrants.

The onus placed on the JRC leadership and the sense of duty felt by those responsible is echoed in the community weekly: "In accordance with the decree, the Prague Jewish Community is now headed by a governing body [*Leitung*] to whose jurisdiction all communities in the country are subordinated as well. The authority [to be] exercised by this body derives from the competence of the Zentralstelle. The very existence of such an authority is [a] new [phenomenon] in the history of the Jewish Diaspora. It is the profound wish and the firm hope of the governing body that this authority will be used solely for the benefit of the community."[108]

In due course the functions of the JRC were expanded and redefined to include collection of fees and taxes, aid for the needy, gathering statistical data, emigration, implementation of the orders for forced labor, and assistance to deportees.[109] (As earlier noted, Jews had to work as assigned by the Labor Exchange, and the JRC now had jurisdiction over all congregations in the Protectorate and all individual Jews.)

In order to cope with these new functions, a huge bureaucratic apparatus of thirty-two sections with a total of approximately twenty-six hundred employees was set up.[110] During 1940 the public kitchens of the JRC in Prague provided over one million meals to its now destitute beneficiaries: occupants of five homes for the aged, two orphan asylums, and ten children's homes, with a total of nine hundred residents. It ran two hospitals, a dispensary, and a home for the mentally ill.[111] Similar institutions were run in two other major cities: Brno and Moravská Ostrava. Bank accounts held by Jews were blocked; only small amounts (500 crowns) could be withdrawn each month.

Eventually with German approval a special fund was launched by Otto Zucker under the slogan "Give! Build! Live!" and endowed by affluent Jews who transferred funds from their personal bank accounts.[112] This made it possible for the JRC to care for the needy members of the congregation, to provide them with clothing, to open up soup kitchens and infirmaries, and to run vocational training classes and foreign language courses for prospective emigrants. Official fund-raisers, mostly former lawyers and other professionals ousted from their positions, were engaged by the JRC. They visited provincial areas to solicit contributions from well-to-do Jews.

The writer Norbert Frýd, who was active in this campaign, related in his memoirs his experiences in the city of Mladá Boleslav.[113] It was there that he first encountered the misery of the Jews who had been evicted from their homes and crowded into a dilapidated old castle outside the city. Everything was in chaos as these families arrived with their sparse belongings. On his second visit Frýd was gratified to discover that the castle had been made habitable with plumbing, showers, and bathrooms. The "Give! Build! Live!" campaign, Otto Zucker's initiative and endeavors "to keep the desperate Jewish community above water" were a formidable project, he wrote.[114]

The Jewish issue was making headlines in the press and on the radio and remained consistently in the public eye. The Nazis employed various devices to fan anti-Jewish sentiments, some of which held the threat of punishment for Czechs who associated with or tried to assist Jews.

Arijský boj in its column "Reflector" carried the following item: "Židomil (Jew-lover): The minor J. K. has been frequently observed visiting Jewish homes, bringing food parcels and spending some time there. Such activity can only be seen as Jew-loving, which we in this paper have so often castigated. For the meanwhile let this be a warning! However, should there be need for it we shall take forceful steps against J. K. who cannot be excused even by reason of his young age. In the meantime let this be a warning!"[115]

It has been argued that the Nazis made two basic errors with regard to anti-Jewish propaganda: (1) exposing the First Republic—viewed by every Czech as the symbol of independence—as the creation of the Jews; and (2) using every means to discredit Czechoslovak resistance abroad—the only hope of the oppressed Czech people—claiming that it was being financed and led by the Jews.[116]

Although Reichsprotektor von Neurath's policy aimed at incorporating Bohemia and Moravia within the Reich without resorting to arbitrary terror, he managed during his term of office to promulgate a major set of anti-Jewish decrees, making pariahs of the Jews. In addition to the published decrees a host of many oppressive regulations were enforced to torment and dehumanize the Jewish public. Some of these orders were mere subterfuge: on official trading days (Tuesdays and Fridays) Jews were forbidden to walk along Panská Street, where the stock exchange was located, so that they could not "engage" in black market activities.[117] Anyone caught violating this ordinance would be required to pay a fine of five thousand crowns on the spot. Those not able to produce the sum would be handed over to the Gestapo and taken to the Terezín Small Fortress, and if not murdered there in the infamous courtyard, they would be sent on to Auschwitz or Mauthausen.

Hundreds of totally innocent people were fined for crossing streets to which access had been forbidden, for illegally buying fruit, for violating shopping hours fixed for Jews even when this "crime" was a matter of a minute or so.

We have mentioned already the "trips" the members of the JRC were permitted to make abroad as if to encourage Jewish emigration. One of the most crucial episodes relates to March 1941, when Jacob Edelstein and Richard Israel Friedmann traveled together with Hans Günther, head of the Zentralstelle, to Amsterdam. Their "mission" was to encourage the leaders of Dutch Jewry, members of the just established Joodse Raad, to advise them of the benefits accruing from cooperation with Günther's office. "The two gentlemen from Prague," as Jewish sources in Amsterdam referred to them, did just the opposite. "Edelstein's companion, Friedmann, stood shoulder to shoulder with him, demonstrating great courage and self-sacrifice." They issued warnings concerning the fate of the Jews: "They sounded the alarm and prophesied in detail events that took place at a later date."[118]

Edelstein also met with Mrs. Van Tijn, in charge of emigration, and Menachem Pinkhof, one of the heads of the halutzic underground in Holland. Both wrote after the war that he gave voice to his total pessimism with regard to the future of European Jewry should the war not end shortly. At the Eichmann Trial, Dr. Joseph Melkman (Michman) recalled that at the meeting of the Zionist Federation of Holland Edelstein depicted the situation of the Protectorate Jews as very black indeed and stated bluntly: "The Germans intend to kill us all."[119]

In May 1941 the Prague JRC Council had thirty-seven members. Several central positions were filled by veteran Zionist leaders, among them Hanna Steiner, the only woman representative. The main activities centered on the welfare department, which had fourteen subdivisions.[120] By then, most of the Jews were without gainful employment and were thus forced to live from their savings or the proceeds from their liquidated businesses.

Nazi Germany's expansionist policy, as seen in the attack on the Soviet Union on June 22, 1941, engendered a new stage in the solution of the Jewish problem. Newspapers carried articles signed by ordinary citizens demanding that strong measures be taken against "provocative" Jewish behavior. Some of these items might even have been fabricated to demonstrate the public's approval of the anti-Jewish campaign. *Večerní české slovo* of July 5, 1941, for instance, carried an article headlined "Complaints against Jewish Arrogance," reporting the offensive conduct, especially of Jewesses, who had taken up cycling and were frequenting sports events: "This Jewish impudence has to be stopped."[121]

Although the methods of deception, fraud, camouflage, and innocuous language were still employed to mask the true intentions of the anti-Jewish policies, there was a notable change in the wording of the directives. Heydrich's instructions to the *Einsatzgruppen* (mobile killing units) in Poland on September 21, 1939 referred vaguely to the "final objective" (*Endziel*). However, the new order issued by Goering and addressed to Heydrich on July 31, 1941, spoke of a "total solution" (*Gesamtlösung*) to be implemented in all areas under German influence.

Early in September 1941, in view of the forthcoming events, Hans Günther ordered the JRC to prepare a statistical breakdown of the Jewish population of the Protectorate by age, labor capacity, family status, health, etc. The census yielded a total of 88,105 persons.[122] The urgency of the demand to dejudaize Bohemia and Moravia was reinforced by Himmler's unequivocal pronouncement: "The Führer demands that the Reich and the Protectorate, from west to east, be liberated from the Jews as soon as possible."[123]

The impact of the invasion of the Soviet Union and the escalation of resistance activities in the Protectorate area brought about Neurath's sudden removal. On September 24, 1941, Hitler appointed SS *Obergruppenführer* Reinhard Heydrich, the man with the iron heart, as acting Reichsprotektor to "scare the Czechs." "This region must become German and the Czechs in this region have after all no right to be here . . . The task of the near future is dictated by the needs of waging war. I therefore need peace in this region so that the workers may make full use of their labor to support the German war effort . . . This means, of course, that the Czech workers must be given the grub (*Fressen*)"[124]

Heydrich's arrival in Prague on September 27 sounded the beginning of a new line of policy, based upon three principal aims: Germanization of the Protectorate, wiping out Czech resistance, and launching the "Final Solution"—the wholesale deportation of the Jews. It is symbolic that one of the first ordinances he issued, on September 29, was the closing of all the synagogues and houses of prayer.

Two weeks later, on October 10, Heydrich convened a meeting at Hradčany Castle, attended by Karl Hermann Frank, Horst Böhme, Eichmann, Maurer, Hans Günther, Wolfram von Wolmar, and Dr. Karl Freiherr von Gregory, to discuss the "solution of the Jewish problem."[125] As a first move about five thousand Jews were to be "evacuated" from the Protectorate within the next few weeks. It was also decided to concentrate the remaining population of Jews in Terezín and then, once their numbers had been considerably depleted by death, to send them on "to the East."

After the meeting Heydrich held a press conference in which he raised the issue of the resistance movement in the Protectorate, warning the Czech populace against associating with underground groups. Commenting on the anti-Jewish measures, namely the concentration of Jews in a ghetto (Terezín not specified), Heydrich termed this measure to be an integral part of a planned step-by-step policy meant to be only an "interim solution." Following this crucial meeting, Günther summoned the representatives of the Prague JRC to his office and ordered them to submit plans for the location of one or more "labor ghettos" in certain localities in Bohemia and Moravia that could be suitable for such purposes.[126]

Another top secret meeting took place a week later on October 17, after the first transport of Jews to Łódý (Litzmanstadt) had already left, to plan forthcoming activities—depoliticization of the Czech population and other issues. He announced that four additional transports would follow to the same destination (altogether five thousand Jews), others would be dispatched to Minsk and Riga, and the bulk, around fifty to sixty thousand, to Theresienstadt. Also on the agenda were the issue of intimidation of the Czech populace and the evacuation of the original inhabitants of Terezín to make room for the Jews.

On October 24, 1941, Heydrich received a delegation of workers, promising to raise their wages and provide other benefits, such as additional rations of fat "from the stores of the Reich." The delegation of workers presented him a written memorandum promising "to continue their fight against the war-profiteers and Jews." They bluntly declared that exploiters and good-for-nothings were unwanted in the Protectorate and "no honest worker will feel sorry for them being removed."[127]

The SS chieftains knew full well what awaited Jews at their destination. The minutes of the infamous meeting at Hradčany detailed the new living accommodations in the spirit of Heydrich: "Die Juden haben sich die Wohnung in die Erde hinab zu schaffen" (The Jews will have to erect their dwellings under the ground).[128]

It was the first time that the people of Prague witnessed the exodus of their Jewish neighbors. The public reaction to one of the transports leaving for Łódý at the end of October 1941 was described after the war by a survivor: "The marching column, consisting of old and young people as well as of small children, made its way during the day to the railway station, closely guarded by SS men and Czech gendarmes. They were watched by crowds who filled the pavements on both sides of the street, the men demonstratively removing their hats, many of the women weeping."[129]

The transports to Łodý made up five trainloads.[130] The core of the people deported to Łodý consisted of Prague's industrial and professional elite, who had previously been robbed of their possessions. The transport that left on October 26, 1941, included the bulk leather industrialist Quido Bergmann and his wife, who before parting wrote letters to their sons. The following passage reflects the mental state of anxious parents leaving for an unknown destination: "Please, do not try to follow us under any circumstances . . . We do not want it . . . The consequences would be disastrous . . . My life concerns solely your well-being: you brought us joy. Now it bears upon us heavily that your youth has been ruined . . . I thank 'Messrs. boss and the manager' for all they have done for you and I ask them to remain favorably inclined to you also henceforth. May God compensate them for all their goodness. (Destroy the letter!)"[131]

Upon reaching the Łodý ghetto the 5,000 new arrivals from Prague, together with fifteen thousand Jews from Central Europe (Austria and Germany), were assigned to workshops already crammed with native Polish Jews. They were put up in dilapidated houses abandoned by their previous inhabitants. In effect, those among them able to work were exploited inhumanely until they were selected a year later for their next destination—the Chelmno death camp.[132]

On November 16, 1941, a few days before the great removal to Terezín began, a thousand Jews from Brno were dispatched to Minsk. This transport was made up mainly of persons supported by the JRC, the majority being Austrian emigrants and Polish subjects who were interned at the Spilberk Fortress. They perished in the infamous Minsk massacre; only a dozen of them survived.

Although the ss had already made the actual decision with regard to Terezín (it was in fact referred to in Heydrich's conference at Hradčany), nevertheless, in line with their tactics of make-believe, they allowed the JRC to think Jewish leaders alone would choose a suitable location. The former garrison town of Terezín near Litoměřice, sixty kilometers northwest of Prague, had but a small number of easily removable inhabitants and could be sealed off and controlled with ready-made housing and barracks.

The Jewish leaders, mainly Weidmann, Edelstein, Friedmann, and Zucker, guided by the idea of avoiding transports to the "East," were in favor of cities located in the heart of overwhelmingly Czech-populated areas. A committee of fourteen experts set to work to draw up a detailed memorandum on the "Ghettoization of Jews within the Protectorate of Bohemia and Moravia," hoping that such a solution would forestall transportation to the East.[133] They proposed over a dozen mostly industrial small towns such as Kyjov, Ivančice, Německý

Brod, Beroun, Čáslav, Hlinsko, Choceň, Turnov, and Roudnice nad Labem, each only to be rejected on some pretext or other: Čáslav for example, was "too beautiful," others "too close to Prague" or "too good for the Jews."

Finally, Terezín was officially announced. Objections raised by the community officials were swept aside and a date was set for the first Jewish work detail (*Aufbaukommando*) to leave and prepare Terezín for the deportees.[134] The officials of the Zentralstelle succeeded in "pacifying" the concerned leaders with the empty promise that there would be no further deportations to the East. Considering the alternatives, Edelstein viewed this development as a "lesser evil." His whole theory of a working strategy and thus the rescue of the younger generation rested upon Terezín as a self-contained, self-governing community engaged in industrial production badly needed for the war machine. He viewed this as an interim solution, a "night shelter" in Nordau's famous phrase, until the war was over.[135]

In an effort to enforce full cooperation on the part of the JRC leadership, the Zentralstelle tightened its control with a view to eliminating any sort of obstruction. (A method of eliminating members of Jewish councils demonstrating a certain degree of independence was practised in other occupied countries.) Günther's deputy, *Obersturmführer* Karl Rahm, devised the following intimidation.[136] Upon learning that registration was proceeding too slowly and that in the first two days the contingent of one thousand Jews had not reported in full, he summoned the two officials responsible, Hanuš Bonn and his deputy Erich Kafka. He then notified them of their forthcoming deportation. (According to another source this occurred after Bonn had argued that the registration could not be carried out as quickly as demanded.) Rumor has it that before sending them off to their fate the "infuriated" Rahm tore down their pictures from the bulletin board displaying photographs and personal details of JRC officials (who themselves jestingly referred to it as the "death board"—*Sterbetafel*—sensing its ultimate purpose).[137] The death certificates of the two men were sent from Mauthausen and soon received in Prague with an attached warning that a similar fate would be in store for anyone attempting to obstruct German orders. This was not the only incident: Dr. Neuwirth of the administrative department and his deputy were also punished on charges of having purchased goods to be sent to the Terezín ghetto. They were shipped to a concentration camp never to return.[138]

Upon Zucker's suggestion, supported by the other members of the Prague JRC, a special network called Department G was set up, officially charged with providing as well as purchasing some essential goods for the ghetto. This enabled them to maintain contacts with the inmates of the ghetto. After Zucker's departure to Terezín it was mainly Richard Israel Friedmann who, with relentless work and inventiveness, managed to utilize every opportunity to smuggle into the ghetto the most important necessities. With the straw and building material they were officially permitted to send, he and his aides managed to dispatch sanitary and other sorely needed items.[139]

The deportation measures were not publicized over the radio or through the official *Verordnungsblatt* (Law gazette) but were transmitted verbally to the JRC representatives. Evidence of this can be found in the minutes of the crucial meeting of February 19, 1942, a month after the Wannsee Conference on the "Final Solution," during which Eichmann briefed the representatives of the JRC of Prague, Vienna, and Berlin on the forthcoming mass deportations from the "Greater Reich" to the "East" and to Terezín.[140]

Initially certain categories (children of mixed marriages, Jewish spouses of non-Jews, families or persons employed by the JRC, etc.) were exempted from deportation. The Zentralstelle in charge of the deportations prepared the lists (on the basis of the records), picking twelve to thirteen hundred names from the card files and handing these to the JRC, which in turn notified the deportees by sending out the summonses. These were usually delivered at night, along with a sheet of instructions about the day and hour they were to report at the assembly points. Special instructions were given on how to handle household pets including cats, dogs, and birds.

Each week beginning on November 24, 1941, transports left for Terezín from Prague, Pilsen, Brno, and other cities. The agony and calvary of the community's uprooting is described in a huge corpus of survivors' testimony. The chaos was immense. Hanna Steiner's office at the JRC served as a clandestine "postal depot," conveying messages and instructions of all sorts. Moreover, it was thanks to her that the old and helpless were attended in their dire need. She organized teams of pioneer youth groups and scouts to assist the elderly and helpless people in packing their belongings and carrying them to the assembly point.[141]

In Prague a group of wooden shacks on the premises of the Trade Fair grounds at Holešovice, with dirty walls and no sanitary facilities, served as the deportees' assembly point. (There were outdoor latrines located some distance away.) The area was guarded by Czech police outside and SS units inside. Upon arrival on the Trade Fair grounds, each person was allotted "living space," a tiny piece of bare ground in one of the shacks on which to sleep. Individually they were called to the desks to fill in numerous forms, including a declaration of personal assets (*Vermögenserklärung*) and to hand over the keys, ration cards, home fuel ration certificate, valuables, cash, and personal documents. This "processing" lasted about three days. Many of the deportees were subjected to exhaustive questioning, during which standard SS methods were employed. Those who collapsed under torture were taken to the Prague Jewish hospital, which was forced to certify that they had died of some illness.

Once registered properly, after their three-day sojourn, they were escorted by SS guards, police, or even Czech gendarmes and thus marched to the nearby Holešovice railroad station to be taken to Terezín. The boarding of the deportation trains took several hours, and after a two- to three-hour trip they arrived at Bohušovice station, where they were received with shouts and beatings. There they were again checked (extra belongings were confiscated) before finally being marched to Terezín.

In the provincial towns large halls, mainly community centers, schools, and synagogues, were selected as assembly points for the· processing of the deportees. The abuses reported from there were similar to those perpetrated in Prague.

In Moravia, as of mid-July 1942, prior to their deportation to Terezín, Jews were summoned to special assembly points. Only in rare cases did families dare to escape and hide to avoid deportation. A unique example is that of the family of Cantor Bertold Wolf (his wife Rosalia, daughter Felicitas-Lici, and young son Otto), who did not comply with the summonses. Instead of reporting to the school that served as the assembly point for Jews they took the road to a secret prearranged hiding place in the forest of Tršice, near Olomouc. Otto Wolf, aged seventeen, recorded the start of their venture in his diary on July 22, 1942.[142] "We walked on tirelessly until a quarter to twelve at night, taking one rest for about an hour or so. Around seven o'clock in the evening we passed Velký Týnec, reaching the forest at midnight. Sl. [Jaroslav Zdařil][143] who had been waiting for us with knapsacks, left because we were late and he returned to his home . . . We can hardly fall asleep and just lie around like dummies."[144]

Before the deportation of Jews from the provinces began on March 27, 1942, all Jewish religious congregations were dissolved. The JRC made a proposal to the Zentralstelle to collect historically valuable material—books, ritual objects, and artifacts—from the various abandoned communities and thus save them from being looted or destroyed randomly.[145] An appeal was launched to the Zentralstelle, stressing the high historic and artistic value of the objects and proposing to concentrate them in Prague. Officially the Zentralmuseum began to function on August 3, 1942. Individuals specially selected by the JRC traveled to the various localities to draw up inventories of the collections. A letter dated June 17, 1942, addressed to SS Sturmführer Rahm, reports on the progress made by the staff responsible for compiling the inventory.[146] Mention is made of the collections received from Budweiss, Gross-Meseritch, Klattau, Leipnik, and Pilsen and their storage at the Museum in Prague V, Luythongasse 243. Another paragraph relates to the Pardubice community where the collection of about two hundred volumes housed in the synagogue was inaccessible, since the building was occupied by the military. From other places the collections reached their destination safely and were stored in the community premises. Work on this assignment continued until fall 1944, when the museum staff was sent to Auschwitz.

One member of the team assigned by the community to register the books was the noted humorist Karel Poláček, a great favorite of the public. In letters written from the various places he visited to his wife Dr. Dora Voňáčková, still in Prague, he recorded some of his experiences with a sardonic touch.[147] While working on the lists of libraries in Jewish possession—defined by the Nazis as "returned books," implying that they were "stolen Jewish property"—often freezing and famished, he had time to reflect on this tragicomic situation. He recorded how proceeding by train, day and night, from city to city, with a yellow star pinned to his jacket, he occasionally stayed overnight in the homes of very hospitable Jewish families.

Some of his asides relate to the local scene and the people he met. In one scathing remark Poláček referred to liquidated Jewish households, noting with sarcasm how some peasants on the street, "farm laborers carrying with notable exhilaration Jewish cupboards and iron desks" evoked in him sad associations from the past. With benevolent humor, he also relates how his loyal readers, both Jews and Gentiles, would call on him while he was working, bringing his novels and respectfully pleading with him to autograph them. Even in this macabre situation, it seems, he was more than willing to sign, for "this is a *Kovet*" (a great honor) at all times, he confided.[148]

At the beginning of the deportations the so-called *Treuhandstelle*, dubbed the "Krämer Department," was established within the JRC to handle the property and valuables left behind by the Jews. It was headed by Salo Krämer, former chairman of the JRC of Moravská Ostrava, and employed several hundred skilled workmen.[149] Accumulated possessions such as furniture, glassware, textiles, furs, and rugs were "processed" carefully: books were cleaned, bookplates removed and the former owner's names erased, monograms on silverware and table linen were taken off. Select items were sent to the Reich or sold to Nazi officials and clerks eager to obtain these household effects. In January 1944 there were still fifty-four large warehouses left, which were housed in former synagogues or other Jewish premises.

It is important to note that items from these stores of the Treuhandstelle were eventually channeled clandestinely to the ghetto by Department G. The funds required for this campaign came from several Jewish organizations abroad (the HeHalutz Center and the JDC in Geneva, the Rescue Committee in Istanbul).[150] In addition, the JRC sent hundreds of parcels to the Czech deportees starving in Łódý and Lublin and to other camps, with the assistance of a network of individuals and organizations in neutral countries.[151] Although these parcels were but a drop in the bucket, they were a source of succor and, mainly, moral support. A record from the chronicle of the Łódý ghetto relates to this assistance rendered to Prague Jews still in the ghetto in 1944 "who have a significantly better chance of holding out especially now, because of the frequent arrival of food packages from their homeland."[152]

On January 28, 1943, the tenth anniversary of the establishment of the Third Reich, the JRC of Prague was abolished, as were its counterparts in Berlin and Vienna, and in its place the Jewish Council of Elders (Ältestenrat der Juden in Prag; Židovská rada starších, or ŽRS) came into being.[153] Weidmann, Dr. Franz Kahn, and Richard Israel Friedmann, the outgoing officials, were deported to Terezín to be sent later to their death in Auschwitz.

The new Council of Elders, headed by Salo Krämer and his deputy Herbert Langer, was but short-lived. It officiated for only five months (until July 1943); František Friedmann and his aide Erich Kraus, who replaced them, were to be the last elders, serving until the end of the war.[154] The last transports of *Volljuden* (full Jews) left Prague during that summer.

The reduced staff of the newly established Ältestenrat was made up of officials protected by Aryan family ties (*Arisch-versippten*). Aside from the small circle of the Council of Elders, the Jewish remnant in Prague consisted of half-Jews, partners of mixed marriages, and 1,081 "disputable cases," some involving persons under arrest or in hiding.[155] Jewish partners in mixed marriages were periodically required to prove that their Aryan spouses were still alive (and still married to them) in order to safeguard their privileged status. Pressure was applied to encourage the Aryan partners to divorce their Jewish spouses, but not many did so.[156]

During 1943 several letters were smuggled out of Prague via Geneva signed by Heinz Schuster and Lazar Moldovan, in charge of the HeHalutz youth center and addressed to Nathan Schwalb and the Va'ad Hahatzalah, the Istanbul-based Rescue Committee. Written partially in hints, the letters contain information on conditions both in the city of Prague and in Ghetto Terezín. One such message, dispatched from Prague on June 19, 1943, conveys greetings to the Yishuv in Palestine and indicates that the cash reached them safely, as did packages from Wenia (Pomerantz) from Istanbul.[157] It also mentions that the money is being used for purchasing goods and foodstuffs for the detainees in Terezín; the ghetto itself, the letter stresses, is totally isolated and so "a visit there is under no circumstances possible."

The following coded message with interspersed Hebrew words was dispatched clandestinely from Prague through a special courier on May 20, 1943.[158] Addressed to "Friends" (*Haverim*) in Palestine, it reached destinations in Geneva and Istanbul.

Dear Friends,

We cannot tell you what a pleasure it was to have received news from you. It would have been a happy day for us even if the enclosed 30,000 [*Reichsmark*] had not been enclosed. We are going to use it to provide some essential goods for our comrades who live with Jakob [Terezín], since this is permitted. There is only a small remnant left here, altogether about 10,000 souls, a greater part of whom had previously not belonged to us and still do not consider themselves as part of us. There are six times as many people at Jakob's, of whom half come from Aron [Vienna, Austria] and Alfred [Old Reich] as well as some children and aged folk from Van Tijn [Holland]. Together with Jakob are Otto [Zucker], Franz [Kahn], Juval-Erich [Munk], Leo [Janowicz] [Beck], Aron [Manczer-Wien], Kaspi funds [money received], Gert [Koerbel], and many others, such as Eng. Robert [Stricker] and Desider [Friedmann]. We were pleased to hear that food parcels can be sent from your country. Since we have to comply with the regulations we are not allowed to buy meat, milk, white flour, baked goods, eggs, fruit, vegetables, fish, cheese, sweets, and jam. We also had to give up smoking. Still we can enjoy our children, who cannot attend school. We are not able to gather a *Minyan* so we cannot offer you a *Misheberach* [grateful blessing]. Nevertheless we are better off than the greater part [of our people] who are with Geler [in Poland].[159] We cannot receive any news from them. However, what we do hear makes us feel very, very sad. Only a small number of our compatriots are still with Jakob, the majority have been sent on to Geler's.

Although we hear from you that you are well and the same goes for Moledet [Eretz Israel], you can imagine how happy we would be to be with you; you should bear in mind that we here have to endure hardships that only the toughest will be able to overcome. Sooner or later everyone will have to move to Jakob. Many have died there, especially the old people. We enjoy every bit of news from Moledet, although we miss more detailed reports. We were also very pleased to receive a few lines from Balus [Barlas?]. With Béla [Hungary] we have no contact; we cannot visit him or talk to him about

Aliya. We do not have here any Hachshara, or Plugot either; there is still a Merkaz [HeHalutz Center] which is still active and does what it can with your and Nathan [Schwalb]'s help. Also Willi Sm. [Sweden] and his family are very kind. Jakob's children are learning the language and are working hard in workshops, gardens, and fields and thus make use of their training. They also still have a Merkaz with its routine work. Nathan's missives [gift parcels] that you and Willi prepared were forwarded immediately and more are eagerly awaited. Since Jakob has left we have neither seen him nor spoken to him, for this, as well as corresponding, has been made difficult—in fact, impossible. Jakob continues to be in a leading position, together with his good friends. His task is not an easy one; however, he keeps on and is most popular. The youth movements there as well as here give us much pleasure in our daily life. The halutzic youth also keep close together. Your task is not an easy one, everyone knows it, and nobody harbors any hard feelings against you; we have great confidence in you and in Moledet. With your help, strength, and mutual assistance we hope to remain healthy and to be able to survive. Once again many thanks, we feel stronger and more hopeful. Keep strong and united.

Heinz [Schuster] and Lazar [Moldovan]

The messages, hidden between the lines, were amply understood in Geneva and Istanbul as well as in Palestine, and henceforth efforts were made to find avenues for establishing contact with the remnant community in Prague and Terezín. However, it took some time before this could be put into effect. This occurred only in May 1944 after the occupation of Hungary by the German Army, in the wake of which the fate of Hungarian Jewry was sealed.

During the secret negotiations held between the Budapest Relief and Rescue Committee and Heinrich Himmler's representatives for the so-called Blood for Trucks deal, Dr. Rezső (Israel) Kastner asked Dieter Wisliceny, Eichmann's representative in Hungary, to set up contact for him with Dr. František Friedmann, head of the Jewish Council of Elders in Prague, as well as with his Zionist friends in Terezín.[160]

Consequently, with Eichmann's approval, *Hauptsturmführer* Klausnitzer was dispatched with letters and the sum of ten thousand U.S. dollars from the Istanbul-based Rescue Committee destined for the inmates of the ghetto of Terezín. It is noteworthy that Friedmann's answer to Kastner, sent from Prague on May 24, 1944, and censored by the ss, overflowed with praise for the achievements in all the spheres of life in Terezín, just like the one sent a day earlier from the ghetto.[161] A single sentence in Friedmann's letter stands out conspicuously:

"Schuster devotes his time primarily to his little daughter."[162] It must have been inserted with the specific aim of revealing the fact that more Jews had been deported from Prague to Terezín, including Heinz Schuster, his close associate. This was the only covert message that Friedmann dared pass along. The innocuous sentence about Schuster's "little daughter" evidently escaped the attention of the German censors.[163]

By December 31, 1944, there were still 6,795 Jews left in the Protectorate. However, in late 1944, the Germans had caught up with mixed marriages too; the Czech partners were sent to labor camps in Bystřice near Benešov or to Postoloprty.[164] The Jewish husbands were enlisted as a work force and moved to Prague, where they were quartered in the barracks that had once housed the Hagibor Jewish Athletic Club.

The turning of the tide of war and the approach of the Red Army spurred the Nazis to send members of the work squads composed of husbands of mixed marriages to Terezín as well. Their calamity is described in a report of February 8, 1945, compiled by Friedmann on behalf of the Council of Elders of Prague, addressed to ss Obersturmführer Girczik of the Zentralamt.[165] The first part of the report sums up the execution of the previous transports dispatched to Terezín (on January 31 and February 4), using the prescribed briefing formulas, such as: the boarding of the train, the number of the deportees, the technical difficulties, "discipline," and "mood."

Outstanding is the closing paragraph, deviating from routine content and wording altogether. Friedmann underlines the difficulties anticipated during the impending transport of 913 men to be carried out within two days (on the night of February 11). The dispatch was also to include council members, who were ordered to assist at the railway station as technical staff. The main problem, however, revolved around the order to include in the transport of the Jewish men small "Jewish" children of Aryan spouses. The youngsters were to be deported with their fathers, but the fathers had already been separated from their families for more than two years and were complete strangers to their children. All this, Friedmann states, led to panic, hysterical outbursts, and incidents of suicide. The council was stormed by desperate mothers pleading for their children: "It is humanely impossible (*menschlich unmöglich*), to make [the mothers] grasp that such a [Draconian] order had in fact been handed down." The closing sentence of the report encapsulates the helpless and desperate situation of the Jewish elder: "Whatever the difficulties, the transport would be carried out as ordered (*ordnungsgemäss abgewickelt*)."[166]

During January and February 1945, around 3,570 persons were deported to Terezín, along with the staff of the Jewish Council of Elders, leaving behind altogether 2,803 officially registered Jews. Between November 24, 1941, and March 16, 1945, a total of 122 trains were dispatched from the Protectorate to Terezín, containing 73,608 persons altogether.[167]

It is noteworthy that whereas the chairmen of the Jewish councils (*Judenräte*) in East European countries were as a rule sent to their deaths after the ghetto was liquidated, the last of the Prague Council of Elders, František Friedmann and his deputy Erich Kraus (both with Aryan family ties) were left in their positions to the end—the day of liberation in May 1945. Whether this was connected with the functioning of the ghetto at Theresienstadt or a premeditated act intended to maintain appearances vis-à-vis the International Committee of the Red Cross (ICRC) has yet to be investigated.

It is apparent, however, that couriers employed by the Jewish underground, especially those in Bratislava, were instrumental in conveying messages and information to Jewish organizations abroad, using the good offices of the Geneva-based Dr. Jaromír Kopecký. Owing to these contacts the inmates of Terezín were enabled to exchange letters and receive gift packages from overseas.[168]

As of June 1944 the ICRC began to take an interest in the fate of the Jewish inmates in the ghetto of Terezín, under pressure from Jewish organizations in Switzerland and elsewhere. The results of this noticeable change in ICRC policy were the pathetic "inspection visits" to the ghetto made by its representatives in June 1944 and April 1945, discussed in detail later.[169]

It is hardly possible for a historian to pass an unequivocal judgment on such a complex issue, as some aspects belong to the realms of ethics and psychology (humane behavior *in extremis*, "coping mechanisms," etc.). From the outset the crux of the problem pivoted upon the ominous tasks the Nazis imposed on the Jewish councils in compelling them to prepare the deportation lists—as Raul Hilberg phrased it, "to serve as a conduit" in carrying out the Nazi policy of destruction.[170] The leadership, traditionally charged with the duty of building up the community and "protecting its interests vis-à-vis the authorities," had to act as accomplices, eliciting contempt and hatred in the eyes of their own people.

It is important to distinguish between three different periods. During the first—1939–41, the chaotic span of anti-Jewish measures when people were under constant threat and intimidation and suffering indignities and corporal punishment—the JRC leaders were still active in various spheres of constructive help, such as maintaining secret contacts with Jewish organizations in the free world, alleviating the plight of the community as a whole, and enabling close to thirty thousand people to emigrate overseas (legally and illegally).[171] All their energy was vested in winning concessions, boosting morale, and seeking ways to overcome the plight and misery that engulfed the community.

There is evidence that very early on, some of the leading persons in the JRC of Prague realized that they were being used to carry out the design of their oppressors. Was it their duty to stay at the helm, to continue in their position? Could they have acted otherwise?

A basic change in their situation occurred in late summer of 1941. From testimony written in 1945 by Dr. Cecilie Friedmann, the widow of Dr. Richard Israel Friedmann, it transpires that her husband recognized the radical change in the German authorities' approach and their dealings.[172] He sensed that the time of "negotiations and retardation tactics," had come to an end. The rescue of one person actually had to be "bought" with the life of another human being. He viewed the approaching deportation campaign as "the collapse of their long-term policy of retardation" and thus realized that from that point forward the Gestapo would use the Jewish leaders solely as "executive organs." Friedmann made up his mind not to obey, wrote his widow in her testimony: "He himself refused to act as a member of the 'Transport Committee,' deciding about who would live and who would die." However, he told her that he too intervened in certain cases in order to save from deportation some of his close friends and their children as well as some noted personalities. "To act according to moral criteria in such a situation . . . would demand a society formed from superhuman idealists . . . when the issue was a matter of life or death."[173]

Thus it was in the second stage, during the period of the mortal blow of the transports of 1941–43 and in the shadow of incessant arrests and terror, that the leadership was reduced to total compliance. Those who continued with their functions as the last Ältestenrat (1943–45) concentrated on two constructive aims: clandestinely providing aid to the inmates of Terezín; and pursuing the task of saving the historic relics, "the precious legacy" of the Jewish enclave in Bohemia and Moravia. The latter effort, crowned by success, has earned them lasting acclaim.

We may presume, however, that the Prague JRC leaders, like members of Jewish councils in other countries, must have assuaged their conscience with a whole range of rationalizations. Foremost among these were acting as a buffer between the SS and the community members; alleviating the plight of the needy through welfare institutions and social assistance; and clandestinely handling secret funds for the benefit of the Terezín inmates.

The first to assess the activities of the Jewish Council in Theresienstadt in a balanced way was the rabbi of Kolín, Dr. Richard Feder, a survivor of the ghetto. His monograph published after the war expresses fresh memories of his experiences. He was restrained with regard to the Ältestenrat of the ghetto, although he referred with scorn to Dr. Murmelstein. Rabbi Feder acknowledged the efforts of those ensuring the undisturbed functioning of the camp and care for the inmates, the sick, and the old. He also recorded the help that reached them from outside: "Some of the credit must certainly be given to the supplies and help reaching the ghetto from Prague."[174]

H. G. Adler, the great authority on Theresienstadt, is known for the severity of his criticism of the Jewish council. Discussing the initial phase of the JRC in Prague, Adler claimed that from the beginning there were two possibilities: to disband the Jewish communities and destroy the registers and documents or to negotiate cleverly in order to alleviate the situation. He observed that "the latter road was followed to the bitter end." Years later, under the pressure of his former fellow inmates, he mitigated his judgment: "The men responsible must not be condemned blindly. Some of them demonstrated the virtues of goodwill and self-sacrifice."[175]

Rezső Kastner, a leading figure of the Hungarian Relief and Rescue Committee, had this to say about the conduct of the Jewish councils: "Nearly everywhere in Europe, the *Judenrat* followed the same road. Step by step, they were made tractable. In the beginning relatively unimportant things . . . Later, however, the personal freedom of human beings was demanded. Finally, the Nazis asked for life itself. For this, it was the task of the Judenrat to decide who would go first, who later . . . The road the Judenrat took was tortuous, and led nearly always to the abyss."[176]

Erich Kraus, the former deputy of the last Judenältester František Friedmann, commented on the issue of staying at the helm in his "Observations," compiled in 1980: "Every individual had in the back of his mind (the question of whether to resign his post) whenever a serious decision had to be made . . . On certain occasions, collective action was also considered. However, it always transpired that this would be a pathetic, unrealistic gesture that could neither slow down developments nor reverse their occurrence."[177]

This issue will remain a point of ongoing discourse, it seems, and two other more down-to-earth views merit consideration. Erich Kraus claims that the sheer existence of the ŽNO, or after 1943 of the ŽRS—that is, of the JRC and the Jewish Council of Elders—"created [sorely needed] venues for self-help—a place to meet and exchange information without being endangered . . . as well as to overcome the total solitude."[178] Humorist Karel Poláček came to a similar conclusion, commenting on these institutions in his macabre, scathing way. While commuting between the various localities of the Protectorate he was well acquainted with the *mis-en-scène* and the prevailing mood. In a letter of March 21, 1943, Poláček wrote from Olomouc to his wife in Prague: "Here I am sitting in the community offices, which are open here, as everywhere, on Sundays: the *k'hillah* and the cemetery are the only available places of rendezvous left for the Jewish intelligentsia."[179]

Kraus also addressed the "critics and moralists" of our day, who deal with this issue in total disregard of the 1940s context. Recalling the unprecedented situation under which abandoned people had to exist, bare handed and totally stripped of their basic rights, exposed to wanton despotism and sadism, he stresses: "The leaders themselves were, in addition, responsible for all the actions undertaken on behalf of the community, without having any chance of appeal, reasoning, or defense. It was not a time for heroic gestures and exalted deeds."[180]

Several important questions demand clarification in this context: How much help, if any, had been extended to the Council of Jewish Elders in Prague by the local factors, eventually the various underground groups? When and how much information relating to the deportation of the Jewish population was provided to the Czechoslovak Government-in-Exile? And last, to what extent was the local population influenced by the Protectorate government's anti-Jewish policies?

5

The Protectorate Governments and the "Final Solution"

The role of the native, so-called quisling governments installed in Nazi-occupied countries, either upon German demand or with their blessing, is doubtless one of the most intriguing issues of World War II history. Although they shared some common characteristics, there was certainly no uniformity either in their overall conduct or in their stance with regard to the solution of the Jewish problem. Thus each requires individual evaluation. The Czech case certainly stands out with its special geopolitical and local traits.[1] Curiously enough even during the war years the "home front" held a somewhat different view from that of the Czech Government-in-Exile in London, both with regard to the activities of the Protectorate governments and regarding the stance taken by President Hácha. It seems that now, more than fifty years later, on the basis of documentation, research, and memoir literature at our disposal, we may form a more definitive view on the relevant issues.

The discussion began early on. In 1943, while still in exile in London, Jaromír Smutný, the *chef de cabinet* of President Beneš, published an article on the subject. He stated clearly that "the problem of Hácha is as specific as are similar problems of Pétain, Laval, Darlan and other politicians." At the same time, he advised that judgment should be reserved for a later date, when these issues could be examined in a broader context and "without passion."[2]

Indeed, while Emil Hácha, the protectorate state president, is described in historiography as a case of "clear-cut collaboration," the posture of the premier of the Czech government, General Alois Eliáš, is still one of the most intriguing riddles of World War II history.[3] His unique policy of retardation and "double dealing" as well as his tragic fate have no analogy. Eliáš was the only prime minister to be tried by the Nazis for high treason; he was executed in June 1942.

The American scholar Stanley Hoffmann in his perceptive study "Self-

Ensnared: Collaboration with Nazi Germany," analyzing the wartime Vichy government, distinguishes between "state collaboration"—that is, safeguarding of interests in interstate relationships between the vanquished state and the victor—and collaboration with the Nazis, an openly desired cooperation imitating the German regime, prompted either by career advancement or on ideological grounds. Most of these persons were motivated by anti-Semitism, xenophobia, or hatred of Communism.[4]

Hoffmann's conclusions can be applied differentially to the conditions in the Protectorate and to the case of Czech quislings. In general, we could assert that none of the puppet governments either in the Nazi-occupied countries or in the satellite states put the rescue of Jews on their agenda. This axiom also applies to the Protectorate Government.

From the available research on the role of collaborationist governments we learn that their members recruited for the most part from the ranks of fascist organizations and extreme rightist parties. Moreover, the satellite states' treatment of the Jews demonstrated their loyalty vis-à-vis the Third Reich. Nevertheless, we may assert that their posture concerning "the Final Solution of the Jewish Question" was influenced to some extent by the degree of dependence on the Reich and, in the course of time, by developments at the front.

Of note, from this standpoint, is the case of the clero-fascist government in Slovakia, which aside from initiating the deportation of its Jews in early 1942, paid the Germans a sum of five hundred Reichsmarks for each "evacuee" as a "settlement allowance." However, in mid-1942–43, in the wake of the German debacle at Stalingrad and following the renewed intervention of the Holy See against the expulsion of Jews (reflecting the influence of the illegal Bratislava "working group" upon the local clergy), the Slovaks decided to put a halt to the deportation campaign.[5]

Another example is that of the Vichy government of Marshal Philippe Pétain, known for its ideological leanings toward Nazism and its own brand of racial policy in "state anti-Semitism." On its own initiative this government issued Les statuts des Juifs (October 3, 1940; and June 2, 1941).[6] The French police demonstrated rampant readiness to collaborate with the Germans in the deportation of Jews. However, the cruel scenes in the roundups of Jews in the summer of 1942 had a boomerang effect on the public.[7] The Jewish underground movements engaged thereafter in rescue operations met with willing assistance from ordinary people and farmers. The Church, both Catholic and Protestant, also began to reveal more readiness to assist with ways and means for hiding and to provide false baptismal certificates. Owing to the pressure of the Resistance and popular domestic opposition, the French authorities were forced to make concessions. As a result three-quarters of French Jews were saved. (Most of those who perished were either foreigners or naturalized Jews.[8])

As with Vichy, the Czech Protectorate Government did not arise in a vacuum. Following the Austrian *Anschluss* there were some disturbing signs of aggressive anti-Jewish notions and frequent slander in the press; some Czech newspapers even began reprinting articles from Streicher's *Der Stürmer*.[9] Curiously enough this new tendency is also evident in the May 5, 1938, letter of the Czechoslovak consul general in New York to the foreign ministry in Prague, in which he transmitted a protest against the anti-Semitic article published in the magazine *Česká výzva* on April 4, 1938. The complaint was registered by the well-known Jewish leader Dr. Stephen G. Wise, a friend and supporter of T. G. Masaryk, and thus required a speedy reply. After the issue was duly discussed by the Czech authorities, the minister of the interior advised the head of the Presidium of the district administration to adopt the consulate general's recommendation: "to act possibly in such a way that the anti-Jewish utterances would not surpass the measure desirable to Czech interests, especially in the United States."[10]

As far as the initial economic measures against Jews are concerned, these date back to the post-Munich Second Republic plagued by deep political crisis and chaos. Even though at this stage the rightist Beran government, known for its alacrity in "accommodating" the Third Reich, kept demonstrating a certain restraint, anti-Jewish excesses occurred in several localities.[11] The question of Jewish property came more and more to the fore. It was clear that Jewish assets were to be exploited for the stabilization of the economy as compensation for the losses suffered in the cession of territories. The prevailing atmosphere is reflected in the report the British chargé d'affaires, J. M. Troutbeck, dispatched from Prague to his government: "There is a diversity of views among unprejudiced persons as to how far anti-Jewish measures are being forced upon Czechs from Germany and how far the Czechs are merely alleging German pressure as an excuse for taking action which they themselves desire . . . there are Czechs of the younger generation particularly in the liberal professions, who beat the anti-Semitic drum—they are indeed particularly active in the legal profession, but in general anti-Semitism is foreign to the Czech temperament."[12]

Still anti-Semitic agitation became the order of the day. The by now socially segregated Jewish population found itself engulfed in "sorrow and uncertainty."[13]

The occupation of the Czech lands by the Wehrmacht came as a surprise to all and signaled the approaching peril and calamity. The aims of Nazi policy in the Protectorate of Bohemia and Moravia (proclaimed by Hitler himself on March 16, 1939, the day after the occupation) were developed against the background of the centuries-long Czech-German conflict and within the framework of Hitler's *Drang nach Osten* policy. As a matter of fact, from 1939 onward several schemes had been conceived by the leaders of the Third Reich aiming at the final liquidation of the idea of Czech sovereignty. The Nazis firmly believed that after their victory the Czech lands would again become an enclave ("heartpiece") within the greater German Reich.

Initially the terror unleashed in the Protectorate, unlike that in Poland, was not all-pervasive. Given the exigencies of the war, "the solution of the Czech question" was a long-range target and, as such, was subordinated to total exploitation of resources, heavy industry, and the working capacity of the population, in a drive to meet economic requirements. The Czech lands were to be the granary of the Reich; the laborers providing arms, tools, and services for the war effort were to be given preferential treatment.[14]

Eliáš assumed office as prime minister of the Protectorate Government on April 27, 1939, and held this office throughout the so-called pacification period of Reichsprotektor Konstantin von Neurath. These were the two most critical years for both anti-Jewish legislation and emigration overseas (and the first experiment in deportation). The Germans, eager to consolidate the political situation and to carry out the militarization of Czech economy and industry, obviously considered General Eliáš to be the proper choice to reconcile the unruly strata of the Czech population.[15]

In a special directive attention was given to the type of government they meant to have: "What we need is a weak Czech government, able to reshape the Czech nation in a way that it should never rise against Germany but strong enough to prevent the opposition from taking over." The Germans also established a "governmental body of troops" with a total strength of seven thousand men including 280 officers, all Czech nationals, whose commander in chief became the state president. This "army" was to maintain internal order in the Protectorate.[16]

In what way did the Protectorate Government differ from quislings in other states, and what are the particular characteristics in the Czech case? Without doubt the most striking phenomenon of the Protectorate Government was the dominant figure of Premier General Alois Eliáš. A former World War I legionnaire and later an associate of Beneš, he had acted between 1926 and 1931 as delegate to the League of Nations. In the post-Munich government of Rudolf Beran he served as minister of transport. After the German seizure of the Czech lands, Eliáš became a leading member of the secret military organization Obrana národa (Defense of the nation). To all intents and purposes his foremost aim was the renewal of sovereignty. Thus from the very beginning he cooperated closely with the Czechoslovak National Committee formed abroad and later with the Government-in-Exile in London.[17]

One of the earliest documents reflecting on General Eliáš's responsibility and unrelenting commitment to his homeland is dated October 11. 1939; it is addressed to his deputy Dr. Jiří Havelka, who also acted as secretary to the state president. Expressing disagreement over the content and tone of a letter addressed to Hitler, Eliáš urged him to make some corrections: "The more I read it, the more grievous is my impression. It seems to me that this letter could hardly stand, either currently or eventually later, before [the judgment] of history and would thus serve to the condemnation of the old man . . . Please, do weaken whatever is possible; cut from the letter everything that refers to March 15 directly or indirectly. I think thereby we shall at least be able to express something."[18]

Needless to say, the first Czech government was not monolithic; while some of its members, active figures of the *ancien régime*, were ready to adapt to the new conditions, others secretly supported the prime minister. Two of the ministers, Ladislav Feierabend and Jaromír Nečas, made a successful escape in January 1940 (with Eliáš's knowledge), to join the Czechoslovak resistance abroad and later acted as members of the Government-in-Exile.[19]

While we do not have solid information about Eliáš's personal attitude toward the Jewish community, we may surmise that as an enlightened Czech patriot and former member of the "Truth Prevails" Freemason Lodge, he had no prejudice. We may assume that he was aware of the murderous aims of Nazi policy very early on.[20] It was to František Chvalkovský, the Czechoslovak foreign minister, during his visit to Berlin on January 21, 1939, that Hitler revealed in passing: "Here in Germany we are destroying the Jews."[21]

In the pursuit of his main goal as of mid-1939, Premier Eliáš took part in the organized escape of soldiers and airmen via Budapest. This campaign, indeed, contributed greatly to the forming of the first Czechoslovak army units in France and England. By means of telegraph and courier service, he kept in contact with the representatives of the National Committee in Paris, primarily with the head of intelligence, General František Moravec. Later he also maintained communication with Beneš himself. It is interesting that during Beneš's stay in America, Eliáš's link to him was the noted historian and diplomat George F. Kennan.[22] Kennan arrived in Prague in August 1938, as second secretary to the U.S. Legation, and thus became an eyewitness to and reporter on the drama of post-Munich Czechoslovakia. His skillful briefings "with their three-dimensional quality" (flair, substance, and atmosphere) constitute a unique contribution to historiography.[23]

One of the marked characteristics of German rule in the Bohemian lands was the harsh treatment and humiliation meted out to the Czech government by the German Security Services. The latter were constantly monitoring and scrutinizing the moves of the premier and of some other government members. From the first days of the occupation, while still under military administration, the government needed special approval for each plenary session. Dr. Friedrich Bachmann, representing Konrad Henlein, the head of civil administration, had to be present at all government meetings.[24] Later on, as we know, the Reichsprotektor himself interfered in government meetings, issuing instructions phrased as orders.

Even though President Hácha remained at his post, all vestiges of Czech sovereignty were abolished after March 15, 1939. Two days later Beran's government held its first session, during which it passed a set of anti-Jewish measures excluding Jews from public life.[25] Already at this stage the fifty-member Committee of National Solidarity (*Národní souručenství*), a quasi-parliamentary body established upon the initiative of the president, became especially active in appointing trustees and commissars to non-Aryan factories and concerns.[26]

On April 27, 1939, Hácha reorganized the cabinet, appointing Eliáš as prime minister. One of the first targets of the new premier became to pursue "intensely" the preparation of an outline defining the legal status of Jews in public life. We should assert that Eliáš's intention in dealing with the question of anti-Jewish legislation was first and foremost utilitarian, as it was aimed at preventing the transfer of Jewish property into German hands, thus safeguarding Czech interests for the benefit of the national economy.[27] In effect, by the exclusion of Jews from various sectors of economic and public life Eliáš meant to solve the problem of massive unemployment that was plaguing the country as an outcome of the disintegration of the former Czechoslovakia. The large numbers of Czech officials and army personnel who had lost their positions after the cession of territories to Germany and Hungary needed new jobs and a source of livelihood.

As a matter of fact, the occupation authorities did not demand the introduction of the Nuremberg Laws, already in force in both Germany and Austria: this decision was left to the Czech government. It appears, however, that Neurath believed that this could be achieved as a result of "the given dynamics"—that is, the pressure of the various fascist groups, which clamored for the racial Nuremberg Laws.[28] (At this stage in neighboring Hungary and Slovakia Jews were defined according to religious belief and not by race.)

We may presume that Premier Eliáš discussed this issue with leading Czech representatives abroad. From the notes of Chancellor Smutný we learn that very early on, in his messages to the Home Resistance, Beneš kept referring to the international political situation, warning them not to fraternize with Nazis since "pro-German activities at home are most harmful."[29]

"The Situation in Bohemia and Moravia up to June 1939," a secret report compiled by "Citoyen" (pseudonym) and dispatched from Prague to London by the clandestine military intelligence, refers to the dilatory tactics of Prime Minister Eliáš in the matter of the draft of the anti-Jewish Law. The report suggests that "the government is not ready 'to bite fully into this sour apple' and therefore the draft of the law keeps cheerfully running to and fro between the government and the Reichsprotektor."[30]

Indeed, in his effort to find a modus vivendi for the exclusion of Jews from the economy, Eliáš kept postponing the issue until at last, on May 11, 1939, the final draft was submitted for the Reichsprotektor's review. However, notwithstanding the pressure of the extreme fascist organization Vlajka (the flag) and some members of National Solidarity, the draft law was based on religious criteria.[31] Consequently on May 22, a meeting was called at the Reichsprotektor's office with participants from all interested sectors. The discussion centered mainly on clause 2, "who should be considered a Jew," and clause 8, "the exemption from the law upon the proposal of the State President." Both clauses were severely criticized for their "mild nature." In the end no decision was made. The government's draft proposal was circulated among various public officials and also sent to some authorities in Berlin for their comments.

On June 21, 1939, the Reichsprotektor took the Czech government by surprise in issuing his own comprehensive decree on Jewish property (Verordnungen des Reichprotektors über das jüdische Vermögen), effective retroactively to March 15, defining Jews according to the criteria of the Nuremberg Laws.[32] In practice this meant the addition of some 5 to 6 percent to the 105,000 Protectorate Jews, according to the government's proposal, who would otherwise have been exempted from the law.[33] The Reichsprotektor retained full authority in the enforcement of the drastic economic measures. Neurath's decree introduced a wide definition of the term "Jewish firm" so as to include a broad range of potential cases, enabling owners of German factories and concerns to Aryanize firms where Jews held even a negligible proportion of shares.[34] However, this step ensured that the process of despoiling the Jews would harm the Czechs as well, reaching far beyond the ostensible purpose.

It became obviously clear that the property of the Jewish population in Bohemia and Moravia [estimated at roughly 20 billion crowns] was intended to strengthen German ethnicity in the Czech lands. Most instructive is the secret directive issued on the very day the Wehrmacht entered Prague: "Jüdisches

Vermögen wird Volksgut" ("Jewish assets become the people's property").[35] In effect, the "Jewish question" had become directly connected to the "Czech question," forming a cornerstone in the Germanization process of the erstwhile Bohemian lands. Neurath's decision also made it abundantly clear who "are the masters of the house," and the Czech establishment came to recognize the gross offense and infringement of the legal basis of the country's autonomy. On July 3, 1939, the U.S. consul in Prague briefed the State Department that the legislative authority of the Protectorate "must be considered as already abandoned in everything but name."[36]

With the promulgation of the law on Jewish property, the Reichsprotektor assumed *de jure* full authority over the Jewish community. Adolf Eichmann's arrival in Prague at the end of June 1939 as delegate of the Jewish Section of the Berlin Reichssicherheitshauptamt (RSHA) was well timed. He became instrumental in establishing the Zentralstelle für jüdische Auswanderung (Central office for Jewish emigration), upon the Vienna pattern. As noted in chapter 4, Eichmann's deputy, SS Hauptsturmführer Hans Günther, was placed in charge of the office.[37] Günther remained in this position until the end of the war. Even though a whole set of laws and anti-Jewish measures issued in the first years (1939–40) carry the imprimatur of the Protectorate Government, in reality the Czech authorities ceased to be a responsible factor in decisions regarding the fate of the Jews.

Shortly after Eichmann's arrival, an order was issued to the Jewish community to make arrangements for a "resettlement" campaign of all Jews living in the Protectorate. As a first step provincial Jews were to be concentrated in Prague, prior to their shipment abroad. The news caused great panic. Following are passages from two insightful reports of police chiefs, who attended *ex officio* the meetings held by the Jewish community functionaries.

The first report, compiled by Police Commissar Dr. Miloš Šebor and addressed to the Ministry of Interior, records the meeting at the Prague Jewish Town Hall on July 30, 1939, addressing the crucial issue of forced emigration. The gathering was attended by the representatives of the Prague community, all provincial Jewish communities, and the leading members of the Zionist organizations, headed by Dr. Franz Kahn, who also chaired the session. The report reveals, on the one hand, the desperate mood of the Jewish leadership and its unprecedented situation, and on the other hand we learn of the ignominious stance of Šebor, the "intervening officer," who represented the Czech Government.

The first participant asking to comment was Leo Singer, representing as chairman the community of Jindřichův Hradec . . . he complained that these meetings are arranged with long delays even though the emigration of Jews has to take place in an accelerated way . . . Before every meeting we have to come to terms with the head of the district office and there [the appeal] lies for a fortnight. Then it is sent to the *Oberlandrat* and the Oberlandrat [Šebor, the intervening officer] lets it lie about . . . After this utterance I called right away upon the chairman to reprimand the speaker for the way he spoke out, asking to stop [him] at once. Even before Singer made his pronouncement, according to my routine, I took his personal data. The chairman [Kahn] thereupon closed the session with a short announcement made in Czech . . . in his closing words he stressed that every Jew has to believe in the eternal existence of the nation. The participants dispersed in a composed way. I did not note the presence of the representative of the German Reich authorities.[38]

The second "very urgent" report, sent by the Police Directorate of České Budějovice to the Presidium of the Ministry of Interior in Prague, dated August 7, 1939, differs in both content and tone from the account quoted. Describing the session at the Jewish community of České Budějovice, which was attended by seventeen representatives, Police Commissar Nečásek summed up the arguments raised on the planned evacuation thus: "It was evident that the Jews are fully crushed by this decision and for the time being seem to be totally helpless. During the debate, one of the questions posed pointed out that there will not be anybody to take care of the old and sick Jews [left behind]. For it is doubtful whether their own community could take care of them . . . I asked Rabbi Dr. Ferda to keep me informed about the continuing developments, in case he will have a chance to do so."[39]

Following the intervention of the Czech district authorities and mainly that of the Ministry of Industry, Commerce and Trade, arguing that this move would endanger the economy, the campaign of concentration of provincial Jews was eventually suspended for the time being.[40] However, soon after the outbreak of war and the occupation of Poland, a new campaign devised by Reichsführer ss Himmler for the strengthening of Germandom called for the resettlement of the Jews of the Katowice region, Moravská Ostrava, and Vienna in the General Government. The function of this "reserve"—in Himmler's words "a bin for rubbish"—was to absorb around one million Jews.[41]

Reichsprotektor von Neurath gave his ready consent for the deportation of the Jews of the Protectorate. Known in historiography as the Nisko plan, this campaign became the first Nazi experiment prior to the deportations to "Lublinland."[42] The 1939–40 Nisko-Lublin plan was an attempted territorial solution to the Jewish question, the intent being to deport all Jews of the expanding

Reich territories to the Lublin area of Nazi-occupied Poland. Deportation commenced in 1940, but the overall plan was ultimately abandoned.

The outbreak of war generated a new optimistic atmosphere among the Czechs, and the security services promptly began scrutinizing the activities of the various resistance groups; during Operation Albrecht I several hundred former army officers were arrested. In October 1939 the first group of members of the clandestine Obrana národa (ON) and Politické ústředí (PÚ; Political center), who engaged in intelligence gathering, were arrested. Among them was Dr. Zdeněk Schmoranz, head of the Czech press department in the prime minister's office.[43] Another wave of arrests included a whole range of journalists connected with the illegal *V boj* (Into battle), the most popular underground paper printed in the Protectorate.

Eliáš's situation became even more precarious after the students' demonstrations of November 17. On December 2, 1939, the first alarm was sounded from Nazi headquarters with regard to the premier's involvement. State Secretary Karl H. Frank, in his speech at the Old Town Square, announced that Germany would not tolerate any opposition and would employ the most severe measures: "The Czech government and the Czech leaders should abandon all ambiguity and double-talk."[44]

Eliáš, it seems, retreated to a sanatorium for a few days. His anguish is perceived in two contradictory moves he made on December 8, 1939. While meeting with the German press bureau, Eliáš declared full loyalty to the Reich, welcoming the harmonious symbiosis of the Czech and German nations. He also stressed that "the only representative of the Czech people was the Protectorate Government." Moreover, Eliáš condemned the activities of the National Committee abroad, terming his relations with Beneš "clearly negative."[45] On that very day, however, after consultations with Ministers Feierabend and Klumpar, he dispatched a message to President Beneš in London, assuring him of the government's loyalty and asking for his a priori consent "in such opportunistic political moves as would help in evading national or economic disaster."[46] It seems that for this and similar tactics and announcements the head of the Prague Gestapo, Geschke, described him as "the Janus-faced premier."[47]

An illuminating instance of how powerless the Czech government indeed became as of autumn 1939 is the case of the so-called privileged Jews and their exemption from the anti-Jewish law. This category included individuals recognized for outstanding services rendered to the fields of science, literature, the arts, and sport or as men with outstanding military careers. In the Protectorate this became a case *sui generis*, arousing prompt opposition. The possibility that State President Hácha could grant recognition to an individual as a non-Jew was questioned outright. Most enlightening are the comments of the chief of the Security Police, Stahlecker, on June 1, 1939, arguing why this would simply be "unacceptable." In effect, he said, this rule of exception would doubtless include the category of "well-established Jews with good connections, on whose marking as Jews special importance should be laid."[48]

The original roster of one thousand persons for "presidential exemptions" compiled by Eliáš's government included a stratum of long-established families known for their major contributions to Czech economic and public life. It is noteworthy that the NSDAP had warned von Neurath (who was to authorize each case himself) that "the persons proposed by the president for exemption would be the most rabid anti-German elements in the Czech camp."[49]

After protracted dealings and cynical comments from German quarters, Hácha assured the Reichsprotektor that "the main criteria will henceforth be the applicant's own attitude to Germandom or his family's," including the relationship of his forebears to the Aryan world.[50] Specifications for the respective candidates were carefully prepared by the government and issued on July 4, 1940.[51] Finally, the reduced list of forty-one applicants (twenty-seven men and fourteen women who were Jewish wives of Aryan husbands) was presented to the Reichsprotektor on November 21, 1940. However, even this minute number would not pass. Undersecretary of State von Burgsdorff bluntly informed Premier Eliáš on January 14, 1941, that the list of individuals "could not convince him that there exists any public interest to exempt them from the applicability of the law."[52]

Even Hácha's personal appeal to Karl Hermann Frank to exempt Professor Hugo Siebenschein from the anti-Jewish law failed. His argument that the applicant's mother stemmed from an old German Protestant family and that "Siebenschein is engaged in compiling the Czech-German standard dictionary" did not impress Frank, who stated simply that "he was not able to help."[53] The definitive answer was given by Reinhard Heydrich on October 4, 1941, asserting that "in principle no one could be exempted."[54]

The political situation in the Protectorate in the summer of 1940 was influenced greatly by two major events: the defeat of France and Britain's recognition of the provisional Czechoslovak Government-in-Exile. The fall of Paris had a grave psychological impact upon public opinion the world over. In the Czech lands apprehension rose as rumors circulated that certain files of the Czechoslovak National Committee in Paris had fallen into the hands of the Gestapo.[55] This was demonstrated by the massive arrests of Czech activists, conducted according to ready-made lists: followers of Beneš, leftist social democrats, communists, teachers, priests, and intellectuals. Among those arrested was Dr. Otakar Klapka, the mayor of Prague and Eliáš's associate, whose functions included the allocation of financial support for families of Resistance activists.[56]

The German authorities' surveillance of Premier Eliáš's activities is also reflected in the July 1940 monthly report of the Security Police. Reviewing the political developments in the Protectorate (and the *Angstpsychose*, the all-pervasive fear prevalent among the public), the report refers to the last government meeting, sarcastically alluding to Eliáš's "playing the role of a neutral arbitrator."[57]

It is not without interest that among the Czech files the Nazis discovered in Paris were several documents touching upon the negotiations conducted after the outbreak of the war between the World Jewish Congress representative and President Beneš.[58] The main issue in these documents was the offer of a $5 million loan by friendly North American Jewish banks for the new "building up of the Republic."[59]

The victory of the Wehrmacht in western Europe brought about the ostracism of the Jewish population. On October 9, 1940, with no German prompting whatsoever, Josef Nebeský, on behalf of the National Solidarity, asked the government to propose the introduction of the law "for the defense of Czech Aryan honor and blood." The Reich authorities, however, took no notice of the government's draft of October 24.[60] Thus the prime minister had to apply for the second time. On April 3, 1941, in a letter addressed to K. H. Frank, Eliáš asked for his consent to the proposal. He claimed that his government was being criticized over the fact that "the Jewish question has not yet been solved in certain aspects and that thus far Jews were not forbidden to marry non-Jewish persons or prevented from having extramarital sexual relations with them."[61] Even though Eliáš openly indicated that he was being pressured by certain circles, his ostentatious backing of the proposal makes one wonder: Did he believe that this was an empty gesture—an "opportunistic" overture—or was he signaling more flexibility and readiness to fall into line?

The premier's situation at this point became quite precarious for new evidence on his involvement in underground activities reached the German Security Services. In February 1940 some of his contacts in Budapest, who were assisting Czech military personnel in their flight abroad, were tracked down by local security forces. The Hungarian authorities promptly briefed the German government on the case.[62] Moreover, after Klapka and other members of the Resistance had been interrogated, Eliáš realized that his life hung in the balance. It appears that in late 1940 he made up his mind to flee via Belgrade to London, but because of the political changes in Yugoslavia (in early 1941) he had to cancel his plan.[63] Eliáš's fate was obviously sealed by that time; the Germans, however, continued postponing his final ouster for reasons of their own (probably to maintain the necessary tranquility within the Protectorate).

A special routine employed by the German authorities was to make use of intimidation, plots, and intrigues to provoke personal feuds and animosity among the ministers, creating tension and uncertainty as far as their term of office was concerned. This situation is reflected in messages the Home Resistance sent to London as early as February 1940. One special dispatch intimated: "If they [the government] will not act the way they are meant to they [the Germans] will install their own Vlajka government."[64]

The German invasion of the Soviet Union on June 22, 1941, generated a new situation, and in the Protectorate a wave of sympathy and hope arose in the Czech population. Sabotage activities also became frequent. At the same time, anti-Soviet proclamations and utterances by the fascist groups and State President Hácha could also be heard; even Beneš was attacked.[65] These attacks, of course, ran counter to the new line of policy and requirements of the "family" or "pseudofamily," as the Czech president kept referring to his allies at home.

Upon reassessing the impact of the latest activities of Hácha and even those of Premier Eliáš, Beneš found them counterproductive and in many ways harmful. He thus sent a special message on June 24, 1941, requesting their immediate resignation. "Let them create a quisling government" or "Let them abolish the Protectorate, it would be all the same."[66]

Although Beneš had earlier asked his contacts at home not to cross the Rubicon in their deeds and proclamations, after official recognition of the Czechoslovak Government-in-Exile by Britain (July 18, 1941) he became more resolute in his demands.[67] In his message dispatched to Prague, Beneš expressed his appreciation to General Eliáš for having contributed greatly to his work in England, paving the way to the recognition of the exile government. However, at the same time, he advised Eliáš to consider abdication, convinced that the Government-in-Exile would only profit by this step.[68]

In response, in his last message sent to London on August 7, 1941, Eliáš assured Beneš he would resign "should the Germans try to impose new burdens, unbearable to the nation."[69] The crucial question then poses itself: Why did Eliáš's government not resign—what made the premier go back on his promise?

Let us recall that the launching of Operation Barbarossa and the Soviet Union's entry into the war engendered elation and a new kind of rapprochement among the various sections of the Home Resistance and naturally also with the illegal but effective Communist cells. It is important to note that Eliáš had twice asked Beneš to brief him on the issue of the Red Army and his own relations with the Soviet Union.[70] After the outbreak of the war Eliáš held regular contacts with some leading figures of the Prague Central Committee (CCP) of the illegal Czech Communist Party (ÚV KSČ).[71] Of special importance were his clandestine meetings in public parks and cemeteries with Milan Reiman (a Jew), who served as liaison between Eliáš and Kurt Beer-Konrád, linked at that time to the Soviet Consulate General in Prague.[72] Premier Eliáš met Reiman for the last time on August 10, 1941, before Reiman went into hiding, alarmed by the mass arrests of leading members of the CCP. During this meeting Reiman left Eliáš with a memorandum (symbolically folded into Kamil Krofta's book *The Immortal Nation*), urging him "to turn East . . . the final victory of socialism under the aegis of the Soviet Union is a path preferable to the Western way of domination."[73]

It is known that while held at the notorious Pankrác prison Eliáš did his utmost to pass a message to Dr. František Berdych, a leading Communist activist also held there, asking him not to disclose to interrogators the identity of "Novotný" (one of the aliases of Milan Reiman), as he was sought by the Gestapo.[74]

On September 27, 1941, the very day Heydrich arrived in Prague as acting Reichsprotektor, Eliáš was arrested and removed from office.[75] We know that even before reaching his new destination, Heydrich had met with *Brigadeführer* Judge Otto Thierack, president of the Berlin People's Court (*Volksgerichtshof*), who agreed to preside at Eliáš's trial. Three days later, on October 1, 1941, Eliáš was tried by a people's court in Prague and sentenced to death for high treason.[76] Helmut Heiber in his study "Der Fall Eliáš," records how insidious was the indictment put together by Heydrich with the assistance of the security service.[77] Eliáš's removal had to be a deterrent, signaling to the Czech people the new line of policy: Germanization, the destruction of the Czech Resistance cells, and the launching of mass deportation for systematic decimation of the Jews.[78]

Before the death sentence was pronounced, Eliáš was threatened with the mass execution of Czechs and thus, under duress, signed a proclamation recommending to his nation "sincere loyalty to German hegemony" as the sole way to future existence.[79] This "legacy" was widely publicized in the press and on the radio. Eliáš's execution was delayed for special purposes and was not carried out until eight months later, on June 19, 1942, during the retaliation for Heydrich's assassination. Perhaps it was some solace for the defiant legionnaire that he lived to learn of his arch-enemy's death. Before his execution Eliáš managed to smuggle out of jail a message to his wife: "We shall prevail" (Zvítězíme!).[80]

Perusing the verdict of Eliáš's trial I came across a statement made by the defendant that, surprisingly, the censor did not delete but that has not thus far been given proper appraisal. Eliáš seems to have formulated with the utmost care two sentences obviously meant for posterity, as a disavowal of the very essence of Nazi policy: "[Eliáš] found himself in a dilemma while having to choose between the moral imperative of humanness [Menschlichkeit] and the interests of the Reich. He thus decided to harm the Reich."[81] Eliáš's strategy and his "double game" (as he himself described it to the court) were analyzed in the perceptive studies of Tomáš Pasák and more recently in a new biography; however, some questions remain without definitive answers.

Milan Reiman, Eliáš's key liaison, was arrested during the Moscow-masterminded Slánský trials (directed against "bourgeois nationalism," Trots-kyism, and Zionism), which took place in Prague in 1950–52. Reiman was charged as an "imperialist agent" and was tortured to death by his jailors.[82] He was probably one of the few who could have shed some light on the subject. The other liaison, Dr. Zdeněk Bořek-Dohalský of the PÚ, who delivered Beneš's last message to Eliáš in late September 1941, was arrested soon thereafter by the Nazis.[83] He was executed at Terezín on February 7, 1945.[84]

With Heydrich's arrival a civil state of emergency was proclaimed through-out the country (it would last until the end of November 1941), followed by curfews and draconian measures, culminating in mass executions. Arrests became the order of the day with four to five thousand people being apprehended and around four hundred put to death, among them many Jews; others were sent to concentration camps.[85] At the same time the wholesale cleansing of the Jewish population got under way.

On the eve of the mass deportation in October 1941, the National Solidarity, the acting Czech government, together with President Hácha, eager to share in the Jewish spoils, made a last joint effort and demanded full participation in the confiscation and isolation of the deportees. This, however, was summarily denied. A cynical note dated November 3, 1941, ridiculing their alacrity, bluntly advised the president and government that "it is solely the Reich authorities who are empowered to carry out anti-Jewish measures."[86]

Heydrich's "Report on the Situation in the Protectorate" on November 16, 1941, addressed to Bormann, outlined the basic principles for the reorganiza-tion of the German and Czech administration: "It is imperative to scrape holes into the autonomy, without, however, jeopardizing the facade" (die Autonomie auszuhöhlen, ohne die Fasade zu gefährden).[87] The new government, installed on January 19, 1942, was dominated by two vociferous collaborationists: law professor Dr. Jaroslav Krejčí as chairman or *Regierungsvorsitzender* (the office of the prime minister had ceased to exist), and Colonel Emanuel Moravec, the minister of education. Both men expressed their readiness to pursue Heydrich's political program in three areas: close cooperation in the solution of all problems; the reorientation of Czech education; and the reeducation of the Czech population. The last clause referred to the suppression of the people's will for self-determination and the indoctrination of the youth with the notion of the Greater Reich. Several institutions and organizations were established for this purpose. Thus the new ministers became, in Heydrich's phrase, "an extended arm of the Reichsprotektor."[88]

Hand in hand with the effort to win over certain segments of the Czech population, dissemination of propaganda and indoctrination with Nazism increased.[89] On the model of the German *Kraft durch Freude* (Strength through joy), a new movement called *Radost ze života* was founded to provide recreation opportunities. The most important official organization of this nature was the Kuratorium pro výchovu mládeže v Čechách a na Moravě (Council for the education of youth in Bohemia and Moravia), which as of May 1942 made all Aryan youth between ten and eighteen years of age subject to compulsory service providing "physical, spiritual, and moral education," thereby ensuring early and thorough indoctrination.[90] Another institution was Úřad lidové osvěty (Office of people's enlightenment), which would maintain control over all mass media until the end of the war.[91]

While the Germanization process was being set afoot, a group of parachutists dispatched from London in December 1941 under the code name Operation Anthropoid was preparing to carry out a mission—the elimination of Heydrich. This was accomplished on May 27, 1942, on a street in suburban Prague, giving rise to great alarm at German headquarters.[92] Hitler termed this event "our heaviest loss" and his fury upon learning the details knew no bounds. The frantic advice he gave to Karl H. Frank was "to arrest and execute immediately ten thousand Czechs suspected of anti-German activities"—a warning even his obedient lackey felt to be "too much."[93]

Repercussions, however, were not long in coming: a civil state of emergency in the region of the Prague Oberlandrat, announced over the radio, was soon extended to the entire area of the Protectorate, and the manhunt began. The first aim was to find those who had done the deed. A reward of a million marks was posted for helping disclose the identity of the perpetrators. A warning was issued: anyone who had helped the culprits or provided any active assistance or even knew them but did not report them to the police would be shot, together with his whole family.[94]

During the sweep held on the night of May 27–28, 541 persons, among them several Jews, were arrested in the streets either because they had been unable to reach home in time or because they were not carrying their identity cards. Large posters printed in black on a red background appeared with detailed descriptions of the men who had been seen fleeing from the scene. One of paragraphs read: "The criminals who fled on foot left a woman's bicycle near the spot: it has the mark Moto-Velo J. Krčmár, Teplice, and the manufacturer's number 40.363."[95]

The objects were exhibited at the Bat'a shoestore, 6 Wenceslas Square, and the public was urged to come forward with information. For several weeks the German police were at a loss. Unfortunately one of the Czech parachutists, Karel Čurda, dispatched in fall 1941 from London and living undercover (faithfully looked after by native patriots), gave away his colleagues and all those Czech people who had helped him.[96] Čurda identified some of the assassins' items found at the scene and gave the addresses of safe houses provided by the Resistance. The Gestapo raid in the Žižkov flat of the Moravec family on the morning of June 17, and the threats and the torture of the inhabitants, yielded the first clue as to the whereabouts of the assassins.

The parachutists' secret hiding place in the Orthodox Carl-Borromaeus Church in Prague was thus detected and raided by the ss forces: some died in the fight; others took their own lives when the situation became hopeless. The pastor of the church, its elders, and Bishop Gorazd of the Czech Orthodox Church were later executed.[97]

Among the people arrested for rendering assistance to the assassins was Lydia Holzner, the former owner of the bicycle (bought at Teplice Šanov before the war).[98] She was a nurse and the wife of neurologist Dr. Jiří Bondy, both working at the Prague Vinohrady Jewish hospital. Arrested together with the young couple were Lydia's mother, Jiří's elderly parents Dr. Alexander Bondy and his wife Hilde (née Bergmann), and Hilde's brother Zdenko Bergmann, all of whom were sharing the same small flat in Prague. They were taken to the Terezín Small Fortress. Upon arrival, Jiří Bondy was knocked down and he died some days later.[99]

On September 29, 1942, the German summary court sentenced 254 persons to death, most of them members of the families of Heydrich's assassins and others charged with being involved in various ways in the parachutists' affair.[100] The accused were "tried" in absentia.

Appended to the report of the Prague Secret Police (dated November 3, 1942) listing those condemned, we find the relatives of the parachutists Kubiš and Valčík, involved in the attack. Dr. Milada Fantlová-Reimová, the physician who attended to Kubiš's wounded eye, appears on the list, as do the Nováček family and their fourteen-year-old daughter Jiřina, who upon her mother's request hastily removed the "woman's bicycle" from the scene. Aside from the condemned Jewish "culprits" (Bondy, Holzner, Bergmann), three additional Jewish women figure on the list: Polaková Alžběta (née Weissberger), Soinarová Julie (née Bloch), and Sedláková Julie (née Polák), of whose part in the assassination we know nothing. On the night of October 22, after a month's stay at Terezín, they were brutally herded into a long convoy of prisoners headed for the Mauthausen concentration camp. Some of the elderly perished en route; the rest were shot at two-minute intervals.

One of the survivors of this convoy describes in his testimony how the guards separated the prisoners into two groups: "the parachutists" and the others.

> It was 24 October 1942 . . . Snowflakes fell on our shaved heads; it was terribly cold . . . We went down the steps into the cellars: here there were the baths. SS were waiting: they hit us and beat us. Some of my comrades fell dead. We had to take our clothes off and then we were taken back to the courtyard: it was already covered with snow . . . At that moment the "parachutists" group was taken away: some two hundred and fifty men, women, boys, and girls. Their heads shaved: their bodies bruised all over. They were thrust forward: we could still see them: they vanished. Forever . . . That afternoon thick smoke rose from the tall chimney of the neighboring building . . .[101]

Reinhard Heydrich's death on June 4, 1942, at the Bulovka Prague Sanatorium was the finale to an eight-month rule that shed rivers of innocent blood of men, women, and children. The so-called *heydrichiáda* resulted in the arrest of 13,119 people, many of them Jews. Mass executions occurred daily. The official announcements account for 1,331 executions between May 28 and July 3, 1942. Among those executed were 223 women.[102]

On June 10 a special "penal" transport of one thousand Jews was dispatched from Prague. It consisted mainly of Jews from the area of Kolín (Poděbrady, Nymburk, Kutná Hora, and Čáslav). Most were taken to Ujazdowo in Poland, where they were ordered to dig their own graves before they were executed. Two additional transports followed shortly.[103]

A week later, on June 9–10, the entire male population of the village of Lidice was shot by SS squadrons in retaliation for having given temporary asylum to parachutists responsible for Heydrich's assassination.[104] The village was burned down: 106 houses and the baroque church built in 1729–32 were destroyed, and 205 women were deported to Ravensbrück and other camps. Some of the children were taken by German families to be raised appropriately. Of Lidice's ninety-six children, eighty-one perished in the gas chambers.

The scene of the bloodbath at Lidice was described by some of the Jewish inmates of Ghetto Terezín. Upon the order of the camp commander, Obersturmführer Dr. Seidl, thirty of them—members of the former Work Detail—were quickly mobilized for "earthwork" (to act as grave diggers).[105] They were driven "hanging onto each other" in the direction of Kladno on a green truck, accompanied by a ten-man detachment of gendarmes equipped with shovels, pickaxes, crowbars, and two barrels of quicklime. Arriving at Lidice they were met by personnel of the ss, Gestapo, Kripo, *Schutz polizei* (Schupo), and Security Police (Sipo, formed by merging of the Gestapo and Kripo)—many of them drunk. Before the diggers was a nightmare, the place covered in blackish gray smoke. They were ordered to the spot where they were to dig: "twelve meters long, nine meters wide, and four meters deep." They dug and scraped for thirty-six hours without a break and left blood-soaked in the night, blood running over their clothes, back to the ghetto. Years later one of the men wrote how mattresses and pallets piled up in the background formed the execution wall. "Here the dead lie on the ground. Shot! A colorful carpet bleeding from a thousand wounds . . . they are lying on their backs, on their chests, on the side, caps and hats have fallen off, hands under their bodies or arms outstretched, their eyes glassy . . . the martyrs of Lidice, heroes of Bohemia . . . miners, small householders, peasants and pensioners, the old parish priest, a boy, a dog . . ."[106]

Two weeks later, on June 24, the next German target was the hamlet of Ležáky, where apparently a secret radio transmitter was discovered.

The wounds inflicted upon the Czech nation during and after the *heydrichiáda*, both physical and moral, were immeasurable. As if this was not enough, the collaborationist government of Krejčí made its own extra demoralizing contribution. In an effort at "mourning over the gruesome loss of a leader" (Heydrich), several campaigns and events were organized throughout the country. Among these was a convention of Czech artists at the Prague National Theater and at the Old Town Square.[107] The climax was a demonstration on July 3, 1942, at the equestrian statue of St. Wenceslas, a rallying symbol of Czech revival and statehood, with around 200,000 people avowing their loyalty.[108] The solemn ritual, "The oath of the nation" conducted by Colonel Emanuel Moravec, was attended by President Hácha. This was the most traumatic and pathetic scene ever documented in the history of the occupied Czech capital.

Although the state of emergency was lifted that very day, the reign of terror continued. Lieutenant General Kurt Daluege, head of the German Order Police (*Ordnungs polizei*), who replaced Heydrich as acting Reichsprotektor, issued an order establishing the death penalty for anyone aiding or failing to report persons engaged in activities hostile to the Reich, including giving shelter to Jews.[109]

Additional restrictions on the movements of Jews (use of public transportation, etc.) were issued, which made the life of the Jews still left in the Protectorate totally unbearable. Whoever held a grudge against someone could take his revenge. Scores of Czech people, many of them Jews, were put to death. From a postwar report about the executions in the Lubsky forest (near Klatovy) we learn that the following Jewish persons were put to death on charges of "approving" the assassination of Heydrich: Singer Leopold of Sušice (born 1894), owner of the Klatovy villa (taken over by the Gestapo); Kamila Barthová of Sušice (born 1897); the brothers Leopold and Karel Fürth of Žichovice (born 1903 and 1907). Informing on them was Zdeněk Chadt, caretaker of the Žichovice estate and member of Vlajka.[110]

In September 1942 a special internment camp was set up at Svatobořice near Hodonín (Göding) for relatives of prominent political émigrés in exile and of members of the Resistance living abroad.[111] Among these internees were some Jews who received especially harsh treatment from the camp guards; many were beaten and died in the camp.

Special camps were also erected for Jews of mixed parentage and those *versippt* with Aryans as well as for non-Jewish spouses in Tršovice, Uhlířské Janovice, and Bystřice, working on the nearby exercise grounds for the ss troops. By the end of September 1944 the number of detainees was two hundred: they were mainly employed on the construction of a railway station.[112]

Daluege's tenure was also marked by a change in the legal status of the Jews. Until July 1, 1943, legal cases involving Jews had been handled by German courts; after that date, under the "Reich Citizenship Law" clause 13, Jews accused of a crime were tried and sentenced by the Gestapo.[113] The guillotine installed at the Pankrác prison in the spring of 1943 put an end to the lives of 1,075 men and women before the war ended. Executions were, however, no longer publicized.[114]

On August 20, 1943, the ever-aspiring K. H. Frank was finally nominated by Hitler as all-powerful minister of state for Bohemia and Moravia. Dr. Wilhelm Frick, the last appointed Reichsprotektor, represented the Reich merely as a symbol of the executive power.[115]

There followed a period of relative quiet in the years 1943–44. Owing to the intimidation campaign and the new German policy of recruiting manpower, no major acts of sabotage were carried out. Czech workers were compelled to work in Germany. Thus in the last phase, indeed up until the end of the war, the Protectorate remained the sole territory where the economy and communications kept functioning. Frank, eager to appease the Czech population, even made some pretentious gestures. On June 4, 1944, he offered the order of the "Eagle of Duke Wenceslas" for those Czechs who distinguished themselves in fulfilling their duty and demonstrated preparedness to serve. His fatuous gesture, however, was greeted with concealed derision.[116]

As of fall 1944 guerilla fighting broke out, and along the eastern border of Moravia partisan activities followed suit. Still, Prague witnessed two additional transports of Jews loaded for Terezín. Most of these people were the Jewish husbands of mixed marriages, enlisted as a work force and included in the last groups sent in January and February 1945.[117] By then partisan warfare had spread along the borders. The uprising in Prague erupted on May 5, 1945. Capitulation was on May 8, and on May 9, 1945, the Red Army marched into Prague to the cheers of the population.[118]

The first Czech government, although short-lived, had left some indelible marks. Heydrich himself ironically conferred upon it the epithet "the government of proud silence" (die Regierung des stolzen Schweigens), defining its activities as sheer "connivance" intended to outwit the German authorities.[119] George Kennan, recalling the spirit of "the brave soldier Schweik," added this whimsical characterization of the Czech government's mentality and tactics: "a boggling willingness to comply with any and all demands and an equally baffling ability to execute them in such a way that the effect is quite different from that contemplated by those who did the commanding."[120]

In the first postwar years while General Eliáš was hailed as a hero by both the Western émigrés and the Communist establishment, the members of the second Protectorate government were tried by the Retribution Courts in Prague. (The ailing President Hácha died in prison on June 10, 1945.) Eliáš was posthumously decorated by President Beneš. In paying tribute to his heroism, several leading members of the CCP described his tactics as "Wallenrodism," a reference to the hero of Mickiewicz's epic poem *Pan Tadeusz*, about Konrad Wallenrod, who sought to serve his nation as a "traitor." After the Communist takeover some controversy persisted over Eliáš's past; he was occasionally labeled "a lackey of the Western powers."[121] The definitive evaluation of his role has yet to be written.

In summation, three cardinal issues exemplify the singularity of the solution of the Jewish question in the Protectorate. The first blatant and devious Nazi attempt to lure Premier Eliáš into "adopting" the racial definition failed. This was a significant development, as the Nazis had hoped to demonstrate the Czechs' accommodation with the New Order and to present them in the eyes of the world as the vanguard of racist legislation in Europe, thereby discrediting

Masaryk's republic. Eliáš's rejection of the Nuremberg Laws is therefore meaningful and of special symbolic value.

The intricate issue of exemptions also took a different course in the Protectorate. While Eliáš's government utterly failed in its efforts to release any category or even individuals from the anti-Jewish law, in Vichy France, Slovakia, and Hungary, a certain number of long-time residents and war veterans were granted this favor. In Germany proper, too, there existed a category of "privileged" individuals, as illustrated in the macabre case of the "Prominenten" in Theresienstadt.[122] In this context Heydrich's command on the eve of deportations of the Protectorate Jews is most revealing: "No consideration at all should be given to Jews who possess war decorations" (Es soll keine Rücksicht auf Juden mit Kriegsauszeichnungen genommen werden).[123]

Last, while in all other countries under German tutelage the Nazi chieftains openly encouraged the local authorities' cooperation, both in the process of confiscation of Jewish property and deportation "to the East," the Czechs were barred from sharing the spoils. The second acting government's offer was bluntly rejected, notwithstanding its total loyalty and eagerness to participate in the deportation campaign.

The Czechs paid a heavy price for the killing of Reinhard Heydrich, and in the first postwar years Beneš was severely criticized for the lack of widespread resistance in the Protectorate (in comparison to France and the Low Countries) as well as for the enormous contribution the Home Front made to the German war effort. Beneš confessed to Jaromír Smutný that Heydrich's assassination and "the executions . . . consolidated our state of affairs."[124] He believed that the political consequences would lead to the guaranteeing of the state anew.

6

The Czechoslovak Government-in-Exile in London
Attitudes and Reactions to the Jewish Plight

There is consensus that during the five years of his exile it was Beneš himself who acted as the central figure and architect of his government's policies.[1] His personal secretary in those crucial years, Edvard Táborský, wrote about him: "As of 1939 until in late 1944 nothing of political importance, insofar as it depended on the Czechoslovak Government-in-Exile, could be decided without Beneš."[2] Indeed he was president, premier, foreign minister, and at times ambassador; he maintained contacts with the Czech and the Slovak Home Resistance, the Protectorate Government, the Moscow-backed Czechoslovak Communists, the German emigrants in London, and the Jewish organizations in the free world.[3] Beneš saw the undoing of Munich and its consequences as his *raison d'être*, hence the struggle waged for international recognition for the legal continuity of the First Republic and its pre-Munich boundaries became his objective and obsession; he "kept thinking of it literally day in day out." All through the years spent in exile he went on describing the events as he saw them, and which, in effect, became so fateful in shaping his policy in the postwar years.[4]

Deeper insight into the subject emerges in the diaries of Jaromír Smutný, who served until the end of the war as Beneš's *chef de cabinet* and who meticulously recorded the president's conversations with politicians and other prominent personalities, adding his own comments.[5] From his long personal acquaintance with Beneš, Smutný saw him as a statesman with a pragmatic, realistic approach to international affairs. About his personal character and approach to people, Smutný has the following comment:

Beneš is a brilliant master of tactics and strategy, the greatest Machiavelli of our time, but he is unable to awaken the enthusiasm of the masses . . . He does not inspire confidence. Sensitive people in his presence feel that he always leaves things unsaid, that Beneš exploits them for some purpose of his own, which he does not mention . . . People leave him persuaded, but not feeling entirely with him, full of confidence but without affection . . . and we recognize that he is head and shoulders above us, distinguished by his intelligence, tenacity, and dedication to his aims.[6]

Forty years later Beneš's close associate Prokop Drtina, who acted as Minister of Justice in the postwar government, published a memoir entitled *Czechoslovakia My Fate*, providing interesting insights into Beneš's policy.[7] Throughout the whole of this important memoir and in the documentary literature, the Jewish question is almost entirely absent. In spite of its broad, general implications, the struggle of the national Jewish group for representation on the State Council (*Státní rada*) is scarcely mentioned—and then only as part of the complex problem of the minority issues.[8]

It could be safely asserted that the Jews per se as positive and loyal citizens did not present any problem in the foreign policy of Czechoslovakia in the period of the First Republic (1918–38).[9] Moreover, the freedom and democracy accorded to minorities, including the Jews, was a matter of great satisfaction to world Jewry and augmented the esteem in which the young republic was held.[10]

In the late thirties, however, Beneš was particularly disturbed by the posture of the German and Hungarian minorities, exploited eagerly within the framework of the expansionist propaganda of the Third Reich.[11] Those among the Jewish population who spoke German or Hungarian, or claimed to belong to the latter national entities, lent additional force to the complaints and petitions submitted by these "unruly" ethnic groups to the League of Nations.[12] Beneš viewed the dismemberment of the republic as a personal insult and humiliation; it also determined his attitude to the Jewish question, linked as it was to his global strategy of undoing the wrongs of Munich and preventing any such repetition.

THE "CZECH TRANSFER" AND RECRUITING CZECHOSLOVAK CITIZENS IN PALESTINE

Among the first issues involving the Czechoslovak National Council's representatives in London, both Beneš and Jan Masaryk, were the question of prospective Jewish immigrants stranded in the occupied Protectorate and the mobilization of former Czechoslovak citizens living in Palestine.

The emigration of several thousand Jews in the years 1939–40 came about under the terms of the so-called Czech Transfer.[13] The latter agreement between the Jewish Agency of Palestine and the Czecho-Slovak Government in January 1939 (granted British parliamentary assent in July 1939) provided for the immigration of twenty-five hundred Czechoslovak Jews and the transfer of £500,000 via the Bank of England to Mandatory Palestine. Two groups of immigrants succeeded in reaching the shores of Palestine as a last-minute escape. It was estimated that by the end of 1939 there were altogether six to seven thousand Czechoslovak Jews, holders of Czechoslovak passports, in Palestine.[14]

The starting point was the rehabilitation loan of £10,000,000 granted by the Chamberlain government after the Munich Agreement. The Czechoslovak authorities agreed to allot £500,000 from this loan to the Ha'avara (transfer) Fund to support refugees from various parts of the country who were migrating to Palestine. The conditions of the agreement were set out in a letter from Dr. Kalfus, the Czechoslovak finance minister, to František Friedmann, representing the Jewish Agency.[15] One of the conditions was that the equivalent of the British pounds be paid in Czechoslovakia in local currency. Heading the Transfer Committee in Prague was Dr. Paul D. März, its other members being Friedmann, Jakob Edelstein, Dr. Franz Kahn, and Eng. Otto Zucker. The Transfer Agreement was reconfirmed after the German occupation of Bohemia and Moravia. It made possible the immigration to Palestine of twenty-five hundred to three thousand Jews from Czechoslovakia and some two thousand from Germany and Austria between October 1939 and January 1940. Dr. Leo Herrmann, initiator of the scheme, was instrumental in seeing it through all its stages with the cooperation of mainly Czech and British organizations.[16] Jan Masaryk's support for the rescue of Jews from Nazi clutches and his effective intervention with the British Foreign Office was one of his many accomplishments in the course of his term as ambassador in London and later as Czechoslovak foreign minister.[17]

He is also to be credited with the resolution of the sensitive issue that arose during the first year of the war with the general mobilization of Czechoslovak citizens living in Palestine. This move in the wake of the setting up of the Czechoslovak National Committee in Paris in October 1939 was initiated by the Czechoslovak consul general in Jerusalem, Josef M. Kadlec.[18] (Accredited in 1932 to Palestine, Trans-Jordan, Saudi Arabia, and Aden, he refused to hand over his office to the Germans after the occupation of Bohemia and Moravia on March 15, 1939.)

Understandably, the call to arms raised problems of an exceptional character, which exercised the Jewish leaders in Palestine, most notably Moshe Shertok

(Sharett), head of the Political Department of the Jewish Agency, and Yitzhak Ben-Zvi of the Va'ad Leumi (Jewish National Committee).[19] Leo Herrmann and other Czechoslovak Zionist leaders who had emigrated to Palestine in 1939 (Dr. Angelo Goldstein, Dr. Chaim Kugel, Dr. Josef Rufeisen, and Dr. Paul D. März) likewise confronted these problems.[20] It should be mentioned that Jerusalem became at that time the center of Czechoslovak resistance activities in the Middle East, where press releases and information were issued (*Čechoslovak v Orientě*, Czech and English news sheets, and an official bulletin, *Czechopress*, for the Middle East and Africa).

Immediately after the signing of the agreement between the Czechoslovak National Committee and the French Government (October 2, 1939), providing for the establishment of an independent Czechoslovak army on French soil, Kadlec, the consul general in Jerusalem, summoned Czechoslovak citizens of military age to report for medical examination.[21] The call stated that the mobilization would be voluntary. Some twelve hundred Czechoslovak Jews signed up. The majority of these recent immigrants who had arrived without any means responded spontaneously, driven by the ardent will to fight against Hitler's Germany and to help restore the freedom of the republic. The first battalion of five hundred men (including around forty to fifty non-Jews, among whom were a few monks) left for France on November 12, 1939, and a second group of around two hundred men followed in January 1940, while the third group was held back owing to the French surrender in June 1940.[22]

The Czechoslovak army organized in France consisted mainly of volunteers, among them a great number of Jewish refugees from Paris and other cities. They were stationed at the Agde camp in the south of France. In November 1939 they were joined by the volunteers who had enlisted in Palestine. The new volunteers' arrival at Agde set off demonstrations prompted by strong anti-Jewish sentiments prevalent among Czech officers, who were antagonized by the conspicuous number of Jews within the unit. By December 1939 the Agde camp held four thousand officers and enlisted men, of whom eight hundred were Jews.[23]

The publication on April 4, 1940, of a new issue of the *Information Bulletin* (no. 17) of the Czechoslovak campaign abroad, in which Kadlec proclaimed the compulsory call-up of "Czechoslovak citizens in Palestine," aroused opposition among the Zionist leaders.[24] (It is not without interest that in his cable sent to Beneš on August 8, 1940, Kadlec defended his standpoint by claiming that he had one chance "to make registration binding and summons voluntary.") The case in point was the following clause of the proclamation: "Those who fail to obey this order will be regarded as deserters. The Consulate General also stated that wives and families of Czechoslovak soldiers will receive maintenance allowances according to the standard of living in Palestine. The technical arrangements for the respective payments through the French consular authorities are practically completed."[25]

The consul's threat was viewed as conflicting with Jewish national interest and as a dangerous precedent in the matter of the status of immigrants in Palestine. It must be remembered that this occurred at a time when the Zionist leaders had strong hopes for the formation of a Jewish Army. In pursuit of this aim a persistent political struggle was being waged against the British authorities. The first proposal for a Jewish Brigade, made in autumn 1939, had been rejected on political grounds.[26] As a halfway solution military cooperation with the British had been suggested. The Jewish leadership favored this move both for defense potential and as a moral claim to be taken into account at the end of the war.

The issue of mobilization was widely covered in the daily press, stressing the difference between volunteering and compulsory call-up.[27] Thus, for instance, the *Palestine Post* (April 14, 1940), under the heading "The Czech Summons," reacted to the Consulate's announcement in an adroit manner.

No member State of the League of Nations has given more loyal support to the mandatory system or shown greater sympathy for the Jewish National Home than the Czechoslovakia of President Masaryk and of his successor Beneš. On more than one occasion, they have emphasized their appreciation of the distinctive character of Jewish nationality and of the Jewish national revival in Palestine. Moreover, successive Czechoslovak governments have consistently supported and facilitated the emigration of Jews to Palestine with a view to their permanent settlement here. While it may, therefore, be appropriate that those who wish to offer their services to the Czechoslovak Army in France should be afforded an opportunity of doing so, it is equally clear that those who have come here with the definite intention of becoming members of the Jewish national community have special obligations in this country . . . In the meantime it is clearly imperative that the community should not be depleted of its defense resources through its manpower being dispersed in various foreign military units.

The situation thus created caused a division of opinion within the Organization of Czechoslovaks in Palestine (OCP), where the majority of members accepted the view that new immigrants should exercise their right to assume Palestinian citizenship after two years in the country.[28] The conscription found the new arrivals from Czechoslovakia, still holding passports of their country of origin, in a legal vacuum.[29] It is characteristic that several of the leading Zionists when relinquishing their Czechoslovak citizenship did so by courteously notifying Consul Kadlec of their intentions.[30] The consul general reassured them of his understanding, expressing the hope that they would retain their friendly sentiments toward the old country. However, in his confidential reports sent to President Beneš, he criticized the approach of several of the leading members of the OCP, pointedly focusing on Angelo Goldstein, who, "driven by personal ambitions," was hampering the formation of the unit.[31]

Consequently efforts were made to bridge the conflict of interest between the Czechoslovak consul and the representatives of the Yishuv. A memorandum drafted at the Jewish Agency headquarters clearly delineated the cardinal issues of "allegiance and loyalty":

> . . . It is very evident that this call to arms raises an important question of principle. There is no Jew in Palestine who does not feel deeply for Czecho-slovakia in its present plight and who does not wish to see her established in her former glory. Actually several hundred Czechoslovak Jews have gone to France as volunteers in the Czechoslovak legion, long before the present call to arms was published in Palestine. The Jews of Palestine regard themselves as part of the allied front against Hitlerism and they are prepared and have made this clear on many occasions that they are willing as Jews to make their contribution to the common cause . . .[32]

The leadership of the state-in-the-making was clearly deeply angered by the opportunistic approach of the Czechoslovak consul, carried away in his "patriotic fervor." The memorandum went to great lengths to explain the difference between the status of a Jewish emigrant in Europe and of a settler in Palestine.

> There is in Palestine no room for "Czechs of the Mosaic confession." He is not in Palestine a Czechoslovak "emigrant" as he is in France, or in Switzerland, or in England. He becomes here part and parcel of the Jewish national community, he is no longer a refugee but a citizen among his own people from the moment that he enters the country of the National Home with the intention of becoming one of them. The community that accepts him as a member has made great efforts in order to assure his admission to Palestine. It has excluded other Jews for the sake of enabling him to come here and it is making great efforts to enable him to become economically settled in this country, and in consequence it also has a claim upon his loyalty to his people and to its country. There may be those who regard Palestine merely as a country of transition or as a temporary refuge, but to the Jew who comes here

for the purpose of settling permanently as a member of the Jewish National Home his duty must be clear.

At the same time Professor Lewis M. Namier on behalf of the Executive of the Jewish Agency in London appealed to Jan Masaryk (April 10, 1940) requesting his mediation in the matter: "Kadlec seemed to be pressing on seriously with the calling up for the Czechoslovak Army of Czechoslovak Jews resident in Palestine. I submitted that the position of Jews who had gone back to the Jewish National Home was radically different from that of Jews resident in other countries, and asked whether some instructions could be given to M. Kadlec not to press in the matter of calling them up."[33]

Masaryk's reply, addressed directly to Leo Herrmann, contained instructions for Consul Kadlec advising him in forceful terms to consult with Herrmann on everything "concerning the status of the Jews in Palestine."[34] His wording revealed the dismay he felt over the way this issue was handled. On the question of the loyalty of those who still held Czechoslovak passports, Masaryk's advice was both appeasing and encouraging. He recommended an approach so that "they may fulfill their obligations as Jews and Zionists without their loyalty to their country of origin being doubted." Herrmann, briefing Moshe Shertok on the new developments (November 11, 1940), underscored the fact that Masaryk "raised this point also with Dr. Beneš."[35] Further evidence that the Czechoslovak president grasped the problem from the national Jewish point of view—depletion of the reservoir of active manpower for Zionism—is to be seen in a sentence in Smutný's diary. Speaking of the drafting of recruits in Palestine, Beneš remarked that it was quite reasonable that in Palestine "they were not too pleased" when men were called up for the Czechoslovak Army.[36]

In spite of the confusion and differences of opinion, close relations between the Jewish leadership in Palestine and the central figures in the Czechoslovak Government-in-Exile continued. The sentiments of the Yishuv in Palestine for the young democratic state and its fate were given expression in March 1940, on the ninetieth anniversary of the birth of T. G. Masaryk: the foundation stone was laid for a new agricultural settlement in the Zebulun Plain, named Kfar Masaryk, founded by members of the HaShomer HaTza'ir who hailed from Czechoslovakia.[37]

Kadlec, who enjoyed the confidence of the British and was supported by the military authorities in his mobilization campaign as well (prior to the official recognition of the Czechoslovak provisional government), had his way in securing admission for some of the "illegal" refugees stranded in Syria. The close cooperation that existed between Kadlec and the British Mandatory authorities with regard to the issue of mobilization and in drafting of volunteers is best illustrated in a letter from the Czech consul general in Jerusalem (July 5, 1940) to the chief secretary of the government of Palestine:

Sir,

I have the honour to refer to the kind interest you have shown for the group of our 200 Czechoslovak volunteers and to inform you about the contents of an Aid-Memory I handed over to Brigadier S. Brunskill with whom I dealt with the question of our soldiers after their entrance to Palestine. In the enclosure you will find the copy of the Aid-Memory.

At the occasion of my personal visit in the provisional camp of the Czechoslovak soldiers in As Sumaria I could make a list of personal details of the volunteers which I gave to the disposal of Brigadier S. Brunskill. Owing to the arrival of the Czechoslovak Liaison Officer Staff Captain SIMAN from Beyrouth on these days to Jerusalem, the characteristics of all officers and soldiers of the detachment in As Sumaria was offered by me to British Headquarters in Jerusalem where the question of reliability of the Czechoslovak soldiers is of special importance . . . I have informed by a telegram from the 3rd inst. H. E. Dr. Eduard Beneš about the arrival of the Czechoslovak volunteers from Syria.

I have the honour to appeal to His Excellency the High Commissioner and to the Government of Palestine to use this occasion of the presence of more than 200 Czechoslovak soldiers on the soil of Palestine for a formation of a Czechoslovak unit which would with greatest enthusiasm fight in the frame of the British Army against common enemies. The group of As Sumaria could be completed by Czechoslovak volunteers from this country and eventually from Egypt and Iran if it would be desirable so that this detachment could grow from the actual state of one company to one battalion.

Thanking you for everything you would do in this matter,

[unsigned][38]

Following representations by the Government-in-Exile made on the recommendation of Kadlec in late 1940, the Mandatory authorities permitted a number of ships to land their "illegal" passengers, who then joined the Czechoslovak Army.[39] After the arrival of a group of two hundred Czech volunteers, including thirty-five Jews, from the Balkan countries via Syria, an independent Czechoslovak battalion had been formed in Palestine in August 1940.[40] They were joined by the detainees held in the camps at Athlit and Sarafand and later by Czechoslovak nationals from Mauritius (deported there from Palestine by the

British in 1940 as "illegal" immigrants).[41] This battalion fought at Tobruk and in Libya and after the opening of the Second Front joined the Czechoslovak forces in Britain.[42]

It was during a visit to Jerusalem of the Czechoslovak minister of national defense, General Sergey Ingr (on June 19, 1942) that the status of the immigrants from Czechoslovakia was finally settled.[43] In the minutes of a meeting between General Ingr, Moshe Shertok, and Leo Herrmann (attended by Consul General Kadlec and Lt. Col. Kalla, the military attaché), it was concluded that "all Jews who have come to this country with the intention of making it their and their children's home should join the British Army, while those who had come for a temporary stay and intended eventually to return to Czechoslovakia belonged in the Czechoslovak Army."[44]

In the final analysis, those Jewish immigrants in Palestine who responded in autumn 1939 to the first call to arms constituted the nucleus of the Czechoslovak Army on French soil, prior to the recognition of the Czechoslovak provisional government by the Allied powers. By volunteering they contributed to the prestige of the Czechoslovak cause at a time when there was a dire need for recruits.

STRUGGLE OF THE NATIONAL JEWS FOR REPRESENTATION ON THE STATE COUNCIL

Arriving in London after his resignation in October 1938, Beneš and his wife Hana took up residence in Putney, leading a quiet life. Until the outbreak of war, the British treated Beneš as a private person facing difficulties of various sorts. This attitude transpires from a record of August 1939 relating to Beneš's first public lecture in Britain, at the Liberal summer school in Cambridge. The British Foreign Office requested that Czechoslovakia not be mentioned in the address and that the discussion of democracy should be the general topic.[45]

Even after the outbreak of the war Beneš was treated, especially by the French, as *persona non grata*. In those days he used to refer to them bitterly as "munichois" and to the British as "munichites."[46]

In fact Beneš was accorded his first ovation as a statesman during the opening of the Czechoslovak pavilion at the 1939 New York World's Fair. Upon his arrival on February 10, he and Mme. Beneš were met by Mayor Fiorello LaGuardia, who staged a motorcade to City Hall for his guests.[47] At the inauguration ceremony the flag was flown at half mast with the famous passage of Komenský's Bequest on the flagpole: "After the passing of the storm of wrath, the rule of your own affairs will be restored to thee, O Czech people." Over the entrance to the pavilion hung the inscription: "Begun by the Czechoslovak Republic, unfinished, but maintained by its friends in America." Moreover, as of 1939, various Jewish circles offered Beneš both moral and material encouragement.[48]

Negotiations for the recognition of a Czechoslovak Government-in-Exile began immediately after the outbreak of war; however, for political reasons these were held up by both the French and the British for almost two years. A French-Czechoslovak agreement providing for the creation of a Czechoslovak army in France was nevertheless signed on October 2, 1939. A further development occurred when Beneš was recognized as the head of the "Czechoslovak National Committee" by the French on November 14, 1939, and by the British on December 20, 1939.

> For two years, then, there was a breach in Czecho-Russian relations . . . But
> when Hitler attacked Soviet Russia in June 1941, and Britain offered Russia
> her alliance, Dr. Beneš lost not a moment in asking Moscow to resume
> relations—in his own words, "at the point where those relations were inter-
> rupted after Munich." Moscow does not do things by halves, and on 18 July
> 1941 Czechoslovakia and Soviet Russia signed a new Treaty, on the basis of
> qualified recognition and of the pre-Munich frontiers. It was only a matter of
> time that Britain also should accord Czechoslovakia full recognition, and the
> Anglo-Soviet Alliance of June 1942 led quite logically in June 1943 to Brit-
> ain's complete repudiation of the whole Munich settlement.[49]

Only on July 21, 1940, did the British Government extend recognition to the Czechoslovak provisional government with Beneš as president. This recognition set an official, legal seal on the continuity of the State—though the question of its previous boundaries remained open. The same day the president issued a decree setting up a *Státní rada* (State Council) as a controlling and advisory body.[50] It was intended to provide wide political representation though not on the basis of party platforms. Moreover, it was to act as a unifying center for resistance abroad (*zahraniční odboj*) in all its forms.

The State Council, its forty members appointed for a year at a time, was founded to take the place of the parliament, which for obvious reasons could not be constituted abroad. At the same time it had the task of uniting all the prominent political representation of Czechoslovakia to embody the continuity of the republic.

According to an estimate by the Government-in-Exile, there were in Britain some nine thousand Czechoslovak citizens, no fewer than seven thousand of them Jews and Germans.[51] The great majority of the refugees were from the

Sudeten area, victims of the Munich Agreement (some of whom had been active in the Social Democratic and Communist parties), whose immigration Britain had facilitated in the autumn of 1938, *locus standi*, in payment of a moral debt.[52]

With the establishment of the provisional parliament the split among the Jewish immigrants in London began to reveal itself openly. The principal organizations among them were the Federation of Orthodox Jews from Czechoslovakia (Federace Orthodoxních Židů z Československa) and the Central Council of National Jews from Czechoslovakia (Ústřední rada národních Židů z Československa, hereafter referred to as National Jews).[53] While the Orthodox Jews engaged mainly in welfare and relief work among the refugees, the National Jews (formerly members of either the Jewish Party or the Social Democratic Jewish Party—Poaley Zion in Czechoslovakia), headed by Dr. Leo Zelmanovits, insisted first and foremost on political activity.[54] The assimilationist Union of Czech Jews (Svaz Čechů-židů), centered around businessman Milan Kodíček, apparently emerged ad hoc, in an attempt to forestall the nomination of a Zionist representative to the State Council.[55]

At the beginning of December 1939, after the establishment of the Council of National Jews, its representatives Leo Zelmanovits and Rabbi Dr. Hugo Stránský visited Beneš's residence at Putney in London, presenting him with a memorandum offering their full cooperation in the struggle for the renewal of Czechoslovakia.[56]

Evidently Beneš had already set out his views clearly on the minority question. It is not without interest that in a speech delivered in November 1939, while enumerating the minorities of the republic, Beneš omitted to mention the Jews.[57] His endeavor to gain Western support for the idea of a massive postwar population transfer was first aired in public in a major speech at the Royal Empire Society in London on January 23, 1940.[58] In a report by Sir Bruce Lockhart, British representative to the Czechoslovak provisional government, based on lengthy conversations with Beneš on the subject of the reestablishment of the Czechoslovak state after the war, it is explicitly stated: "With regard to internal reconstruction, President Beneš's aim is to re-create a state which will be *as homogeneous as possible*. It is his ambition to rid the country of those minority problems which proved so disastrous to the former Republic" (italics mine).[59] Beneš clearly stated in his memoirs that the problem of minorities and especially the problem of the Germans would have to be solved radically and definitively. "The small Czechoslovak nation cannot live with a German revolver permanently against its breast."[60] He also bore serious grudges against the Slovaks. During a conversation with Jaroslav Stránský in London on April 11, 1940, Beneš remarked: "We always had two guns pointed against us;

one from the Sudeten and the other from Slovakia. The very minute we would not give in to one of them, they were confronting us with threats. One party threatened to annex themselves to the Germans, the other to break away from us. These two guns we have to eliminate."[61]

The Home Resistance had been kept informed about Beneš's new conception on minority issues and the ongoing debate with regard to envisaged post-war policy.[62] Thus in the first half of 1941 they sent messages to London protesting the plan proposing to concentrate the German population within three designated areas in Bohemia. This plan and the president's readiness to accept eventual border amendments also met with criticism on the part of some of the ministers as well as members of the State Council. Noteworthy is the nonconformist position adopted by Jaroslav Stránský: although he too opposed the idea of border amendments, Stránský bluntly spoke out against the planned transfer of the German population, describing it as an appalling Nazi invention.[63]

At first, all the Jewish organizations that had emerged in London saw themselves as candidates for representation in the State Council, and they negotiated individually with President Beneš and other members of the government. In spite of this, there was no official Jewish representative among the thirty-two council members appointed. Consequently, the National Jews refused to take part in the opening ceremony of the State Council on December 11, 1940, and issued a resolution of protest, expressing their great disappointment over the fact that the Czechoslovak State Council was convening without any Jewish representatives.[64]

It seems that President Beneš deliberately delayed the appointment of a Jewish representative to the State Council. In conversations with various delegations he justified this by citing the lack of unity among the Jewish organizations and their inability to put forward a joint candidate. He even offered his services in bridging their differences. It was however the National Jews, who alone had had their party members in Parliament in Prague until 1938, who persisted in their demands, and the true reason for the delay lay in the fact that the president viewed the problem of the Jewish minority as part of the general minority question and, curiously enough, that of the German minority in particular. He discussed this more than once with the head of his office, Smutný, and put it clearly: "The Germans as a minority are not yet represented on the council and therefore I cannot solve the Jewish problem."[65] Another reason he gave was that "he was daily being attacked by the Germans in Czechoslovakia, who were accusing him of being a tool of the Jews, and if only for the sake of contradicting this propaganda he felt bound to settle all minority representation at the same time."[66] Discussing the problem with the Jewish delegation, Beneš emphasized that the great majority of the Czech-Jewish emigrants in England were German-speaking Jews and that there had long existed a mistrust of these German Jews among the Czech population in the small towns and villages. He could thus deal with Jewish representation on the minority basis only after the two other minorities (German and Hungarian) had been given representation. He accepted the argument of the Jewish representatives that "there was no territorial nation behind the Jews," and that hence there was an inherent difference between the two issues; but Beneš nevertheless insisted that the minority problem be simultaneously settled in all its aspects.[67]

Moreover, according to Bruce Lockhart's report, President Beneš held the view that "if he agreed to Zionist representation in the Council, he would be faced with similar demands for representation from other small groups. The Council would then bear some resemblance to the former Czechoslovak Parliament with its numerous parties, and for obvious reasons this is most undesirable."[68]

Beneš's position was much strengthened following Nazi Germany's attack on the Soviet Union on June 22, 1941, and the recognition soon accorded the Czechoslovak Government-in-Exile by Britain and the Soviet Union (July 18) and the United States (July 31). Beneš expanded the State Council by appointing six Communist representatives (one being Karel Kreibich, who had been a deputy for the Sudeten region in the Czechoslovak Parliament). These events— and also, it would seem, the influence of the Board of Deputies of British Jews and the London Section of the World Jewish Congress—induced Beneš to act with greater flexibility. Members of delegations from these two Jewish bodies laid stress on the moral value that Jewish circles ascribed to representation on the State Council, in view of the fact that enemies had begun a whispering campaign to tell the non-Jewish world that "even their friends the Czechs had abandoned them."[69]

The newly developing anti-Semitism was first discussed between Lewis Namier and Bruce Lockhart. The latter concurred that there existed some discrimination against the Jews in the army. He explained this phenomenon by the fact that Jewish refugees from Czechoslovakia were the first to escape, and some of them, at least, had succeeded in transferring certain sums of money to Britain. Lockhart stressed that "President Beneš himself has taken strong measures to check anti-Semitic sentiments among the Czechoslovak officers."[70]

There was tension and prejudice among the Czechoslovak troops evacuated from France to England and housed in a tent camp at Cholmondeley Park near Chester. The situation of the Jewish soldiers there became intolerable. A soldiers' committee was formed to seek help from the Central Council of National Jews as well as the Jewish Agency in London.[71] A memorandum composed by the council—addressed to Selig Brodetsky, president of the Board of Deputies of British Jews, on July 31, 1940, and enumerating the anti-Jewish statements and insults leveled by the officer's corps—requested amendments and negotiations with the military authorities.[72] The final outcome of the protracted interventions with the president and Army Command led to the dismissal of some of the officers and to a certain *modus vivendi*.[73]

Beneš's sensitivity to world Jewish opinion spurred him to bring the matter of Jewish representation to a conclusion before arriving at a solution for the general problem of minorities.[74] The president's original choice was Dr. Angelo Goldstein, a former deputy of the Jewish Party in the Prague Parliament, who appealed to him "as a man of conviction." (In 1939 Goldstein emigrated to Palestine and not to London, as did Zelmanovits and some others.)[75] At a meeting with Sydney S. Silverman and Dr. Noah Barou on April 17, 1941, Beneš made reference to his choice and also pointed out that Goldstein's candidacy encountered considerable opposition within Jewish circles. Beneš later changed his mind due to the position Goldstein adopted over the conscription of Czechoslovak recruits: "Some trouble had arisen between the representative of the Czech forces in Palestine over the question of mobilization of Czech nationals. There had been a serious difference of policy, though this difference may have been exaggerated . . . but, said Dr. Beneš, Dr. Goldstein could not be on the State Council and at the same time pursue a policy not in accordance with such representation."[76]

In fact Goldstein was rather reluctant to accept this offer, which would have entailed leaving Palestine.[77] After several months Zelmanovits finally suggested that Ernst (Arnošt) Frischer, former chairman of the Jewish Party in Czechoslovakia and a civil engineer by profession, be nominated to this position.[78] (Zelmanovits was fully aware that he himself stood no chance of receiving the president's nomination.) Frischer, who also reached Palestine with the last group of Zionist activists in 1939, accepted the candidacy. On November 18, 1941, he was appointed a member of the State Council *ad personam*, not as a representative of his party. Ernst Frischer took on his duties at the end of November and soon became an active member of the parliament-in-exile, assuming the burden of providing relief and rescue for those suffering under the Nazi oppression.

As an experienced statesman, Beneš could immediately pinpoint problems as events unfolded and viewed them as part of a global picture. He understood the question of Palestine; it did not elude him that a new status for the Jews in the Diaspora could be expected to result from the establishment of a Jewish state.

He had already expressed his views frankly on the subject early in 1941 to Jewish leaders, when he said: "The granting of minority rights will not need to be taken into account as far as the Jews are concerned . . . After the establishment of a Jewish State it will be up to the Jews in the countries where they live to decide whether they are for Palestine or for assimilation (in the national sense) into the people of the country where they live."[79] Obviously at the time neither Beneš nor the Jewish leaders could have known of the German plan for the physical liquidation of European Jewry or that the remnant of Jews returning to Czechoslovakia would be too small to justify any claim to national rights. To Beneš's credit it must be said that already in April 1941 he openly expressed support for the establishment of a Jewish state, in the hope that "the civilized world would find a reasonable settlement of the Jewish question after the war and he and his government would do their best to facilitate this."[80]

In conversation with Zionist leaders in May 1943 Beneš expressed "serious doubts concerning the wisdom of simultaneously demanding a Jewish State and minority rights in the countries where Jews live."[81] His declaration aroused dissatisfaction in the World Jewish Congress, whose spokesmen saw it as a deviation from his erstwhile position, as Dr. Nahum Goldmann pointed out— views "difficult to identify with the liberal ideas that he had always upheld."[82]

It should be noted that in his comment on a discussion Goldmann, Beneš, and Dr. Stephen Wise held on May 21, 1943, on the subject of the future of Czechoslovak Jewry, Frischer moved closer to Beneš's views and rejected Goldmann's demand for the renewal of minority rights in the reconstituted republic after the war. To add weight to his opinion he resorted to quoting the disadvantages implied in the minority clause as far as Jews were concerned:

> In Czechoslovakia, a minority had to have at least 20 percent in order to be subject to the minority rights, namely to be allowed to use their own language in State Offices and in the Law Courts, which was considered the most important of these rights. The percentage of Jews in Bohemia and Moravia [as] against the other population was 1 percent, in Slovakia 4 percent and in Carpatho-Russia 13 percent. The average percentage of Jewish population [as] against the whole population was only 2 percent. Naturally, after the war, the percentage will be even less favorable.[83]

In contrast to Stránský's view Frischer also favored Beneš's conception on the issue of the German transfer. Frischer at the same time underlined that the Germans "who will have proved that they had kept faith with the Republic, will be permitted to stay on, and those of them who were forced to go abroad will be allowed to return to Czechoslovakia."[84]

The struggle of the National Jews in London for the right of representation on the Czechoslovak State Council recalls in some way the entangled prewar election campaigns for the Prague Parliament. It is paradoxical that Beneš, the man who stood by the cradle of the League of Nations and who as a foremost politician and statesman had been identified as the upholder par excellence of the concept of minority rights, had become a determined opponent of this very principle.

In an article written in 1942 Beneš bluntly stated that the prewar system for the protection of minorities had broken down. He maintained, therefore, that in the future it should work primarily in defense of human democratic rights and not of national rights. "Minorities in individual states must never again be given the character of internationally recognized political and legal units, with the possibility of again becoming sources of disturbance. On the other hand, it is necessary to facilitate emigration from one state to another, so that if national minorities do not want to live in a foreign state they may gradually unite with their own people in neighboring states."[85]

INTELLIGENCE AND INTERVENTION

The dramatic escape to England on March 14, 1939, of the Czechoslovak military intelligence chief Colonel František Moravec and his staff made headlines in the international press.[86] Already known from its activities in Prague, it was a welcome asset to the Western orbit threatened by Hitler's aggressive policy. From the very outset Czech Intelligence had received regular briefings on current issues in occupied Europe from the Home Resistance and various confidential sources operating in the Protectorate. It maintained close connections and exchanged information with British counterparts. As a result the Czechoslovak Government-in-Exile in London was regarded as the best informed source of intelligence.

As of 1941 the Home Resistance was in radio contact with London, operating several stations. Although occasionally interrupted, transmissions were maintained until June 1942.[87] Henceforth contact was mainly through a network of couriers operating between Prague and London, via Geneva and Istanbul. Because of its proximity to and good relations with independent Slovakia, Switzerland played an important role as a meeting place. The connections were maintained by Slovak underground groups in Bratislava and coordinated by Dr. Jaromír Kopecký, the Czechoslovak representative at the League of Nations in Geneva.[88]

In Istanbul a Czechoslovak military group consisting of some ten members transmitted regular reports and news to London.[89] Special importance attaches to the briefings compiled by Dr. Miloš Hanák, who served as a diplomatic representative in Turkey before the war. The military cooperated closely with the local Czech colony at Istanbul, made up for the most part of Jewish businessmen and professionals and some musicians and artists, who had escaped from Czechoslovakia before Nazi persecution. (Among them were Maximilian Rose, Ota Shick, and Dr. Stephen Kertesz.)

One of the earliest "messages from home" (*Zprávy z domova*) touching upon the topic of collaboration was sent by the Central Leadership of Home Resistance (ÚVOD, discussed in chapter 7) in July 1940, pointing out:

At the head of the Czech nation are cowards and opportunists (*chlebíčkáři*). We who carry the onerous burden of the assignments which you expect us to accomplish are in a pitiable situation. We are forced to hide ourselves away like criminals . . . You would do well if, for the strengthening of the spirit of the resistance against the Germans and their accomplices as well as the Czech renegades, you would time and again issue a warning; threaten with reckoning for treacherous activities those indifferent [persons] who take no interest nor care about our common struggle.[90]

Another message relating to the same issue described the despicable situation and high percentage of those complying with the government's policies: "Hácha and his government are complying; the Association for Cooperation with the Germans (*Svaz pro spolupráci s Němci*) functions well. *Vlajka* [meekly] acts upon every order, would perform any foul act, arrest whoever they choose. Nobody protests so as not to irritate the Germans and in order to save their own positions, be it in the government or elsewhere . . . Altogether there is too much moral denigration, even though on the whole the nation remains healthy. For us, however, numbering eight million, the percentage of those who are despicable is too high."[91]

A dispatch sent from Prague on October 1, 1940, involves the Aryanization of Jewish property, maintaining that this is solely a pretext for its transfer into German hands and that it would be advisable to warn the Czech population emphatically against requesting to be part of such sequestration: "If the Germans win the war, nothing will be left—the expropriation of Czech property would follow that of the Jews. In the case of German defeat, for which we sincerely pray, all the stolen property would have to be returned. A warning should be issued over the radio that everything that has been expropriated from the legionnaires, the Red Cross, etc., as well will be considered stolen [property] and therefore will have to be returned. There is no need to specify this [warning] solely with regard to the Jews."[92]

One of the earliest and most crucial items of information received by Czech Intelligence concerning murderous Nazi policy was the briefing of the famous agent A-54, Paul Thümmel (René), on June 21, 1941: "The driver of the Prague Gestapo chief, who returned from the eastern front, reports that in the Ukraine the Jewish question is radically solved. Immediately upon the occupation of a location, the Jewish men are summoned to forced labor and under the pretense of preparing fortifications they are to dig pits. When these are long and deep enough they are being shot and covered with earth."[93]

Additional information was provided by refugees and escapees who made their way to the West. A detailed report thus received in June 1942 from a teacher contained no reference to the fate of the Jews but did explicitly mention Auschwitz and poison gas.[94] Bruce Lockhart, head of the Political Warfare Executive (PWE) regularly received news from Czech Intelligence sources on conditions inside the Protectorate and Slovakia. Needless to say, the Government-in-Exile Information Department monitored German and Protectorate press as well as communiqués issued by various news agencies.[95] All these carried sporadic items on the wholesale deportations of Czech Jews that were launched after Heydrich's arrival in Prague.

As far as the fate of Jews from Slovakia was concerned, the Czechoslovak Government-in-Exile was fully informed about anti-Jewish measures introduced by the Bratislava government and as of April 1942 had its own liaison officer stationed in the Slovak capital.[96] In reaction to the mass deportation in Slovakia the Government-in-Exile even decided on July 6, 1942, to approach the Catholic bishop of London to use his influence with the Vatican. An official delegation composed of Dr. Juraj Slavík, former Czechoslovak ambassador to Poland and a member of the government, Ernst Frischer, and Dr. Viktor Fischl called on Bishop Meyers of London and handed him an aide-mémoire addressed to Cardinal Hinsley, archbishop of Westminster. The notes requesting intervention by the Holy See referred to "at least 48,000 Slovak Jews who had already been deported," in contravention of "principles of Christian ethics," which act was "an outrage upon humanity."[97]

Furthermore, in July 1942 a special government emissary was sent from England to Bratislava to negotiate with Dr. Anton Vašek (in charge of "Department XIV," responsible for the deportation of Slovak Jews), whom he met again five months later at the Hotel Bristol in Budapest.[98] Both news and rumors trickled in constantly, supplying data on the general situation as well as about the predicament of the Jewish population both in Slovakia and in the Protectorate.

It is not surprising therefore that already in late June Frischer appeared at a press conference in London, together with Ignacy Schwartzbart and Sydney S. Silverman.[99] At the meeting Frischer spoke of organized wholesale killing. His written report describing the situation in detail was handed over to Anthony J. Drexel Biddle Jr., U.S. ambassador to the allied governments-in-exile in London, who on August 26 forwarded it to the State Department.[100] The ambassador found the contents of the memorandum so important that he dispatched a copy of it directly to the White House. The gist of Frischer's warning read: "There is no precedent for such organized *wholesale dying* in all Jewish history, nor indeed in the whole history of mankind" (italics his). He further stressed the crucial outcome of this "nonconventional war," arguing the moral obligation "of putting a stop to boundless, unscrupulous destruction."[101] Although not indicated, it is highly probable that Frischer gleaned his information from Czech as well as Slovak secret sources that must have been made available at the same time to President Beneš. Colonel Moravec himself claimed that the president saw him every day: "Indeed, I was his first daily visitor throughout the war. He demanded from the start that all messages from home, military, economic, political or intelligence, be presented to him alone."[102]

At this point emphasis should be laid on the secret report received in July 1942 by the World Jewish Congress representative in Geneva, Dr. Gerhard Riegner, revealing the German plan for the total extermination of European Jewry. On August 8, 1942, Riegner transmitted this information to London and Washington.[103] (The Czechoslovak Government-in-Exile received this report on September 14, 1942.) It should be emphasized that the State Department, although in possession of a continuous flow of earlier information from its own representatives abroad, did not immediately release the so-called Riegner telegram but suppressed it for a period of three months.[104] Meanwhile President Beneš, known to have the "best intelligence" at his disposal, was approached on September 29 by representatives of the WJC, Dr. Noah Barou and Alexander L. Easterman, who sought proof of this staggering evidence.[105] Most surprisingly, Beneš expressed doubts as to its veracity and suggested withholding the report for the time being. (In reality as of May 27, 1942, the date of Reichsprotektor Reinhard Heydrich's assassination by the parachutists sent from England, there was an ongoing retaliation campaign in the Protectorate, with daily announcements of executions of culprits connected with the affair!)

As time passed and no news was forthcoming from Beneš, on November 6, 1942, Easterman once again asked for an answer as to whether the result of his inquiry "enabled him to form any definitive conclusions upon the authenticity of the report."[106] President Beneš, in his belated reply to Easterman of November 11, mentioned that he had obtained two replies to his inquiries, both "rather negative in sense," implying that no special plan existed for a wholesale extermination of all the Jews. He thus seems to have endorsed the American and British claim "to have no information bearing on or confirming the story."[107] It is noteworthy that the day before the president addressed his reply to Easterman, Ernst Frischer, the Jewish representative on the State Council, discussed the issue with him. What is stunning is that in describing the situation of the Jews in the Protectorate Beneš omitted mentioning the wholesale deportation, which continued unabated as of mid-October 1941.

Dear Mr. Easterman,

I was just about to inform you of the results of my enquiries, when I received your letter of November 6th.

As I told Mr. Frischer already when he came to see me yesterday, I obtained two replies to my enquiries and both were rather in a negative sense. According to my reports there seem to be no positive indications that the Germans should be preparing a plan for a wholesale extermination of all the Jews. From the reports which I have at present at hand, it would appear that such a plan does not exist and I therefore cannot give you any confirmation of the information which you received in this matter.

This of course, does not mean to say that the Germans are not going perhaps to proceed against the Jews with ever growing brutality. Indeed, the more they see that they themselves are lost, the more will their fury and their terror increase—against the Jews as well as against other subjugated peoples. But this has, in my opinion, nothing to do with any special plan such as you mentioned when you and your delegation came to see me. And my doubts regarding the existence of any such plan are further strengthened by the fact that although innumerable Jews are being terribly persecuted and practically starved, there are others, however small their number may be, who still remain in their original places and even are almost unhindered.

I shall continue, however, to follow the matter and I shall let you know any further information which I might obtain in the matter.

Yours sincerely,

(s.) E. Beneš[108]

It has been suggested that Beneš could have been misled by his own intelligence sources. This, however, is questionable in view of the massive amount of information from Czech and Slovak sources disseminated the world over as well as the alarming memorandum Frischer issued. By the same token we could cite the intervention by the Czechoslovak Government-in-Exile in July 1942 in the matter of deportations in Slovakia. It would appear that Beneš's enigmatic and evasive reply could have been influenced by the stance of Foreign Minister Anthony Eden, as is indicated by the fact that "sensitive" evidence touching upon the early mass killings was long kept under lock and key. Another possible influence could have been the prevailing war tactics and strategy of the Allies, on whose agenda "the fate of an ethnic or religious minority did not figure high."[109]

The clue may be found in a letter Winston Churchill wrote to Lady Reading on February 21, 1943, explaining why there was no possibility of reaching out to the persecuted by evacuating them. "The lines of escape pass almost entirely through war areas where our requirements are predominantly military, and which must therefore in *the interests of our final victory* receive precedence."[110]

Of note is that the Polish Government-in-Exile also somewhat delayed publicizing the fact of genocide against Jews on Polish soil. One claim is that they began to do so when it dawned on them that the Poles might be next in line, and they hoped "if the world turned its attention to Polish Jews," calamity for Polish gentiles could be prevented.[111]

Messages were sent back and forth from London to Prague. Closely following events in the Protectorate (under various pseudonyms such as "Sezima," "Svoboda," etc.), Beneš often addressed questions to members of the Home Resistance about issues that exercised him. Thus on January 3, 1943, he requested information about how the Socialists, the Communists, the conservatives, wealthy people, and so on were conducting themselves.[112]

From a message the Government-in-Exile received from Istanbul on August 23, 1943 (conveyed by Hanák), we learn about the political and economic conditions in the Protectorate. It refers succinctly to the situation of the various strata of the population: workers were accorded better advantages than clerks; the agricultural sector was the most prosperous of all sectors; the intelligentsia carried the heaviest burden of the new order, making the greatest sacrifices. Another comment relates to the Communists, whose activities are described as better and more extensive than those of all other political parties. They had their own people and excellent contacts and said what Moscow told them to say. The people in general were kept informed through chain-letters disseminated by the Communists. Hatred toward the Germans was most prevalent among the middle class.

Beneš also wanted an estimate of the number of victims—aside from Jews—either executed or dying as a consequence of persecution. How many people were incarcerated in concentration camps, and how many were performing forced labor in Germany? The answer received in Geneva on June 21, 1943, written by Kamil Krofta and E. Lány, gave the following estimate: the total number of Czechs killed amounted to fifty thousand without the Jews. Two hundred thousand were imprisoned, and half a million people were employed in forced labor in Germany and other occupied territories.[113]

An additional remark by Beneš concerning the Jews in Terezín, made during his meeting with WJC representatives Dr. Wise and Dr. Goldmann on May 21, 1943, is no less astounding:

> Discussing subsequently the Jewish situation in Europe, President Beneš expressed his conviction that we would find more Jews alive after this war than we think. According to his information, there are some 50–60,000 Jews in Terezín, thousands either in hiding or else posing as non-Jews; there are furthermore certain small townships where the small number of Jews play no role at all and from where they were not deported. As for the fear that the Jews concentrated in ghettos and camps would be exterminated the moment the Germans realize their doom, he thinks there will not be time enough for them to accomplish their wicked purpose.[114]

It is noteworthy that Ernst Frischer, to whom this conversation was conveyed, made no response in his reply of June 21, 1943, to the passage relating to Beneš's estimate of Jewish survivors.[115] In July 1943, Barou and Easterman called again on President Beneš on behalf of the British Section of the WJC, urgently asking him to intervene, together with the queen of the Netherlands, the premier of the Polish Government-in-Exile, and the king of Norway, with President Roosevelt to take energetic steps toward rescuing European Jews.[116]

Beneš reacted to this proposition with considerable reservation, requesting that the delegation first ascertain from the American ambassador in London whether such intervention was at all desirable and how it would be received. His savoir faire in state affairs prompted him to add: "To meet with refusal would result in an unfortunate loss of prestige and this the Heads of State could not risk."[117]

This approach, however, would present only one side of the coin. After the shocking truth of the German plan aimed at the total annihilation of European Jewry had been officially confirmed by Allied headquarters, the Czechoslovak National Council held a special session in London on December 14, 1942. During the meeting a strongly worded declaration was read by Jožka David, the deputy chairman, condemning Nazi barbarism against Jewry, urging that "Allied governments already today should make a clear declaration on behalf of all decent people in the world. A common protest has to be made and a declaration of common responsibility of all those who take part in whatever way in the realization of the plans of the German devils. It is necessary also to attempt relief actions wherever possible."[118]

Indeed, in due course the representatives of the Czechoslovak Government-in-Exile in neutral European capitals (Geneva, Stockholm, and Lisbon) were instructed to assist in rescue campaigns trying to save individuals. Funds were also allocated to alleviate the fate of starving inmates in the ghetto of Terezín; food parcels were sent through the International Committee of the Red Cross to the camps in Poland.[119]

The relations between the Czechoslovak Government-in-Exile and the leadership of the state-in-the-making in Palestine remained close and friendly all through the war years. There was even a close and intimate friendship between Chaim Weizmann and Jan Masaryk. Ardent belief in Allied victory and hope for a better future reinforced their solidarity and feeling of fellowship. Moshe Shertok's message of congratulations to President Beneš on the Day of National Independence in October 1942 expressed these sentiments:

> On the occasion of the celebration of the Day of Czech National Independence, the heart of every Jew who is concerned for the fate of his own people goes out in solidarity and fellow-feeling to the Czech nation. The freedom of many peoples has been trampled on in our day but only that people which of its own accord abandons the struggle for freedom loses it, while those who continue the fight remain free in spirit and will live to see their independence established. The birth pangs of liberation are hard at all times but doubly so for peoples suppressed for centuries like the Czechs or for thousands of years like the Jews. The heroic efforts made in the last war for the creation of the Czechoslovak state, and the struggle today for the restoration of its independence destroyed by Nazi tyranny, are but two stages in one war of liberation. Victory in this struggle, as in the war as a whole, will come to those who are fighting for freedom.[120]

ტ ა ა We know relatively very little about the instructions and advice communicated through Czechoslovak official channels to the Home Resistance with regard to how the local population in general or those actively engaged in underground work were to react to the persecution of the Jews. Beneš tended to be cautious in general, fearing for the sheer biological survival of the nation. We do know that the official line given to the Home Resistance, transmitted in several messages, was: "No hazardous ventures entailing the sacrifice of hundreds or thousands of lives should be undertaken without ensuring a major contribution to Allied warfare"; people were to "keep calm," were "not to be provoked," and were to "await the day of reckoning and revenge."[121]

As of late 1941, however, Beneš changed this line owing to the increased pressure from Moscow, now arguing that "the Protectorate is the most peaceful of all the occupied territories." He altogether began to "play the Russian card," even advising the British to come to terms with the Russians with regard to Central Europe.[122] Thus, in the late fall Operation Anthropoid, the most spectacular action conceived by the Government-in-Exile, was launched with the dispatch of the parachutists to the Protectorate to assassinate Heydrich.[123] This policy meant an outright change from the previous general advice. It would be sheer speculation to connect these warnings with the issue of "sheltering Jews" or extending them assistance. Suffice it to recall Heydrich's threat issued to the Czech population on the eve of the expulsions and the punishments meted out to individuals who reached out to Jews, trying to assist them.[124] Still, sad as it may be, during the height of the Jewish deportations there was a tacit acceptance of their disappearance from the streets.

Jaroslav Smutný in a mid-1943 article for the London *Observer* on quislings—spurred by comments in the British press about the role of Hácha and General Eliáš—underlined that this phenomenon was more common among the Slovaks.[125] Smutný singled out the Slovak premier Dr. Vojtěch Tuka as a prime example, insinuating that he was more a Magyar than a Slovak (Tuka was accused of being a paid agent; his trial for treason in 1929 provoked a great outcry in Czechoslovakia). Moreover, Smutný claimed that only "a scant number" among the Czechs was ready to collaborate. For some reason he omitted to mention the members of the second acting Protectorate government, who eagerly took over their tasks, ready to help in the liquidation of the Jewish population. Some of them were given long-term sentences after the war: Gustav Kliment and especially Colonel Emanuel Moravec, the minister of education and the head of the so-called Office for Public Enlightenment, functioned as propagandists of the Third Reich.[126] In the eyes of members of the Home Resistance, Moravec, once a member of the Czechoslovak Legion and a Czech nationalist, was "collaboration personified."[127] From the messages sent to London, it transpires that the underground leaders suggested to Beneš that Moravec be assassinated instead of Heydrich.[128] The president, however, dismissed this proposal, viewing Heydrich's assassination as an act "essential both politically and internationally for the recovery of the destiny of the nation, even if it should entail great sacrifices."[129]

The situation that evolved in the Protectorate was much more complicated in those days of stark terror: courage, empathy, and dedication were required to render assistance to individuals desperately seeking shelter. In their broadcasts over the BBC some representatives of the Czechoslovak Government in London urged their listeners to extend help to the Jews. Jan Masaryk emotionally exhorted them to reach out to "the most wretched of the wretched" in every way possible, so that after the liberation the Czechs would be able to tell the world that during the horror of the German regime "we remained decent people."[130]

In one of his public speeches in New York, on June 18, 1942, Masaryk outlined his profound understanding and positive approach for Jewish statehood thus: "To reinstate the people of Israel, to make them feel safe, to give them social and economic security, to try to repay them for the sacrifice they brought for the cause of freedom, to solve the Jewish problem in all its complexity, is the duty of every public-spirited man and woman, regardless of race, color and nationality."[131]

Alarming are the reports transmitted in August 1943 to the Government-in-Exile by Hanák stationed at Istanbul. It can be assumed that these were written in response to an inquiry as to what the public anticipated after the war in the social and political spheres. The message from the Protectorate spoke of Jews with hostility reminiscent of the post-Munich atmosphere:

> Much apprehension [exists] that the Czechoslovak government will upon its return to the country bring back all the Jewish émigrés and will return them to their erstwhile and, possibly, even better positions. To our own [native] Jews, people are extending help wherever they can, prompted by sheer humanitarian motives. Otherwise they do not wish their return. They feel alienated from them and are pleased not to encounter them any more. It is not forgotten that with few exceptions Jews have not assimilated and that they sided with the Germans whenever this was advantageous to them, causing damage to the Czech people . . . It should be taken into consideration that after the war anti-Semitism will grow substantially, and that all those who will try to ease and assist the return of the Jews will meet with opposition.[132]

Another message focused bluntly on the economic issue, anticipating the advent of the new socialist era: "Anti-Semitism will probably be the only thing we shall partially adopt from the Nazi ideology. Our people do not agree with the bestial methods of the Germans. Nevertheless they are of the opinion that most of the Jews deserve what is happening to them. After the war, in the New Republic, our people hope that the Jews will not be able to profit from our labor as they did before the war. They think that the property taken from them during the German rule should not be returned."[133]

These views were proliferating in the occupied territories in Bohemia and

Moravia. It may be surmised that they may have exerted some influence on President Beneš as he was formulating his conception on the status envisaged for Jews in postwar Czechoslovakia.

Upon his return to the liberated homeland on April 5, 1945, Beneš proclaimed the establishment of a binational state of Czechs and Slovaks, with freedom of religion and full equality of rights for all citizens and no discrimination based on race.[134] The newly established republic took decisive steps to preserve its homogeneous national character: the problem of the German and Hungarian minorities was solved by the transfer of a majority of these ethnic groups to their own homelands, while the problem of the Ruthenians was solved by the annexation of Transcarpathian Ukraine (Zakarpatská Ukrajina) to the USSR, under the Czechoslovak-Soviet Treaty of June 29, 1945.[135] The Jewish remnants who returned to Czechoslovakia were given the choice of declaring themselves of either Czech or Slovak nationality.

True to his convictions, after the war Beneš continued to support Jewish national aspirations. On August 12, 1947, a Conference of European Zionist Federations took place in Karlovy Vary, attended by the Palestine Jewish Agency Executive. At the opening session Beneš's special message to this conference was read out: "It will, first of all, be necessary to put a radical and permanent end to racism and anti-Semitism. At the same time your aspirations for an independent homeland should be fulfilled. I regard the creation of a Jewish state in Palestine as the only just and possible solution of the world Jewish problem. I promise that whenever and wherever an opportunity offers itself, I shall help promote this solution."[136]

Beneš's presidency lasted no more than three years; it came to an end with his abdication in June 1948. These were fateful years for the Jewish entity in Palestine struggling for independence. It is no secret that during this period the Czechoslovak Republic gave the fledgling state decisive help.[137]

Early postwar historiography addressed President Beneš's role with scathing criticism, mainly with regard to his stance during the Munich period and on account of the treaties he concluded with the Soviet Union.[138] Both Jaromír Smutný and Prokop Drtina, his closest associates during those years, disclaimed Beneš's assertion "that it was the Czechoslovak Government that made the fateful decision about Munich."[139] Táborský drew this conclusion: "Actual decision making in all major policy matters, and even some minor ones, remained in Beneš's hands."[140]

Especially as of the 1989 Revolution, Beneš's stance in the crucial Munich days has earned him condemnation anew. He is also being castigated for his decision leading to the German transfer (1946–47).[141]

However, in spite of all this sharp critique, one aspect supersedes all others: the central axis of his wartime policy. He was looked upon as the leader of the Resistance movement, both by the Czechoslovak army units fighting abroad and by various groupings of the Home Resistance. Although Beneš lost much of his popularity after the war, mainly because of his flawed judgment of Soviet policy, he is still credited for the role he played in the reconstruction of the state.

7

Jews in the Czech Home Resistance

From the onset of the Hitler era and especially as of the late thirties Jewish intellectuals were deeply involved in the anti-Nazi campaign, together with their Czech counterparts. They participated in public demonstrations, international rallies, and discussions and wrote widely in the press, unraveling the Nazi menace. As early as 1935 the Prague writer and journalist Dr. Oscar Singer published his anti-Nazi play *Herren der Welt*, forewarning of the approaching catastrophe.[1]

Nevertheless, the Jews of the Protectorate never mounted any full-scale resistance operation of their own. The absence of any separate organized underground movement or armed resistance can be ascribed to the historical development of this enclave, its political and geographic circumstances, the prevailing mentality, and other factors. Still a solid number of intellectuals, leftist socialists, and young students, overcoming the various difficulties, found their ways to various groups of the Home Resistance.[2]

The Nazi policy of coercion and intimidation *ab ovo* made it clear that any obstruction would be regarded as sabotage, punishable by death. This is reflected in a communication issued by the leadership of the Jewish Religious Congregation, reminding the public in categorical terms about obedience to the law and thus dismissing "any thought of active opposition or hostile acts against the ruling authorities."[3]

Already during the first mass arrests in the fall of 1939 many Jewish intellectuals and notables were taken hostage.[4] As political detainees they were treated during their interrogation with such cruelty that several of them preferred to put an end to their lives. Such was the case of Dr. K. Bachrach, the noted representative of the Czech liquor production and agricultural cooperative, who committed suicide while in custody.[5]

Among the early victims liquidated by the Nazis were two leading figures of the Czech-Jewish movement. Dr. Otto Stross, the last head of this organization, perished in 1941 in Buchenwald. Dr. Zdeněk Thon, a young lawyer from Louny who served for some time on the staff of the JRC, was arrested on charges of maintaining contacts with the Resistance movement abroad and was tortured to death.[6]

The bulk of Jewish participants in the Home Resistance naturally consisted of people already deeply engaged with Czech society, including some members of the National Organization for Physical Culture—known as Sokol—whose ideological and social involvement dated back to prewar days. Another category was their teenage sons, ardent patriots and avid resistance fighters, who fully identified with the Masaryk's republic and democracy. Last we should mention a colorful group of Zionist youngsters of leftist orientation, mainly belonging to HaShomer HaTza'ir, including some who had come from Slovakia and Subcarpathian Ruthenia to attend vocational training courses and had been stranded in the Protectorate after the German occupation.

The question of Jewish identity became a subject of discussion during the "thaw" in the late sixties, in the light of a major project set afoot by the academic authorities to record the history of the Second World War in all its aspects. When attention was devoted to the clandestine organizations the question of Jewish participation emerged, and a nationwide campaign was launched in an effort to gather testimony and all available evidence held in private collections or by the surviving relatives of the resistance fighters.[7]

An interesting comment on the matter of Jewish identity is contained in a letter from Heda Kaufmannová, sister of Dr. Viktor Kaufmann of the PVVZ (We Remain Faithful) clandestine group: "The members of PVVZ, insofar as they were of Jewish origin, joined the struggle as Czechs. Their Czechness (češství) was to them as natural as breathing; [ethnic] origin or religion played no role whatsoever. Only the Nazis literally beat this [latter] fact into their heads. Thus, in the Dresden trial they separated them from the other accused, turning them over to the Gestapo."[8]

This is, however, but one side of the coin. Our attribution of their positive Jewishness derives from the fact that specifically Jewish issues—the persecution of their families, friends, and the community as a whole—could not but have affected their basic outlook, weighing heavily in their reactions, decisions, and attitudes.[9] We know only too well that they were regarded as Jews not only by their Nazi persecutors but even by people around them, their closest associates in the underground cells. Most revealing on this complex issue are the comments on the Czech-Jewish relationship appearing in the illegal press in the wake of the mass deportation of the Jews.[10] Moreover, they were tried, tortured, and sentenced to death (mostly by hanging) specifically as members of that race.

And, ironically, in postwar Czechoslovakia many of them were overlooked while the president of the republic accorded recognition and honor to their fellow combatants.[11]

Henry Michel, the foremost expert on the European Resistance movement, also poses the question of whether "this action by Jews within the Resistance can properly be called Jewish resistance." Although his answer is ambiguous, he admits that the anti-Jewish measures "stirred their sense of nationhood."[12] In this context it is worth noting another statement of Michel's referring to the subject of European Jewish resistance and its unique features: "Jewish resistance was the outcome of despair: it was doomed to failure from the outset, since it lacked all the conditions necessary to an enduring resistance, which could grow and on occasion be victorious. In all countries the clandestine resistance was only one aspect of national resistance; the other into which it had to dovetail, was the resistance outside the country concerned."[13]

It would be an exaggeration to view the various rescue organizations that sprang up in London, Geneva, Istanbul, and New York as representing the Jewish state-in-the-making in terms of an exile government. The Zionist leaders lacked a priori the authority of recognized statehood; limited in the scope of their activities, they were mainly concerned to assist the doomed communities in Nazi-occupied Europe. They focused primarily on arousing public opinion by uncovering the atrocities and systematic extermination carried out in the death camps, addressing vigorous protests to the Allied governments and intervening to obtain immigration permits.[14] The various Jewish rescue organizations nevertheless did serve as reliable channels for clandestine communications, mostly for Zionist groups active in Poland, Hungary, and Slovakia and to a much lesser extent in the Protectorate; last but not least, they provided a source of material and moral succor.[15]

Ústřední vedení odboje domácího (ÚVOD, the Central Leadership of Home Resistance) received its orders from the London Government-in-Exile, whereas the Communist Party underground was directed from Moscow.[16] Several sources reveal that leaders of the Home Resistance were careful not to include Jews among its members and apparently issued a secret directive to this effect. But there was obviously tacit endorsement of exceptions.[17] It should further be remembered that during the first years of the war the official line openly dictated by London was to refrain from risky undertakings: "no hazardous ventures entailing the sacrifice of hundreds or thousands of lives should be undertaken."[18]

The line of Moscow-inspired Czech propaganda, emerging following the German onslaught upon Russia on June 22, 1941, was radically different: it advocated sabotage and underground activities on a broad scale. Simultaneously the party leadership moderated its policy of strict seclusion in an effort to win wider public support.[19] Consequently, it was the left-oriented groups that were more lenient in the matter of Jewish cooperation. Among them were veteran combatants from the Spanish International Brigade who reached the Protectorate via Germany carrying forged identification papers.[20] Ignoring the directives they joined forces with Jewish individuals, often providing them with food and shelter. This cooperation entailed considerable risk, for if by sheer chance the Jewish partner was tracked down and his identity disclosed, the punishment was harsher, the torture was unbearable, and the whole resistance cell was jeopardized. Jewish resistance fighters were fully aware of what was in store for them if detected. Many of them always carried loaded pistols or poison capsules. "There was no chance of survival for them. Those among our Jewish friends who joined our ranks in illegal activity were from the very start real heroes."[21]

Finally, in assessing the participation of Jews on the home front, one encounters still another hurdle—the tendency of German records to exaggerate the Jewish role in subversive activities, as part of the global aims of Nazi propaganda. The Jews are presented there as the true culprits, inciting sabotage, spreading rumors and false information, and playing a prominent part in underground activities. In numerous instances, especially during the Heydrich terror, Jews were executed on trumped-up charges, such as "aiming to undertake acts of sabotage," or "hoping to cause discontent and famine in the country."[22] Records of this nature, of course, require careful scrutiny.

As indicated, this attempt at surveying Jewish participation on the home front is prompted by the desire to bring the subject into focus, without regard for political or party allegiance. The battle waged against the Nazis manifested itself in diverse activities: political-ideological struggle; intelligence and sabotage; and acts of defiance.

POLITICAL AND IDEOLOGICAL STRUGGLE AND THE ILLEGAL PRESS

The initial clandestine activities began in the wake of the Munich crisis and were facilitated by several favorable factors. President Beneš, who resigned his post after the Munich Agreement, urged his associates before his departure abroad in October 1938 to create suitable channels of communication.[23] Later, the escape to London of the chief of military intelligence František Moravec together with eleven members of his staff, on the very day German troops crossed the Czech border, fired the imagination of pilots and army officers, who anxiously sought for escape routes to freedom.[24]

Even after the breaking up of the Second Czecho-Slovak Republic and the establishment of "independent" Slovakia, the close-knit ties among the populations of these regions persisted and created certain opportunities for cooperation in finding escape routes, sheltering escapees, and engineering illegal departures to the West.[25] Consequently, spontaneous and often haphazard enterprises initiated in a combined effort by antifascist elements in both the Protectorate and Slovakia aided figures of the *ancien régime* and officers of the Czechoslovak Army, as well as leftist party functionaries, in their escape to freedom. The situation changed after the occupation of Poland. From that time onward the crossing point shifted to Hungary, where the escapees were less welcome.

The Hungarian authorities' attitude toward the fleeing refugees was "not too benevolent," and thus an interim station had to be set up to enable the flight toward the south, to Yugoslavia via Budapest. The French authorities, eager to gather intelligence about the military moves in the Protectorate and Slovakia, made the premises of the embassy in Budapest available for this purpose, issuing a "laissez-passer" enabling people to reach Yugoslavia. It was Miloš Otto Bondy, known for his prewar arms dealing activities and connections, who was entrusted with this special intelligence mission. He left Paris on December 5, 1939, with a French passport in the assumed name Michel Bonis, launching the project and also financing it partially himself. Up to the day of his arrest on February 19, 1940, 850 Czechoslovak refugees passed via Budapest, their real aim being to join the foreign legion; most were officers, pilots, mechanics, and technicians. Miloš Bondy's arrest by the Hungarian police occurred upon the instruction of German counter espionage. First dispatched to Prague and later tried by the Berlin Senate Court, he was condemned to death on August 10, 1942, and was executed shortly thereafter.

The Czech population numbering around twenty-nine thousand in Slovakia formed an important link with the Czechoslovak resistance abroad, many of them cooperating closely with the local Jews.[26] As earlier noted, clandestine material of the PVVZ, written for the most part by Dr. Josef Fischer, was dispatched from Prague to London via Bratislava. These pouches were handled by railway workers in the mail and sleeper trains en route to Belgrade.[27]

The Maccabi athletic organization in the Czech historic lands, together with its sister organization in Slovakia, managed to smuggle out several hundred of its youngsters via Yugoslavia and Hungary on their way to Palestine. A greater part of these individuals enlisted in the army, formed in late 1939.[28] Other groups were sent from Prague and Brno to Poland, many becoming part of the Czechoslovak unit in the Soviet Union. Close cooperation existed in the gathering of intelligence. In all these activities there were numerous Jewish participants, as revealed in the Bratislava trial of Zibrín and his associates in the clandestine group Demec.[29]

The nucleus of organized resistance dates back to the post-Munich days when a group of leftist intellectuals who opposed the political line adopted by Prime Minister Beran issued the writers' manifesto "We Remain Faithful." It was essentially from this group that the clandestine PVVZ emerged after March 15, 1939.[30] The illegal Národní hnutí pracující mládeže (National Movement of Working Youth) derived from the same core.[31]

At the beginning of the occupation, aside from the Central Committee of the illegal Czechoslovak Communist Party (CCP), there existed three major underground organizations in the Protectorate. The first was Politické ústředí (PÚ; Political center), which formed after Beneš's departure abroad. Initially it was this group that furnished the valuable situation reports known as "message from the homeland" (*zprávy z domova*). Their couriers, mostly businessmen, traveled frequently between Prague and London with urgent dispatches. One of the early dispatches (February–March 1940) conveyed the alarming information that there were signs "the Germans were about to launch a chemical war; they removed from the Kolín chemical works 150 wagon-loads of sodium cyanide salts (NaCN)."[32]

The second group was Obrana národa (ON; Defense of the nation), made up of veteran officers from the Czechoslovak armed forces and hereafter called the Army Organization.[33] The chief aim of this organization was to provide the skeleton for a future secret army. The officers ran a technical group that maintained regular radio-telegraph communications with the London Government-in-Exile as well as with military headquarters in the USSR. Some of the members were apprehended as early as 1939. It has been stated that between March 1939 and November 1940, 1,172 of these men were imprisoned.[34]

The third and most important civilian clandestine group, Petiční výbor "Věrni zůstaneme" (PVVZ) was left-wing and had the broadest Jewish participation.[35] The overwhelming majority of its members consisted of young Social Democrats, Communists, and Freemasons who had been associated with the Workers' Academy (Dělnická akademie) in prewar days. Consequently, it had a broad infrastructure throughout the country.[36]

The Czechoslovak Army had few high-ranking Jewish officers during the interwar period. It is thus symbolic that the first victim of military persecution was Major Bohumil Klein, killed by the Gestapo on October 14, 1939.[37] The former military attaché in Budapest was arrested by the Germans in Moravia for allegedly maintaining contacts with foreign agencies. A similar fate awaited military attaché Major Braun, who served on the embassy staff in Bucharest.[38]

The news of Major Klein's martyrdom was brought to London by the visiting head of the secret Army Organization, who related the details to Bruce Lockhart. The latter recorded in his memoirs: "Major Klein was imprisoned in the sinister Spielburg in Brno and tortured in order to make him speak. He had been kept on the rack for two days. The Germans had put red-hot needles into his testicles. He died without opening his lips."[39]

After the flight of some of the key members of these clandestine organizations, ÚVOD—the Central Leadership of Home Resistance—came into being in late 1939–40, with the aim of bringing all the remaining members of the three resistance groups under one umbrella. A coordinating committee was formed representing the three organizations (PÚ, ON, and PVVZ), with an editorial board that issued the illegal monthly *V boj*, the publication most in demand in the Protectorate during the war years.[40]

The role played by the illegal Czechoslovak Communist Party—the only party that survived throughout all the war years—has been the subject of numerous studies.[41] Although the participation of Jews is not dealt with as a separate topic, some authors occasionally refer to the double danger they had to run, both as "illegals" and because of their racial origin. The majority of the Communist leaders (Gottwald, Šverma, Kopecký, Krosnář, Široký, Slánský, Appelt), together with the German and antifascist émigrés who had taken refuge in Czechoslovakia, were among the first to escape after the Munich Agreement, mainly to the Soviet Union and to France. However, other party functionaries stayed behind, many of them Jews well known to the Gestapo from their activities, such as Otto Synek, Kurt Beer-Konrád, Dr. Jan Frank, and František Taussig, who were later to form the first illegal Central Committee.[42] (Otto Synek's brother Viktor, a journalist and youth leader who had actually left for the Soviet Union, returned after a short period to organize the resistance network.)[43]

The first illegal Central Committee operated in the ideologically chaotic period of the Berlin-Moscow rapprochement. The Nazi-Soviet Non-Aggression Pact of August 23, 1939, and the German victories produced political apathy among the rank-and-file party members. The dilemma plaguing the Communist leadership is reflected in contradictory statements issued in the illegal *Rudé Právo* of that period.[44] An interesting case illustrating the confusion is the story of Gerhard Fuchs and his wife Valerie, both members of the CP and ardent Marxists.[45] Fuchs (cover name Fink), a capable publicist, spent several years in Berlin. Because of their objections to the policy of the Soviet Union on the eve of the war and after the Non-Aggression Pact the two were expelled from the party after the occupation of Bohemia and Moravia. Gerhard Fuchs nevertheless engaged in underground activities. As of autumn 1941, together with his comrade Arnošt Lorenz (whose father was a Jew), he established a secret press. They managed to acquire a typewriter from the Prague Jewish community offices and, using a duplicating machine in a student attic, produced the magazine *Svět proti Hitlerovi* (The world against Hitler), closely cooperating with Julius Fučík. The modest apartment in the heart of the city was shared by Lorenz and his Jewish girlfriend Margareta Baumgarten. By the beginning of 1942 the magazine's circulation reached two thousand copies. On February 25, 1942, Fuchs was arrested in the workshop together with Lorenz, and after cruel torture and an abortive attempt at escape, Fuchs was executed on July 1, 1942 at Prague-Kobylisy, during the Heydrich reprisal campaign. Lorenz was executed in 1944 at the Terezín Small Fortress.

In February 1941 almost the entire Communist Party leadership was uncovered, and during the state of emergency Heydrich declared in September 1941, all were executed.[46] The remaining Jewish rank-and-file party members as well as sympathizers were active until late summer of 1942.

A secret report compiled by Walter Schellenberg (June 10, 1941), addressed to the *Reichsführer* of the SS, Himmler, dealt with the destructive activities of the third Communist International (Comintern) and its underground work directed against National Socialism.[47] It pointed out that prior to the outbreak of war, several Communist functionaries from former Czecho-Slovakia had been sent to the Lenin School in Moscow, where they had trained in military political studies and civilian and terrorist warfare, in both theory and practice. The report contains the following informative passage about the Protectorate and singles out Kurt Beer(-Konrád), a leading theoretician of the Communist Party and former editor of the weekly *Tvorba*. (Until August 23, 1939—the signing of the German-Soviet Pact—he had acted officially as press officer at the USSR Consulate General in Prague.)

The competent functionaries were activated upon the establishment of the Protectorate. They immediately began setting up and expanding the illegal Communist Party [KPD—sic]. Contact with the Comintern and surveillance of Party work were carried out and maintained through the Consulate General of the USSR in Prague. The TASS correspondent and the press officer at the Soviet Consulate General, Kurt Beer (*Jude!*), served as liaison with the Soviet Consulate General. In the course of his duties he received from the diplomatic representation Russian newspapers and Communist propaganda material which he was instructed to pass along to the ranking functionaries of the Communist Party. He was also an intermediary [disposing] of enormous sums of money destined for the maintenance and support of illegal party work.[48]

The report elaborates on the radio contacts with Moscow and the briefings on decisions, situation surveys, and two-way communication all aimed at bringing about the destruction of National Socialism; it also lists the widespread activities throughout Europe. This organization along with others distributed anti-German leaflets. At the end of May 1941, several of these functionaries were arrested.[49]

WE REMAIN FAITHFUL

The PVVZ built up a nationwide underground network with branches in Brno, Moravská Ostrava, Chrudim, and Hradec Králové. In spring 1940 a plan was prepared for a general uprising to commence in Prague.

The organization intended to expand its scope with channels to the Sudeten area and Slovakia with a view to gathering intelligence. At the initial stage it operated radio transmitters at various places. The PVVZ issued leaflets and organized national rallies and pilgrimages that were marked by spontaneous outbursts of patriotic feeling. The leadership exploited these rallies as cover for clandestine meetings and deliberations.

Their primary concern was the reconstruction of the republic—both national and social reforms on the broadest possible scale.[50] Their tenets were formulated in the elaborate program *Za svobodu* (For Freedom), compiled by the leading figures of this organization: Josef Pešek, Professor Wolfgang Jankovec, Dr. Karel Bondy, Eng. Josef Friedl, Dr. K. J. Beneš, and Colonel Churavý. The bulk of the wording is ascribed to Josef Fischer, doubtless the ideological leader of the group, whose erudition in philosophy, social theory and public affairs was widely acclaimed.[51]

Already in 1933 with Hitler's advent to power, Fischer had thus formulated the political line to be pursued with regard to the German issue: "We have to employ every possible means in our work to destroy the Hitler regime . . . Nevertheless we ourselves should not yield to extreme Czech nationalism: it must be clear that the struggle is not waged against the German people or against their natural rights but against the menacing psychosis; against the people themselves only in so far as they are willing to espouse this outlook. One has to differentiate between two Germanys."[52]

In 1935 he published his "War and Peace in Ancient Philosophy." As of spring 1940 he lived in hiding in Prague under the name Antonín Hübschmann, in the home of the Palatý couple, who faithfully attended to all his needs. Until his last days (he was sentenced to death by the Volksgericht on November 15, 1944) he continued to formulate the political program with unrelenting spirit. A passage from the courtroom evidence illustrates his moral stamina: "In prison the condemned was engaged in translating the [seized] archives of the movement into German. Thus, in 1942 he made an attempt to smuggle out portions of the material to his fellow comrades who were still free. Even while in detention he continued formulating the political program [For Freedom: Toward a new Czechoslovak Republic] and managed to smuggle out his tracts and other writings in false containers with the help of disloyal (sic) jailors, who in turn passed them on to his acquaintances."[53]

Fischer's spouse Milena, née Balcarová, was also arrested; she was executed on March 5, 1945, at Ravensbrück. The *For Freedom* program was printed clandestinely in September 1941 in an edition of three thousand copies by the Prague Aubrecht press, mimeographed by Dr. Jiří Baum in the form of a booklet and dispatched to the Czechoslovak Government-in-Exile in London.[54]

Apart from Fischer five additional leading Jewish intellectuals were in the PVVZ: Dr. Karel Bondy, Dr. Viktor Kaufmann, Anna Pollertová and her brother Dr. Jiří Baum, and Jiřina Picková, all well known in their professional fields. Bondy, a lawyer, had been active in the trade unions and in the Pravda vítězí (Truth prevails) Freemason Lodge in the prewar years, where he cooperated closely with General Alois Eliáš (later the prime minister).[55] Along with other activities, he was in charge of building up the organization in Moravia by joining the existing underground cells. Kaufmann, an outstanding physician, was an accomplished linguist (he knew more than twelve languages) and a fine musician.[56] Together with Dr. F. Pascuala he translated Karel Čapek's *White Plague* into Spanish (1937). Pollertová was a public figure associated with Národní rada žen (the National Council of Women). Picková, a teacher and educator, was a prewar member of the Communist Party, active in student organizations. During the war she compiled a textbook on psychology. Baum was an expert in the natural sciences; he wrote several books and travelogues.[57] With his technical skill and expertise in mimeographing he prepared photographs for fake documents and identity cards supplied to PVVZ members.[58] All of them had been active before the war and were involved in the campaign "For the Aid of Spain" and in other humanitarian and welfare committees that assisted refugees from Germany.[59] One of the first undertakings of the PVVZ was the "crown campaign" to raise money for refugees. Thousands of metal coins that poured in were taken by Kaufmann and Pollertová to the Moravian–Slovak border.[60]

From the outset concern about persecution of the Jews is implied in some of their messages sent to London. It appears that as early as January 1940 the PVVZ foresaw the possibility of wholesale deportation and endeavored to counteract it: "With regard to certain measures it is advisable to demand American reprisals and to launch a campaign toward this aim; nothing else can help. One cannot stand by passively and watch things happen. For instance if it should come to mobilization, drafting for forced labor, *mass deportation of Jews*, public opinion has to be prepared so that the campaign may be launched if necessary" (italics mine).[61]

More detailed information is available on Bondy, thanks to the notes he managed to pass to his jailor Kolínský, who smuggled them out of the Pankrác prison.[62] (Incidentally, this same Kolínský was instrumental in saving Julius Fučík's "secret slips," which became widely known after the war as *Notes from the Gallows*.) Bondy's notes lack the insight of the professional writer but are permeated with clear thinking and genuine soul-searching. Apart from recording physical endurance in the face of the special torture meted out to Jewish prisoners at the "Wailing Wall" of the notorious Pankrác prison, he gives a full account of the PVVZ's aims and activities and of the objective reasons for its failures and final dismemberment.[63]

Most painful, but of historical value, are his comments on the informers who were instrumental in denouncing the organization.[64] With the precision and detachment of an attorney he penned his "indictment" of *prstýnkáři*, the group identified by identical finger rings.[65] While in prison Bondy witnessed their comings and goings, their dealings with the Gestapo, their "narrow treacherous acts." He described their motivations as "human frailties and weaknesses . . . animosity, envy or vengefulness, in other cases they acted out of venal lust or sheer egoism."[66] Most scathing is Bondy's concluding remark: "Were it not for the treachery of some of our Czech people, many, many of our friends, if not the overwhelming majority, could have been spared incarceration, execution, the horror of jail and dying." This criticism is corroborated by Milena Jesenská, who in early 1940 also managed to smuggle a message out of the prison at Pankrác, penciled on her underwear sent to the laundry and addressed to her friend Rokyta Illnerová: "The worst of all is to observe the Czech character. It is, Rokyta, horrible, outrageous. Two thirds of the people [prison staff] here are [used] as informants on the Czechs."[67]

Bondy himself was a scion of an old Prague family. His grandfather Filip Bondy was the first rabbi to use the Czech language in synagogue services as early as the 1860s. His father Dr. Max Bondy was among the founders of the Kapper Czech-Jewish Student Association, which strove for close cooperation with the Czech nation. Dr. Bondy himself gave up his profession as a lawyer after the occupation and divorced his non-Jewish wife to spare her daily harassments; he devoted all his time to underground work.[68] Although in possession of entry visas to England and France, he never considered emigrating. He was in charge of contacts with members in the regional groups, "a kind of Secretary-General."[69] This function entailed frequent train journeys, which caused him considerable inconvenience because he was Jewish.

On the range of activities Bondy carried out, Veselý-Štainer's memoirs are most illuminating.[70] The latter recalls how after the dispersal of Colonel Mašín's group, radio-telegraph contact with London was disrupted. On July 20, 1941, Veselý-Štainer met with Bondy, who described how after a lapse of three weeks he had managed to restore communications. There is also a reference to Bondy's liaison with parachutists:

> During the deliberations of the PVVZ with the trade unionists, while the devastating news came through over the radio about the execution of the generals [the victims shot on October 1 included several high-ranking officers], Dr. Bondy informed us of the forthcoming arrival of parachutists and that actual preparations had been made for this event in the Pardubice area. And indeed, some time on October 3, 1941, while our deliberations were dragging on into the night, we were thrilled to hear the sound of sirens followed by anti-aircraft fire, proof that the pilots were about to drop the expected parachutists with the promised material.[71]

❦❦❦ A different task was entrusted to Anna Pollertová (née Baum, May 7, 1899), the daughter of an established Jewish family in Prague. The house at number 7 Ve Pštrosce (now ulice Anny Letenské) that played a unique role in the PVVZ clandestine movement as both shelter and workshop was part of her dowry.[72] Today the house bears a plaque inscribed with twenty-six names of PVVZ leading members who perished at the hands of the Nazis.

It appears that in 1939 Pollertová mortgaged her property for 2.5 million Czech crowns, which she clearly used for underground activities.[73] At least two other inhabitants of this house are worthy of note. In the attic lived Jiřina Picková, who was associated with various resistance acts. She is credited with the rescue of the secret Army Archives. Gusta Fučíková recorded their meeting at the Pankrác prison thus: "She was arrested in January 1943 and beaten so severely that her legs up to the waist were one continuous black bruise. She suffered from an inflammation of the veins . . . [she] never disclosed the source from which she received the pistols for the resistance."[74]

Another PVVZ member, Eng. J. Kochta, married to a cousin of Anna Pollertová, occupied one of the apartments, which was equipped with a mimeograph machine operated by a "Mr. Skřivánek." The meetings held at Pollertová's were called banquets; the guests were served by Zdena, housekeeper and confidante.[75] It was to her that Anna confided her last will and testament before she went underground. Pátková assumed custody of both of Pollertová's children—Irena, aged 17, and Jaromír Herbert, aged 15—after their mother's arrest.[76]

Pollertová also provided hiding places for several members of the organization. It was she who rented, in Pátková's name, numerous apartments in various parts of town, where Bondy, Professor Čížek, Fischer, General Čihák, and others living under assumed names occasionally spent single nights. Another shelter utilized for this purpose was the apartment of Anna Pollertová's parents, the Baums.[77]

Pollertová cooperated closely with Dr. Milada Horáková-Králová of the National Council of Women as well as with Mastníková, Eng. Friedl, Čížek, Andršt (Malina), and other members of the secret Army Organization.[78] One of her assignments was to take care of the first parachutists from Britain who landed in the Protectorate. She looked after the families of arrested patriots and provided them with money and advice. Her courage knew no limits. According to the testimony of her associates, she succeeded in making off with a suitcase holding incriminating evidence from the house of Colonel Churavý (cover name Vlk) after his arrest.[79] It is symbolic that Pollertová was arrested near the apartment of the writer and editor Vincy Schwartz and his non-Jewish wife Anna, while on her way to warn them of impending danger. (Actually both had been apprehended by the police the day before, on October 20, 1941).[80]

The PVVZ employed couriers and messengers who regularly distributed clandestine leaflets and directives, pasting them on doors or dropping them into letterboxes. They also disseminated news, especially items broadcast over the BBC, and issued warnings to collaborators and informers working with the Gestapo; they distributed by the thousands "detective stories" that, under an authentic jacket, were actually anti-Nazi literature, carefully selected for the purpose.[81] Full use was made of the Czech sense of humor. Aside from whimsical rhymes (written by the poet František Halas), current political events, jokes, and cartoons in response to Reich propaganda all for the readers' amusement, the back cover of every issue of the detective stories carried, in lieu of the printer or publisher, names such as: Šaňo Mach, Konrad Henlein, G. E. Stapo, etc.[82]

All these seemingly minor tasks required dedicated people who were ready to run risks. Among the aides was Anka Rottová (daughter of Vitězslav Stein, a noted Social Democrat and trade unionist), who before her deportation to Auschwitz was in charge of a shelter for small children in Prague run by the JRC.[83] She perished in Auschwitz during the liquidation of the "Czech family-camp" in Terezín. Similarly Professor Čížek's student Hanka Fuchsová (aged twenty) served as his driver and helped him in setting up the PVVZ network.[84] In April 1942 she was deported to Terezín and from there to Zamošč, where she perished.

As of 1939 the PVVZ benefited from the cooperation of Otto Gall, who was secretary of the "Civil Resistance" [Movement] Criminal Section of the Prague Gestapo.[85] A *Reichsdeutsche*, Gall had earlier held a position in Aussig (Ústí nad Labem), where he became disillusioned with National Socialism. It was there that he met Herta Bauer, whose father Dr. František Bauer was a Jew and whose mother was a Czech Aryan. Some foremost Czech figures in the Home Resistance such as Anna Dohalská, wife of Zdeněk Bořek-Dohalský, became involved in the effort to assemble proof of the Czech Aryan descent of Gall's fiancée.[86] Dohalská later acted as contact between Gall and the Resistance, meeting with him weekly or even more often. Gall reported on the Gestapo actions planned against several organizations (Sokol, the Union of the Legionnaires, the Communists, and the Freemasons). He also informed them about the arrival of parachutists and managed to arrange the release of some members of the Czech Resistance from prison. Gall was instrumental in procuring posts as maintenance workers for Fischer and Jankovec in Pankrác prison and, later, as clerks.[87]

The PVVZ went through various stages of reorganization and change in leadership. Most of its leading members were uncovered in October 1941 owing to denunciations. Of the forty-two arrested only eleven survived the war. Fischer, Bondy, Kaufmann, and Pollertová were kept for years in various prisons. On November 11, 1944, they were put on trial in Dresden, then separated from their Czech comrades, charged by the Volksgericht with high treason, and sentenced to death.[88] Their execution took place in January and February 1945 at Winterfeldhalle, Brandenburg, and in Berlin. Picková (arrested in January 1943) was shot on November 16, 1943, in Auschwitz. Jiří Baum was deported to Terezín and subsequently taken to Warsaw, where he perished in 1944.

The farewell letters—scraps of paper hidden in the clothes returned to the families of the resistance fighters—convey the last laconic message: loyalty and an unwavering belief in the justice of their cause. "The rest is silence."[89]

THE VRŠOVICE YOUTH GROUP

A unique resistance group evolved at the end of 1939–40 around the Kodaňská Street Gymnasium of Vršovice.[90] Most of the members came from well-to-do middle-class families. Motivated by an innate sense of social justice and freedom, they were among the first to voice protests against the Nazis. Some of them had contacts with prewar Communists or left-wing socialists and from an ideological point of view were merely sympathizers; others were avowed Communist Party members. Young, romantic, and highly talented, they often employed their ready wit and unfailing Czech humor in anti-Nazi propaganda activities—writing leaflets and drawing cartoons.

The Vršovice group convened in discussion circles in private homes and under the influence of their politically mature comrades joined the illegal resistance cells. The most active among them were Karel Renner, Jiří Kysela, Hanuš Polák, Ladislav Polák, Drahomír Barta, Stanislav Bálek, Olga Tvrdková, Hanuš Škába, Helena Ellnerová, Zdeňka Rennerová, Věra Bálkova, Věra Aubrechtová, and Věra Andrlová. Of these Jiří Kysela and the Poláks, who were cousins, were Jews. Věra Aubrechtová's devotion to and solidarity with the Kysela family, for which she paid with her life, deserve special mention.[91]

The group's activities gathered momentum after June 1941 with Germany's attack on the Soviet Union. At this stage a number of Jewish youngsters found their way to this network, presumably through the mediation of the leading Jewish resistance fighters Jiří Kysela and Ladislav and Hanuš Polák, all three born to well-to-do families in Prague.[92] Ladislav Polák, a medical student whose father was a well-known physician, joined after the experience of a few months' stay in Sachsenhausen in 1939. His cousin Hanuš had a wide circle of friends and acquaintances—his father, Eugen Polák, owned a delicatessen store in the Karlín district. Through his contacts and winning personality Hanuš recruited more sympathizers for the cause who were ready to provide financial support. One of the staunch supporters of the group was Dr. Vladimír Polák, a relative from the Žižkov district.[93]

Most active on the ideological level was Jiří Kysela, son of noted sculptor František Kysela, who was a close friend of the philosopher and scholar Zdeněk Nejedlý. Jiří's family belonged to the progressive elite, maintaining good connections with the Soviet Consulate in Prague.[94]

These young people copied, duplicated, and disseminated Marxist literature and pasted up slogans advocating sabotage and go-slow campaigns in factories. Their main aspiration was to organize armed resistance, and to this end they cooperated closely with the group of physicians and various workers' cells. In October 1941, when the systematic deportation of Jews from the Protectorate began, the Jewish members of the group decided to go underground and live under assumed names. (They either skillfully changed their own identity cards or acquired Aryan papers with the help of their comrades.)[95] It appears that every two or three cells shared a single head; members of one cell were kept in ignorance of the others. We know of two cells that had numerous Jewish members, namely those of Ladislav Polák and Helena Ellnerová.[96] The first included Vojtěch Feuerstein (Fai) of the HaShomer HaTza'ir youth organization as well as the Lederer brothers, Miloš and Pavel.[97] The second cell included Jiří Heller, Grünthal, Eva Králová, Eva Langerová, and Alena Voglová. Our information on "Fai" derives from various sources.[98] He evidently acted as contact man for a group of youths who, contrary to the guidelines of the Zionist leadership, went into hiding; this was the subject of many heated discussions, HeHalutz objecting to any sort of deserting or "running away" and insisting on standing by the masses of the Jewish people at the moment of their greatest affliction.[99] Contrary to this conception Fai and his *Af-al-pi-khen* (In spite of all) group took up the challenge of taking their own course, finding their way to the clandestine movement.[100] We know of the hardships in hiding and the struggle for survival from the report sent to the Geneva HeHalutz Center by one of the survivors of this group, Dr. Arnošt (Ephraim) Neumann.[101] He succeeded in escaping from Prague to his native Slovakia in the late summer of 1943 with the help of the illegal Slovak branch of the movement.

The passage of Neumann's report dealing with his contacts with the Vršovice group reads as follows: "We have established contact with Communists to fight a common enemy, and they have recognized our political integrity. Consequently, for the time being, they regard the debates on ideological issues as academic, and they promised to lend us their support within the framework of their overall organization. They advised us not to report for transports and provided us with a source for acquiring baptismal certificates that enabled us to live [in this country]. Our friend Benzion [Vojtěch] Feuerstein acted as liaison between them and ourselves."[102]

Another report, dispatched from Budapest on February 27, 1944, and signed by Hede Türk-Neumann (who reached Slovakia two months after her husband, in October 1943), stresses the assistance rendered to them by various Czech individuals while they were in hiding in Prague and in the countryside.[103] She also comments on the fact that Communist resistance groups adamantly refused to include them in any activities because of the danger inherent in such cooperation: "there was, however, a clandestine group, whose members were closer to us and more lenient about cooperating.[104] Although they did not know anything personal about us they were aware of our outlook. Cooperation was such that they helped us with identity papers and hiding; in return we organized an ideological seminar for two of their comrades and provided them with socialist literature; we had somehow managed to keep a copy of every important book. Thus we had Marx, Engels, Krupskaya, Stalin, Ulrych, Lunatscharky and so on."[105]

From the testimony of Miloš Hájek and M. Petránková-Šimková we learn further details about this unusual cooperation.[106] According to them a group of HaShomer youth regularly participated in meetings that took place at the house of Dr. Šimek in Vinohrady. They studied together, distributed antifascist leaflets, and procured work permits for patriots who lived in hiding.

The main task of the Czech clandestine cell called *Přehledy* (Surveys), was to compile for its members overall reports on the current political situation.[107] They undertook to render assistance to the Jewish comrades by furnishing them with identity cards (*Kennkarte*), baptismal certificates, etc., and often "under dramatic circumstances transmitted to them messages, letters and food."[108]

We may assume that it was partly thanks to contacts with this clandestine group that about twenty young men and women listed in Neumann's report could actually evade deportation, finding various avenues of escape and in 1942 "volunteering" for labor in Germany proper and enlisting together with other young Czech draftees.[109] Others found jobs as railway employees, stagehands, electricians, supervisors, and teachers of German language courses.[110]

The members of the Vršovice group survived the first wave of arrests following the imposition of martial law after Heydrich's assassination, during which period it was primarily resistance groups directed from London that became the main target of persecution. However, at the beginning of June 1942, following denunciation by a paid Czech informer, some of the leading members of the group were apprehended.[111] On June 8, 1942, Ladislav Polák was arrested; at his father's clinic the Gestapo uncovered a notebook with lists of names and other evidence, which apparently led to further arrests of the members of the Vršovice group. Altogether fifty people were arrested and after interrogation at the Small Fortress of Terezín were sent to Mauthausen or Auschwitz.[112] Only about half of these youngsters survived the war; Jiří Kysela perished in Auschwitz and Hanuš Polák, Vojtěch Feuerstein (Fai), and Miloš Lederer in Mauthausen.[113] Miraculously, Ladislav Polák survived.[114] Three of the girls, Eva Stichová, Králová, and Langerová, returned from Mauthausen after the war.[115]

INTELLIGENCE AND SABOTAGE

In the first years of the occupation the various clandestine groups and mainly the secret Army Organization (ON) concentrated on gathering intelligence. The contribution of the Czech underground to the Allied war effort (information on Axis troop movements, situation reports, data on industrial output, etc.) has been described in memoirs as well as in wartime reports. It is estimated that from March 1939 to October 1941 more than fourteen thousand messages were exchanged between the Protectorate and the exile centers in Paris and London.[116] As noted, special channels for conveying information were established via Istanbul and Switzerland, which functioned up to the end of the war.

Kurt Beer-Konrád played an important role. Until his arrest on August 23, 1941, he continued to work on the staff of the USSR Consulate.[117] Konrád's intellect and sense of social justice crystallized early. Upon graduating from high school he was already a mature and balanced person, corresponding with Romain Rolland. The latter gave him the following advice in 1926, which Konrád fully espoused: "You should fight courageously and with patience. Life is a struggle; I love it therefore and believe that one of the most effective means of helping people is to set them an example of a man who adheres to [principles] and who tenaciously holds on and perseveres to the last."[118]

In the thirties, during his university studies, he devoted much of his time to public and party activities. He wrote to various papers and review magazines about cultural-political issues. As a historian he took an interest in the Spanish Civil War and the meaning of Czech history. He was the first to attempt interpreting the Hussite era from a Marxist vantage point, viewing it as a social revolution. One of his contact men was Dr. Jan Frank (Arnošt), secretary of the Communist Party of Bohemia.[119] A second was Eng. Milan Reiman (M. Novotný).[120] Thanks to these well-placed sources, intelligence of major significance streamed into Konrád's office: briefings on the activities of the Protectorate Government from National Solidarity headquarters, guidelines issued in the Reich for the mass media, and copies of maps printed for the German Military Cartographic Institute.[121] Through Reiman, Konrád maintained contact with Prime Minister Eliáš, who met with Reiman at various places in the city.[122]

We learn of an additional intelligence source from the memoirs of Gusta Fučíková.[123] She relates a chance meeting with Kurt Glaser, a former Communist Party member, who as a Jew in the compulsory labor service worked in a brigade demolishing a bridge in the center of Prague. Glaser told her of his daily meetings with a former Sudeten German schoolmate from the Wehrmacht Intelligence who briefed him on current affairs.[124] Julius Fučík, learning from his wife of the matter, requested Glaser to brief the CCP regularly on his meetings, and in 1942 when the mass deportations began, Glaser was instructed not to report for transport.[125]

Acts of sabotage such as derailing military trains and cutting telephone lines occurred sporadically as of the earliest stages of occupation. According to an official announcement in the Czech press on January 31, 1940, "the Jew Bauer together with Kulka were tried and executed in Brno."[126] In June 1940 there was another case of sabotage in the armaments industry.[127] A special unit for sabotage and other acts was commended by ON officers.

The activities of the various underground movements were stepped up after the German attack on the Soviet Union. The Communist Party, emerging from its isolation, began vigorous promotion of acts of resistance: illegal newssheets and leaflets were circulated in factories and workshops, calling for strikes and sabotage.[128] The Czech-language broadcasts from London called for a go-slow (*pracuj pomalu*) campaign. During the week of September 14, the Czechs staged an effective boycott of the official press, an action instigated by ÚVOD and assisted by the BBC from London.[129]

By the fall of 1941, two years after the occupation, the German Security Services could boast of having nipped in the bud any wide-ranging clandestine network in the Czech lands. The core of the leadership—top-ranking army officers, intellectuals, political liberals, leftist socialists, and freemasons—had been either executed or imprisoned. This constituted a severe blow to the Czech nation and was to have profound implications on the postwar political scene.

The collapse of national resistance and its aftermath affected the Jewish population in their hour of direst need—on the eve of mass deportations. With the arrival of the new acting Reichsprotektor Reinhard Heydrich on September 28, 1941, the campaign for extermination of the Jews of the Czech lands began.

It has been asserted that Heydrich's appointment in September 1941 followed Hitler's receipt of reports on the alarming 20 percent decrease in the production of war materiel in Czech factories. Heydrich thus arrived on the scene with the primary goal of breaking the will and the strength of the resistance movements.[130] Upon his arrival a state of emergency and martial law were declared. The prime minister, General Eliáš, was arrested and sentenced to death.[131] Executions for high treason, sabotage, and other offenses were the order of the day. The verdicts of the special courts set up in Prague and Brno were made public in the press.

Otto Synek, Communist member of Parliament, was shot on September 29, 1941, to be followed by the others. The next day Jiří Spitzer and Leo Schwartz from Prague, members of a resistance group, were executed (Schwartz, a former legionnaire, was associated with the Credit Institute of the Czechoslovak Legions). Chemist Emil Feuerstein, a Social Democrat who subsequently joined the Communist Party, was condemned to death for membership in a clandestine group, the main functions of which were smuggling out former legionnaires and collecting intelligence.[132]

The group associated with the National Movement of Working Youth in the Žižkov district, under the guidance of Eng. Oldřich Štancl, proprietor of a small mechanical workshop in Prague, commenced activities in early 1941.[133] The team numbered five members, among them Jiří Stricker, who acted as foreman. At the end of September they carried out several acts of sabotage in Prague and the surroundings, using homemade explosives. The report of the RSHA security headquarters in Berlin reads: "At the end of October 1941, a Communist terrorist group was discovered which, led by a Jew, started the industrial production of incendiary materials and explosive bombs. Production was taken over by the Czech owner of an armaments factory. In November 1941 members of this group including Jiří Stricker were executed in Prague."[134] As that report notes: "Fráňa Stricker, his brother, also charged with sabotage, was sent to Mauthausen at the beginning of January 1942 and put to death the following day."[135]

According to *Dienst aus Deutschland* of October 3, 1941, fifteen persons were condemned to death by shooting and four Jews by hanging for planning high treason, for economic sabotage, and for illicit hoarding of arms. As a rule, Jews were described as ringleaders of an illegal Communist organization and were charged with playing a part in the reconstruction of the Communist Party— distributing leaflets, producing and distributing Communist tracts, collecting membership fees.

Heydrich's assassination on May 27, 1942, was followed by the harshest retaliatory policy, eliminating yet another stratum of courageous and dedicated Czech patriots, potential allies for any possible support and cooperation. Among the first victims executed were some Jewish intellectuals and public figures, the pillars of Czech-Jewish symbiosis.

Several trials that took place in the German People's Court in 1943 dealt with cases of Jews who had donated money for the illegal Communist Party in 1941–42 and who had carried out the fund-raising campaign. According to a People's Court verdict of January 14, 1943, the accused Smetana, Polák, Rosenfeld, Dr. Zuckermann, and Adler were charged with making preparations for "treason and collaboration with the enemy" and were sentenced to death by hanging. They were also accused of "plotting to set up a Czechoslovak-Soviet state and the breakaway of the Protectorate from the Reich."[136] We know of additional victims executed on similar charges: Jindřich Fest (October 4, 1941), Arnošt Freund (August 31, 1942), Václav Wolf (November 24, 1942), Pavel Kohn and Bedřich Weiner (January 1943), and Josef Weiss (April 28, 1943).[137] Other Jewish resistance fighters were handed over to the Gestapo and shipped to concentration camps, never to return.[138] Particularly revealing are the logbooks of Mauthausen and Auschwitz, which at this period show instances of massive executions and deaths from various causes such as "shot during attempted escape."[139]

Jewish involvement in resistance decreased by the end of 1942, but we have definite knowledge of some more young Jews engaged in resistance activities in the last years of the war. Milan Weiss, charged with stockpiling arms, was beheaded at Pankrác prison on September 10, 1943.[140] Dr. Otakar Weisel, executed at the Small Fortress, was connected with the underground group associated with Jaroslav Kvapil.[141] In January 1944 Dr. Heřmann Freund was killed by agents of the Security Police while trying to escape after having lived illegally in a summer hut in the area of Nové Město na Moravě.[142] Another victim was Jiří Kohn, former secretary of the Šalda Committee for the Assistance of Refugees. The coordinator between the clandestine cells of the Avia factory and the central Social Security Office in Prague, he was arrested in March 1944.[143] Some additional instances of Jews participating in partisan units have been recorded at even later dates.[144]

One of the aspects of the Czech Home Resistance touches upon the new social order envisaged by the Communist resistance cells for the postwar years. This transpires clearly from the illegal press and leaflets issued in the Protectorate in 1943 as well as from messages transmitted by various underground groups to the Government-in-Exile. Most of these dealt at length with the Jewish question in Bohemia, making critical references to the state of affairs in the pre-Munich republic, putting the blame for all the misfortune on the "treacherous bourgeois elements" aligning themselves with the Western powers. Statements collated from articles written in a most hostile vein project some blatant views with regard to Jews' siding with the Germans in the past (Germanization, social oppression). The future policy and socioeconomic plans in the newly constructed state were envisaged thus: "No one will be asked why he suffered, and there will be no merit awards for 'martyrdom,' but each and every individual will be asked: how did you conduct yourself in the interest of your nation, whom did you support and whom did you oppress today, yesterday and even before that? And to these questions there will be simple responses, which *per se* will straight away resolve this very unpleasant Jewish question as well."[145]

The reports penned by Miloš Hanák, transmitted in August 1943 from Istanbul to the Government-in-Exile and citing views held by the Czech population, in effect concur with the views orchestrated from Moscow anticipating the new social and political order after the war.

In September 1944 Václav Kopecký, a leading Communist functionary who spent the war years in the USSR and who would become minister of information in the postwar government, discussed this issue in the same vein in an article entitled "On the Question of Anti-Semitism."[146] Kopecký delineated the criteria of granting Czechoslovak citizenship (to be based upon the 1930 census) and how these would apply to those Jews who adhered to German or Hungarian nationality: "Each emigrant of Jewish origin will be strictly examined as to how he conducted himself from the national point of view in the past, what his attitude was toward German and Hungarian nationalism, eventually toward irredentism, what his attitude was to the Czech nation and to other Slavic nations. In the same way his conduct during the Second Republic and during the German occupation will be strictly examined."

Even more dogmatic was his reference to the return of Jewish property confiscated by the Nazis:

> To suppress anti-Semitism does not mean, for example, at the same time to safeguard Jewish [financial] magnates à la Petschek, Weinmann, Rothschild, Gutmann, etc. [to condone their] return to the liberated republic so that they may eventually take over their former property and continue their [blood]sucking . . . No, never! Jewish magnates (*velkoboháči*) who like Petschek, Weinmann, Rothschild, Gutmann, etc. knew how to run away from the country prior to the critical period of the defense struggle of the republic; who knew [how to make arrangements] to handle their property by transferring it of their own volition to the Germans, who knew how to give up Czechoslovak citizenship and acquire instead foreign citizenship—such panicking Jewish overlords should never return to the republic! And their former property will not be returned to them.[147]

MAGNANIMITY IN DISTRESS; WRITING UNDER PSEUDONYMS

After Hitler's ascent to power the Czechoslovak state in general and the Czech intellectuals in particular earned themselves worldwide acclaim for generously reaching out to the German émigrés who found refuge in their midst. This welcoming gesture was a spontaneous outcry against rising fascism. Reflecting on the long-term effects of this outreach, Pavel Eisner likened it to "building blocks upon which a cultural bridge could be erected."[148] The Nazis, on the other hand, from the very beginning led a virulent campaign in the media against Czechoslovak artists (especially actors and theatrical directors), angered by their activities on behalf of refugees.

One has to recall the headlines in the mid-thirties reporting on the escape of several illustrious exiles who found asylum in Czechoslovakia. The warm reception extended to Thomas Mann and his brother Heinrich Mann is well-known, as is the sad story of Professor Theodor Lessing, a philosopher engaged in the history of ideas, whose life ended abruptly in August 1933 at the hands of an assassin dispatched from Germany to murder him in a Marienbad hotel.[149]

The initial move of the intellectuals was to organize aid for the refugees and stir the interest and involvement of the public the world over. Among the names that figured prominently in announcement of the setting up of F. X. Šalda's Committee for the Assistance of Refugees in April 1933 were Henri Barbusse, André Gide, G. B. Shaw, H. G. Wells, Aldous Huxley, Hugh Walpole, and Lewis Golding.[150] The Prague International Exhibition of Caricature held in April 1934—disclosing the true face of Nazism—was greeted by letters of encouragement from Henri Barbusse, Louis Aragon, Jean Cocteau, and Oscar Kokoschka.

One should add that aside from the Šalda Committee, other associations mushroomed, supported by notable Czech writers, artists, and public figures. On June 8, 1935, the community of Czechoslovak writers, together with the Union of Progressive Students, organized in Prague an exhibition called "The Burned Book" in response to the Berlin auto-da-fé. In his opening address, the poet Josef Hora described that event as a perversity signaling "the overall destruction of culture."[151]

However, this was but a prelude to the real tragedy that ensued in the wake of the Munich *Diktat* and after the occupation of the Czech lands by the Nazis. The overwhelming grief over the loss of freedom generated apathy among the general public, calling into question some basic issues such as identity and nationhood. The significance and the value of literature, music, theater, and paintings as a guarantee of strength and hope for the future of a nation "robbed of its 'soul' " was expressed in October 1939 in Josef Hora's poem "Flight into the Book."[152]

The occupation put an end to the flourishing cultural life in music, art, and especially literature. One of the outcomes was a sharp decline in published works. A further indication was the prohibition and removal of literature produced by prominent Czech national writers. Around three thousand of the finest literary works were taken off library shelves and destroyed.[153] These included the works of Komenský, Palacký, Jirásek, the brothers Čapek, Vančura, Olbracht, and others as well as everything authored by Jewish writers and composers, who were the first to be silenced. Most of them had to write, create, and compose clandestinely, hiding their literary output for better days.

An amusing episode of "Jew hunting" is associated with the celebrated writer Erich Maria Remarque, who was hated by the Germans and whose novels (*All Quiet on the Western Front* and *The Road Back*) were banned because of their pacifist ideas. The writer recounted after the war to Julius Firt, who visited him at his Swiss residence, his own version of the story.[154] He recalled with bitter humor how the scrupulous Nazis in their search for Jewish names banned his books, taking Remarque for "Kramer" written in reverse.

It is an established fact that the Hitlerite cohorts never forgave those who challenged their ideology; humanist writers were the first to be entered on their blacklists and rosters. It is symbolic that for the collective "guilt" of the Czech literary community Vladislav Vančura, the nestor of the Czech literati, "the cream of a gifted generation," had to pay with his life.[155] Vančura (1891–1942), a master of artistic expression and language, left in his legacy his own protest against Nazi persecution of the Jews by rendering a new version of Josef Jiří Kolár's popular historical drama "The Prague Jew" (1871). Fallu Eliab, the central figure who was ready to sacrifice his life for his Czech fatherland after the Battle of the White Mountain, became in Vančura's version an ardent fighter defying barbarian fascism.

In the gloomy atmosphere of suppression the Czech cultural elite demonstrated a rare solidarity unparalleled elsewhere in occupied Europe. Several magnanimous Czech writers, spurred by a sense of resistance and compassion, enabled Jewish colleagues to publish under fictitious or disguised names, even lending their own names. They often did this with the complete connivance of the publishers, who printed the work under various pseudonyms. Most of the literati in Prague could guess at the real identity of the writers. Apart from providing a modest income, the publication of their work became the sole source of moral succor to these Jewish writers.

Somebody humorously suggested that this kind of negligence might eventually have arisen from "Slavica non leguntur" (Slavic literature is not read). However, from the reminiscences of the poet Josef Hiršal, it transpires that it was thanks to Vilém Kostka, former major of the Czechoslovak Army, that this special kind of gesture worked.[156]

The most illustrious example is that of young Jiří Orten, who saw his first poems printed under the pen names "Karel Jílek" or "Jiří Jakub."[157] His friends Boněk Březovský, Zdeněk Urbánek, Kamil Bednář, and others, acknowledging his unusual talents, willingly supported him in these efforts.[158] Václav Černý and František Halas were also aware of his enormous creative capacity.[159] Neither the decree against publishing work by Jews nor the various evils imposed upon Jews could silence his magical poetic soul. It was during this period that, in his free time, Orten indulged in reading the entire works of Shakespeare and rediscovered his attachment to the Bible. He wrote the three-volume diaries and elegies conveying his passionate yearning for freedom, love, and humanity. From his posthumous work we learn of his awe for and devotion to the creative world, of his intuitive sense that time was running out. Orten foresaw his impending death and alluded to it repeatedly. According to Pavel Eisner it was his *amor fati* that imbued him "with the urge to create and bear witness, recording man's inhumanity to man." The night before his tragic accident (he was run over by a German vehicle on the Rašín embankment) he wrote his last poem, wishing he could have yet another moment to look at the sky.[160] In a Czech underground newspaper, in 1941, he earned the tribute of "the greatest young talent in modern Czech poetry."[161]

Another important representative of this generation of Jewish poets was Orten's bosom friend Hanuš Bonn, already well known in the late thirties. He published his work under the pseudonym "Josef Kohout." Both wrote under Otokar Fischer's influence, drawing on biblical sources, underscoring their close ties with their ancestral heritage. The two young poets sensed the threat of impending destruction, as is revealed in their posthumous work. In 1936 Bonn envisaged "fiery crosses in the sky" and later he predicted his own approaching death:

So many landscapes I shall never see
to say to myself one day I know the world
So many nights will never cover me
to discern all their mysteries . . .[162]

Bonn perished tragically, as the first victim of the staff of the JRC, before the mass deportation of Czech Jewry began (October 1941). He was tortured to death at Mauthausen. These two untimely deaths symbolically marked the beginning of the wholesale expulsion of the Jewish population to the death camps.

Several other writers succeeded in publishing their works either while protected by non-Jewish spouses or while living in disguise under assumed names. Thus, for instance, in 1940 poet and editor Vincy Schwartz published an anthology of foreign writers on Prague under the title *Město vidím veliké* (I see a great city), which was put out by the Fr. Borový publishing house. Hana Volavková managed to publish under her non-Jewish husband's name the following works on art and Czech painters: *Mácha and Graphic Arts* (1940); *New Works of Max Švabinský for the St. Vitus' Cathedral* (1940); and *Literary Heritage of Karel Purkyně* (as late as 1944).

Vojtěch Jirát gave his name to the new edition of Otokar Fischer's translation of Goethe's *Faust*, which appeared in 1940, published by Fr. Borový.[163]

Eric A. Saudek, the foremost Shakespearean translator, remained in Prague throughout the war, moving from one address to another across the city.[164] He lived under the constant threat of deportation, illegally and in anonymity, ailing and in dire need, earning his bread wherever he could, against all odds; his hope never died. It became his lot to see his friends and colleagues deported—among them the composers Rafael Schächter and the young Gideon Klein, architect František Zelenka, and his parents, who never returned.

Saudek's translations of Kleist, Molière, and Shakespeare were proscribed; some of his former translations of plays, including *Hamlet*, were staged even so under the name of Aloys Skoumal, although the identity of the translator was common knowledge in theatrical circles. Saudek persisted in his work, translating a selection of German baroque poems entitled *Růži ran* (Frailty of roses), evoking omens of tyranny. The book appeared with Jan Reimoser named as author, with the knowledge and approval of the director of the publishing house, Josef Träger. Nevertheless Saudek, like others who managed to survive in hiding, also sustained many disappointments from friends and acquaintances, some of whom pretended not to know him. He consoled himself with the goodness of individuals who remained loyal friends up to the day of liberation, among them some distinguished Czech poets.

The famous linguist and translator Pavel Eisner took pride in outwitting the German censor by using the pseudonyms Karel Kořínek and Jan Šebor.[165] In those "years of hell" he succeeded in writing seven original pieces and translating twenty-five volumes of poetry from the universal repertoire.

Humorist Karel Poláček published "The Inn at the Stone Table" in 1941 under the name of the Czech painter Vlastimil Rada, who also illustrated the book.[166] Prior to his deportation František Zelenka worked in 1941 for the Prague Vinohrady Theater under a wide range of pseudonyms, designing sets for some of Shakespeare's comedies. Later he became the leading spirit in the theatrical enterprises in Terezín.[167]

Jiří Weil did not comply with the summons to deportation.[168] He escaped from prison assisted by a Czech police official, and after his "suicide" was duly reported he went underground and thus managed to survive. The writer Norbert Frýd used the pseudonym Emil Junek while still in Prague. Fate caught up with him and he spent several years in Dachau.[169]

There is a general consensus that to create in those years demanded much strength and courage. Several authors lived to see their writing in print, prior to their deportation. Karel Strass, a lawyer, was sent to Terezín and from there to Auschwitz. Before his deportation he managed to publish *Tales from All over Africa* under the pseudonym Jan Alexander, with a preface by writer and art critic Jaromír John, known for his anti-Nazi novel *Wise Engelbert*, warning against resignation.[170]

Dr. Emil Neumann, born in Prague in 1904, a close relative of the writer Vojtěch Rakous, was a physician and an author. As a doctor he worked first in the district of Smíchov and later in the Jewish hospital. He wrote several short stories and a selection of poetry. and during the occupation he wrote novels, one of them *Zlé noci* (Bad nights) under the pseudonym Jan Simon, published in installments in a magazine and illustrated by Jiří Trnka. In 1942 he was arrested by the Gestapo together with his wife and sent to the Small Fortress of Terezín, where he was tortured to death by ss Commander Rojko.[171]

The assistance extended to Jewish writers by their Czech colleagues is probably one of the most inspiring aspects of the dark chapter of the occupation, projecting hope and faith. One of the legacies is doubtless the issue of persisting with creative work under difficult conditions of physical discomfort and mental tension, circumstances T. S. Eliot characterized as "the man who suffers and the mind which creates."[172] Psychologists describe the phenomenon of creative writing during the years of Nazi occupation as exemplifying the need for self-assertion. This intensive use of the spirit, imagination, and will became an act of defiance, the ultimate aim of which was to regain individual dignity.

The last unparalleled and most symbolic act of defiance was the scheme undertaken by a group of resolute men and women to save the Jewish cultural heritage and art treasures created in the Czech lands. This idea was born while mass deportation was reaching its peak in the spring of 1942. The deserted provincial synagogues, communal halls, and libraries with their precious art and book collections amassed over centuries lay open to looting and destruction. Upon the suggestion of the foremost artists of the Prague Gallery—architect František Zelenka, Dr. Tobias Jakobovits, and Dr. Josef Polák—a plan was submitted to the Zentralamt by Dr. Karel Stein, head of the JRC department for provincial communities, stressing the value of the ritual and art objects and the possibility of expert cataloguing and preservation.[173]

The Nazi chieftains gave their consent to the project with a view to exploiting it for their own nefarious plans and propaganda purposes. Their ultimate aim was to create a museum after their victory, demonstrating the inferior characteristics "of the extinct Jewish race."[174] Practically overnight a magnificent collection of textiles was amassed, priceless fabrics in the Renaissance, baroque, and rococo styles, together with a variety of ritual objects as well as Torah mantles sparkling with gold, embroidery, and jewels. Some of these precious items (such as Torah binders made from the swaddling cloths of newborn boys) had been donated by families as votive gifts to their synagogues on various festive occasions over the centuries. The Central Jewish Museum began to function in August 1942.

The ritual objects and artifacts gathered from the uprooted communities amounted to 199,000 items stemming from the various localities of the country. The collection included an immense range of alms boxes, etchings, medallions, silver cups, engraved glass jugs, and about ten thousand Torah ark hangings (*parochet*) and Torah mantles illustrating the evolution of fabrics and craftsmanship through the centuries.

The museum staff (specialists in the field of museology, Jewish studies, general history, and art), set themselves far more comprehensive goals. Under constant threat of deportation they were anxious to document every period and event in the life of this enclave. This endeavor transpires from the program prepared by Dr. Josef Polák in November 1942, aiming to achieve the objective of "characterizing as fully as possible and to the greatest degree the social, economic and cultural development . . . of the Jews in the Protectorate. An earlier circular sent to the provincial communities requested photographic records of synagogue interiors in their original state, with all their furniture, draperies, etc., before the removal of any scrolls and other ritual objects."[175]

In November 1942 plans for an exhibition entitled "Jewish Life from the Cradle to the Grave," designed by Polák and architect Zelenka to be installed at the Klaus Synagogue, were approved by the Nazis. The designers chose the sixth commandment, "Thou shall not kill," as a motto, a silent reminder that the owners of the ritual objects and artifacts on display were being bestially murdered. The minutes of the museum planning committee in 1943 reflect the conflicts between the staff and the Nazi authorities on conceptual issues.

The scheme of saving the Jewish past was supported in all its stages by the Czech art historian Dr. Zdeněk Wirth at the State Institute for the Preservation of Monuments, who by his courageous stand jeopardized his own life.[176] The staff was headed by Jakobovits and included Polák, Zelenka, Dr. Salomon Hugo Lieben (who died at the end of 1942), Dr. Moses Woskin-Nahartabi, Dr. Alfred Engel, Dr. Simon Adler, Dr. Hana Frankensteinová-Volavková, and Dr. Otto Muneles. Only the last two survived the war.[177] All did their utmost to preserve the Jewish past for posterity. The Nazis took care to ship several of the museum workers in October 1944 in one of the last transports bound for Auschwitz.

It is an established fact that the majority of Jews involved in resistance activities were fully aware of the inherent dangers; nevertheless, as individuals they were resolute, initiating and carrying out acts of sabotage and defiance at a time when the tide of German victories was reaching its peak.

In general terms we can speak of Jewish individuals' participation within the Home Resistance until late summer 1942, while a quasi-orderly community structure still functioned. Though harassed and disgraced, Jewish families could still provide shelter for daring individuals. They could mingle and communicate with the outside world and, most important, could hide at the opportune moment before treacherous denunciations reached police headquarters. The situation changed radically after the deportations, when those in hiding became totally dependent on the assistance and mercy of the local population.

As far as the participants are concerned we can discern two generations, both characterized by their awareness of impending doom, yet imbued with a heroic spirit and determinist rationale: "One should die proudly when it is no longer possible to live proudly."

In retrospect, among the many acts of defiance, the salvaging of the Czech-Jewish cultural heritage conjures up immense awe and admiration. The Jewish Museum inaugurated after the war is the most poignant testimony of Jewish existence in Central Europe, portraying by means of loving craftsmanship the continuous evolution of the life and spirit of Bohemian and Moravian Jewry.

8

The "Righteous" and the Brave
Compassion and Solidarity with the Persecuted

Resentment toward Nazism was naturally more pronounced in Czechoslovakia than in other neighboring countries. Hitler's anti-Czech tirades and the growing antagonism among the Sudeten Germans generated widespread apprehension and fear of Nazi expansion. Only quite recently did it become known that it was actually President Masaryk himself who initially reviewed Hitler's *Mein Kampf* (1933) in the *Prager Presse*.[1] He did so under the title "Hitler's Credo," using the initials V.S., warning the world against the insanity of such chauvinistic and racist ideas. From the very beginning many noted Czech intellectuals actively participated at international conventions, raising their voices of foreboding against National Socialism, fascism, and the totalitarian rule in Germany, foreshadowing in their works and plays the approaching catastrophe. Suffice it to recall Karel Čapek's *White Plague*, which won worldwide recognition. Another Prague publicist and journalist, Dr. Oscar Singer, wrote his anti-Nazi play *Herren der Welt* as early as 1935.[2]

The Czechoslovak section of the Paris-based Ligue International contre l'Antisémitisme (International League against Anti-Semitism) warrants special acknowledgment. Under its auspices the *Věstník čsl. ligy proti antisemitismu* (Bulletin of the Czechoslovak League against Anti-Semitism) made its appearance as of 1936. The national chairman of this organization was Pastor Bohumil Vančura of the Church of Bohemian Brethren. The head of the Brno section, Professor Maxmilian Ryšánek, publisher and owner of the press service Tribuna tisková korespondence or Tri-Kor, cooperated closely with the League against Anti-Semitism in extracting features from the Nazi press for distribution at no charge to newspapers and weeklies in Bohemia and Moravia (in both Czech and German). The objective was to make readers aware of Nazi methods, racial theories, and treatment of the Jews in Germany and at the same time make people cognizant of their freedom in a democratic country.[3]

However, this type of activity gradually petered out following the Munich Agreement and the short-lived Second Republic. After the Ides of March both physical and spiritual resources were channeled to rescue efforts: last-minute escapes and emigration overseas. The outbreak of war on September 1, 1939, put an end to free emigration from the Protectorate and later (as of 1941) made it difficult, if not virtually impossible for individuals to leave the country legally. Altogether around 80 percent of the Jewish population remained in the Protectorate, deprived of basic human rights and, in effect, segregated as outcasts.

Examining the issue of human solidarity and help extended to the persecuted Jews by their gentile fellow citizens, we should take into account the policies of the Nazi authorities in this enclave (in comparison to the circumstances prevalent in other occupied countries) during the various phases of the war. Germany's system of administration and ruling in conquered Europe varied from country to country. Punishment meted out to gentile individuals for various modes of help, such as supplying false papers and ration cards, entailed far less danger in some countries than in others. Ultimately the nature and extent of German control were the primary factors determining the toll of Jewish lives.

The conduct of the Nazi authorities vis-à-vis the Jewish entity in the Czech lands differed somewhat from the pattern adopted elsewhere. The main reasons for this were the centuries-old Czech-German conflict and Hitler's long-range policy aimed at "the solution of the Czech question."[4] As indicated in chapter 5, the goal of this policy was incorporation of the lands of Bohemia and Moravia into greater Germany as a "heartpiece" of the Reich.

The persecution of the Jews, however, was carried out with more subtlety than in Eastern Europe during the first months of "appeasement": no street attacks upon Jews were forthcoming, aside from those instigated by rabid Volksdeutsche and the Czech fascists in Brno, Jihlava, and some other localities. Initially, the arrests of political and public figures were also made selectively, on ideological grounds and according to prepared lists (Czech patriots, legionnaires, Socialists, Communists, etc.) In this period of general confusion the anti-Semitic discrimination seemed to be just one plank of the Nazi oppression.

A watershed was the promulgation of the decree on the legal status of the Jews (*Rechtstellung der Juden*) issued by Reichsprotektor von Neurath on June 21, 1939, wresting full control over the Jewish communities. The decree introduced a regime of drastic economic measures, and the Reichsprotektor reserved full authority for enforcement of the law ousting Jews from every sphere of economic and public life. Now the Protectorate Government learned in one fell swoop who ruled the country. It soon transpired that Aryanized Jewish property was targeted exclusively for the strengthening of German ethnicity in the Czech lands.

In the Protectorate there was no organized network to provide aid to Jews; there was no entity comparable to the Warsaw-based Žegota council established toward the end of 1942 and aided by the Polish Government-in-Exile and various Jewish organizations in the free world. One of that council's assigned tasks was to undertake a rapid and systematic campaign against the informers, blackmailers, robbers, and extortionists who were endangering Jewish lives.[5] In Western Europe various national organizations had been formed specially to reach out to Jews by locating suitable hiding places and providing food.

We cannot, however, overlook the first Protectorate government's attempt to exempt a stratum of old established and outstanding Jewish persons from the effectiveness of the anti-Jewish legislation.[6] The list of candidates for so-called presidential exemptions, after having been gradually reduced from one thousand to a mere forty-one, had been an effort that dragged on for some time, only to be totally rejected in the end. The "autonomous" Czech government was informed that "as a matter of principle," Jews could not be exempted.

We may distinguish three periods in the approach to Jews:

(1) During 1939–41, in the initial phase of curtailment of rights in the Protectorate, aid could have been provided with more ease and less risk to individuals and groups eager to flee abroad for political reasons.

(2) As of fall 1941, the beginning of the mass evictions, aid provided by gentiles to Jews "evading deportations" was viewed as "sabotaging the final solution" and as such was considered an activity "hostile to the Reich," entailing punishment by death.

(3) In 1943–45 came the period of escalated Jew hunting; Jews living under false names or in hiding were eagerly tracked down through the aid of paid informants and Nazi agents.

Gentiles who risked their lives to save Jews during the Nazi era for no ulterior motives have been recognized as of the mid-fifties as "Righteous among the Nations" by the Yad Vashem Holocaust Memorial in Jerusalem.[7] However, the established criteria nominally do not include those rescuers whose attempts to save Jewish individuals or groups failed for some reason (bad luck, denunciations, or the like). Indeed, because of the strict police surveillance we know of a relatively high number of protagonists involved in daring rescue enterprises who were caught by the Gestapo. These individuals were tried by Special

Courts (*Sondergerichte*) and executed on charges of treason, together with the Jewish victims they intended to save. People in this "gray zone" and gentiles who received some kind of remuneration to cover expenditures involved in sheltering Jews have hitherto not been recognized.

Sadly enough, because of the political situation that evolved after the Nazi era abated, with the onset of the Communist regime research on the "Righteous" was altogether neglected for almost forty years. Moreover, as of the fifties the Czech Security Service manipulated the files of Nazi courts for their own callous purposes. In the late seventies the Jewish victims of the war were officially subsumed as losses incurred by Czechoslovakia. This and other false notions and interpretations brought about the dissemination of obscene anti-Jewish pamphlets, blaming the Jewish leadership for collaboration and distorting the Jewish tragedy altogether.

Consequently, free scholarly investigation of this and other issues related to the fate of the Jewish population eventually began to surface only after the collapse of the Communist regime. As an outcome of this situation we lack some basic data, mainly the testimony of people involved in such cases, who have passed on without recording their activities as rescuers. We know also that during this trying period most people were not keen to reveal their activities as "Jew-lovers" and thus receive public recognition in Israel. Many survivors were hesitant to give away their secrets to a regime overtly hostile to Judaism and religious tradition.

The most telling example is the case of Bertold Wolf of Olomouc, who with his wife Rosalia, daughter Felicitas (aged twenty-five), and son Otto (aged seventeen) ran away from the transport and lived in hiding for more than three years. They found shelter in a shack in the forest near the village of Tršice (in the district of Olomouc) and were supported by the dentist Ludmila Tichá, the gardener Jaroslav Zdařil, and several other villagers, who provided them with food and other necessities. During the three years of their hiding (1942–45) Otto penned a diary describing their daily experiences, vicissitudes, and hopes.[8]

The diary portrays minutely the heroic struggle of a pious Jewish family who did not abandon their faith even while they lived as outcasts in the forest for three long years, finding spiritual succor and hope even in the harshest conditions. They kept observing ancient Jewish rites, celebrating traditional holidays, praying for the return of their elder son from the battlefield and for the end of the war. Unfortunately, only Bertold Wolf, his wife, and their daughter managed to survive the war and thus save Otto's precious diary. The diarist himself perished tragically.[9]

The diminished Wolf family returned after the liberation to Olomouc, where

Bertold acted as the cantor of the postwar Jewish community until his death in 1962. (In 1950 a street was named in memory of his two sons: the officer Dr. Kurt Wolf, who fell in the Battle of Sokolov in 1943, and Otto, tortured to death and burned alive by the bandits of the German-sponsored General Vlassov's Army of Liberation in April 1945).

Because of the prevalent political atmosphere and anti-Semitism during the Communist regime, not much could be done toward the publication of this diary; although it was deciphered and copied in 1952, no publisher was interested to print it until 1997.[10]

Flight abroad began soon after the successful escape to London of the chief of military intelligence, Colonel František Moravec, and his staff of eleven members. This widely publicized event no doubt influenced some young soldiers and civilians eager to leave the country. The favored destination became Poland via the Moravian border. A solid section of the Jewish population managed to emigrate legally in the wake of the occupation, in 1939–40. Others, for various reasons, managed to leave the country illegally.

Along these routes the initial escapes of political fugitives and young pilots took place, organized with the assistance of the courageous and popular journalist Milena Krejcarová-Jesenská.[11] Working with her was Joachim von Zedtwitz, a scion of long-established German-Bohemian nobility and a medical student at Charles University.[12] He was known as a member of the activist German Christian Democratic club Die Tat in Prague (closed on March 16, 1939).

Jesenská and von Zedtwitz, through the cooperation of the paid assistants they hired, made it also possible for a number of Jewish individuals to cross the borders and reach safe shores. Years later Dr. Zedtwitz described how upon Jesenská's instruction he drove these people in his sports car from Prague to Moravská Ostrava, whence hired smugglers assisted them in crossing to Poland. (Some spent the night before their flight at Jesenská's apartment.) Among them were several people whose names he remembered, including Walter Tschuppik, the former publisher of *Prager Montag,* and members of the Petschek family as well as Eugen Klinger, Jesenská's life partner, who emerged on the political scene after the war.[13] Both these rescuers were arrested on political grounds by the Nazis. Jesenská was apprehended in November 1939 for supporting the military resistance group ON and because her writing was considered incitement. Somewhat later von Zedtwitz was taken into custody.[14]

From early on there existed close ties between the Czech and Slovak antifascists, especially Zibrín and his associates in the clandestine group Demec, in finding escape routes via Slovakia for illegal departures to the West. Numerous figures of the ancien régime and officers of the Czechoslovak Army as well as leftist party functionaries succeeded in escaping. It was through this channel that several hundred Jewish youngsters from Bohemia and Moravia, members of the Maccabi athletic organization, made their last-minute escape abroad thanks to the cooperation of the Bratislava-based Maccabi youths and went via Yugoslavia and Hungary to Palestine.[15] Other groups of youngsters were sent from Prague and Brno to Poland. These youths were among the first to enlist in the Czechoslovak army unit abroad in late 1939.

In comparison, with the aid provided by the churches in other countries of occupied Europe, the assistance of clergy in the Protectorate was negligible. None of the foremost representatives of the Catholic Church protested publicly against the introduction of the Nuremberg Laws.[16]

There is evidence that in the first years of the occupation several clergymen were arrested and tried for assisting Jews by procuring false baptismal certificates to prove their Aryan origin.[17] Overall, however, the record of the Church in the sphere of rescue is less impressive than in other countries. A classic example of failure is the case of Dr. Alfred Fuchs, a convert and a leading Catholic theologian and philosopher who wrote under the pen name "Draf." Although he was given sanctuary in the Franciscan monastery of the Virgin Mary in Prague, in October 1940 he was arrested and deported to Dachau, where he died a most gruesome death.[18]

Eng. Milan Reiman (alias Miloš Novotný and "Pospíšil"), the main contact between the leadership of the CCP and Prime Minister General Alois Eliáš, managed to survive the war. In late summer 1941 when the leading members of illegal CCP were caught, he decided to "submerge." He found shelter through the help of Father Jozef Fiala of the parish of Saint Jakub, in the heart of Prague's Old Town. He kept working as a joiner, distributing illegal publications, producing false identity cards, contributing to the illegal *Rudé Právo*, and gathering intelligence until the end of the war. Ironically, it was during the Slánský trials (1950–52) that he perished, tortured to death in prison for his activities as a cosmopolitan "imperialist."[19]

Noted Czech philanthropist and educator Dr. Přemysl Pitter (1895-1976) was associated with the Church of Czech Brethren. As of 1922 he acted as the director of Milič House in Prague, erected at his initiative to shelter abandoned children. In his journal *Sbratření* (Brotherhood) he wrote articles about human bonding and equality. In the late thirties he cooperated with Pastor Vančura, head of the League against Anti-Semitism.[20] Following the German occupation of the Czech lands and the exclusion of the Jewish children from education, the Jewish pupils of his institution could not stay at Milič-House. He nevertheless maintained contact with them. Pitter also regularly sent fresh milk to the Jewish Orphanage in Prague. He visited former pupils privately, distributing to them fruit and sweets from the gift packages that reached him from Swiss aid organizations.[21]

Pitter used his sermons in the Church of Czech Brethren at Smíchov to remind believers of the miserable situation of the Jews, urging people to help by sharing rations with them. His humanistic activities after the war centered on gathering surviving children from concentration camps as well as abandoned German children into educational homes that he established for them. A number of fine Bohemian castles around the country served as recreation homes for "Pitter's children." Upon receiving the title of "Righteous among the Nations" in 1964, he said his care for the Jewish children was intended as reciprocation, a grateful acknowledgement of all he had learned from the great teachers, the Jewish prophets.[22] His deeds have been internationally acclaimed; in 1995 UNESCO chose Pitter as "man of the year."

In the wake of Germany's onslaught on Soviet Russia in June 1941, the leading Czechoslovak Communists in Moscow, eager to win wider public support, began to campaign for broad-scale resistance activities. As a matter of course they also became more lenient in the matter of Jewish cooperation. In Prague as well as other localities members of the Resistance formed the core group revealing greater readiness, on ideological grounds, to help their Jewish comrades stay above water: they were instrumental in providing links for legalizing identity (so that "illegals" could register with the police) and in finding them shelter and shielding them in jobs.[23]

The crucial period of intimidation began with the arrival of the new acting Reichsprotektor Heydrich (September 27, 1941) and the proclamation of the state of emergency: razzias in public places and arrests of activists of various political hues occurred daily. The beginning of October saw the first wave of mass executions of political opponents and individuals engaged in sabotage.[24]

The Jewish issue came into the forefront in mid-October with the mass deportation of several thousand Jews from Prague to annihilation camps. But before the campaign was launched a communiqué was issued to the press with a special warning to the Czech population that "those converging with Jews would be evacuated too."[25] In face of these threats, courage and dedication were required of gentiles willing to assist their Jewish friends. We shall refer to several special cases in which groups of people were engaged in rescue efforts.

A case that stands out is that of Gerhard Fuchs and Arnošt Lorenz, engaged as of September 1941 in issuing the clandestine information bulletin *Svět proti Hitlerovi* (The world against Hitler). Both were arrested on April 25, 1942. From the notes of Joseph Böhm, the Prague Gestapo commissar (written in prison after the war), it transpires that Fuchs's former employer, the manager of the firm Praga-textil, together with several other employees, made an attempt to free Fuchs by offering a bribe of 150,000 crowns to Kallus, commissar of the Pankrác prison.[26] (A note attached to the check indicated that the same sum would be placed at his disposal after their comrade was set free.) Fuchs was caught during an abortive attempt to run away and was tortured severely. Half dead, he was taken to Kobylisy, where he was hanged on July 1, 1942. Executed with him were Václav Kotlár, the manager of Praga-textil, and its employees František Šulc, Alois Trunečka, and Rudolf Finger, for their attempt to free Fuchs.[27]

The Vršovice left-wing resistance group, known to have had several Jewish youngsters as leading members, reached out to a group of HaShomer HaTza'ir Zionist youths who lived in hiding in Prague. Through the Vršovice group's help baptismal certificates were acquired, which enabled the Zionist youths to stay on in the Protectorate.[28]

After Heydrich's assassination on May 27, 1942, with the new state of emergency proclaimed across the country, the Protectorate became the most dangerous soil for the Jews in hiding. During a meeting with Hitler the day after the attack upon Heydrich, K. H. Frank presented a seven-point emergency program. One of the issues referred to was the award to be allotted to informers: "High to highest remunerations to all those Czech people who contributed to the uncovering of a case tending to prevent or dissolve further activities hostile to the Reich."[29]

Soon executions for high treason, sabotage, and other offenses were taking place. The Special Courts (*Sondergerichte*) set up in Prague and Brno regularly made public in the press the names of the victims.[30] Among these were several cases of so-called Jew-lovers—individuals who were assisting Jews to escape from the deportation trains to Terezín.[31] A group of people who sheltered Jihlava's popular doctor Rudolf Goldmann had to pay for this with their lives. Denounced during the *heydrichiáda*, three couples from Kamenice and KameniČka in the Jihlava area—the Čipeks, Pospíšils, and Plašils—were executed at the Kounice student attics on June 24, 1942. Dr. Goldmann himself, aged eighty-two, and his relatives, the Králíček family from Jihlava, were sentenced to death and hanged.[32]

Another announcement referred to Říčany police agent Josef Palička, aged thirty-three, who was executed on June 26, 1942. He was charged with abusing his official position to enable the Jew Walter Stein to reside in Prague as an Aryan.[33]

Public places in Prague and other cities were swarming with informants. It was at this period that the Protectorate Government addressed the public, warning people not to provide shelter to parachutists or to individuals living in hiding but to report their whereabouts to the police.[34] In those gruesome days whoever could do so made efforts to flee to a safer abode. Ironically the most coveted places became the neighboring Germany, Austria, and Slovakia.

Thanks to Miloš Hájek, the leading figure of the Czech clandestine cell called *Přehledy* (Surveys,) and his contact man Milan Pažout, who procured several false baptismal certificates, about twenty young men and women living under false identities could actually evade deportation, finding various avenues of escape. Several among them enlisted, together with other Czech draftees, for labor in Germany proper.[35] Two of them, the previously mentioned Arnošt Neumann and his wife Hede Türk-Neumann, managed to make their way separately back to Slovakia in 1943 and, with the aid of the Slovak Jewish underground, proceeded to Budapest.[36]

The situation in the Protectorate became even more strained following the massacres of the population of Lidice and Ležáky and the constant police surveillance and daily arrests. The Nazi method of turning captives into "confidants" and informants, practiced as of 1939, was given a new legal basis on July 3, 1942, when the new acting Reichsprotektor, Kurt Daluege, issued the decree on "defense against hostile acts committed against the Reich." Henceforth the death sentence was legally sanctioned for aiding traitors and escaped prisoners of war. Considerable numbers of people (among them many Jews) were hanged after being denounced for "approving of" Heydrich's assassination. Although Allied parachutists were the main target, the decree concomitantly encompassed the Jews.[37] We know of several executions from this period, under various charges. Thus for instance the brothers Václav and Karel Heřmánek of Dublovice, aged twenty-seven and twenty-eight, were executed on December 18, 1942, charged with "offenses against the economic order"— giving clothing coupons to Jews.[38]

The most pointed judicial comments are to be found in cases handled by the judges at the Prague Special Court. The statement appended to the death sentence pronounced on May 18, 1943, against a group of eighteen so-called destructive elements (*Volksschädlingen*) led by Marianne Goltz-Goldlust reads as follows:

A Jew who evades evacuation is an enemy of the Reich. The Jews comprise in National Socialist Germany an entity of a political nature. They are part and parcel (*Bestandteil*) of international Jewry, which confronts the German Reich as an enemy power . . . An opportune means to meet this threat that

Jewry presents is the evacuation of Jews and their concentration in certain places, erected specially for this purpose. When a Jew evades compliance with such a measure, he cannot possibly remain just a latent enemy of the state . . . since otherwise he could not reach his ultimate goal . . . The Jewish fugitive can expect help only from elements who also nurture hostility toward the state.[39]

The campaign piloted by the Viennese actress, singer, and journalist Marianne Goltz was one of the most daring enterprises known to us during these crucial years. She was of mixed parentage: her mother was Czech and her father a Pole. In the late twenties she married the Jewish journalist Hans Goltz, from Berlin, with whom she fled to Czechoslovakia in 1933.[40] Shortly after the occupation Goltz escaped to London, while Marianne decided to stay on. In 1943 she was arrested together with partners she had managed to recruit for the rescue team, most of them Czechs, but some were Austrian nationals. They were charged with *Beihilfe zu Menschenschmugel*: harboring a number of Jews in Prague, helping them to acquire false documents, and thus facilitating their crossing the border to Germany and Vienna.

It transpires that Marianne Goltz's family in Vienna tried in vain to procure an attorney in Prague willing to take up her defense. (German advocates were expressly prohibited from undertaking the defense of Jews, Gypsies, and Poles and could do so only in exceptional cases by virtue of a special decree.)[41] Finally a brave Czech woman attorney, Dr. Marie Schrámek, took it upon herself to plead Marianne's case, describing her deeds as "an act of charity."[42]

Ten persons among the accused in the Goltz case were sentenced to death in July 1943: Walter Lewit, Yvonne Lewit, Joseph Goldschmidt, and Ervin Samek as Jews, for trying to evade deportation, and Marianne Goltz, Otakar Zápotocký, Emilie Funk, Ladislav Dlesk, Svatopluk Cila, and Václav Dryák for helping them hide and cross frontiers to Austria and Germany and for finding them lodgings and places of work. The ten were beheaded (by guillotine) on the same day at Pankrác prison. Five other persons involved in the case were given lighter sentences.[43]

While in prison Marianne Goltz and the Czech artist-designer Václav Dryák (who actually worked in Germany) secretly exchanged messages with fellow prisoners and also managed to smuggle several letters out of Pankrác to relatives.[44] The salvaged correspondence together with Dryak's caricatures drawn on prison life provide enlightening asides on the Nazi judicial system, the "defending counsel," and other aspects of human suffering during these crucial years. Thus for instance the German daily *Der neue Tag* listed on April 10, without names, the executions for crimes including not denouncing an enemy of the Reich, black market offenses, giving food to escaped prisoners of war, hiding politically active Jews, and disseminating enemy broadcasts.

The following individuals were executed in the second half of 1943 by the Special Court of the Prague Landgericht for harboring Jewish individuals:

> *František Černý*, born 29.9.1890, Ouřezím, district Prostějov, executed 1.7.1943, for actuating his anti-Reich feelings by helping Jews who resided in Prague without being registered, to evade evacuation; *Vlasta Hellerová*, born 4.7.1909, Prague, executed 1.7.1943 for offering shelter to elements hostile to the Reich; *Jaroslav Klemeš*, born 1896, Sudoměřice, executed 5.11.1943, for helping Jewish people to escape abroad, thus sabotaging the German orders for the solution of the Jewish question in Bohemia and Moravia; *František Kučera*, born 1909, Prague-Strašnice, executed 5.11.1943 for helping Jewish people to escape abroad, thus sabotaging the German orders for the solution of the Jewish question in Bohemia and Moravia; *Josef Malý*, born 1904, Malešice near Prague, executed 1.10.1943 for providing false personal documents to a Jew who lived for years by illegal trading in Prague and wished to flee abroad; *Vilemína Pruchová*, born 23.9.1899, Česká Skalice, executed 1.7.1943, for offering shelter to elements hostile to the Reich; *Petr Řiháček*, born 1907 Strašnice, executed 5.11.1943, for helping Jewish people to escape abroad, thus sabotaging the German order for the solution of the Jewish question in Bohemia and Moravia: and his brother; *Tomáš Řiháček*, born 1902, Strašnice, executed 5.11.1943, on the same count; *Jan Sádlo*, born 1904, Radlice, executed 5.11.1943, for helping in the escape of Jewish people abroad, thus sabotaging the German order for the solution of the Jewish question in Bohemia and Moravia; *František Šedivý*, born 1896, Prague, executed 5.11.1943, for helping Jewish people to escape abroad, thus sabotaging the German order for the solution of the Jewish question in Bohemia and Moravia; *Oldřich Smetana*, born 28.7.1909, Holiče, municipal official, executed 13.1.1943, for misappropriating a considerable number of food cards, giving them mainly to Jews; *Elsa Tausigová*, born 1885, Prague, executed 5.11.1943, for helping Jewish people to escape abroad, thus sabotaging the German order for the solution of the Jewish question in Bohemia and Moravia.[45]

The high number of individuals the Nazis managed to recruit by force, bribes, or other methods to act as informants is mentioned in a report ÚVOD sent to the Government-in-Exile in London, referring to the "cowards, opportunists and Czech renegades."[46]

In spring 1944, following events on the eastern front and expectations for the opening of a second front in the West, a new wave of intimidation was launched. The state president himself issued a warning on April 14, 1944, reminding the population that the Reichsprotektor's decree of July 3, 1942, was still in force and that whoever harbored elements hostile to the state would be punished by death. The Protectorate Government made its own contribution, calling upon the public not to provide shelter for parachutists and those living illegally but to report their whereabouts immediately to the authorities.[47]

The following individuals were sentenced to death by the Special Court of the German Landgericht in Prague in the spring of 1944 for harboring Jews: "*Bauerová née Košatová*, born 1910, Prague, executed 28.4.1944, for harboring together with *Max Michl*, born 1891, Prague, two Jews who were wanted by the Gestapo for illegal political activities and supporting them with food and necessities; *Jan Fleischmann*, born 1903, Prague, executed 26.5.1944, for helping Jews by providing forged documents to camouflage their origin and descent."[48]

HELP AND SYMPATHY IN THE TEREZÍN GHETTO AND THE SMALL FORTRESS

Expressions of human solidarity occurred also within the walls of Ghetto Terezín. The Czech gendarmerie unit in there deserves special note. Fourteen of its 150 members were imprisoned for extending help or having contact with Jews (*Verkehr mit Juden*). Two of these Czech guards, Vilém Vach and Jiří Černý, were transferred to the Small Fortress on the order of Commandant Rahm and perished there.[49] There is evidence that several gendarmes reached out to the inmates by providing them contact with the outer world or procuring for them sorely needed necessities.

Jews who were transferred by the camp commandant from the ghetto as a punishment (for violating camp regulations) were sent to the Small Fortress, which served as an auxiliary prison. They were singled out for cruel treatment, never to return alive. So were some of the political prisoners sent there by the Prague Gestapo. As a routine Jews were made to work, but upon their return to the tiny Jewish cell (sixteen square meters, with two buckets for excrement for about fifty people) they had no possibility whatsoever of lying down. They were forced to sleep squatting down after a long day's labor. Many of the prisoners were whipped to death on the work site. The half-dead victims and the wounded were taken on wheel-barrows to the cell, or directly to the morgue, as recorded by eyewitnesses after the war.

There was no end to the cruelty: as a pastime the notorious Jöckl periodically held boxing "matches." In September 1944 several Jewish prisoners were driven out into a ditch near the morgue, where a muddy, stinking inundation canal ran. They were given sticks and pitchforks and had to fight for their lives until one dropped dead. From a little bridge nearby Jöckl and the guards watched: their satanic laughter was heard in the adjoining prison cells.

The encouragement and aid secretly provided to the cruelly tortured Jewish pariahs by some of their fellow prisoners at the Small Fortress, especially those daring Czech physicians who attended to their wounds or managed to smuggle them some medications, evokes deep admiration.

The Catholic priest Dr. Jan Merell, liberated in Dachau in the spring of 1945 (he would serve after the war as dean of the Faculty of Divinity at Litoměřice), can be credited for some of these authentic descriptions of martyrdom. He spent a year and a half at this hell. While in the Small Fortress, urged by his heart, he saw it as his foremost duty to record some of the terrible scenes he witnessed: "Remembering those who can no longer speak for themselves . . . to bow our heads before the suffering of the Jews."[50]

> I shall never forget the emaciated, physically and mentally exhausted figures of the Jews destined for death, whose suffering we were only rarely able to lighten. Sometimes a fleeting, compassionate glance from us may have been of some comfort to them . . .
>
> . . . I worked for a rather long period of time at the camp laundry. Once we secretly took over some vermin-infected Jewish laundry to be washed . . . A fellow prisoner and myself were transporting the laundry on a little cart. As misfortune would have it, the cart suddenly overturned, and what was still more unfortunate, the infamous Jöckl saw us. He came running . . . and when he found out that we were carting Jewish laundry, which we were not allowed to wash, he began to curse us . . . He got hold of the stick we used to stir the laundry in the boilers and began to rain blows on me, hitting me wherever he could, till he broke the stick. To this very day I bear the results of the blows on my spine.

The horrors of the last months of the war and the notorious death marches brought to the Czech borders many columns of hungry and desperate people. Several eyewitness accounts written in this period recorded how "reaching the Czech populated areas they immediately sensed an outpouring of sympathy"; ordinary people offered bread and warm drinks to the emaciated victims.[51] One of the most moving cases is that of the teenager Eva Erben, born in Prague in

1930, who was saved by the Czech farming couple Kryštof and Ludmila Jahn in the village of Postřekov in South Bohemia.[52]

After tribulations at Terezín and later in Auschwitz, Eva was to witness her mother's death during the death march. When her group was ordered by the ss guards to spend the night in a barn, she waited until everyone fell asleep, then burrowed into a huge pile of hay and remained there when the column moved on. For three days she walked alone along the railroad tracks until she reached a Czech village.[53] Kryštof found her lying in his clover field. He and his wife resuscitated the girl, taking care of her with great love. They kept her in an improvised hiding place under the kitchen floor until liberation.

Zdeněk Urbánek, doyen of Czech writers, known for his devoted friendship with Jiří Orten, whose literary legacy he saved for posterity, tried from the beginning of the occupation to ease the suffering of his acquaintances and colleagues.[54] His modest two-room Prague apartment, where he lived with his wife and two children, served as a mail depot for food packages dispatched to friends at Ghetto Terezín.[55] Several Jewish people found temporary refuge at his home before being taken to safer abodes. His last act of rescue occurred in January 1945, when one night eight Czech-Jewish girls with shaven heads knocked at his door, asking for his help. They recorded how during the evacuation of the camp at Kurzbach (in the General Government), while heading with their guards for the Gross Rosen camp, they decided to step aside from the marching column and thus escaped.

An intriguing manifestation of solidarity arose in the cases of three enigmatic German political opponents, each shrouded in some kind of mystery. We shall venture to name the first—Prague's "anonymous" Armin Wegner. On November 27, 1941, a letter signed by "Prof. Dr. Armin Hergeth" reached the chancellery of the acting Reichsprotektor Reinhard Heydrich, protesting against the deportation of the Czech Jews.[56] From the briefing of the head of Security Police (Sicherheitsdienst, SD) in Prague (January 14, 1942), it transpired that no such person resided in Prague and that "this could be an assumed name."[57] Obviously there was no interest on the part of Undersecretary von Burgsdorff, who looked into the matter, in launching a further inquiry.

Our assumption is that the writer of this protest letter must have had knowledge of Armin T. Wegner's now famous "Warning," addressed to Reich Chancellor Adolf Hitler in Berlin on Easter Monday, April 11, 1933.[58] Wegner's lengthy 1933 letter of protest was in response to Hitler's proclamation of March 29, signaling the beginning of Jewish persecution. Several key sentences of Wegner's warning resonate in Hergeth's protest: "American newspapers call these deportations of Jews as well as their ghettoization organized robbery, committed upon a defenseless nation that is driven out naked into suffering. A barbarism that recalls the darkest middle ages. Urgent reprisals are demanded against the Germans in America . . . *As a good German, who loves his nation, my soul aches to see what false paths are taken to reach the ideal that spurs all of us . . .* Our German brothers are at stake, Your Excellency!" (italics mine).[59] Whoever was behind the signature of "Prof. Dr. Armin Hergeth" clearly deserves designation as a voice crying in the wilderness.[60]

One of the most famous cases in wartime espionage involves the role played by the German *Abwehr* agent Paul Thümmel, A-54, known also as René, who worked for Czechoslovak Military Intelligence as of 1936.[61]

Originally trained as a baker, Thümmel was employed as of 1928 by the NSDAP and as of 1933 by the military espionage section of the German Security Service. In 1934 he became chief officer of the Dresden *Abwehrstelle*. After the occupation of Bohemia and Moravia he was stationed at Prague heading the Abwehr agency. He was the only high-ranking officer who collaborated directly with the Allied intelligence organizations in the years 1938–41, via his famous Czech liaison Colonel František Moravec, head of military intelligence for Beneš's Government-in-Exile. Thümmel provided the Secret Intelligence Service (SIS) with first-class political and military intelligence—advance notice of Germany's plans for intervention, orders of battle and mobilization plans, equipment of the German Army, the German entry into Prague, and the attack on Poland, among other things.[62]

What qualifies Paul Thümmel to be included in the category of the "Brave" is his gruesome message conveyed from Prague to London on July 26, 1941 (coded "René" to "Pavel"), about the mass executions.[63]

There are various views and evaluations of Thümmel's motivation for his services rendered to the Allies. The overriding question is to ascertain whether he volunteered his services driven by principle—that is, opposition to the Hitlerite regime—or for material gain. In 1946 experts of Department no. 5 of the General Staff of the Czechoslovak Army, headed by Lieutenant-Colonel Bedřich Reicín, conducted a thorough evaluation.[64] They described Thümmel as "a giant and shrewd confidant of worldly profile" who offered his help to the Czechoslovak intelligence service not for monetary gain but rather as an opponent of the Nazi regime.[65]

Why research examining the first information reaching the free world about the mass executions of Jews has not up to now focused on his early and important firsthand report is certainly incomprehensible.[66] The fact that Thümmel found it imperative to reveal at the very beginning the massacres of the Jews by the *Einsatzgruppen* is momentous. Another point of utmost importance is that this item of information had reached the SIS in London in July 1941 yet was not exploited by the recipients.[67]

Thümmel was arrested twice in 1942, then set free, but was arrested again on charges of high treason. After being held at the Terezín Small Fortress he was executed upon the special order of Willy Leimer of the anti-parachutist section of the Gestapo in Prague on April 27, 1945.[68]

The case of Otto Gall remains a riddle to this day. He was the Gestapo contact man of one of the most important clandestine groups, the civilian PVVZ, which had the broadest participation of Jewish members in its leadership. Gall began to cooperate with the group as early as 1939, while serving as secretary of the criminal "civilian" section of the Gestapo in Prague. It is known that a year earlier, during his service at Aussig (Ústí nad Laben), Gall became disenchanted with Nazism. He became aware of the plight of the Jewish population through his fiancée, Herta, whose father, Dr. František Bauer, was a Jew; her mother was a Czech Aryan.[69] Thanks to Bauer this important contact had been gained for the Czech underground. Bauer himself and Anna Dohalská, wife of Count Zdeněk Bořek Dohalsky, were regularly meeting with Otto Gall on behalf of the PVVZ.[70] He would brief them about the various activities and operations planned by the Gestapo against Czech organizations identified as opponents of the regime. Owing to Gall's assistance, several of the PVVZ members arrested by the Gestapo were set free and other leading members were allotted preferential tasks in prison, alleviating their situation. It may be assumed that it was through Gall that the underground PVVZ learned as early as January 1940 about the possibility of forthcoming expulsions of Jews. In one PVVZ message the Czechoslovak Government-in-Exile was urged to launch a campaign in the free world, especially in the United States, to thwart this aim.[71]

The PVVZ contacts with Otto Gall lasted until the end of the war, when his activities were unveiled; he was arrested and taken to the Terezín Small Fortress, never to be seen again. (Rumor has it that he may have been taken prisoner by the Russians).[72]

There is an old adage that bad times harden people's hearts. Zdeněk Urbánek, upon receiving the title of the "Righteous among the Nations," declared that "assistance provided to Jewish friends remains one of the most important mainstays of his life." He also expressed his humble and genuine regrets that no more had been done on behalf of Jewish fellow citizens: "I feel ashamed of how small and inadequate was the help or defense we, meaning the Czech community of the time, and myself, succeeded in offering our Jewish compatriots and friends . . . Even now I believe the Munich Agreement should not have been accepted by Mr. Beneš for the sole reason, if not for any other, of the murderous Nazi anti-Semitism."[73]

As recent inquiry into the gray zone indicates, numerous noble-minded individuals did try to bring succor to the persecuted Jews in spite of the great risk involved. Alas, many paid for their deeds with their lives. Their significance transcends their actual numbers, for they are the ones who in an era of inhumanity carried the torch of light and hope for future generations.

9

Gateway to Death
The Unique Character of Ghetto Terezín (Theresienstadt)

The ghettoization of the Jews within the Protectorate of Bohemia and Moravia was part of the global Nazi policy meant to serve several interim aims. The hopes nurtured by the Jewish leadership that it would forestall deportation "to the East" were shattered early on. Nevertheless, despite all odds, the struggle for the community's survival continued in various ways to the last.

Research focusing on the totality of Hitler's racial policy underlines the fact that victory in war and the annihilation of the Jews were parallel aims.[1] Thus any plans or projects on the part of Jewish leaders or organizations to bring about a change were doomed to failure from the start. With hindsight we may assert, however, that there was still one important factor with some bearing upon the total execution of the "Final Solution": the time coefficient, bringing the turning of the tide of war.[2]

Unlike other concentration camps, Theresienstadt had a dual role from the moment of its establishment in the fall of 1941: it was to serve both as *Siedlungsgebiet* (settlement) and *Sammellager* (assembly camp) and, as such, as a means for decimation of its population.[3] After the Wannsee Conference on the "solution of the Jewish question," held on January 20, 1942, a third function was added: it was to act as an alibi—to camouflage the ongoing annihilation process before the eyes of the free world. A special paragraph of the minutes referred to Theresienstadt euphemistically as an "old-age ghetto": "It is intended not to evacuate Jews above the age of sixty-five but rather to remove them (*überstellen*) to an Altersghetto. Theresienstadt is under consideration [for this purpose]. Along with them Jews seriously wounded during the war [World War I] and Jews with military decorations (Iron Cross, First Class), will be taken to the old people's ghetto."[4]

Consequently, the many disguised names used in the Nazi nomenclature reflect the varied functions this camp was to fulfill during its four-year existence. In retrospect, each of these designations is both meaningful and evocative, exemplifying the deceptive aims of Nazi policy at various stages of the war. Terezín was called the *Altersghetto* (old-age ghetto) or alternatively *Prominentenghetto* (ghetto for the privileged) or *Musterghetto* (model ghetto). In 1945 it was called a *Judenstaat* (miniature Jewish state), a term cynically coined by Adolf Eichmann himself to impress the visiting delegation of the International Committee of the Red Cross (ICRC) during their inspection visit on April 6, 1945.[5]

Theresienstadt occupies therefore a special place on the map of concentration camps of the Third Reich. Located sixty kilometers northwest of Prague and formerly known as a garrison (originally established by Joseph II in 1780 and named in memory of his mother, Empress Maria Theresa), it became a concentration camp for Jews in fall 1941. The townlet had eleven barracks, 218 civilian houses, and a large number of military installations including the Small Fortress (Malá pevnost). In 1940 its Czech population—amounting to more than 7,000 people (3,500 soldiers and 3,700 civilians employed by the army)—had to be evacuated to make room for the deportees. Within the confines of this small town with streets a mere 700 meters long, laid out in a rigid grid, 60,000 inmates were crammed by September 1942. The Small Fortress complex built on the opposite bank of the River Ohře came to be used as a prison of the Prague Gestapo with a strong SS guard division, mainly for non-Jewish political prisoners but also for Jewish "culprits," most of whom were tortured to death.[6]

An in-depth scrutiny of the available documentation proves beyond doubt that the Germans never seriously regarded Terezín as a permanent camp for detainees or a labor ghetto but used it at every stage to pursue their annihilation policy. This is abundantly clear from the minutes of Heydrich's Prague Conference (October 10, 1941), delineating its real function as a transit camp: "The number of Jews in this temporary *Sammellager* would be substantially reduced. Evacuation to Eastern territories would follow and then the whole area might be used for a model German settlement."[7]

Subsequently, developments in the ghetto were determined mainly by decisions made by Nazi higher echelons, in conformity with the changing international situation. During the first stage of its existence the camp was supervised by camp commander SS Obersturmführer Siegfried Seidl. It was tightly sealed off and guarded by a Czech gendarmerie unit of 170 men under the command of Captain Theodor Janetschek, a rabid anti-Semite whose conduct toward the inmates was outrageous, sometimes surpassing the SS guards in cruelty.[8] His men performing patrol duty and other functions had the strictest instructions for the handling of the Jews. They were to deal with these people "with absolute disregard, brutality and cruelty for they were destined for extermination (*zur Ausrottung bestimmt*). Contact with Jews (*Verkehr mit Juden*) was strictly forbidden and punishable. Upon meeting the gendarmes, the inmates of the ghetto were obliged to take off their hats and bow respectfully.

The first Jewish Council of Elders (*Ältestenrat* or *Židovská rada starších*), appointed on December 4, 1941, was composed of former leading functionaries of the Prague JRC, who took on the task of their own volition. Upon learning of the designation of the camp at Terezín, Dr. František Weidmann (head of the JRC) and Jacob Edelstein agreed between themselves—realizing that this function would be a dangerous commitment—that whoever was elected would take along his closest co-workers.[9] Thus after the Germans appointed Edelstein as head of the "self-administration" (*Selbstverwaltung*) of the camp, it was composed of twelve men: six Zionists, three Czech assimilationists, and three specialists. It is noteworthy that among the first transports reaching Terezín were Jews from the Moravian capital Brno, where the Zionist element was much stronger than among the Bohemian Jews.

Jacob Edelstein and his entourage, including Otto Zucker, arrived in the ghetto on December 4, 1941, with a mission. Edelstein strongly believed that in this desperate situation it was his duty as a Jewish leader to stand between the SS and his own community, trying to exploit every possible opportunity for alleviating its burdens. His ultimate aim was to save as many Jewish lives as possible. In this endeavor he was assisted by several of his associates, namely Zucker, Dr. Franz Kahn, and Dr. Leo Janowitz and a team of skilled craftsmen, engineers, physicians, and other workers—the so-called Work Detail (*Aufbaukommando*), who were the first to reach the ghetto on November 24 (numbering 340 men) and December 4, 1941 (one thousand men).

After the gruesome experience at Nisko, Edelstein and his associates were determined to do their utmost to avoid further transports "to the East." Thus, upon leaving Prague, they embarked on their new mission as a close-knit unit with the aim of organizing a self-sustaining, productive community, which through its work for the German war machine could survive the war. In fact, they became the only Zionist-oriented leadership in Nazi-occupied Europe acting as a Jewish Council of Elders.

The Jewish self-administration was to function both as a quasi-municipal authority with a large bureaucratic apparatus and as the administration of a labor camp. It was to carry out the onerous task of providing the population with municipal services, such as housing, lighting and water, sewage and sanitation, policing, and religious, judicial, and postal services. At the same time it acted as a central body organizing labor detachments for internal and outside work.

Everyone between the ages of sixteen and sixty-five was obliged to work. "People work day and night, sometimes without a break," wrote a diarist. Many women were engaged in the kitchen (peeling potatoes, cleaning soup vats); others swept courtyards, washed stairs and latrines. The luckier worked in vegetable gardens outside the camp. A solid number of women served in the sick rooms (*Krankenstube*) as nurses or cleaning personnel. The men were assigned to various workshops (carpentry, leather, tailoring, and machine shops), with others assigned to hard work outside the camp in the mines of Kladno and some construction sites; the most unfortunate were working under constant scrutiny of the ss for German military needs.

Thanks to the ingenious activities of the Work Detail the dilapidated and neglected compound was transformed into a setting that was eventually to accommodate an average of forty thousand people. The enormous financial resources required for this enterprise were administered by the Nazis from confiscated Jewish property. The Jewish leadership saw in these investments a positive development, assuming that Terezín would become a full Jewish city, "a night asylum." (They had no inkling whatsoever that the German plan actually meant to turn the place, after the cleansing of the Jews, into a model "German settlement.")

On January 9, 1942, less than two months after its establishment, Terezín witnessed the departure of the first deportation trains: a transport of a thousand camp inmates leaving for the "East," soon to be followed by a second group, bound for Riga, where Jews from Germany and Latvia already lived in an overcrowded ghetto. After this assignment, four additional transports followed. Around sixteen thousand mostly able-bodied young inmates were deported from Terezín "to the East."[10]

The hopes pinned on saving the ghetto's population through work for the German war machine were thus shattered. Still, efforts continued to keep the existing workshops operating. Health and employment services were set up and social, educational, and cultural enterprises were launched (part of which were carried out clandestinely), in an effort to maintain some measure of normal human behavior.

In August 1942, the Nazis made sure of building up the illusion of "autonomy" by issuing a special currency for Theresienstadt through the so-called Bank der jüdischen Selbstverwaltung. These bank notes, never to be circulated outside the ghetto, bore the effigy of Moses holding the tablets of the law and were signed by Jacob Edelstein. A postage stamp depicting a lovely scene of the Theresienstadt panorama was issued.

The second event that caused general outcry and tension was the execution by hanging of nine men on January 10 for violations of the German rules—smuggling out letters to relatives still at large. Members and officials of the Council of Elders had been ordered to watch the execution. Edelstein refused to attend, and his resignation submitted to the camp command was ignored by the ss.

In December 1942, one year after his nomination, Edelstein felt a need to delineate his initial ideological credo as "a halutz," in a letter written to his friends, justifying his decision: "Who if not we should have come forward to reach out [to the people] during moments of unsurpassed agony and fateful decision? I never grasped or interpreted the concept of a pioneer in the narrow sense of the word. To be a pioneer means not only to be a laborer but also to carry the burden of self-fulfillment [of the idea—the Land of Israel] for which the positive must be drawn from the negative in order to create new sources of life for the community."[11]

In the first year of its existence the ghetto thus witnessed, on the one hand, construction work and arrangements to provide the inmates with basic necessities, and on the other hand, the beginning of deportation "to the East" and executions of scores of people for minor transgressions.

The construction activities in the camp and the organization of living conditions are recorded in a historical survey titled "Geschichte des Ghettos Theresienstadt 1941–1943" (unsigned, dated December 31, 1943) with illustrations, charts, and graphs.[12] Although the report was compiled upon the command of the ss, it was evidently not used for any purpose by the camp command. They must have realized the silent heroism of the people resonating between the lines. Authorship is ascribed to Otto Zucker, who used restrained language in order to evade problems of censorship. In one of his letters sent to Fritz Ullmann in Geneva the articulate Zucker described the new serfdom, glossing over the slavery in ancient Egypt: "We are building again Pitom and Ramses and keep recalling the Haggadah."[13]

A careful reading of the text conveys the unprecedented harshness of the situation confronting the Jewish self-administration engaged in organizing, at gunpoint, a ghettoized community amidst a constantly growing and changing population. One becomes aware of the leadership's two-pronged policy for survival, exercised simultaneously on both the physical and spiritual planes: exploitation of the capacity of those able to work, and care for the spiritual needs of the population in order to sustain life.

This goal was pursued within the framework of the *Freizeitgestaltung* (free-time activities), originally instituted at the behest of the ss but in due course becoming a vital factor of self-confidence, boosting morale among the inmates. Music, plays, and readings had an immense effect upon the people: the vigilant audience could always detect comic situations and characters in allegorical plays that mirrored their inner feelings and strengthened their will to struggle for survival.

The concept of rescue though work was not exclusively Edelstein's device. It is known that a number of Judenräte in eastern Upper Silesia, especially in the Łodý and Bialystok ghettos, eagerly translated the productivity program into the language of action. It has been suggested that some form of common strategy might have existed. This assumption is based on the fact that members of the Judenräte—representatives from occupied Poland and from the Berlin *Reichsvereinigung* as well as those of the Vienna and Prague communities, including Jacob Edelstein—were sometimes jointly summoned to Eichmann's offices in Prague and Berlin during the early years of the war. They certainly held some secret consultations of their own.[14]

Coping with the complicated task of management within a coerced, heterogeneous community demanded nerves and guts: running the administrative apparatus, technical staff, economic enterprises, and sanitation system was complex. The art of choosing the right personnel and teams was itself a most complicated affair. Had the professional level of engineers, doctors, technicians, and cooks not been as high, many enterprises would have collapsed in the ghetto management. Edelstein himself recorded that he was fully aware of the difficulties of his unprecedented task. His main goal from the outset was to save the young generation, and he therefore made sure that both the Youth Welfare Department and the Labor Department were managed by the HeHalutz.[15]

As the influx of elderly people from Germany and Austria proceeded, in May 1942 the leadership decided to reduce the bread ration of nonlaborers and "reward" those engaged in heavy physical labor, working sixty to eighty hours a week, and thus keep them going. Depending solely on the meager diet actually meant starvation for the elderly population, who had no chance to barter (bereft of money and jewelry) and no-one to send them food parcels.

The decision on the allotment of "special rations" for hard laborers spurred clashes within the Council of Elders. Another issue generating bad blood was the fact that the so-called Transport Committee was to compile the list of the inmates to be included in the transport "East." The camp command determined only the total number of deportees, variably, guided occasionally by age category, occupation, or country of origin. Although the individuals selected for deportation had the right to ask the Appeal Committee to reexamine their cases, their chances were close to nil.[16]

This system allowed each political group (the Zionists, assimilationists, and Communists) to draw up a list of their own people to be "protected." It is known that Otto Zucker had his own list of artists, writers, and cultural personalities to be saved from deportation. Egon Redlich tackled the dilemma with the utmost honesty in his diary entries of March 13–14, 1942, bluntly asserting the sheer reality: "favoritism was rampant."[17] Every person holding some function tried to help friends and acquaintances. As a result, each list had to be made up several times. Redlich also reflected on this impossible situation from the moral point of view as a Zionist, admitting his doubts: "The appeals of our *chaverim* (affiliates) are also a difficult matter. Do we have the right to do it or not? The difference [between *protekzia*—favoritism—and exempting members of the HeHalutz] is small . . . Do we really have the right to appeal?"[18]

The second half of 1942 saw the arrival of further transports of provincial Jews from Bohemia and Moravia as well as elderly people from Germany and Austria. Before these people embarked on their journey the German authorities employed ruses and false promises to lure the elderly, among them a range of privileged individuals and World War I veterans, into the "resettlement" project. The official "home purchase contract" (*Heimeinkaufsvertrag*) that they had to fill in and sign described the destination as "The Reich's Home for the Aged" or "Theresienbad" (Theresien spa).[19] The authorities charged considerable sums in advance for board and lodging. Many people, believing they were going to a kind of sanatorium, readily signed away their life insurance to the RSHA.

In the fall of 1942 with the new arrivals, Austrian and German Jews came to constitute a dominating element. Dr. Karl Loewenstein, half Jewish by birth, a Protestant by religion, and a naval aide-de-camp to the German crown prince in World War I, arrived in Terezín from Minsk. As commander of the ghetto police in Minsk he enjoyed preferential "detention" and was obviously intended to fulfill some special tasks in his new function. In September 1942 the SS decided to reorganize the ghetto police (*Ghettowache*). Loewenstein took over the command of the Ghetto Guard. A militant Prussian in charge of the four-hundred-man unit in Theresienstadt, he soon became part of the power struggle afflicting the Council of Elders.[20]

The Council of Elders was also reorganized, and upon the camp commander's order four German and five Austrian Jews were assigned to several functions. The most serious shuffle of the leadership was ordered on January 13, 1943, with the arrival of the functionaries of the Reichsvereinigung and of the Vienna Jewish community leadership. Now a triumvirate was established: Rabbi

Dr. Benjamin Murmelstein of Vienna and Dr. Paul Eppstein of Berlin joined Edelstein on the council. This device gave Eichmann an opportunity to create three internal power groups, a recipe for constant confusion and struggle for power.[21]

Upon German command Eppstein took over the task of dealing with the *Kommandantur*, and henceforth Edelstein had to act as Eppstein's deputy. This design was obviously created to evoke quarrels and jealousy by antagonizing the two: Eppstein acted openly as Edelstein's main opponent and rival. Another member joining the council was Loewenstein. It was clear that the scene was set for radical changes.

The German Zionist leader Eppstein was a professor of sociology, an erudite person with many weaknesses, who had already become acquainted with Gestapo methods in the late thirties while imprisoned in Berlin. Zdeněk Lederer wrote of him: "He had neither Edelstein's tough optimism nor Zucker's will to resist."[22]

The stark reality that awaited the transports of the aged from Germany and Austria in the crammed barracks was authentically portrayed in Otto Zucker's survey:

Accommodation of the masses arriving in close succession was a truly insoluble task. The barracks were already fully occupied in July and the buildings were crammed to capacity by August. Most of the elderly and feeble people were not able to use the many-tiered bunks prepared for mass accommodation. Already in August the average net living space per person was 1.6 sq. m., in which [the occupant] had not only to sleep but also to keep his belongings. The only alternative was to make use of the rooms considered hitherto unfit for habitation. Next came attics in a state of total neglect [covered in decades' worth of dust and soot] with no insulation against cold or heat, no wiring for lights, no plumbing, and no lavatories. In the heat of the summer the prevailing temperatures made living there exceptionally hard. In addition many of the feeble and the sick were [physically] unable to use the stairs in order to take refuge from the rooftop quarters during the peak of heat. More than 6,000 persons were put up under the rafters.[23]

In summer 1942, when the whole town was cleared of its erstwhile population, several large houses were allocated for children's homes where the young could be separated from adults and would thus not succumb to demoralization.[24] The teachers and instructors in the homes devoted the utmost care to the young children, untiringly pledging themselves to educating the next generation. They called all their skill and erudition into play to protect the children's sanity, employing modern teaching methods of self-expression and distraction. The children also received better food and had better housing conditions. Large collectives of around two to three hundred children, subdivided into smaller collectives by rooms of boys or girls according to age, had a leader and one or several helpers. Pedagogues were recruited mostly from among former teachers and students; doctors, nurses, and social workers attended to the needs of every home. Teaching took a semiformal shape, with a centrally administered education system.[25] The evening hours, after the parents had been visited, were mostly filled with cultural programs. This is how the "cultural correspondent" of the *Vedem* (We lead) youth magazine sums up activities and cultural events for the last fortnight, on January 15, 1943:

> Sunday, January 3—Recital of Wolker's poems in commemoration of the poet's death . . . Then "Profa" recited the one-act play *Hospital*. On Monday, Míša S. delivered the first part of his successful lecture on the textile industry. On Tuesday, Dr. Zwicker lectured, explaining some basic economic terms to us. On Wednesday lights-out was earlier, at eight-fifteen, because of Laubi, who was seriously ill . . . On Friday Mrs. Klinke came to see us and sang some Hebrew songs for us and one aria from the *Bartered Bride*. Fricek F. came on Monday and spoke fascinatingly about sport and about his own experiences from his sporting career. On Tuesday we read. On Wednesday Sisi E. lectured on chemistry and the food industry. On Thursday Shmuel K. spoke interestingly about modern psychology. Of special importance for our cultural life is the reestablishment of two study circles (Latin and Russian).

Aside from the problems of living space there were other issues facing the newcomers, especially those from Germany proper: the loss of privacy created tense relationships among the inmates.[26] Sad mentions of the delicate issue of ethnic compatibility can be found in diaries and reminiscences of former inmates, notably those from Germany. It transpires that although relations between Austrian and Czech Jews were not always too friendly, there was certainly more understanding between them. The Jews who arrived from Germany, instead of finding fellow sufferers, were received coolly, sometimes even derisively by the Czech inmates, who were irritated by their German. An eighty-year-old Berlin woman recorded her feelings thus: "One would have anticipated a certain bonding and solidarity, since they too had been robbed of home, possessions, and existence, had been separated from their loved ones just as forcibly as we, had also to live in a concentration camp. But nothing of the sort happened. For them we were not persecuted fellow-believers but hated Germans."[27]

In reality, the Czech inmates had some advantages: they could speak both German and Czech, and they felt superior in every way. They were also far better provided for, having friends in nearby Prague and thus occasionally receiving packages of food. After the war František Makovský, one of the sympathetic gendarmes of the camp, recording his own contacts with some of the Czech inmates, referred to the miserable situation of the aged:

> Secretly and with many difficulties I was delivering to some of them packages with groceries, letters, and money [given to me] by relatives and sympathizers. I myself kept supplying goods of all kinds and vegetables, since all of them were suffering from vitamin deficiency (their teeth were falling out, etc.) . . . to ghetto inmates whose allocated food was such that just the look of it made one's stomach turn, these items were fabulous! [The sight of] these unfortunate people, laboriously picking and eating the scant, downtrodden grass in the park as well as potato peels salvaged from the garbage heap to assuage their hunger . . . moved me to tears whenever I saw it.[28]

The delusion of the promised asylum did not last long. In due course, some of the so-called *Prominenten* (privileged) were also dying of enteritis and pneumonia. Corpses remained unburied for days because of a shortage of grave diggers; those in service were unable to cope with the situation. The sight of the funeral cart rattling through the narrow streets loaded with coffins became part of the daily routine. The talented and sensitive youth reporter Petr Ginz recorded his impressions of death and burial in Terezín: "The wooden coffins are stored in the blind alleys of the passageway. Some are full and ready to be hauled away; others are empty. They are waiting for their occupants." [29]

A further development occurred in autumn 1942, when the SS initiated several moves in an effort to create a sense of "normal life" in Terezín, as a "face-saving device for external consumption."[30] As part of this embellishment increased cultural activities were encouraged. At the same time, nine transports comprising eighteen thousand people over the age of sixty-five, many of them only half alive, were herded into deportation trains leaving for the "East." However, constant new arrivals filled the vacated space, and the ghetto continued to be desperately overcrowded.[31]

Occasionally there were collisions and misunderstandings within the SS leadership itself. At the beginning of February 1943 Ernst Kaltenbrunner, head of the RSHA, proposed to Himmler that conditions be eased in the ghetto, where the population at the time amounted to 46,735, by deporting to Auschwitz or to the General Government five thousand people over the age of sixty.[32] He argued that aside from tying down a large number of people who could be employed in useful work for the war effort, they were also the main source of epidemics. At the same time Kaltenbrunner advised including "only such Jews who have no special personal connections or contacts to appeal to, or do not hold high decorations of any kind." Himmler, however, mindful of the newly adopted alibi tactics, rejected the proposal out of hand, claiming that deportation from the old-age ghetto would contradict the implied understanding that "the Jews could live and die in peace" in Theresienstadt.[33]

It seems that Himmler's caution was triggered by the Allied declaration of December 17, 1942, condemning Nazi atrocities and the wholesale extermination of the Jews. Henceforward new steps were taken to transform Terezín with greater intensity into a real model ghetto (*Musterghetto*) for propaganda purposes: a showcase to be displayed to visitors from abroad. This chiefly meant representatives of the International Committee of the Red Cross, who had already expressed interest in inspecting the camp.[34]

At this period several "liberal" instructions were issued by the ss in concert with this trend, allowing inmates to carry on limited though censored postal correspondence and to receive food parcels from relatives and friends in the outside world.[35] Along with this and other relaxations of earlier restrictions came the launch of the *Stadtverschönerung* (town beautification campaign), which persisted until the end of the war.

The changes in leadership position originating from Nazi headquarters gave rise to further strains and tensions among the various national groups (Czech, German, and Austrian) already antagonized by constant intrigue and bickering. Indeed, throughout the existence of the ghetto, there was overt rivalry between Zionists and extreme Czech-Jewish assimilationists. Many of the latter defined themselves as Jews "by origin" (not by religion). Others learned of their Jewishness only as a result of the Nuremberg Laws. (Each national group—Czech, Austrian, and German—included adherents of the Catholic or Protestant faith with no feelings of solidarity whatsoever with the Jewish community.) Unlike in Prague, where the Jewish community abandoned prewar rifts and united in a common effort to overcome the Nazi onslaught, the old conflict between Zionists and assimilationists persisted in Terezín, partly due to the ss tactic of sowing discord among the diverse groups of Jews.[36]

The Czech assimilationists formed the bulk of the working population; among them were numerous leading intellectuals and former officers of the Czechoslovak Army. Aside from their numerical strength, it was their ascendancy in living native culture, an asset shared in common by all the Jews of the Protectorate, that enhanced their self-esteem.[37] Even after the arrival of elderly Jews from Germany and Austria in the fall of 1942, whereupon the Czech Jews no longer constituted the majority of the ghetto population, the Czech cultural elite maintained their prime position until September 1944, when the majority were deported to Auschwitz. After that point the Czech Jews had no political leadership to rally around. In the circumstances until then, many of them viewed Edelstein and Zucker as representing their interests, trying to block the mounting antagonism deriving from the German element.[38] Another marginal social group in the ghetto was the Communists, who were described as an "ideologically coherent unit" excelling in organization and secrecy.[39]

Amidst all these activities came a bolt from the blue on November 9, 1943: the news spread that Edelstein had been arrested together with the head of the central registry, Leo Foltýn, and two other clerks, Alfred Goldschmid and Egon Deutsch. This occurred on the very day when Lager Commandant Anton Burger paid a surprise visit, seizing some of the registry records. Charges were raised against the staff involving manipulation: errors and "discrepancies" in the lists. Edelstein was accused of trying to cover up the absence of fifty-five inmates who had escaped. He and the registry personnel were taken to the cellar of the command and kept there under strict isolation up until their deportation to Auschwitz (on December 15, 1943).[40]

The day after Edelstein's arrest the camp command decided to check the identities of the inmates. A great census (*Zählappel*) took place on November 11. The ghetto's old and young inhabitants were marched to the open field near Bohušovice that had once served as a military campground. Only the very sick were spared; Redlich recorded some details on the tragic event: "Children two years old went with old people of seventy. They went and stood all day, from 7 a.m. till 11 p.m. They went and were counted. As if we were cattle or sheep. Darkness came, and the Jews planned to spend the night in the open field. Thirty-six thousand people, docile as little children or lambs, standing and waiting."[41]

By the time the Nazis' counting was over around three hundred persons had died of fatigue and exhaustion in the field. At last, late at night, they were marched back to their bunks in the ghetto. A month later (December 15–18) about five thousand of them were to embark on their road to Auschwitz. As already indicated, at this stage Terezín was in a state of grand rehearsal, being prepared to go on show. Paradoxically, in the year of 1944 cultural life and theatrical activity were so rich that even in peacetime the average city could not boast as many theater performances as took place in the ghetto.

It is noteworthy that two of the famous representatives of the cultural elite of the ghetto, Victor Ullmann and H. G. Adler (the latter became widely known only after the war through his monumental works on Terezín), looked differently upon the avid, unprecedented cultural activity. Adler, known for his ambivalent attitude toward Judaism in general and his animosity toward Zionism in particular, viewed with derision the blooming cultural life "initiated by the SS." In contrast, Victor Ullmann, in his essay "Goethe and Ghetto," adroitly expressed the value of creative activity as a tool of self-preservation and a spark of humanity.[42]

The first inspection visit of the ICRC delegates took place on June 23, 1944, under the guidance of the "burgomaster" Dr. Eppstein. This was at a time of major developments in the larger world. The inmates, as we learn from some diaries, knew that the Allied invasion of Normandy had begun and that the German armies were in retreat on all fronts. "And here in the ghetto (it's forbidden to say "ghetto"), we play a big game. They built a Potemkin village. The Red Cross Committee inspected it," noted Redlich in his diary.[43]

On July 20, 1944, the news spread that a group of artists had been arrested and taken to an unknown place. Their crime was their art, the way they surreptitiously sketched the true face of life in the ghetto, which of course did not suit the aims of the "beautification" campaign. These works were found in the possession of an art collector named František Strass, who was sending them to his gentile in-laws in Prague. Other works of art had already been sent off to Switzerland. The affair of the artists (Fritta, Ungar, Bloch, and Haas) enraged the SS. The artists were summoned before Eichmann, Günther, Möhs, and Rahm for interrogation. Charged with *Greuelpropaganda*, they were taken to the Small Fortress for torture.[44]

Eppstein's term as head of the Council of Elders came to an end on September 27, 1944, while several massive transports were being prepared to be sent to Auschwitz. These dispatches of Terezín inmates included the core of construction workers and some leading members of the council (including Zucker and Robert Stricker). An accusation of transgressing "the regulations" of the ghetto was leveled against Eppstein, and he was shot by the SS at the Small Fortress that very day.[45] Rabbi Dr. Benjamin Murmelstein was nominated as the new (third) senior Jewish elder, and he served in this position until the liberation of the camp on May 8, 1945.

The tragic fate of the autumn 1944 deportees was described after the liberation by a survivor of one of these transports:

In Auschwitz I [heard] that all our leading personalities with their families, wives, and children were, immediately after their arrival, killed by gas. Every transport had a separate carriage, the first with leading persons of Terezín dispatched by a special order of the Nazis. So perished Otto Zucker and his wife, Franz and Olga Kahn, Philipp Kozower and his whole family, Erwin Elbert and his family—only his old mother lives now in Hodonín—Karl Schliesser and family, Julius Grünberger and wife, Dr. Weidmann, who was already killed by an ss-man in Bohušovice, at the railway station of Terezín, Dr. Desider Friedmann and Robert Stricker with their wives, and many, many others.[46]

By that time, the national structure of the ghetto population had undergone great changes: after the Dutch Jews were brought to the ghetto in April 1943, a group of Danish Jews arrived in October that year, and in December 1944, the first transport of Slovak Jews arrived from Sered after the crushing of the Slovak National Uprising. Three further groups of deportees from Slovakia followed in January, March, and on April 7, 1945. Finally, just prior to the end of the war, on the threshold of liberation, Terezín saw an influx of emaciated evacuees from various concentration camps and survivors of the death marches, causing chaos and epidemics.[47]

After the October 1944 deportations and the influx of newcomers the Germans decided to stabilize life in the ghetto. No more transports were to leave, with the exception of the two special groups that left for freedom. In February 1945 twelve hundred people left for Switzerland as an outcome of the Himmler-Musy negotiations.[48] The second "gesture" of the Nazi henchmen toward the Danes resulted in the freeing of 350 Danish Jews, who were "repatriated" to their country. Both events were contrived to buttress the alibi idea.

On April 6, 1945, another ICRC visit took place, the delegates led by Dr. Otto Lehner and Paul Dunant. The last person to visit the camp before liberation was Dr. Rezső Kastner of the Jewish Relief and Rescue Committee of Budapest, together with ss Haupsturmführer Krumey, who was to deliver Himmler's message about the handing over of the ghetto to the Red Cross representative, Dunant.[49]

In the last months, until the day of liberation, a reorganized Council of Elders representing the inmates according to their country of origin was in charge of affairs. Next to Murmelstein, who remained the head, four other executives were added: Rabbi Leo Baeck for the German Jews; Dr. Alfred Meissner, who had served as minister of justice and later social welfare in prewar Czechoslovakia; Dr. Edward Maurice Meijers, a famous Dutch lawyer and former high court justice in the Hague; and Heinrich Klang, an authority on civil law and a university professor at Vienna.

With the arrival of the evacuation transports (cleared from concentration camps before the advancing Allied forces), epidemics and various contagious diseases were spreading throughout the camp. In the last phase the total number of inmates grew to thirty thousand.

On May 2, 1945 the ss flag was hauled down from the abandoned headquarters and the International Red Cross took over the camp. On May 11 medical units of the Red Army entered the camp to alleviate the situation. After two weeks of strict quarantine the evacuation of the liberated inmates began: by August 17, 1945, repatriation of all the nationalities to their homelands was accomplished.

Following the liberation by the Red Army, Murmelstein resigned and the "Council of Four" came to run the place. On May 12, 1945, Jiří Vogel, a Czech Jew and a Communist, was appointed as head of the liberated community by all the national groups. Theresienstadt was the only ghetto to be freed with a significant number of survivors on the day of liberation; they numbered 17,320. Among them was the seventeen-year-old Dagmar Hilarová. After the agonizing experiences of four years, her life had just begun. Echoing Karel Hynek Mácha's famous love poem, she expressed her response in her "May 1945":

The bitter years had passed.
The breeze of spring
whiffed away the last pain from the heart.
It was May
and everything opened up to freedom.[50]

Terezín's uniqueness within the history of Nazi concentration camps rests on three salient characteristics: its window-dressing function as a cynical tableau disguising the extermination campaign, and the broader implications of this; the disgraceful role played by the International Committee of the Red Cross; and the spiritual resilience and creativity of its imprisoned population.

THE ROLE OF THE INTERNATIONAL COMMITTEE OF THE RED CROSS: INSPECTIONS OF THE *MUSTERGHETTO* (1944–45)

The fate of the Jewish inmates in the ghetto of Terezín can be considered the touchstone of the negative role of the ICRC during World War II. However, the secrecy and the "neutral" stance adopted by this institution up until the summer of 1944 cannot be viewed as an isolated, separate issue.[51] There were other factors bearing influence on the overall course of this institution, namely the stance of the neutral states, especially Switzerland, and to no less a degree the policies of the Allied governments.

It is an established fact that Swiss neutrality during World War II and the policy of the Swiss government were based on friendly relationships with the Third Reich and with the Axis-controlled satellite states. These circumstances a priori bore a direct influence upon the Geneva-based ICRC activities. It was only natural that economic ties with Germany and Italy, the countries with which most Swiss commerce was conducted, were of vital importance in maintaining good relationships, material advantages, and interests. In addition, it should be remembered that among the two hundred thousand German and Italian citizens of Switzerland there were many Nazis and fascists, members of pro-fascist political parties whose influence upon public opinion was considerable.

The Red Cross organization was generally regarded by the people of Europe, including the Jews, as a means of salvation for the suffering and persecuted, and the ICRC as an institution safeguarding humanitarian laws, *conditio humana*, during periods of war and distress, as proclaimed by its founders in 1863.[52] As early as 1939 the ICRC encountered difficulties when the Allied powers rejected the proposal to include civilians under the protection of the draft Tokyo Convention. In later years the Allies posed difficulties about lifting their blockade and allowing the passage of relief supplies for civilian victims, lest this interfere with their overall policies.

The leading members of the ICRC were Swiss citizens. Professor Max Huber, a distinguished expert in the field of international law, was its president, and Professor Carl J. Burckhardt—diplomat, historian, and student of literature— filled the role of the "foreign minister." Together with Jacques Chenevière and Frederic Barbey, Burckhardt acted as a member of the Central (Co-ordination) Commission established in 1940. They supervised committees dealing with prisoners of war, relief, legal questions, and the like.[53]

We should also bear in mind that from the beginning of the war, ICRC headquarters was the best-informed entity next to the Vatican, constantly receiving firsthand information from delegates in the occupied European countries. According to Dr. Marcel Junod, the special delegate of the ICRC, it was in October 1939 that he secretly received from the Swiss Embassy in Berlin the earliest information on the "Organization of a 'Jewish Reservat Plan,'" dated September 1939. With it was an undated secret report compiled by the Jewish community in Moravská Ostrava (Mährisch Ostrau), describing the harsh realities of the first deportation to Nisko (southeast of Lublin in occupied Poland), which began on October 17, 1939.[54] Had such knowledge been shared with other countries, it could perhaps have influenced their handling of refugee issues and provoked relaxing of stringent restrictions.

It is noteworthy that Jan Masaryk, at a meeting in London in September 1941, advised the representatives of the SJC that a joint approach should be made to the ICRC but at the same time suggested that "a special approach should be made to the American Red Cross in Washington." Masaryk also promised to urge the Czechoslovak ambassador in Washington to act jointly in this matter with the SJC Executive in New York and with the Yugoslav minister.[55] He obviously believed that if the proper approach were made to the American Red Cross, this organization would be able to render considerable help.

More recently Jacques Moreillon, director-general of the ICRC, claimed that this institution "had mostly indirect and incomplete information" and that it was not conscious at the time (meaning October 1942) of Hitler's "Final Solution."[56] This claim is easily refuted. A cursory look into the relevant documentation published by the Vatican as well as other reliable sources, information that must have reached the ICRC, provides ample evidence on the matter. The most important information sources on the persecution of the Jews were accumulated by representatives of several organizations—such as Dr. Gerhard Riegner, Dr. Jaromír Kopecký, Nathan Schwalb, Dr. Fritz Ullmann, and Dr. Abraham Silberschein—all stationed in Geneva.[57]

We learn a stunning piece of information about the cardinal question of how much the ICRC leadership knew in 1941 about Hitler's extermination aims from a conversation that took place between Dr. Carl J. Burckhardt, ICRC's foreign minister, and Paul C. Squire, the American consul in Switzerland, on November 17, 1942.[58] Upon the advice of Leland Harrison, Squire asked Burckhardt directly: What did he know of a written order signed by Hitler, at the beginning of 1941, about the extermination of Jews? Burckhardt responded that although he himself did not see this order he could *confidentially* confirm that Hitler had signed an order at the beginning of 1941 that Germany should be *judenfrei* (free of Jews) by the end of 1942. He underlined that he had received this information from two "very well informed Germans" in whom he had full confidence. Squire also asked about the real connection between *Vernichtung* (extermination) and *judenfrei*, and Burckhardt argued thus: "Since there is no place where these Jews could be disposed of, in order to cleanse the territory from this race, the final result is obvious."[59]

The ICRC had delegates in all European countries and was regularly briefed on the current state of affairs in Hungary, Slovakia, Rumania, and Croatia either through permanent delegates or through emissaries who visited the various countries.[60] The massacres that took place in these countries were reported by some of these delegates as early as of the fall of 1941, with alarming comments. In one case, René de Weck, the Swiss minister in Bucharest, wrote in a private letter to Jacques Chenevière (November 29, 1941) about the plight of the Rumanian Jews, claiming that "the Armenian massacres that had shaken the European conscience at the beginning of the century were mere child's play in comparison." In a postscript, he also pointed out that the basic tendency was "the physical destruction of the Jews."[61]

Briefings of similar content must also have reached the ICRC from American sources. Paul T. Culbertson of the State Department's Division of European Affairs informed the American JDC on September 26, 1941, of the massacres at Kamenetz Podolsk of "stateless" Jews deported from Hungary. This information, gained "from a trustworthy Hungarian officer, an eyewitness" read: "The number killed is placed as high as 15,000 according to other reports. Fleeing people and praying Jews in synagogues were machine-gunned. Corpses are reported floating down the Dniester River . . . The efforts of the Hungarian Red Cross to alleviate the situation have been quite ineffective. We believe that the situation should be made known to the International Red Cross and other groups."[62]

The general secretary of the World Council of Churches, Visser t'Hooft, wrote a letter on October 29, 1941, to Professors Max Huber and Carl Burckhardt, asking them to pay special attention to the situation in the Warthegau and the General Government.[63] He enclosed a "Memorandum on the Situation in Poland," which described recent deportations from Polish cities and ghettos. Visser t'Hooft justified WCC's activities on behalf of the Jews thus: "On the whole, Jewish organizations are no longer able to act effectively on behalf of their people. The Jewish question is related to the heart of the Christian message; if the Church failed to raise its voice in order to protest and to warn and if it failed to do its best to help, it would not be obedient to its Lord. It is therefore the duty of the Christian Churches and especially of their ecumenical representative, the WCC in the process of formation, to act as the spokesman of the persecuted."[64]

The WCC general secretary also suggested setting up a special Red Cross mission to Poland to investigate the situation. The answer received from the ICRC clearly deferred to the prevailing attitude: "The members of the Committee were convinced—and we could not prove that they were wrong—that actions on behalf of the Jews whom Hitler hated would endanger the indispensable work of the Red Cross for millions of Allied prisoners of war."[65]

Other sporadic but weighty reports on deportations, including a report by the head of the national Slovak Red Cross, Skotnický (June 9, 1942), referred directly to Auschwitz.[66] "Hauswith" is also mentioned by Colonel Gartesier, the representative of the French Red Cross, who notified ICRC headquarters that the deportees were never heard of again; they were not permitted to write or receive letters (June 2, 1942).

Most revealing is the exchange of letters between Miss Warner and Miss Campion of the British Red Cross and Mlle. Suzanne Ferrière in Geneva. The British correspondents inquired about the fate of the German and Czech Jews who were deported and whether it was true that these people were sent to Poland and Russia. The answer from Geneva said that although there was no reliable information, it actually happened all over Europe. Ferrière added that it was tragic but "we cannot do anything about it."[67]

Hence, while in late autumn 1942 information was pouring in from official quarters and private individuals as well as from some escapees from the notorious extermination camps, the draft appeal being prepared by Professor Huber and his staff, although incorporating the essential principles of *ius gentium*, was cautiously worded.[68] It avoided outright condemnation, simply demanding that citizens should be treated humanely. The members were divided about the wording; some thought stronger language should be used. The decisive plenary meeting chaired by Jacques Chenevière (owing to Huber's illness), took place in October 14, 1942.[69]

Philip Etter, representing the Swiss Government (in the 1930s he had served as foreign minister), vehemently objected to the proposed draft, arguing that it could be interpreted as a violation of neutrality. His judgment was endorsed, and the Red Cross appeal was not made public.

At this stage help came from an unexpected source; the evidence on the massacre of the Jews accumulated at ICRC Geneva headquarters was passed along by at least two of its highly placed officials: Professor Carl Burckhardt and presumably André de Pilar, a Baltic baron who had become a Swiss citizen. As members of the Commission mix de secours, both were in constant touch with German colleagues and diplomats. Burckhardt's intimation in October 1942 to his Jewish friend and colleague Professor Paul Guggenheim of the Geneva Center of Advanced Studies and in November to Paul S. Squire, the American consul in Geneva [November 7, 1942], was of special significance: using the term *judenrein* in this connection, he corroborated the content of the August Riegner telegram on the Final Solution plan.[70]

One could speculate on what prompted Burckhardt to share his inside information with other official representatives at that point.[71] Riegner's notes on his meetings with ICRC functionaries in 1942–43 with regard to assistance to be extended to Terezín inmates refer to de Pilar's assertion (February 2, 1943) on the status of Jewish detainees, claiming that the ICRC would be able to provide help to the Jews in the occupied territories if "an official ruling on behalf of the American, British and eventually other Allied governments were forthcoming."[72] The acceptance of such a rule, however, was questionable since the

Geneva Convention does not embody such provisions. On July 6, 1943, Gerhard Riegner noted another meeting with several officials in connection with America's recognition of the Jews as hostile civilian detainees in an effort to include them in a relief campaign led by the Red Cross.[73]

Thus even after the mass murder of Jews became known and had been verified by many reliable sources, the conspiracy of silence continued over a long period. It has been suggested that one of the cardinal reasons for this could have been the fear of a general impression that the war was being waged in order to save the Jews, which of course could only harm the Allies' war effort.

On March 4, 1943, in response to the inquiry by the ICRC about the feasibility of a dispatch of food and drugs to Terezín, the German Red Cross in Berlin stated that "no such dispatches are possible for the time being."[74]

Three months later, on June 27 or 28, 1943, the German Red Cross delegation visited the ghetto to ascertain the conditions of the inmates there. One should point out that the National Committee of the German Red Cross was headed by Dr. Grawitz and Professor Gebhardt, leading members of the SS associated with the invention of gas chambers and experimental medicine used in the death camps.[75] It is therefore amazing that the only more or less accurate outside record of the situation prevailing in the ghetto should come from this source. The report authored by Walter Hartmann was unfavorable; the delegation found Theresienstadt dreadful (*grausam*), "frightfully overcrowded," the inmates severely undernourished, and the medical care entirely inadequate.[76]

It was only as of June 1943 that the ICRC made efforts to conduct an inspection visit to Terezín, spurred by negative information gleaned from the German Red Cross report. Burckhardt had pressured the German Red Cross into visiting Terezín, anxious to find out whether the inmates were to remain there or eventually be deported to other camps.[77] Actually the designation of Terezín as a "transit point" was known fairly early both in Washington and in the Vatican. President Roosevelt's special envoy to the Holy See, Myron C. Taylor, in a note to Cardinal Maglione on September 26, 1942, informing him of the Nazi extermination plan, said the following about Terezín: "This place, however, is only an interim station and the people there await the same fate [as all the others]."[78]

In July 1943 Cardinal Maglione instructed Orsenigo, the Papal Nuncio in Berlin, to apply for permission to visit the ghetto of Theresienstadt. More than two months passed before Maglione received a response on September 28, informing him that such a request had been "categorically denied" by the foreign minister.[79]

Six months after the first visit by the German Red Cross, ICRC headquarters at Geneva received a letter signed by Eppstein and Murmelstein, dated November 30, 1943, when the Terezín death toll had peaked and medicines were sorely needed, carrying this astounding message: "We respectfully acknowledge receipt of your letter of September 30, 1943, notifying us of your dispatch of medications. We again allow ourselves to point out that the care provided for the Jews under our responsibility, especially in the matter of medications, is so satisfactory that it would be advisable to refrain from further shipments. The state of health of Jews entrusted to our authority can, as before, generally be described as favorable."[80]

Almost a year went by before finally, in a letter to the RSHA dated March 14, 1944, Hauptsturmführer Niehaus, the representative of the German Red Cross for external affairs, probed the possibility of an ICRC visit to the old-age ghetto in Theresienstadt."[81] At that point he also made reference to a discussion held with Günther and Eichmann a week earlier about visiting "a Jewish labor or penal camp," in the presence of an RSHA official. Niehaus suggested holding a special roll-call of inmates during which parcels of food and medical supplies would be handed out "spontaneously" to the sick inmates (*Starkungsmittel für Kranke*). This, of course, would enable the German Red Cross representative to see for himself the distribution of gift parcels and thus personally confirm their receipt to the Joint Relief Committee in Geneva. The letter concludes that such an act seemed "highly advisable considering the rise in the number of foreign inquiries about the various Jewish camps."

It therefore transpires that only as of the middle of 1943, once the outcome of the war had become clear, did the ICRC began to reexamine the application of humanitarian principles and of the Geneva Convention to civilian populations. This was no doubt an outcome of the pressure on the part of the Allied governments and of the intervention of the World Jewish Congress, the JDC, and some noted personalities. A. L. Easterman, political secretary of the SJC, spurred by the Allied Declaration of December 17, 1942, addressed President Huber on January 6, 1943, in a letter asking for his immediate intervention:

The outrages of which our fellow-Jews, men, women and children, are the victims, have recently attained unparalleled horror . . . The humanitarian principles which 80 years ago inspired the foundation of the Red Cross Movement and its symbol, have since then protected not only the victims of war but also those who have suffered in belligerent countries, without distinction of race or religion . . . We invoke the aid of the one international body which has authority to approach governments and to enlist the cooperation of the National Red Cross Societies, in support of our approach to these neutral states.[82]

Henceforth new instructions were given to representatives of this institution in occupied Europe, and a permanent delegate was even sent to Hungary (after pleading to this effect had gone unheeded for some years) in the person of Jean de Bavier, who arrived in Budapest in October 1943.[83]

A clue to the change in policy can be found in the records of the secret negotiations conducted between Allen Welsh Dulles and Count Egon Hohenlohe-Langenburg, Himmler's and Schellenberg's emissary, in early 1943.[84] Dulles (SD code-named Mr. Bull), having been in Switzerland since November 1942 with his aide Myron C. Taylor (code-named Roberts), held several meetings with Hohenlohe (Pauls) and Reinhard Spitzy (Bauer).[85] According to the minutes of the final talk, which took place on March 21, 1943, reference was made to how to ameliorate the German position in America. Roberts recommended that the Nazis should deal in a more sensible way with the Jewish question "so that even the hatred of the Jews can be overcome," using methods that would lead to practical results "without evoking outrage and leaving themselves open to attack."[86] It is noteworthy that the same Roberts regarded the Nazi extermination of the Jews and Poles as a *fait accompli*. He even commented that he considered this annihilation drive unrealistic for the simple reason that "an enormous percentage of Jews and Poles live outside the German sphere of influence."

Yielding to Dulles's recommendation in an attempt to open up new vistas for further developments, in March 1943 Himmler ordered that Bergen-Belsen be set up for "exchange Jews" (people to be ransomed), and almost simultaneously Terezín was transformed into a "model ghetto."[87]

It is of interest to recall that in due course the Terezín beautification campaign was indeed put into motion. In addition to Burckhardt's inquiry, the deportation of 450 Danish Jews in October 1943 triggered an urgent demand for the ICRC's visit.[88] The Danish Red Cross, following the intervention of King Christian X of Denmark, the bishop of Copenhagen, and the chancellors of Danish universities, immediately appealed to its German counterpart, submitting a request for such a visit.[89] Another factor of importance was a trip to Denmark in November 1943 by Eichmann, who, under pressure, agreed in principle to the visit of a delegation. He was, however, adamant that this could not take place before the spring of 1944.[90]

Eichmann obviously needed some time to prepare the setting for such an event. One aspect of this endeavor was to provide suitable accommodation for the *Prominenten* as well as for the Danish Jews whose evidence to the Danish Red Cross delegates would be of paramount importance.[91] Many of them were moved to new quarters furnished with the ultimate in luxury (lampshades, curtains, potted plants). The Jews were instructed on how they were to dress, where they were to be stationed, and what they were to say when spoken to. Children too were coached. Ailing, emaciated, ragged, and crippled Jews were warned to remain on the upper storey of the barracks and to keep out of sight of the guided tour.

The streets were cleaned and flowers planted, benches were installed in the square, and a music pavilion was erected. In addition a special playground for children and a recreation hall were set up. The morgue was equipped with signs in Hebrew and the name of the ghetto was changed to Jüdisches Siedlungsgebiet (Jewish Settlement Area). Abandoned buildings in poor condition were torn down and elegant shops with charming outdoor signs reading "grocery," "bakery," "pharmacy," and "perfumery" were opened and stocked with the appropriate merchandise to authenticate the fraud. A café with sidewalk tables was to enhance the idyllic setting. Every corner of the camp was cleaned and scrubbed. The streets previously marked by the letters "L" and "Q" were given pastoral names. Now several cultural events took place daily: lectures, concerts, theater, cabaret, and sports. Once or twice a day the town band played in the square, like at any holiday resort, and there were also musical interludes at the café.

In May 1944 in the midst of the ongoing beautification campaign, for the first time a message from Budapest reached the Council of Elders in Terezín, transmitted by the ss. It was spurred by the Istanbul-based representatives of the Yishuv in Palestine, who, on learning from clandestine sources of the plight of the population in the ghetto, were eager to extend financial support to boost their morale.

The choice fell on the Budapest Relief and Rescue Committee engaged in negotiations with the ss chiefs about the "Blood for Trucks" ransom deal. Dr. Kastner, on behalf of the Rescue Committee, eagerly took on the role of go-between. Consequently he asked Dieter Wisliceny to transmit his letters to Dr. František Friedmann in Prague and to his Zionist friends at Terezín.[92] After Eichmann's approval was received ss Hauptsturmführer Klausnitzer was dispatched with the two letters and with the sum of ten thousand dollars to be delivered to Friedmann (who, in his capacity as senior Jewish elder in Prague, was in charge of the financial affairs of ghetto Terezín). Kastner's note to the Jewish elder in Terezín contained "greetings from the Yishuv and from American Jewry, "expressing hope for their eventual *aliyah*."

The answers were not long in coming. Letters dated May 23 and May 24 were dispatched from Prague and Terezín to Kastner in Budapest, obviously dictated by the ss and almost identical in content.[93] The letter from the ghetto carried the signatures of Dr. Franz Kahn, Dr. Paul Eppstein, Dr. Erich Österreicher, Dr. Erich Munk, Eng. Otto Zucker, and Gert Körbel and was adorned with a charming letterhead—a lithograph of Terezín by the Dutch artist Jo Spier. In both letters the ghetto was depicted as a pastoral place—"a veritable Jewish city in which all work is done by Jews" with vibrant cultural and social activities, library, coffee house, and musical offerings—all this at a time when almost seventy thousand inmates had already been deported to extermination camps.[94]

Kastner's letter dispatched from Budapest and other positive signs reaching Terezín from the outside world, together with the hectic preparations for the Red Cross officials' visit, generated a certain measure of optimism in the population.[95] They also had news about how the tide of war had turned; newspapers smuggled into the ghetto by Czech gendarmes, many of whom acted as messengers between the ghetto and the Czech population, boosted their hopes.

On May 16 Himmler himself, pressured by various organizations including the Swedish Red Cross, gave his consent. Finally on June 13, 1944, eight months after the arrival of Danish Jews, the RSHA informed the Red Cross that the date for the visit had been set for June 23, 1944.[96] It is worth noting that Werner Best, German plenipotentiary in Denmark, reassured the Danish officials on the eve of the roundup of Jews in Copenhagen that no harm would befall anyone taken into custody and that the aged and those incapable of working would be sent to Theresienstadt, "where the Jews enjoyed self-government and lived in decent conditions." However, when Best witnessed the Danes' outrage following the deportations, he promptly notified the German Foreign Office, recommending that "such a visit will have a calming effect in Denmark."[97]

It appears that the Danes were the driving force behind the ICRC's request for a visit to Terezín. The Danes even launched a shipment of parcels before permission was granted to do so, sending around seven hundred parcels to the Danish inmates in Terezín on a monthly basis.[98]

The delegation visiting Terezín on June 23, 1944 was composed of Frants Hvass, head of the Political Department of the Danish Foreign Office; Dr. Juel Hennigsen, representative of the Danish Red Cross; and Swiss physician Dr. Maurice Rossel, representative of the ICRC in Berlin.[99] German escorts were Rolf Günther and Ernst Möhs, representatives of the RSHA, Eberhard von Thadden of the Foreign Ministry, and Dr. Heidenkampf of the German Red Cross. The only Jew attached to the delegation accompanying the guests inside the ghetto was Eppstein, head of the Ältestenrat. He wore a top hat suitable for a "burgomaster"; an automobile and chauffeur were placed at his disposal. The chauffeur (an SS man in civilian clothing) occasionally raised his cap with due respect. En route the delegation stopped at the town hall, renamed Haus der jüdischen Selbstverwaltung, which housed the Ältestenrat. Its interior was decorated with beautiful carpets placed there for the occasion. There Eppstein delivered his speech, which had been carefully phrased by the ss commanders. (Eppstein's face still bore a black and blue mark under his eye from a beating by the camp commander Karl Rahm a few days earlier.) Eppstein described life in Theresienstadt and the activities of the Jewish self-administration in most favorable terms. To make his address sound authentic he spoke derisively about the harshness of the Jewish Police generating ill feeling and making them "unpopular" among the inmates. Eppstein gave the number of inmates as 37,000–40,000, of whom 94 percent came from Germany and the Protectorate, 5 percent from Holland, and 1 percent from Denmark. In the course of his description he also mentioned that tobacco and alcohol were forbidden.

As part of the well-prepared program, the ICRC entourage was briefed about the legal and judicial status prevailing in the camp. To illustrate the work performed by the Jewish judges, a play within the play was staged. As if by chance the delegation witnessed a mock trial in which a case of petty theft was brought before the bench. The lecture ended with the ss officer's benevolent assertion that the Council of Elders was empowered to pardon the culprit.

During the eight-hour visit the delegates had a break for a meal with the Nazi entourage, to which "burgomaster" Eppstein was not invited. On their way to the dining hall they could not miss noticing that football was being played on the grounds, attended by cheering crowds, and that the children's opera *Brundibar* was being performed in the newly erected Community Hall.[100]

The Red Cross delegation saw a "free city" bearing no resemblance to the crowded and filthy Polish ghettos with their emaciated population. Moreover there were no signs of armed policemen.[101] The Czech gendarmes had been withdrawn to avoid their passing embarrassing information to the visitors.[102]

As instructed by the ss chiefs, Eppstein proclaimed that there were no deportations from Terezín, and Rossel recorded unequivocally in his report that "Terezín is a final camp and whoever reaches this place was not to be sent any further."[103] This is all the more surprising given that well-informed ICRC sources in Geneva were in possession of evidence testifying to the continuous deportation of Jews from Terezín to Auschwitz; the information was probably passed along to Rossel.[104]

The most telling testimony was the letter Leo Janowitz addressed to Fritz Ullmann in Geneva (October 1943). This message was obviously dispatched upon the instruction of the camp administration at Auschwitz, which had its own ulterior motives. Janowitz told of his arrival in Birkenau together with eighteen hundred deportees, claiming that he himself was in charge of the newly set up "labor camp," and requested gift parcels to be addressed to individuals (according to a list of names) as well as collective shipments.[105] In a cable dispatched from Geneva on October 15, 1943, Jaromír Kopecký informed the Czechoslovak Government-in-Exile in London of the contents of Janowitz's letter.[106] (The transport lingered for six months at the Birkenau "family camp," and all but a few individuals were gassed on the night of March 8, 1944.)

Upon their return from Terezín the ICRC delegates reported on July 19, 1944, to the Danish Legation in Stockholm and to a group of Jews, among them representatives of the Committee for the Aid of Persons Deported from Denmark. The general impression was that their main concern was to serve the interests of the Danish Jews and their well-being. The Danish representatives, though cautious in their assessment, praised the Jews for creating their own self-administration and for their will to live. In his report Havass nevertheless noted that the question of great importance—whether the stay of the ghetto population would be temporary—still remained open.[107]

Von Thadden's observations referred to a talk with the artist Jo Spier, who "very willingly gave information" took him and his entourage to the kitchen where they were offered a taste of food, and then showed them a few of his paintings.[108]

During a brief exchange of words between Rossel and Eppstein, the ICRC delegate asked the Jewish elder what he thought would be the ultimate fate of the ghetto population. Eppstein answered that he had no response to this question but added that he personally "saw no way out." However, this communication implying the utterly hopeless situation of the inmates fell on deaf ears. Rossel's report to the ICRC lauded the Jewish administration and the living conditions, clearly asserting that the camp was an *Endlager*—a final camp. Moreover, in his conclusion he pointed out that "Ghetto Theresienstadt is a communist society, headed by a "Stalin' of high qualities: Eppstein."[109]

No wonder the RSHA and the German Red Cross received Rossel's briefing with "unqualified satisfaction."[110] In contrast to those of the Danish delegates, Rossel's report was phrased in positive terms, falling in line with German propaganda. He acknowledged the German argument that Jews were better off in the ghetto than non-Jews were in the Protectorate, for "certain articles available in the ghetto are almost impossible to find in Prague." He also noticed "smart women wearing hats and scarves" and flashily dressed young men. In summing up, Rossel pointed out that "certainly there are few populations whose health is as carefully looked after as in Theresienstadt." In his concluding paragraph he even made an attempt to dispel the rumor circulating in the free world about the annihilation of the Jews: "Our report will change nobody's opinion. Everyone is free to condemn the Reich's attitude toward the solution of the Jewish problem. However, if this report could contribute in some small measure to dispel the mystery surrounding the Theresienstadt ghetto we shall be satisfied."[111]

It is revealing that Niehaus of the German Red Cross immediately informed Dr. Hartmann, his colleague in Switzerland, on the matter: "The inspection in Terezín was conducted in a very satisfactory manner from every angle. I am convinced that the representatives from abroad will submit a favorable report."[112]

On the day after the visit *Lagerkommandant* Rahm, obviously pleased with the progress of the well-staged comedy, rewarded the inmates for their participation with an official day and a half break from work.[113] But if the public at large was bemused by the upheaval the visit created, to others it turned out to be a great disappointment. Leo Baeck's comments testify to the bitter aftertaste it left with them: "The [members of the delegation] appeared to be completely taken in by the false front put up for their benefit . . . Perhaps they knew the real conditions—but it looked as if they did not want to know the truth. The effect on our morale was devastating. We felt forgotten and forsaken."[114]

The photographs Rossel took and attached to his report were made public only in 1990. Some of the contents of his briefing did, however, reach the SJC in Geneva. In protest against the misleading information, the SJC demanded an additional inspection of Terezín by the ICRC. For this, however, they had to wait almost another year.

After the visitors' departure there followed a short period of quiet and inertia, described by a survivor, the lawyer Dr. Arnošt Wald of Prostějov: "The summer of 1944 was the best time we had in Terezín. Nobody thought of new transports. Suddenly—at the end of September—an order was issued to prepare a transport of 5,000 men, aged between 16 and 65."[115]

During that summer a sham "documentary" film was produced on Terezín, portraying the "honorable" members of the Ältestenrat deliberating at ease in the conference room. Shortly thereafter, on September 23, 1944, Paul Eppstein, Otto Zucker, and Benjamin Murmelstein were summoned to the camp commander's office and told resolutely that an inspection of the workshops had proved that their work for the war effort was inadequate. Consequently the decision had been made to deport five thousand men to a new labor camp to be erected under Zucker's supervision. And indeed three transports were sent off on September 28 and 29 and October 2, taking 5,499 prisoners straight to Auschwitz. Zucker left with the first dispatch with some of his Work Detail staff. Upon their arrival on the platform at Birkenau, Zucker, blindfolded, was led straight to the gas chamber.

It has been suggested that these special transports consisting of the core of Jewish manpower, many of whom were former officers of the Czechoslovak Army, were targeted with the intent of weakening the resistance potential of Terezín. The timing coincided with the outbreak of the Slovak National Uprising at Bánská Bystrica (August 29, 1944), which caused panic in the Protectorate high echelons. This is documented by urgent appeals of State Secretary K. H. Frank and Konrad Henlein, demanding Hitler's immediate help.[116]

On the eve of the dispatch of the first transport Eppstein was arrested (September 27, 1944), and he was shot in the back at the Small Fortress the same day. There are several speculations as to what led the SS to bring about his liquidation. It has been surmised that when asked to cooperate in preparing the forthcoming transport, he refused to do so. Some other testimonies, however, refer to Eppstein's New Year address (*Neujahrsgedanken*—5705) delivered on September 19, 1944, obviously under the impact of the Allied landings, suggesting that this might have angered the SS. Eppstein used this parable in his address: "We are like a boat that from a distance catches a glimpse of the coveted harbor. We deem that we can already discern our friends [waiting] on the beach. However, we still have to navigate our way through invisible obstacles and therefore should be cautious and not be lured by untimely signals of welcome for we have yet to overcome dangers that still lie ahead."[117]

The new Ältestenrat nominated on December 15 and headed by Murmelstein—Baeck eventually became his deputy—remained in office until the liberation of the ghetto. According to Zdeněk Lederer, Murmelstein was "a domineering, harsh individual" who saw himself as another Josephus Flavius: "undeterred by the vociferous contempt of his people, [he] worked for its salvation," continuing with some variations the policy of his predecessors. He was, however, "very sly and particularly clever with his German superiors."[118]

Throughout 1944 the ICRC received numerous items of information from Jewish organizations as well as individuals implying that Terezín was in a state of liquidation or that the Jews were being deported from there to other extermination camps.[119] The most desperate message reached Fritz Ullmann from Birkenau on March 10, 1944, sent by his good friend Jacob Edelstein's wife Mirjam, who managed to convey an SOS call to save her husband.[120] She used the simplest device to evade the censor, intimating that her husband was separated from her and her fourteen-year-old son Arjeh after their arrival from Terezín in December 1943. All this time, Edelstein had been held incarcerated in the infamous "death block," Block 11, in total seclusion.

Dear Ully,

Husband, Arjeh, and myself are here together with Leo [Janowitz]. We are all healthy and that is the most important [thing]. From Jaikew [the Yiddish diminutive for Jacob] I unfortunately do not have any information. Perhaps you have more luck. I am convinced that you will do everything for him. Perhaps you can do something for the Jacob Hahlafa family [*hahlafa* means "exchange" in Hebrew]. Please help them as much as you can. How are Max and Bertl? Have you any news about them? Heartfelt greetings to you and your wife from your

Mirjam [Edelstein]

Heinz Prossnitz in Prague received two postcards from Mirjam Edelstein expressing thanks for gift parcels. Jacob Edelstein was permitted to send letters to Terezín. The Nazis, it seems, were anxious that both the outside world and the leadership in Theresienstadt be informed that the "family" was doing "well."[121]

Two months later the family was joined together in death. Before Edelstein was shot on June 20, 1944, in Auschwitz he was to witness the execution of his son, his wife, and his mother-in-law, Jente Oliner.[122]

On June 16, 1944, one week before the first infamous visit of the ICRC delegation had taken place in Theresienstadt, the following bulletin was broadcast on all the BBC European Services, at noon, about the forthcoming massacres ordered by the Germans to take place at the gas chambers at Birkenau "on or about" June 20: "These Jews were transported to Birkenau from the concentration camp of Theresienstadt on the Elbe, last December. Four thousand Czech Jews who were taken from Theresienstadt to Birkenau in September 1943 were massacred in the gas chambers on March 7th."[123]

The BBC bulletin warned the German authorities that full information had been received in London about the massacres in Birkenau and that "all those responsible for such massacres from the top onwards, will be called to account."[124]

On February 5, 1945, several weeks before the second visit of the ICRC delegates took place, twelve hundred inmates were released from Terezín, as earlier mentioned. With Himmler's consent they were sent by train to Switzerland as an outcome of the negotiations conducted by Dr. Jean-Marie Musy, former president of the Swiss Confederation.[125] Their release received wide publicity both in Berne and in New York (*New York Times*). The so-called Operation Musy, however, was discontinued when it was brought to Hitler's knowledge. The new arrivals were warmly received in Switzerland. They described the real conditions in Terezín, claiming that the reports of the ICRC delegates were "far from the truth" and that the "show" in the camp had been staged for the exclusive benefit of the visitors.[126]

At that time the contents of the Auschwitz Protocol became widely known and excerpts of it had been published by the Swiss press. An open letter referring to the Auschwitz Report sent on July 17, 1944, to the Swiss Confederation by the Lebensrettung-Gesellschaft (Life-saving society) and the University of Zurich student body, implored the Bundesrat in the name of Christianity to save the remnant of Jewry from such a fate.[127]

In response to the pressure exerted by the Jewish organizations a new visit of inspection took place on April 6, 1945, with Dr. Otto Lehner and Paul Dunant representing the ICRC. During the visit Lehner was offered a special treat; he was shown the documentary film *Heimstätte für Juden* (Homes for Jews).[128] The artists who had worked on the film were by then dead—they had been gassed in Auschwitz in October 1944. Both gentlemen, especially Lehner, were expressly satisfied with conditions in the ghetto.[129]

It is difficult to conceive of how at this point such "enlightened" officials could have been misled to this extent. It looks rather as if their main interest lay in presenting further supporting evidence to the ICRC delegates' earlier reports. There is a passage corroborating this approach in Lehner's letter: "The overall impression made by the camp was very favorable; we also refer to the [former] report of Dr. Rossel and we may add that nothing has changed in the meantime . . . The elder of the Jews is currently Herr Murmelstein. The former elder of the Jews, Dr. Eppstein, was transferred to the East six months ago. According to the testimony of the elder of the Jews as well as of the German authorities, no deportations have taken place recently: 10,000 Jews were dispatched to the camps in the East, especially to Auschwitz."[130]

It is indeed pathetic that the representatives of the ICRC were once again hoodwinked when inspecting the camp on the threshold of Germany's surrender. They were escorted by Adolf Eichmann, and while touring the ghetto Dunant spoke to Murmelstein and later continued his negotiations in Prague with Karl Hermann Frank. At a soirée hosted for the honored guests at Hradčany Castle, they engaged in vivid conversation with Eichmann and Dr. Rudolph Weinmann, head of the SD in Prague.[131] Dunant, it seems, was not entirely taken in by the latter's inflated rhetoric. The report he sent to Geneva brings the core issue into focus: "More interesting than the actual living conditions and installations in the ghetto of Theresienstadt was the question whether it had indeed served merely as a transit camp for the Jews and how many deportations to the East had taken place [from there]."[132]

Lehner's report on Terezín culminates in the passage referring to the ghetto as a "Zionist experiment" for a future Jewish state—a devilish invention of Eichmann's brain. (He did not repeat this "prophetic vision" during his trial in Jerusalem.) Lehner took it at face value, and thus reported in earnest: "The idea of the Reich government in establishing Theresienstadt was [prompted by the desire] to create a Jewish community to be run by its self-government, which would serve as a practical experiment [*element* in the original] on a small scale, for the future Jewish state to which a certain strip of land should be allotted after the war. The miniature Jewish state in Theresienstadt rests on the principle of collective economy. There exists a kind of elite communism, which is strongly reflected in the overall structure."[133]

Lehner also referred to Weinmann's statement stressing that most of those deported from Terezín "are engaged in enlarging the camp in Auschwitz, others are employed in administration."[134] In reality Auschwitz had been liberated by then and all those "employees" had been reduced to ashes.

At this point it is of interest to mention Kastner's visit to Terezín on April 16, 1945, in the company of Krumey and several other SS men.[135] After meeting Murmelstein and listening to his monotonous lecture about the development of Terezín, Kastner asked to speak with Dr. Eppstein. When he learned that the latter was not available he asked to see Franz Kahn, and was informed that he too was not available. Then he insisted on seeing one of the signatories of the letter sent to him to Budapest in May 1944. Murmelstein named Leo Baeck (who actually had not signed that letter), whom Kastner later met and to whom he proffered some words of encouragement.

Following his second visit to Terezín (April 21, 1945) Paul Dunant also found it imperative, just as Lehner had earlier, to substantiate the report of their previous mission in an attempt to refute the charges leveled against them for being led astray by the Nazis: "I report that my present impression is identical with that we gained during our visit on April 6, and [express] the conviction that no special *mis-en-scène* had been prepared for our reception."[136]

The record of the ICRC took a different course only right at the end. The Swedish Red Cross after due negotiations arrived with a convoy of buses on April 15 and thus the Danish Jews were safely taken to Sweden.

In the last tragic days of the ghetto, Terezín was flooded with many thousands of camp evacuees, remnants of the death marches, directed there by the SS before the advancing Allied armies. The outbreak of a typhoid epidemic was the final blow inflicted upon the weak and emaciated population. After the breakup of the SS authority, Paul Dunant took over the ghetto on May 2, flying the flag of the ICRC. Terezín was liberated by the Red Army on May 11, 1945.[137] From his headquarters in Prague, Dunant kept providing succor to the survivors of the camp.

For many years after the war the ICRC documentation was not accessible to the public, and official publications contained only selective material on the Jewish issue. A summary of the ICRC's activities published in 1947 in *Inter Arma Caritas* is perhaps the most telling evidence of its ambiguous attitude: "Once, but only once, after a year's struggle, they were allowed to visit a camp: the town of Terezín. *Not the fortress of evil memory, but only the town, which was to be a model ghetto*" (emphasis mine]). But the report went on: "At Auschwitz and Ravensbrück, they penetrated as far as the camp office quarters, but could not enter the camp itself, for they must not be allowed to see *what nobody must see*" (emphasis in the original)."[138]

The Spiritual Legacy of
the Terezín Inmates

Both revolt and spiritual resistance in the struggle against the Nazis are indisputably topics for which the parameters have become palpable only in the course of the past half century. In the immediate postwar period the glorification of armed combat persisted, and public interest focused primarily on events such as the Warsaw Ghetto Uprising, concentration camp revolts, and escapes from the camps. Today, perhaps as a result of chronological distance and constant interaction between past and present, we can offer more profound and articulate conclusions in this area of research.

Spiritual resistance is without question *fons et origo*, the source of every single act of rebellion and resistance. For many centuries books, creative activity, and above all writing constituted traditional Jewish sources of self-preservation. No wonder, therefore, that in the time of the European catastrophe so many people striving for survival gave expression to their revolt in words, documenting their ghastly experiences in the ghettoes, concentration camps, and Nazi torture chambers through poetry, songs, satirical verses, drawings, and caricatures.

In his treatise "Goethe und Ghetto" pondering the moral significance of creativity in the Terezín ghetto, Victor Ullmann wrote: "By no means did we sit weeping by the rivers of Babylon; our endeavors in the arts were commensurate with our will to live."[1]

What took place in Terezín is undoubtedly a unique phenomenon: culture became the elixir of life for the ghetto inmates. At issue are the activities of thousands of artists, both professional and amateur, spectators and listeners, concerts and performances of the highest standard, poetry readings, other creative activities, and above all the composition of musical works, an outpouring unparalleled in the life of the concentration camps. All this was an outcome of the secret Nazi design, the dual mission of this camp: it was intended for the decimation of its inhabitants as part of the overall extermination design but was simultaneously creating an instrument of propaganda for a false alibi.

For this reason special conditions and facilities were provided for performances and cultural activities, which in turn afforded the inmates certain advantages and concessions. Although the people in Terezín lived in the shadow of constantly threatened deportations, in appalling housing conditions and pervading hunger, compared with other concentration camps the situation in Terezín had a certain degree of "decency." The inmates themselves called this *Leben als ob* (life as if), the phrase deriving from an ironic couplet by Leo Strauss. People did in fact have their modest corner for their private possessions; they wore their own clothes, and occasionally correspondence was even allowed.

Terezín was the only concentration camp where religious life was practiced undisturbed: Jewish rites were observed and the festivals celebrated. Religious burial was permitted to a certain degree. It is noteworthy that many of the more religious communities, mainly Moravian, had brought with them their Torah, Megillah, Shofar, Kiddush goblets, and candelabra. Some individuals managed to bring prayer books, Passover Haggadah, festival *machzorim, tallis, tefillin*, and *tachrichim* (shrouds) for their last journey.[2] Religious services and rituals were observed from the very beginning. With the arrival of the first rabbis, the Council of Elders chairman Jacob Edelstein, himself a religious Jew, appointed the chief rabbi of Brno, Zikmund Unger, together with Erich Weiner of Pilsen and Vojtěch Schön of Brno as his assistants, as a kind of Beth Din (religious court). In effect, this body was incorporated into the *Beerdigungswesen* (funeral team) that attended to the deceased. Rabbi Richard Feder, reminiscing on this sacred duty, wrote: "Our hardest work was to officiate at funerals. This was truly exhausting work, which was also the reason why we performed this duty only once a week . . . The bodies of the dead were washed by God-fearing people well-versed in the rites. By order of the German command it was forbidden to place any textiles in the coffins but we had paper shrouds to clothe the dead before laying them in the wooden coffins. Up to August 1942 every corpse was interred in a separate grave. Then mass graves were dug to receive as many as thirty-six coffins."[3]

Curiously enough, neither Nazi censorship nor the ban on performing Jewish music applied in the ghetto. The foremost factor in the development of cultural life was the leadership of the Terezín Jewish self-administration. In close cooperation with artists and educators from the Youth Welfare Department, the leaders exploited existing conditions for clandestine cultural and educational activities to give hope to the ghetto population.[4] Another important factor was the large number of well-known artists, cultural figures, and musicians from the Protectorate who were among the first to arrive at Terezín, together with the Work Detail (*Aufbaukommando*), on November 24 and December 4, 1941. Among them were the musicians Gideon Klein, Rafael Schächter, Karel Švenk, and others. Significantly, they all brought their musical instruments as part of the limited amount of "necessities" they were allowed to bring. Later, with the arrival of transports from Germany and Austria (and later from Holland and Denmark as well), their numbers were augmented with artists from these countries.

According to survivors' testimony, as early as the first week of December 1941 "social evenings" took place in the garrets and other billets first inhabited, in the dark or by the light of a single candle.[5] It was in this atmosphere that the first Hanukkah evening was celebrated in late December, led by the choir conducted by Karl Fischer, cantor from Teplitz-Schönau, performing psalms and other liturgical melodies mourning for the freedom they had lost. This and other choirs later became an integral part of the ceremonies and celebrations of the Jewish holidays that were held in all the barracks and makeshift prayer rooms.[6]

At the beginning all cultural events were mounted spontaneously. However, with time, activities came to be organized under the aegis of the self-administration within the context of the official "free-time activities" (*Freizeitgestaltung*). Secular music was composed, choirs were formed, skits were performed satirizing the Nazi New Order, and popular couplets sprang up commenting with pointed irony on the inmates' life and the various misdemeanors of the camp.[7] The musical entertainments encouraged optimism; many of the songs and couplets were sung throughout Terezín, while people worked or peeled potatoes as well as on the stage. Their effect is echoed in the telling refrain from Karel Švenk's "Terezín March," which became the camp anthem.[8] As of December 1943, with the issuing of the regulation on town beautification (*Stadtverschönerung*), the camp command became actively involved in the quality of concerts and the level of performances.[9] At the same time, however, dozens of people were dying daily and the transports eastward to the extermination camps were continuing. Simultaneously, for "aesthetic" reasons, the people selected for the transports were the elderly, the starving, and the sick. This took place prior to the memorable inspection visit of the ICRC on June 23, 1944.

Although there was no visual evidence in the camp of brutish terror, the hopeless situation of the elderly emaciated by hunger and of the sick moaning in their garrets could not be overlooked. Evidence of the death toll was provided by the hearses daily conveying coffins to the mortuary. In the prevailing circumstances, it was only natural that large numbers of artists sank into apathy and depression. Many of them spent their whole day performing a variety of physically exhausting tasks. It demanded considerable mental stamina to prevent acceptance and resignation and to rise above the gloom of daily life and personal bitterness.

The shock already experienced by the Jews prior to deportation, both as individuals and as a community uprooted and degraded, left them deeply scarred. The national identity crisis was mirrored throughout all strata of Jewish society. Hanuš Hachenburg, aged fourteen, expressed the issue succinctly in his poem: "To which people do I belong? . . . Will Bohemia, will the world be my home?"[10] This dilemma is reflected in the creative work throughout the years of captivity. Compared with other inmates, however, for the Jews of Bohemia and Moravia their removal to Terezín was less agonizing. The proximity of Prague and the "home pastures" of Bohemia gave them the feeling that their stay was but a temporary one and that they would soon return "home." It was thanks to these circumstances and their creative vigor that they assumed the leading position in all cultural spheres.

The Jews from Germany and Austria, in contrast, found themselves in an alien, antagonistic environment, in grim physical conditions, and in spiritual chaos.[11] Moreover, utterly shattering was the realization that they had been uprooted and driven out from a people with whom they had identified linguistically and culturally for many centuries. Nevertheless, with the help of sarcastic humor most of the creative artists managed to come to terms with the appalling situation in which they found themselves. The literary satirical cabarets and couplets of the Jews from Germany and Vienna (Hans Hofer and Leo Strauss) are characterized by self-mockery and a macabre wit.[12]

Spiritual resistance seeks expression in the religious sphere, in the field of literary, musical, and plastic arts, and in culture in a broader sense. Essentially, there were two kinds of cultural activity in the ghetto: culture and entertainment for the inmates in the interests of self-preservation, and purely creative activities—artists' emotional expression as a personal avowal and a way of defying the enemy. It goes without saying that attachment to one's native country and culture as well as belief in the future were the most vital factors. Here we shall limit ourselves to citing only the outstanding accomplishments of a selection of artists whose works are inextricably linked with the Terezín phenomenon.

It is amazing that neither the daily difficulties and problems nor the fear of the transports succeeded in permanently silencing people's creative talents. Artistic effort in such conditions, particularly composing music in a concentration camp, demanded immense intellectual and spiritual strength, which only a few musicians were able to summon up. That certain individuals did manage to do this testified above all to their tenacity, reflected in the motifs that inspired

them: first and foremost home and family and a longing for freedom and for a ⟩ ⟩
return to traditional Jewish roots.

It is interesting to note that no really outstanding works of prose emerged. It was as if writers had lost their footing. Even an outstanding writer like Karel Poláček did not manage to produce anything remarkable during the time of his detention. In his diary, Miloš Salus made some interesting observations about why Terezín primarily inspired amateurs and chroniclers: "I provide them [the authors] with pencils, paper, inform them about events, all in vain . . . Perhaps they have learned to interpret the world only as a stimulus for their own imagination. Yet life in Terezín leads to the growth of blossoms of such strange shapes, such profound beauty, such terrible profundity, that it exceeds even the artist's imagination."[13]

In poetry, too, we cannot speak of a high creative level. Many inmates turned to poetry as a temporary solace, driven by the desire to document their sorrow and the will to overcome their loneliness. A number of theories—not mutually exclusive—have been advanced about this phenomenon. Two of the standard assessments (by Adler and Lederer—both former Terezín inmates) concur on this issue. Adler viewed these poems as "average products of Terezín verse-illness," prompted both by their authors' will to live and by boredom. Lederer's critique is milder, although he too believes that the standard was mediocre: "Though most of the writers and poets were adults, their work bore the mark of immaturity . . . The style of the writers was conventional; the older generation clung to the patterns established by the literature of the nineteenth century, while the younger poets paraphrased the well-worn Socialist catchwords of the twenties . . . Genuine and strong as were their sentiments, their poems were spiritless and conventional."[14]

The ghetto library was a unique phenomenon and deserves special mention.[15] After the war Emil Utitz, former head of the *Ghettobücherei*, commented on the birth of the library and its role. With regard to its holdings, he noted the lack of works of fiction. To compensate for this state of affairs, he prided himself, "we had over 10,000 valuable Hebrew works, and also some very rare literature." The Germans, he said, "regarded our entire work in general as a kind of cultural decoration that fundamentally did not interest them. For us, however, it was bitterly serious to supply the camp with spiritual fare."[16]

To understand this pride and joy we need to mention another unique cultural enterprise—the "open university." An echo of its existence is provided by the October 17, 1942, diary entry by Egon Redlich: "26 years old—last year [of the war] 10 months in Terezín. Wedding." That very day, while reflecting on "developing HeHalutz" to meet the future and the "Hebrew circle," he mentions the phenomenon of the open university operating in Terezín and compares it to the Czech Enlightenment, which heralded the rebirth of the nation and the establishment of the Czechoslovak Republic: "A Hebrew circle. Many people participate in it, a great number of experts. Indeed, it gives the impression of an assembly of Czech cultural activities during the period of the Enlightenment. We are 150 years behind."[17]

There is evidence to the effect that 2,309 lectures were delivered on culture, art, music, science, medicine, and economics. A total of 489 individuals are said to have been involved in giving lectures. Of these, more than four hundred were devoted to Jewish topics within the "Jewish Academy," covering three main categories: Judaism, general Jewish history, and Zionism (Palestine and the Hebrew language).[18]

Jewish life in the Diaspora was illustrated in a wide chronological and geographical range of presentations from the Babylonian Exile down to European and American Jewry in modern times. The most popular issues discussed, it seems, were the history of the Jews in Bohemia and Moravia as well as of the Jewish communities in Prague, Berlin, and Vienna. There was no lack of sophisticated topics: messianic movements in Judaism; Jewish monuments and tombs; Jewish sects and ancient inscriptions; Jewish spirit, humor, names (humor in the Talmud), German humor, French *ésprit*, and Jewish *Witz;* women's studies; mysticism; Judaism and other religions—Moses and Buddha, Moses and Mohammed, Moses and Paul; and Athens, Rome, and Jerusalem.

Philip Manes's moving eyewitness account of the open university can be considered one of the main sources on and guidebooks to this enterprise. He was an unusual, devoted "old gentleman who spent all his free time persistently writing his entries in the chronicle at his bare table in the garret," recorded a fellow inmate. "Everything that had happened to him during his long time there, his artistic work, the work of others, the people with whom art brought him together, his pen captures everything in detailed reports."[19]

It is generally held that chamber music played the prime role. Knowing no language barriers, it could touch people deeply and afford emotional and spiritual upliftment. This was also the sphere in which most cooperation took place—the artistic mainstays of Karel Ančerl's string orchestra were professional musicians from Bohemia, Germany, Holland, and Vienna.

By the same token, all kinds of music were highly popular among the Terezín inmates. Many survivors agree that apart from Verdi's *Requiem*, Hans Krása's children's opera *Brundibár*, and the folk play *Esther*, the most memorable and stirring cultural event was the première of *The Bartered Bride*. They treasure vivid memories of the festive yet surrealistic appearance of Rafael Schächter's choir on November 25, 1942, in the gymnasium of the former school.[20] The soloists had yellow stars sewn onto their clothes, with the choir standing behind them. The audience sat on the floor, perched on gymnastic equipment or windowsills, or stood in the doorways—wherever there was room. And Schächter, the "Spiritus rector," the resourceful conductor and stage director, sat on a vaulting horse at the broken-down piano. Egon Redlich recorded in an animated diary entry the immense response the performance generated.[21]

Another outstanding individual was Ilse Weber, who personifies the Terezín creative paradigm with her activities for the inmates and contributions both literary and musical.[22] Her language was German, and for many years her contribution was overlooked; she was criticized as simplistic. She wrote spontaneously about and for children. Her favorite topics were stories about happy children's lives, little animals, and nature, and she excelled at tender lullabies.

As a nurse, Ilse Weber looked after the sick children in the camp. Part of her therapy was music: she played the guitar, taught poems, and even set up a choir among the children. She wrote more than a hundred poems, the power of which derives from her frank observation and rendering of the experiences, realities, and horrors of life. In some of her poems she expresses criticism of social inequality and a call for human feeling. Her lyrics center on the motifs of the mother, family, home, identity, and human solidarity. Since she spoke to everybody from her soul, her influence was strong in bonding people together.

"Home," so beautiful a word,
my heart cries out aloud.
They took my home away from me,
and now I am without.[23]

Two of her poems stand out as being of historic importance: "The Lidice Sheep" ("Die Schäfe von Lidice") and "Avowal of Belief" ("Bekenntnis"). The first, written in the days of the *heydrichiáda*, echoes her ardent relationship with and sympathy for the suffering Czech people and her native country:

The little village in Bohemia,
and so much misery and suffering.
The little houses,
dwellings of peace—destroyed,
An entire village wiped out,
and only the cattle mercifully spared.[24]

In the second she proudly asserts her Jewish identity and her identification with the suffering of her own people in good times as well as bad.

The longing for freedom and rescue was naturally one of the most frequent themes. This is reflected in programs prepared by authors who wrote in Yiddish and whose theatrical performances made them famous in the camp. Especially popular with the Yiddish-speaking public were programs prepared by Irene Dodal and Eugen Weiss, whose hallmark was a preference for Jewish themes.[25] Dramatic works by I. L. Peretz and Sholom Aleichem were mostly presented by the Jidishe Bühne troupe with participation by composer Ullmann, with his arrangements of Jewish folk melodies, and by artists Bedřich Fritta and František Zelenka, who painted the sets. Transcending linguistic boundaries, these programs were enjoyed by inmates from Austria, Germany, Denmark, and Holland.

In the field of fine arts reference must again be made to the academic painter Bedřich Fritta, whose real name was Fritz Taussig and who headed the Art Department within the framework of the Jewish self-administration.[26] He worked with a group of the best artists and illustrators who had come to Terezín: painters Leo Haas, Otto Ungar, Petr Kien, Felix Bloch, and Dr. Leo Heilbronn and architect Norbert Troller.[27] It was their task when so ordered by the camp commander to illustrate the allocation of the work force, living conditions, and so on by means of graphs, sketches, and drawings. But German intentions aside, the artists set themselves the task of recording in drawings and paintings the real nature of this monstrous town, in order to uncover its farcical setup and the wretched life it afforded. They selected topics and types, the physiognomy of human beings broken by the ravages of age, hunger, and disease and the dramatic day-to-day images of the camp's miserable existence. All these were perpetuated in pictures such as "Night Transport," "Living in a Garret," "Abandoned Luggage," and "Autumn," symbols of human suffering and dying. Fritta's cycle of black and white "still lifes" and his ironic contrasts ("Symbol of Parting—Israel and Sarah," "Prayer Room and Theater") stand out for their timelessness and emotional intensity.

The heroic actions of Fritta and several of his fellow artists in exposing to the free world the true face of Terezín had disastrous consequences: they cruelly were punished for their offense.[28] Their art and courage affect us profoundly, even after the passage of more than fifty years. Some of the artists became known only many years later, after their work was discovered and publicly displayed. Special mention must be made of the work of Max Plaček, who before being removed to Terezín had worked on the staff of the Prague Jewish community and had produced a series of portraits of the community's leading personalities. Although Plaček spent but a year in the ghetto (September 1942– December 1943), he managed to create a collection worthy of an entire lifetime with his portraits of 550 of the most interesting images from all walks of life. Some are sketches in caricature style, emphasizing naked reality. At his express wish, his fellow inmates added to his signature their own names and comments. This "double signature" of fascinating comments affords us a glimpse into the spiritual world of the cultural elite, a most original and dignified memento of the time and place.[29]

A remarkable representative of the young generation who grew to maturity during the war years was Petr Kien, a brilliant twenty-two year old.[30] He was one of the first artists to come to Terezín, and right from the beginning he attracted attention with his imaginative talent. Kien had an innate all-round artistic soul. He wrote poetry before the war and produced over a hundred poems, among them "I Love You, Prague" ("Ich lieb' dich Prag"), reflecting his profound attachment to this city. Many of Kien's verses deal with doubt, never-ending restlessness and uncertainty. Like his talented contemporaries Bonn and Orten, he had premonitions of danger and impending death.

In addition to his allocated work in the ghetto, Kien sought out subjects to paint that were meaningful for him in the spheres of theater, art, and music. Thanks to him a whole gallery of important personalities from the Terezín intellectual elite has been preserved for posterity, each of these portraits depicting the characteristic expressions of the subject. One of the best examples is the portrait of his close friend, the artist Gustav Schorsch: "Both fresh and mature in technique, this was the portrait in which he probably came closest to a synthesis of modern realism."[31]

Kien was active in the literary sphere as well. His most important work was the poetry cycle *The Plague City* (*Die Peststadt*, also translated into Czech and set to music under the title *Mor* by his friend Gideon Klein). The poem is a unique lyrical document of firsthand experiences in the camp, describing the Jewish people's pitiful situation in allegorical reflections and metaphors. Darkness and death in the camp, "The corpses unburied . . . Without breath, bare, torn shirt." His images from the plague city are one of a kind in this genre:

Without breath, bare, with rear thrashed black and blue
Distress tightens the thumb-screws on us
And dulls its blade on our flesh
Yet nobody can rob us of our dreams.[32]

The brilliant young poet's imagery, conjuring up horror and sorrow, is reminiscent of the works of today's most celebrated postwar Holocaust poets, in particular Paul Celan and Nelly Sachs, as pointedly described in Ludvík Václavek's study.[33]

Of the musical works created in Terezín, the achievements of the most distinguished composers, Victor Ullmann, Pavel Haas, and Zikmund Schul, are touched upon here. First place in musical life undoubtedly goes to Victor Ullmann, who had studied with Arnold Schönberg and had already been well-known before the war as a conductor, pianist, choir master, and music critic. Within the framework of free-time activities, he also organized the Studio for Contemporary Music.[34]

Ullmann became involved in creative artistic work and composing soon after arriving in Terezín. In his letter of June 1, 1943, to Otto Zucker he complained that during his nine-month stay, not one single note of his works had been heard in the ghetto—the result of a total silencing (*Totschweigen*) of his music. To Ullmann's satisfaction, Zucker immediately took steps to remedy the situation, as we learn from Ullmann's response of June 7, 1943, warmly thanking him for his assistance.[35]

Within two years Ullmann was able to write more than twenty musical works, although some remained unfinished. In addition to his basic repertoire, Ullmann created *Drei Kinderchöre* using Hebrew texts (1. Hora; 2. Halleluyah; 3. Hedad, hedad, gina ktana). Using Yiddish texts he wrote for male choir *Drei Männerchöre* (1. Yome, mome, spil mir; 2. Du solst nischt geyn; 3. Du meydele, du scheyns). He also wrote two Hassidic choral works for women, *Hala Yarden* and *Drei Männerchöre a capella* (1. As der Rebe; 2. Scha shtill; 3. Fregz die Welt) and two compositions for a capella mixed choir, *Eliahu Hanavi* and *Anu Olim*.[36]

Sonata No. 7, which is considered his last and most demanding work, was completed in August 1944 but not performed in the ghetto. In its finale, in addition to the motifs from the Hussite hymn and the Slovak and Czech national anthem *Kde domov můj*, there can also be distinguished both Luther's *Wir danken alle Gott* and the strains of Rachel's Hebrew poetry of the 1930s, as set to music by Yehuda Sharett.[37] It is the biblical figure of Rachel the matriarch, whom Rachel the poetess evokes: "Her blood, which flows in mine, her voice, which sounds in mine." The choice of motifs and the date of composition, during the years of hardship in riot-torn Palestine, convey to us "the message of consolation and of hope."[38]

Ullmann's most important work is undoubtedly the opera "The Emperor of Atlantis or: Death Resigns" (*Der Kaiser von Atlantis; oder Der Tod dankt ab*), composed with a German libretto written in 1943 by Peter Kien.[39] It is a satirical allegory on the Third Reich, with allusions to Hitler's tyranny. The musical imagery includes a motif from the German national anthem. The opera ends with an adaptation of Martin Luther's famous hymn "A Mighty Fortress Is Our God." This work, unique both for its substance and in quality, was rehearsed at Terezín in September 1944. However, it was never performed, apparently at the suggestion of the self-administration; the leaders were troubled by its powerful symbolic and rebellious content.

The first to use a motif from *Deutschland, Deutschland über alles* in a parody was the composer Carlo S. Taube in the *Theresienstädter Symphonie*, performed in the Magdeburg Barracks a year earlier. From reminiscences of survivors we learn that on May 3, in the same Magdeburg Barracks, a program called "Ghetto Lullaby" was performed within the framework of Taube's "Ghetto Suite" for orchestra and alto soloist.[40] One of the inmates recalled the shattering effect of the third movement, the recitation of Erika Taube with a pianissimo obligato from the orchestra. The lullaby of a Jewish mother was reminiscent of Hebraic chants. The climax was unforgettable: "There followed a turbulent finale in which the first four bars of *Deutschland über alles* were repeated over and over again in more and more wrathful spasms, until the last outcry . . . '*Deutschland, Deutschland*' . . . did not continue to "*über alles*,' but died out in a terrible dissonance."[41]

Already at that time the public had a clear grasp of the profound meaning of the piece and of Taube's courage.[42]

Alas, the score of Taube's work has been lost. (Another of his compositions, found after the war, was the lullaby *Ein jüdisches Kind*, with words written by his wife Erika Taube and music by Taube himself. Dated November 4, 1942, it was dedicated to the great music lover Otto Zucker.) "Most of the artists and musicians involved in preparing the production of the *Kaiser von Atlantis* perished in late October 1944 in the Auschwitz gas chambers as the last victims."

Before his deportation, Ullmann left his work with Prof. Dr. Emil Utitz, asking Utitz to pass it on to his friend Dr. H. G. Adler, should he not return from the camp. (Ullmann set to music Adler's poem cycle *Der Mensch und sein Tag*.) Why Adler failed to fulfill his dead friend's last wish is a mystery: Ullmann's Theresienstadt legacy remained stored "in safe-keeping" in Adler's archives in London for over thirty years. It was Kerry Woodward of the BBC Music Department who by pure chance discovered the existence of the score. In 1975, the opera finally had its festive premicre in Amsterdam under Woodward's baton.[43] By that time, sadly, Ullmann's reputation as a composer had fallen into oblivion. The opera was subsequently performed in other European cities, in Israel, and also in America and in Prague, being exceptionally well received. Ullmann's work was hailed as the pinnacle of artistic creation and at the same time as the most ardent protest against war and Nazi barbarism.

It is noteworthy, however, that in referring to the most important composers in Terezín, Adler mentioned Victor Ullmann first; next were Karl Reiner, who survived the war, Pavel Haas, Hans Krása, Zikmund Schul, and Gideon Klein.[44] It is also interesting that while Adler frequently drew on Ullmann's music criticism; he made only passing reference to the *Kaiser von Atlantis*.[45] Strangely, in the alphabetical listing he referred to the score under the letter K (= Kien), asserting that the work "had scarcely any allusions to Theresienstadt."[46] He omitted to indicate, however, that Ullmann's Theresienstadt legacy was in his archives. For many years it was therefore believed that the scores were irretrievably lost.

In this connection it is relevant to note that Adler and Ullmann differed in their views with regard to the ethical significance and value of cultural activities in Terezín. Ullmann summed up his views on the *Freizeitgestaltung*, incisively defining his own "shaping of the material in the Terezín conditions," as follows:

> Terezín was and is for me the school of form . . . In Terezín I have written a fair amount of new music, mainly to meet the needs and wishes of conductors, stage directors, pianists and singers, and hence the needs of the *Freizeitgestaltung* of the ghetto . . . However, it must be emphasized that Terezín has served to enhance . . . not to impede my musical activities, that by no means did we sit weeping by the rivers of Babylon, . . . our determination in the cultural sphere was commensurate with our will to live. And I am convinced that all those who, in life and in art, were fighting to force form upon resisting matter will agree with me.[47]

In contrast to this view, Adler commented negatively on the cultural activities that took place "at the initiative of the Nazis." Indeed, he viewed them as a "loss of a sense of reality" and even as self-deception: "One benumbed oneself, denied the present and, worst of all, unsuspectingly willingly carried out the wishes of the ss . . . The intended deception of [outside] visitors became the self-deception of the prisoners."[48]

It is also characteristic that Adler, who must have been aware of how Pavel Haas and Victor Ullmann metamorphosed in Terezín, described their ties with Judaism thus: "As a Czech he felt as remote from Judaism as Ullmann did as a German. Haas was a cheerful, carefree person . . . in total contrast to Ullmann's metaphysical broodings."[49]

It was known that Ullmann's father, a high-ranking Austrian officer, had converted to gain promotion in his military career; Ullmann himself as a youth had converted from Catholicism to Protestantism and later, under the influence of his friend Albert Steffen, became an adherent of Rudolf Steiner's anthroposophical teachings.[50] He drew closer to Judaism only after his second return to the Bohemian capital, shortly after Hitler's rise to power, mixing primarily with Jewish intellectuals. Ullmann expressed his personal fate after the Wehrmacht's occupation of Bohemia and Moravia in the composition *Aus der Tiefe rufe ich, Herr, zu dir* (Psalm 130).[51] Since his efforts to emigrate were unsuccessful, he remained in Prague, where he made a living for his family by teaching music in the retraining courses organized by the Jewish Religious Community for future emigrants, as did other Jewish musicians.[52] Something of a change occurred in his attitude to Judaism as the war began. It was only natural that an artist with such firm ethical principles as Ullmann could not remain indifferent to the fate of his family and people. In the last portion of his life, in Terezín, his view intensified. Paul Nettl wrote about Ullmann that he "was one of the most talented musicians of his time as well as a man of high ethical principles."[53]

Pavel Haas, already known before the war as a leading student of Leoš Janáček, reached Terezín from Brno with the first transports. As we know, he was never alienated from Judaism: synagogue melodies and biblical motifs had always inspired him.[54] After his arrival in the ghetto he remained apathetic and unproductive for months and in impaired health. However, encouraged by friends, above all by Gideon Klein, he nevertheless managed to find a new source of inspiration. His first composition was *Al S'fod* (Do not lament), an arrangement for string orchestra of a Hebrew text, completed on November 30, 1942. The text was written by the poet David Shimoni during the period of the Jewish settlers' struggles in Palestine in 1928–29 (originally set to music by J. Milet).

The essence of the composition is the spirit of rebellion against oppression. In the concluding hymn section, the nation is called to new life: "The blood calls the soul of the people"; "Be rejuvenated and create! Free yourself and redeem!" This composition bears additional symbolism: it was preserved as part of a special collection of commemorative scores by a number of composers (dated November 30 and December 4, 1942) compiled on the occasion of the anniversary of the ghetto's founding.[55] Also notable is the Hebrew cryptogram on the title page of *Al S'fod*. The Hebrew text, enciphered by Haas to appear as musical notes, reads: "Memento of the first and [may] it [also be] the last anniversary in the Terezín exile—end (*Mazkeret leyom hashana harishon vehu haacharon begalut Terezín—sof*), composed in Terezin, 30.11.1942 for male choir to Hebrew words by Pavel Haas, dedicated by the author to Eng. Otto Zucker."[56]

It is touching that through this unique gesture, Haas expressed his appreciation of his fellow Brno townsman, the art connoisseur Zucker, for Zucker's devoted support of cultural life in the ghetto.

Lubomír Peduzzi, Haas's former student and biographer, commented on

Adler's description of Haas's nature: "He obviously did not belong to the circle of Haas's friends."[57] In Peduzzi's view, and also according to the evidence of contemporaries, it is clear that in the last years of his life Haas "was very pathetic, pale, anticipating horrors." As far as his national affiliations were concerned, also reflected in his musical work, we read in Peduzzi's biography: "And there are *loci communes* connecting Haas's melodic phrases, consciously derived from Hebraic songs, through the Gregorian chant with the song of St. Wenceslas. This is a connection symbolizing the lot that befell the composer, as determined by his belonging to the Jewish race as well as to the Czech nation."[58]

Haas's principal work, *Vier Lieder auf Worte der chinesischen Poesie* (Four songs to the text of Chinese poetry), written with the encouragement of Karel Berman, was called a "gem of lyrical composition."[59] Its first performance at Terezín took place on June 22, 1944, sung by Karel Berman with piano accompaniment by Rafael Schächter. The third part of the work is the emotional climax. It conveys suffering, pain, and a loneliness that cannot be described in words, expressed by Haas through simple repetition: "My hands, my hands, how empty you are, to say all that, to say all that."[60]

The connecting link among all the songs is the fourth one: the vision of the happy return home, a motif derived from the Old Czech St. Wenceslas' chorale. *Vier Lieder* was exceptionally well received: Victor Ullmann honored the composition by calling it a "masterpiece."[61]

Zikmund Schul focused primarily on Jewish liturgical music in Terezín. He was from Kassel and had studied in Prague with Paul Hindemith and Alois Hába before the war. At that time he often visited the Lieben family, under whose influence he began to develop an interest in medieval music and Cabbalism. In Terezín he composed the *Divertimento Ebraico* for string orchestra and *Zwei chassidische Tänze* for violin and cello as well as liturgical songs for a boys' choir and cantorial melodies. Also preserved is a one-page fragment of his composition *Finale di Cantata Judaica*, based on the daily prayer—"Teka, teka, teka be-shofar gadol lecherutenu"—evoking liberation.[62] Schul died in Terezín in June 1944, aged twenty-eight. Having become friendly with Victor Ullmann in the ghetto, he entrusted his musical legacy to Ullmann. Ullmann was profoundly affected by Schul's death and wrote an obituary and an elegiac poem to the "uniquely gifted artist," who was "more than a hope" at the beginning of his musical career.[63]

Terezín is known for the careful attention given to the children and their welfare. Indeed, it may be said that the children's homes and education of the young were one of the self-administration's greatest achievements in its "race against time" approach.

The situation of children and youngsters as well as the educational activities provided by their teachers have been abundantly described in the literature. The high standard of the efforts is reflected in the numerous youth magazines put out by the various children's homes, which mirror the reality of Terezín while also reflecting the internal debate: criticism of the bureaucracy and of the prevailing conditions.[64]

The work and devotion of educators and instructors from different backgrounds and outlooks (Czech-Jewish, assimilationist-oriented, Communist, and Zionist) still await a sociologist's analysis. The youth collectives "were quasi-islands for the moral continuity of the young people's ideals," enhancing their spiritual growth and influencing their outlook.[65] The instructors led the children to think independently and to undertake literary activities on their own.

Until recently the prevailing view was that the culture and education were predominantly left-wing oriented, influenced mainly by Communist ideas. On the whole, mention of the Zionist-influenced children's homes (Maccabi HaTza'ir, HeHalutz, and HaShomer HaTza'ir) was either omitted or portrayed in negative terms. It is not without interest that in these communes, the modes of daily life were influenced by the tradition of the Jewish scout movement, and thus in many respects, one may perceive in their group cohesion and educational ideology some likeness to the genesis of the kibbutzim in Palestine.[66] In addition there was a Hebrew circle where the Hebrew language was taught in preparation for life in Eretz Israel.[67] Educational activities intensified in the years 1943–44, when cultural life reached its peak. A major contribution in this sphere was made by Dr. Franz Kahn, who played a leading part in the free-time activities after arriving from Prague in January 1943. By way of illustration, from July 10 to 16, 1944, he organized a "commemorative week" marking the fortieth anniversary of Theodor Herzl's death, highlighting the Zionist leader's personality and thinking.[68]

At the end of 1943 and mainly during 1944, influenced by events unfolding on the Eastern Front, the Marxist instructors and educators intensively disseminated Communist ideology.[69] In essence it can be stated, however, that regardless of their ideological affiliation, all teachers who devoted themselves to their young charges' education bolstered the youngsters' will, adding fervor to their perseverance. In his work addressing the polarity of Jewish existence, Professor Ernst Simon provided a striking portrayal of the educational activities during the Nazi reign of terror, viewing them as the epitome of all intellectual and spiritual efforts to retain a human countenance.[70]

It seems that under the impact of the massive revelations about the creative cultural activities of the children's homes, Adler mellowed his critical views. In 1972, on the occasion of an exhibition in London of paintings by the internationally acclaimed Yehuda Bacon, it was Adler who saluted the artist. In his *Profile* he described Bacon's "phenomenal variety of means of expression" and "grippingly forceful images." At the same time he underlined the positive role and "the strangely salutary atmosphere of Jewish and Zionist idealism," which in fact helped people "spiritually in overcoming the horror and the deprivation."[71]

The Vienna artist Friedl Dicker-Brandeis, already known for her artistic work before the war, devoted all her time and skill to the education of the children. In the ghetto she gave drawing lessons using the advanced therapeutic method. This innovative approach tended to reduce the abnormal psychological pressures and burdens to which the children were subject.[72] Her method and her creative instruction, immortalized in the celebrated drawings of the children of Terezín, earned the artist international recognition.

It has been asserted that the influence of the communal and cultural activities had the effect of producing cohesion among the Terezín detainees, adults and youngsters alike. This intense experience of community bonding they took with them when most of them were deported in September 1943 to Birkenau, where the Czech "family camp" was erected.[73] Thus even in the conditions of Auschwitz, in the shadow of the chimneys of the nearby crematoria, this collective of prisoners was able to form a new human and social entity. Here too the high point was reached in the activities of the children's block, to which a group of devoted instructors and teachers made a major contribution, led by the famous youth leader Fredy Hirsch.[74] They battled daily with the brutal surroundings, teaching the children clandestinely and singing Czech and Hebrew songs with them.

There is poetic justice in the fact that the courageous behavior of this special Terezín transport has been preserved in writing. From the dramatic description of Salmen Gradowski, a member of the Sonderkommando and a witness to the murder of the Czech transport, we learn of the women's dignified conduct on that night in their final moments in the very bowels of hell.[75] They resisted to their last breath, singing in the gas chambers the Czech national anthem "Kde domov můj," "Hatikvah," the Internationale, and the song of the Soviet partisans. It is thus no coincidence that it was a young poetess imbued with the communal spirit of Terezín who left her message to the civilized world in a lyrical poem written before the gassing in Auschwitz: *Wir tote klagen an* (We, the dead, accuse).[76]

Faith and religious observance in the ghetto present complex issues; theologians have wrestled with these for more than half a century. In Terezín, with its pluralistic, imposed society of various religious shades—including a spectrum of denominations of the Christian faith—there were certain phenomena that may lead to surprising conclusions in comparison with other camps.[77] We should mention, however, that the believers mostly belonged to the ranks of the elderly, primarily Jews from Austria and Germany. Those young people in the ghetto who identified with Judaism were motivated mainly on national-historic grounds. The festivals—Purim, Pesach, Shavuot, Rosh Hashana, Yom Kippur, and Hanukkah—were mostly observed in Zionist youth homes, primarily in a historical context.[78]

Several testimonies relate that on the Sabbath, summer and winter alike, people gathered in improvised locales, in crowded garrets and in catacombs, most of them standing, listening to the rabbis' sermons and fervently reciting Hebrew prayers.[79]

Reflecting on the issue of religion, Emil Utitz came to the conclusion that "despite all the trials and tribulations, devoutness certainly did not diminish." On the eve of the High Holy Days, he noted, "candles burned in many houses— God knows where people got them—and men and women prayed, immersed in thought. Somehow they maintained an awareness that God . . . would protect them from destruction and reverence for the impenetrability of His ways."[80]

We also know that most of the rabbis participated in the activities of the Freizeitgestaltung as consultants and advisers, as teachers of the Bible and Talmud, and primarily as comforters, easing the personal suffering of adults and children. Above all two rabbis played a prominent role: the much beloved rabbi of Kolín, Dr. Richard Feder, and the rabbi Dr. Leo Baeck, who with his universal view of the Jewish faith also turned his attention to Christians of Jewish extraction and comforted them in their grim situation.[81]

There is grim irony in the fact that the coexistence of the three ethnic elements died out in Terezín. For several hundred years the Czech, German, and Jewish peoples and cultures had mutually influenced and enriched one another on Bohemian soil. In the extreme setting of German hegemony under the Nazis and the ambiguous circumstances of this ghetto, the ethnic rapprochement of centuries was stripped away to a narrow core. After the war, Karl Ančerl observed: "Indeed, the Nazis practically managed to wipe out the Jews. But what they did not succeed in doing, and could never manage to do, was to destroy the idea of what is human in humanity."[82]

It is indeed a paradox, but thanks to the creative drive of its inmates hovering between life and death, Terezín has entered the general consciousness as a double entendre, an oxymoron. The contrasts and dual associations hold fast on both the intellectual and emotional level: *Peststadt* (plague city) was also *Kulturstadt* (the city of culture), the sole spot on the map of German concentration camps that, like a satiric couplet, can simultaneously elicit a mocking smile and a tear. One cannot but grieve that most of the inmates and creative artists, including the children, perished in the last months of the war. At the same time Terezín will always be remembered as the only place in Europe where spiritual strength prevailed and where the monster was defeated.

The closing words of the finale of the children's opera *Brundibár* exemplify this sweeping message: "Brundibár is defeated! . . . the barbarian . . . everybody join 'our song of victory!' Whoever has seen this play will keep in mind: how one fights back together, and thus breaks the power of evil."[83]

Terezín saw the completion of Leo Baeck's historical work *Dieses Volk*, chronicling the tenacity of the Jewish people. It was there that Gideon Klein composed his piano sonatas and his trio, paying homage to his Moravian birthplace. There echoed first the strains of Haas's nostalgic dreaming of homecoming, the emotive power of which will forever remain comforting. It was Victor Ullmann who recognized their beauty and universal value when he wrote: "As soon as one has heard them, one can no longer do without them, wishing to live with them in intimate companionship."[84] It was in Terezín that *Der Kaiser von Atlantis* was created—the most illustrious emblem of the Holocaust's spiritual legacy.

Reminiscing about the cultural activities, the prominent baritone soloist Karel Berman of the Prague National Theater predicted that one day, after everything about the ghetto of Terezín had been recorded, humanity would be amazed at how "adults and children, in constant expectation of death, lived a full, noble life, between pain and anxiety," how among people, "mussulmans" [those more dead than alive], in hunger and misery . . . lived a life that was a miracle under the given conditions."[85]

The most precious legacy handed down to posterity is, of course, the collection of drawings and paintings by the children of Terezín.[86] These little prisoners expressed their dreams and hopes in their artwork. From their living quarters they saw the hills of Bohemia, the beautiful landscape and the road leading to Prague, so near and yet so far! They drew flowers, fields, graceful princesses, colored butterflies—but also the stark reality: a funeral procession and an execution by hanging. A number of the drawings portray the Seder night with touching simplicity: the family sitting around the table, laid in the traditional manner, the illustrated Haggadah relating the Exodus of the Children of

Israel from Egypt, reverberating with the promise: from slavery to freedom. Alas, only a few of them lived to see this wish come true.

The new millennium has seen a reappraisal of the historiography of Terezín and publication of several studies dealing mainly with cultural aspects and the open university.[87] It seems that the unique phenomenon of this ghetto will keep engaging historians, educators, and artists in forthcoming decades.

Epilogue
Between 1945 and the Velvet
Revolution of 1989

Historians term the immediate postwar years (1945–48) the period of "pseudo-democracy" to indicate that the reconstructed state was not a continuation of the pre-Munich First Republic. In spite of certain similarities and the fact that President Beneš was reinstated, from the outset both internal and external affairs took a different turn. In the wake of the Teheran and Yalta agreements determining the "division of spheres of influence," Czechoslovakia was occupied by Russian troops; only Budějovice, Pilsen, and some other localities in western Bohemia were for a short time under American occupation.

The so-called Košice program of the new government of April 4, 1945, delineated domestic policy according to a draft meticulously drawn up by leading Czech Communist exiles in Moscow with a view to changing the social order.[1] They were to occupy key posts in the cabinet of Prime Minister Klement Gottwald, who would become the new president after Beneš's resignation in June 1948. While President Beneš's ambiguous attitude toward the Jews during his years of exile in London has received adequate attention, his attitudes and policy after the end of the war have not so far been appraised.

As a true disciple of Masaryk, Beneš remained a staunch supporter of Zionism during the war years while he was head of the Czechoslovak Government-in-Exile. This is clear from his declaration made on April 17, 1941, to the World Jewish Congress delegation visiting his home in Putney: "He was sure that the civilized world would find a reasonable settlement of the Jewish question after the war and that he and his Government would do their best to facilitate this."[2]

On the occasion of a mass rally organized by the Zionist Federation in London on October 30, 1942, to mark the twenty-fifth anniversary of the Balfour Declaration, both President Beneš and Jan Masaryk sent messages of encouragement to Chaim Weizmann. Beneš recalled events in 1917–18 and the connections that had existed between the two nations in their struggle for liberation: "We Czechoslovaks have always been following with sympathies the Zionist efforts for the creation of a Jewish National Home in Palestine. My great predecessor and teacher, T. G. Masaryk, recalls in his Memoirs how deeply impressed he was in November 1917 by the manifestation of 150,000 Jews in Kiev who gathered in front of the British Consulate in order to express their thanks for the Balfour Declaration. He also recalls the conference of small nations, which under Masaryk's chairmanship took place in Philadelphia in October 1918."[3]

Beneš was convinced that with the establishment of a new Jewish homeland it would be up to the Jews to decide "whether they are for [emigration to] Palestine or for assimilation (in the national sense) into the nation of the country where they live."[4] Beneš lived to see the birth of the state of Israel and the elation generated among Jewish survivors in Czechoslovakia following the United Nations resolution of November 29, 1947, as expressed in demonstrations of joy in Prague and throughout the country.[5] However, because of his illness (he resigned on June 6, 1948), it was Klement Gottwald who extended official recognition to the State of Israel on May 18, 1948.

As a result of the transfer of the German minority and the mass exchange of population with Hungary, the prewar multinational state became almost entirely homogeneous, the Czechs and Slovaks constituting over 94 percent of the population. In keeping with the newly adopted national and minority policy the status of the Jewish entity was no longer recognized. Henceforth Jews could adhere to either Czech or Slovak nationality.

The hallmarks of the newly reconstructed republic became nationalization of industries and land reform, which augured ill for industrial plant owners whose property had been Aryanized by the Nazis. The enforcement of the initial laws concerning indemnity and restitution of property encountered many encroachments by extreme nationalists as well as fanatical Communists seeking ways of placing the Nazi-expropriated Jewish assets under national administration.[6] A definitive Law of Restitution (128/1946) was promulgated on May 16, 1946.

The first laws enacted by presidential decree set up special "people's courts" to bring to justice traitors and Nazi collaborators. It is a sad fact, however, that these trials were greatly influenced by the ongoing strife between the members of the London emigration and the Communist activists who spent the war years in Moscow. The courts were mainly concerned with political offenses, "the collaboration of members of the Protectorate government with the arch enemy, during the period of the greatest menace."[7] The judges themselves related to the Jewish issues marginally. The anti-Jewish legislation was dealt with solely in the trials of the Nazi chieftains, first and foremost in the trials of State Secretary Karl H. Frank and the commandants and guards of the ghetto of Terezín.[8]

During the first postwar years Czechoslovakia played a unique role in the building up of the Jewish entity: the liberated country became the transit point for thousands of survivors of the Holocaust and refugees from neighboring countries who reached its borders desperately seeking passage to their coveted destination, Palestine. As early as mid-October 1945 Foreign Minister Masaryk allocated Ehud Avriel, representing the Brihah branch of the Haganah, nine trains to be used to transport escapees from Poland and Austria to the American occupation zone in Germany, where they were put up in displaced persons' camps.[9]

In the course of time a massive exodus of Jewish survivors from Poland, Rumania, and Hungary passed across the Czechoslovak borders to Germany. In July 1946 Brihah had been granted official recognition by the Czechoslovak Government as a rescue agency for survivors, and the organization had begun cooperating closely with the Ministry of Social Welfare. The Haganah head-quarters set up at 7 Josefovská Street, in the heart of the ancient Jewish ghetto in Prague, expanded its activities as the outpost of the army procurement unit (Rehesh), headed by Uriel Doron (Dr. Otto Felix—a former Czechoslovak citizen who had emigrated to Palestine before the war).

The first arms deal between Czechoslovakia and the Jewish state-in-the-making was concluded on December 1, 1947, two days after the adoption of the United Nations resolution on the establishment of a Jewish state in Palestine. Czechoslovakia was at that time "the only country to facilitate an open transaction of arms at reasonable, even low prices," wrote the mastermind behind this significant deal, Ehud Avriel, many years later.[10]

On May 18, 1948, Czechoslovakia was among the first countries following the Soviet Union to recognize the State of Israel. Moreover, some hours prior to David Ben-Gurion's historic announcement of the declaration of the Jewish state a cable of congratulations from the mayor of Prague was received by the mayor of Tel Aviv.[11]

Ehud Avriel became the first diplomatic representative of the State of Israel: he arrived in Prague on May 21, and on July 28, 1948, he presented his credentials to President Klement Gottwald. The first Czechoslovak minister to Israel, Professor Eduard Goldstücker, a leading intellectual and member of the Communist Party, arrived to Tel Aviv in 1950. (Two years later during the Slánský Trials he was recalled from his post and was subsequently arrested and sentenced to a lengthy prison term.)[12]

Sympathetic attitudes toward the fledgling State of Israel were expressed in official declarations as well as in trade and cultural relations, and there was open friendliness and goodwill in the air both in the higher echelons and among the ordinary people.[13] At the same time some political leaders kept alluding to the issue of Jewish allegiance. Thus Minister Václav Kopecký, ostensibly following the Communist party line but in reality an opportunist known for his anti-Jewish declarations, made this double-edged statement: "This is a historical moment which has no equal in human history. Only now is the Jewish nation being born, because it is finally acquiring all the conditions of national existence as defined by Stalin [!]. Jews have to choose between total assimilation and joining their nation in helping to build up Palestine."[14]

The Communist takeover in February 1948 and the death of Jan Masaryk two weeks later made Israeli leaders apprehensive as far as future cooperation was concerned. However, Vlado Clementis, the new foreign minister, pursued his predecessor's line in giving his consent to various Israeli requests for arms, thus responding to Ben-Gurion's urgent demand that arms be dispatched by air in order to avoid British interception at sea. For this purpose the military airfield at Žatec, some seventy-five kilometers west of Prague (code-named Etzion Base), was placed at the disposal of the Haganah under the command of Yehuda (Brieger) Ben Chorin, a member of Kibbutz Hazorea. It was there that rifles, machine guns, mortars, and even fighter planes (repaired or reequipped) were hastily loaded to be flown to their destination—Israel.[15]

A special role in the Žatec episode was played by Gordon Levett, an Englishman who served his country in World War II in the Royal Air Force and joined the Israeli Mahal unit (overseas volunteers) early in 1948, together with a handful of Jewish pilots from Britain, to fight for Israel in the War of Independence. He was charged with secretly flying numerous dismantled Messerschmitt 109 fighter planes, supplied by Czechoslovakia, from the Žatec base to the Ekron aerodrome in the Negev. This key airlift, code-named Balak, lasted three months, during which Levett managed to ferry out tons of arms as well as ammunition and personnel.[16]

A unique enterprise was the two-month-long undercover parachutists course organized with the assistance of the Czechoslovak authorities and run by the Israeli poet Chaim Guri, an officer of the Palmach holding the rank of captain. Its main objective was the preparation of trainees for the future Israeli air force.[17] Czechoslovak authorities and President Gottwald personally gave permission for the formation of a brigade of auxiliaries and pioneers, popularly known as "the Gottwald Brigade." The agreement was signed on June 25, 1948, by Staff Captain Šimon Šachta, a member of the general staff, and Israel's minister to Prague, Ehud Avriel.[18]

A marked change in the policy of the Czechoslovak Government occurred in the fall of 1948, shortly before the first elections in Israel, in which the Communists scored little success. The friendly attitude vanished from government offices: the national press became hostile overnight. The League of Friends of Jewish Palestine, established on April 27, 1948, ceased its activities. In its place the government-sponsored Czechoslovak-Israel Friendship League came into being on December 11, 1948, headed by the former Sudeten German Communist leader Karel Kreibich, who subsequently launched a campaign to "replace" the Zionist Federation.[19]

It has often been pointed out that the Czechoslovak Government was simultaneously selling arms to the Arab countries; particularly large quantities of weaponry were sold to Syria, in keeping with Czechoslovakia's policy of arms balance in the Middle East. (A portion of these were skillfully channeled to Israel.)[20] These facts are unquestionably outweighed by the manifold efforts of the Czechoslovak Government to reinforce the state-in-the-making. The arms purchased by the Haganah from Czechoslovakia reached Tel Aviv on a small steamship via Yugoslavia; the *SS Nora* arrived in April 1948 at a time when arms were desperately needed. They were deployed in Operation Nahshon, which opened the road to besieged Jerusalem and thus facilitated the liberation of the city by Israeli troops.[21]

Finally, Czechoslovakia made it possible for its Jewish population to emigrate to Israel. As a result around nineteen thousand persons moved to Israel in the first two years after the establishment of the state.[22] Thus the "lucky accident that springs from the inner logic of life and history," to use one of Masaryk's famous phrases about the momentous events of thirty years earlier, spawned in 1948 a new course unrivaled in history for its intricacy.[23]

By the end of the war there were altogether about twenty-four thousand Jews in Bohemia and Moravia, of whom the "optants"—a special civic status accorded to those who left Subcarpathian Ruthenia and opted for Czechoslovak citizenship—constituted about one third. The onerous task of spiritual reconstruction of the devastated Jewish community made up of survivors and returning émigrés was taken over in 1947 by the newly appointed chief rabbi of Prague, Dr. Gustav Sicher.[24] Both Sicher and his successor, Dr. Richard Feder, contributed greatly to the renewal of the decimated community through their moral and religious guidance.[25]

The Communist coup in 1948 and the ensuing shift in policy of the Soviet Union toward Israel in the early 1950s brought about a radical change in the life of the community diminished by aging, assimilation, and emigration. Many Jews holding important positions were purged from political, economic, and cultural life, and a great number of them were imprisoned. The notorious Slánský Trials and the vicious diatribes against Zionism, Judaism, and cosmopolitanism marred Czech-Jewish interaction for the ensuing five decades.

The early sixties, however, witnessed a thaw in the political climate, ushering in a respite of liberalization in every facet of creative life, which culminated in the Reform Movement of the Prague Spring of 1968.[26] The year 1963 saw a remarkable anniversary: the eightieth birthday of Franz Kafka and his countryman Jaroslav Hašek, author of *The Good Soldier Schweik*, widely celebrated by the cultured world. Articles and discussions about Kafka's oeuvre peaked in a seminal conference held at Chateau Liblice under the auspices of the Academy of Sciences, attended by participants from both East and West.[27] One should bear in mind that for several decades Kafka had been proscribed in the East European countries, being considered by Communist ideologists as the embodiment of formalism, decadence, and pessimism. The moving force behind the Liblice literary encounter was Professor Eduard Goldstücker, an authority on German literature. He would chair the writers' union during Prague Spring and would later be accused by the Soviets of contriving this campaign, using Kafka's writings for political objectives.

On the eve of the Six-Day War, following intense Arab agitation, an anti-Jewish campaign was launched throughout Czechoslovakia. However, the one-sided attitude toward Israel and the massive official support for the Arab states generated widespread disapproval and overt protest, especially in Czech intellectual circles and among students, who did not succumb to the vicious propaganda.[28] The Union of Czech Writers took an especially courageous stand by issuing a proclamation in support of Israel. Writer Pavel Kohout, repudiating the charges of Israeli aggression, compared the position of Israel threatened by Arab "genocide" with that of the situation in Czechoslovakia in 1938.

The leadership of the Jewish community, which had been controlled by the authorities and subdued for four decades, rose to the occasion, spurred by the dawning of freedom. Its chairman František Fuchs and Dr. Benjamin Eichler, head of the Central Council of Jewish Communities in Slovakia, issued the following declaration in Prague on April 6, 1968: "We wish to take this opportunity to declare that we shall never agree to the destruction of the State of Israel and to the murder of its population. It is in that country, the cradle of our religion, that the refugees found a haven. It is there that our brothers and sisters, fellow prisoners from the concentration camps and combatants in the resistance against Nazism, live . . . We welcome the efforts of our people for the renewal of our democracy, and believe that they will bring beneficial results for our republic and our people."[29]

In spite of the liberal upheaval and the fact that "public opinion almost unanimously sided with Israel," there was an outpouring of anonymous letters written by extremely hostile individuals in an anti-Semitic and anti-Zionist vein, reminiscent of the trials of the fifties.[30] One of the most virulent anonymous letters was addressed to Goldstücker.[31]

It has been suggested that the campaign unleashed in the press against Jews was one of the factors prompting publication of Ludvík Vaculík's now famous statement on June 27, 1968, in *Literární listy*: "2,000 Words to Workers, Farmers, Scientists, Artists and Everyone," a scathing critique of Communist bureaucracy and the prevailing state of affairs, advocating spontaneous initiatives to force out remaining conservatives who had misused their power.[32]

A curious episode evolved around the planned celebrations of the millennium of Jewish settlement in Prague and the seven-hundredth anniversary of the Prague Old-New Synagogue, originally scheduled for 1966. The date was to be marked with the issue of a series of postage stamps, the motifs carefully selected from the State Jewish Museum's collection of memorabilia.[33] On May 22, 1967, the colorful series was finally released for circulation and immediately gained wide acclaim in philatelist circles. However, its distribution lasted only a short time. At the beginning of June 1967, after the outbreak of the Six-Day War and upon the intervention of the Ministry of Foreign Affairs, the stamps were withdrawn. It transpired that this occurred under pressure from the Arab states, which viewed the printing of a Judaica series as a demonstration of pro-Israeli attitudes. The source of the Arab reaction stemmed from Lebanon, where the suspicious director of communications detected on one of the stamps—bearing the emblem of the Prague Jewish Printers' Guild of 1530—an alarming inscription: "He giveth power to the faint; and to them that have no might he increaseth strength" (Isaiah 40:29).[34]

The large-scale millennium celebrations planned for Prague for 1966 had to be postponed following the internal political problems generated by Prague Spring. Finally, in July 1969, the authorities turned the occasion into a local and purely religious affair.

With the outbreak of the Arab-Israeli war in the summer of 1967, the Soviets severed diplomatic relations with Israel. Czechoslovakia too recalled its diplomats from Tel Aviv, thus cutting off ties for many years to come. Following the invasion of Czechoslovakia by the armies of the Warsaw Pact and the presence of Soviet troops in the territory of the republic, the ensuing two decades can be described as a time of government-sponsored chicanery and suppression, accompanied by virulent anti-Semitism and marked by the preoccupation of the mass media with Israel.[35]

It is estimated that between 1968 and 1971 some six thousand Jews left the country, along with a wide assortment of Czech intellectuals and professionals. Henceforward the reduced Jewish community suffered from intensified atheist and anti-religious measures; these affected the Christian denominations as well. Jewish life was reduced to synagogue worship and religious observance, and any manifestations of broader Jewish cultural expression, including ties to Israel and even Hebrew songs, were discouraged or directly prohibited.

The Jewish communal organization was expected to function in line with the requirements of the regime—the Communist Party, the State Security police, or the Ministry of Church Affairs, to which it was subordinate. While the president of the communities was elected by his peers (with governmental approval), the secretary-general was directly appointed by the authorities and became the *totum factum*, the focus of real power, receiving orders from the party or the police and obliged to render slavish obedience. The head of the community himself had to provide information, such as lists of members attending synagogue and of visitors from abroad, and had to publish anti-Israel statements in the pages of the community bulletin. There was no chance of remaining untainted within the existing totalitarian system, and for most communal leaders life became an endless series of harrowing pressures and unsavory compromises. Those officials who were not sufficiently obedient or spoke out on a "sensitive issue" were immediately replaced. Such was the case of František Fuchs, president of the Jewish communities, defending the stance of the wartime leadership in Prague.[36] Addressing a memorial rally he claimed that they "did their utmost to halt the deportations to the death camps," for which statement he was suspended from his post.

As of the seventies the State Jewish Museum of Prague, the most important of the cultural institutions, restricted its contacts with the community. The museum journal *Judaica Bohemiae* launched during the liberalization period (1965) presented its articles in German, French, English, and Russian intended for distribution abroad. A Czech version of its contents was never made available.

Even more paradoxical is the fact that the Jewish community was denied access to its cultural heritage: the unique resources of the museum, the vast libraries of rare Judaica, the bequests of famous scholars, were under lock and key, stored in some of the synagogues used as depositories. This and other practices instituted by the regime were part of the overall policy obviously intended to deflate Jewish self-esteem.[37]

Eloquent testimony to this pitiable state of affairs may be found in the issues of *Věstník*, the community monthly, which over the course of four decades engaged mainly in reporting or reflecting upon the traumatic events of the Holocaust—death, memorial meetings, and wreath-laying ceremonies. Indeed, the issue of the Holocaust served as an outlet for some noted Jewish writers, survivors of concentration camps as well as veterans in the Czechoslovak army units abroad (Ota Kraus, František Kafka, Jiří Weil, František Gottlieb).

Traditional Jewish communal life diminished during the Communist era; a new type of anti-Semitism flourished, viewing the Jews as parasites, cosmopolitan aliens, conspiring against the proletarians. This trend was evident even in the "official" articles and reports of the community bulletin. The only exceptions were the weekly homilies of the chief rabbi Dr. Sicher. He skillfully selected passages from the midrash and homiletic tales of the Talmud meant to enlighten the reader about the true concepts of Judaism, to remind people that the study (of Torah) combined with physical work (*avodah*) is the basic idea of life.[38]

In the mid-seventies the State Security disinformation department in Prague stepped up attacks against "the main threats to peace"—American imperialists, West German militarists, and world Jewry. It disseminated rumors and invented plots linking Czechoslovak Jews, famous Jewish personalities, and former Czech citizens in Israel with fraudulent activities aimed at the overthrow of the socialist order.[39] The gloomy atmosphere that characterized the so-called normalization period was echoed in *samizdat* literature smuggled abroad.

Throughout the years of overt hostility and denigration, a new type of interaction between the various Christian Church organizations and the Jewish community developed *sub rosa*, reflecting both understanding and solidarity. This can be demonstrated by frequent articles on Jewish topics printed in periodicals issued by the Christian communities, some of these touching upon Jewish martyrdom and the Holocaust, others commemorating great Jewish figures in Czech history. For instance *Český zápas*, organ of the Czechoslovak Hussite Church, in its issue of November 5, 1959, included a tribute "In Memory of the Exalted Rabbi Loew" (on the occasion of the 350th anniversary of his birth). The article dwelt on the symbolic value of the sculpture of the rabbi placed at the entrance to the new Prague Town Hall, viewed as one of the pillars upon which the ancient tradition of the Czech capital rests: "A shield to the entrance of the building." Alluding to Rabbi Loew's transcendental faculties, he "who witnessed both good and bad times in the history of the city," the article concludes thus: "In those dark days of the Hitlerian assault he heard the grievous laments of his desperate flock."[40]

Noteworthy is the article published in *Věstník* in 1982, written by the Reverend Jan Amos Dvořáček, an evangelical parson in Sternberk, summarizing a series of four articles originally published in *Kostnické jiskry*.[41] Addressing the issue of the "unrequited debt" of Christianity incurred by the thousand years of suffering and persecution of the Jews, Dvořáček advocates, in ecumenical spirit, a thorough revision of Christian attitudes.

The void in postwar Jewish historiography can be attributed to both objective and subjective causes, the most important of which was the political situation that developed in postwar Czechoslovakia. The years 1945-48 were too close to the horrors of the Second World War, and documentation was still being processed and was only partially available. After the Communist takeover in 1948 and with the ensuing anti-Semitic climate in the wake of the Slánský Trials, conditions were not conducive to the pursuit of any such study. Later the respite of the more liberal period preceding Prague Spring (1965–68) was too brief to afford in-depth long-range study.

Following the suppression of Prague Spring, the invasion of Warsaw Pact troops, and the UN resolution of November 1975 equating Zionism with racism, a widespread propaganda program was launched in the press and on the radio denigrating the issue of the Holocaust.[42]

A turning point in public affairs in the next decade was the formation of Charter 77, signed in 1975 in the aftermath of the Helsinki Final Act on Human Rights. Charter 77 provided a legal foundation for peacefully defending human rights in the struggle against totalitarianism, and it developed in the course of events into Czechoslovakia's foremost dissident movement. Among its three founding spokesmen were Professor Jan Patočka, Václav Havel, and Jiří Hájek.

In the wake of *glasnost* in 1989 and spearheaded by Václav Havel, Charter 77 became the nucleus of the Civic Forum, heralding the revolution by advocating reform and a new social democratic order. It was during this period that the Jewish issue was directly referred to in two important documents: the first was titled "An Open Letter to the Leadership of the Council of Jewish Communities in the Czech Lands" (February 19, 1989), signed by Dr. Leo Pavlát and twenty-four other signatories, and the second was "A Critique on the Devastation of Jewish Cultural Monuments and the Tacit Disregard of the Role of Jews in Czechoslovak History."[43]

Analyzing the dearth of research on Czech-Jewish interaction during World War II in postwar Czechoslovak historiography we are faced with a special phenomenon: for various reasons the traumatic events created a barrier, both for those historians who emigrated to the free Western world to pursue their research and for those who remained in their native Czechoslovakia. Thus topics such as the attitudes of the Czech population during the period of the post-

Munich Second Republic and during the Nazi occupation, or the part played by Jews in the Home Resistance and the resistance abroad, have been given little attention. Only a few students of Czech history—among them Tomáš Pasák, Bohumil Černý, Jan Křen, and Ivan Pfaff—have touched some topics.[44]

Josef Träger, writer, publisher, and well-known personality of the prewar cultural scene, summarized the Czech-Jewish intellectual interaction astutely in insightful observations penned in a tone of reverence. Although he was discussing only "Jews of Czech-Jewish milieu," centering first and foremost on his friend Egon Hostovský (in contrast to the Prague German environment!), he spoke highly of the great value of Jewish contributions to the literary scene:

> At this point it would be fitting to recall how much this generation is in-debted to the impact of the Jews. I am not stressing this for my own sake *ad usum Delphini* for indeed we are at present witnesses to an anti-Semitic hysteria that has also engulfed the so-called Marxist camp. Long ago we discussed this with František Hrubín and concurred that in our youth we were lucky to have been exposed to the continuous benefits gained through our contacts with our Jewish surroundings . . . The Jewish spirit introduced us to analysis, led us to profound knowledge, and drew us in its great sagacity to viewing humanity from a distant perspective.[45]

It seems, however, that other views were gaining currency. The great surprise was Václav Černý's important volume of recollections on the Home Resistance and postwar events. Černý, professor of modern French literature and one of the leading Czech intellectuals, voiced a sharp attack on Jews, arousing a continuous debate.[46]

His book was widely acclaimed but also vehemently criticized for the slanderous and malicious portrayal of some prominent figures.[47] As far as the Jewish aspect is concerned, aside from several of his friends (Hostovský, Eisner, Firt) whom he graciously spared his venom, all others (Czech Jews, German Jews, Communists) were treated with harsh criticism and occasionally racist definitions and other uncomplimentary epithets such as *semit* (Semite), *hebrejčík* (petty Hebrew), or Bolshevik, all identified with Zionism. The gist of his accusation centers around the Communist Slánský Trials in the fifties, condensed in the following scathing attack: "Together with Slánský, our Jews have become indebted to us for many years to come; this should be obvious to everyone. It is not them to whom we owe moral credit; on the contrary they remain indebted to us: let them not forget this."[48]

In retrospect the exaggerated role attributed to the Jews in the advent of Communism and the takeover in 1948 is questionable. Both the ideological and political Czech elite constituted the first-rank leadership; could not the coup have taken place without Jewish involvement?

After the Jewish issue had been absent for several decades the publication in 1975 of Christopher Stölzl's perceptive study *Kafkas böses Böhmen* (in Munich) opened up a heated debate. As a result several studies emerged, of which Jan Křen's insightful essay published first in the Paris-based *Svědectví* was most valuable. It raised the question of why the so-called third nation in the Czech lands, the Bohemian Jews, had disappeared from the scene of contemporary history: "The annals of the Czech lands without this element remain incomplete; its omission especially distorts the panoramic view of Czech national history."[49] He also pointed out that the Jewish contribution to German and Czech culture cannot be overlooked for several reasons as Jewish people "were the moving force of the economic wonder of this part of Europe," constituting the source and main link with the outside world and a major factor behind the process of putting an end to provincialism.

Křen argued that this lacuna in Czech history can be ascribed partly to the fact that anti-Semitism always lurked under the surface and never disappeared from the Czech surroundings—note its vestiges in the fifties; it survived even the Nazi era, which essentially obliterated the Jewish element in the Czech lands. "This ignorance of historiography does not stem from sentiments of tact. If this is not non-interest or rather non-conscience, but a relic of anti-Semitism, so it is a failing of scholarly qualification, which if destined to endure forever is unbearable . . . The Jewish question and anti-Semitism remain a great civil and scholarly debt of our historiography."[50]

As of November 1989 the Czech nation embarked on the road to recovery after the long nightmare of the destructive years of Nazism and the tyranny of the Communist regime. The sweeping changes brought about in the wake of the Velvet Revolution gave the minute Jewish community a new lease of life.[51] The devastated synagogues and community buildings throughout the country once again came to be attended after forty years of misuse and neglect. On the walls of the Pinkas Synagogue the names of those who perished during the Holocaust have been inscribed. Prague's ancient Jewish historic sites and the Jewish Museum entered a new era of reverence and admiration.

More recently, under the aegis of the Czech government, a "Working Committee" examined the issue of the Nazi-confiscated gold, silver, precious stones, and other "lost" valuables of Jews in the Czech lands in the years 1939–45. The committee's résumé stresses the part of the Soviet authorities, which bluntly announced in 1946 that "the losses" should be ascribed to "the exigencies of the war."[52]

After decades of dogmatic management the State Jewish Museum is once again called the Jewish Museum. Under the leadership of the learned scholar Dr. Leo Pavlát, the museum's permanent exhibitions launched as of 1994 present the precious ancient collections of ritual objects and works of art not merely as accessions but in the very context of Jewish history and religious life. The museum's Educational and Cultural Center, headed since 1998 by Dr. Miloš Pojar, offers a variety of programs enhancing Prague's immense spiritual spectrum. The ancient historic sites and the Old Jewish Cemetery as well as the renovated buildings—the Klaus, Maisel, and Spanish synagogues—became memorials to the Jews of Bohemia and Moravia who perished during the Holocaust and testimony to the spiritual values of the Jewish people and their continuity: Central Europe's special legacy.

One should bear in mind that the process of revival in all spheres of cultural and social activities will be protracted in a society depleted by the massive emigration of its technical and intellectual talents. It will take many a decade to overcome the internal problems so as to shake off the totalitarian system and erase the consequences it imposed over the course of forty years. Nevertheless, with "the return to history" as of 1989, a new era has commenced in the Czech lands.[53]

Conclusions

The centuries-old Jewish presence in the Czech historic lands, richly expressed in architecture, crafts, sculpture, and literature, is a unique segment of European history. The thrust of my work deals with the years 1939–45, the last tragic chapter of persecution and suffering that brought about the demise of the once-blooming Jewish communities and their renowned institutions. To understand the focal issues fully it seemed to me imperative to survey the radical transformation of the Jewish community in the nineteenth century, following the Enlightenment, the Emancipation, the process of modernization, the Czech national awakening, and mainly the impact of the Czech-German national conflict. One of its marked aspects was the assimilation of the Jews and their gradual adoption of the official and compulsory German language. This process of Germanization ultimately evolved into a firm attachment to German education and culture, generating sharp antagonism during the bitter nationality struggles between Czechs and Germans.

In the course of time the firmly rooted, devout Jewry split into a number of factions: German Jews, Czech Jews, national or Zionist-oriented Jews, agnostics, and even a category who defined themselves as "Jews by origin."

It is certainly remarkable that despite their extremely low percentage in the total population (estimated at 1.01 percent at the beginning of the twentieth century), Jews were the moving force behind the Bohemian "economic wonder"—the development of trade, industry, and crafts. At the same time, assimilation and progress penetrated all strata of life. The situation was somewhat different in Moravia, where the "autonomous" Jewish community, thanks to the constant influx of fugitives from the east, retained a greater hold upon its traditionally religious members.

The Prague Jewish community, which constituted half of Bohemian Jewry, had become especially affluent and acculturated. Much has been written about the unprecedented generation of creative talents at the fin de siècle, the famous Prague Circle (Kafka, Werfel, Brod, Rilke, Kisch, etc.), enriching Central European culture so forcefully. This galaxy of poets, writers, and philosophers went down in history as the Prague "cultural phenomenon."

There is general consensus that the First Czechoslovak Republic (1918-38) was a model democracy among the neighboring successor states, even though the original Swiss pattern envisaged by its founders had not materialized. One should bear in mind that while in Poland Marshal Pilsudski headed a military dictatorship, and Hungary prided herself on the authoritarian ruler Admiral Horthy, at the helm of Czechoslovakia stood the humanist president Thomas Garrigue Masaryk.

Notwithstanding its frailties and weaknesses as a multiethnic state—despite the "canker at her heart," as A. J. P. Taylor put it—Czech rule over national groups was remarkably benign. It was in many respects tolerant and more sensitive to its minorities than were other progressive countries. The judicial system was generally viewed as one of the country's finest achievements. Spheres such as organization of labor legislation, unemployment compensation, economic welfare, health benefits, and recreation surpassed those in many a Western country. And last but not least, the education system afforded growth and progress to all the minority groups.

As far as overall progress is concerned, in both social and economic spheres Czech Jewry reached its zenith during the era of the First Czechoslovak Republic. The Jewish population was one of the major beneficiaries of the advances in education. The unique opportunity together with traditional Jewish attachment to education generated a twenty-year-long interlude with a literary and intellectual climate that excelled in creativity, penetrating every cultural frontier. For the first time in the history of the Czech lands there emerged a distinctive range of Jewish politicians and literati, who identified themselves fully with the Czech nation and who became foremost representatives of the state hierarchy.

With Hitler's rise to power, the Nazi-streamed propaganda, and the escalating Sudeten German agitation against the republic, the anti-Semitic campaign became a permanent issue in the press. Time and again the language issue came to the forefront, becoming once again the bone of contention between Czechs and Jews. Sorrow and uncertainty engulfed the community as a whole: Jews using the German language were blamed by the press even for the territorial losses of the Munich Agreement. Most alarming of all was the faltering of some of the writers, journalists, and other members of the Czech intelligentsia during and after the Munich crisis, in a pathetic attempt to seek some sort of *modus vivendi* with the Germans. The worst was to follow.

The occupation of the Czech lands by the Wehrmacht on the Ides of March and the proclamation of the Protectorate of Bohemia and Moravia by the Führer in Prague, on March 16, 1939, marked the onset of the most tragic chapter for the population in general and for the Jewish enclave in particular.

From the perspective of fifty years, we may safely assert that the persecution of the Jews in the initial phase of the Protectorate of Bohemia and Moravia, during the so-called pacification period (1939–41) under Reichsprotektor von Neurath, was carried out with more subtlety and cunning than in Eastern Europe. The main reasons behind this policy were, first, the Czech workers' contribution toward the war effort and, second, the exploitation of the country's technical and agricultural capacity.

However, it soon became obvious that the total "de-Czechization of the Bohemian-Moravian space," intended at the highest level (Hitler, Heydrich, Frederici) for the postwar period, was directly connected to the Jewish question. The first target of the anti-Jewish legislation was economic: the quick and smooth transfer of Jewish property (estimated before World War II as one third of all industrial and banking capital) into German hands for the strengthening of the ethnic German element. Thus the Jewish question had become part and parcel of the Germanization process of the erstwhile Bohemian lands, firmly bound up with Hitler's long-range policy: "the solution of the Czech question" and incorporation of the lands of Bohemia and Moravia into greater Germany after the war.

As of July 1939, with the promulgation of the anti-Jewish decrees according to the criteria of the Nuremberg Laws, Reichsprotektor von Neurath assumed full authority and jurisdiction over the Jewish community. This meant that the SS-supervised Zentralstelle für jüdische Auswanderung (Central office for Jewish emigration, later renamed Central office for the solution of the Jewish question), an outpost of the Reich's main security office in Berlin, took over responsibility for the fate of the Jewish entity.

General Eliáš's government known for its double game—feigning support for the Nazi line while actually cooperating with the Home Resistance and the exile government—can be credited with the symbolic act of rejecting the introduction of the Nuremberg Laws. Although his conduct was prompted primarily by economic interest, Eliáš was at the same time cautious not to "cross the Rubicon," ostensibly adopting the New Order. It is an established fact, however, that after his removal in September 1941, the second Acting Protectorate Government meekly collaborated with the Nazis. Indeed, during the launching of the deportation campaign the acting head of the Protectorate Government and President Hácha asked to take part in the isolation of the Jews and in sharing the spoils. This offer was rejected outright by the Nazis on the ground that only the

Reich authorities were empowered to carry out anti-Jewish measures. Between 1941 and 1943 the majority of the Jewish population was deported to annihilation camps, several transports going directly "to the East"; others were first dispatched to the Theresienstadt ghetto and from there to other death camps, mainly to Auschwitz.

Jews did not have any separate organized underground movement in the Protectorate. Still, individuals joined several resistance organizations in the first years of the war, some in leading positions. However, the ongoing arrests and the strict police surveillance precluded the growth of a large-scale resistance movement.

Already in the late summer of 1941, two years after the Nazi occupation, the German Security Services boasted of having nipped in the bud the clandestine network in the Czech lands. The failure of national resistance and Heydrich's reign of terror brought to an end the activities of Jewish individuals within the various underground groups. Most of the leading members were caught, tried in German courts, and later hanged.

Luckier were all those Jewish men and women who managed to escape to the USSR and Great Britain, where they joined the Czechoslovak army units, returning at the end of the war with the liberating armed forces. Jewish volunteers enlisting in 1939 in Mandatory Palestine were among the first to offer their services, thus doubtless contributing to the prestige of the London-based Czechoslovak Government-in-Exile.

Heydrich's iron hand, the civil state of emergency, and the special warning issued to the Czech population at the beginning of the mass deportations not to side with the Jews certainly had a deterring effect. Needless to say in the Protectorate, as everywhere, the Nazi hierarchy was mindful that the local rabble would also derive material benefit; the expulsions were accompanied by looting of the remains of Jewish households.

In assessing Czech attitudes toward the plight of the Jews during WW II we are faced with inconsistencies in the stance of the Protectorate Government, the various resistance groups, the population at large, and the Government-in-Exile in London.

Jan Tesař, the most outstanding analyst of this period, takes issue with the main strategy of wartime Czech policy, formulated by President Beneš himself as sheer ethnic survival. Tesař draws a direct line from the "Munichites"—the reactionary elements openly demonstrating their loyalty to Nazi Germany—to the members of the Protectorate Government, maintaining that it was this overall concern that actually led "to a further blind alley of legal and loyal patriotism, a patriotism bereft of human content, indifferent to the dehumanization, ignoring the totalitarianization process also pursued by prominent national leaders."[1] What is astonishing is the fact that this attitude, in effect, engulfed some groups of the Home Resistance as well.

In the present research I have stressed the fact that during the first stage of the war the main concern of President Beneš's Government-in-Exile was the rescinding of the Munich Agreement and restoration of the prewar boundaries of Czechoslovakia. One of the serious failures ascribed to Beneš was his odd reaction to the inquiry by the World Jewish Congress (in September 1942) about the ongoing extermination of Jews. In spite of having the best informed sources, his belated reply of November 11, 1942, implying that he was unable to form any "definitive conclusions" on the authenticity of the report, aroused many questions. One reason could have been the advice of the Foreign Office. Some intelligence files declassified by the British in 1993 indicate that the most "sensitive" evidence about the earlier mass killing of Jews in occupied Poland had been suppressed for both political and military reasons.

The calamity of the Jewish population of Bohemia and Moravia is marked by some distinctive features stemming from geopolitical and local particularities. The Jewish leadership became aware early on of the murderous German policy. The first hints may have originated from sympathetic highly placed officials of the Czech hierarchy. One need only recall the conversation between Foreign Minister Chvalkovský and Hitler in January 1939 (which, according to hearsay, rendered Chvalkovský speechless). Even stronger than rumor was the harrowing experience in Nisko: the trials and tribulations of Jacob Edelstein and Richard Israel Friedmann in the fall of 1939. It is no exaggeration to claim that the leaders of the Prague JRC, during their mission to occupied Holland initiated by the SS in the spring of 1941, were the first to uncover the Nazi intention of "destroying the Jews, body and soul." By informing the Jewish leadership of Amsterdam and some leading figures of the Jewish Agency in Palestine, they became the first messengers foretelling the catastrophe.

Painful as it may be, in his memoirs Nahum Goldmann revealed some serious doubts about the posture of the Jewish leadership in the free world: "Yet for a people and its leaders short-sightedly to refuse to believe in our imminent catastrophe or to have denied the truth because they feared it, is indubitably a sign of inadequacy and an inability to face facts."[2]

As far as the role of the Jewish community leaders and their strategy are concerned, we may distinguish two different periods. During the initial years (1939–41), although under constant threat and intimidation, the JRC leaders still revealed feverish activities in various spheres, seeking ways to overcome the sudden chaos and misery that befell them. The main aim was alleviating the plight of the besieged community by a large-scale vocational reorientation and by helping with emigration overseas. The result was that more than twenty-seven thousand Jews managed to emigrate legally. It may be estimated that an additional thousand, mainly young people, escaped illegally. The second phase (1941–43) came with Heydrich's mass expulsion campaign; in the shadow of incessant terror and arrests, the intimidated leadership was gradually reduced to total compliance.

This was the saddest chapter in the history of this ancient community. From memoirs and postwar testimonies it transpires that some of the leading representatives of the JRC had become aware by the summer of 1941 that they were being exploited as tools by the enemy. The worst was soon upon them: their involvement under German orders in the task of filling the quotas for the projected deportations and in working up the list of the so-called privileged Jews to be exempted. The latter issue caused bad blood, friction, and sorrow within the coerced society. In addition the Jewish leadership had to function in an atmosphere of constant intimidation, intrigue, and machinations by the SS camp command, which was plotting incidents and was eager to generate personal feuds and demoralization.

Every discussion probing the task of the Judenräte poses the crucial question: Did the balance of their positive actions indeed justify the notion of remaining at the helm? Cui bono?

Two initiatives of the Czech Jewish leadership stand out as unique in this chapter of history: the "race against time" strategy in the struggle for the survival of the community, in the ardent belief that the establishment of the ghetto of Terezín might eventually forestall deportation of the Jews of Bohemia and Moravia "to the East"; and the scheme to save the ancient ritual and art objects of the uprooted communities and thus to preserve the historic past. This last mute but symbolic effort calls into question the myth of "Jewish passivity" and demonstrates above all the innate commitment to spiritual values.

In the summer of 1942, at the height of the deportation of the provincial Jews, the JRC appealed to the SS in a memorandum, claiming that the priceless books, ritual objects, and artifacts assembled over the course of centuries—lying derelict in the emptied communities—could be saved by assembling them in Prague for storage. The "storage" project brought about the preservation of the precious legacy, the ancient Jewish heritage, and its bequest to posterity.

The unique character of Ghetto Terezín, its changing role during its four-year existence, and the spiritual legacy of the inmates add a special dimension to the tragedy of Central European Jews in general and of the Jews of Bohemia and Moravia in particular.

The stance of the International Committee of the Red Cross is documented in two testimonies describing inspection visits by ICRC delegations on June 23, 1944, and April 6, 1945. Kept under lock and key for more than four decades, these records were made accessible in full only in 1994. The documents prove beyond doubt the gruesome fact that instead of "caritas inter arma"—ICRC's traditional motto—this institution served as a tool of Nazi extermination policy. Its president, Professor Carl J. Burckhardt, himself a close friend and admirer of Hitler, had been among those fully informed about the planned extermination process as early as the spring of 1941.

There is no monograph analyzing the conduct of the various segments of the local populace during the Nazi occupation. Reports of the Secret Police indicate that it was mainly the upper class of the society (*die Oberschichte*) that demonstrated solidarity with the Jews. The questionable stance of the workers and the agricultural sector, both favored by the regime for their crucial contribution to the German war effort, has not as yet been evaluated. Most instructive, however, is a short remark made by Foreign Minister Dr. Hubert Ripka during a session of the postwar Czechoslovak government (October 2, 1945), discussing the issue of the pogrom against returning survivors in the city of Trnava after the liberation of Slovakia. He recalled that he and Jan Masaryk, in response to their appeals over the BBC pleading for sympathy toward Jewish suffering, kept receiving letters from both Czechs and Slovaks demanding that they not extend any help to Jewish compatriots.

Nevertheless, in contrast to the situation in other East European nations, atrocities and bestial or vicious anti-Semitism were alien to the Czech mentality. This can be viewed as one of the most striking achievements of the democratic spirit that prevailed in the First Republic. Some noted experts on Czech history (F. X. Šalda, O. Donath, E. Wiskemann, P. Tigrid, B. Černý) speak of the "spasmodic" nature of Czech anti-Semitism, erupting in times of social ferment and national calamity. But on the whole Czech anti-Semitism was lacking in two basic elements common to rabid Jew baiters: racism and bigoted religious hatred. In general, Czechs tended to be more tolerant, many of them priding themselves on the Hussite tradition of liberty of conscience.

As of September 27, 1941, the date of Heydrich's arrival, and especially during the *heydrichiáda* retaliation campaign following his assassination on May 27, 1942, Czechs lived with a sword hanging over their heads, in stress and anxiety, under the constant threat of death. In spite of this, we know of scores of Czech people who were tried by summary courts and put to death for rendering assistance to Jews. It is interesting to note that Czechs residing outside the Protectorate—some of them in Volhynia, or in "independent" Slovakia, where assistance rendered to Jews did not entail punishment by death—displayed more readiness to assist their Jewish acquaintances.

It is worth noting that the period at the height of the war and the peak of mass deportation of Czech Jewry to the death camps was also the period of the highest degree of military cooperation between Czechs and Jews, in defiance of the common Nazi oppressor and tormentor. The massive participation of Jewish men and women volunteers, constituting the nucleus of the Czechoslovak army units abroad, testifies to the Jewish minority's genuine feeling of solidarity with and loyalty to the republic.

Paradoxically enough, Beneš's policy was later increasingly influenced by the vociferous Communist resistance group guided by Moscow—the only underground group to survive throughout the war years. As of summer 1943 messages from the homeland dispatched to the Government-in-Exile amply reflect the policy envisaged for the new postwar social order. It transpires that it was under the pressure of the Home Resistance that Beneš adopted the total transfer of the German minority, viewed as the main cause for the dismemberment of the First Republic. The issue of Jewish minority rights had to fall in line with the newly embraced ethnic policies; henceforth Jews were not recognized as a minority but had to adhere to either Slovak or Czech nationality.

Among other things, the Communist leadership prepared guidelines of differential criteria for granting citizenship to Jewish returnees (from the camps and from overseas) as well as proposals on the issue of Jewish property confiscated by the Nazis. It is evident that the Central Committee of the Czechoslovak Communist Party in Moscow hastened to survey the Aryanized Jewish property, the seizure of which was a prerequisite for their future aims and plans.

In every country under Nazi occupation there were specific conditions that ultimately determined the situation of the Jews and their fate. Even satellite countries can be classified according to the differing degrees of independence and their stance vis-à-vis Germany's demands. Perhaps the most crucial point was the degree of intimidation and the punishment meted out by the Nazis to gentiles who were ready to extend assistance to the persecuted Jews. As we have seen, several dozen individuals in the Protectorate were charged by Nazi special courts and sentenced to death at Pankrác prison in 1943–44 for thus "sabotaging the Final Solution"; those assisting Jewish individuals or helping them cross frontiers (*Beihilfe in Menschenschmugel*) were described as "destructive elements" (*Volksschädlinge*).

The concerned attitude and helpfulness of the Czech population toward the emaciated survivors of the death marches during evacuation of the concentration camps in the last months of the war are therefore noteworthy. Memoirs and recollections relating to this period contain heartrending descriptions of survivors' experiences upon reaching the Czech countryside. Time and again these wretched people were approached by courageous Czech women and men who dared to hand them a drink or a piece of bread, demonstrating thereby their deep empathy and solidarity.

During the Second World War the Czechs lost their national sovereignty and were thus absolved from having to make their own decision on the fate of the Jewish population. The crucial question still remains: Did the Czechs as a nation live up to their reputation as the model democracy in Central Europe whose standards were set by the great philosopher-president T. G. Masaryk?

The role of society in crisis-ridden situations is basically a sociological or an ethical enquiry. There is, however, no cultural code or appropriate hierarchy of values to guide rank-and-file citizenry about conduct in extreme situations. In his treatise *Modernity and the Holocaust*, probing the moral dimensions of complicity, Zygmunt Bauman makes some subtle observations on the issue of responsibility.

Each generation views historical events through its own set of spectacles. Recently, following the volte-face in Eastern Europe, the issue of moral responsibility has gained new regard. After long decades of silence, statesmen in Slovakia and Hungary and also in France have made open confessions of their involvement as accomplices in the perpetration of the Final Solution. The Czech nation as a whole escaped this stigma. It was the Reichsprotektor who assumed jurisdiction over the Jewish community: the German executive organs were the entities eagerly carrying out the mass deportation of Jews to the death camps. This line of strategy in the Protectorate was consistent with Hitler's ultimate aim, the postwar solution of the Czech question—incorporation of Bohemia and Moravia into the thousand-year Reich.

The intermezzo of the immediate postwar period (1945–48) was too short and too close in time to allow investigation of the most sensitive issues of the fateful years of World War II. The Czechs were more than mere witnesses to the uprooting of the Jews: they themselves were also victims. Suffice it to recall the *heydrichiáda* and the ensuing destruction of the villages of Lidice and Ležáky.

It has been asserted that the scars inflicted on the nation's psyche in general and on the Jewish survivors in particular played an important role in shaping postwar public opinion and attitudes. The September 1938 Munich crisis—the abandonment by Western allies as well as the faltering of bourgeois society—were doubtless the main reasons behind the mass conversion to Communism both in the immediate postwar years and after the 1948 takeover. As a result the

Czechoslovak Communist Party became the largest one in the world, its membership reaching one million in the early fifties.

The treatment of minorities after 1945 and the attitude toward the Jewish entity during the Communist era merit separate research and scrutiny. We shall nevertheless touch upon two significant events that took place in the crucial year of 1948, which may be regarded as the last chords in the final movement of Czech-Jewish coexistence.

The first is the massive support Czechoslovakia extended for establishment of the Jewish state between 1945 and 1948—the brightest thread in the dark fabric of that gruesome decade. Aside from the political and ideological aims of Moscow headquarters, the goodwill and commitment on the part of numerous Czech statesmen and the military involved in the campaign were of immense value. These reflect the traditional support for the national aspirations of the Jews and compassion for their suffering in the Hitlerite era.

The year 1948 also saw the ill-fated coup d'état, which became the most controversial postwar issue, followed by the political show trials staged in Prague in 1951–52 against Rudolf Slánský and accomplices—"Zionist conspirators, plotting with Western cosmopolitans"—who were sentenced to death by hanging. (During the late sixties, in the wake of the liberalization process, they were rehabilitated.)

As noted, at the onset of the Stalinist era in 1949 the bulk of the Jewish survivors, numbering around nineteen thousand people, migrated from Czechoslovakia to Israel and other countries in the free world. Those who stayed behind were to endure four long decades of Moscow-orchestrated anti-Semitism and discrimination. One of the outcomes of this predicament was accelerated assimilation of Jews. Thus while the millennium of the first Jewish settlement in Bohemia, marked in 1966, saw but a minute Jewish remnant—a pale shadow of the vibrant prewar community—two decades later the Velvet Revolution of 1989 found the Jewish community on the verge of extinction.

The politically charged first postwar years and the ensuing forty years of the Communist era with its manipulated history did not allow coming to terms with the past or with the moral dilemmas that the war had seared into Czech consciousness. Only the last decade has at last afforded open discussion after the long hiatus. One hopeful sign is the ongoing large-scale restoration of the synagogues and ancient Jewish historic buildings, encouraged by state authorities and financially supported by Jewish philanthropy the world over.

With the collapse of the Communist regime and the newly regained freedom, the absence of the once-flourishing Jewish community became more conspicuous. The void created by its absence became a recurring theme in contemporary literature. Oscar Jászi's dictum on Austrian Jewry's role as "the chief bearer of the Austrian state idea," cementing the nationalities of the prewar monarchy, achieved new dimension and focus in several studies published in the mid-eighties about the perished Jewry of Central Europe, recalling with nostalgia the absence of the Jewish spirit as an integrating element and intellectual glue. Milan Šimečka, while stressing the fact that "it was Nazism, after all, that so effectively silenced the 'Jewish genius,' which had been part and parcel of Central Europe's spiritual evolution," also points out that the role of Soviet Communism and its effect upon a section of the native people cannot be overlooked: "Our spiritual Biafra bore an indelible local trademark."[3]

Reflecting in the late fifties on the constantly diminishing, aged, and assimilated Jewish community in the Czech lands, Pavel Eisner, insightful as ever, gave a rather pessimistic prognosis. In his view it was unlikely that in future generations a talented Jewish writer could ever emerge on the Czech scene "with direct awareness of his origin." Nevertheless, it is to be hoped that the assimilated and mainly culture-oriented Jewish community—torn away from the more religiously rooted Slovak Jewry as of January 1993—will be able to maintain its group identity.

Czech intellectuals view the last fifty years of their annals as an incursion, a discontinuity in the centuries-old evolution on national, economic, religious, and cultural planes. For indeed, with the disruption of the erstwhile triple society of Czechs, Germans, and Jews, a society known for its contrasts and cultural sophistication, the physiognomy of Prague and of the Czech lands altogether has ultimately changed. The incursion of two totalitarian regimes has irreversibly sealed the historical continuity of the triple society that gave rise to the Prague cultural phenomenon in which the Jewish element was so preeminent.

Abbreviations

ALM	Archives of the Labor Movement, Tel Aviv
APT	Archiv památníku Terezín
BEBCA	Böhmische Escompte Bank (Bohemian discount bank)
BCE	before the Christian era
CCP	Czechoslovak Communist Party
CEO	Central European Observer
ČsČH	Československý časopis historický, Praha
CZA	Central Zionist Archives, Jerusalem
DBFP	Documents on British Foreign Policy
DHČP	Dokumenty historie československé politiky
ECE	East Central Europe
FFUK	Filozofická Fakulta University Karlovy, Praha
GFHA	Ghetto Fighters' House Archives
HIAS	Hebrew Imigration Aid Society
HICEM	composite of HIAS, ICA, and Emig[ration]-direct
ICA	Jewish Colonization Association
ICRC	International Committee of the Red Cross, Geneva
IMT	International Military Tribunal
JB	*Judaica Bohemiae*, Praha
JDC	Joint Distribution Committee, New York
JGG–	Jahrbuch der Gesellschaft für die Geschichte der Juden in der
JČR	Čechoslovakischen Republik, Prag
JNBL	Jüdisches Nachrichtenblatt
JRC	Jewish Religious Congregation(s), Prague
KČŽ	Kalendář česko-židovský, Praha
LBIYB	*Leo Baeck Institute Yearbook*, London
NA	U.S. National Archives, Washington DC
NHPM	Národní hnutí pracující mládeže
OCP	Organization of Czechoslovaks in Palestine
ON	Obrana národa
PRO	Public Record Office, London
PÚ	Politické ústředí
PVVZ	Petiční výbor "Věrni zůstaneme," We Remain Faithful
PWE	Political Warfare Executive
RSHA	Reichsicherheitshauptamt
SČAŽ	Spolek českých akademiků židů, Praha
SDP	Sudeten German Party
SOAL	Státní oblastní archiv, Litoměřice

SÚA	Státní ústřední archiv ministerstva vnitra, Praha
ÚŘP	Úřad říšského protektora
ÚVOD	Ústřední vedení odboje domácího
VŽONP	Věstník židovské obce náboženské v Praze
VHA	Vojenský historický archiv, Praha
WIZO	Women's International Zionist Organization
WJC	(WJCA)World Jewish Congress (Archives), London
YIVO	YIVO Archives, New York
YVA	Yad Vashem Archives, Jerusalem
YVS	Yad Vashem Studies
VfZ	Verordnungsblatt des Reichsprotektors in Böhmen und Mähren
ŽM	Židovské muzeum, Praha
ŽNO	Židovská náboženská obec
ŽRS	Židovská rada starších

Notes

Prologue

1. For an illustrated volume on Jewish monuments in Czechoslovakia see Salomon H. Lieben, ed., *Die jüdischen Denkmäler in der Tschechoslowakei*; Hana Volavková, *Zmizelá Praha* (Prague, 1947); Hana Volavková, ed., *Jewish Monuments in Bohemia and Moravia* (Prague, 1952); J. Lion and L. Lukas, *Das Prager Ghetto* (Prague, 1959); Jiří Fiedler, *Jewish Sights of Bohemia and Moravia* (Prague, 1991).

2. In her short story "The Lifted Veil" (1859) George Eliot refers to her visit to Prague, which in fact spurred the initial change in her attitude toward Judaism. See Edward Alexander, "George Eliot's Rabbi," in *Commentary* 92 (July 1991), p. 29.

3. Zdenka Münzer, "The Old-New Synagogue in Prague: Its Architectural History," in *The Jews of Czechoslovakia: Historical Studies and Surveys*, vol. 2, pp. 520–46; the three-volume work (Philadelphia, 1968, 1971, 1984) is hereafter cited as *Jews of CS* with volume and page numbers. See also Milada Vilímková, "Seven Hundred Years of the Old-New Synagogue," in *Judaica Bohemiae* 1 (1969), pp. 72–83 (hereafter cited as JB); Alexander Putík, "The Origins and Symbols of the Prague Jewish Town," in JB 30–31 (1994–95), pp. 7–46.

4. See Herzl, *The Diaries of Theodor Herzl*, entry for August 30, 1899.

5. František Bílek (1872–1941), the foremost representative of the symbolistic trend of his generation. The sculpture was hidden by caring persons during the Nazi occupation. See Ctibor Rybár, *Židovská Praha* (Prague, 1991), p. 330.

6. Ladislav Šaloun (1870–1946), foremost representative of secessive sculpting. His most famous sculpture is that of Master Jan Hus, at the Old Town Square. See Rybár, *Židovská Praha*; Ladislaus Šaloun, "Das Denkmal des Hohen Rabbi Loew am Prager Neuen Rathause," interview in *Das jüdische Prag: Eine Sammelschrift* (Prague, 1917; 2nd ed. with introduction by Robert Weltsch, Kronberg, 1978), p. 40; J. B. Čapek, "Velký rabbi pražský," in *Kostnické jiskry* 14, no. 30 (20.10.1960).

7. Oskar Donath, *Židé a židovství v české literatuře 19. a 20. století*, 2 vols. (Brno, 1923–30); Pavel Eisner, "Jews in the Literature of the Czech Lands," in *Jewish Studies*, ed. Rudolf Iltis (Prague, 1955), p. 51; see Livie Rothkirchenová, "Exil a návrat; historické analogie v českém a hebrejském písemnictví," in *Pocta 650. výročí založení Univerzity Karlovy v Praze* (Prague, 1998), pp. 163–73.

8. See Roman Jakobson, "Řeč a písemnictví českých Židů v době přemyslovské," in *Židovská ročenka* (hereafter ŽR), 1992–93

9. A collection of religious hymns, prayers and missals including the famous Hussite song "Ye Who Are God's Warriors"—discovered in South Bohemia in 1872, in the parish of Jistebnice. First to announce the sensational find of the student Lepold Katz publicly was his gymnasium teacher Martin Kolář, in an article entitled "Hussite Songs, Discovered

and Reviewed by M. Kolář," in *Památky archeologické a místopisné* 9 (1873), p. 825.

10. J. B. Čapek, "Velký rabbi pražský."

11. A. F. Kleinberger, "The Didactics of Rabbi Loew of Prague," in *Scripta Hyerosoly-mitana* 13 (Jerusalem, 1963); Hugo Stránský, "Rabbi Judah Loew of Prague and Jan Amos Comenius: Two Reformers in Education," and Karel Vrána, "The Ecumenical Sense of Culture in J. A. Comenius," both in *Comenius*, ed. Vratislav Bušek, pp. 112, 165 respectively.

12. See Stanislav Segert, "The Unity of the New-Covenant—the Unity of Brethren: A Comparison of Two Religious Communities," in *Jewish Studies*, ed., Rudolf Iltis (Prague, 1955), pp. 71–80.

13. Segert, "Unity."

14. Ruth Kestenberg-Gladstein, "Čechen und Juden in altväterischer Zeit," in JB4, no. 1 (1968), pp. 64–68.

15. Written in 1564 in Leszno in Czech: "Kšaft umírající matky Jednoty Bratrské"; see Jan Amos Comenius, *The Bequest of the Unity of Brethren*, ed. Matthew Spinka (Chicago, 1940).

16. See William F. Albright, "Israel—Prophetic Vision and Historical Fulfillment," in Moshe Davis, *Israel: Its Role in Civilization* (New York, 1956), pp. 31–38.

17. Count Franz von Lützow, *Bohemia: An Historical Sketch* (London, 1939), pp. 328–29.

18. Cf. Song of Solomon (2:11–12); for the English translation of Mácha's "May" by Hugh Hamilton McGovern, see *Translation*, ed. N. Braybrooke and E. Icing (London, 1947), p. 86.

19. See František Gottlieb, "Julius Zeyer (1841–1901)," in ŽR 5730 (1970–71), pp. 109–19; A. M. Píša, *Ivan Olbracht* (Prague, 1982), pp. 115–16; (the memoirs of) Jaroslav Seifert, *Všechny krásy světa* (Prague, 1982).

20. See Milada and Erich Einhorn, eds., *Golden Prague*, p. 28.

21. *Píseň Písní*, translated from the 1937 Stuttgart Hebrew edition of *Shir HaShirim* by Jaroslav Seifert and Stanislav Segert, with illustrations by Arnošt Paderlík (Prague, 1958; rev. ed. 1963).

22. See Bernard Lewis, "Jews and Judaism between Two Cultures. Palimpsests of Jewish History: Christian, Muslim and Secular Diaspora," in Papers from the Tenth World Congress of Jewish Studies, see *Jewish Studies* 30 (1990), pp. 7–13.

23. Felix Weltsch, "Masaryk and Zionism," in *Thomas G. Masaryk and the Jews*, ed. Ernst Rychnovský, transl. B. R. Epstein (New York, 1941), p. 77; Weltsch stresses the point that Masaryk as early as 1883 (in a review of Ernest Renan's *Le Judaisme comme race et comme religion*) unequivocally asserted that the Jews constitute a nation.

24. Ahad Ha'Am (Asher Ginsberg, 1856–1927) bore a strong influence upon Prague Zionists. His "cultural" conception identified as an antithesis to Herzl's political Zionism was presented in two essays: "The Jewish State and the Jewish Problem" (1897) and "Flesh and Spirit" (1904), discussing the modern Jewish national movement focused on its spiritual dimension. For a discussion of his thesis see Shlomo Avineri, *The Making of Modern Zionism* (New York, 1981), pp. 112–24.

25. See Josef Penížek, "Masaryk and the Jewish Czechs," in Rychnovský, ed., *Masaryk and the Jews*, pp. 118, 123.

26. Tomas G. Masaryk, *The Making of a State: Memoirs and Observations, 1914–1918* (New York, 1927); Karel Čapek, *President Masaryk Tells His Story* (London, 1935), p. 256.

27. Masaryk, *Making of a State*, pp. 207, 222.

28. T. G. Masaryk, *Národnostní filosofie* (Prague, 1905), p. 14; cf. Weltsch, "Masaryk and Zionism," pp. 77–79; Hillel J. Kieval, *The Making of Czech Jewry: National Conflict and Jewish Society in Bohemia 1870–1918* (New York, Oxford, 1988), p. 110.

29. Cf. chapter 2; see Lev Vohryzek, "Masaryk a Židé," in *Věstník židovské obce náboženské* (hereafter VŽONP), 28.2.1935, pp. 4–5.

30. See Otakar Odložilík, "Jan Amos Komenský," in *Comenius*, p. 37.

31. Vladimir Jabotinsky, "Tribute to T. G. Masaryk's 80th Birthday," in *Jewish Daily Bulletin*, 7.3.1930.

32. F. X. Šalda, "Genius řecký a genius židovský," in *Zápisník* 3 (1931); on his attitudes toward the Jews see Oskar Donath, "F. X. Šalda a židovství," in VŽONP, 30.4.1937.

33. Eisner, among others, claimed that "the main point is that the Prague genius loci operates in Kafka"; see Pavel Eisner, *Franz Kafka in Prague* (New York, 1950), p. 14; see also Eduard Goldstücker et al., eds., *Franz Kafka aus Prager Sicht* (Prague, 1965).

34. František Kautman, "Kafka, Hašek, Weiner a Jesenská," in *Svědectví* 69 (1983), p. 98.

35. Robert Weltsch, *Max Brod and His Age*, Leo Baeck Memorial Lecture 13 (New York, 1970), p. 8.

36. Rabbi Gustav Sicher (1880–1960), who served as spiritual leader of the postwar Jewish community of Bohemia, Moravia, and Silesia, can be considered the last and most articulate representative of Czech-Jewish interaction. For a tribute to his wide-ranging work and the literary treatises written in his honor see *Jewish Studies: Essays in Honor of the Very Reverend Dr. Gustav Sicher Chief Rabbi of Prague*, ed. Rudolf Iltis (Prague, 1955). See also Rabbi Sicher's treatises and essays, *Volte život* (Prague, 1975).

37. For the full text of his reinstatement address see VŽONP, 1.8.1947.

38. See "A Message from Václav Havel," in *Where Cultures Meet*, ed. Natalia Berger (Tel Aviv, 1990), p. 12.

1. The Historical Setting

1. My data on early history are gleaned from the following works: A. C. Adams, *The History of the Jews from the War with Rome to the Present Time* (London, 1887), p. 271; Václav Vladivoj Tomek, *Dějepis města Prahy*, 2 vols. (Prague, 1855); Gottlieb Bondy and Franz Dworsky, *Zur Geschichte der Jüden in Böhmen, Mähren und Schlesien von 906 bis 1620* (Prague, 1906); Jaromír Čelakovský, "Příspěvky k dějinám židů v době Jagellonské," in *Časopis Českého Musea* 13 (1898), p. 386; *Jahrbuch der Gesellschaft für Geschichte der Juden in der Čechoslovakischen Republik*, ed. Samuel Steinherz, 9 vols. (Prague, 1929–38; hereafter cited as JGGJČR); Bertold Bretholz, *Geschichte der Juden in Mähren im Mittelalter* (Brünn, 1934), and *Quellen zur Geschichte der Juden im Mähren* (Prague, 1935); Tomáš Pěkný, *Dějiny Židů v Čechách a na Moravě* (Prague, 1993).

2. See Samuel Steinherz, "Die Einwanderung der Juden in Böhmen," in *Die Juden in Prag* (Prague, 1927), pp. 35, 53.

3. Hana Volavková, "Výmluvný dokument," in Žr 5721 (1960–61), pp. 77–84.

4. See entry in *Slavonic Encyclopedia*, ed. Joseph S. Rouček (New York, 1949), p. 528, citing "Description of Slavonic Lands" in Obaid alBekri, *Book of Roads and Lands* (1066) as well as later publications and translations.

5. Tomek, *Dějepis města Prahy*, 1:150; see also Emil Spira, "K dějinám Židů v Čechách: Doba válek křižáckých a posledních Přemyslovců," in *Kalendář česko-židovský* (hereafter KČŽ), 1900–1901), p. 123.

6. František Palacký, *Dějiny národu českého v Čechách a na Moravě*, vol. 1 (Prague, 1968), p. 283, refers to the prudent farmer "taking away the surplus of honey from the bees at an opportune moment."

7. For a most detailed study on the period of the rule of the Jagellonian dynasty see Čelakovský, "Příspěvky k dějinám židů," pp. 385–484; Jan Heřman, "The Conflict between the Jewish and non-Jewish Population in Bohemia before the 1541 Banishment," in JB 6, no. 2 (1970), pp. 39–54.

8. The main Jewish source for the description of the pogrom is Avigdor Kara, whose penitential poems (*Slihot*) on this event are included in a special collection of prayers edited by Shimon Bernfeld, *Sefer haDemaoth*, vol. 2 (Berlin, 1924), pp. 159–61. See also František Graus, "Prag 1389–1419–1422," in *Struktur und Geschichte, Vorträge und Vorschungen* 7 (Singmaringen, 1971), pp. 45–60.

9. František M. Bartoš, "Židé v Čechách v době Husově," in KČŽ 35 (1915–16), pp. 154–63, bases his theory upon the tractate *De usura* by Jakoubek ze Stříbra (Jacobellus de Misa), a theologian and a towering figure of Hussitism. This work was written in 1414 in the wake of the bloody Easter night pogrom in Prague. Jacobellus leveled horrendous charges against the usurers and their lascivious way of life, exhorting the Jews to work in forests and fields, earning their livelihood as artisans and laborers, and thus to avoid falling prey to the cruelty of their enemies.

10. See Otto Muneles and Jan Heřman, eds., *Prague Ghetto in the Renaissance Period* (Prague, 1965); Volavková, *Jewish Monuments*, vol. 4; J. Spěváček, *Rudolf II a jeho doba* (Prague, 1987).

11. André Neher, *Le puits de l'exil* (Paris, 1987); Vladimír Sadek, "Rabi Loew: Sa vie, héritage pédagogique et sa legende," in JB 15 (1979), pp. 27–41.

12. The reference is to Jirásek's classic novel *Temno* ("The darkness"); cf. M. Čapek, "Comenius and the Moral Problem," in *Comenius*, pp. 43–44.

13. See M. Čapek, "Comenius," pp. 35–36.

14. Jan Heřman, "The Evolution of Jewish Population in Bohemia and Moravia, 1754–1953," in *Papers in Jewish Demography, 1977* (Jerusalem, 1980), pp. 53–67.

15. See John Toland, "Reasons for Naturalizing the Jews in Great Britain and Ireland: On the Same Foot with All Other Nations," in Mendes-Flohr and Reinharz, *The Jew in the Modern World*, pp. 12–16. "A Defence of the Jews against All Vulgar Prejudices in All Countries" (London, 1714) is also reproduced in this volume; see pp. 6, 10–15, 17, 20, 39–46.

16. See Ruth Kestenberg-Gladstein, *Neuere Geschichte der Juden in den böhmischen Ländern*, Erster Teil: *Das Zeitalter der Aufklärung, 1780–1830* (Tübingen, 1969), pp. 1–4; Anita Franková, "Erfassung der jüdischen Bevölkerung in Böhmen im 18 und in der ersten Hälfte des 19 Jahrhunderts," in JB 6 (1970), pp. 55–69.

17. Josef Bergl, "Die Ausweisung der Juden aus Prag im Jahre 1744," in *Die Juden in Prag*; Salomon Hugo Lieben, "Briefe von 1744–1748 uber die Austreibung der Juden aus Prag," in JGGJČR 4 (1932), pp. 367–70; for "Letters on the Expulsion of the Jews from Prague," see also Wilma A. Iggers, *The Jews of Bohemia and Moravia: A Historical Reader* (Detroit, 1992), pp. 36–38.

18. See Mendes-Flohr and Reinharz, *The Jew in the Modern World*, pp. 34–36.

19. Kestenberg-Gladstein, *Neuere Geschichte*, pp. 95–112; Eduard Goldstücker, "Jews between Czechs and Germans around 1848," in *The Czech National Revival, the Germans and the Jews* (Los Angeles, 1972), pp. 17–29.

20. Jan Havránek, "The Development of Czech Nationalism," in *Austrian History Yearbook*, vol. 3, pt. 2 (1967), pp. 223 60.

21. William O. McCagg Jr., *A History of Habsburg Jews, 1670–1918* (Bloomington, 1989), pp. 75–77; Gustav Otruba, "Der Anteil der Juden am Wirtschaftsleben der böhmischen Länder seit dem Beginn der Industrialisierung," in *Die Juden in den böhmischen Ländern*, Vorträge der Tagung des Collegium Carolinum in Bad Wiessee vom 27.–29. November 1981, ed. Ferdinand Seibt (München, Wien, 1983), pp. 209–68.

22. This attitude was aptly reflected in Czech literature. See Donath, *Židé a židovství*; Avigdor Dagan, "Jewish Themes in Czech Literature," in *Jews of CS* 1:456–57.

23. Alfred Meissner, *Geschichte meines Lebens* (Wien-Teschen, 1884), cited in Christoph Stölzl, *Kafka's böses Böhmen: Zur Sozialgeschichte eines Prager Juden* (München, 1975), p. 29; Eduard Goldstücker, "Prague German Literature: Its Socio-Historical Setting," in *The Czech National Revival*, pp. 31–43.

24. Josef Vyskočil, "Die tschechisch-jüdische Bewegung," in JB 3, no. 1 (1967), pp. 36–55; Egon Hostovský, "The Czech-Jewish Movement," in *Jews of CS* 2:148–54.

25. Donath, *Židé a židovství*, p. 11.

26. Moritz Hartmann, "Böhmische Elegien," cf. Jan Patočka, *Co jsou Češi?* (Prague, 1990), p. 90; Oskar Donath, "Siegfried Kapper," in JGGJČR 6 (1934), pp. 323–442.

27. Guido Kisch, *In Search of Freedom: A History of American Jews from Czechoslovakia* (London, 1949), pp. 26–44.

28. Kisch, *In Search*, p. 39.

29. Kestenberg-Gladstein, *Neuere Geschichte*, pp. 126, 263–65, 315–16; Jiří Kuděla, "Pražští židovští knihtiskaři, knihkupci a antikváři v 17. až 19. století," in *Documenta Pragensia* 9 (1990), and "Mojžíš Israel Landau (1788–1852): Nové poznatky k biografii významných osobností pražského ghetta," lecture presented on January 29, 1990, at the Prague Jewish Community, 19 pp. plus appendices, copy in possession of the author.

30. See Guido Kisch, *Die Prager Universität und die Juden, 1348–1848* (Moravská Ostrava, 1935; 2nd ed. Amsterdam, 1969).

31. See Kieval, *Making of Czech Jewry*, p. 69.

32. See Michal Frankl, "Can We, the Czech Catholics Be Antisemites? Antisemitism, at the Dawn of the Czech Christian Socialist Movement," in JB 23 (1997), pp. 47–71.

33. Vyskočil, "Die tschechisch-jüdische Bewegung," p. 42.

34. Lützow, *Bohemia*, p. 352.

35. Vyskočil, "Die tschechisch-jüdische Bewegung," pp. 36–55.

36. The first *Siddur* issued by Hynek Kraus, published in Vienna in 1847, was replaced

by a novel Czech-Hebrew prayer book, compiled by Augustín Stein, *Maarche-Lev: Modlitby Israelitův* (Prague, 1884); see J. S. Kraus, "Or-Tomid: Spolek českých židů pro pěstování bohoslužby jazykem českým a hebrejským," in κČŽ 4 (1884–85), pp. 111–13.

37. For a fresh appraisal see Helena Krejčová, "Kalendář českožidovský 1881–1938," in ŽR 5750 (1989–90), pp. 127 ff.

38. It was Karel Fischer who inspired Jaroslav Vrchlický to write his famous epic "Bar Kochba" (1897).

39. See introduction by Robert Weltsch to the new edition of *Das Jüdische Prag*, p. vii.

40. On the intense life in the Lese und Redehalle deutscher Studenten and the casino, see Guido Kisch, *Der Lebensweg eines Rechthistorikers: Erinnerungen* (Singmaringen, 1975), p. 45; Gary B. Cohen, *The Politics of Ethnic Survival: Germans in Prague, 1861–1914* (Princeton NJ, 1981), pp. 177–78.

41. Kieval, *Making of Czech Jewry*, pp. 24, 49–50.

42. Frankl, "Can We Be Antisemites?" pp. 50–54.

43. Frankl, "Can We Be Antisemites?" p. 52.

44. Frankl, "Can We Be Antisemites?" pp. 60–62.

45. Robert Neuschl, *Křest'anská sociologie*, vol. 11 (Brno, 1898), p. 188.

46. For Rudolf Vrba's activities and pamphlets, see Frankl, "Can We Be Antisemites?" pp. 63–65.

47. Stölzl, *Kafkas böses Böhmen*, p. 35, quotes František Pravda and the priest's vicious portrayal of Jews. See also Fred Hahn, "The Jews among the Nations in Bohemia and Moravia," in *Religion and Nationalism in Eastern Europe and the Soviet Union* (Boulder, London, 1987), pp. 45, 48–49.

48. Michael A. Riff, "Czech Anti-Semitism and the Jewish Response before 1914," in *Wiener Library Bulletin* 29 (1976), pp. 9–10.

49. *Hilsnerova aféra a česká společnost 1899–1999*, Sborník přednášek na Univerzitě Karlově v Praze ve dnech 24.–26. listopadu 1999, ed. Miloš Pojar (Prague 1999); Michal Frankl, "The Background of the Hilsner Case: Political Antisemitism and Allegation of Ritual Murder 1896–1900," in JB 34 (2000), pp. 34–118.

50. Lederer, "Memories of Masaryk," in Rychnovský, ed., *Masaryk and the Jews*, p. 275. A close friend of Masaryk wrote of this period, "1899 and 1900—terrible years, years of blood and darkness . . . Czech intelligence hit a lamentable low in this intelligence test . . . which left us with a sad augur for our future"; see Jan Herben, "T. G. Masaryk über Juden and Antisemitismus," in *Masaryk und das Judentum*, ed. Ernst Rychnovský (Prague, 1931), pp. 274–99.

51. See Viktor Vohryzek, "Epištoly k českým židům" in *Českožidovské listy*, 15.3.1900, reprinted in Vohryzek, *K židovské otázce* (Prague, 1923), pp. 15–16.

52. Eduard Lederer, *Žid v dnešní společnosti* (Prague, 1902); for a detailed discussion see Kieval, *Making of Czech Jewry*, pp. 88–89.

53. Viktor Vohryzek, "Několik slov úvodem," in *Rozvoj* (Pardubice, 1904), reprinted in *K židovské otázce*, p. 42.

54. For his discussion with Dr. Teytz see "Rozmluva s prof. Masarykem," in *Rozvoj*, 9.9.1909; Felix Weltsch, "Masaryk and Zionism," pp. 77–79.

55. See Vohryzek, "Masaryk a židé," pp. 4–5.

56. Cohen, "Jews in German Society: Prague 1860–1914," *Central European History* 10 (1977), p. 38, and "Ethnicity and Urban Population Growth: The Decline of the Prague Germans, 1880–1910," in *Studies in East European Social History*, ed. Keith Hitchins, vol. 2 (Leiden, 1981), pp. 3–26. Cohen gives the breakdown for the 1900 census for Bohemia, p. 14, as follows: Czechs 50,080; Germans 40,521; others 177. For the city of Prague: Czechs 9,880; Germans 8,230.

57. Both parties attached great importance to such symbolic acts; see Cohen, *Politics of Ethnic Survival*, p. 18.

58. *Encyclopaedia Judaica*, vol. 13, col. 304; Hugo Gold, *Die Juden und Judengemeinden Mährens in Vergangheit und Gegenwart* (Brno, 1929); *Židé a Morava*, Sborník příspěvků přednesených na konferenci konané 12. listopadu 1997 v Kroměříži (Kroměříž, 1998).

59. See Cohen, *Politics of Ethnic Survival*; Kestenberg-Gladstein, *Neuere Geschichte*.

60. V. Zeman, "Bez židův a proti židům," in KČŽ, 35 (1915–16), p. 132, refers to Zucker's articles published in KČŽ and in *Českožidovské listy*.

61. Zeman, "Bez židův a proti židům," p. 133.

62. Viktor Teytz, "Bohumil Bondy," in KČŽ 27 (1907–8), pp. 81–84.

63. Jaroslav Rokycana, "Za Leonem Bondym," in KČŽ 46 (1924–25), pp. 4–5.

64. Emanuel Svoboda, "Mikoláš Aleš u Alexandra Brandeise," in KČŽ 34 (1914–15), pp. 72–76; Hana Volavková, "Alexander Brandeis a jeho přátelé," in ŽR 5722 (1961–62), pp. 73–77; R. I. Kronbauer, "Alexander Brandeis a jeho přátelské styky s českými umělci výtvarnými," in KČŽ 22 (1902–3), p. 78.

65. Ladislav Škroup wrote the first Czech opera, *Dráteník* (The tinker), and gained fame as the composer of the Czech national anthem "Kde domov můj." See "Židovská hudební kultura v Čechách," in VŽONP (May 1983), pp. 4–5.

66. See Franz Kafka, *Dearest Father: Stories and Other Writings*, transl. E. Kaiser and E. Wilkins (New York, 1954), pp. 171–72; Franz Kafka, *Brief an den Vater* (München, 1960), pp. 38–40.

67. See Heřman, "Evolution," pp. 255–65; for a description of internal conditions and developments in the Jewish community see Ruth Kestenberg-Gladstein, "The Jews between Czechs and Germans in the Historic Lands, 1848–1918," in *Jews of CS* 1:21–71.

68. For Maccabi's appeal to gymnasium students, see "Aufruf der Prager Makabea" (June 1894), reproduced in N. M. Gelber, "Kavim leKidmat Toldoteha shel haZionut beBohemia uMoravia," in *Prag ve Yerushalaim*, ed. Felix Weltsch (Jerusalem, 1954), pp. 48–49.

69. See Theodor Herzl, "Die Jagd in Böhmen," originally printed in *Die Welt* (November 5, 1897), Czech translation in *Židovský kalendář* 1938–39, pp. 118–19.

70. Irma Polak, "The Zionist Women's Movement," in *Jews of CS* 2:137.

71. On the occasion of the twentieth anniversary of the establishment of *Selbstwehr*, Zdeněk Landes discusses the role of the weekly at various stages in *Židovské zprávy*, 26.3.1926.

72. The papers of Leo Herrmann are deposited in the Central Zionist Archives in Jerusalem (hereafter CZA), A140; for a tribute see *Prag ve Yerushalayim*.

73. For discussion see Kieval, *Making of Czech Jewry*, "Bar Kochba under Leo Herrmann," pp. 124–36.

74. Buber's addresses in English: *On Judaism*, ed. Nahum N. Glatzer (New York, 1967); in Czech: *Tři řeči o židovství* (Prague, 1912).

75. Oskar K. Rabinowicz, "Czechoslovak Zionism: Analecta to a History," in *Jews of CS* 2:20.

76. Rabinowicz, "Czechoslovak Zionism," 20.

77. Hugo Herrmann, "Zur čechisch-jüdischen Frage," in *Selbstwehr*, 7.4.1911.

78. For a reference on Buber's impact see Šalda, "Genius."

79. Arne Novák, author of the monumental *Přehledné dějiny literatury české od nejstarších dob až do naše dny*, 4 vols. (Olomouc, 1936–39), dealt with the Jewish-Zionist issue in public speeches, addresses, etc.; see chapter 2.

80. *Rozvoj*, 27.7.1906; Machar's letter is referred to in *Židovská otázka a její řešení*, 2nd ed. (Prague, 1912), p. 10.

81. František Krejčí, "Assimilation und Zionismus vom ethischen Stadpunkt," in *Selbstwehr*, 11.6.1909.

82. The reference is to Christoph Stölzl's emphatic assertion that Kafka's year of birth (1883) coincided with "a mass outpouring of anti-Semitic popular literature in the German and Czech languages." See Stölzl, *Kafka's böses Böhmen*, p. 47.

83. Johannes Urzidil, underscoring the spiritual element prevailing in the work of the Prague writers, termed this milieu a "universal megalopolis, much more brilliant than many a larger European metropolis." See Urzidil, *There Goes Kafka*, trans. Harold A. Besilius (Detroit, 1968), p. 13.

84. See the essay of Hans Tramer, "Prague—City of Three Peoples," in *Leo Baeck Institute Yearbook*, London (herefter cited as LBIYB) 9 (1964), pp. 305–9. For an excerpt of the paper read at the Liblice Conference of 1963, see Kautman, "Kafka, Hašek, Weiner a Jesenská," pp. 97–103.

85. Pavel Eisner, "Kapitola o česko-německém soužití," in *Přítomnost* 4, 19.5.1927, p. 295; see also Eve Bock, "The German-Jewish Writers of Prague: Interpreters of Czech Literature," in LBIYB 23 (1978), pp. 239–46; Harry Zohn, "Participation in German Literature," in Jews of CS 1:487–88; Wilma A. Iggers, "The Flexible National Identities of Bohemian Jewry," in *East Central Europe* 7, no. 1 (1980), pp. 39–48.

86. "Our heart feels "connational' with all the oppressed nations," wrote Werfel in his introduction. See Peter Stephan Jungk, *Franz Werfel, Eine Lebensgeschichte* (Frankfurt, 1987), p. 75.

87. Dr. Viktor Teytz, editor of *Rozvoj*, claimed that they considered themselves "in memory Jews," having completely merged with the Czech present. Cf. Kieval, *Making of Czech Jewry*, p. 156.

88. Max Brod recalls Masaryk's warnings in his *Streitbares Leben 1884–1968* (Munich, 1969), pp. 95–98; Masaryk met several Czech-Jewish activists (Max Pleschner, Dr. Otakar Guth, Dr. Josef Beck, and others), consulting with them on how to prevent riots in Prague. He also asked them to warn the German Jews to refrain from expressing their sympathies publicly; see Okatar Guth, "1918 (28.10) 1938," in KČŽ 57 (1938–39), p. 17.

89. See Siegmund Kaznelson, "Erinnerungen an gemeinsame Kampfjahre," in *Dichter, Denker, Helfer: Max Brod zum 50. Geburstag*, ed. Felix Weltsch (Moravská Ostrava, 1934),

p. 53; Max Brod, "Prag-Wien-Erinnerungen," in *The Jews of Austria*, ed. Josef Frankel (London, 1967), pp. 241–42.

90. Ludvík Singer, "Naše cíle," in *Židovské zprávy*, 5.4.1918, pp. 1–2.

91. The intellectual and halutzic activities of the new "olim" proved a solid asset to the building up of the Yishuv in Palestine. See Hans Kohn, "Before 1918 in the Historic Lands," in *Jews of CS* 1:20.

92. See Rabinowicz, "Czechoslovak Zionism," pp. 20, 110.

2. Years of Challenge and Growth

1. See Robert Kvaček, "The Rise and Fall of Democracy," in *Bohemia in History*, ed. Mikuláš Teich (Cambridge, 1998), p. 246.

2. The most useful surveys of the First Republic in the English language are: Jan Opočenský, *The Collapse of the Austro-Hungarian Monarchy and the Rise of the Czechoslovak State* (Prague, 1928); Robert J. Kerner (ed.), *Czechoslovakia: Twenty Years of Independence* (Berkeley, Los Angeles, 1940); Věra Olivová, *The Doomed Democracy: Czechoslovakia in a Disrupted Republic, 1914–1948* (London, 1972); Victor S. Mamatey and Radomír Luža, eds., *A History of the Czechoslovak Republic, 1918–1948* (Princeton NJ, 1973); Josef Korbel, *Twentieth Century Czechoslovakia: The Meaning of its History* (New York, 1977).

3. Cited in A. Brož, *The Rise of the Czechoslovak Republic* (London, 1919), p. 8.

4. Brož, *Rise of the Republic*, p. 13.

5. Aharon Moshe Rabinowicz, "The Jewish Minority," in *Jews of CS* 1:155–61.

6. Rabinowicz, "Jewish Minority," pp. 193–96.

7. The chief rabbi of Prague, Dr. I. Brody, composed a special prayer in Hebrew on the occasion of the establishment of the republic, with blessings for Masaryk, the great man who became its head. Noteworthy is the last passage of the prayer: "Be merciful to us and give solace, the remaining people of Israel, the remnant of the House of Jacob! Gather us again, the dispersed and the scattered and let us live to see in our lifetime a redeemed Jerusalem." *Židovské zprávy*, 9.11.1923.

8. See *Jüdische Rundschau*, 26.11.1918.

9. Josef Svátek, "Pogromy v Holešově v letech 1774–1918," in ŽR 5740 (1920), pp. 41–43.

10. *Neue Freie Presse*, 19.11.1920.

11. Kafka noted: "Mounted police, gendarmerie ready for a bayonet charge, a screaming crowd is dispersing"; Franz Kafka, *Letters to Milena*, ed. Willi Haas (New York, 1953), p. 213.

12. The Czechoslovak Constitution was based on several democratic constitutions of the world and mainly on that of the French Third Republic. The opening words of the text, "We, the Czechoslovak nation," were reminiscent of the preamble of the United States constitution. Apparently the final wording was greatly influenced by the Czech politicians' experience in the Vienna *Reichsrat*. See Vaclav L. Beneš, "Czechoslovak Democracy and Its Problems, 1918–1920," in *A History of the Czechoslovak Republic 1918–1948*, pp. 92–93.

13. Aharon Moshe Rabinowicz, "The Jewish Party: A Struggle for National Recognition, Representation and Autonomy," in *Jews of CS* 2:253–319.

14. About the launching of *Tribuna* and Peroutka's activities see Milan Otáhal, "Ferdinand Peroutka: Muž Přítomnosti," in *Svědectví* 18, no. 70–71 (1973), pp. 339–41; see also chapter 3.

15. Of the 93,000 Jews living in Subcarpathian Ruthenia in 1921, 80,000 (87 percent) declared themselves to be of Jewish nationality while in 1930 of the 101,000 Jews, 94,000 (93 percent) did so.

16. František Friedmann, *Einige Zahlen über die Tschechoslowakischen Juden* (Prague, 1933). For a most illuminating analysis of the nationality and language issues prevailing amidst the Jews of the First Republic, see Jaroslav Bubeník and Jiří Křesýan, "Zjišťování národnosti a židovská otázka," in *Postavení a osudy židovského obyvatelstva v Čechách a na Moravě v letech 1939–1945*, ed. Helena Krejčová and Jana Svobodová (Prague, 1998), pp. 11–39.

17. For an overall view of various aspects of life in the three enclaves see *The Jews of Czechoslovakia*, vols. 1–3.

18. For comments on the refugees see Josef B. Nežárecký, *Židé v minulosti a přítomnosti* (Prague, 1919), pp. 3, 4.

19. Max Brod, "Erfahrung in Ostjudischen Schulwerk," in *Der Jude* (1916–17), pp. 32–34.

20. Rabinowicz, "Czechoslovak Zionism," pp. 19–123.

21. Josef Chmelář, *Political Parties in Czechoslovakia* (Prague, 1926); Charles Hoch, *The Political Parties in Czechoslovakia*, Czechoslovak Sources and Documents, no. 9 (Prague, 1936).

22. See Beneš, "Czechoslovak Democracy," p. 96.

23. Rabinowicz, "Jewish Minority," pp. 193, 210–13.

24. Rabinowicz, "Jewish Minority," pp. 283–84.

25. In the late thirties Dr. Emil Margulies (1877–1943), head of the Jewish Party (1920–29), together with Leo Motzkin brought the case of Franz Bernheim, the so-called Bernheim petition, to the League of Nations. See Nahum Goldmann, "Recollections of Czech Jewry," *Review of the Society for the History of Czechoslovak Jews* 1 (1987), p. 160.

26. Rabinowicz, "Jewish Party," p. 295. For Frischer's activities as member of the National Council see "The Czechoslovak Government-in-Exile," chapter 6.

27. Rabinowicz, "Jewish Party," pp. 295–96.

28. *Těsnopisecké zprávy o schůzích Národního shromáždění republiky československé 1918–1938*, Session no. 266 (Prague, 1919–39), 27.4.1933, pp. 25–29.

29. For a concise survey of the Czech-Jewish movement see Josef Vyskočil, "Českožidovské hnutí," in *Dějiny a současnost*, no. 4 (1966), pp. 18–20; Hostovský, "Czech-Jewish Movement," pp. 148–54.

30. Hostovský, "Czech-Jewish Movement," p. 152.

31. See František Friedmann, *Mravnost či oportunita: Několik poznámek k anketě akad. spolku "Kapper" v Brně* (Prague, 1927), p. 3.

32. Friedmann, *Mravnost či oportunita*, p. 7.

33. Richard Weiner, "Neviditelné ghetto," in *Přítomnost* 3 (1926), p. 698.

34. This new element reinforced the small minority of traditional Jews in some of the cities, constituting a spirited opposition to the liberal majority. For a detailed de-

scription see Hugo Stránský, "The Religious Life in the Historic Lands," in *Jews of CS* 1:340.

35. Jan Martinec, "Doktor chudých," in ŽR 5739 (1978–79), pp. 115–19.

36. See Gustav Fleischmann, "The Religious Congregation, 1918–1938," in *Jews of CS* 1:278.

37. Fleischmann, "Religious Congregation," p. 308.

38. Fleischmann, "Religious Congregation," pp. 315–16.

39. Fleischmann, "Religious Congregation," pp. 314–15.

40. Fleischmann, "Religious Congregation," pp. 320–25.

41. Goldstein's report in the parliament was reproduced in the community bulletin; see VŽONP, 31.1.1937.

42. For a review of the activities of B'nai B'rith see Meir Färber, "Jewish Lodges and Fraternal Orders Prior to World War II," in *Jews of CS* 2:229–40.

43. See Guido Kisch, "Jewish Historiography in Bohemia, Moravia, Silesia," in *Jews of CS* 1:6–7.

44. Kisch, "Jewish Historiography," p. 7.

45. See statistical table, Friedmann, *Einige Zahlen*, pp. 27–54; Jan Heřman, "The Development of Bohemian and Moravian Jewry, 1918–1938," in U. O. Schmelz, P. Glikson, and S. Della Pergola, eds., *Papers in Jewish Demography, 1969* (Jerusalem, 1973), pp. 191–206.

46. Friedmann, *Einige Zahlen*, p. 15; Heřman, "Evolution," pp. 255–65.

47. See VŽONP, 11.11.1938.

48. See Heřman, "Development," p. 200.

49. Bruno Blau, "Yidn in der Tshekhoslovakay," in *Yiddishe Ekonomik* 3 (1939), pp. 27–54; Ezra Mendelsohn, *The Jews in East Central Europe between the World Wars* (Bloomington, 1983), pp. 142–45.

50. For details see Lucian Benda, *Židé v našem hospodářství* (Prague, 1939); Václav Král, *Otázky hospodářského a socialního vývoje v českých zemích v letech 1938–1945*, 3 vols. (Prague, 1957–59); Joseph C. Pick, "The Economy," in *Jews of CS* 1:359–435.

51. See *Těsnopisecké zprávy o schůzích Prozatimního Národního shromáždění republiky československé*, Tisky 1930 II (210), pp. 167–68; VŽONP, 14.5.1934.

52. See Willy Schönfeld, ed., *Přeškolování: Malá nauka o povolání pro praksi* (Prague, 1940), p. 1.

53. For the listing of names of professors later ousted at German establishments see "Die entlassene jüdische Professoren," in *Medina Ivrit*, 20.1.1939, as follows: Faculty of Law 5, Faculty of Medicine 35, Faculty of Philosophy 8, Faculty of Natural Sciences 13, Technical Institutions 4.

54. Wolfgang Johann Bruegel, "Jews in Political Life," in *Jews of CS* 2:243–52.

55. Bruegel, "Jews in Political Life," p. 245.

56. Bruegel, "Jews in Political Life," p. 246. In 1942, Dr. Meissner together with his wife was deported to Terezín where he survived the war.

57. Bruegel, "Jews in Political Life," p. 249.

58. Bruegel, "Jews in Political Life," p. 246.

59. Dr. Gustav Winter died in 1943 in London; Bruegel, "Jews in Political Life," pp. 246–47.

60. Bruegel, "Jews in Political Life," p. 247. Arnošt Winter perished in one of the concentration camps during the war.

61. Bruegel, "Jews in Political Life," p. 247. Robert Klein perished in Buchenwald in 1941.

62. After the German occupation Firt managed to escape illegally to France and later reached London. He became a member of the State Council of the Czechoslovak Government-in-Exile. After the war, upon his return to Prague, he became a member of Parliament on behalf of the Czech National Party and was active in public affairs until the Communist coup. In the last years of his life he lived in Germany, heading the Czechoslovak section of Radio Free Europe in Munich. See Julius Firt, *Knihy a osudy* (Köln, 1972).

63. For a survey of journalists and authors see Hostovský, "Participation in Modern Czech Literature," in *Jews of CS* 2:441, 446–48; Avigdor Dagan, "The Press," pp. 523–27; Peter Heumos and Peter Becher, eds., *Drehscheibe Prag—Staging Point Prague: German Exiles 1933–1939* (München, 1989), pp. 95–102. On Weiner, see Hostovský, "Participation," p. 442.

64. Jaroslav Hasek, *The Good Soldier Svejk*, transl. Cecil Parrott (London: Penguin Books, 1973), xvi–xvii.

65. The most promising poets were Jiří Langer (1894–1943) and František Gottlieb (1904–74). Gottlieb was regarded as one of Otokar Fischer's closest disciples: his lyrical poetry dealt with themes such as the return to the "Promised Land," "The Road to Canaan," etc. See Donath, "Jüdisches in der neuen tschechischen Literatur," in *Jahrbuch der Gezellschaft für Geschichte der Juden in der Čechoslovakischen Republik* 3 (1931), pp. 130–35.

66. Together with Prof. Arnošt Kraus, Fischer established the Czech Germanic studies department at Charles University. For an assessment of his work in this field see Pavel Eisner, "Host Otokar Fischer," in KČŽ 57 (1938–39), p. 70.

67. See Hostovský, "Participation," p. 443; for an in-depth discussion of Fischer's "return," see Hans Kohn, "Stimmen," in *Der Jude* (1923), pp. 552–56.

68. See Fischer, *Slovo a svět* (Prague, 1938), chapter 3.

69. Fischer's *Slovo a svět* was reviewed in *Židovské zprávy*, 18.2.1938; his first collection of essays, *Duše a svět* (The soul and the word), was published in 1929.

70. It is noteworthy that a clandestine issue of *Přítomnost* (3.2.1943) that castigated Jews on the score of "Germanization" and social oppression singled out Otokar Fischer and others like him "whom every Czech would more than willingly acknowledge for their work and merits."

71. See Eisner, "Host Otokar Fischer," p. 72.

72. Langer described his years in exile in France and England in an essay entitled "Za války," in *Vzpomínky českých divadelníků na německou okupaci a druhou světovou válku*, ed. František Černý (Prague, 1965), pp. 278–88.

73. For a short biographical sketch of the two Langer brothers, František and Jiří, see *Encyclopedia Judaica*, vol. 15, cols. 1418–20.

74. The Czech version of his foreword under the title "My Brother Jiří," written for the English edition (published in New York, 1961), is included in František Langer's essay collection *Byli a bylo* with a perceptive preface by Josef Träger, "František Langer pamět-

ník" (Prague, 1963). More recently it was also included in the new Czech edition of Jiří Langer's *Devět Bran aneb chasidů tajemství* (Prague, 1992).

75. Jiří Langer died of pneumonia in March 1943 in Tel Aviv as a consequence of a harrowing three-month trip aboard a refugee ship sailing from Bratislava to Palestine. After all his tribulations the new homeland brought him some surcease from pain as reflected in his last volume of poetry, written in Hebrew as *Me'at Tsori* ("A Little Balm"), published in Tel Aviv shortly after his death.

76. Avigdor Dagan's tribute on the one hundreth anniversary of his birth, "The Jewish Identity of Frantisek Langer," in the *Review of the Society for the History of Czechoslovak Jews* 2 (1988–89), pp. 25–32. The essay contains excerpts from Langer's letters from Prague written to the Dagans in Jerusalem.

77. František Kafka, "Odešel František Langer," in VŽONP, 1.9.1965.

78. F. X. Šalda, *Šaldův zápisník* 8 (April 1936). For an assessment of Hostovský's impact on his Czech contemporaries see Josef Träger's view, written in 1969 and reproduced in *Egon Hostovský: Vzpomínky, studie a dokumenty o jeho díle a osudu*, ed. Rudolf Sturm (Toronto, 1973), p. 134.

79. Václav Černý, *Paměti* (Toronto, 1982), p. 245; Antonín J. Liehm, "Egon Hostovský" in *Generace* (Prague, 1988), pp. 372–97.

80. Liehm, "Egon Hostovský."

81. *Letters from Exile* was translated from the Czech by Ann Křtil (London, 1942), pp. 120–22. It includes Hostovský's apotheosis to his homeland: "My One and All" (Má jediná)—a confession of faith and loyalty clothed in magnificent expression, described as "a most poetic and faithful prayer through which Hostovský sought to save his soul." See František Langer's review of the book in *Obzory* (January 1942).

82. Cf. chapter 4.

83. See Jan Havránek, "Fascism in Czechoslovakia," and Joseph F. Žáček, "Czechoslovak Fascisms," both in *Native Fascism in the Successor States, 1918–1945*, ed. Peter F. Sugar (Santa Barbara CA: 1971), pp. 47–55, 56–62.

84. See Hugo Gold, ed., "Samuel Steinherz, zum 80 Geburtstage," in Steinherz Festschrift, *Zeitschrift für die Geschichte der Juden in der Tschechoslowakei* 5, no.2 (Prague, 1938), pp. 51–55. For some interesting comments on the initial "racial disturbances" and the case of Prof. Samuel Steinherz, see Alena Míšková, "Von Schönerer zum Genozid?" in *Židé v Sudetech: Die Juden im Sudetenland* (Prague, 2000), pp. 65–81.

85. *Selbstwehr*, 26.9.1924.

86. *Selbstwehr*, 26.9.1924.

87. Žáček, "Czechoslovak Fascisms," p. 61.

88. The same author translated into Czech *The Protocols of the Elders of Zion*. See Karel Relink, *Spása světa, ubozí pronásledovaní židé* (Prague, 1926), and *Nenažranski, ministr: humanista filistr* (Prague, 1927).

89. KČŽ 44 (1924–25), p. 225.

90. Z. L. [Zdeněk Landes], "O antisemitismu u nás," in *Židovské zprávy*, 30.6.1926; 7.9.1926.

91. See chapter 3.

92. Šalda's principal works, *Boje o zítřek* (Battles for tomorrow) and *Rozum a práce*

(Mind and work), and his famous "Notebooks" exerted immense influence upon his contemporaries and are being reissued now, after the lapse of around six decades; see also František Kautman, *Masaryk, Šalda, Patočka* (Prague, 1990), pp. 8–9.

93. F. X. Šalda, "Požáry," in *Listy pro umění a kritiku* 3 (1935); for an assessment of his attitudes toward the Jews see Donath, "F. X. Šalda a židovství."

94. See chapter 3.

95. *Židovské zprávy*, 5.2.1926.

96. *Židovské zprávy*, 29.9.1926.

97. *Židovské zprávy*, 9.4.1926.

98. *Židovské zprávy*, 9.4.1926.

99. *Židovské zprávy*, 24.12.1926.

100. *Židovské zprávy*, 7.9.1926; a special supplement "Nová Palestýna"; 22.9.1926; no. 40, 29.9.1926.

101. Donath, "Jüdisches in der neuen tschechischen Literatur," pp. 84–86.

102. Cited in Donath, "Jüdisches in der neuen tschechischen Literatur," pp. 84–86.

103. *Doar Hayom* carried an article by the editor in chief, Itamar Ben Avi, reminiscing about the Congress of Mid-European Nations in Philadelphia (October 26, 1918), during which he befriended Masaryk. Upon his arrival in Jerusalem, the only journalist the president invited to call upon him at the Notre Dame de Paris convent was Itamar Ben Avi. See *Doar Hayom*, 11.4.1927; *Davar*, 13.4.1927; *Hagalil*, 8.4.1927.

104. *Židovské zprávy*, 4.3.1927.

105. *Židovské zprávy*, 15.4.1927.

106. For a description of this historic visit see S. Hugo Bergmann, "Masaryk in Palestine," in Rychnovský, ed., *Masaryk and the Jews*, pp. 268–71; Koloman Gajan, "Postoj T. G. Masaryka k židovství a sionismu za první republiky," and Miloš Pojar, "Masarykova návštěva Palestiny v r. 1927," both in *Hilsnerova aféra a česká společnost*, pp. 129–37; pp. 138–42.

107. Pojar, "Masarykova návštěva Palestiny."

108. George F. Kennan, *From Prague after Munich: Diplomatic Papers 1938–1940* (Princeton NJ, 1968), p. 37.

109. See Donath, "F. X. Šalda a židovství," pp. 45–46.

110. J. W. Bruegel, "The Germans in Pre-war Czechoslovakia," in *A History of the Czechoslovak Republic 1918–1948*, pp. 180–81, 183.

111. Dr. Ludwig Czech was highly regarded by all parliamentarians and the public within his lifetime. He was deported in 1942 to Terezín and perished there (20.8.1942). On 20.8.1993 a solemn state ceremony attended by Czech and German statesmen took place on the premises of the former ghetto, during which a plaque was unveiled to Dr. Czech's memory. See Czech, *Symbolischer Staatsakt fur einen unbeugsamen Demokraten* (München, 1993).

112. Havránek, "Fascism in Czechoslovakia," p. 52; Žáček, "Czechoslovak Fascisms," p. 57.

113. See F. Gregory Campbell, *Confrontation in Central Europe* (Chicago, London, 1975), pp. 260–61.

114. Koch's report to the German Foreign Ministry of May 3, 1933, quoted by Bruegel, "Jews in Political Life," p. 243.

115. Fritz Jellinek, *Die Kriese des Bürgers* (Zürich, 1936), pp. 25–28; cf. Bruegel, "Jews in Political Life," pp. 243–44.

116. For an in-depth survey see Elizabeth Wiskemann, *Czechs and Germans: A Study of the Struggle in the Historic Provinces of Bohemia and Moravia* (London, New York, Toronto, 1938); Bruegel, "The Germans in Pre-war Czechoslovakia," pp. 167–87.

117. Havránek, "Fascism in Czechoslovakia," p. 50.

118. Karel Čapek, "Promluvíme si o tom," in *Lidové noviny*, 2.12.1934.

119. Karel Čapek, "Návrat k malosti," in *Lidové noviny*, 16.12.1934.

120. Josef Popper, "Work for Refugees," in *In Memoriam Marie Schmolka* (London, 1944), reissued Tel Aviv, 1970, pp. 22–25; Bohumil Černý, *Most k novému životu* (Prague, 1967); Kurt R. Grossmann, "Refugees to and from Czechoslovakia," and Manfred George, Refugees in Prague 1933–1938," both in *Jews of CS* 2:565–71, 582–88. For further details see chapter 3.

121. Grossmann, "Refugees," pp. 566–67.

122. Černý, *Most k novému životu*," p. 178.

123. Černý, *Most k novému životu*," pp. 23–24.

124. Grossmann, "Refugees," p. 568.

125. See report "Jak žijí emigranti," in *Věstník židovské obce náboženské v Praze* (hereafter VŽNOP), 28.5.1937.

126. Rabinowicz, "Jewish Party," p. 301.

127. KČŽ, 57 (1935–36), p. 195.

128. The interpellations recorded in *Tisky* (1935) XVI, document 2871, March 26, 1935.

129. *Tisky* (1935) XVI (2871), 26.3.1935, interpellation by Dr. Angelo Goldstein and Dr. Chayim Kugel.

130. For the proclamation see Rabinowicz, "Jewish Party," p. 298.

131. See *Selbstwehr*, 4.10.1935; Fleischmann, "Religious Congregation," p. 317.

132. Nahum Goldmann, *Memories: The Autobiography of Nahum Goldmann: Sixty Years of Jewish Life*, transl. Helen Sebba (London, 1969), pp. 148–49.

133. Rabinowicz, "Jewish Party," pp. 300–301.

134. Wiskemann, *Czechs and Germans*, p. 143; Bruegel, "The Germans in Pre-War Czechoslovakia," p. 180.

135. Karol Sidor, *Slovenská politika na pôde pražského snemu 1918–1938* (Bratislava, 1943), 2 vols.

136. Korbel, *Twentieth Century Czechoslovakia*, p. 122; Alena Gajanová, *Dvojí tvář předmnichovského fašismu* (Prague, 1962), pp. 154–78.

137. For a succinct survey of developments in Slovakia see Livia Rothkirchen, "Slovakia: II, 1918–1938," in *Jews of CS* 2:108–9; Eduard Nižňanský, *Židovská komunita na Slovensku medzi československou parlamentnou demokráciou a slovenským štátom v stredoeuropskom kontexte* (Prešov, 1999).

138. Fleischmann, "Religious Congregation," p. 317. From the total amount of 480 million crowns, 80 million were raised by the Jews of Bohemia and Moravia; see Helena Krejčová, "Českožidovská asimilace," in Rybár, *Židovská Praha*, p. 142.

139. Appeal reproduced in Walter Jacobi, *Golem, metlo Čechů: Rozklad českého nacionalizmu* (Prague, 1941), p. 48.

140. Jacobi, *Golem, metlo Čechů.*

141. Wiskemann, *Czechs and Germans*, p. 226.

142. Wiskemann, *Czechs and Germans*, pp. 225–26; cf. note 128.

143. "Fear and opportunism were sneaking across the country"; see Firt, *Knihy a osudy*, pp. 255–56.

144. See *Věstník čsl. ligy proti antisemitizmu* (January, May 1937).

145. *Židovské zprávy*, 28.1.1938.

146. *Věstník čsl. ligy* (January 1937); cf. chapter 8.

147. See Egon Hostovský, "Czech-Jewish Movement," p. 153; Hostovský nevertheless believed that the ideas as formulated by the founding fathers of the Czech-Jewish movement "still have not lost all their validity."

148. More than six hundred Czech-Jewish legionnaires participated in the struggle for Czech independence, among them Otto Gutfreund, František Langer, Dr. Baumel, Dr. Rudolf Guth, and Dr. Josef Beck; see Guth, "1918 (28.10) 1938," pp. 17, 20.

149. Hostovský, "Participation," p. 449.

150. VŽONP, 30.4.1937; *Židovské zprávy*, 28.1.1938.

151. VŽONP, 25.3.1937.

152. Rabinowicz, "Jewish Party," p. 309.

153. See Igor Lukeš, "Czech Partial Mobilization in May 1938," *Journal for Contemporary History* 31, no. 4 (1996), p. 701; refers to the leaflets (12.3.1938) to be found in the Archives of the National Museum, box 38.

154. Bohumil Bílek, *Fifth Column at Work* (London, 1945), pp. 36–58; Wiskemann, *Czechs and Germans*, p. 228.

155. For a case study based on Runciman's papers more recently made accessible at the Public Record Office, see Vaughan Burdin Baker, "Selective Inattention: The Runciman Mission to Czechoslovakia, 1938," in *East European Quarterly* 24, no. 4 (January 1991), pp. 425–45.

156. Baker, "Selective Inattention," pp. 435–36, passages of the memorandum submitted by the Council of the Jewish Communities in Bohemia of 10.9.1938, Runciman Papers, Public Record Office, London (hereafter PRO), FO 800/306. Originally written in German, as "Memorandum der jüdischen Kultusgemeinde Prag zur Verfolgung der Juden durch die Henlein-Bewegung in den Sudeten-deutschen Gebieten" (dated August 1938), it was translated by the Board of Deputies of British Jews into English and dispatched to several Jewish organizations the world over. The full text of the memorandum was printed in Peter Heumos and Peter Becher, eds., *Die Emigration aus der Tschechoslowakei nach Westeuropa und den Nahen Osten 1938–1945* (München, 1989), pp. 278–81.

157. See chapter 3.

3. The Aftermath of Munich

1. The description is Kennan's, in *From Prague*, p. 7.

2. The bibliography dealing with the various aspects of the Munich period is extensive. A select and annotated bibliography can be found in "Munich 1938 from the Czech Perspective," arranged and edited by Stanley B. Winters, in *East Central Europe* 8, nos. 1–2

(1981), pp. 62–96; the first attempt to analyze the situation after the Munich Agreement was made by Heinrich Bodensieck, "Das Dritte Reich und die Lage der Juden in der Tschechoslowakei nach München," in *Vierteljahrshefte für Zeitgeschichte* (hereafter VZ) 9 (1961), pp. 249–61; see also Otto D. Kulka's masters paper at the Hebrew University (Jerusalem, 1963) in its abbreviated version "Hayehadut haTschechit be'pros haShoah" (Ghetto in an annihilation camp, hereafter cited thus), in *Gesher*, Quarterly Review of the Nation's Problems, 2–3 (September 1969), pp. 143–50; Jan Rataj, *O autoritativní národní stát: Ideologické proměny české politiky v Druhé republice 1938–1939* (Prague, 1997).

3. The most important memoirs are Edvard Beneš, *Mnichovské dny: Paměti* (Prague, 1968); Ladislav Feierabend, *Ve vládách druhé republiky* (New York, 1961); Firt, *Knihy a osudy*; Václav Černý, *Kultur im Widerstand 1938–1942*, I, translated from the Czech original, *Pláč Koruny české* (Bremen, 1979); Prokop Drtina, *Československo můj osud*, 2 vols. in 4, vol. 1, pts. 1 and 2; vol. 2, pts. 1 and 2 (Toronto, 1982).

4. See Bruegel, "The Germans in Pre-war Czechoslovakia," pp. 167–215.

5. Milena Jesenská, "Poslední dny Karla Čapka," in *Přítomnost* 16, 11.1.1939, pp. 23–25.

6. Karel Čapek in his eulogy, "Smrt dne 12. brežna 1938," in *Lidové noviny*, 13.3.1938, named four reasons for Fischer's sudden death: his sensitivity as a Czech, a Jew, a universalist, and a Germanist scholar.

7. Willy Schlamm, "Proč zemřel Karel Čapek," in *Přítomnost* 16, 25.1.1939, pp. 56–57; see also Willy Schlamm, "Why Did Karel Čapek Die," in *Saturday Review of Literature* (January 1939). In his reminiscences, Dr. Karel Steinbach (called "Kadelík" by his friends), an intimate friend of the Čapeks who spent the last fateful days and nights at his bedside, said after his death: "He died because at that time there were no antibiotics or sulfa-medicaments. However, there is much truth in the claim of those who maintain that he died as a result of the tragedy of Munich." See *Dr. Karel Steinbach: Svědek téměř stoletý*, ed. Viktor Fischl (Köln, 1988), p. 66.

8. Korbel, *Twentieth Century Czechoslovakia*, p. 123; Beneš's wavering policy and the tension that engulfed the "Castle" is described by Prokop Drtina, one of the secretaries of the president's cabinet, in his memoir, see *Československo můj osud*, vol. 1, pt. 1, chapters 10–12.

9. See Beneš, *Mnichovské dny*, p. 262; Korbel, *Twentieth Century Czechoslovakia*, p. 124.

10. The Communists' protest against the Munich Agreement was the loudest. Gottwald's patriotic speech in the National Assembly on October 11, 1938, denouncing "the treason of the capitalist governments," was the strongest call for open resistance to Nazism. Even if delivered *post factum* and gratuitous in wording, it triggered wide sympathy and support for the Communist Party. Although it was tarnished by the Molotov-Ribbentrop Pact (August 1939), it became a great asset for the party in later years. See Klement Gottwald, *Deset let* (Prague, 1947), pp. 126–27.

11. The motto is taken from Dr. Beneš's pledge of loyalty; closing words of the funeral oration at the burial of President T. G. Masaryk on September 21, 1937: "President-Liberator, *We remain faithful* to the heritage which you have laid in our hands." See also Jan Kuklík, *K problematice vzniku národní fronty v domácím odboji* (Prague, 1976), pp. 26, 34.

12. For details see Korbel, *Twentieth Century Czechoslovakia*, pp. 123–28.

13. Kennan, *From Prague*, p. 7.

14. Frederic W. Nielsen, *Reminiszenzen 1934–1979: Ein Beitrag zur Gegenwartsbewaltigung* (Stuttgart, 1980), pp. 43–50.

15. Nielsen, *Reminiszenzen*, p. 46.

16. On the role of the Czech nobility during the first republic see Jiří Doležal, "Úvahy o české šlechtě v času První Republiky," in *Svědectví* 77 (1986), pp. 39–62.

17. The Executive Committee of the World Jewish Congress, convening in London, issued a proclamation expressing its sympathies with the grave fate that had befallen the Czech nation, calling upon the Jews of all the countries to do their utmost to support the growth of the Czechoslovak economy. *Židovské zprávy*, 2.12.1938.

18. For details see Heinrich Hermelink, *Kirche im Kampf* (Tübingen, Stuttgart, 1950), pp. 453–55.

19. Jungk, *Franz Werfel*, p. 258.

20. Jungk, *Franz Werfel*, p. 258.

21. Jan Kuklík, "Antifašistická kultura proti Mnichovu," in *Mnichov 1938* (Prague, 1988), vol. 1, p. 60.

22. Kuklík, "Antifašistická," pp. 64–67.

23. Entry of 2.12.1921 in *The Diaries of Franz Kafka 1914–1923* (New York, 1965), p. 200.

24. Milena Jesenská, "Jak tato doba zahrála s našími nervy," in *Přítomnost* 15 (1938), pp. 734–36.

25. Margaret Buber-Neumann, *Mistress to Kafka: The Life and Death of Milena* (London, 1966). This was the first attempt at a detailed description of her personality, her courageous struggle, and her death in May 1944 in the concentration camp of Ravensbrück, and about their "death-defying friendship" (Arthur Koestler). A more recent biography from the pen of Jesenská's daughter, Jana Černá, *Milena Jesenská* (Frankfurt, 1985), was translated from the original Czech edition by Reinhard Fischer, *Adresát Milena Jesenská* (Prague, 1969).

26. Firt, *Knihy a osudy*, p. 48.

27. Vočadlo's open letter signed O. V., in *New Statesman and Nation*, 15.10.1938, pp. 564–65.

28. Prof. Vočadlo, in one of his letters written to me on 28.6.1967, related how he managed to annoy the Nazis by writing a "pseudoscientific" article: "Are the Germans Aryans?" He was, in fact, among the first hostages arrested by the Gestapo in Prague on September 1, 1939. After Heydrich's assassination in May 1942, he was again arrested and sent to Auschwitz. In May 1945 he was liberated in Buchenwald. See M. C. Bradbrook, "Otakar Vočadlo 1895–1974," in *Slavonic and East European Review* 53, no. 133 (October 1975), pp. 579–81.

29. Doreen Warriner, "Document: Winter in Prague," in *Slavonic and East European Review* 62, no. 2 (April 1984), p. 210.

30. Milena Jesenská, "Nad naše síly," in *Přítomnost* 15, 10.10.1938, pp. 650–51.

31. Jesenská, "Nad naše síly," pp. 650–51.

32. Wilbur J. Carr was appointed in June 1937 by President Roosevelt as minister to Czechoslovakia. His situation reports and memoranda sent from Prague on refugee questions are written with great empathy and understanding. See U.S. National Archives

(hereafter NA), 860F.48/52, 19.3.1939. Most of these were included in Kennan's *From Prague*.

33. Published first in Czech in *Lidové noviny*, 22.9.1938; for the English translation see Kerner, ed., *Czechoslovakia: Twenty Years of Independence*, pp. 448–49.

34. Joseph Rothschild, *East Central Europe between the Two World Wars* (Seattle, 1974), pp. 132–33; Korbel, *Twentieth Century Czechoslovakia*, p. 151.

35. A letter of "protest" sent from Prague to London, *Documents on British Foreign Policy 1919–1939*, ed. E. L. Woodward and Rohan Butler, 3rd series, vols. 1–10: 1938–39 (London, 1946–70), 2:518–19.

36. Ilse Weber (1903–44), who hailed from Vítkovice, is known as "the poetess of Terezín." While in the ghetto she worked as a nurse in the children's sick room, performing little miracles. In October 1944 together with her little son Tommy she voluntarily followed her husband Vilém to Auschwitz and perished there. The letter is reproduced here by courtesy of her brother; see Oskar A. Mareni, "The *Erbrichterei* and Its Children" (Jerusalem, 1987–88), unpublished, pp. 123–25. The original letter written in German is in the Yad Vashem Archives (hereafter YVA), 07/7-1.

37. Olivová, *Doomed Democracy*.

38. *The Testament of Adolf Hitler*, ed., Francois Genond (London, 1960), pp. 84–85.

39. Korbel, *Twentieth Century Czechoslovakia*, p. 152.

40. Marie Pujmanová, "Zase na světle božím," in *Kritický měsíčník* 1 (1945), p. 40; for an illuminating account of the ideological changes within Czech society, especially the loud rightist groups, see Rataj, *O autoritativní národní stát*, pp. 91–129.

41. Leopold Chmela, *The Economic Aspects of the German Occupation of Czechoslovakia: Sources and Documents* (Prague, 1948), pp. 56–57.

42. Manfred George, "Refugees in Prague, 1933–1938," in *Jews of CS* 2:582–88.

43. Hansjorg Schneider et al., *Exil in der Tschechoslowakei in Grossbritannien, Skandinavien und in Palestina*, vol. 5 (Leipzig, 1980), p. 30.

44. Grossmann, "Refugees," p. 568; see also Manfred George, "Refugees in Prague," in *Exil in der Tschechoslowakei*, pp. 582–88. Of the approximately 4,000 refugees who reached Prague by November 1934 there were only about 300 left. "K problému židovské sociální péče v Praze," in VŽONP, 16.11.1934.

45. Ivan Pfaff, "Německá kultura v českém exilu 1933–1958," in *Svědectví* 18, 70–71 (1983), p. 482.

46. Pfaff, "Německá kultura," p. 484.

47. Letter addressed to the Legal Adviser of the State Department; with the attached two laws (nos. 51 and 52), NA, 860F.III/59; III/60.

48. Letter to Legal Advisor, NA 860F.III/59; III/60.

49. Theodor Lessing was murdered in Marienbad on August 30, 1933; Schneider, *Exil in der Tschechoslowakei*, p. 29; see also chapter 6.

50. Formis, an expert on radio transmission, had fled to Czechoslovakia after the Nazi takeover and had become involved with Gregor Strasser and his clandestine underground network. The Nazis sent Alfred Naujocks, a companion of Heydrich, of the SD on a "special assignment" to murder engineer Formis in his room at Hotel Záhoří, near Prague (23.1.1935). See Černý, *Most k novému životu*, pp. 138–51.

51. Pfaff, "Německá kultura," p. 488.

52. See Gerhard L. Weinberg, "Secret Hitler-Beneš Negotiations in 1936–1937," in *Journal of Central European Affairs* 19 (January 1960); A. Šnejdárek, "Tajné rozhovory Beneše s Německem," in *Československý časopis historický*, Praha (hereafter ČsČH) 9 (1961), pp. 112–16; František Uhlíř, *Prague and Berlin, 1918–1938* (London, 1941), pp. 58–59.

53. Weinberg, "Secret Negotiations," p. 366; J. W. Bruegel, *Czechoslovakia before Munich: The German Minority Problem and the British Appeasement Policy* (Cambridge, London, 1973), pp. 179–83.

54. Beneš's request is in Weinberg, "Secret Negotiations," p. 368.

55. Weinberg, "Secret Negotiations," p. 370; Šnejdárek, "Tajné rozhovory," p. 114.

56. Memorandum, 10.11.1937, *Documents on German Foreign Policy 1918–1945, from the Archives of the German Foreign Ministry*, Series D, 13 vols. (Washington DC, 1949–66), vol. 1, pp. 35.

57. In 1937 the Ministries of Internal Affairs and National Defense announced plans to transfer refugees from the border area and Prague to eight districts of the Czech-Moravian highlands (Českomoravská vysočina). In an effort to prevent this step, Marie Schmolka lodged a protest on behalf of the Coordinating Committee, and thanks to the support rendered by the press and protests by the public, the plan was canceled. See Černý, *Most k novému životu*, p. 176.

58. Pfaff, "Německá kultura," p. 488.

59. Pfaff, "Německá kultura," p. 482.

60. See "Lidé na výspě," in *Přítomnost* 15, no. 43, 1937, p. 685.

61. "Lidé na výspě," pp. 686–87.

62. Kurt Weisskopf, *The Agony of Czechoslovakia, '38–'68* (London, 1968), pp. 60–61.

63. Buber-Neumann, *Mistress to Kafka*, pp. 130–31.

64. Milena Jesenská gave a harrowing description of the brutalities of the Austrian population toward Jewish citizens in her article "Statisíce hledají zemi nikoho," in *Přítomnost* 15, 20.7.1938, pp. 477–79.

65. Kennan's report to the U.S. Secretary of State, "The Jewish Problem in the New Czechoslovakia," 17.2.1939, NA, 860F.4016/68, pp. 9–10.

66. Wilbur J. Carr, "Review of Czechoslovak Internal Developments since Munich," Prague, December 20, 1938, NA, box 375, record group 165, no. 301.

67. Václav Černý, viewing this demoralization, referred to Czech individuals who "with the advent of Munich evaporated from Czech public life, crept into places of hiding, from where it was captivating to watch how the heads of real heroes were rolling," see *Proměny* (January 1983), pp. 3–6.

68. Buber-Neumann, *Mistress to Kafka*, pp. 130–31.

69. Buber-Neumann, *Mistress to Kafka*, pp. 130–31.

70. See *Documents on British Foreign Policy*, 3rd series, vol. 3, pp. 631–38 (hereafter cited as DBFP with volume and page numbers).

71. See Král, *Otázky hospodářského*.

72. Karel Poláček, *Poslední dopisy Doře*, ed. Martin Jelinovicz (Toronto, 1984), p. 7.

73. Milena Jesenská, "Pověz kam utíkáš—povím ti, kdo jsi," in *Přítomnost* 15, 14.9.1938, p. 594.

74. Jesenská, "Nad naše síly," pp. 650–51.

75. "V zemi nikoho," in *Přítomnost* 15, 29.12.1938, p. 829.

76. "V zemi nikoho," p. 827, quoted by Jesenská, who relates with great admiration to "Mařka Schmolková" and her work on behalf of the refugees. See also *In Memoriam Marie Schmolka* (London, 1944).

77. Wilbur J. Carr, cable to U.S. Secretary of State, Prague, 23.11.1938 (NA, 860–.48) cites the Red Cross, probably relying on the report of the British representative on refugee matters; see R. J. Stopford, MS, "Prague 1938/39," part 2, Central Zionist Archives (CZA), Jerusalem.

78. Joint Distribution Committee Report, 28.11.1938, American Joint Distribution Committee Archives, New York (hereafter cited as JDC Archives).

79. Wilbur J. Carr, Prague, 12.10.1938, to the Secretary of State, NA, 860F.918/13.

80. Sir Ronald Maclay served in 1927–29 as minister in Prague. For details on the activities of the various refugee organizations in London see Heumos and Becher, *Emigration*, especially documents 2–3, pp. 282–89.

81. See Carr's report of 12.10.1938.

82. See Max Brod's reminiscences, "A Home in Prague," in *In Memoriam Marie Schmolka*, p. 14.

83. *Přítomnost* 15, 12.12.1938.

84. *Mnichov 1938*, vol. 2, pp. 77, 91, 117, 163, 173; "Reichskristallnacht" in the Sudeten area, see Ludomír Kocourek, "Das Schicksal der Juden in Sudetengau im Licht der erhaltenen Quellen," in *Theresienstädter Studien und Dokumente 1997*, ed. Miroslav Kárný, Raimund Kemper, and Margita Kárná (Prague, 1997), pp. 88–97.

85. Testimony of Edita Stützová (Levinsohnová) of Karlovy Vary, Czech collection in YVA, I/18.

86. See Grossmann, "Refugees," p. 572.

87. Grossmann, "Refugees," p. 572.

88. Grossmann, "Refugees," p. 572. However, it is an established fact that neither these refugees nor Communists (including members of the International Brigade: Germans, Hungarians, Poles, etc., who fought in Spain and were directly dispatched by the Soviet government) were given shelter or allowed to return to the Soviet Union. In fact, only leading Communist functionaries eventually found refuge in the Soviet Union. For an in-depth discussion see Milena Jesenská, "Dobrá rada nad zlato," in *Přítomnost* 16, 8.3.1939, pp. 151–52; Josef Novotný, "Činnost KSČ v letech 1938–1941," in *Odboj a revoluce* 4, no. 4 (1966), pp. 84–85.

89. See Grossmann, "Refugees," p. 574; Kennan report, 17.2.1939, NA, 860F.4016/68.

90. The final negotiations in London were summed up under the title "Anglo-French Conscience Money," in *New Statesman and Nation*, Comments, 4.2.1939, p. 158.

91. For details on the transfer agreement see chapter 5.

92. Grossmann, "Refugees," p. 576.

93. Vera Gissing, *Pearls of Childhood* (London, 1988), p. 10.

94. See Friedmann, *Einige Zahlen*.

95. See Samuel Maimann, *Das Mährische Jerusalem* (Prostějov; Selbstverlag, 1937), p. 4, cited by Hahn, "The Dilemma," p. 31.

96. Fleischmann, "Religious Congregation," pp. 267–329.

97. Rabinowicz, "Jewish Party," pp. 317–18.

98. Theodor Procházka, "The Second Republic, 1938–1939," in *A History of the Czechoslovak Republic 1918–1948*, pp. 255–70.

99. The Czech-language community weekly *Věstník židovské obce náboženské v Praze* (VŽONP), first issued in Prague on 7.2.1934, appeared under that name until fall 1939, when it became bilingual and censored by the Gestapo; see chapter 4.

100. As of 1939 among the persons resigning their membership, mostly young professionals were listed in the bulletin. The "desertion" was castigated by leading figures of the community, who viewed the decline of religion as an outcome of the emancipation. See Rabbi A. Bass, "Ze židovské obce náboženské vystoupili," VŽONP, 6.12.1938.

101. Of the total of 709 conversions, 506 were recorded during the three months following the Munich Agreement. See VŽONP, 11.11.1938.

102. See "Uprchlíci," in VŽONP, 9.11.1938.

103. Dr. Emil Kafka, a leading figure of the Czech-Jewish movement, was elected to head the community after Dr. Maxim Reiner's death in 1937; see VŽONP, 30.4.1937.

104. The community leadership had already appealed to the Jewish public earlier to use the Czech language instead of German. See VŽONP, 23.5.1938.

105. Reference is to a declaration issued by a group of Czech intellectuals including the following statement: "In our new national state the influence of other entities and non-Aryans should strictly correspond to their percentage in the population, provided they will be absolutely loyal to the state." For a reaction to the declaration of the intelligentsia, see Viktor Fischl, "Líc a rub," *Židovské zprávy*, 4.11.1938.

106. See VŽONP, 9.11.1938.

107. Wilbur J. Carr's cables, NA, 860F.918/13, 12.10.1938; 860F.4016/61, 25.11.1938.

108. See "Něco o Českém národu a o Židech," in *Přítomnost* 15, 19.1.1938.

109. Some newspapers, such as the Social Democratic *Právo lidu* as well as the organ of the Evangelical Church, *Křesťanská revue*, condemned the anti-Semitic wave in Rumania. See *Židovské zprávy*, 4.2.1938, 11.2.1938, 18.2.1938.

110. On Peroutka's activities in *Tribuna* (1919–23), and later in *Přítomnost* (1924–39), see Otáhal, "Ferdinand Peroutka," pp. 339–90. The author sides with Julius Firt, a colleague and close associate of Peroutka, who maintains (p. 380) that it was "most probably, the German background of Peroutka's mother that shaped his outlook on the Czech-German rapprochement."

111. An editorial in *Nedělní listy*, 31.7.1938, pointed out that the ratio of Jewish employees in the civil service was too high. (In reality it was in most branches around 70 percent less than would correspond to their quota.) *Národní politika*, which had the largest circulation in Czechoslovakia, carried an article entitled *Židé mezi námi* (The Jews in our midst) accusing the Jews of "exploiting other races," "lacking consideration," and even of "spreading unrest and revolt wherever they may be." See "Ein antisemitischer Ausbruch der *Národní politika*," in *Selbstwehr*, 5.8.1938. For a survey of anti-Semitic press during the Second Republic see Petr Bednařík, "Antisemitismus v denících "Venkov" a "Večer" v období Druhé Republiky," in *Postavení a osudy židovského obyvatelstva*, pp. 118–44.

112. The massive influx of Subcarpathian Jews, most of whom resided in Prague and

lived in deplorable conditions, caused further socioeconomic problems to the already plagued community; it is estimated that the number of Slovak Jews residing in Bohemia and Moravia in 1939 was around 2,500; see Jan Rychlík, *Češi a Slováci ve 20. století: Československé vztahy 1914–1945* (Bratislava, 1997), pp. 206–12.

113. *Rozvoj*, 21.1.1938.

114. *Rozvoj*, 7.3.1938.

115. Benda, *Židé v našém hospodářství*.

116. The report by police counsel Dr. Antonín Jakubec to the Presidium of the Ministry of Interior of 3.11.1938; see Státní ústřední archiv ministerstva vnitra, Praha *(hereafter* SÚA) 225–1324–1.

117. See *Medina Iwrit*, 6.1.1939; see also *Židovské zprávy*, 13.1.1939.

118. Zbyněk A. B. Zeman, *Nazi Propaganda* (London, 1964).

119. *Documents on German Foreign Policy 1918–1945, from the Archives of the German Foreign Ministry*, Series D, vol. 4, pp. 69–72.

120. Wilbur J. Carr's cable of 25.11. 1938, NA, 860F.4016/65.

121. Report of B. C. Newton, Prague, to Viscount Halifax, PRO, FO C15720/2475/12; see also Drtina, *Československo můj osud*, vol. 1, pt. 1, pp. 284–85, describes the brave stance taken by Rašín in that period. In the January issue of *Národní myšlenky* Dr. Rašín published a letter written to him by a Czech man, reacting to his speech in Parliament against anti-Semitism. Thanking him for his "manly and prudent words," the man ends his letter: "The Republic is not lost. It will live again!" *Židovské zprávy*, 27.1.1939.

122. Halifax to Newton 6.12.1938; Newton to Halifax, 8.12.1938, DBFP 3:631–38.

123. Francois de Lacroix, *Le livre jaune francaise: Documents diplomatiques 1938–1939* (Paris, 1939), pp. 60–62; DBFP 3:407–14.

124. Walter Jacobi, *Země zaslíbená* (Prague, 1943), p. 155.

125. See DBFP 3:631.

126. Newton to Halifax, 8.12.1938, 9.12.1938, DBFP 3:407–14.

127. "Rasismus i u nás?" in *Věstník čsl. ligy proti antisemitismu*, no. 1 (January 1937).

128. Pavel Haas, born in 1899, was a composer of the Janáček school, working on Moravian folksongs and also on Jewish melodies. He was active in the ghetto of Terezín, composing songs and fantasies on Jewish themes, and he worked on Czech and Hebrew texts and a "Requiem for the Martyrs." He perished in Auschwitz in October 1944.

129. See František Černý, ed., *Vzpomínky českých divadelníků* (Prague, 1965), pp. 14–15.

130. Černý, *Vzpomínky českých divadelníků*, pp. 14–15.

131. Hanuš Thein, *Žil jsem operou Národního divadla* (Prague, 1975), p. 60.

132. The poster, dated October 13, 1938, is reproduced in Thein, *Žil jsem operou*, p. 60.

133. According to *Židovské zprávy*, 30.12.1938, a "technical" trick was used to outwit the Jewish members by notifying them by mail to pay their membership dues. Those who did not comply within three days to this demand were arbitrarily excluded from the club.

134. The story was reorded by Čapek's widow in her memoirs; see Olga Scheinpflugová, *Český román* (Prague, 1946), p. 521.

135. Poláček, *Poslední dopisy Doře*, p. 8.

136. On Hromádka's activities see *Židovské zprávy*, 27.1.1939.

137. Josef B. Foerster, composer and music critic, was a great admirer of Gustav Mahler.

In an inspiring eulogy evaluating his creative work, Pavel Eisner described him as one of the greatest Czech composers and greatest Czech men of his era. See Pavel Eisner, "Položte tam kytičku," in VŽONP, 1.5.1956.

138. See Dr. I. [Iltis], "K osmdesátým sedmým narozeninám J. B. Foerstra," in VŽONP, 15.1.1947.

139. "Křesýané a židé," published in *Křesýanská revue*, quoted in *Židovské zprávy*, 24.2.1939; A. M. Píša commented in *Směry* on his embarrassment over the new situation: It would be terrible if a nation defenseless and afflicted would be ready to compensate by inflicting [trouble] upon those who are even more defenseless.

140. *Židovské zprávy*, 27.1.1939.

141. *Akten zur deutschen auswärtigen Politik 1918–1945*, Series D, vol. 4, Oktober 1938– März 1939 (Berlin, 1951), document 158, p. 170.

142. See Bílek, *Fifth Column*.

143. Kennan report, 17.2.1939, cf. note 65.

144. Jaroslav Stránský (1884–73) of the Czech National Socialists, a close associate of Beneš, was among the first political figures to flee to London after the occupation. He related the circumstances of this grim episode in his life to Jaromír Smutný. During the war Stránský served in the Government-in-Exile and in 1945–48 as deputy premier, minister of justice, and minister of education. In 1948 he returned to London, where he lived until his death. See entry of Smutný of 5.6.1941, Dokumenty historie československé politiky, doc. 181, vol. 1, p. 225 (hereafter cited as DHČP with volume and page numbers); Bruegel, "Jews in Political Life," p. 245.

145. Wilbur Carr's report of February 2, 1939, NA, 860F.4016.

146. Kennan report, 17.2.1939, pp. 5–6.

147. Kennan report, 17.2.1939, pp. 5–6.

148. Under the title "The Great Migration of Jews," *Národní listy* of 25.11.1938 states: "Those Jews who always have sided with us, felt and lived with us and endured good and bad times, we fully recognize as members of our nation."

149. The following categories were to be applied: (1) Jews converted at least until 31.12.1937, (2) Jews who in the 1930 census adhered to the Czech nation, and (3) all the Jewish legionnaires; see "Židé a strana národní jednoty," in *Přítomnost* 15, 7.12.1938, p. 84.

150. "Češi, Němci a židé," in *Přítomnost* 15, 22.2.1939; 16, 1.3.1939, p. 144; Zdeněk Landes, analyzing Peroutka's double standard in his assessment of the Jewish problem, calls him "a petty witness" in contrast to "great defendants" the Jews knew in their past. See "Přítomnost svědčí," in *Židovské zprávy*, 24.2.1939.

151. The tendency to minimize the overall Jewish contribution to Czech culture transpires in another article dealing with the role of the Jews in the Czech press: "Židé v českém tisku" by Eduard Bass, highlighting the merit of several individuals "whose exit would not only weaken the paper itself but its Czechness too."*Přítomnost* 16, 19.1.1939, pp. 36–37.

152. Peroutka, however, rejected outright the proposal to launch anew his *Přítomnost* as a vehicle of Nazi policy and was among the first intellectuals to be sent in autumn 1939 to a concentration camp, where he spent six years; see Otáhal, "Ferdinand Peroutka," pp. 339–90.

153. *Sbírka zákonů a nařízení Československé Republiky* 1, no. 1415/1939; 10.2.1939; DBFP 3:100.

154. It has been estimated that Jewish property amounted in Bohemia and Moravia to around one third of the total. See Chmela, *Economic Aspects*, pp. 64–65; Kennan, *From Prague*, p. 189.

155. Julien Benda, *The Treason of the Intellectuals* (New York, 1978), p. 193.

156. F. X. Šalda, "Fašismus a kultura," 9.3.1933, referred to by Pfaff, "Německá kultura," p. 490.

157. Pfaff, "Německá kultura," p. 490.

158. For an in-depth analysis see David W. Paul, *The Cultural Limits of Revolutionary Politics: Change and Continuity in Socialist Czechoslovakia* (New York, 1979). In 1924 Ferdinand Peroutka published a treatise about the character of the Czechs, entitled *Jací jsme* (How we are). Pavel Tigrid enhanced this topic by discussing the crucial landmarks in Czech history of 1938, 1948, and 1968 in his essay "Jací jsme když je zle" (How we are when it's bad), see *Svědectví* 12 (1973), pp. 303–19.

159. Finally it was the Church that saved the situation and graciously embraced Čapek's remains, enabling the public to pay its last tribute to the great man and author. See Milena Jesenská, "Poslední dny Karla Čapka," in *Přítomnost* 16, 11.1.1939, pp. 23–25; Firt, *Knihy a osudy*, pp. 255–56.

160. Jaroslav Seifert's poetry "Zhasněte světla" (Put out the light), published weekly in the last issues of *Přítomnost*, reflected the public mood; Theodor Procházka views this period as "the most lamentable episode in modern Czech history." See "Munich 1938 from the Czech Perspective," *East Central Europe* 8, nos. 1–2 (1981), p. 93.

161. Drtina, *Československo můj osud*, vol. 1, pt. 1, chapters 10–12.

162. Liehm, "Poslední rozhovor," pp. 160–91.

163. Kuklík, *K problematice*, p. 17.

164. Milena Jesenská, "Denní zprávy na posledních stránkách," in *Přítomnost* 15, 12.10.1938, p. 671.

165. Milena Jesenská, "Proč nemluvíte mladí?" in *Přítomnost* 16, 25.1.1939, p. 53. Until her arrest in fall 1939 Jesenská was a pillar of the underground paper *V boj* and also instrumental in the rescue of Czech officers and airmen as well as in assisting a number of her Jewish friends and acquaintances in their escape abroad. See Jaroslav Dressler, "Kafkova Milena" in *Milena, Cesta k jednoduchosti* (Engelfelden, 1982), pp. 93–121.

166. Milena Jesenská, "O umění zůstat stát," *Přítomnost* 16, 5.4.1939, pp. 205–6; cf. Derek Sayer, *The Coasts of Bohemia: A Czech History*, translated from Czech by Alena Sayer (Princeton NJ, 1998), pp. 368–69.

167. See chapter 4.

168. Kusin, *The Intellectual Origins of the Prague Spring* (Cambridge University Press, 2002).

169. Kusin, *Intellectual Origins*.

170. Beneš, *Mnichovské dny*, pp. 340–42; Drtina, *Československo můj osud*, vol. 1, pt. 1, chapters 10–12.

171. There were 457 German officers, among them one general, in the Czechoslovak Army. This was 7 percent of the active officer corps: the proportion of Germans in the Officer Reserve must certainly have been higher, but no figures are available. Bruegel, *Czechoslovakia before Munich*, p. 149.

172. Hubert Ripka, *Munich: Before and After* (London, 1939), pp. 212 ff. Ripka refers to Professor Bernard Lavergue, in *l'Année politique francaise et etrangere* (November 1938).

173. Quoted in Winston S. Churchill, *The Second World War*, vol. 1: *The Gathering Storm*, 7th ed. (London, 1953), pp. 281–82.

174. See Milan Hauner, Radomír V. Luža, Theodor Procházka, Stanley B. Winters, and Jonathan Zorach in "Munich 1938 from the Czech Perspective," roundtable, in *East Central Europe* 8, nos. 1–2 (1981).

175. Hauner et al., in "Munich 1938," p. 76.

176. Hauner et al., in "Munich 1938," p. 77.

177. See Patočka, *Was sind die Tschechen?* pp. 220–21.

4. Under German Occupation

1. František Bauer, *Můj boj: Hitler o sobě a o svých cílech* (Prague, 1936).

2. As of March 11, 1938—the *Anschluss* of Austria—German troops ringed western Czechoslovakia on three sides.

3. Walter Schellenberg, *The Labyrinth: Memoirs of Walter Schellenberg* (London, 1956), p. 57.

4. For details on the Protectorate during Neurath's tenure, see John L. Heinemann, *Hitler's First Foreign Minister, Constantin Freiherr von Neurath: Diplomat and Statesman* (London, 1979), mainly chapter 13; Gotthold Rhode, "The Protectorate of Bohemia and Moravia," in *A History of the Czechoslovak Republic 1918–1948*, pp. 198–310; Mastný, *Czechs under Nazi Rule* (New York, 1971); Detlef Brandes, *Die Tschechen unter deutschem Protektorat*, I. *Besatzungspolitik, Kollaboration und Widerstand im Protektorat Böhmen und Mähren bis Heydrichs Tod (1939–1942)* (Munich, 1969); Livia Rothkirchen, "The Protectorate Government and the 'Jewish Question,'" in Yad Vashem Studies *(hereafter* YVS) 27 (1999), pp. 331–62.

5. The Committee of the National Solidarity comprised 97 percent of the male population of various party affiliations, some of whom acted as opposition and others as a restraining factor. See Tomáš Pasák, "K problematice české kolaborace a fašismu za druhé světove války," in *Příspěvky k dějinám fašismu v Československu a v Maïarsku* (Bratislava, 1969), p. 137.

6. For a dramatic description of Hácha's visit to Hitler's chancellery on 15.3.1939, see John W. Wheeler Bennett, *Munich: Prologue to Tragedy* (New York, 1948), pp. 344–45.

7. Wilbur Carr's telegram from Prague to Secretary of State, Washington, 19.3.1939, NA, 860F.48.

8. Carr telegram, 19.3.1939; attached is the aide-mémoire of March 17, 1939, of the British Embassy at Washington.

9. František Lón, Zdeněk Filip, and Karel Sommer, "Príšpěvek k historickému boji komunistů olomouckého kraje za vytvoření národní fronty proti okupaci v letech 1939–1941," in Acta Universitatis Palackianae Olomucensis, *Historica* 1 (1960), p. 229.

10. Hanna Steiner was soon released. On her activities see note 141 to this chapter. Marie Schmolka was released through the intervention of Senator Františka Plamínková, former president of the Czechoslovak Women's Council (executed during the Heydrich

terror). Schmolka managed to leave for London but died there on March 27, 1940, following a heart attack. See *In Memoriam Marie Schmolka*.

11. Mastný, *Czechs under Nazi Rule*, p. 80; Brandes, *Die Tschechen*, 1:45–46.

12. Jan Rys, *Hilsneriáda a T.G.M. 1899–1939* (Prague: Weisner, 1939)—highlighting Masaryk's role in the Hilsner Trial (1899); see Tomáš Pasák, "Der tschechische Faschismus," in *Fascism and Europe: An International Symposium* (Prague, August 28–29, 1969), p. 107.

13. Pasák, "Der tschechische Faschismus," p. 107.

14. Such actions would continue. According to the local chronicle the synagogue at Holešov (dedicated on 3.9.1893) was ignited by Vlajka members on the night of August 11–12, 1942. The farmers of the surrounding villages bought up the bricks and other building materials—a wagon-load for 3–5 crowns. See Svátek, "Pogromy v Holešově, p. 43.

15. See Max Steiner, "The Rise and Fall of a Jewish Community in Bohemia," in *YIVO Annual* 12 (1958–1959), p. 257.

16. The American Consul, I. N. Linnel's dispatch, no. 160, 22.6.1939 (enclosure 2), NA, box 4895, 860F.4016/73.

17. The custodian of the Altneu synagogue related that on Sunday night 12.1.1943 at 1:00 A.M. he was woken up by a policeman because light could be seen inside the synagogue. After a search it transpired that the insulating wires, affected by humidity, had lit up the eternal lamp, dimly illuminating the synagogue. The Czech duty officer said that "this was a good omen . . . the ray of light was the sign of divine blessing." Testimony of Franz Fischof, 17.9.1945, Zeev Shek collection, YVA, 0–64.

18. Fischof testimony, 17.9.1945.

19. According to another source some of the community leaders had to participate in the staged "service," clad in prayer shawls; holding the prayer books their hands trembled and their voices quavered. Supervising the scene, next to the cameraman, stood Günther. See Hana Volavková, *Das Schicksal des jüdischen Museums in Prag* (Prague, 1965), p. 126; Susan Tegen, " 'The Demonic Effect': Veit Harlan's Use of Jewish Extras in Jud Süss" (1940), in *Holocaust and Genocide Studies* 14, no.2 (Fall 2000), pp. 215–41, especially pp. 230–33.

20. See Volavková, *Schicksal*, p. 16.

21. Report on Bohemia and Moravia, File "Czechoslovakia 1939–1940," JDC Archives.

22. Report of Josef Fischer of 21–28.5.1939, describing the internal political and economic situation, sent by the underground (*Politické Ústředí*, PÚ), to the Czechoslovak Government-in-Exile in London. See DHČP, 2:428.

23. Fischer report, DHČP, 2:435.

24. Personal communication to this writer by his daughter Ilse (Drexler) Maier, now living in Los Angeles, in June 1980; Tomáš Pasák, "Český antisemitismus na počátku okupace," in *Věda a život* (Brno, March 1969), p. 150, refers to two additional victims beaten up during this attack: K. Rosenberg (director of a sugar plant) and Leo Neubauer, who, stripped of his clothing and wounded, sought refuge at the police station. An additional victim was O. Weissmantl, a Jew, who apparently was brought to the police station under the protection of A. Bourdet, an SA-man "to save him from the Czechs' beatings."

25. Pasák, "Český antisemitismus," pp. 147–51.

26. Fischer report, 29.5.1939, DHČP, 2:433–39.

27. In Olomouc members of the Svatopluk guard and some of the Fascists (Pavlík, Novák, and others) distributed fliers demanding the abolition of the Protectorate and its annexation to the Third Reich. See Lón et al., "Příspěvek," p. 231.

28. Alice Teichová, "The Protectorate of Bohemia and Moravia (1939–1945): The economic dimension," in *Bohemia in History*, ed. Mikuláš Teich (Cambridge, 1998), pp. 267–305.

29. Pasák, "Český antisemitismus," p. 149.

30. Karel Fremund, *Konec pražského gestapa* (Prague, 1972), pp. 6–7.

31. On the circumstances of its establishment (the visit of Adolph Eichmann and the approval of Reinhard Heydrich, 21.6.1939, and of Premier Eliáš, 15.7.1939, see Hans Safrian, *Die Eichmann-Männer* (Wien, Zürich, 1995), p. 73, 84; Jaroslava Milotová, "Die Zentralstelle für jüdische Auswanderung in Prag: Genesis und Tatigkeit bis zum Anfang des Jahres 1940," in *Theresienstädter Studien und Dokumente 1997*, ed. Miroslav Kárný, Raimund Kemper, and Margita Kárná (Prague, 1997), pp. 2–30.

32. On the tasks and role of the Zentralstelle as well as Zentralamt see also chapter 5.

33. "The Czechs must get out from Central Europe"; see Herman Rauschning, *Gespräche mit Hitler* (New York, 1940), p. 43. See also Heinemann, *Hitler's First Foreign Minister*, pp. 205–12.

34. *Šest let okupace Prahy* (Prague, 1946), p. 24; "Humiliation of the Czech Lands Continues," in *Czechoslovak Informations*, Letters to Friends (London, March 15, 1940).

35. Memorandum "On the Czech Problem," by General Friderici, Plenipotentiary of the Defense Forces with the Reich Protector, 12.7.1939; see *Anatomie okupační politiky hitlerovského Německa v "Protektorátu Čechy a Morava*," Sborník k problematice dějin imperialismu, 21 (Prague, 1987), ed. Miroslav Kárný, Jaroslava Milotová, and Dagmar Moravcová, doc. 13, pp. 50–52.

36. See International Military Tribunal, 33, doc. 3859-PS, pp. 269–70. Cf. Henry Buxbaum Brompton, "The Politics of the German Occupation in the Protectorate of Bohemia and Moravia: A Case Study of a Totalitarian Breakthrough," unpublished dissertation at the University of Southern California at Ann Arbor (1974), p. 93.

37. Bernhard R. Kroener, Rolf-Dieter Müller, and Hans Umbreit, *Das Deutsche Reich und der Zweite Weltkrieg: Organisation und Mobilisierung des Deutschen Machtbereichs* (Stuttgart, 1988), vol. 5, pt. 1, p. 23.

38. Dispatch of 19.6.1939, addressed to the State Department, NA, 860F.50–110.

39. Dispatch of 19.6.1939.

40. According to Walter Utermöhle and Herbert Schmerling of the Office of the Reich Protector, there were in the territory of Bohemia and Moravia about 30,000 establishments, factories, and shops in Jewish ownership with a total value of about 17 billion crowns. For a systematic survey of anti-Jewish legislation enacted up to August 15, 1940, compiled by these two officials, see *Právní postavení židů v Protektorátu Čechy a Morava* (Prague, 1940), p. 13; Chmela, *Economic Aspects*, p. 104.

41. For a detailed account, see Raul Hilberg, *The Destruction of European Jews: A Documented Narrative History* (Chicago, 1961), pp. 66–81; Cf. Teichová, "The Protectorate," p. 285.

42. Teichová, "The Protectorate," p. 285.

43. See report of the Böhmische Escompte Bank in Prague on Aryanizations carried out in Bohemia and Moravia from March 1939 to April 1941 (Prague, August 1941), in *Trials of War Criminals before the Nuremberg Military Tribunals* (NID-13463), vol. 13, pp. 671–74.

44. Jungk, *Franz Werfel*, p. 415.

45. See Miroslav Kárný, "Die Judenfrage in der nazistischen Okupationspolitik," in *Historica* 21 (Prague, 1982), pp. 137–92.

46. "Sinn und Zweck der Gründung der Treuhandstelle in Rahmen der Erfassung des jüdischen Vermögens," see YVA, 07/1-1.

47. See Kárný, "Judenfrage."

48. *New York Times*, 14.5.1939; see Moses Moskowits, "The Jewish Situation in the Protectorate of Bohemia-Moravia," in *Jewish Social Studies* 4 (January 1942), p. 34; Tomáš Pasák views Eliáš's policy as "restraining." He quotes Rabbi (sic) Dr. Friedmann, claiming that Eliáš rejected introducing the Nuremberg Laws in the Protectorate in 1939; see "Český antisemitismus," p. 147. See also Tomáš Pasák, "Aktivističtí novináři a postoj generala Eliáše v roce 1941," in ČsČH, 15, no. 2 (1967), p. 185.

49. *Sbírka zákonů a nařízení*, no. 87/1939; see also Stanislav Jurášek, *Předpisy o židovském majetku a další předpisy Židů se tykající* (Prague, 1940), pp. 61–62. For details on the Germanization scheme see Václav Král, ed., *Lesson from History: Documents Concerning Nazi Policies for Germanization and Extermination* (Prague, 1961), pp. 119–20.

50. See Kárný, "Judenfrage," p. 141.

51. Kárný, "Judenfrage," p. 167.

52. Kárný, "Judenfrage," p. 167.

53. Ordinance of 21.6.1939 in *Verordnungsblatt des Reichsprotektors in Böhmen und Mähren* (hereafter VOBl); see also DHČP, doc. 365, 2:464.

54. See Král, *Otázky hospodářského* 1:76 (table 14.7), the first report of Devisenschutzkommando to Reichsbank concerning confiscated Jewish property in "Protectorate Bohemia and Moravia" (saving deposits, cash, foreign exchange, and securities) by October 14, 1941; (table 14.8) the second report summarizes the value of movable and immovable assets by July 1, 1942. Reproduced in Teichová, "The Protectorate," pp. 290–92.

55. See Norman Rich, *Hitler's War Aims: The Establishment of the New Order* (London, 1974), vol. 2, p. 35.

56. Jurášek, *Předpisy*. For a survey of anti-Jewish legislation see John G. Lexa, "Anti-Jewish Laws and Regulations in the Protectorate of Bohemia and Moravia," in *Jews of CS* 3:75–103.

57. *Šest let okupace*, p. 24; Kennan, *From Prague*, p. 233.

58. Kárný, "Judenfrage," p. 167.

59. Fremund, *Konec pražského gestapa*, p. 16.

60. See Kárný et al., *Anatomie*, doc. 15, pp. 57, 58.

61. Feierabend, *Ve vládě druhé republiky*, p. 62.

62. Brandes, *Die Tschechen*, 1:199.

63. See Oscar Mareni, "The "Erbrichterei'" (unpublished), p. 129; the original letter is in YVA, 07/7-1.

64. *Master of Spies: The Memoirs of General František Moravec* (London, 1975), p. 184, describes the assailants as "newly-killed concentration camp inmates."

65. See Eugen V. Erdely, "Das erste jüdische Konzentrationslager," in *Informationsbulletin*, no. 4 (1979).

66. Richard Feder, *Židovská tragédie, dějství poslední* (Kolín, 1947), p. 22, 29; DHČP, 2:428; Testimony of Margit Galat (neé Hutter), YVA, E2. For the tragic fate of Rabbi Grünfeld see Ladislav Vilímek, "Jihlavský rabín Dr. Grünfeld," in *Židé a Morava*, pp. 66–70.

67. For the documentation of the Gestapo in Moravská Ostrava see *Nazi Dokumente sprechen* (Kroměříž, 1998); for the file of the RSHA on the Nisko campaign, YVA, DN/30–1. Of the 1,291 men sent to Nisko from Moravská Ostrava, 460 returned when the camp was dissolved in April 1940. Two years later these were deported to Terezín and from there to the East. See Karel Lagus and Josef Polák, *Město za mřížemi* (Prague, 1964), p. 300.

68. For Salo Krämer's secret report, dated October 27, 1939 (found in the military archives Vojenský historický archiv in Prague, hereafter cited as VHA, 37–91–1), dispatched as part of "The Situation in Bohemia and Moravia" to the National Committee abroad, see Stanislav Kokoška, "Zwei unbekannte Berichte aus dem besetzten Prag über die Lage der jüdischen Bevölkerung des Protektorats," in *Theresienstädter Studien und Dokumente 1997*, ed. Miroslav Kárný, Raimund Kemper, and Margita Kárná (Prague, 1997), pp. 32–33, 44–45; for details on Marcel Junod's enquiry on the ICRC's early information, see chapter 9.

69. See J. Zehngut, *Dějiny židovstva ostravského* (Ostrava, 1952); for an in-depth analysis see Zeev Goshen, "Eichmann und die Nisko-Aktion in Oktober 1939: Eine Fallstudie zur NS-Judenpolitik in der letzten Etappe vor der 'Endlösung,'" in *INVZ* 29 (1981), pp. 74–96; Měčislav Borák, *Transport do tmy: První deportace evropských Židů* (Ostrava, 1994). On the third transport of "stateless" Jews and those holding Polish citizenship, dispatched from Prague on November 1, 1939, see Lukáš Přibyl, "Osud třetího protektorátního transportu do Niska," in *Terezínské studie a dokumenty 2000*, pp. 309–46.

70. For a more detailed account about Edelstein's harrowing experiences as reproduced in Moshe (Shertok) Sharett's diary (entry for February 2, 1940), see my article, "The Zionist Character of the Self-Government in Terezín," in *YVS* 11 (1976), pp. 61–70; Ludmila Nesládková, ed., *Nisko 1939–1994: The Case of Nisko in the History of the "Final Solution of the Jewish Problem"* (Ostrava, 1995).

71. Nesládková, *Nisko 1939–1994*, p. 69.

72. For Edelstein's letter addressed to Eliahu Dobkin, 12.12.1939, see CZA, S25/2379.

73. During his visit to Yad Vashem in 1958 (accompanied by Prof. Jacob Talmon), Prof. Louis Namier revealed to this author that he was actually the "correspondent" who authored the article "The Nazi Plan: A Stony Road to Extermination," *Times*, 16.12.1939. Moshe Sharett also referred to this issue in his diary; see CZA, S25/2371.

74. Sharett diary, CZA, S25/2371.

75. See T/37 (8), Report on Eichmann's study trip to Palestine; 4.11.1937, 54 pages (B06–2, Statement, p. 431); see also State of Israel, *The Trial of Adolf Eichmann*.

76. See Rothkirchen, "Zionist Character," p. 68.

77. About Nisko and participation of Ostrava Jews in the Czechoslovak Army, see Erich Kulka, "Nisko a účast ostravských Židů v boji československých vojsk proti nacistickému

Německu v druhé světové válce," and Bedřich Kopold, "Nejen utrpení také i odplata," both in *Nisko 1939–1994*, pp. 191–205, 207–12.

78. The article "The Czech Revolt," in the *Times*, 22.9.1939, also reported that Czechs living in exile are "flocking in their thousands to the colors of the Czech legions formed in the Allied countries."

79. Drtina, *Československo můj osud*, vol. 1, pt. 1, p. 438.

80. "Intractable Czechs," in *Times*, 17.10.1939, also gave this amusing comment: "The grimmest jokes are now current in polite society. Now that the question has arisen of renaming Prague streets Czechs have suggested among themselves that Hrdlořezy ('Cut-throat') Street should be renamed 'Es kommt der Tag,' that Podhořelec ('The Burned') Street should be called Hitler Street and in a lighter vein that Klamovka ('Mystification') Street should be renamed German Press Agency."

81. Some operas such as *Braniboři v Čechách* and *Jakobín* were banned for their patriotic attributes; see *Šest let okupace*, p. 70.

82. Brandes, *Die Tschechen*, 1:199, relies on SD (Security) reports.

83. The flier distributed to the journalists was entitled "Pravda zvítězí" (Truth prevails); see Feierabend, *Ve vládě druhé republiky*, p. 151.

84. Linnel's report to Washington of March 30, 1940. See NA, box 4895, 860F.00/947.

85. K. H. Frank's memorandum (*Denkschrift*) to Hitler of August 18, 1940, became the basis of a long-term policy of Germanization. See "Denkschrift über die Behandlung des Tschechen-Problems und die zukunftige Gestaltung des Böhmisch-Mährischen Raumes." Cf. DHČP, doc. 315, 1:459.

86. Entry of 27.10.1940, in *Deníky Jiřího Ortena: Poesie—myšlenky—zápisky* (Prague, 1958), p. 304; Pavel Eisner, "Jinoch Exodus," in ŽR 5719 (1958–59), p. 84.

87. See Marie Rut Křížková, "Básník smrti a lásky," in ŽR 5733 (1972–73), pp. 93–102. According to the author, already in August 1938 Orten envisaged an act of suicide for his twentieth birthday.

88. Josef Hiršal, *Vínek vzpomínek* (Prague, 1990), p. 105, claims that it was Orten's tremendous love and jealousy that inspired him to write his unique lyrics and sombre elegies.

89. See Ota Ornest in an epilogue to his brother's diaries, *Deníky*, pp. 459–68, and his "Jiří Orten—básník i clovek," in ŽR 5740 (1980), pp. 83–85.

90. Ornest, *Deníky*, and "Jiří Orten."

91. Our information on the activities of the JRC are for the most part gleaned from the reports in the weekly, monthly, and overall situation reports (*Wochenberichte, Monatsberichte, and Lageberichte*) submitted to the Zentralstelle between July 1939 and December 1942, to be found in YVA, 07/10–1; cf. statistical table between March 15, 1939, and June 15, 1942, in *Židé v protektorátu: Die Juden im Protektorat Böhmen und Mähren: Hlášení Židovské náboženské obce v roce 1942, dokumenty*, ed. Helena Krejčová, Jana Svobodová, and Anna Hyndráková (Prague, 1997), pp. 51–63.

92. At this stage there were altogether thirty-seven members on the JRC. From the report submitted to the Zentralstelle it transpires that the overall number of Jews by 31.3.1941 was 74,417. Those of "non-Mosaic" faith (12,168) were enumerated thus: without confession 5,611, Catholics 4,818, Evangelics of Augsburg confession 909, Bohemian-

Moravian Church 542, Bohemian Brothers' community 446, old-Catholics 192, Anglicans 52, *rechtglaubig* 44, Greek Orthodox 17, Unitarians 24, Helvetian confession 17, and Bohemian Reformed Church 8; see YVA 07/112.

93. "Die Juden zur Zeit des Protektorates in Böhmen und Mähren-Schlesien," recorded by Dr. Friedrich Thieberger after a series of interviews with Dr. Karel Stein, chairman of the JRC of Prague after the war. Stein emigrated to Israel in 1949 and died in Jerusalem in 1961. (Stein MS, 22 pp).

94. Erich Kraus acted as deputy of the last Judenältester Dr. František Friedmann. In 1955, upon the demand of the Prague State Security, he wrote a résumé of observations on the Prague Jewish leadership in the years 1939–45, "Cíle ŽNO a ŽRS" (The aims of ŽNO and ŽRS), which he made available to the New-York-based Society for the History of the Czechoslovak Jews after his emigration to Switzerland in 1980. A copy of his résumé is in the author's possession.

95. See "Report on Bohemia and Moravia 1939–1940," in JDC Archives, p. 10.

96. "Report on Bohemia and Moravia," p. 3: "The Czechs are for the most part helpful and have maintained a praiseworthy attitude."

97. JRC Weekly report 23–29.8.1939, see YVA, 07/10–1.

98. The fund-raising campaign yielded a total of $1,062,199, most of which sum was contributed by the JDC. See Lagebericht, April 1, 1941, YVA, 07/11–2.

99. The JRC annual reports, compiled in the format of an album, are to be found in YVA, 07; see also the report of Schönfeld on the "Vocation Campaign"(in his *Přeškolování*).

100. According to a survey in the JRC Annual Report for 1940, the community bulletin *Jüdisches Nachrichtenblatt* (JNBL) was issued in 1939 in a press run of 9,300 copies and in 1940 it reached 13,000 copies.

101. For an in-depth study on the role of the weekly see "Židovské listy v letech 1939–1944," an unpublished dissertation by Zdeněk Jirotka, Faculty of Journalism, Prague Charles University.

102. Oscar Singer, publicist and writer, worked as a journalist first for the *Prager Tagblatt, Der Montag, Selbstwehr,* and *Jüdischer Volksblatt* and at last for the JNBL. In 1935 he published his three-act anti-Nazi play *Herren der Welt.* Singer's tragic fate in the Łodý ghetto and his important contribution documenting events of daily life there is recorded in *The Chronicles of the Łodý Ghetto 1941–1944,* ed. Lucjan Dobroszycki (New Haven, London, 1984), pp. xiii–xvi.

103. Within a period of a year and a half, the HeHalutz pioneering organization succeeded in registering 3,000 young people for emigration to Palestine. Of these, 1,908 were engaged in *hahsharah.* They were assigned in small groups to jobs on the lands of Czech farmers but were later sent to concentration camps. See Shlomo Schmiedt, "HeHalutz in Theresienstadt: Its Influence and Educational Activities," in YVS 7 (1968), pp. 107–25.

104. JNBL, no. 1, 24.11.1939.

105. One of these vignettes in Hebrew read: "Do not despair and do not lament!" (*Lo tevoshi—ve'lo tikolmi*), in JNBL, no. 15, 12.4.1940.

106. JNBL, no. 13, 29.3.1940.

107. JNBL, no. 16, 19.4.1940. The oldest Czech and German translation by Karel Jugl of the two Passover songs describing Jewish customs and beliefs, *Chad Gadja* and *Echad mi*

Jodea, are among the holdings of the National Museum in Prague (sign. I.E.9). See Čeněk Zíbrt, *Ohlas obřadních písní velikonočních Haggadah* (Prague, 1928), p. 86.

108. JNBL, no. 30, 26.7.1940.

109. Cf. Franz Friedmann, *Rechtstellung der Juden im Protektorat Böhmen und Mähren*, Stand am 31.7.1942, pp. 232–34.

110. For the structure of the JRC, the various sections, and the list of functionaries (and their family members) see note 92 to this chapter and Krejčová et al., *Die Juden im Protektorat*; see also Philip Friedmann,"Aspects of the Jewish Communal Crisis in the Period of the Nazi Regime," in *Essays on Jewish Life and Thought* (New York, 1959), pp. 200–230.

111. See "Soziale Fürsorge" and "Krankenfürsorge," in Krejčová et al., *Die Juden im Protektorat*, pp. 67–84, 85–96; cf. Kraus, Observations; Stein MS (note 93), p. 10.

112. Darovat—budovat—žít!, announced in JNBL, no. 1, 24.11.1939.

113. Norbert Frýd, *Lahvová pošta, aneb konec posledních sto let* (Prague, 1971), pp. 116–17.

114. Frýd, *Lahvová pošta*, p. 116.

115. J(an) K(ojan) many years later was reminiscing under his own name. See "Z paměti židomila," in ŽR 5740 (1979–80), pp. 127–31.

116. See Zdenka Neumannová, "Protižidovská propaganda," in *Šest let okupace Prahy*, pp. 114–24.

117. Neumannová, "Protižidovská propaganda," p. 124.

118. The visit of the "two gentlemen from Prague" is documented in the minutes of the Amsterdam Joodse Raad; see Jacob Presser, *Ashes in the Wind: The Destruction of Dutch Jewry* (London, 1965), p. 343.

119. See Rothkirchen, "Zionist Character," p. 72. For the testimony of Dr. Joseph Melkman (Michman), see State of Israel, *The Trial of Adolf Eichmann*, Record of Proceedings in the District Court of Jerusalem (Jerusalem, 1992), vol. 2, pp. 611–12.

120. Cf. "Soziale Fürsorge," note 111.

121. Neumannová, "Protižidovská propaganda," p. 124.

122. See Heydrich's report of 11.10.1941, dispatched to the chief of the NSDAP office, Martin Bormann, in *Deutsche Politik im "Protektorat, Böhmen und Mähren" unter Reinhard Heydrich 1941–1942: Eine Dokumentation*, ed. Miroslav Kárný, Jaroslava Milotová, and Margita Kárná (Berlin, 1997), doc. 30, pp. 144–45; see also JRC Annual Report 1941, quoted in VŽONP, no. 51–52, 1951.

123. In his letter dated September 18, 1941, Himmler entrusted Heydrich with carrying out the proposed evacuations.

124. For the fundamental line of policy as outlined by the Führer, in Heydrich's speech of October 1941, see Král, *Lesson from History*, pp. 129–30.

125. See DHČP, 2:632–34; Kárný et al., *Deutsche Politik im Protektorat*, doc. 29, pp. 137–41.

126. Lágus and Polák, *Město za mřížemi*, p. 60.

127. For the workers' declaration see YVA, M58/5, 105–8.

128. Heydrich's witticism might have been spurred by one of his "knowledgeable" assistants' reference to the sixteenth-century chronicler Hájek's description of Jews build-

ing their houses in the old Oujezd district of Prague, "*dolů do země do lochu*" (in the bowels of the earth). The Prague "Protomedicus" called the Jewish quarters *Mordgruben* (death-pits); see JGGJČR 5 (1933), p. 339.

129. Testimony of Margit Galat (nee Hutter), YVA, E2. Subsequently the Nazis made sure to avoid any occurrence of commotion amidst the Czech population by directing the convoys to the railway station under the screen of darkness, before dawn or late at night.

130. The five transports were made up of Prague Jews whose arrival was duly registered by the Litzmanstadt Stapo IIB4—signed Dr. Schefe (or Fuchs)—between 17.10 and 3.11.1941. See YVA microfilm collection, JM/807.

131. The letter was addressed to Bergmann's elder son Karel, who was later arrested in Prague and executed in Mauthausen in May 1942. See (unpublished) reminiscences of the younger son, Dáša Bergmann, who survived the war. (He was sent in 1939 with a Zionist youth group to Denmark and from there reached England, where he joined the Czechoslovak Army units.)

132. See Dobroszycki, *Chronicles*; Michal Unger, ed., *The Last Ghetto: Life in the Łodý Ghetto 1940–1944* (Jerusalem, 1991).

133. See Fuchs,"Die tschechish-jüdische Widerstandsbewegung in Theresienstadt," in *Theresienstädter Studien und Dokumente 1997*, ed. Miroslav Kárný Raimund Kemper, and Margita Kárná (Prague, 1997), p. 149.

134. See Fuchs,"Die tschechish-jüdische Widerstandsbewegung," pp. 15–16; Zdeněk Lederer, *Ghetto Theresienstadt* (London, 1953), pp. 12–14.

135. See Schmiedt, "HeHalutz in Theresienstadt," pp. 107–25.

136. See VŽONP, nos. 12 and 17, 1947, referring to the Trial of Karl Rahm; Kraus, Observations, pp. 12–13.

137. Kraus, Observations, p. 7.

138. Kraus, Observations, p. 7.

139. About the dedicated work of Richard Israel Friedmann on behalf of the Terezín inmates, see Fuchs, "Die tschechisch-jüdische Widerstandsbewegung," p. 155.

140. See H. G. Adler, *Die verheimlichte Wahrheit: Theresienstädter Dokumente* (Tübingen, 1958), p. 11.

141. Under the guidance of Hanna Steiner a group of around two to three hundred young volunteers assisted the deportees, providing them with clothes, food, and medicine before boarding the trains. See testimonies in Zeev Shek Collection, YVA, 0–64/85; Stein MS, p. 10.

142. Otto Wolf's diary describes the hardships of the family: foraging for food in the forest, living under constant threat. It also reveals the close-knit family life of observant, religious Jews, who despite the harsh circumstances observe holidays and pray daily for the return of the elder son, Captain Kurt Wolf (who fought and fell at Sokolovo, March 1943). See Miroslav Kárný and Ludvík Václavek, "Deník Otto Wolfa z let 1942–1943," in *Okresní archív v Olomouci* (1987), pp. 31–41, and their "Otto Wolfs Tagebuch 1942–1943," in *Germanistisches Jahrbuch* DDR-ČSSR (1987–88), pp. 133–44.

143. The farmer (sl. = Slávka), Jaroslav Zdařil, made the initial arrangements for their hiding place, but it was mainly the dentist Ludmila Tichá and other villagers who helped them survive.

144. See *Deník Otty Wolfa* (Prague, 1997), introduction by Ludvík Václavek and Ivan Klíma, p. 33; only the parents and the daughter survived the war. During a razzia in April 1945, young Otto was taken hostage along with other villagers by a unit of the Vlasov army, attached to the Gestapo. On April 20 they were shot in the forest near the village of Kyjanica. During the interrogation Otto never revealed his name nor the hiding place of his parents.

145. See Stein MS, pp. 8–9; Hana Volavková, "The Jewish Museum of Prague," in *Jews of CS* 3:568–77.

146. The letter was signed by František Weidmann; see Volavková, *Schicksal*, pp. 60–62.

147. Poláček's letters to Dora in Prague contain laconic and whimsical comments on the situation: "To work with books is elevating. Today books are definitely better [friends] than living beings. God knows how disgusted I am with the human race." See Poláček, *Poslední dopisy Doře*, p. 14.

148. Poláček, *Poslední dopisy Doře*, p. 14.

149. As of 28.2.1943, after the deportation of Dr. Weidmann and other members of the JRC to Terezín, Salo Krämer served for less than six months as the elder of the Jewish council. For an account of the activities of the *Treuhandstelle* see Adler, *Verheimlichte Wahrheit*, pp. 77–85; Krejčová et al., *Die Juden im Protektorat*, pp. 345–50.

150. From the letters smuggled out of Prague to the HeHalutz center in Geneva it is clear that some funds reached the Prague JRC, and these were used for the purchase of food and other necessities that were forwarded to Terezín. (The ghetto was referred to as Ir Jakov or Jakobstadt, meaning Jacob Edelstein's town.) These letters of the various Jewish organizations are now available in several Israeli archives: CZA, ALM, and YVA.

151. Within the first half year twelve hundred of the Protectorate deportees died of starvation in the Łodý ghetto. Their situation was later somewhat less extreme, owing to the gift parcels sent from Prague and the Jewish organizations abroad. See Heinz Prossnitz's correspondence, YVA, 07 / 1819: cf. chapter 8.

152. Dobroszycki, *Chronicles*, p. 508: in the fall of 1944 the majority of the inmates were sent to Auschwitz. It is estimated that of the 5,000 deportees from Prague about 5 percent, 253 persons, survived. The Red Army liberated Łodý on 19.1.1945, finding 878 people alive there, of whom nine were survivors of the Prague transports. See Eva Stehlíková, "Proč mi bývá smutno," in vŽONP (October 1981); according to the *Terezín Memorialbook* (Prague, 1996), p. 100, altogether 276 persons survived.

153. See "Ältestenrat der Juden in Prag," after April 1, 1943, in Krejčová et al., *Die Juden im Protektorat*, pp. 356–86.

154. Cf. Kraus, Observations.

155. There are minor discrepancies in the various statistical sources. According to an official German estimate of January 31, 1945, altogether there remained 6,446 Jews left in the Protectorate: 3,060 living in Prague and 3,386 in the provinces. Another estimate refers to 6,621 "arisch versippt," part Jews. Of these 4,243 persons were deported during January and February 1945 to Theresienstadt. At the end of war altogether 2,803 persons remained in Prague and other localities. See Statistical Surveys, YVA, 0–64.

156. Feder, *Židovská tragédie*, p. 211.

157. This letter is one of the documents (no. 29) microfilmed upon my request by

courtesy of Elizabeth Maier of the World Jewish Congress, New York, now to be found in YVA, JM/1698.

158. The letter was originally written in German, translation mine; see CZA, S25/2374.

159. The reference is to the fate of the deportees from the Protectorate, some of whom managed to smuggle out cryptic messages that reached the Prague JRC about the mass murder carried out in Poland.

160. For a brief description see Rudolf Kastner, Der Bericht des jüdischen Rettungs-komitees aus Budapest 1942–1945, typescript (Geneva, 1946), p. 36; see also H. G. Adler, *Theresienstadt 1941–1945: Das Antlitz einer zwangsgemeinschaft*, rev. ed., (Tübingen: J. C. B. Mohr–Paul Siebeck, 1960), pp. 169–71.

161. Reproduced in Kastner, Bericht, pp. 195–96.

162. Kastner, Bericht, pp. 195–96.

163. See passage from a letter of Heinz Schuster reproduced earlier.

164. Jana Grňová, *Svatobořický tábor* (Brno, 1948); Jan Marek, "Sonderlager," in ŽR 5741 (1981), pp. 39–45.

165. Report of the Ältestenrat der Juden in Prag to the Zentralamt für die Regelung der Judenfrage in Böhmen und Mähren, prepared on the order of Obersturmführer Girczik, YVA, 0–64; cf. Livia Rothkirchen, "Czech and Slovak Wartime Leadership: Variants in Strategy and Tactics," in *Holocaust and History*, ed. Michael Berenbaum and J. Abraham Peck (Bloomington, 1998), pp. 630–45.

166. Report of the Ältestenrat.

167. See note 155.

168. For the rescue activities of Fritz Ullmann in Geneva and his contacts with Jaromír Kopecký and other personalities see the Ullmann collection in CZA, A320; see also Miroslav Kryl, "Fritz Ullmann und seine Hilfe fur die Theresienstädter Häftlinge," in *Theresie-städter Studien und Dokumente 1997*, ed. Miroslav Kárný, Raimund Kemper, and Margita Kárná (Prague, 1997), pp. 184–215.

169. For an overall discussion of the subject see chapter 9.

170. See Raul Hilberg, "The Judenrat as a Conscious or Unconscious Tool," in *Patterns of Jewish Leadership in Nazi Europe, 1933–1945. Proceedings of the Third Yad Vashem International Conference, April 1977*, ed. Yisrael Gutman and Cynthia J. Haft (Jerusalem, 1979), p. 39.

171. Regarding secret contacts, see Livia Rothkirchen, "Die Repräsentanten der There-sienstädter Selbstverwaltung; Differenzierung der Ansichten," in *Theresienstädter Studien und Dokumente 1996*, pp. 114–26.

172. For Cecilie Friedmann's testimony see Protokoll, Manuscript, DA Prag, 1945. Passages from this MS were first published in Adler, *Theresienstadt*, pp. 737–38.

173. Friedmann testimony.

174. Feder, *Židovská tragédie*. See chapter 9 for more about Murmelstein.

175. Adler, *Theresienstadt*, pp. 19–20.

176. Kastner, Bericht, pp. 67–68.

177. Kraus, Observations, p. 8.

178. Kraus, Observations, p. 8.

179. Poláček, *Poslední dopisy Doře*, p. 44.

180. Kraus, Observations, p. 10.

5. The Protectorate Governments and the "Final Solution"

1. Tomáš Pasák, "General Alois Eliáš a odboj," in *Slovo k historii* 2, no. 27 (Prague: Melantrich, 1995); Robert Kvaček and Dušan Tomášek, *General Alois Eliáš: Jeden český osud* (Prague, 1996); Dušan Tomášek and Robert Kvaček, *Causa Emil Hácha* (Praha, 1995); see Tomáš Pasák, *Judr. Emil Hácha 1938–1945* (Praha, 1997); Dušan Tomášek and Robert Kvaček, *Obžalována je vláda* (Prague, 1999).

2. Smutný's text prepared in mid-1943 for the London *Observer* is printed in Libuše Otáhalová and Milada Červínková, eds., *Dokumenty z historie československé politiky 1939–1943, Acta occupationis Bohemiae et Moraviae*, 2 vols. (Prague, 1966), doc. 339, 1:412.

3. See Livia Rothkirchen, "Protectorate Government," pp. 331–62.

4. See Stanley Hoffmann, *Decline or Renewal? France since the 1930s* (New York, 1974), chapter 2, pp. 26–44.

5. Livia Rothkirchen, "The Slovak Enigma: A Reassessment of the Halt to the Deportations," in *East Central Europe* 10, nos. 1–2 (1983), pp. 313.

6. Denis Peschanski, "The Statutes on Jews October 3, 1940 and June 2, 1941," and Renee Poznanski, "The Jews of France and the Statutes on Jews," both in YVS 22 (1992), pp. 65–88, 115–46.

7. Pierre Laborie, "The Jewish Statutes in Vichy France and Public Opinion," YVS 22 (1992), pp. 89–114.

8. Michael Marrus, "Coming to Terms with Vichy," in *Holocaust and Genocide Studies* 9, no. 1 (Spring 1995), pp. 34–35; Serge Klarsfeld, *Vichy-Auschwitz: Le role de Vichy dans la solution finale de la question juive en France, 1943–1944* (Paris, 1985).

9. Julius Streicher's *Der Stürmer* was a popular anti-Semitic pro-Nazi weekly. In a crude and aggressive style the newspaper promoted the idea that Jews were the enemy of the Reich through allegations of ritual murder, Slovak or world Jewish conspiracy and Jewish sexual crimes, and anti-Semitic cartoons. Even some noted liberal journalists, among them Ferdinand Peroutka, the editor of *Přítomnost*, wrote articles in an anti-Semitic vein, vexing the Jewish public. A kaleidoscope of the anti-Jewish excesses may be found in *Věstník čsl. Ligy proti antisemitismu*, the bulletin of the Czechoslovakian League against Anti-Semitism, published as of 1937. The national chairman of this organization was Pastor Bohumil Vančura of the Church of Bohemian Brethren.

10. The Minister of Interior's instruction of July 25, 1938, to the Presidium of the Provincial Administration, in the matter of the American Jewish Congress' complaint (5 May 1938), Státní Ústřední Archív (Central State Archives, SÚA), MV, 207–1938–5.

11. Minister of Interior's instruction.

12. J. M. Troutbeck, First Secretary of the British Legation in Prague, to Foreign Secretary Lord Halifax, February 9, 1939, see Public Record Office, PRO no. 63, C1868/568.

13. Editorial in VŽONP, 20.12.1938.

14. Speech made by Reinhard Heydrich on October 2, 1941; see Karel Fremund and

Václav Král, eds., *Lesson from History: Documents Concerning Nazi Policies, Germanization and Extermination in Czechoslovakia* (Prague, 1962), doc. 19, p. 118.

15. Heydrich speech, pp. 119–20; Věra Olivová and Robert Kvaček, *Dějiny Československa* (Prague, 1967), vol. 4, p. 354.

16. VOBl, no. 2, 1939, pp. 53–57; Tomášek and Kvaček, *Causa Emil Hácha*, pp. 59–60.

17. Jaroslava Eliášová and Tomáš Pasák, "Poznámky k Benešovým kontaktům s Eliášem ve druhé světové válce" in *Historie a vojenství*, no. 1 (1967), pp. 108–40; Tomáš Pasák, "Činnost protektorátní representace na podzim roku 1939" in ČsČH 17, no. 4 (1969), pp. 553–72.

18. DHČP, doc. 364, Prague, 11.10.1939, 2:454.

19. Ladislav Feierabend, *Ve vládách druhé republiky* (New York, 1961), *Ve vládě protektorátu* (New York, 1962), and *Ve vládě v exilu*, 2 vols (Washington, 1965, 1966).

20. Already in early November 1938 the word spread in higher echelons that the Germans demanded physical attacks against Jews. A report sent from Prague by J. M. Troutbeck to Lord Halifax (15.11.1938) refers to a "conversation between Count Kinský and Robert J. Stopford." See PRO no. 397, C14 188/2475/ (enclosure).

21. "Die Juden würden bei uns vernichtet," Minutes of the conversation of January 21, 1939, see *Akten zur deutschen auswärtigen Politik 1918–1945*, Series D, vol. 4, doc. 158, pp. 170–71.

22. Kvaček and Tomášek, *General Eliáš*, p. 66.

23. Kennan, *From Prague*. For an assessment of Kennan's invaluable contribution, see "Epilogue by Frederick G. Heymann," pp. 241–53.

24. Břetislav Tvarůžek, "Okupace Čech a Moravy a vojenská správa (15. březen az 15. duben 1939)," in *Historie a vojenství* 41, no. 3 (1992), pp. 52–53.

25. Protokoll der Regierungssitzung vom 17.3.1939, Beschlusse IV bis VIII (Beschränkung der Praxis der nichtarischen Ärzte, und Advokaten, Beseitigung der Nichtarier aus den Funktionen der einigen wirtschaftlichen Organisationen und aus allen leitenden Stellen in industriellen Unternehmen und Organisationen, die Bezeichnung rein arischer Geschafte), SÚA, sign. PMR, box 4148; see Miroslav Kárný, "Vorgeschichte des Regierungsverordnung über die Rechtsstellung der Juden im öffentlichen Leben," in JB 30–31 (1996), p. 109.

26. Miroslav Kárný, "Judenfrage," p. 147; for a milder judgement se Pasák, Judr. *Emil Hácha*, pp. 65–80.

27. DHČP, doc. 365, 2:464.

28. Originally it was Hitler who suggested to von Neurath "to leave the decision to the Czechs." See Burgsdorff, "Judengesetze," minutes of 2.5.1939, in Kárný et al., *Anatomie*, doc. 77, pp. 203–5.

29. Cf. Beneš's message from London to Prague, 11.5.1940, Eliášová and Pasák, "Poznámky," p. 123.

30. See Kokoška, "Zwei unbekannte Berichte," pp. 32–33.

31. Cf. Kárný et al., *Anatomie*, doc. 79–84, pp. 205–19.

32. VOBl, no. 6, 7.7.1939.

33. Kárný, "Vorgeschichte," pp. 110–11.

34. DHČP, doc. 379 (enclosure), 3.1.1940, 2:500.

35. "Sinn und Zweck der Gründung der Treuhandstelle im Rahmen der Erfassung des judischen Vermögens, der 15. März 1939," YVA, 07/1-1, pp. 151, 156; DHČP, doc. 365, 2:464–65.

36. See "Dispatch of July 3, 1939, from Consul General Linnell to the Department of State on General Conditions in Bohemia and Moravia," in Kennan, *From Prague*, pp. 188–89.

37. Wochenbericht der Jüdischen Kultusgemeinde in Prag, 23–29.7.1939.

38. See the report of Police Commissar Šebor, 30.7.1939, SÚA, sign. PMR, 225-1323-1-8.

39. In the same set of documents is the report of Police Commissar Nečásek; the full text of this report was printed (as doc. 3, pp. 174–75) in a selection of pertinent documents published by Otto D. Kulka, "Le berur mediniut hayehudit shel ha-S.D. bearzot kvushot harishonot," in *Yalkut Moreshet*, no. 18 (November 1974), pp. 163–84.

40. Kárný, "Judenfrage," p. 147.

41. Heinrich Himmler, *Geheimreden 1933 bis 1945 und andere Ansprachen*, ed. B. F. Smith and A. F. Peterson (Frankfurt, Wien, 1974), pp. 128–29.

42. See Nesládková, *Nisko 1939–1994*; see also Borák, *Transport do tmy*.

43. See indictment of Alois Eliáš, Nuremberg Document NG-081; indictment of Zdeněk Schmoranz, NG-699.41.

44. For the autumn arrests see Detlef Brandes, *Die Tschechen* 1:98.

45. DHČP, doc. 376, 8.12.1939, 1:493–94.

46. For an analysis see Pasák, "Aktivističtí," fn. 6, p. 175.

47. SS-Obersturmbannführer Dr. Hans Ullrich Geschke, head of the Gestapo in Prague, had been collecting discriminating evidence on Eliáš as of autumn 1939. Pasák, "Aktivističtí," p. 174; Kvaček and Tomášek, *Generál Eliáš*, p. 53.

48. Kárný et al., *Anatomie*, doc. 84, p. 218.

49. Communication of the office of NSDAP to the Reichsprotektor (4.7.1939); see Miroslav Kárný, "*Konečné řešení*": *Genocida českých židů v německé protektorátní politice* (Prague, 1991), p. 58.

50. Hácha's response to von Neurath, 19.7.1940, see SÚA, sign. ÚŘP, I-3b-5801, box 388.

51. Comments on the government draft proposal, 4.7.1939, SÚA, sign. PMR-S, 1590/7-1040, vol. 1, box 589.

52. Undersecretary of State von Burgsdorff to Premier Eliáš, 14.1.1941, SÚA, sign. PMR-S, 1590/7-1040, vol. 1, box 589.

53. Tomášek and Kvaček, *Causa Emil Hácha*, p. 100.

54. It was Dr. Walter Fuchs who on behalf of the Reichsprotektor wrote the definitive answer to Acting Prime Minister Krejčí, dated 4.10.1941; SÚA, sign. PMR-S, 1590/7 1941, vol. 2, box 594.

55. DHČP, doc. 404, 1.7.1940, 2:544.

56. Pasák, "Generál Alois Eliáš," pp. 9–10; Kvaček and Tomášek, *Generál Eliáš*, p. 62, 71.

57. Monatsbericht Juli 1940, Sicherheitsdienst RFSS, SD-Leitabschnitt Prag, SÚA, sign. ÚŘP-d, box 32.

58. The offer was made through Siegmund Amarant, during Beneš's stay in Paris. See Jacobi, *Země zaslíbená*, pp. 9–11.

59. Jacobi, *Země zaslíbená*, pp. 9–11.

60. Minutes of the session of the cabinet, 24.10.1940, SÚA, sign. PMR, box 4155.

61. Eliáš to K. H. Frank, 3.4.1941, SÚA, sign. ÚŘP, I-36–5880, box 390.

62. Ernst von Weizsäcker on 27.3.1940 claimed that Eliáš headed the clandestine organization; SÚA, sign. AA, 489807–489810, box 32a.

63. See Pasák, "Generál Alois Eliáš," pp. 9–10; Kvaček and Tomášek, Generál Eliáš, p. 70.

64. DHČP, doc. 383, February–March, 2:510–11; David Kelly, The Czech Fascist Movement 1922–1942 (New York: Columbia University Press, 1995), mainly "The Unwanted Collaborators," pp. 168–75.

65. Message to Prague, 11.5.1940, see Eliášová and Pasák, "Poznámky," pp. 122–23; DHČP, doc. 444, 3.6.1941, 2:609.

66. DHČP, doc. 447, 24.6.1941, 2:614; see also Beneš's explanations to Smutný (25.6.1941) regarding why Hácha and Eliáš should resign, DHČP, doc. 448, 2:615.

67. As of fall 1941 Hácha's stance vis-à-vis the London government became rude and venomous. In one of his notorious proclamations he blamed Beneš's Jewish milieu thus: "While under the genial command of the Führer the new European Order is being construed, the former President Beneš in London, obviously influenced by his Jewish milieu, is heralding the lost case of the Reich's enemies." See DHČP, doc. 469, 4.12.1941, 2:644–45.

68. For Beneš's message to Hácha and Eliáš of 26.7.1941, see Eliášová and Pasák, "Poznámky," pp. 138–39.

69. Eliáš's last message from Prague, 7.8.1941, Eliášová and Pasák, "Poznámky," p. 140.

70. Pasák, "Generál Alois Eliáš," p. 27.

71. Eliášová and Pasák, "Poznámky," pp. 112–14.

72. See chapter 7.

73. Eliášová and Pasák, "Poznámky," p. 114.

74. Pasák, "Generál Alois Eliáš," pp. 25–26.

75. For Heydrich's cable to Himmler of 27.9.1941, on the arrest of Gen. Eliáš, see Kárný et al., Deutsche Politik im Protektorat, doc. 12, p. 94.

76. Heydrich's cable to Bormann regarding the trial of Eliáš, 1.10.1941, see Kárný et al., Deutsche Politik im Protektorat, doc. 20, pp. 102–6.

77. Helmut Heiber, "Zur Justitz im Dritten Reich: Der Fall Eliáš," in VZ 3 (1955), pp. 275–96.

78. For Heydrich's exposé about future plans in the Protectorate, 17.10.1941, see Kárný et al., Deutsche Politik im Protektorat, doc. 33, pp. 147–57.

79. During his 1946 trial at the People's Court in Prague, Karl H. Frank admitted that he threatened to kill twenty thousand Czechs if Eliáš would not issue his proclamation. See Český národ soudí K. H. Franka (Prague, Orbis, 1947), p. 90.

80. Pasák, "Generál Alois Eliáš," p. 37.

81. See Nuremberg Document NG-147, "Abschrift des Urteils des Volksgerichtes vom 1. Oktober 1941," p. 25.

82. Eliášová and Pasák, "Poznámky," pp. 112–13.

83. Heydrich's letter to Hácha, referring to Bořek-Dohalský's last meeting with Premier Eliáš (before his arrest), DHČP, doc. 464, 15.11.1941, 2:640.

84. Jaroslav Drábek, Z časů dobrých a zlých (Prague, 1992), p. 91.

85. For an alphabetical list of those executed during the first state of emergency (with an analytic commentary), see Zlatuše Kukánová, "Seznam osob popravených za prvního stanného práva ve dnech 28. září až do 28. listopadu 1941," in *Sborník historick* 18 (Prague, 1985), pp. 98–126.

86. For an exchange of letters see Kárný et al., *Deutsche Politik im Protektorat*, docs. 24 and 44, pp. 128–29, 174.

87. Heydrich's report to Bormann about the situation in the Protectorate, 16.11.1941, doc. 51, p. 189.

88. See Heydrich's situation report sent to Reichsleiter Bormann, Prag, 22.1.1942, and Heydrich's secret speech of 4.2.1942, both printed in R. Amort, *Heydrichiáda* (Prague, 1964). Cf. Brandes, *Die Tschechen*, 1:217–19.

89. The last report about the situation in the Protectorate, sent by Heydrich to Bormann, 18.5.1942 (instructions for the re-education of the Czech youth); see Kárný et al., *Deutsche Politik im Protektorat*, doc. 98, pp. 266–68.

90. On the Germanization policy and the re-education of youth see Petr Němec, "Das tschechische Volk und die nationalsozialistische Germanisierung des Raumes," in *Bohemia* (1991), pp. 424–55.

91. Jan Doležal, *Česká kultura za Protektorátu: Školství, písemnictví, kinematografie* (Prague, 1996), pp. 47–58.

92. For a survey of the dispatches of parachutists from the West to the Protectorate in 1941–45, see Oldřich Sládek, *Přicházeli z nebe* (Prague, 1993), pp. 234–40. For data on Anthropoid (Kubiš and Gabčík, dispatched on 28 and 29. 12. 1941), see p. 234.

93. For the telephone conversation between Frank and Hitler on Heydrich's assassination on May 27, 1942, see Kárný et al., *Deutsche Politik im Protektorat*, doc. 105, pp. 281–82.

94. About the forthcoming repercussions, see summary of Frank's visit to Hitler's headquarters on 28.5.1942 in Kárný et al., *Deutsche Politik im Protektorat*, doc. 106, pp. 282–90.

95. Abschlussbericht. Attentat auf ss-Obergruppenführer Heydrich am 27.5.1942 in Prag, YIVO, New York; Occ E7 (a) 5, p. 10; Jaroslav Drábek, "The Assassination of Reinhard Heydrich," in *Czechoslovakia Past and Present*, ed. Miloslav Rechcígl, vol. 1 (The Hague, Paris, 1968), p. 766; Stanislav F. Bertoň, "Das Attentat auf Reinhard Heydrich vom 27. Mai 1942: ein Bericht des Kriminalrats Heinz Pannwitz," in vz 4 (1985), pp. 668–706. Miroslav Ivanov, *The Assassination of Reinhard Heydrich, May 27, 1942* (London, 1973), pp. 206–8; Jan Gebhart and Jan Kuklík, *Dramatické i všední dny Protektorátu* (Prague, 1996), pp. 218–24.

96. On the betrayal of the parachutist Karel Čurda, see Ivanov, *Assassination*, pp. 246–47.

97. For a description of the discovery of the parachutists hiding in the Carl-Borromaeus Church, see Berton, "Das Attentat"; Callum MacDonald, *The Killing of* ss *Oberruppenführer Reinhard Heydrich* (New York, 1989), chapter 10, ending, pp. 191–97.

98. The information about the fate of the Bondy-Holzner-Bergmann family was given first to their surviving nephew, Dáša Bergmann, by two of his Prague acquaintances, Božena Štiplová and Václav Lukeš, with whom his uncle Zdenko Bergmann exchanged notes while held at the Terezín Small Fortress. See Adolf (Dáša) Bergmann's "Memoirs," pp. 115–16; cf. Jaroslav Čvančara, "Atentát na Heydricha; od hypotéz k faktům; Transport z ráje," in *Týden* (June 1995), *Mladý svět* (September 1994).

99. Among the listed victims are also the members of the Bondy-Bergmann-Holzner family. Their ordeal was recorded in the diary of a close relative, the renowned Prof. Shmuel Hugo Bergmann of Jerusalem. See *Tagebücher & Briefe*, Band 1, 1901–48, ed. Miriam Sambursky (Königstein, 1985), entry of 2.8.1945, pp. 677–78.

100. Ivanov, *Assassination*, pp. 288–90; Sládek, *Přicházeli z nebe*, photo annex, p. 160; for the full list of the 254 victims executed at Mauthausen (listing also three additional Jewish women), I am indebted to Dr. Zdeněk Klíma of the Central State Archives, Prague.

101. This unique eyewitness account on the demise of the members of the parachutists' families and others "involved" in the assassination was given by Antonín Nováček, one of the survivors of the convoy of prisoners deported from Terezín to Mauthausen. See Ivanov, *Assassination*, pp. 289–90.

102. Altogether 1,331 persons were executed during the second state of emergency (27.5.1942–3.7.1942) in Prague and Brno. Of these 201 were women; see Bertoň, "Das Attentat," p. 705. For the list of the women executed, with a commentary on their whereabouts, see Zlatuše Kukánová, "Seznam žen popravených z rozhodnutí stanného soudu v Praze, ve dnech 30. května až 3. července 1942," in *Sborník historick* 23 (Prague, 1990), pp. 72–86.

103. Altogether three thousand Jews were dispatched as "penal" transports to their deaths. See Feder *Židovská tragédie*, p. 91; Lagus and Polák, *Město za mřížemi*, pp. 310–11.

104. Cf. "Abschlussbericht uber den Mordanschlag auf ss-Obergruppenführer Heydrich," the report of Kurt Daluege to Martin Bormann on the destruction of the villages Lidice (June 10, 1942) and Ležáky (June 18, 1942), the murder of the male population, the deportation of women to concentration camps, and "the adoption" of children, printed in DHČP, doc. 385, 1:486–89; see also B. Huták, *With Blood and Iron: The Lidice Story* (London, 1957); Amort, *Heydrichiáda*, pp. 212–15, 247.

105. See letter of ss Standartenführer Horst Böhme to the head of the Security Police of June 12, 1942, in Amort, *Heydrichiáda*, p. 304. On the brigade of grave-diggers brought from the ghetto of Terezín, see testimony of F. R. Kraus, "But Lidice Is in Europe," in *Terezín, 1941–1945*, ed. František Ehrmann, Otto Heitlinger, and Rudolf Iltis (Prague, 1965), pp. 143–48. (The edited volume is hereafter cited simply as *Terezín*.)

106. Kraus, "But Lidice Is in Europe," p. 144, 148.

107. On the manifestation of 30.6.1942, see Tomášek and Kvaček, *Causa Emil Hácha*, pp. 153, 157.

108. Cf. Pasák, *Judr. Emil Hácha*, pp. 212–13.

109. "Verordnung zum Abwehr der Unterstützung reichsfeindlicher Handlungen," see VOBl, no. 27, 30.7.1942, pp. 181, 182; Gerhard Jacobi, *Racial State: The German Nationalities Policy in the Protectorate of Bohemia-Moravia* (New York: Institute of Jewish Affairs, 1944), p. 257.

110. For the executions by Gestapo at Klatovy, see *Klatovské listy*, no. 32, 8.8.1942, p. 35; see also unpublished MS "Tak jsme žili," describing the life of the Jews in Klatovy during WW II, YVA, 07/24-2, p. 38.

111. Grňová, *Svatobořický tábor*; see also mimeographed copy on Umschulungslager Linde (Lípa), 1940–1945, compiled by survivors of this labor camp, 24 pp., copy in the author's possession.

112. See Marek, "Sonderlager," pp. 39–45.

113. VOBl, no. 20, 31.7.1943, p. 103,114. Kurt Daluege was sentenced to death in Prague and executed there on October 20, 1946; see also International Military Tribunal, PS-391.

114. Karel R(ameš), *Žaluji: Pankrácká kalvárie* (Prague, 1946), vol. 2, pp. 862–63; see also chapter 8 of the present volume.

115. For the last phase of the war, see Rhode, "Protectorate," pp. 315–21; Jiří Doležal, *Jediná cesta* (Prague, 1966).

116. Rhode, "Protectorate," p. 317.

117. Transports to Terezín dispatched between January 26 and March 16, 1945, numbering altogether 3,657 persons (liberated on May 11, 1945), see *Terezín Memorialbook*, p. 108.

118. For a comprehensive account of the activities of the Home Resistance over seven years, see Josef Grňa, *Sedm roků na domácí frontě* (Brno, 1968).

119. See Heydrich's letter to Bormann of January 22, 1942; Heydrich's secret talk of February 4, 1942, in Amort, *Heydrichiáda*; cf. Brandes, *Die Tschechen*, 1:217–19.

120. Kennan, *From Prague*, pp. 117–18.

121. Eliášová and Pasák, *Poznámky*, pp. 110–14.

122. The list of "prominents" and other documentation appear in Anna Hyndráková, Helena Krejčová, and Jana Svobodová, eds., *Prominenti v ghettu Terezín 1942–1945: Dokumenty* (Prague, 1996).

123. For minutes of the talks at Heydrich's office in Prague about "the Final Solution of the Jewish Question in the Protectorate," 10.10.1941, see Kárný et al., *Deutsche Politik im Protektorat*, doc. 29, p. 138.

124. Especially after June 22, 1941, President Beneš was exposed to complaints from Moscow, arguing that the Protectorate "was the most peaceful of all the occupied territories." Dr. Beneš confessed to Jaromír Smutný his fears and hopes concerning the effects of Heydrich's assassination. See MacDonald, *The Killing*, pp. 201–2; Moravec, in *Master of Spies*, p. 211, claims that Czechoslovak intelligence planned forty-six operations and carried out thirty-seven of them, among these Operation Anthropoid, upon Beneš's direct order.

6. *The Czechoslovak Government-in-Exile in London*

1. Dr. Edvard Beneš acted in 1918–35 as foreign minister of Czechoslovakia. As of 1936, for two years, he held the office of president, from which he resigned in October 1938. During World War II he headed the Czechoslovak Government-in-Exile in London and acted as the leader of the Resistance movement. Between 1945 and 1948 Beneš served as president of the liberated Czechoslovakia. After his resignation (7.6.1948) he lived at his summer residence in Sezimovo Ústí, where he died on 3.9.1948.

2. Edvard Táborský, "Politics in Exile," in *The History of the Czechoslovak Republic*, pp. 322–23; see also his *Czechoslovak Democracy at Work* (London, 1945); *Pravda zvítězila* (Prague, 1947); and "Beneš a náš osud," in *Svědectví* 23, nos. 89–90 (Spring 1990), pp. 117–18.

3. Livia Rothkirchen, "The Czechoslovak Government-in-Exile: Jewish and Palestinian Aspects in the Light of Documents," in YVS 9 (1973), pp. 157–99.

4. Edvard Beneš, *Šest let exilu a druhé světové války: Řeči, projevy a dokumenty z r. 1938–1945* (Prague, 1946); see also his *Od Mnichova k nové válce a k novému vítězství* (Prague, 1947); *The Memoirs of Dr. Edvard Beneš: From Munich to New War and New Victory*, transl. Godfrey Lias (London, 1954); and *Mnichovské dny: Paměti* (Prague, 1968).

5. Smutný's diaries and other source material were included in the volume of documents *Dokumenty z historie československé* edited by Otáhalová and Červínková.

6. See Smutný's entry dated March 22, 1940, DHČP, doc. 69, 1:91.

7. See Drtina, *Československo můj osud*, mainly vol. 1, pt. 2, and vol. 2, pt. 1.

8. The collections of documents consulted were PRO, FO (London); World Jewish Congress Archives (hereafter WJCA), London; SÚA MV (Prague); VHA (Prague); CZA (Jerusalem); YVA (Jerusalem); and bequests of public figures associated with the topic.

9. During the years of the republic the usage of the languages among the Jewish population has changed.

10. On the struggle of the Jewish leadership for recognition after World War I, see chapter 2 and Rabinowicz, "Jewish Minority," pp. 155–265.

11. According to an estimate (A. Hora, 1938) the Jewish population was divided as follows: Jewish nationality 206,962 (58.0%), Czecho-Slovak nationality 87,424 (24.5%), German nationality 45,674 (12.8%), Hungarian nationality 16,770 (4.7%). See memorandum dated February 4, 1941, The Legal Position of the Jews in Czechoslovakia, CZA, A280.

12. These demands of Sudeten Germans and Hungarian irredentists became vociferous in the late thirties, when a drastic reduction was noticeable in the number of Jews declaring themselves German or Hungarian. See Bruegel, *Czechoslovakia before Munich*; Rothkirchen, "Slovakia: II, 1918–1938," p. 103.

13. See address by Dr. Leo Herrmann, founder and secretary-general of Keren ha-Yesod (Palestine Foundation Fund), on 11.8.1940 to the Organization of Czechoslovak Immigrants on the subject "The Prague Transfer" (copy in author's possession). See also Paul D. März, "Haha'avara Hachekhit—hatzala be'sha'at tzara," in *Prag ve Yerushalaim*, pp. 160–79, and his "Trumat Yehudey Tshekhoslovakia Lebinyan Haaretz," in *Gesher* 2–3 (September 1969), pp. 251–59.

14. This estimate is taken from the press; see "Mitnadvim Letzava Hachekhi," in *Ha'aretz*, 9.11.1939. The figure does not include immigrants who arrived during various periods and the "illegals" of the year 1940. Altogether some seventeen thousand Czechoslovak Jews entered Palestine prior to the establishment of the state. See also Fini Brada, "Emigration to Palestine," in *Jews of CS* 2:589–98.

15. CZA, Z4/20 377/I; März, in a communication to this author, viewed this as the first bilateral agreement of the Jewish state-in-the-making.

16. Particularly valuable help was given by R. J. Stopford of the British Treasury, who did a great deal in helping to rescue Czechoslovak refugees. See his collection in CZA.

17. For Masaryk's letter of 27.9.1939, addressed to the Under Secretary of State for Foreign Affairs, see CZA, Z4/20 377/I.

18. For his reminiscences from the war years, see Josef M. Kadlec, *Svatá země v československém odboji* (Prague, 1947).

19. As of 1948 Moshe Shertok was known by his Hebraicized name—Sharett. He was Israel's first foreign minister (1948), became prime minister (1954–55), and died in Jerusalem in 1965. Ben-Zvi was a member and later chairman of the Jewish National Committee. In 1952 he was elected (second) president of Israel. He died in Jerusalem in 1963.

20. Chaim Kugel earned himself great popularity as director of the Hebrew Gymnasium in Mukačevo and parliamentary deputy for the Jewish Party in Subcarpathian Ruthenia. He immigrated to Palestine in 1938; was among the founders of the city of Holon and its first mayor; and died in Holon in 1956. Rufeisen was chairman of the Zionist Executive of Czechoslovakia and a founder of the Jewish Party. In 1939 he immigrated to Palestine; he died in Tel Aviv in 1948. Paul März was one of the founders of the Jewish Party, immigrated to Palestine in 1939, held high public office, and died in Jerusalem in 1981.

21. For details see Kadlec, *Svatá země*, pp. 51–71; Gershon Swet, "Mitnadvim LeTzava HaTshekhi," in *Ha'aretz*, 9.11.1939, and his "400 Local Czecho-Slovaks for France to Join Up," in *Palestine Post*, 3.11.1939; see also "The Birth of an Army, Jews Responding to Czechoslovakia's Call," in *Palestine Post*, 24.11.1939.

22. See Otakar Spaniel, *Československá armáda druhého odboje* (Chicago, 1941), p. 30; Kadlec, *Svatá země*, p. 71.

23. See Toman Brod and Eduard Čejka, *Na západní frontě* (Prague, 1963), pp. 84–88; Toman Brod, *Tobrucké krysy* (Prague, 1967), pp. 27–28.

24. See CZA, Z4/20 376.

25. See VHA, fond 40, sign. XVIII, Palestina 2, BL 320/92.

26. For details of the political struggle see Yehuda Bauer, *From Diplomacy to Resistance: A History of Jewish Palestine* (Philadelphia, 1970). It was only after Winston Churchill's intervention (17.8.1944) that the British War Ministry authorized the raising of the Jewish Brigade. The Jews of Palestine provided a total of twenty-six thousand men and women for the British Army, including commandos. See J. Gil (Lipshitz), *A History of the Jewish Infantry Brigade Group* (Tel Aviv, 1950); Zerubavel Gilead, ed., *Magen baSeter: Palestinian Underground Activities in World War II* (Hebrew, Jerusalem, 1952).

27. "Proclamation of General Mobilization of Czechoslovak Citizens in Palestine," CZA, S25/4813.

28. Founded in 1921, it had its name changed in 1938 to Hitachdut Oley Tshekhoslovakia (Association of Czechoslovak Immigrants). During the war its chairman was Dr. František Seidmann.

29. A great part of the volunteers among these many students who reached Palestine without any means preferred to enlist in the Czechoslovak Army instead of the British because of the rate of maintenance allowances, which were paid according to French standards and were considerably higher.

30. Chaim Kugel, Josef Rufeisen, and Paul März set personal examples by being the first to become naturalized. The letter of Consul Kadlec to Kugel, dated January 23, 1942, was reproduced in my article "The Czechoslovak Government-in-Exile: Jewish and Palestinian Aspects in the Light of the Documents," in YVS 9 (1973), p. 157.

31. Kadlec's letter to President Beneš of 15.8.1940, VHA, BL 320/92.

32. For the two-page memorandum see CZA, S25/4813.

33. Namier urged Masaryk that Kadlec receive telegraphic instructions. See letter reproduced in my article "Czechoslovak Government-in-Exile," (doc. 2), p. 178. Namier was known for his sympathetic attitude toward Czechoslovakia. He wrote a number of essays on the subject and two books: *The Case for Bohemia* (1919) and *Diplomatic Prelude 1938–1939* (1948).

34. Herrmann's letter to Shertok, 2.8.1940, CZA, A140, reproduced in my article, "Czechoslovak Government-in-Exile" (doc. 4), pp. 179–80, reveals that Herrmann called on Kadlec to deliver to him personally Masaryk's instructions.

35. Herrmann to Shertok, 11.11.1940, CZA, A145/10; an account of his visit to Consul Kadlec is reproduced in my "Czechoslovak Government-in-Exile," (doc. 5), p. 181.

36. DHČP, 1:145–46.

37. Leo Herrmann's letter to Jan Masaryk, 18.2.1940, announcing the establishment of Kfar Masaryk, an agricultural settlement, CZA, Z4/20 376/I. For a description of President Masaryk's visit in 1927 see chapter 2, note 106.

38. According to the enclosed aide-mémoire of 3.7.1940 (copy in author's possession), "two transports of Czechoslovaks [Jews] from Palestine whose transportation to the Syrian frontier [en route to France] was undertaken by the British Army."

39. Herrmann's letter to Shertok of 2.8.1940, CZA, A140.

40. At the same time (August 1940) an agreement was entered into between the two governments in London concerning the Czechoslovak forces in territories of the British Empire, thereby establishing the status of the units in the Middle East. See Kadlec, *Svatá země*, p. 13; Brod and Čejka, *Na západni frontě*; Karel Klapálek, *Ozvěny bojů—vzpomínky z druhé světové války* (Prague, 1966).

41. Herrmann's letter to Shertok of 2.8.1940, CZA, A140; Aharon Zwergbaum, "Exile in Mauritius," in YVS 4 (1960), pp. 191–257.

42. See Kadlec, *Svatá země*, p. 13.

43. The meeting took place at the King David Hotel. See CZA, S25/6585; the minutes are reproduced in my article, "Czechoslovak Government-in-Exile," (doc. 11), pp. 196–99.

44. Rothkirchen, "Czechoslovak Government-in-Exile," p. 198.

45. Táborský, "Politics in Exile," p. 325.

46. Táborský, "Beneš a náš osud," pp. 117–18.

47. Feierabend, *Ve vládě*, p. 51; see Compton Mackenzie, *Dr. Beneš* (London, 1946), p. 242.

48. In his entry of 21.9.1942 Smutný notes financial support of prominent Czech-Jewish figures such as Steuer, who was received by the president and presented him with a £1,000 check to be used for a special fund. Another donor not mentioned by name, the son of a former well-to-do Czechoslovak citizen, was living in England and also presented a £1,000 check, offering Dr. Beneš the use of his home in Oxford as a residence. See DHČP, 1:297.

49. See Táborský, "Politics in Exile," pp. 325–26; for an illuminating passage on the "signing of the Czechoslovak-Soviet Treaty Alliance on 12 December 1943" see doc. 220 in "R. W. Seton-Watson and His Relations with Czechs and Slovaks," *Documents—Dokumenty 1906–1951*, vol. 1, ed. Jan Rychlík, Thomas D. Marzík, and Miroslav Bielik (Prague, 1995), pp. 631–34.

50. Printed in Beneš, *The Memoirs*, pp. 128–29.

51. Referred to by Beneš during an interview with the WJC delegation, 17.4.1941, Schwartzbart collection, YVA, M-2.

52. For details regarding the refugees from the Sudeten area, see PRO, FO 371 / 21587; on German refugees in London, see Eva Schmidt-Hartmann, "Die deutschsprachige jüdische Emigration aus der Tschechoslowakei nach Grossbritannien, 1938–1945," in *Die Juden in den böhmischen Landern*, ed. F. Seubt, pp. 297–311; Heumos and Becher, *Emigration*, chapter 4, pp. 205–72; Rudolf M. Wlaschek, *Juden in Böhmen: Beiträge zur Geschichte des europäischen Judentums im 19. und 20. Jahrhundert* (München, 1990), chapter 8, "Im Exil," pp. 139–50.

53. On the federation see Gertrud Hirschler, "The History of Agudath Israel," in *Jews of CS* 2:155–72. For minutes of meetings, regulations, and details of the work of the Central Council of National Jews see CZA, A280.

54. For details concerning the Jewish Party, see Rabinowicz, "Jewish Party," pp. 253–346. Before the war Zelmanovits acted as the secretary-general of the Jewish Party in Czechoslovakia.

55. See Avigdor Dagan, "The Czechoslovak Government-in-Exile and the Jews," in *Jews of CS* 3:455.

56. Memorandum dated December 4, 1939, CZA, Z4 / 20 376.

57. See Beneš, *Šest let exilu*, p. 72.

58. Cf. Táborský, "Politics in Exile," p. 335; in an address at Oxford University (23.5.1941) and discussion that followed, Beneš recommended a massive population transfer as the best solution for the Central European minorities' problem. He spelled out this idea again in *The Nineteenth Century and After* 30 (September, 1941), 150 ff.

59. Report of Bruce Lockhart of 7.10.1940, PRO, FO 371 / 24289.

60. In a letter to Wenzel Jaksch, the exiled leader of the Sudeten German Social Democrats. Beneš, *The Memoirs*, p. 210.

61. Smutný's entry 11.4.1941, DHČP, doc. 153, 1:199–200.

62. See Smutný's entries of 3 and 11.4.1941, 11.6.1941, DHČP, docs. 149, 153, 1:196, 198; Feierabend, *Ve vládě*, p. 46f; cf. Detlef Brandes, *Menschen im Exil: Eine Dokumentation der Sudetendeutschen Sozial-demokratischen Emigration von 1938 bis 1945* (Stuttgart, 1974).

63. Detlef Brandes, "Das Problem der deutschen Minderheiten in der Politik der Alliierten in den Jahren 1940–1945: Das tschechische Beispiel," in J. Křen, V. Kural, D. Brandes, *Integration oder Ausgrenzung* (Bremen, 1986), p. 110.

64. See enclosure (dated 10.12.1940) to Bruce Lockhart's Report, addressed to Viscount Halifax, 17.12.1940, PRO, FO 371 / 24.289, reproduced in my "Czechoslovak Government-in-Exile," doc. 7, pp. 184–87.

65. See entry of November 25, 1940, in Smutný's diary, DHČP, 1:145–46.

66. See interview with WJC delegation (17.4.1941), Schwartzbart collection, YVA, M-2.

67. Interview with WJC delegation.

68. Lockhart's report, 17.12.1940; see also R. H. B. Lockhart, *Comes the Reckoning* (London, 1947).

69. Interview with WJC delegation.

70. Lockhart's report, 17.12.1940; anti-Semitic tendencies were also noticeable in Czechoslovak publications in Britain: According to an ex-serviceman, the Czech language official organ of the Government-in-Exile, *Czechoslovak*, as well as the army's news bulletin

Naše vojsko posed the question whether the Jews viewed Czechoslovakia as their homeland or whether they were not able to "acclimatize" in any country. See testimony of F. Beer, YVA, 059–2.

71. The members of the committee included Capt. Brichta, Lieutenant Fleischmann, Sec. Lt. Kraus, Private Dr. Stephen Barber, and Private Dr. Rudolf Braun.

72. For the text of the memorandum see Heumos and Becher, *Emigration*, pp. 344–46; see testimony of Alex Kraus and of Drs. Rudolf Braun and Mirek Kerner, YVA, 0–59–50. See also correspondence between Zelmanovits and members of the committee, 30.7.1940, CZA, A280/11. For a detailed account on the topic see Erich Kulka, "Jews in the Czechoslovak Armed Forces during World War II," in *Jews of CS* 3:331–448; Jan Stříbrný "Židovští vojenští duchovní v Československém vojsku na západě v letech 1939 1945," in *Postavení a osudy židovského obyvatelstva*, pp. 162–218.

73. Lockhart's report, 17.12.1940.

74. The problem of German representation was the subject of lengthy discussion and correspondence between Beneš and Wenzel Jaksch, former deputy for the Social Democratic Party in the Czechoslovak Parliament, who also came as a refugee to London. No decision was ever reached. See Beneš, *The Memoirs*, pp. 213–19, 320–34.

75. See DHČP, 1:145–46; Angelo Goldstein lived from 1939 in Palestine, where he practiced as a lawyer and was active in the Association of Czechoslovak Immigrants. He died in Tel Aviv in 1947.

76. Interview with WJC delegation; see also letter of Consul Kadlec to President Beneš of 29.10.1941, strongly criticizing Angelo Goldstein and Chaim Kugel for hampering the formation of the military unit, VHA, fond 40, sign. XVIII.

77. See Dagan, "The Czechoslovak Government-in-Exile," p. 463.

78. Frischer returned to Czechoslovakia at the end of World War II and until 1948 acted as chairman of the Council of Jewish Religious Communities in Bohemia and Moravia. From 1949 till his death in 1954 Frischer lived in London.

79. Quoted from a letter sent to New York by Dr. Zelmanovits to Dr. Aryeh Tartakower, member of the World Jewish Congress, 8.3.1941, CZA, A280/28.

80. Interview with WJC delegation.

81. Details of the conversation are given in a letter from New York, 24.5.1943, from Dr. A. L. Kubowitzky, Secretary of the World Jewish Congress (later head of the Rescue Department), to Ernst Frischer, CZA, A280/28.

82. Kubowitzky to Frischer, 24.5.1943.

83. Frischer to Kubowitzky, 21.6.1943, CZA, A280/28.

84. See *Czechoslovakia and the Czechoslovak Jews*, addresses delivered at the Meeting of the Czechoslovak Jewish Representative Committee affiliated with the WJC, 18.11.1944 (New York, 1945), p. 23, referred to in Heumos and Becher, *Emigration*, p. 251.

85. See Edvard Beneš, "The Organization of Postwar Europe," in *Foreign Affairs*, an American Quarterly Review (January 1942), p. 16.

86. Moravec, *Master of Spies*.

87. For details on radio-telegraphic contacts see Karel Veselý-Štainer, *Cestou národního odboje: Bojový vývoj domácího odbojového hnutí v letech 1938–1945* (Prague, 1947), pp. 80, 84.

88. The contacts between Bratislava and Geneva during the period of the Heydrich

retaliation drive up until August 1944 (the Slovak National Uprising) were especially frequent. Detailed accounts about persecution and arrests were transmitted from Prague via Bratislava underground groups to Dr. Kopecký, who passed them along to London. Kopecký's significant role in resistance was summed up in an article written in honor of his seventieth birthday in the Slovak *Práce*, entitled "Cesty vedly přes Ženevu," and reproduced in *Hlas revoluce*, 15.8.1969; cf. chapter 7.

89. See Jozef Jablonický, *Z ilegality do povstania, kapitoly z občianského odboja* (Bratislava, 1969), pp. 63, 78.

90. DHČP, 2:553–54.

91. DHČP, 2:575.

92. DHČP, 2:573.

93. See "René an Pavel" (Krajina to Drtina), 26.7.1941–T77, R1050, referred to in Detlef Brandes, *Grossbritannien und seine osteuropäischen Alliierten 1939–1943* (München, 1988), pp. 201–2.

94. Walter Laqueur, *The Terrible Secret: Suppression of the Truth about Hitler's "Final Solution"* (Boston, Toronto, London, 1980), p. 164.

95. *Dienst aus Deutschland*, 29.10.1941, reported: "48,000 Jews from Prague deported to East"; see also *Nová doba*, 16.1.1942, about the deportation of all Jews from Pilsen.

96. Testimony from the trial of Dr. Anton Vašek, YVA, M-5/137.

97. Dagan, "The Czechoslovak Government-in-Exile," pp. 464–65.

98. Testimony from the trial of Vašek.

99. Laqueur, *Terrible Secret*, p. 81.

100. Arthur D. Morse, *While Six Million Died* (New York, 1968), p. 10.

101. Morse, *Six Million*, pp. 10, 11.

102. Moravec, *Master of Spies*, p. 165.

103. Laqueur, *Terrible Secret*, pp. 162–63.

104. For a detailed description see "A Plan for Murder," in Morse, *Six Million*.

105. WJCA, London.

106. WJCA.

107. Comment from the cable sent by Richard Law of the British Foreign Office to Sydney S. Silverman, 17.8.1942, see PRO, FO 371/30917: 7853/61/18.

108. WJCA; also to be found in the archives of the Military Institute in Prague, VHA, BL 320/92, box 26.

109. See Laqueur, *Terrible Secret*, p. 65; see Richard Breitman, *Official Secrets: What the Nazis Planned, What the British and Americans Knew* (London, New York, 1998), especially chapter 6, British Restraint, pp. 88–109, 129–30.

110. WJCA; see Breitman, *Official Secrets*, chapter 10, Reactions to Publicity, pp. 171–74.

111. See David Engel, *In the Shadow of Auschwitz: The Polish Government-in-Exile and the Jews 1939–1942* (Chapel Hill NC, 1987).

112. DHČP, 2:705.

113. DHČP, 2:715.

114. See letter of Kubowitzky to Frischer, 24.5.1943, CZA, A280/28.

115. Frischer's answer (21.6.1943) to Kubowitzky on the issue of "minority rights," CZA, A280/28.

116. WJCA, box 1943/2; note of a conversation between President Edvard Beneš and Dr. Noah Barou and Alexander L. Easterman, 23.7.1943, quoted in Heumos and Becher, *Emigration*, p. 268.

117. Heumos and Becher, *Emigration*, p. 268.

118. Dagan, "The Czechoslovak Government-in-Exile," p. 468.

119. Red Cross parcels had to be addressed to persons. By the time they reached the so-called family camp in Auschwitz-Birkenau the inmates to whom they had been sent had already been gassed. The bulk of the Red Cross parcels and other sources dispatched from Geneva, Lisbon, and Istanbul were stolen by the SS. There is, however, evidence that parcels were received by the inmates of Terezín. See Miroslav Kárný, "Terezínské balíčky ve světle archívních dokumentů," in *Vlastivědný sborník Litoměřicko* 23 (1987), pp. 195–210.

120. See CZA, S25/6585.

121. DHČP, 1:373, 2:721.

122. See Zbyněk Zeman and Antonín Klímek, *The Life of Edvard Beneš 1884–1948: Czechoslovakia in Peace and War* (Oxford, 1997), pp. 183–84.

123. On Heydrich's assassination see chapter 5.

124. Cf. *Verbrecher in Richterroben* (Prague, 1960), pp. 58–59, 85, 128–29, citing trials of a number of Czechs who were punished by death for extending help to Jews in the Protectorate.

125. Smutný's comments in DHČP, 1:412; on the role of Hácha and Eliáš, see chapter 5.

126. Aside from members of the government several Czech journalists (Werner, Novák, and Krychtálek) were tried by the National Tribunal and sentenced to death by hanging. See Drtina, *Československo můj osud*, vol. 2, pt. 2, p. 280; Kaplan, *Dva retribuční procesy: Komentované dokumenty 1946–1947* (Prague, 1994); Borák, *Spravedlnost podle dekretu* (Ostrava, 1998).

127. To escape punishment, Moravec committed suicide on 5.5.1945. His son, actually drafted to the SS, was sentenced to death by hanging.

128. It was the secret Sokol organization leader Vaněk ("Jindra") who dispatched the plea to Beneš; see Král, *Otázky hospodářského*, 3:242–43; cf. chapter 5.

129. Král, *Otázky hospodářského*, 3:242–43.

130. Jan Masaryk, *Speaking to My Country* (London, 1944), pp. 119, 141. Masaryk's appeal to the Czech people was on the occasion of the Jewish New Year 5704 (1943).

131. Masaryk's address in New York, 18.6.1942.

132. DHČP, 2:721.

133. Pasák, "Český antisemitismus," pp. 147–51.

134. See Program of the Czechoslovak Government of the National Front of Czechs and Slovaks, agreed to at the first government meeting in Košice on 5.4.1945. *Bulletin of the Ministry of Information*.

135. For the background see Radomír Luža, *The Transfer of the Sudeten Germans: A Study of Czech-German Relations, 1933–1962* (New York, London, 1964); Association Hongroise des Affaires Étrangeres, *La déportation des Hongrois de Slovaquie* (Budapest, 1947); Ludvík Němec, "Solution of the Minorities Problem," in *A History of the Czechoslovak Republic 1918–1948*, pp. 416–27.

136. Cited from VŽONP, 1.9.1947.

137. See epilogue.

138. For a discussion see "Munich 1938 from the Czech Perspective," in *East Central Europe* 8, nos. 1–2 (1981), pp. 62–96.

139. Smutný's entries, London, 28.9.1943 and 17.10.1943, DHČP, 1:310, 399–400; cf. Karel Novotný, "O pamětech Beneše," in *České země a Československo v Evropě XIX. a XX. století*, ed. Jindřich Dejmek and Josef Hamzal (Prague, 1997), pp. 438–39.

140. One of his harshest critics was the philosopher Jan Patočka, who severely condemned his Munich policy, claiming that in those trying days he utterly failed; see Patočka, *Was sind die Tschechen?* pp. 220–21.

141. Theodor Schieder, ed., *Dokumentation der Vertreibung der Deutschen Bevölkerung aus der Tschechoslowakei* (München, 1984); see Černý et al., eds., *Češi, Němci a odsun* (Prague, 1990); Tomáš Staněk, *Odsun Němců z Československa 1945–1947* (Prague, 1991).

7. Jews in the Czech Home Resistance

1. Dr. Oscar Singer, editor of the JRC bilingual community weekly *Jüdisches Nachrichtenblatt* between 1939 and 1941, was deported in October 1941 to the Łodý Ghetto and perished there in 1944. For his activities see chapter 4.

2. The Home Resistance was also called the "Inside Front"; in Czech *domácí odboj* is employed in contrast to *zahraniční odboj*, the term used for the resistance movement abroad. See my article "Židé v domácím odboji (1938–1942)," in *Židé v novodobých dějinách: Soubor přednášek na FF ÚK*, ed. Václav Veber (Prague, 1997), pp. 95–123.

3. See chapter 4.

4. The first contingent of sixty political detainees, "Communists and other subversive elements," from Brno reached Auschwitz on June 6, 1941, and the second group from Prague in November 1941. See Kalendarium 1941, in *Hefte von Auschwitz* 2 (1959), p. 109. In that first group was Eng. Egon Glas from Brno, whose "death notice" dated December 1941 was sent by the camp authorities to the Glas family in Brno. By courtesy of his sons, Pavel and Tomáš Glas of Jerusalem, this document was printed in my "The Defiant Few," in YVS 14. See also the lists of victims in two publications printed by the Government-in-Exile: *Memorandum of the Czechoslovak Government on the Reign of Terror in Bohemia and Moravia under the Regime of Reinhard Heydrich* (London: Czechoslovak Ministry of Foreign Affairs, c. 1942), and *Heroes and Victims* (London, 1945).

5. See Feierabend, *Ve vládě*, p. 50.

6. Rybár, *Židovská Praha*, p. 142; *Československý zpravodaj*, Informační Bulletin Čsl. generálního konsulátu v Jerusalemě pro čechoslováky v Palestině, Iráku a Iránu, no. 19/4, 6.8.1941.

7. This historical project, however, never came to fruition. See Jan Marek, "Zápisky z boje," unpublished MS, compiled in 1968 (by courtesy of Marek of Děčín, a copy is in the author's possession); letter of Heda Kaufmann to Jan Marek, Marek MS, p. 14.

8. In spite of the fact that Heda Kaufmannová was obliged to wear a yellow star and was marked by a highly visible physical defect, she succeeded in mediating contacts between Dr. Kaufmann and Prof. J. Fischer even while he was incarcerated in the Gestapo prison at Karlovo Square. She did not comply with the deportation summons and with the help of

some Czech families managed to survive the war. Her memoir was published in two parts in the *samizdat* issue *Historické Studie*, nos. 21 and 22, 21.6.1987, 22.1.1988.

9. On the various problems of Jewish resistance, especially valuable are Helmut Eschwege, "Resistance of German Jews against the Nazi Regime," in LBIYB 15 (1970), pp. 143–80; Arnold Pauker, "Some Notes on Resistance," in LBIYB 16 (1971), pp. 239–47; and Konrad Kwiet, "Problems of Jewish Resistance Historiography," in LBIYB 24 (1979), pp. 37–45.

10. Some of these comments were sympathetic, as in *Komsomol*, 15.10.1941: "One of the latest crimes of the Nazi 'culture-bearers' is the deportation of our Jewish fellow-citizens to Poland . . . Jewish friends and comrades! We are behind you with all our heart and all our might . . . Our hearts were heavy when we saw you on Monday morning, leaving with knapsacks and bundles. It was even more distressing than seeing you with a yellow star for the first time. But this too shall pass. And therefore we cry out to you: may we soon meet again."

11. Out of the Jewish leading figures of the PVVŽ only Josef Fischer was accorded the distinction of "Řád práce" (good work). See "Docent Dr. Josef Fischer *In memoriam*," in VŽONP, no. 11 (November 1968).

12. Henry Michel, *The Shadow War: Resistance in Europe 1939–1945* (London, 1972), p. 178.

13. Michel, *Shadow War*, p. 179; see also his "Jewish Resistance and the European Resistance Movement," in YVS 7 (1968), pp. 1–18.

14. See *Rescue Attempts during the Holocaust*, Proceedings of the Second Yad Vashem International Historical Conference, ed. Yisrael Gutman and Efraim Zuroff (Jerusalem, 1977).

15. For evidence on contacts with Prague see letters and postcards confirming receipt of packages, money, and messages transmitted through couriers, to be found in the files of the CZA; "Istanbul" files—folders of the HeHalutz Committee of the Kibbutz haMe'uhad, now in the archives of the Ghetto Fighters' House (GFHA), Z/1063-Th; and in the YVA, 07/18–1; E199.

16. See Radomír Luža, "The Czech Resistance Movement," in *A History of the Czechoslovak Republic 1918–1948*, pp. 343–61; Brandes, *Die Tschechen*, 1:173–88.

17. See report of the Hede Türk-Neumann of 17.2.1944 sent from Budapest to the Rescue Committee in Istanbul, GFHA, Z/1063-Th.-10; YVA, E199.

18. DHČP, 1:373, 375; message from Gen. Sergej Ingr urging "to concentrate all the strength for the end of the war," DHČP, 1:701.

19. For the guidelines see František Janáček, *Dva směry v začiatkoch národného odboja: October 1938–June 1940* (Bratislava, 1962), pp. 283–87.

20. Vlastimila Kladivová, "K historii činnosti ilegální KSČ v Praze v letech 1939–1942," in *Acta Universitatis Carolinae Philosophica et Historica*, no. 1, Proti fašismu a válce (1962), p. 162; Karel Bondy's notes in Marek MS, p. 160.

21. Communication to the author by Václav Berdych, one of the outstanding figures in the Prague resistance organization.

22. Compare People's Court verdicts, cited in contemporary press reports; see also *Memorandum of the Czechoslovak Government* and *Heroes and Victims*.

23. *Memoirs of Dr. Edvard Beneš*, p. 52; Veselý-Štainer, *Cestou národního odboje*, p. 22.

24. Cf. Moravec, *Master of Spies*.

25. For a detailed analysis of the Budapest enterprise, based on correspondence between Paris and Budapest in late 1939–40, see Jan Gebhart, "Někteří z mnohých, k činnosti Josefa Fischera, Karla Bondyho a Miloše Otto Bondyho v českém odboji za druhé světové války," in *Postavení a osudy židovského obyvatelstva*, pp. 158–61; see also Anton Rašla, *Civilista v armádě: Spomienky na roky 1938–1945* (Bratislava, 1967), p. 58; Anna Josko, "The Slovak Resistance Movement," in *A History of the Czechoslovak Republic 1918–1948*, p. 365.

26. DHČP, 2:725.

27. Jaroslav and Stanislav Kokoškovi, *Spor o agenta A-54* (Prague, 1994), pp. 251–53.

28. The following Maccabi members were decorated for their underground activities after the war: Julius Baláž, Ervin Diamant, Eng. Leopold Drucker, Mikuláš Kanner, Moric Kohn, Eng. František Weiss, and Dr. Lev Kraus. See "Slavnostní dekorování členů odbojové skupiny "Svazu Makabi,"' in VŽONP, 1.9.1947.

29. About the discovery of the Slovak secret sender, installed in the house of Dr. Frei, see Kokoškovi and Kokoškovi, *Spor o agenta A-54*, pp. 251–53; According to the proceedings of the District Court of Bratislava the members of this conspiracy, recruited overwhelmingly from the professional educated class, were mainly Jews. The following were sentenced by the court: Dr. Stefan Laufer, Fridrich Fischer, Alexander Herz, Dr. Frei, Eugen Freund, and Pavel Feller (many of them inhabitants of Topolčany). See indictment, 30.5.1942, pp. 1–9; verdict 13.5.1943, pp. 21–22, YVA, M5 14–5/120.

30. For the genesis of the Home Resistance see the volume of studies edited by Oldřich Janoušek, *Z počátku odboje 1938–1941* (Prague, 1969); for the history of PVVZ, see the article by Václav Vrabec in the same volume.

31. Miloslav Moulis, *Mládež proti okupantům* (Prague, 1966).

32. A selection of these dispatches was printed in DHČP, 2; for the warning concerning chemical war, see 2:511.

33. Veselý-Štainer, *Cestou národního odboje*; Mastný, *Czechs under Nazi Rule*, pp. 145–48; Jan Křen, "Vojenský odboj na počátku okupace Československa 1938–1940," in *Historie a vojenství* (1961), vol. 10, pp. 271–313.

34. Brandes, *Die Tschechen*, 1:58.

35. There is extensive literature on the PVVZ; however, the private collections of some of the leading figures and their notes smuggled out of prison have not yet been fully exploited. One study emphasizes the ideological maturity of the leadership, which advocated radical reforms and nationwide cooperation and thus laid the ground for the postwar National Front. See Kuklík, *K problematice*.

36. According to the political section of II-BM-1, in 1942 Otto Gall, commissar of the Prague Gestapo, estimated the number of organized members in Bohemia and Moravia at three thousand; see Václav Vrabec, "Petiční výbor 'Věrni zůstaneme,' " in *Odboj a revoluce* (1967), pp. 21–37.

37. *Heroes and Victims*, p. 67. According to another source he was tortured to death at Pankrác prison and buried in Prague on October 22, 1939. See Eugen V. Erdely, *Germany's First European Protectorate: The Fate of Czechs and Slovaks* (London, 1942), p. 69.

38. Erdely, *Germany's First*.

39. Lockhart, *Comes the Reckoning*, p. 73.

40. It had a press run of two thousand copies. For details see Arnošt Polavský, *V boj: Třebechovice pod Orebem* (Dědourek, 1946), pp. 114–15.

41. Oldřich Sládek and Jaroslav Žižka, eds., *KSČ proti nacismu* (Prague, 1971); *Odboj a revoluce 1938–1945: Nástin dějin československého odboje* (Prague, 1965); Radomír Luža, "The Communist Party of Czechoslovakia and the Czech Resistance, 1939–1945," in *Slavic Review* 28 (December 1969), pp. 561–76; *Rudé právo 1939–1945* (Prague, 1971).

42. Apparently it was Klement Gottwald who made the choice of the major figures who were to remain in the republic. See Josef Novotný, "Činnost KSČ," pp. 84–85.

43. See "Československý odboj po 15 březnu 1939," in *Hlas revoluce*, no. 14, 8.4.1972.

44. According to Mastný (*Czechs under Nazi Rule*, p. 151, fn. 41), in a message to Moscow on September 6, the Prague Central Committee protested against what it termed "the rotten bureaucratism" of the Moscow radio broadcasts.

45. Alena Hájková and František Janáček, "Na okraj motáků: Vysvětlivky a komentáře," in Julius Fučík, *Reportáž psaná na oprátce: První úplně kritické a komentované vydání*, ed. František Janáček et al. (Prague, 1995), pp. 88, 125, 129, 131, 232, 233, 240.

46. Kurt Beer-Konrád committed suicide in Dresden (29.8.1941); Dr. Jan Frank, František Taussig, and Otto Synek (29.9.1941) were executed in Prague; Otto's brother, Victor Synek, was the first victim of martial law declared in 1942. Julius Fučík in his *Notes from the Gallows* (New York, 1948), pp. 71–72, wrote: "They take him to Mauthausen for the bump-off as their elegant expression is."

47. Walter Schellenberg, *Memoiren* (Köln, 1956), pp. 377–80; the English translation *The Labyrinth* does not include this secret report.

48. Schellenberg, *Memoiren*, p. 380.

49. Schellenberg, *Memoiren*, p. 379.

50. Veselý-Štainer, *Cestou národního odboje*, p. 52.

51. For the conclusions of Jan Kuklík see "Petiční výbor "Věrni zůstaneme' v odbobí Mnichova a za druhé Republiky," in *ČsČH* 17, no. 5 (1969), pp. 681–710; see also indictment of Fischer and Pešek, NG1897, in YVA microfilm collection, JM/02021.

52. *Dělnická osvěta* 19, no. 7 (1933), p. 231; Pfaff, "Německá kultura," pp. 482–95; Fischer changed his view after the occupation. In December 1939 he wrote that the widely prevailing view is that "the only solution could be the expulsion of the Germans"; see Černý et al., *Češi, Němci a odsun*, pp. 16–17, p. 305.

53. See indictment (note 51).

54. Marek MS, p. 163.

55. Bondy's pseudonyms: Březina, Doucha, Dusil, Čermák. About his stature and human qualities see Josef Grňa-Vlk, *Partyzánské historky* (Brno, 1946); E. Brokešová, *Ty a já* (Prague, 1947); Jan Šach, "Judr. Karel Bondy," in *Historie a vojenství*, no. 1 (1994), pp. 142–60.

56. Kaufmann wrote an analysis of *Mein Kampf* from the medical point of view and diagnosed Hitler as paranoic. His study was sent abroad secretly. According to Antonín Machta in *Pankrác-Terezín* (Prague, 1946, p. 130), it was discussed at a special session of the British Parliament. For his assistance to his fellow prisoners and description of his personality see Machta, *Pankrác-Terezín*; Pavel Eisner, *Svobodný zítřek*, 14.2.1946; *Hlas revoluce*,

11.4.1951. Kaufmann's sister Heda, who survived the war, described his activities in detail; see note 8 to the present chapter.

57. Accounts of Baum's worldwide journeys in search of spiders and beetles were published in collaboration with his wife, the writer Růžena Fikejsová. Pollertová addressed her farewell letter from the prison to Fikejsová, her sister-in-law. See note 76.

58. Marek MS, p. 163.

59. See Kuklík, "Petiční výbor."

60. See *Věrni jsme zůstali* (Prague, 1947), p. 40.

61. See DHČP, 2:500.

62. Marek MS, pp. 11–12.

63. Marek MS, pp. 11–12; Šach, "Judr. Karel Bondy," p. 153–54.

64. The subject was treated in a special study by Lubomír Lehár, "Gestapo a odbojová skupina PVVZ," in *Historie a vojenství*, nos. 6–7 (1968), pp. 1034–35; it was asserted that one of the most important confidants was Antonín Nerad, formerly on the staff of the Ministry of Defense.

65. They used the rings as an identity mark; some of them later became victims of the Gestapo.

66. Marek MS, p. 143; see also Veselý-Štainer, *Cestou národního odboje*, p. 92.

67. Jaroslav Švanda, "Deset adres Mileny Jesenské," in *Svědectví* 20, no. 80 (1987), p. 919; see also "Rakovina a udavačství: Dokumentace z nacistické okupace," compiled by Jaroslav Švanda (Prague, 1984), Židovské muzeum (hereafter ŽM) 1, no. 80.

68. Bondy's widow Dr. Zdena Müllerová was among the right-wing Social Democrats charged in 1954 with subversive activities. In 1966 their sentence was revoked and in 1968 the group was exonerated.

69. Reference in Dr. K. J. Beneš's letter of 18.11.1967, Marek MS, p. 133.

70. Veselý-Štainer, *Cestou národního odboje*, p. 80.

71. Veselý-Štainer, *Cestou národního odboje*, p. 84; we have knowledge about the landing of another group of parachutists somewhat earlier. During the night of March 31–April 1, 1941, it was reported that four parachutists landed not far from the hamlet of Hradčany; one of them was immediately arrested. From the report of the district *landrat* it transpires that during interrogation the captured man revealed the names of the other members of the group, listed as: Pfeiffer (184 cm), Polák, aged 28 (176 cm), Čech, aged twenty-seven, all dressed in civilian clothes and armed with pistols and automatic weapons. They were discovered by a patrol of German storm troopers, two of whom were killed during the clash. Josef Král, *Parašutisté: Reportáže z okupace* (Liberec, 1967), p. 25.

72. The street was named after the actress Letenská-Čalounová of the Vinohrady Theater; together with her husband, she was executed in Mauthausen on October 24, 1942, for help rendered to the assassins of Heydrich.

73. Records in the Prague National Administration of Land Registry and the Emigration Fund (Národní správa majetkových podstat a vystěhovaleckého fondu, Praha 1, Haštalská 20), data received through the courtesy of Václav Berdych.

74. Gusta Fučíková, *Vzpomínky na Julia Fučíka* (Prague, 1961), p. 370; on her activities see also Kladivová, "K historii," p. 165.

75. Photographs and information on the whereabouts of the Pollert and Baum families

as well as the inhabitants of the house at 7 Ve Pštrosce were obtained by courtesy of Zdena Pátková, Prague.

76. Both children were deported to Terezín on July 2, 1942 (registration numbers AA1236 and AA1237)—whence they were sent on September 28, 1944, to Auschwitz with transport EK 874. Pollertová's daughter apparently survived and lives in north Bohemia.

77. Pollertová's parents, Josef and Frantiáka Baum, lived in the near vicinity (Prague, Vinohrady); they were deported in 1941 to Terezín and from there in 1943 to Treblinka. Information received from Václav Berdych (21.1.1981).

78. Dr. Milada Horáková spent five years in Nazi concentration camps. In 1950 she was arrested by the Czechoslovak Security Services, tried for subversive activities against the republic, and executed. She recorded her activities within the PVVZ in a six-page report. See *Proces s vedením záškodnického spiknutí proti republice: Horáková a společníci* (Prague, 1950).

79. Pollertová's involvement in helping parachutists who landed on 4.10.1940 is referred to in an RSHA report. See "Židé v protifašistickém odboji" (Dokumenty sebrané Egonem Jiříčkem, 1940–1945), ŽM 1, no. 51.

80. Dates and information from Pátková (note 75).

81. Veselý-Štainer, *Cestou národního odboje*, p. 42.

82. Kuklík, "Petiční výbor," p. 55. Following the "heydrichiáda" and the massive arrest of the members of the resistance organizations, news and secret information were transmitted by word of mouth and Czech radio broadcasts from abroad, mainly by the BBC. See Jan Kuklík, "Kontrapropaganda v ilegálním tisku v letech 1939–1941," in *Historie a vojenství*, no. 1 (2000), p. 101, 112.

83. Marek MS, p. 183.

84. Marek MS, p. 183.

85. Václav Černý, *Kultur im Widerstand: Prague 1938–1945*, vol. 1 (Köln, 1979), pp. 291–92.

86. Zdeněk Bořek Dohalský actcd as contact between Dr. Beneš and Premier Eliáš; he was jailed during the Heydrich retaliation, held at the Terezín Small Fortress, and executed a day before the liberation. See Firt, *Knihy a osudy*, p. 42; ŽM 1, no. 51.

87. Toward the end of the war Otto Gall was denounced and incarcerated in the Terezín Small Fortress. In May 1945 all trace of him was lost; according to one source he was liquidated by the Gestapo. Others claimed that he was taken captive by the Soviet Army. Černý, *Kultur im Widerstand*, pp. 291–92; Drábek, *Z časů*, p. 99.

88. For the death sentence of Docent Josef Israel Fischer see indictment of Fischer and Pešek NG-1897; YVA, JM02021.

89. From the farewell letter of Dr. Bondy to his sister Ruda Havránková (22.1.1945), Marek MS, p. 139; see also Šach, "Judr. Karel Bondy," p. 159.

90. The background of the development of this group was fully recorded in Kladivová, "K historii," pp. 121–74.

91. Aubrechtová was an only child and a highly gifted art student, responsible for designing many brochure covers and other illustrations produced by the illegal press. On June 24, 1942, in the crucial days of the Heydrich retaliation campaign, she went into hiding in the countryside with her friend Jiří Kysela. They were both discovered and taken

to the Terezín Small Fortress, where she insisted on joining Jiří's mother, Olga Kyselová, who as a Jewess was held in a special cell under harsh conditions. After beatings Aubrechtová was granted this special "favor" by the SS. On November 20, 1942, she was sent to Auschwitz and as a "Jewess" put in the Jewish block: she perished in the gas chambers on December 24, 1942. The notification of her death in Auschwitz was sent to the JRC in Prague. See Kladivová, "K historii," p. 170.

92. Cf. reminiscences of Ernst Kruh, originally from Moravská Ostrava, a member of Kibbutz Givat Haim Meuhad; (Arnošt Lemberger) Moshe Leshem's experiences communicated to this author. See note 95; see also Alena Hájková, "Die sieben Tapferen," in *Theresienstadt in der "Endlösung der Judenfrage,"* ed. Miroslav Kárný, Vojtěch Blodig, and Margita Kárná (Prague, 1992), pp. 202–12.

93. Judging by the numerous "Poláks" (listed with successive numbers) in the Mauthausen logbook during October–November 1942, we assume that apart from Hanuš and Eugen Polák, other members of the family were arrested and perished there; Hanuš Polák's death was recorded on November 19, 1942, Mauthausen logbook, Arolsen, BD, MA 6.

94. See Kladivová, "K historii," p. 170.

95. Valuable information on this aspect is contained in the reminiscences of Kruh, an engraver by profession, who lived illegally in Prague until 1942. He left for Germany as a forced laborer but kept visiting Prague in 1943–44, being assisted by some Czech underground members. His group (about six people) used linoleum stamps for forging documents and altering identity cards. Thus he changed Kruh to Mach and later to Machar, and under these names registered with the Prague Police.

96. Ellnerová, aged twenty-one, a student of medicine and one of the most active members of the group, cooperated closely with the Jewish resistance fighters. She perished in Auschwitz on March 28, 1943; see Kladivová, "K historii," p. 168.

97. Miloš Lederer, aged nineteen, perished in Mauthausen on November 8, 1942; the traces of his brother Pavel, aged seventeen, disappeared in Auschwitz. Their father, Viktor Lederer, a noted member of the Czech-Jewish movement who survived the war, wrote with pride that the names of his two sons, who like himself were members of the Sokol organization, are engraved in the Tyrš House in Prague. See VŽONP, 1.3.1947.

98. Feuerstein was born in Královský Chlumec (Slovakia) on March 13, 1921. He graduated from the Hebrew Gymnasium of Mukačevo and after 1938 came to Bohemia to organize Zionist youth work. From the Small Fortress of Terezín he was sent to Mauthausen with other members of the Vršovice group, among them twenty Jews, on October 22, 1942, and perished there on November 4, 1942. The personal data in our possession draw on a communication from his brother Asher Avinur (Feuerstein), now living in Tivon (Israel); the Hebrew booklet *Theresienstadt,* ed. Y. Reznitschenko (Tel Aviv, 1947); and the Mauthausen logbook, Arolsen, BD, MA 6.

99. See *Theresienstadt,* pp. 14, 23–26; see also *Sefer haShomer haTza'ir,* vol. 1 (Merhavia, 1956), pp. 758, 759.

100. *Theresienstadt,* pp. 23–26.

101. Dated September 5, 1943, this unique document is to be found in the Schwalb collection, Archives of the Labor Movement (ALM), Tel Aviv; information supplemented

by the report of his wife, see note 17. Arnošt Neumann-Hájek (the name he assumed after the war) commenced his studies in medicine in 1937 and received his doctorate in the postwar years. He worked as a gynecologist in Prague until his emigration to London in 1969 with his wife Hede Türk. I wish to thank Dr. Alena Divišová-Hájková for providing me with additional information on this clandestine group.

102. Neumann also recorded after the war his experiences living with Aryan papers, describing in great detail his contacts with various Communist resistance fighters. This record (undated), is now deposited in the VHA archives of military history in Prague.

103. See note 17 to this chapter (passages of this important document are partly illegible). Hede Türk-Neumann supported herself as a foreign correspondent and secretary, working with a Prague firm. She mentions a Czech family in Moravia who assisted her and her husband in registration with the police. Another member of this group, Ernst Kruh (see note 95) mentions the mayor of Nové Město na Moravě, who was instrumental in arranging his registration with the police.

104. In the original text, *Mafia* (designating an underground revolutionary organization of the Czechoslovaks, during World War I).

105. Türk-Neumann report.

106. Moulis, *Mládež proti okupantům*, p. 123.

107. Moulis, *Mládež proti okupantům*, p. 123; another source refers to this group as "intellectuals" who were later associated with Lumír Čivrný and Vladimír Koucký; see Brandes, *Die Tschechen*, 2:80.

108. Moulis, *Mládež proti okupantům*, p. 123.

109. The Labor Office (administered mainly by Czechs) was by 1942 encountering increasing difficulties in filling the quota imposed on the Protectorate. For a lump sum of about five thousand crowns it was possible to settle the enlistment. HeHalutz members were aided by clandestine groups in acquiring documents for this purpose; communication of (Lemberger) Leshem to this author. For enlistment in forced labor in the Protectorate see František Mainus, *Totální nasazení* (Brno, 1970).

110. From the reminiscences of Kruh and Leshem we know additional facts about them: Jasha Berger from Subcarpathian Ruthenia was the first to "submerge" and procure the help of a Czech Communist cell. Kruh, Neumann, and Lemberger (Limberský) acted as inspectors and teachers of German in a Prague language school. Through Jani Lebowitz's friend Alena Divišová they maintained contact with an underground group, collecting intelligence. Endre (Yona) Farkas volunteered as a "foreign laborer" and became an employee of the German State Railway in Breslau; Elie Friedmann, Vojtěch Narcissenfeld, and František Voříšek were employed as stagehands and electricians in a Viennese theater; Hede Türk-Neumann worked in Prague as a translator and correspondent; Abraham Grünberger (Zdeněk Vaněk) worked in Weimar as a shipping clerk; Ernst Kruh worked as an engraver and later as a laborer in a Berlin factory; Jani Lebowitz was caught in Prague and tortured to death by the Gestapo. See also notes 95, 101, 103.

111. Kladivová, "K historii," p. 166.

112. Kladivová, "K historii," p. 166; for details about their fate in Mauthausen see Václav Berdych, *Mauthausen* (Prague, 1959).

113. Jiří Kysela's personal effects and clothes (prison number 78811) were sent after his

"death" in Auschwitz to the parents of Věra Aubrechtová. See Kladivová, "K historii," p. 166 (cf. note 91).

114. When the transport was ready to leave the Small Fortress Ladislav Polák had an outbreak of boils and the sympathetic German doctor advised against including him. He was later sent to another concentration camp and thus survived.

115. Alena Voglová was shipped to Auschwitz, where she perished.

116. Mastný, *Czechs under Nazi Rule*, p. 146. Another source asserts that between 1940 and 1942, twenty thousand messages were passed on to Allied Headquarters; see Henri Michel, *La guerre de l'ombre: La résistance en Europe* (Paris, 1970), p. 122.

117. For Konrád's activities see notes 46, 48; see Jan Skutil, "Kurt Konrád, spolutvůrce pokrokové kulturní politiky a literární kritiky na Moravě v letech 1918–1938," in *Vlasti-vědný věstník moravský* 41 (1989), pp. 104–5.

118. Kurt Konrád lived and died according to these principles. A slip of paper hidden in his clothes, sent to the family after he committed suicide in Dresden (26.9.1941), read: "I am dying honorably, K." See *Hlas revoluce*, no. 38, 18.9.1971.

119. Frank broke down under Gestapo torture and apparently gave away the names of some of his comrades. See Kladivová, "K historii," pp. 143–44.

120. Konrád's widow described Reiman as "the best intelligence contact" of Kurt Beer-Konrád. He also cooperated with Generals Bílý and Vojta from ON. See *Hlas revoluce*, no. 24, 12.6.1970; on Reiman's contacts with General Eliáš, see chapter 5.

121. It was Václav Berdych who furnished this information to Jan Frank. Berdych worked at the Weekly Film Flashes "Aktualita" and was briefed in secret by a sympathetic Reichsdeutsche, V. Hamm (communication to this author). From another source it appears that on April 23, 1941, ÚVOD reported to London that maps of Soviet territory were extensively printed in the Military Cartographic Institute in Prague. Compare Mastný, *Czechs under Nazi Rule*, p. 168 (NA, Oberkommando der Wehrmacht, T-17, 1050, 6526050).

122. At one of his meetings with Prime Minister Eliáš, Reiman received an envelope that contained money for resistance purposes.

123. See Fučíková, *Vzpomínky*, p. 203.

124. In January 1942 Glaser reported that according to Oberkommando der Wehrmacht (High command of the armed forces) headquarters, the Protectorate Government would be instructed to order general mobilization in the Czech lands (units to be deployed in Norway and Finland). In protest against the envisaged plan, Fučík, commissioned by the CCP, prepared an illegal leaflet also signed by ÚVOD. See Fučíková, *Vzpomínky*, pp. 234–35.

125. Kurt Glaser and his family were deported in the summer of 1942, never to return, Fučíková, *Vzpomínky*, p. 207.

126. See *Heroes and Victims*, p. 13.

127. See Brandes, *Die Tschechen*, 1:80.

128. See *Za svobodu českého a slovenského národa: Sborník dokumentů k dějinám KSČ v letech 1938–1945* (Prague, 1956), pp. 161–72.

129. Luža, "Czech Resistance," p. 350.

130. See Heydrich's speech at the press conference, 10.10.1941, DHČP, 2:632.

131. General Eliáš was executed on 19.6.1942; see chapter 5.

132. See *Heroes and Victims*.

133. Jiří Doležal and Jan Křen, *Czechoslovakia's Fight 1938–1945: Documents on the Resistance Movement of the Czechoslovak People* (Prague, 1964), p. 54. See also Karel Lágus, "Židé v boji proti hitlerismu," VŽONP, 1.5.1965.

134. Doležal and Křen, *Czechoslovakia's Fight*, p. 54; see also ŽM 1, no. 51.

135. Fráňa Stricker's imaginative tales were published in 1946, edited by Josef Spilka, under the title *Chléb se dělá ze zlata* (Prague, 1946).

136. See "In Namen des Deutschen Volkes," *Todesurteile des Volksgerichthofs* (Luchterhand, 1981), pp. 70, 72.

137. See *Heroes and Victims*, p. 70; *Hlas revoluce* (May 1980).

138. *Heroes and Victims*, p. 70; *Hlas revoluce* (May 1980).

139. See Mauthausen logbook 1941–42, Arolsen BD, MA 6.

140. Milan Weiss was born in Prague. See R(ameš), *Žaluji: Pankrácká kalvárie* (Prague, 1946), vol. 2, p. 281.

141. Dr. Otakar Weisel, who lived until the occupation in Moravská Ostrava, was a lawyer. In March 1939 he moved to Prague and lived (unregistered) illegally. For his tragic story see Alena Hájková, "Příběh skupiny Otakara Weisla," in *Nisko 1939–1994*, pp. 266–75.

142. While in hiding, Dr. Heřman Freund had been assisted by the head of the local gendarmerie, Tulis. For details on his contacts with a Prague resistance group and his fate see Rudolf Iltis, "Tragédie vlastenecké rodiny," in VŽONP, 20.2.1948.

143. See situation report 1.4.1944, signed by Dr. Gerke, printed in Oldřich and Žižka, *KSČ proti nacismu*, p. 284.

144. For an example see the case of Karel Körper-Marek, VŽONP, 15.6.1947.

145. See "The Jewish Question in Bohemia," signed K. J., in *Přítomnost*, no. 3, 3.2.1943.

146. Václav Kopecký, "K otázce antisemitismu," Problémy našeho boje za svobodu a budování lidové demokratické republiky, in *Cesta k svobodě*, no. 2 (London, September 1944), p. 64.

147. Kopecký, "K otázce antisemitismu," p. 64.

148. See Pavel Eisner, *Rozpravy Aventina*, 14.9.1933, referred to in Pfaff, "Německá kultura," p. 494. Eisner's words were vindicated in an exhibition opened in 1990 in the Prague city museum under the title "Transit Station: Prague, German Emigration 1933–1939," dedicated to the antifascist German emigrants who found sanctuary in Czechoslovakia. It was the first exhibition organized by the Munich-based Adalbert Stifter Society and the Friedrich Ebert Fund of Bonn after the Prague "Velvet Revolution."

149. See chapter 3; for entry on Theodor Lessing (signed S. L.), *Encyclopedia Judaica*, vol. 2, col. 50.

150. Pfaff, "Německá kultura," p. 494.

151. Pfaff, "Německá kultura," p. 491.

152. Černý, *Paměti*, vol. 4, p. 313.

153. *Šest let okupace Prahy*, p. 67.

154. Firt, *Knihy a osudy*, p. 87.

155. Vladislav Vančura was executed on June 1, 1942, after Heydrich's assassination, during the second civil state of emergency (see Kukanová's "List of the executed," no. 220).

156. The poet Josef Hiršal in his reminiscences, *Vínek vzpomínek* (p. 136), claims that Vilém Kostka is to be credited for this leniency. In his capacity as assistant to the censor Dr.

Augustin von Hoop (the former editor of *Prager Presse*), Kostka saw to it that these books slipped through unnoticed.

157. On Orten's poetry see Eisner, "Jinoch Exodus," pp. 79–93; Ota Ornest "Zapomenutý básník," in ŽR 5742 (1981–82), pp. 48–55.

158. Zdeněk Urbánek supported Orten, maintained contact with him, and salvaged his poetry for posterity. Hiršal, *Vínek vzpomínek*.

159. The collected works of Jiří Orten and Hanuš Bonn were first published in Prague in 1947, with an introduction by Václav Černý; see also Zdeněk Koňák, "Jiří Orten," in *Hlas revoluce*, no. 18, 2.9.1966.

160. Eisner, "Jinoch Exodus"; Orten's diaries were published with introductory essays by Jan Grossmann and Zdeněk Urbánek and a closing note by his brother Ota Ornest: *Deníky Jiřího Ortena* (Prague, 1958).

161. "We Shall Cherish the Memory of Jiří Orten," in *Svět proti Hitlerovi*, no. 3, 15.9.1941.

162. Bonn's poem was translated from Czech by Karel Offer, in *Translation*, Second Series, edited by Neville Braybroke and Elizabeth King (London, 1947), pp. 98–99.

163. See Václav Černý, *Kultur im Widerstand*, pp. 145, 313.

164. See Aloys Skoumal, "S Erikem A. Saudkem," in *Vzpomínky českých divadelníků*, pp. 70–73.

165. Eisner exchanged several letters with Viktor Fischl in June 1939, using his pen name Karel Kořínek. He informed Fischl of the difficulties he had encountered in his efforts to emigrate to America. Eisner survived the war in Prague and continued in his literary activities. Among other works he wrote *Chrám i tvrz* (Cathedral and fortress), a monumental study of the Czech language. For his letters to Fischl (Avigdor Dagan) see Department of Manuscripts, Jewish National and University Library of Jerusalem, Vav.581.

166. Václav Vondra on Karel Poláček, *Práce*, 19.10.1974; Jiří Franěk, "Fragezeichen um Karel Poláček," in *Theresienstädter Studien und Dokumente 1997*, ed. Miroslav Kárný, Raimund Kemper, and Margita Kárná (Prague, 1997), pp. 290–307.

167. On 28.8.1939 Zelenka wrote to Viktor Fischl in London of his difficulties in emigrating. Though he had obtained a certificate for Palestine he could not exploit it due to lack of means. The affidavit sent to him by the writer Gerhard S. Kaufmann was actually entered on 24.2.1939 on the "artistic preference quota" waiting list. All he required was a visa for a temporary stay in England. See Jewish National and University Library, Vav.581; see also Ehrmann et al., *Terezín*, p. 326; Volavková, "Jewish Museum," pp. 569–72.

168. Jiří Weil wrote several works on his experience during the war, some of which were translated to English.

169. After the war, Frýd served in the diplomatic corps; he wrote several novels on his experiences in the concentration camps. See *Láhvová pošta, aneb konec posledních sto let* (Prague, 1971). He died in 1976. See ŽR 5742 (1981–82), pp. 57–58.

170. On Karel Strass see František Kafka, "Od zašlápnutých výhonků k mrtvým tvůrcům," in ŽR 5725 (1964–65), pp. 97–102.

171. Kafka, "Od zašlápnutých výhonků."

172. See Thomas S. Eliot, "Tradition and the Individual Talent," in *The Sacred Wood*

(London, 1934), p. 54; for some interesting comments about the writers of the Protectorate see A. French, *Czech Writers and Politics 1945–1969* (Boulder CO, 1982), pp. 19–21.

173. For a description of this initiative see Stein MS, pp. 7–11; see also Volavková, *Schicksal*; Vladimír Sadek, "From the Documents Related to the War-time Central Jewish Museum in Prague," JB 16, no. 1, special issue (1950–80), pp. 5–8; Markéta Petrášová, "Collections of the Central Jewish Museum 1942–1945," JB 24 (1988), pp. 23–36; VŽONP 6, no. 35 (June 1993), p. 3. For a more recent study on this subject see Dirk Rupnow, " 'Ihr must sein auch wenn Ihr nicht mehr seid': The Jewish Central Museum in Prague and Historical Memory in the Third Reich," in *Holocaust and Genocide Studies* 16, no. 1 (Spring 2002), pp. 23–53.

174. In Egon Erwin Kisch's words: "The murderers built a mausoleum for their victims," see *Tales from Seven Ghettos* (London, 1948), p. 210.

175. Petrášová, "Collections," pp. 26–28.

176. Stein MS, p. 8.

177. See Arno Pařík, "Hana Volavková on Jewish Art and Monuments in Bohemia and Moravia," in JB 25, no. 1 (1989), p. 33; Dr. Otto Muneles dedicated his last years to a variety of topics in Jewish studies and bibliography. See Vladimír Sadek, "Dr. Otto Muneles und sein wissentschaftliches Werk," in JB 3 (1967), pp. 73–78. For the fate of the other leading personalities of the museum staff, see Volavková, *Schicksal*.

8. The "Righteous" and the Brave

1. Jaroslav Opat, "Masarykův realismus a naše nová státnost," in *Masarykova idea Československé státnosti ve světle kritiky dějin*, Sborník příspěvků z konference konané ve dnech 24. a 25. září 1992 v aule obchodní akademie v Hodoníně (Prague, 1993), p. 182.

2. Oskar Singer's *Herren der Welt*, with an introduction by Walter Tschuppik, was published in Prague, Vienna, and Zürich, evoking wide interest.

3. Founded in August 1936 under the aegis of the World Jewish Congress, it cooperated with the "Bulletin of the Czechoslovak League against Anti-Semitism" and had sections in the major cities of Czechoslovakia; communication from Dr. Stephen Barber. The head of the Brno section, Maxmilian Ryšánek, was arrested with the hostages of 1939 and again in 1941 and was executed on June 11, 1942 "for harboring persons who were engaged in activities hostile to the Reich." See *Heroes and Victims*, p. 122.

4. For a more detailed discussion on the subject see chapter 5.

5. See Joseph Kermish, "The Activities of the Council for Aid to Jews, Žegota," in *Rescue Attempts during the Holocaust*, pp. 380–81; see also Beate Kosmala, "Ungleiche Opfer in extremer Situation. Die Schwierigkeit der Solidarität in okkupierten Polen," in Wolfgang Benz and Julianne Wetzel, eds., *Solidarität und Hilfe für Juden während der NS-Zeit, Regionalstudien* 1 (Berlin, 1996), p. 77 ff.

6. For details on the issue of "presidential exemptions," see Kárný, *"Konečné řešení": Genocida*, pp. 58–60; cf. chapter 5 of the present volume.

7. Cited from the law of the Yad Vashem Memorial enacted by the Knesset in Jerusalem in 1953.

8. *Deník Otty Wolfa 1942–1945*, with introduction by Ludvík Václavek and Ivan Klíma (Prague, 1997).

9. For the description of the history of the family and the fate of the diary and diarist see introduction to *Deník Otty Wolfa*, pp. 20–21.

10. Cf. chapter 4.

11. On Jesenská's journalistic activities during the crucial Munich period, see chapter 3.

12. For the rescue campaign piloted by Jesenská and von Zedtwitz, see testimonies at Yad Vashem Archives, YVA, M-31/6319; see also Marie Jirásková, "Stručná zpráva o trojí volbě" (M. Jesenská, J. von Zedtwitz a J. Nachtmann v roce 1939 a v čase následujícím), in *Literární Noviny*, no. 40, 5.10.1995, p. 16.

13. Zedtwitz testimony.

14. Zedtwitz testimony.

15. See VŽONP, 1.9.1947.

16. There is no evidence that the Catholic cardinal of Prague, Karel Kašpar, protested from his sickbed against the intention of promulgating anti-Jewish legislation, as some historians claim. See Jan Rataj, *O autoritativní národní stát*, pp. 104–5, and "Český antisemitismus v proměnách let 1918–1945," in *Židé v české a polské občanské společnosti*, ed. Jerzy Tomaszewski and Jaroslav Valenta (Prague, 1999), p. 57.

17. Kárný, *"Konečné řešení": Genocida*, p. 111.

18. Jan Podlešák, "Mučedník za židovství a křesýanství: Život, dílo a smrt Alfreda Fuchse," in *ŽR* 5751 (1990–91), pp. 16–23.

19. See Eliášová and Pasák, "Poznámky," p. 112; intimation to the author by Dr. Alena Hájková.

20. See testimony of Přemysl Pitter, Department of the Righteous among the Nations, YVA, M-31/93, and Pitter's *Unter dem Rad der Geschichte: Ein Leben mit den Geringsten* (Zürich, 1970).

21. Testimony of Otta Ginz of 20.5.1963.

22. Quoted from Přemysl Pitter's letter, sent from Affoltern am Albis (Switzerland) and addressed to Judge Moshe Landau, chairman of the Yad Vashem Committee of the Righteous among the Nations, 19.11.1961, YVA, M-31/93.

23. Cf. chapter 7.

24. Kukánová, "Seznam osob popravených . . . listopadu 1941."

25. Cf. *Deutsche Politik im Protektorat*, doc. 33, October 17, 1941, p. 150.

26. See Alena Hájková and Františck Janáčck, "Na okraj motáků," in Julius Fučík, *Reportáž psaná na oprátce: První úplné, kritické a komentované vydání* (Prague, 1995), p. 88, 125, 129.

27. Fučík, *Reportáž*, pp. 232–33.

28. Cf. Kladivová, "K historii," pp. 121–74; see also reminiscences of Arnošt Lemberger (Moshe Leshem) in chapter 7.

29. K. H. Frank, 28.5.1942, protocol from the meeting with Hitler, see *Protektorátní politika*, p. 272.

30. See *Verbrecher in Richterroben*.

31. See A. Šimka, *Národněosvobozenecký boj na Jihlavsku* (Brno, 1963), p. 58.

32. Šimka, *Národněosvobozeneck*, pp. 62–63.

33. *Heroes and Victims*; the list of those executed by shooting, beheading or hanging is, however, not complete.

34. Cf. chapter 5.

35. See Alena Hájková and Miloš Hájek, O přátelství a solidaritě v letech nejhorších. A copy of the joint testimony of the two engaged in the rescue campaign, written in 1996, is in the author's possession.

36. On the contacts with various Communist resistance fighters, see chapter 7.

37. See Sládek, *Přicházeli z nebe*.

38. *Verbrecher*; *Heroes and Victims*.

39. Marie Golz-Godlust, *Der grosse Tag* (Stuttgart, 1988), pp. 20–21; see also *Verbrecher*, p. 85.

40. Golz, *Der grosse Tag*, 20–21; *Verbrecher*, p. 85.

41. See *Deutsches Recht*, May 13, 1944, cited in *Heroes and Victims*, p. 7.

42. Golz, *Der Grosse Tag*, p. 53.

43. *Verbrecher*, p. 85.

44. Published first in R(ameš), *Žaluji: Pankrácká kalvárie* (Prague, 1946), vol. 1.

45. See *Heroes and Victims*; cited are only persons whose crimes are referred to as "harboring Jews."

46. DHČP, 2:575; see also Lubomír Lehár, "Gestapo a odbojová skupina PVVZ," in *Historie a vojenství*, nos. 6–7 (1968), pp. 1034–35; "Rakovina a udavačství: Dokumentace z nacistické okupace," compiled by Jaroslav Švanda (Prague, 1984), ŽM 1, no. 80.

47. Tomášek and Kvaček, *Causa Emil Hácha*, p. 189.

48. *Heroes and Victims*.

49. See Kárný, "Zvláštní četnický oddíl," pp. 43–44; Leo Haas, "Die Affäre der Theresienstädter Maler," in *Terezín*, pp. 171–76.

50. See Jan Merell, "How They Suffered and Died: A Catholic Priest Testifies to the Suffering of the Jews in the Little Fortress of Terezín," in *Terezín*, pp. 268–71; see also testimony of Pater Dr. Miloš Bič, pastor of the Church of Czech Brethren at Domažlice, in *Terezín*, pp. 273–75.

51. Ample evidence of this may be found in memoir literature and reminiscences held at Yad Vashem Archives.

52. Eva Erben, *Mich hat man vergessen: Erinnerungen eines jüdischen Mädchens* (Weinheim, Basel, 1996).

53. Erben, *Mich hat man vergessen*, pp. 37–38, 56–57.

54. Testimony of Věra Bednářová, YVA, M-31/6923; YVA, M-31/5474; testimony of Anita Hiršalová, YVA, M-31/6923; letter of Zdeněk Urbánek (Prague) addressed to Yad Vashem, to Dr. Paldiel, 2.6.1991.

55. Cf. Bednářová testimony.

56. Prof. Dr. Armin Hergeth's letter of protest to Acting Reichsprotektor Reinhard Heydrich, Prague, 25.11.1941, Bd S IV-9725/41, YVA, M-58/25.

57. The result of the inquiry of the Security Police and the SD, 14.1.1942, YVA, M-58/25.

58. Poet and lawyer Armin Theophil Wegner, the solitary champion of his time, was awarded the Medal of Honor after the war by the Federal Republic of Germany and was also acknowledged as "Righteous among the Nations" by Yad Vashem. See Wolfgang

Gerlach, "Document: Armin T. Wegner's Letter to German Chancellor Adolf Hitler, Berlin, Easter Monday, April 11, 1933," in *Holocaust and Genocide Studies* 8, no.3 (Winter 1944), pp. 395–409.

59. Wegner's letter: "The fate of Germany is also at stake! For whom must the blow now directed against the Jews ultimately strike—whom but ourselves?"

60. Thus far the identity of Prof. Dr. Hergeth has not been disclosed.

61. Kokoškovi and Kokoškovi, *Spor o Agenta* A54, p. 313; see also F. H. Hinsley, *British Intelligence in the Second World War*, vol. 1 (London, 1979), pp. 58–59.

62. Hinsley, *British Intelligence*, pp. 58–59; see also pp. 462–63.

63. First referred to by Detlef Brandes, *Grossbritanien*, pp. 201–2. Cf. chapter 6 of the present work.

64. Kokoškovi and Kokoškovi, *Spor o Agenta* A-54, refer to the final summary of Reicin, dated August 17, 1946, p. 314.

65. Kokoškovi and Kokoškovi, *Spor o Agenta* A-54, pp. 314, 316.

66. Until recently, none of the research dealing with this issue mentioned Thümmel's message of 26.7.1941; Kokoškovi and Kokoškovi, *Spor o Agenta* A54, chapter 26, pp. 305–17, emphasize his "double game" and the abandonment of his Czech partners, members of the clandestine Army Organization (ON). Cf. David Bankier, "The Germans and the Holocaust: What Did They Know?" in YVS 20 (1990), pp. 69–98; see Breitman, *Official Secrets*, p. 95, 275, fn. 31.

67. As far we know there was no reaction at all either by Beneš or by the Allies to the crucial message received as early as July 23, 1941.

68. Cf. Kokoškovi and Kokoškovi, *Spor o agenta* A54, p. 314.

69. See Václav Černý, *Křik koruny české, 1938–1945* (Brno, 1992), pp. 306–7 (German edition: *Kultur im Widerstand*).

70. Zdeněk Bořek-Dohalský, the noted journalist who acted as liaison between the Czechoslovak Government-in-Exile and Prime Minister Eliáš, was executed (following Gall's arrest) on February 7, 1945. See Drábek, *Z časů*, p. 91.

71. DHČP, 2:500.

72. Černý, *Křik koruny české*, p. 307; Drábek, *Z časů*, p. 99.

73. Quoted from Zdeněk Urbánek's letter of June 2, 1991, addressed to Yad Vashem, cited in note 54.

9. Gateway to Death

1. Eberhard Jäckel, *Hitlers Weltanschauung* (Tübingen, 1969); Karl Dietrich Bracher, *The German Dictatorship: The Origin, Structure and Effects of National Socialism* (London, 1971).

2. See Rothkirchen, "Czech and Slovak Wartime Jewish Leadership," in *Holocaust and History*, pp. 63–84.

3. Kárný et al., *Deutsche Politik im Protektorat*, doc. 29, p. 139; see also Fremund et al., *Lesson from History*, doc. 20, pp. 139–40.

4. Kárný et al., *Deutsche Politik im Protektorat*, doc. 29.

5. See Otto Lehner's report on his inspection visit to Theresienstadt on April 6, 1945, in

Documents sur l'activité du Comité International de la Croix-Rouge concernant le Ghetto de Theresienstadt, Geneva, 26.6.1990, Annex 25.

6. The Small Fortress was used as a prison during Austro-Hungarian rule and also in the era of the Czechoslovak Republic. As of March 1939 many Czech political detainees were held there, and numerous Jews on various charges were transferred to the fortress by the Prague Gestapo as well as from the Terezín Ghetto as a punishment for "transgressions."

7. Cf. Kárný et al., *Deutsche Politik im Protektorat*, doc. 29, p. 139; and Fremund et al., *Lesson from History*, doc. 20, pp. 139–40.

8. František Makovský, who served in this gendarmerie unit, gave a description about its function as well as his own activities on behalf of the Jewish inmates. A copy of his report is in the author's possession; Makovský's postwar reminiscences are deposited in SÚA, ZCV, box 1006, H210.

9. Survey written by Dr. Josef Bor in the sixties. See "Stručný přehled o českožidovské organizaci v Terezíně," no. 27, undated, 6p., copy in the author's possession.

10. A majority of these deportees was exterminated in the concentration camp of Salaspils, in the proximity of Riga, through hard labor, torture, and starvation. The second transport was liquidated in the woods outside Riga by SS killing squads, and at fort No. 9 at Kovno. See Lederer, *Ghetto Theresienstadt*, pp. 199–242.

11. Edelstein sent this letter clandestinely to his former associates, probably in an effort to counterbalance the one dispatched to Geneva on October 19, 1942, to his friend Dr. Fritz Ullmann—the contents of which were obviously prescribed to him by the SS. His opening sentence: "Letters are not philosophical epistles . . ." was well understood by the recipients, who realized that it was meant to sound an alarm. See collection of Fritz Ullmann, CZA, A370/5.

12. The fifty-two-page unsigned report was identified after the war by Zeev Shek as Otto Zucker's writing. It contains illustrations designed by Otto Ungar. The original report is deposited in the Zeev Shek collection, YVA, 0-64/7. A major part of it was reproduced under the title "Otto Zucker: Theresienstadt 1941–1943," in *Theresienstädter Studien and Dokumente 1995*, pp. 264–71.

13. See Kryl, "Fritz Ullmann und seine Hilfe," p. 191.

14. Their strategy was based on the rational assumption that the Reich needed the goods produced by Jewish workers, which included war materiel as well as everyday items such as clothing, brushes, etc. This view was first aired by Isaiah Trunk during the colloquium on the Judenräte; see Trunk, "Discussion," in *Imposed Jewish Governing Bodies under Nazi Rule*, YIVO Colloquium, December 2–5, 1967 (New York, 1972), p. 83.

15. Egon Redlich, a member of the Jewish Council and in charge of the Youth Welfare Department, described with utmost honesty the prevailing antagonism and the crucial problems that confronted the *Ältestenrat*: petty politics, ethical impropriety, and favoritism; his diary was discovered in the attic of a Terezín building in 1967. See *The Terezín Diary of Egon Redlich*, ed. Saul S. Friedmann, translated from Czech by Laurence Kutler (Lexington 1992); see also Schmiedt, "HeHalutz in Theresienstadt," pp. 107–25.

16. See Livia Rothkirchen, "Die Representanten der Theresienstädter Selbstverwaltung," in *Theresienstädte Studien und Dokumente 1996*, pp. 119–21.

17. Rothkirchen, "Die Representanten," on the Appeal Committee; cf. *Terezín Diary of Egon Redlich*, p. 27.

18. *Terezín Diary of Egon Redlich*, p. 27.

19. Rita Meyhofer, "Berliner Juden und Theresienstadt," in *Theresienstädter Studien und Dokumente 1996*, pp. 42–43.

20. Loewenstein survived the war and recorded the events in Minsk as "he saw them"; see Karl Loewenstein, *Minsk: Im Lager der deutschen Juden* (Bonn, 1961). His reminiscences about Terezín are in the Terezín Memorial, Archiv památníku Terezín (APT), A1225/3.

21. This trend of animosity was "inspired" by the highest echelons. Himmler, while visiting Mussolini in mid-October 1942, mentioned the issue of Theresienstadt, cheerfully pointing out: "The Jews quarrel there in a very vivid way amongst themselves." See "Himmler's Vermerk über seinen Besuch bei Mussolini," vz 4 (1956), pp. 424–26.

22. Lederer, "Terezín," p. 119. However, views about Dr. Eppstein differed: Emil Utitz recalled Eppstein's "court": his vanity, ambition, and "megalomania," in *Psychologie des Leben im Theresienstädter Konzentrationslager* (Vienna, 1948), p. 3. For a more positive view see "Gedenkblatt für Dr. Paul Eppstein," reprinted in *Jüdische Sozialarbeit*, Frankfurt, Jahrgang 4, no. 3–4, 9.18.1959.

23. Sickness raged especially in the lodgings of the aged, the consequence of which was the rising death toll. In April, May, and June 1942 the death toll generally did not exceed ten per day, but in the ensuing months it rose to extreme heights; by July 1942 there were more than fifty deaths some days; in August mortality reached 113 cases and in September 1942 the daily death toll came to 156. See Zucker's report, yva, 0-64/7, p. 39.

24. On education and care of children, see Erik Polak, "Die Bedeutung der Zeitschrifte im Leben der Theresienstädter Kinder und Jugend," in *Theresienstadt in der "Endlösung,"* pp. 164–72.

25. Hanuš Schimmerling, "Jüdische Jugend im Widerstand," in *Theresienstadt in der "Endlösung,"* p. 181.

26. The problem of coexistence between Czech and German Jews and the effort made by the Jewish Elders to create grounds for cooperation is touched upon in the exchange of letters between Edelstein and Eppstein; see Miroslav Kárný, "Jakob Edelsteins letzte Briefe," in *Theresienstädter Studien und Dokumente 1997*, pp. 217–18.

27. See Ruth Schwertfeger, *Women in Theresienstadt: Voices from a Concentration Camp* (Oxford, New York, Hamburg, 1989), pp. 34–37.

28. František Makovský's report about his assistance addressed to the Israeli Consulate at Prague, 1.3.1951, copy in the author's possession.

29. "Strolls through Theresienstadt—A Visit to the Morgue"; see Peter Ginz and Chava Pressburger, *The Road through Theresienstadt* (exhibition catalogue), Yad Vashem (Art Museum), 1984, p. 12.

30. "Nach aussen das Gesicht zu waren"; see notes taken at a meeting held in Eichmann's office on March 6, 1942, in Adler, *Verheimlichte Wahrheit*, p. 9.

31. While on July 1, 1942, the total population amounted to 21,304, at the end of the month following a massive influx of transports, the number rose to 43,403; the peak was reached in September 1942 with 58,491 inmates. Through several dispatches to the "East"

the number diminished again by February 1943 (to 44,672, according to Zucker's report, p. 26).

32. For Kaltenbrunner's *Schnellbrief* and Himmler's answer of February 16, 1943, see YIVO Archives, New York (reproduced from the collection of the Manuscripts Division, Library of Congress).

33. Kaltenbrunner's *Schnellbrief* and Himmler's answer.

34. The role of the ICRC is further discussed later.

35. It is estimated that about three thousand parcels were sent monthly to Terezín by the Czech population as an act of encouragement and sympathy. On the involvement of the Geneva-based organizations, see Kryl, "Fritz Ullmann und seine Hilfe," p. 191.

36. About the political education of youth, see a special report compiled at Terezín by Gideon Klein, "O tak zvané politické výchově mládeže," APT, K 4/gh. A1238.

37. The passing of Dr. Edvard Lederer (Leda), one of the pillars of the Czech-Jewish movement, was marked by a solemn memorial gathering (14.7.1944) attended by fifteen hundred inmates. See Bor's survey, p. 5; cf. chapter 10.

38. See Anna Auředničková, *Tři léta v Terezíně* (Prague, 1947).

39. See Utitz, *Psychologie*, p. 57.

40. *Terezín Diary of Egon Redlich*, entries of November 10, 1943, and January 1, 1944, pp. 134, 139; briefings of the ICRC delegates are discussed later.

41. *Terezín Diary of Egon Redlich*, entry of November 14, 1943, p. 135.

42. See Otakar Tyl and Tana Kulišová, *Terezín: Malá pevnost-Ghetto* (Terezín: The small fortress ghetto; Prague, 1955), pp. 85, 91; Eva Šormová, *Divadlo v Terezíně 1941–1945*, (Ústí nad Labem, 1973). Cf. chapter 10.

43. *Terezín Diary of Egon Redlich*, entry of June 23, 1944.

44. Haas, "Die Affäre,"

45. Lederer, *Ghetto Theresienstadt*, pp. 150–51.

46. See Dr. Arnošt Wald's letter sent after the war from Prostějov to Dr. Fritz Ullmann in Geneva, CZA, S26/1281. Lederer refers to eleven transports sent to Auschwitz, numbering over eighteen thousand persons; see "Terezín," pp. 140–41; and see Miroslav Kárný, "Die Theresienstädter Herbsttransporte," in *Theresienstädter Studien und Dokumente 1997*, pp. 7–37.

47. Vojtěch Blodig, "Die letzte Phase der Entwicklung des Ghetto Theresienstadt," in *Theresienstadt in der "Endlösung,"* p. 277.

48. The negotiations were initiated by Agudath Israel and the Union of Orthodox Rabbis of the United States and Canada; an important part was played by the brothers Sternbuch of Montreux, whose contact was Jean-Marie Musy. For details see Schellenberg, *Labyrinth*, p. 430; see also Adler, *Verheimlichte Wahrheit*, pp. 106–7; Jean-Claude Favez, *Das Internationale Rote Kreuz und das Dritte Reich* (Zürich, 1989), pp. 489, 494.

49. Blodig, "Die letzte Phase," pp. 274, 277; see also Kastner, Bericht, pp. 323–27.

50. Blodig, "Die letzte Phase," pp. 274, 277 For Hilerová's poem see Miep Diekmann and Dagmar Hilerová, *Ich habe keinen Namen aus dem Tagebuch ernis Fúnfzehnjárngin* (Wúrzbach, 1987).

51. For a comprehensive report see *Rapport du Comité International de la Croix Rouge sur son activité pendant la Seconde Guerre Mondiale* (1er septembre 1939–30ieme juin 1947), 3 vols. (Geneva, 1948).

52. For an astute survey of the activities of the ICRC see Friedrich Forrer, "Hundert Jahre Rotes Kreuz," in *Der Monat*, no. 181 (October 1963), pp. 44–50.

53. Favez, *Rote Kreuz*, pp. 27–29.

54. Favez, *Rote Kreuz*, pp. 122–29.

55. Letter of Noach Barou, London, 5.9.1941, to Dr. Abraham Silberschein, Geneva, WJCA.

56. Moreillon's article entitled "Red Cross Knew in 1942 of Massacre of Jews but Kept Silent," in *Jerusalem Post*, 31.8.1988, was written in answer to David Horovitz's report (28.8.1988).

57. Dr. Abraham Silberschein acted as head of the "Committee of Relief for the War-Stricken Jewish Population—Relico" and as such was in contact with Dr. Jaromír Kopecký. Silberschein's collection of documents is at the Yad Vashem Archives.

58. For Paul C. Squire's Memorandum of 7.11.1942, see Favez, *Rote Kreuz*, Document XI, pp. 137–38.

59. Squire memorandum.

60. See Favez, *Rote Kreuz*, pp. 109–36.

61. For valuable data see Laqueur, *Terrible Secret*, pp. 60–62.

62. The information was received by Paul T. Culbertson of the State Department from the representatives of the JDC in Budapest (Jacobson and Blum); see annex to my article "Deep-Rooted Yet Alien: Some Aspects of the History of the Jews in Subcarpathian Ruthenia," in YVS) 12 (1977), pp. 177–78, doc. 8, pp. 190–91.

63. The WCC began its work in 1938 in Geneva when two ecumenical organizations—the World Conference on Faith and Order and the Universal Christian Council for Life and Work—adopted a constitution for a World Council of Churches. Some of their activities were devoted to assistance for non-Aryan refugees. For a detailed description see Armin Boyens, "The World Council of Churches and Its Activities on Behalf of the Jews in the Nazi Period," in *Judaism and Christianity under the Impact of National Socialism, 1919–1945*, ed. Otto D. Kulka and Paul R. Mendes-Flohr (Jerusalem, 1987), pp. 454–55.

64. Boyens, "World Council of Churches," p. 458.

65. Boyens, "World Council of Churches," p. 459. The committee's basic concern was limited to care for prisoners of war.

66. Laqueur, *Terrible Secret*, pp. 61–62; see also Favez, *Rote Kreuz*, pp. 196–98.

67. Favez, *Rote Kreuz*, p. 120.

68. Laqueur, *Terrible Secret*, pp. 62–63. On information from extermination camp escapees, Laqueur mentions that "Burckhardt was a cautious man . . . he did not leave a report of this talk."

69. Riegner's record of the talk was sent with a covering letter on 18.11.1942 by Richard Lichtheim of the Jewish Agency Geneva Office to Dr. Lauterbach of the Zionist Executive in Jerusalem. Lichtheim mentioned that prior to the meeting Riegner consulted him on some of the issues and the way he should react: "müsse man aktiv reagieren und nicht nur passiv die Nachrichten von Deportierten registrieren." According to Riegner, it was at this point in their talk that Professor Burckhardt suggested addressing "in the wake of new political development" the German Foreign Ministry in Berlin and insisting upon the visit

of the ICRC delegates to the General Gouvernement, Theresienstadt, and eventually to Transnistria. See CZA, 1 22/3.

70. Cf. Squire memorandum, note 58; the Riegner telegram is discussed in chapter 6. See also Gerhart M. Riegner, *Ne jamais désesperer: Soixante années ou service du peuple juif et des droits de l'homme* (Paris, 1998), pp. 74–75.

71. Burckhardt was one of the best informed men in the free world, with excellent contacts in Germany. Von Hassell's diary mentions that Carl Burckhardt intimated in May 1941 that a confidant of Himmler (probably Carl Langbehn) had queried if he thought that Britain would make peace with Himmler, if not with Hitler. *The Von Hassell Diaries 1938–1944: The Story of the Forces against Hitler inside Germany as Recorded by Ambassador Ulrich von Hassell, a Leader of the Movement* (London, 1948), pp. 205, 223.

72. Gerhard M. Riegner, "Die Beziehung des Roten Kreuzes zu Theresienstadt in der Endphase des Krieges," in *Theresienstädter Studien und Dokumente 1996*, pp. 19–30.

73. Riegner, "Die Beziehung," p. 23.

74. See Kulka, "Ghetto in an Annihilation Camp," p. 328.

75. During a conversation in 1943 with the president of the Swedish Red Cross, Folke Bernadotte, Grawitz made it clear that "humanitarianism per se is emotional drowsiness and has to be replaced by the ideal of gallantry—that has to be applied, naturally, only in relation to Aryans or racially equal persons." See Forrer, "Hundert Jahre Rote Kreuz," p. 46.

76. Aside from Hartmann of the German Red Cross, the other two participants were L. Niehaus (representative of the RSHA), in charge of external contacts, and Eberhard von Thadden, of the "Inland II" department of the German Foreign Ministry. According to Forrer, Hartmann spoke frankly to de Pilar in a one-on-one meeting. See Forrer, "Hundert Jahre Rote Kreuz," p. 47.

77. Forrer, "Hundert Jahre Rote Kreuz," p. 47.

78. Myron Taylor's information relied on the Geneva Office of the Jewish Agency for Palestine. It also stated that Jews from Slovakia were being sent to the east "to be butchered." The Vatican's reply stated that "reports of severe measures taken against non-Aryans have also reached the Holy See from other sources but that up to the present time it has not been possible to verify the accuracy thereof." See Minister of Switzerland (Harrison) to Secretary of State, Berne, 16.10.1942, Foreign Relations of the United States, 1942 (Washington DC, 1961), vol. 3, pp. 775–77.

79. *Actes et Documents du Saint Siège relatifs à la Seconde Guerre Mondiale*, vol. 9, Le Saint Siège et les Victimes de la Guerre, Janvier–Decembre 1943 (Vatican, 1975), pp. 491–92.

80. Quoted in Adler, *Theresienstadt*, p. 802.

81. YVA, JM/700; Kulka, "Ghetto in an Annihilation Camp," pp. 328–29.

82. Easterman's letter is printed in Arieh Ben-Tov, *Facing the Holocaust in Budapest: the International Committee of the Red Cross and the Jews in Hungary, 1943–1945* (Dordrecht, 1988), pp. 83–84.

83. Ben-Tov, *Facing the Holocaust*, pp. 91–92.

84. See Allen Dulles, *Germany's Underground* (New York, 1947).

85. Czechoslovak circles eagerly followed the news about the contacts taken up by Hohenlohe-Langenburg (the erstwhile liaison between Henlein and Lord Runciman in

pre-Munich days). They knew of the continuous negotiations about a separate peace by the United States, without the knowledge of the Soviet Union, in autumn 1942 in Lisbon, Geneva, and Stockholm. See DHČP, 1:284, 287.

86. See Dulles, *Germany's Underground.*

87. For a detailed description see Eberhard Kolb, *Bergen-Belsen: Geschichte des "Aufenthaltlagers" 1943–1945* (Hannover, 1962), pp. 366–67; Miroslav Kárný, *Tajemství a legendy Třetí říše* (Prague, 1983), p. 131.

88. Adler, *Theresienstadt,* p. 803.

89. Lederer, "Terezín," p. 135.

90. Adler, *Theresienstadt,* p. 84.

91. Lederer, "Terezín," pp. 134–36, describes the privileged position of the Danish Jews; see also Leni Yahil, *The Rescue of Danish Jewry: Test of Democracy* (Philadelphia, 1969).

92. For details see Kastner, Bericht; see also Adler, *Theresienstadt,* pp. 169–71.

93. Both letters are reproduced in Kastner, Bericht, pp. 169–71.

94. Kastner, Bericht, pp. 169–71.

95. Zeev Shek's testimony mentions the prevailing optimistic mood, which eventually "stimulated the spirit of resistance and strengthened the will to live," see YVA, 027/13.

96. Adler, *Theresienstadt,* p. 691; Forrer, "Hundert Jahre Rote Kreuz," p. 47.

97. Best's note sent on November 19, 1943, see Adler, *Theresienstadt,* p. 141.

98. Yahil, *Rescue of Danish Jewry,* pp. 291–96.

99. A resume of Maurice Rossel's report was first printed in H. G. Adler's *Verheimlichte Wahrheit,* pp. 312–14. For Rossel's full version, see *Documents du Comité International,* published in 1990. For a description of Rossel's visit (with comments) see "Besuch im Ghetto," in *Theresienstädter Studien und Dokumente 1996,* pp. 284–320.

100. *Brundibár,* written before the war by Hoffmeister and Krása, was performed uncensored by the children of the ghetto. For details about the artists and the production see Šormová, *Divadlo,* pp. 73–74.

101. The Danish representative Hwass mentioned in his comments that some Czech gendarmes were standing on guard outside the ghetto. According to the briefing of the SS, altogether fifteen "German Aryans" were in charge of surveillance of the city as well as maintaining contact with the outside world. Adler, *Theresienstadt,* p. 718.

102. František Makovský was posthumously acknowledged in 1994 as "Righteous among the Nations." A copy of his collection of documents is in the possession of the author.

103. See Rossel's report in *Documents du Comité International.*

104. A letter dated 1.1.1944 from Bratislava (in Hebrew), was received by Nathan Schwalb from members of the HeHalutz organization stating that "the situation in Terezín is very bad. The camp is about to be liquidated and people are already being transferred to Zivia [Poland]. Unfortunately Jacob [Edelstein] too is no longer there." See CZA, S26/1285.

105. In the letter addressed to Dr. Fritz Ullmann in Geneva, Janowitz spoke of a "labor transport" (around five thousand deportees), a great part of whom were made up of the Terezín "work details" (AK I and II) especially selected by the *Lagerkommandant,* Anton Burger. See Lederer, "Terezín," p. 133.

106. For the cooperation of Dr. Jaromír Kopecký, who acted as the delegate of the Bureau Permanent de la République Tchéchoslovaque pres la Société des Nations, with the Jewish organizations and his help in fall 1944 in procuring food parcels and other aid to Terezín, see Riegner, "Die Beziehungen," pp. 26–29, and his *Ne jamais désesperer*, pp. 153–56.

107. See Adler, *Theresienstadt*, pp. 752–53.

108. Spier, a Dutch Jew, was apparently chosen by the ss because of his idyllic portrayal of the ghetto. He survived the war.

109. Rossel's summation of 23.6.1944; see note 99 to this chapter.

110. The German Red Cross representative Heydekampf reported to Niehaus, his superior in Berlin, that he himself saw the report and personally briefed Hauptsturmführer Möhs, who was completely satisfied with its contents. See Kulka, "Ghetto in Annihilation Camp," p. 329.

111. Adler, *Verheimlichte Wahrheit*, p. 312.

112. Adler, *Verheimlichte Wahrheit*, p. 312.

113. Adler, *Verheimlichte Wahrheit*, p. 179.

114. See Leo Baeck, "A People Stands before its God," in Eric H. Boehm, ed., *We Survived: The Stories of the Hidden and the Hunted in Nazi Germany* (New Haven, 1949), pp. 293–94.

115. Cf. Wald's letter, note 46.

116. Kárný, "Theresienstädter Herbsttransporte 1944," pp. 7–37.

117. For Eppstein's New Year's address see Feder, *Židovská tragédie*, p. 85; The Diary of Eva Roubíčková, entry September 1944, APT, Collection of Reminiscences, No. 65.

118. Cf. Lederer, "Terezín," pp. 119, 135. Rabbi Dr. Murmelstein, the only survivor on the Council of Elders in Terezín, was arraigned by Czechoslovak authorities but later released. After his emigration to Italy, he was tried in Rome in August 1948, by the civil court of the Organization of Jewish Displaced Persons in Italy, charged with alleged collaboration; but the case was dismissed. See Murmelstein's "Historical Account" (*Geschichtlicher Überblick*) of events in Terezín from its establishment to its termination in May 1945, compiled in fall 1945. YVA, M41 / 145, 146. See also VŽNOP, 28.10.1945.

119. Cf. note 104.

120. Miriam Edelstein's letter was written in German with several key words inserted in Yiddish. See CZA, S26 / 1281.

121. On February 29, 1944, while chairing the meeting of the *Freizeitgestaltung*, Herr Henschel read out to the participants passages from a letter conveying personal greetings from Edelstein. See minutes of 29.2.1944, YVA, P15, III, 44.

122. See testimony of Yehuda Bacon in State of Israel, *Trial of Adolf Eichmann*, vol. 3, pp. 1245–46; together with Edelstein, Leo Foltýn, Alfred Goldschmid, and Egon Deutsch (of the Terezín Registry) and their families were shot. See Ruth Bondy, *Elder of the Jews: Jakob Edelstein of Theresienstadt*, trans. Evelyn Abel (New York: Grove, 1989).

123. See Jeremy D. Harris, "Broadcasting the Massacres: An Analysis of the BBC's Contemporary Coverage of the Holocaust," in YVS 25 (1996), p. 75.

124. Harris, "Broadcasting the Massacres."

125. Adler, *Verheimlichte Wahrheit*, pp. 105–7; see Blodig, "Die letzte Phase," pp. 267–68; cf. note 48.

126. Adler, *Theresienstadt*, p. 806.

127. Excerpts were published in the Swiss press in summer 1944. For the open letter see Ben-Tov, *Facing the Holocaust in Budapest*, annex 4, pp. 403–4.

128. For Lehner's report, see *Documents du Comité International*.

129. Lehner report. Lehner's cynical comment on the film: "a documentary film with a slight touch of propaganda." Its intention was to present the quality of life "Jews were enjoying in Terezín," while German cities were bombed, and the German people were suffering. For a detailed description of the film see Karel Margry, "Theresienstadt (1944–1945): The Nazi Propaganda Film Depicting the Concentration Camp as Paradise," *Historical Journal of Film* 12, no. 2 (1992).

130. Cited in Adler, *Verheimlichte Wahrheit*, p. 357. The number of inmates deported to Auschwitz in September and October 1944 was close to nineteen thousand, see Lederer, "Terezín," pp. 140–41; Kárný "Theresienstädter Herbsttransporte 1944," pp. 7–31.

131. Favez, *Rote Kreuz*, document D XLV, pp. 499–500; see also *Documents du Comité International*.

132. Favez, *Rote Kreuz*, pp. 499–500; *Documents du Comité International*.

133. See Adler, *Verheimlichte Wahrheit*, pp. 355–56.

134. Adler, *Verheimlichte Wahrheit*, pp. 203–4.

135. Kastner, Bericht, pp. 323–27.

136. For Paul Dunant's report see *Documents du Comité International*.

137. Josef Polák, "Facts and Figures," in *Terezín*, pp. 47–50.

138. See *Inter Arma Caritas: The Work of the International Committee of the Red Cross during the Second World War* (Geneva, 1947), p. 72.

10. The Spiritual Legacy of the Terezín Inmates

1. Ingo Schulz, ed., *Viktor Ullmann: 26 Kritiken über Musikalische Veranstaltungen in Theresienstadt*, mit einem Geleitwort von Thomas Mandl (Hamburg, 1993), p. 93.

2. Richard Feder, "Religious Life in Terezín," in *Terezín*, pp. 53–58; Adler, *Theresienstadt*, pp. 609–11.

3. Feder, "Religious Life," p. 54.

4. See *Terezin Diary of Egon Redlich*.

5. One of the first testimonies is the statement given by singer Heda Grab on November 29, 1945. See Ludmila Vrkočová, Hudba terezínského ghetta, *Jazzpetit* 8 (Prague, 1981), pp. 6, 8–9.

6. Arnošt Weiss, "Musical Events in Terezín 1942," in *Terezín*, p. 230; Milan Kuna, *Hudba na hranicích života* (Prague, 1990).

7. Ulrike Migdal, ed., *Und die Musik spielt dazu: Chansons und Satiren aus dem KZ Theresienstadt* (Munich, Zürich, 1986).

8. Karel Švenk, singer and composer, died in January 1945 during the death march. Ullmann called him "our Terezín Aristophanes." He mainly wrote songs for satirical sketches. His play written in the ghetto, "Poslední cyklista" (The last cyclist), was not performed due to its rebellious content. See Šormová, *Divadlo*, pp. 44–49.

9. Rabbi Gustav Weiner, "Die Zeit vor der offiziellen Freizeitgestaltung: November

1941 bis Februar 1942: Entstehung und Anfänge der Freizeitgestaltung Februar 1942 bis Februar 1943," in Migdal, *Und die Musik*, pp. 131–60.

10. "Světélka v noci po nich vztahujeme ruce," in *Terezínske listy* 3 (1973), p. 34.

11. Ruth Schwertfeger, *Women of Theresienstadt: Voices from a Concentration Camp* (Oxford, New York, Hamburg, 1989), pp. 34–37.

12. Migdal, "Texte für das Kabarett," in *Und die Musik*, pp. 59–111.

13. Ludmila Chládková, "Karel Poláček v Terezíně," in *Terezínské listy* 3 (1973), p. 58.

14. Lederer, *Ghetto Theresienstadt*, p. 128.

15. Emil Utitz, "The Central Ghetto Library in the Concentration Camp Terezín," in *Terezín*, pp. 263–67.

16. In 1945 when the time came to disband the library, around one hundred thousand volumes were returned to Prague, whence most had come.

17. *Terezín Diary of Egon Redlich*, p. 78.

18. Karel Herman's collection contains 551 items from Terezín; see Lena Makarová et al., "Die Akademie des Überlebens," in *Theresienstädter Studien und Dokumente 1998*, pp. 213–38.

19. See Claus Leist, "Philipp Manes: A Theresienstadt Chronicle," in *Journal of Holocaust Education* 6, no. 2 (Autumn 1997), pp. 36–79.

20. Karel Berman, "Memories," in *Terezín*, p. 235.

21. *Terezín Diary of Egon Redlich*, entry November 25, 1942, p. 86.

22. Ludvík Václavek, "Terezínské básně Ilsy Weberové," in *Terezínské listy* 5 (1975), pp. 26–34.

23. From the poem "Ich wandere durch Theresienstadt"; see Ilse Weber, *In deinen Mauern wohnt das Leid: Gedichte aus dem KZ Theresienstadt* (Gerlingen, 1991), p. 103; English version "I Wander through Theresienstadt," in *Terezín*, p. 59.

24. This was the first poem written about the Lidice massacre.

25. Šormová, *Divadlo*, pp. 87–90.

26. Marcela Votavová, "Bedřich Fritta: Nástin osobnosti a díla," in *Terezínské listy* 9 (1978), pp. 18–28.

27. Votavová, "Bedřich," p. 22; see also Norbert Troller, *Theresienstadt: Hitler's Gift to the Jews* (Chapel Hill, 1992).

28. Bedřich Fritta and his colleagues, Leo Haas, Felix Bloch, and Otto Ungar, were accused of engaging in "atrocity propaganda and disseminating it abroad." Together with Karel Strass, a former businessman, thanks to whose help and contacts with the Czech gendarmes the pictures had been smuggled abroad, the artists were arrested and tortured in the Little Fortress before their deportation to Auschwitz. Only Leo Haas lived to see the end of the war. The Nazis were not, however, aware that the artists had managed to hide most of their works prior to their arrest. See Gerald Green, *The Artists of Terezín* (New York, 1985), pp. 98–114.

29. Max Plaček, *Double Signature: Portraits of Personalities from the Terezín Ghetto*, Yad Vashem Catalogue (Jerusalem, 1994).

30. Oliva Pechová, "Malířský odkaz Petra Kiena," in *Terezínské listy* 3 (1973), pp. 25–29; Ludvík Václavek, "Der Dichter Petr Kien (1919–1944)," in *Acta Universitatis Palackianae Olomucensis*, Facultas Philosophica, Philologia 66 (1993), pp. 41–55.

31. Pechová, "Malířský odkaz," p. 29.

32. This formal expression of grief, *keriyah*,—that is, the tearing of the hem of one's garment, is still observed by the relatives of a deceased person.

33. Ludvík Václavek, "Literární tvorba Petra Kiena," in *Terezínské listy* 3 (1973), p. 23.

34. Jitka Ludvová, "Viktor Ullmann (1898–1944)," in *Hudební věda* 16 (1979), 2, pp. 99–122; Kuna, *Hudba na hranici života*, pp. 328–45; Joža Karas, *Music in Terezín 1941–1945* (New York, 1985).

35. Both of Ullmann's letters are in the Yad Vashem Archives, 064/94.

36. Kuna, *Hudba na hranici života*, p. 322; David Bloch, "Viktor Ullmann's Yiddish and Hebrew Vocal Arrangements in the Context of Jewish Music Activity in Terezín," in *Viktor Ullmann: Die Referate des Symposions anlässlich des 50. Todestags 14.–16. Oktober 1994 und ergänzende Studien*, ed. Hans-Günter Klein (Hamburg 1996), pp. 79–86.

37. Kuna, *Hudba na hranicích života*, pp. 93–94; Bloch, "Viktor Ullmann's Vocal Arrangements," pp. 80–81.

38. Like the essay "Goethe und Ghetto," Ullmann's opera was composed in August 1944, when people in Terezín already knew about the Allied landings in France and the attack on Hitler. Cf. comments by Thomas Mandl about the information received from Engineer Rust, who had access to a radio. See Schulz, *Viktor Ullmann: 26 Kritiken*, p. 93.

39. André Meyer, "Peter Kiens Libretto zum Kaiser von Atlantis: Ein Text voller Anspielungen," in *Viktor Ullmann, Referate*, pp. 87–96.

40. Weiss, "Musical Events," p. 230.

41. Weiss, "Musical Events," p. 230.

42. Weiss, "Musical Events," p. 230; Vrkočová, *Hudba*, p. 11; Karas, *Music in Terezín*, pp. 125–27.

43. Only in 1987, one year before his death, did H. G. Adler hand over Viktor Ullmann's legacy to the Archiv Goetheana in Dornach, Switzerland. The first symposium took place in 1994, on the occasion of the fiftieth anniversary of Ullmann's death. See Marcus Gerhart, "Vorwort eines des Initiatoren," in *Viktor Ullmann, Referate*, pp. 9–11, 34; Schulz, *Viktor Ullmann: 26 Kritiken*, pp. 12–14, and his, "Wege und Irrwege der Ullmann-Forschung," in *Viktor Ullmann, Referate*, pp. 31–34.

44. Blanka Müllerová, "Hans Krása: Kapitoly ze života a díla skladatele," Ph.D. thesis (Prague, 1966); Milan Slavický, "Gideon Klein—torzo života a díla," in *Hudební věda* 14 (1977), pp. 336–59; Milan Kuna, "Ester—rezistentní hra o záchraně Židů s hudbou Karla Reinera (Terezín 1943/1944)," in *Hudební věda* 31 (1994), pp. 235–71.

45. Adler, *Theresienstadt*, p. 621.

46. In his list of sources, Adler cites (no. 141, p. 761): "Kien P.: Der König von Atlantis oder Der Tod dankt ab. Legend in four pictures, music by Viktor Ullmann, Ms. T. ca. 1943. Scarcely any allusions to T. The music has been preserved (like other compositions by Ullmann from T., which deserve attention)." Under no. 322, p. 841, Adler also lists: "Ullmann, V.: Kritiken musikalischer Veranstaltungen der 'Freizeitgestaltung,'" Ms. T 1944, 27 reviews."

47. "Goethe und Ghetto," p. 93.

48. Adler, *Theresienstadt*, p. 594.

49. Adler, *Theresienstadt*, p. 622.

50. Pamela Tancsik, "Viktor Ullmann: Leben und Werk," in *Kontexte: Musica Judaica 1994*, ed. Vlasta Benetková, Vladimír Karbusický, Jitka Ludvová, and Marta Ottlová (Prague, 1995), pp. 49–61.

51. Bloch, "Viktor Ullmann's Vocal Arrangements," p. 80.

52. Ingo Schulz gives Karl Reiner's memoirs as a source; see *Viktor Ullmann: 26 Kritiken*, p. 18.

53. Paul Nettl, "Music," in *Jews of CS* 1:547–48.

54. Lubomír Peduzzi, *Pavel Haas: Život a dílo skladatele* (Brno 1993), p. 16; Vladimír Karbusický, "Pavel Haas: Vier Lieder auf Worte der chinesischen Poesie," in *Kontexte*, p. 90; Lubomír Peduzzi, "Složeno v Terezíně," in *Hudební rozhledy* 6 (1968), p. 152.

55. Peduzzi, "Složeno v Terezíně," illustration no. 28.

56. The Hebrew word *sof* = "end" enciphered in the violin score has previously been overlooked. It alludes to the "end of the war." Haas wrote this dedication in the fall of 1942, triggered by the news about the German debacle on the Eastern Front.

57. Peduzzi, *Pavel Haas*, p. 12.

58. Peduzzi, *Pavel Haas*, p. 49.

59. Karbusický, "Pavel Haas: Vier Lieder," pp. 90–115.

60. Karbusický, "Pavel Haas: Vier Lieder," p. 103.

61. "Liederabend Karl Bermann," in *Viktor Ullmann: 26 Kritiken*, p. 67.

62. Karas, *Music in Terezín*, pp. 121–24; Bloch, "Viktor Ullmann's Vocal Arrangements," p. 80.

63. Enclosure 1a, "Zikmund Schul," and enclosure 1b, "Bei Betrachtung von Schuls Sarg," in *Viktor Ullmann: 26 Kritiken*, pp. 89–91, 91–92.

64. Erik Polák, "Die Bedeutung der Zeitschriften im Leben der Theresienstädter Kinder und Jugend," in *Theresienstadt in der Endlösung*, pp. 164–72.

65. Hanuš Schimmerling, "Der Jüdische Jugend im Widerstand," in *Theresienstadt in der Endlösung*, p. 181.

66. Schimmerling, "Jüdische Jugend."

67. *Terezín Diary of Egon Redlich*, p. 78; Schmiedt, "Hechaluz in Theresienstadt," pp. 107–25.

68. Rothkirchen, "Zionist Character"; Adler, *Theresienstadt*, p. 589.

69. Polák, "Die Bedeutung der Zeitschriften," p. 171; Schimmerling, "Jüdische Jugend," p. 182.

70. Ernst Simon, "Jewish Adult Education in Nazi Germany as Spiritual Resistance," in LBIYB 1 (1956), pp. 68–104.

71. See *Profile: Yehuda Bacon* by H. G. Adler (London, 1972), 3 p.

72. Elena Makarová, *From Bauhaus to Terezín: Friedl Dicker-Brandeis and Her Pupils* (Jerusalem: Yad Vashem, 1990).

73. Otta Kraus, "Dětský blok v rodinném táboře v Birkenau," in *Terezínské listy* 9 (1978), pp. 18–28.

74. Kraus, "Dětský blok v rodinném."

75. Salmen Gradowski, *In Harts fun Gehinem: A Dokument fun Oyschwitser Sonderkommando* (Jerusalem 1977), pp. 35–92.

76. First publication: Otta Kraus and Erich (Schön) Kulka, *Továrna na smrt* (Prague, 1946), pp. 151–68.

77. Adler, *Theresienstadt*, pp. 609–11.

78. Feder, "Religious Life," pp. 53–58.

79. Utitz, *Psychologie*, pp. 61–62.

80. Utitz, *Psychologie*, p. 62.

81. Albert H. Friedländer, "Leo Baeck in Theresienstadt," and Zdeněk Jelínek, "Richard Feder und das Thesienstädter Ghetto," both in *Theresienstadt in der Endlösung*, pp. 119–30, 131–39.

82. Karel Ančerl, "Music in Terezín," in *Terezín*, p. 238.

83. Rudolf Franěk, "Brundibár," in *Terezín*, p. 256.

84. "15. Liederabend Karl Bermann," in *Viktor Ullmann: 26 Kritiken*, p. 67.

85. Berman, "Memories," p. 237.

86. Hana Volavková, ed., *I Never Saw Another Butterfly: Children's Drawings and Poems, Terezín 1942–1944* (Prague, 1965).

87. For a recent survey of the historiography of the Terezín ghetto, with the author's critical comments, see Miroslav Kryl, *Osud vězňů terezínského ghetta v letech 1941–1945* (Brno, 2000); Elena Makarová, Sergei Makarov, and Victor Kuperman, *University over the Abyss: The Story behind 489 Lectures in KZ Theresienstadt 1942–1944* (Jerusalem, 2000).

Epilogue

1. Vojtech Mastný, "Tradition, Continuity and Discontinuity in Recent Czechoslovak History," in *Die Tschechoslowakei 1945–1970*, ed. Nikolaus Lobkowicz and Friedrich Prinz (München, Wien, 1978), p. 86; Paul E. Zinner, *Communist Strategy and Tactics in Czechoslovakia, 1918–1948* (London, Dunmow, 1963), pp. 186–89.

2. The memorandum is reproduced in Rothkirchen, "Czechoslovak Government-in-Exile," pp. 190–96. For more detailed discussion see chapter 6.

3. See Dagan, "The Czechoslovak Government-in-Exile," pp. 482–83.

4. Quoted from a letter sent by Dr. Leo Zelmanovits addressed to Dr. Aryeh Tartakower, 8.3.1941; see also letter from Dr. Aryeh L. Kubowitzky (Kubovy) to Ernst Frischer, 24.5.1943, and Frischer's reply, 21.6.1943, all in CZA, A280/28.

5. See Kurt Wehle, "The Jews of Bohemia and Moravia, 1945–1948," in *Jews of CS*, 3:525.

6. For details see Peter Meyer et al., *The Jews in the Soviet Satellites* (Syracuse, 1953), pp. 76–92. On the circumstances of the scandalous nationalization, the so-called Varnsdorf affair, the cotton-velvet concern owned originally by Emil Beer, see Drtina, *Československo můj osud*, vol. 2, pt. 2, pp. 422–24; Šárka Nepalová, "Die jüdische Minderheit in Böhmen und Mähren in den Jahren 1945–1948—Restitutionsfälle," in *Theresienstädter Studien und Dokumente 1999*, pp. 341–42, 347.

7. Karel Kaplan, *Dva retribuční procesy*, pp. 31–33; Mečislav Borák, *Spravedlnost podle dekretu*; Tomášek and Kvaček, *Obžalovaná je vláda*.

8. *Český národ soudí K. H. Franka*, Státní oblastní archiv, Litoměřice, sign. LS 86/48.

9. For a full description of the friendly ties of the first postwar years see Ehud Avriel, *Open the Gates: The Dramatic Personal Story of "Illegal" Immigration to Israel* (New York, 1975), and his "Prague and Jerusalem: The Era of Friendship," in *Jews of CS* 3:554–55; *Československo a Izrael v letech 1947–1953*, Studie, ed. Jiří Dufek, Karel Kaplan, and Vladimír Šlosar (Prague, 1993); *Československo a Izrael 1945–1956: Dokumenty*, ed. Marie Bulinová, Jiří Dufek, Karel Kaplan, and Vladimír Šlosar (Prague, 1993).

10. The first arms deal was concluded with the help of Robert Adam, a one-time representative of the Brno Zbrojovka factory in Rumania, through his connection with General Heliodor Pika (formerly Czechoslovakia's military attaché in Rumania). Also instrumental was Uriel Doron (Dr. Otto Felix) of the Haganah. Avriel emphasizes the support of Foreign Minister Jan Masaryk and his deputy Vlado Clementis; see "Prague and Jerusalem," pp. 556–57.

11. Chanan Rosen, "Yahasey Yisrael-Tshekhoslovakia beTmurat haItim," in *Gesher* 2–3 (1959–60), pp. 270.

12. Rudolf Slánský (1901–52), vice-premier of Czechoslovakia and secretary general of the Czechoslovak Communist Party, together with thirteen other leading party functionaries, of whom eleven were Jews, were put on trial in 1950, charged with conspiracy against the state. They were sentenced to death and hanged in 1952. Three were sentenced to life imprisonment and freed in the sixties. All the victims, including Slanský, were posthumously rehabilitated. See Karel Kaplan, *Die politischen Prozesse in der Tschechoslowakei, 1948–1954* (Munich, 1986); Josefa Slánská, *Report on My Husband* (London, 1969); *Československo a Izrael 1947–1953*; *Československo a Izrael 1945–1956*; Meir Cotic, *The Prague Trial: The First Anti-Zionist Show Trial in the Communist Bloc* (New York, London, Toronto, 1987).

13. For a moving description of the historic days of the establishment of Israel's legation in Prague and the ensuing political changes see Ruth Klinger, *Zeugin und Zeit: Ein Lebensbericht* (Zürich, 1979), chapter 21; *Československo a Izrael v letech 1947–1953*, 1. Přátelství, pp. 9–23.

14. Václav Kopecký was known for his changing attitudes and frequent anti-Jewish outbursts, derogatory names—"bearded Solomons," etc., vŽONP 1.4.1947. See also chapter 7.

15. Avriel, "Prague and Jerusalem," p. 559.

16. The epic of these pilots who operated from the Žatec base was revealed in the reminiscences of Lieutenant-Colonel Gordon Levett, *Shabbes Goy* (Tel Aviv, 1990).

17. Avriel, "Prague and Jerusalem," p. 560.

18. A copy of this agreement is in YVA, o–59.

19. See *Documents on the Foreign Policy of Israel, October 1948–April 1949*, ed. Yehoshua Freundlich, vol. 2, doc. 332, 14.1.1949, p. 375; see also doc. 131, letter from Prague by E. Avriel to G. Meyerson, Moscow, 11.11.1948, p. 168; *Československo a Izrael 1945–1953*, 5. Od přátelství k nepřátelství, pp. 81–103.

20. Avriel, "Prague and Jerusalem," pp. 554–55.

21. Avriel, "Prague and Jerusalem," p. 558.

22. See Meyer et al, "Czechoslovakia," especially: "Exodus of 1949," pp. 147–49.

23. Masaryk was referring to the assistance given to him by Jewish and Zionist leaders during his campaign in World War I for the establishment of Czechoslovakia. See *Making of a State*, p. 222.

24. On Dr. Gustav Sicher, chief rabbi of Prague (1947–60) see prologue.

25. Dr. Richard Feder (1875–1970), a well-known teacher and preacher in the town of Kolín, author of *Židé a křesťanství* (Prague, 1919), acted as spiritual leader in Theresienstadt and from 1961 until his death as chief rabbi of Bohemia and Moravia. He compiled a Hebrew primer (*Halelujah*) for his pupils and later an almanac of Jewish stories, entitled *Židovské besídky*; after the war he wrote a book based on his wartime experiences: *Židovská tragédie; dějství poslední* (1947).

26. Kusin, *Intellectual Origins*.

27. For the Liblice conferences see Goldstücker et al., eds., *Franz Kafka aus Prager Sicht*; Eduard Goldstücker, "Die Prager deutsche Literatur als historische Phenomenon," in *Weltfreunde* (Prague, 1965), pp. 21–45.

28. Gordon Skilling, *Czechoslovakia's Interrupted Revolution* (Princeton NJ, 1976), p. 633.

29. Published in VŽONP (May 1968); for the English version see "Jewish Aspects of the Changes in Czechoslovakia," in Institute of Jewish Affairs in association with the World Jewish Congress, Background Paper no. 11 (July 1968), pp. 19–22.

30. Kusin, *Intellectual Origins*, p. 126.

31. For the letter addressed to Goldstücker and his answer see Robin A. Remington, ed., *Winter in Prague: Documents on Czechoslovak Communism in Crisis* (Cambridge, London, 1969), pp. 189–94.

32. See Remington, *Winter in Prague*, pp. 195–98.

33. Vilém Benda, "Byl prorok Isaáš agentem sionismu?" in *Reporter* 6 (1968).

34. Benda, "Byl prorok Isaáš."

35. Since 1971 a campaign has been waged in the press by anti-Zionist propagandists with a view to vilifying the Jewish leadership, charging it with collaboration with the Nazis. See Rothkirchen, "Zionist Character," p. 83.

36. Fuch's courageous address was published in *Věstník* (October 1973). For follow-up on the subject see reports published by the International Council of Jews from Czechoslovakia in its *ICJC Newsletter*, ed. K. Baum (London): no. 1 (January 1972), no. 3 (June 1973), no. 4 (February 1974).

37. See "Kritika devastace židovských kulturních památek v Československu a zamlčování úlohy Židů v čs. dějinách" (5.4.1989; 28/29), signed by Tomáš Hradílek, Dana Němcová, and Saša Vondra, spokesmen of Charter 77, in Vilém Prečan, ed., *Charta 77, 1977–1989: Od morální k demokratické revoluci* (Prague, 1990), pp. 363–70. These documents were reproduced *in extenso* in English. See "Czechoslovakia: Jewish Legacy and Jewish Present," introduced and annotated by Petr Brod, in *Soviet Jewish Affairs* 20, no. 1 (1990), pp. 57–65; Helena Krejčová, "The Czech Lands at the Dawn of the New Age (Czech Anti-Semitism 1945–1948)," in *Anti-Semitism in Post Totalitarian Europe* (Prague, 1993), pp. 115–24.

38. For a memorial tribute see Efraim Sicher, "The Concept of Work in the Writings of Chief Rabbi Dr. Gustav Sicher," in *Shvut*, Studies in Russian and East European history and Culture, Tel Aviv University, 5 (21) 1997, pp. 136–43.

39. See *ICJC Newsletter* (1976).

40. The contents of the article on Rabbi Loew were recorded in the community's German-language *Informationsbulletin* (December 1959).

41. A summary of the four articles written by Dvořáček, printed in *Věstník* upon the request of Dr. Desider Galský, was reproduced in *Informationsbulletin* (September 1982).

42. On lacunae in the historiography of the postwar period, see Livia Rothkirchen, "Czechoslovakia," in *The World Reacts to the Holocaust*, ed. David S. Whyman (Baltimore, 1996), pp. 179–99.

43. See Prečan, *Charta 77, 1977–1989*, n. 37, pp. 66–67.

44. Pasák, "Česky antisemitismus"; Bohumil Černý, *Vražda v Polné* (Prague, 1968), especially his "Závěr k zamýšlení" (Closing words for contemplation), pp. 211–14; Pfaff, "Německá kultura"; Jan Křen, "O Kafkovi, židovské otázce a antisemitismu, také českém," in *Svědectví* 18, no. 69 (1983), pp. 137–42; Milan Hauner, "Hodnoty a hodnocení v naší historiografii," in *150,000 slov* 4, no. 10 (1985), p. 11.

45. Josef Träger, *Egon Hostovský*, p. 134.

46. Černý, *Paměti*, vol. 4.

47. On his blatant anti-Semitic views and references to Jewish personalities, see Robert F. Lambert, "Dlužníci Václava Černého," in *Západ* (April, 1984), pp. 28–29; see also Hanuš Hájek's letter to the editor, in *Svědectví* 18, nos. 70–71 (1983), pp. 583–86.

48. For Václav Černý's accusation of Jews, see *Paměti*, vol. 4, pp. 444–45.

49. Jan Křen, "O Kafkovi," pp. 157–65, see Christoph Stölzl, *Kafkovy zlé Čechy: k sociální historii pražského žida* (Praha, 1997).

50. Stölzl, *Kafkovy zlé Čechy*, p. 142; see also Jan Křen, *Bílá místa v našich dějinách* (Prague, 1990), and his "Czech Historiography at a Turning Point," in *East European Politics and Societies* 6, no. 2 (Spring 1992), pp. 152–69.

51. There is general confusion about the exact number of Jews in the Czech Republic. As a rule the officially quoted number of those registered with the community amounts to around two thousand, one thousand of whom live in Prague. For a brief survey of the initial changes within the Prague Jewish community leadership in the wake of the November 1989 Velvet Revolution see Petr Brod, "Czechoslovakia," in *Institute of Jewish Affairs Research Report*, nos. 2–3 (London, April 1990); see "Interview with Dr. Desider Galský," in *Mladé rozlety*, no. 20, 15.5.1990; Petr Brod "Židé v poválečném Československu," in *Židé v novodobých dějinách*, pp. 147–62.

52. The findings of the Working Committee were published by the Terezín Initiative Institute: *Jewish Gold and Other Precious Metals, Precious Stones and Objects Made of Such Materials: Situation in the Czech Lands in the Years 1939 to 1945* (Prague, 2001), pp. 104–5.

53. See Václav Havel, "The New Year in Prague," in *New York Review of Books* 38, no. 5, 7.3.1991, p. 19.

Conclusions

1. Jan Tesař, *Mnichovský komplex: Jeho příčeny a důsledky* (Český Těšín, 2000).

2. Nahum Goldmann, *Memories: The Autobiography of Nahum Goldmann* (London: Weidenfeld and Nicholson, 1969), p. 145.

3. Oscar Jászi, *The Dissolution of the Habsburg Empire* (Chicago, 1964), p. 173; Milan Šimečka, *Kruhorá Obrana* (Paris, 1985), pp. 176–79.

Bibliography

Published Official Documents
Encyclopedias
Books, Articles, and Dissertations

PUBLISHED OFFICIAL DOCUMENTS

Actes et documents du Saint Siège relatifs à la Seconde Guerre Mondiale, vol. 9, *Le Saint Siège et les Victimes de la Guerre, Janvier–Decembre 1943*, Vatican, 1975.

Akten zur deutschen auswärtigen Politik, 1918–1945, Serie D, 1937–1941, vol. 4, *Die Nachwirkungen von München, Oktober 1938–März 1939*, Berlin, 1951.

Documents on British Foreign Policy (DBFP), 1919–39, vol. 3., ed. E. L. Woodward and Rohan Butler. Third Series, 10 vols., London, 1946–70.

Documents on German Foreign Policy 1918–1945, from the Archives of the German Foreign Ministry. Series D. 13 vols. Washington DC, 1949–66.

Documents on the Foreign Policy of Israel, October 1948–April 1949, vol. 2, ed. Yehoshua Freundlich, Jerusalem, 1984.

Documents sur l'activité du Comité International de la Croix Rouge concernant le Ghetto de Theresienstadt, Geneva, 26.6.1990, Annex 25.

Inter Arma Caritas: The Work of the International Committee of the Red Cross during the Second World War, Geneva, 1947.

Rapport du Comité International de la Croix Rouge sur son activité pendant la Seconde Guerre Mondiale (1er Septembre 1939–30ieme Juin 1947), 3 vols., Geneva, 1948.

Sbírka zákonů a nařízení Československé Republiky 1, no. 1415/1939; 10.2.1939.

State of Israel, Ministry of Justice. *The Trial of Adolf Eichmann*, Record of Proceedings in the District Court of Jerusalem, vols. 2, 3, Jerusalem, 1992, 1993.

Těsnopisecké zprávy o schůzích Národního shromáždění republiky československé 1918–1938, Session no. 266, Prague, 1919–39, 27.4.1933.

Těsnopisecké zprávy o schůzích Prozatimního Národního shromáždění republiky československé, Tisky 1930 II (210).

Trials of War Criminals before the Nuremberg Military Tribunals (NID-13463), vol. 13, 1947–49.

Verbrecher in Richterroben, Dokumente über die verbrecherische Tätigkeit von 230 nazischen Richtern und Staatsanwalten auf dem okkupierten Gebiet der Tschechoslowakischen Republik, die gegenwartig in der westdeutschen Justiz dienen, Prague, 1960.

ENCYCLOPEDIAS

Encyclopedia Judaica, vol. 13, col. 304; vol. 14, cols. 1418–1420, Jerusalem, 1971.

Slavonic Encyclopedia, ed. Joseph S. Rouček, New York, 1949.

BOOKS, ARTICLES, AND DISSERTATIONS

Adams, A. C. *The History of the Jews from the War with Rome to the Present Time*, London, 1887.

Adler, H. G. *Profile: Yehuda Bakon*, London, 1972.

——. *Theresienstadt 1941–1945: Das Antlitz einer zwangsgemeinschaft*, rev. ed., Tübingen: J. C. B. Mohr–Paul Siebeck, 1960.

——. *Die verheimlichte Wahrheit: Theresienstädter Dokumente*, Tübingen, 1958.

Albright, William F. "Israel—Prophetic Vision and Historical Fulfillment," in *Israel: Its Role in Civilization*, ed. Moshe Davis, New York, 1956.

Alexander, Edward. "George Eliot's Rabbi," in *Commentary* 92, July 1991.

Amort, R. *Heydrichiáda*, Prague, 1964.

Ančerl, Karel. "Music in Terezín," in *Terezín, 1941–1945*, ed. František Ehrmann, Otto Heitlinger, and Rudolf Iltis, Prague, 1965.

Association Hongroise des Affaires Étrangères, *La déportation des Hongrois de Slovaquie*, Budapest, 1947.

Auředničková, Anna. *Tři léta v Terezíně*, Prague, 1947.

Avineri, Shlomo. *The Making of Modern Zionism: Intellectual Origins of the Jewish State*, New York, 1981.

Avriel, Ehud. *Open the Gates: The Dramatic Personal Story of "Illegal" Immigration to Israel*, New York, 1975.

——. "Prague and Jerusalem: The Era of Friendship," in *The Jews of Czechoslovakia*, vol. 3, ed. Avigdor Dagan and Lewis Weiner, Philadelphia, 1984.

Baeck, Leo. "A People Stands before its God," in *We Survived: The Stories of the Hidden and the Hunted in Nazi Germany*, ed. Eric H. Boehm, New Haven, 1949.

Baker, Vaughan Burdin. "Selective Inattention: The Runciman Mission to Czechoslovakia, 1938," in *East European Quarterly* 24, no. 4, January 1991.

Bakon, Yehuda. Testimony in *The Trial of Adolf Eichmann*, Session no. 68, vol. 3, Jerusalem, 1993.

Bankier, David. "The Germans and the Holocaust: What Did They Know?" in YVS 20, 1990.

Bartoš, František M. "Židé v Čechách v době Husově," in *KČŽ* 35, 1915–16.

Bass, A. "Ze židovské obce náboženské vystoupili," in VŽONP, 6.12.1938.

Bass, Eduard. "Židé v českém tisku," in *Přítomnost* 16, 19.1.1939.

Bauer, František. *Můj boj, Hitler o sobě a o svých cílech*, Prague, 1936.

Bauer, Yehuda. *From Diplomacy to Resistance: A History of Jewish Palestine*, Philadelphia, 1970.

Bauman, Zygmunt. *Modernity and the Holocaust*. Ithaca: Cornell University Press, 2001.

Bednařík, Petr. "Antisemitismus v denících "Venkov' a "Večer' v období Druhé Republiky," in *Postavení a osudy židovského obyvatelstva v Čechách a na Moravě v letech 1939–1945: Sborník studií*, ed. Helena Krejčová and Jana Svobodová, Prague, 1998.

Benda, Lucian. *Židé v našem hospodářství*, Prague, 1939.

Benda, Julien. *The Treason of the Intellectuals*, New York, 1978.

Benda, Vilém. "Byl prorok Isáš agentem sionismu?" in *Reporter* 6, 1968.

Beneš, Edvard. *The Memoirs of Dr. Edvard Beneš: From Munich to New War and New Victory*, transl. Godfrey Lias, London, 1954.

——. *Mnichovské dny: Paměti*, Prague, 1968.

——. *Od Mnichova k nové válce a k novému vítězství*, Prague, 1947.

——."The Organization of Postwar Europe," in *Foreign Affairs*, an American Quarterly Review, January 1942.

——. *Šest let exilu a druhé světové války: Řeči, projevy a dokumenty z r. 1938–1945*, Prague, 1946.

Beneš, Václav L. "Czechoslovak Democracy and Its Problems, 1918–1920," in *A History of the Czechoslovak Republic 1918–1948*, Princeton NJ, 1973.

Ben-Tov, Arieh. *Facing the Holocaust in Budapest: The International Committee of the Red Cross and the Jews in Hungary, 1943–1945*, Dordrecht, 1988.

Berdych, Václav. *Mauthausen*, Prague, 1959.

Berger, Natalia, ed. *Where Cultures Meet: The Story of the Jews of Czechoslovakia*, Tel Aviv, 1990.

Bergl, Josef. "Die Ausweisung der Juden aus Prag im Jahre 1744," in Samuel Steinherz, *Die Juden in Prag*, Prague, 1927.

Bergmann, S. Hugo. "Masaryk in Palestine," in *Thomas G. Masaryk and the Jews*, ed. Ernst Rychnovsky, New York, 1941.

——. *Tagebücher & Briefe*, Band 1, 1901–48, ed. Miriam Sambursky, Königstein, 1985.

Bernfeld, Shimon. *Sefer haDemaoth*, vol. 2, Berlin, 1924.

Bertoň, Stanislav F. "Das Attentat auf Reinhard Heydrich vom 27. Mai 1942: Ein Bericht des Kriminalrats Heinz Pannwitz," in VZ 4, 1985.

Bílek, Bohumil. *Fifth Column at Work*, London, 1945.

"The Birth of an Army: Jews Responding to Czechoslovakia's Call," in *Palestine Post*, 24.11.1939.

Blau, Bruno. "Yidn in der Tshekhoslovakay," in *Yiddishe ekonomik* 3, 1939.

Bloch, David. "Viktor Ullmann's Yiddish and Hebrew Vocal Arrangements in the Context of Jewish Music Activity in Terezín," in *Viktor Ullmann, Die Referate des Symposions anlässlich des 50. Todestags 14.–16. Oktober 1994 und ergänzende Studien*, ed. Hans-Günter Klein, Hamburg, 1996.

Blodig, Vojtěch. "Die letzte Phase der Entwicklung des Ghetto Theresienstadt," in *Theresienstadt in der "Endlösung der Judenfrage"*, ed. Miroslav Kárný, Vojtěch Blodig, and Margita Kárná, Prague, 1992.

Bock, Eve. "The German-Jewish Writers of Prague: Interpreters of Czech Literature," LBIYB 23, 1978.

Bodensieck, Heinrich. "Das Dritte Reich und die Lage der Juden in der Tschechoslowakei nach München," in VZ 9, 1961.

Bondy, Gottlieb, and Franz Dworsky. *Zur Geschichte der Juden in Böhmen, Mähren und Schlesien von 906 bis 1620*, Prague, 1906.

Bondy, Ruth. *Elder of the Jews: Jakob Edelstein of Theresienstadt*, trans. Evelyn Abel, New York: Grove, 1989.

Bor, Josef. *The Terezín Requiem*, transl. Edith Pargeter, London, 1963.

Borák, Měčislav. *Spravedlnost podle dekretu: Retribuční soudnictví v ČSR a Mimořádný lidový soud v Ostravě 1945–1948*, Ostrava, 1998.

——. *Transport do tmy: První deportace evropských Židů*, Ostrava, 1994.

Boyens, Armin. "The World Council of Churches and Its Activities on Behalf of the Jews in the Nazi Period," in *Judaism and Christianity under the Impact of National Socialism, 1919–1945*, ed. Otto D. Kulka and Paul R. Mendes-Flohr, Jerusalem, 1987.

Bracher, Karl Dietrich. *The German Dictatorship: The Origin, Structure and Effects of National Socialism*, London, 1971.

Brada, Fini. "Emigration to Palestine," in *The Jews of Czechoslovakia*, vol. 2, Philadelphia, 1971.

Bradbrook, M. C. "Otakar Vočadlo 1895–1974," in *Slavonic and East European Review* 53, no. 133, October 1975.

Brandes, Detlef. "Das Problem der deutschen Minderheiten in der Politik der Alliierten in den Jahren 1940–1945: Das tschechische Beispiel," in J. Křen, V. Kural, and D. Brandes, *Integration oder Ausgrenzung: Deutsche und Tschechen 1890–1945*, Bremen, 1986.

———. *Die Tschechen unter deutschem Protektorat*, vol. 1: *Besatzungspolitik, Kollaboration und Widerstand im Protektorat Böhmen und Mähren bis Heydrichs Tod, 1939–1942*, 2 vols., Munich-Vienna, 1969.

———. *Grossbritannien und seine osteuropäischen Alliierten 1939–1943: Die Regierungen Polens, der Tschechoslowakei und Jugoslawiens im Londoner Exil vom Kriegsausbruch bis zur Konferenz von Teheran*, München, 1988.

———. *Menschen im Exil: Eine Dokumentation der Sudetendeutschen Sozial-demokratischen Emigration von 1938 bis 1945*, Stuttgart, 1974.

Breitman, Richard. *Official Secrets: What the Nazis Planned, What the British and Americans Knew*, London, New York, 1998.

Bretholz, Bertold. *Geschichte der Juden in Mähren im Mittelalter*, Brünn, 1934.

———. *Quellen zur Geschichte der Juden im Mähren*, Prague, 1935.

Brod, Max. "Erfahrung in Ostjüdischen Schulwerk," in *Der Jude*, 1916–17.

———. "Prag-Wien-Erinnerungen," in *The Jews of Austria*, ed. Josef Frankel, London, 1967.

———. *Streitbares Leben 1884–1968*, Munich, 1969.

Brod, Petr. "Czechoslovakia," in *Institute of Jewish Affairs Research Report*, nos. 2–3, London, April 1990.

———. "Czechoslovakia: Jewish Legacy and Jewish Present," in *Soviet Jewish Affairs* 20, no. 1, 1990.

———. "Židé v poválečném Československu," in *Židé v novodobých dějinách: Soubor přednášek FF ÚK*, ed. Václav Veber, Prague, 1997.

Brod, Toman. *Tobrucké krysy*, Prague, 1967.

Brod, Toman, and Eduard Čejka. *Na západní frontě*, Prague, 1963.

Brokešová, E. *Ty a já*, Prague, 1947.

Brompton, Henry. *The Politics of the German Occupation in the Protectorate of Bohemia and Moravia: A Case Study of a Totalitarian "Breakthrough,"* University of Southern California, Los Angeles, 1974.

Brož, A. *The Rise of the Czechoslovak Republic*, London, 1919.

Bruegel, Wolfgang Johann. *Czechoslovakia before Munich: The German Minority Problem and the British Appeasement Policy*, Cambridge, London, 1973.

———. "The Germans in Pre-war Czechoslovakia," in *A History of the Czechoslovak Republic 1918–1948*, ed. Victor S. Mamatey and Radomír Luža, Princeton NJ, 1973.

———. "Jews in Political Life," in *The Jews of Czechoslovakia*, vol. 2, Philadelphia, 1971.

Bubeník, Jaroslav, and Jiří Křesýan. "Zjištování národnosti a židovská otázka," in *Postavení a osudy židovského obyvatelstva v Čechách a na Moravě v letech 1939–1945: Sborník studií*, ed. Helcna Krejčová and Jana Svobodová, Prague, 1998.

Buber, Martin. *Drei Reden über Judentum*, Frankfurt, 1916, 1920.

———. *On Judaism*, ed. Nahum N. Glatzer, New York, 1967.

———. *Tři řeči o židovství*, Prague, 1912.

Buber-Neumann, Margaret. *Mistress to Kafka: The Life and Death of Milena*, London, 1966.

Bulinová, Marie, Jiří Dufek, Karel Kaplan, and Vladimír Šlosar, eds. *Československo a Izrael 1945–1956: Dokumenty*, Prague, 1993.

Campbell, F. Gregory. *Confrontation in Central Europe*, Chicago, London, 1975.

Čapek, J. B. "Velký rabbi pražský," in *Kostnické Jiskry* 14, no. 30, 20.10.1960.

Čapek, Karel. *President Masaryk Tells His Story*, London, 1935.

———. "Návrat k malosti," in *Lidové noviny*, 16.12.1934.

———. "Promluvíme si o tom," in *Lidové noviny*, 2.12.1934.

———. "Smrt dne 12. brežna 1938," in *Lidové noviny*, 13.3.1938.

Čapek, M. "Comenius and the Moral Problem," in *Comenius*, ed. Vratislav Bušek, New York, 1972.

Čelakovský, Jaromír. "Příspěvky k dějinám židů v době Jagellonské," in *Časopis Českého Musea* 12, 1898.

Černá, Jana. *Milena Jesenská*, Frankfurt, 1985.

Černý, Bohumil. *Most k novému životu*, Prague, 1967.

———. *Vražda v Polné*, Prague, 1968.

Černý, Bohumil, Jan Křen, Václav Kural, and Milan Otáhal, eds. *Češi, Němci a odsun*, Prague, 1990.

Černý, František, ed. *Vzpomínky českých divadelníků na německou okupaci a druhou světovou válku*, Prague, 1965.

Černý, Václav. *Křik koruny české, 1938–1945*, Brno, 1992.

———. *Kultur im Widerstand*, Köln, 1979.

———. *Kultur im Widerstand: Prag 1938–1945*, vol. 1, ed. F. Boldt. 8 vols. Bremen, 1979.

———. *Paměti*, Toronto, 1982.

Český národ soudí K. H. Franka: Mimořádný lidový soud, Prague, Orbis, 1947.

"Československý odboj po 15 březnu 1939," in *Hlas revoluce*, no. 14, 8.4.1972.

Československý zpravodaj, Informační Bulletin Čsl. gcnerálního konsulátu v Jerusalemě pro čechoslováky v Palestině, Iráku a Iránu, no. 19 / 4, 6.8.1941.

Chládková, Ludmila. "Karel Poláček v Terezíně," in *Terezínské listy* 3, 1973.

Chmela, Leopold. *The Economic Aspects of the German Occupation of Czechoslovakia: Sources and Documents*, Prague, 1948.

Chmelář, Josef. *Political Parties in Czechoslovakia*, Prague, 1926.

Churchill, Winston S. *The Second World War*, vol. 1: *The Gathering Storm*, 7th ed., London, 1953.

Cohen, Gary B. *The Politics of Ethnic Survival: Germans in Prague, 1861–1914*, Princeton NJ, 1981.

——. "Ethnicity and Urban Population Growth: The Decline of the Prague Germans, 1880–1910," ed. Keith Hitchins, in *Studies in East European Social History*, vol. 2, Leiden, 1981.

——. "Jews in German Society: Prague 1860–1914," *Central European History* 10 (1977): 28–54.

Comenius, Jan Amos. *The Bequest of the Unity of Brethren*, ed. Matthew Spinka, Chicago, 1940.

Cotic, Meir. *The Prague Trial: The First Anti-Zionist Show Trial in the Communist Bloc*, New York, London, Toronto, 1987.

Čvančara, Jaroslav. "Atentát na Heydricha; od hypotéz k faktům; Transport z ráje," in *Týden* (June 1995); *Mladý svět* (September 1994).

Czech, Ludwig. *Symbolischer Staatsakt für einen unbeugsamen Demokraten*, München, 1993.

Dagan, Avigdor. "The Czechoslovak Government-in-Exile and the Jews," in *The Jews of Czechoslovakia*, vol. 3, ed. Avigdor Dagan and Lewis Weiner, Philadelphia, 1984.

——. "The Jewish Identity of František Langer," in *Review of the Society for the History of Czechoslovak Jews* 2, ed. Lewis Weiner and Gertrud Hirschler, New York, 1988–89.

——. "Jewish Themes in Czech Literature," in *The Jews of Czechoslovakia*, vol. 1, Philadelphia, 1968.

——. "The Press," in *The Jews of Czechoslovakia*, vol. 1, Philadelphia, 1968.

De Lacroix, François. *Le livre jaune française: Documents diplomatiques 1938–1939*, Paris, 1939.

Deník Otty Wolfa 1942–1945. Introduction by Ludvík Václavek and Ivan Klíma, Prague, 1997.

Deníky Jiřího Ortena: Poesie—myšlenky—zápisky, Prague, 1958.

Dobroszycki, Lucjan, ed., *The Chronicles of the Łodz' Ghetto 1941–1944*, New Haven, London, 1984.

"Docent Dr. Josef Fischer *In memoriam*," in *VŽONP*, no. 11, November 1968.

Doležal, Jan. *Česká kultura za Protektorátu: Školství, písemnictví, kinematografie*, Prague, 1996.

Doležal, Jiří. *Jediná cesta*, Prague, 1966.

——. "Úvahy o české šlechtě v času První Republiky," in *Svědectví* 77, 1986.

Doležal, Jiří, and Jan Křen. *Czechoslovakia's Fight 1938–1945: Documents on the Resistance Movement of the Czechoslovak People*, Prague, 1964.

Donath, Oskar. "F. X. Šalda a židovství," in *VŽONP*, 30.4.1937.

——. "Jüdisches in der neuen tschechischen Literatur," in *Jahrbuch der Gezellschaft für Geschichte der Juden in der Čechoslovakischen Republiek* 3 (1931).

——. "Siegfried Kapper," in *Jahrbuch der Gesellschaft für die Geschichte der Juden in der Čechoslovakischen Republik* 6, 1934.

——. *Židé a židovství v české literatuře 19. a 20. století*, 2 vols., Brno, 1923, 1930.

Drábek, Jaroslav. "The Assassination of Reinhard Heydrich," in *Czechoslovakia Past and Present*, ed. Miloslav Rechcígl, vol. 1, The Hague, Paris, 1968.

——. *Z časů dobrých a zlých*, Prague, 1992.

Dressler, Jaroslav. "Kafkova Milena," in *Milena, Cesta k jednoduchosti*, Engelfelden, 1982.

Drtina, Prokop. *Československo můj osud*, 2 vols., Toronto, 1982.

Dufek, Jiří, Karel Kaplan, and Vladimír Šlosar, eds. *Československo a Izrael v letech 1947–1953*, Prague, 1993.

Dulles, Allen. *Germany's Underground*, New York, 1947.

Ehrmann, František, Otto Heitlinger, and Rudolf Iltis, eds. *Terezín, 1941–1945*, Council of Jewish Communities in the Czech Lands, Prague, 1965.

Einhorn, Milada, and Erich Einhorn, eds. *Golden Prague*, Prague, 1989.

Eisner, Pavel. *Franz Kafka in Prague*, New York, 1950.

——. "Host Otokar Fischer," in *KČŽ* 57, 1938–39.

——. "Jews in the Literature of the Czech Lands," in *Jewish Studies: Essays in Honor of the Very Reverend Dr. Gustav Sicher Chief Rabbi of Prague*, ed. Rudolf Iltis, Prague, 1955.

——. "Jinoch Exodus," in *Židovská ročenka* 5719, 1958–59.

——. "Kapitola o česko-německém soužití," in *Přítomnost* 4, 19.5.1927.

——. "Položte tam kytičku," in *VŽONP*, 1.5.1956.

Eliášová, Jaroslava, and Tomáš Pasák. "Poznámky k Benešovým kontaktům s Eliášem ve druhé světové válce," in *Historie a vojenství*, no. 1, 1967.

Eliot, Thomas S. "Tradition and the Individual Talent," in *The Sacred Wood*, London, 1934.

Engel, David. *In the Shadow of Auschwitz: The Polish Government-in-Exile and the Jews 1939–1942*, Chapel Hill NC, 1987.

Erben, Eva. *Mich hat man vergessen: Erinnerungen eines jüdischen Mädchens*, Weinheim, Basel, 1996.

Erdely, Eugen V. "Das erste jüdische Konzentrationslager," in *Informationsbulletin*, no. 4, 1979.

——. *Germany's First European Protectorate: The Fate of Czechs and Slovaks*, London, 1942.

Eschwege, Helmut. "Resistance of German Jews against the Nazi Regime," in *LBIYB* 15, 1970.

Färber, Meir. "Jewish Lodges and Fraternal Orders Prior to World War II," in *The Jews of Czechoslovakia*, vol. 2, Philadelphia, 1971.

Favez, Jean-Claude. *Das Internationale Rote Kreuz und das Dritte Reich*, Zürich, 1989.

Feder, Richard. "Religious Life in Terezín," in *Terezín 1941–1945*, ed. František Ehrmann, Otto Heitlinger, and Rudolf Iltis, Prague, 1965.

——. *Židé a křest'anství*, Prague, 1919.

——. *Židovská tragédie, dějství poslední*, Kolín, 1947.

Feierabend, Ladislav. *Ve vládách druhé republiky*, New York, 1961.

——. *Ve vládě protektorátu*, New York, 1962.

——. *Ve vládě v exilu*, 2 vols., Washington, 1965, 1966.

Fiedler, Jiří. *Jewish Sights of Bohemia and Moravia*, Prague, 1991.

Firt, Julius. *Knihy a osudy*, Köln, 1972.

Fischer, Otakar. *Duše a svět*, Prague, 1929.

Fischl, Viktor. "Líc a rub," in *Židovské zprávy*, 4.11.1938.

Fischl, Viktor, ed. *Dr. Karel Steinbach: Svědek téměř stoletý*, Köln, 1988.

Fleischmann, Gustav. "The Religious Congregation, 1918–1938," in *The Jews of Czechoslovakia*, vol. 1, Philadelphia, 1968.

Forrer, Friedrich. "Hundert Jahre Rotes Kreuz," in *Der Monat*, no. 181, October 1963.

Franěk, Jiří. "Fragezeichen um Karel Poláček," in *Theresienstädter Studien und Dokumente 1997*, ed. Miroslav Kárný, Raimund Kemper, and Margita Kárná, Prague, 1997.

Franěk, Rudolf. "Brundibár," in *Terezín, 1941–1945*, ed. František Ehrmann, Otto Heitlinger, and Rudolf Iltis, Prague, 1965.

Frankl, Michal. "The Background of the Hilsner Case: Political Antisemitism and Allegation of Ritual Murder 1896–1900," in JB 36, 2000.

———. "Can We, the Czech Catholics be Antisemites? Antisemitism at the Dawn of the Czech Christian-Socialist Movement," in JB 33, 1997.

Franková, Anita. "Erfassung der jüdischen Bevölkerung in Böhmen im 18 und in der ersten Hälfte des 19 Jahrhunderts," in JB 6, 1970.

Fremund, Karel. *Konec pražského gestapa*, Prague, 1972.

Fremund, Karel, and Václav Král, eds. *Lesson from History: Documents Concerning Nazi Policies, Germanization and Extermination in Czechoslovakia*, Prague, 1962.

French, A. *Czech Writers and Politics 1945–1969*, Boulder CO, 1982.

Friedländer, Albert H. "Leo Baeck in Theresienstadt," in *Theresienstadt in der "Endlösung der Judenfrage,"* ed. Miroslav Kárný, Vojtěch Blodig, and Margita Kárná, Prague, 1992.

Friedmann, František. *Einige Zahlen über die tschechoslowakischen Juden*, Schriften für Diskussion des Zionismus, no. 9, Prague, 1933.

———. *Mravnost či oportunita: Několik poznámek k anketě akademického spolku "Kapper" v Brně*, Prague, 1927.

Friedmann, Philip. "Aspects of the Jewish Communal Crisis in the Period of the Nazi Regime," in *Essays on Jewish Life and Thought*, ed. J. L. Blau, New York, 1959.

From a Correspondent. "The Nazi Plan: A Stony Road to Extermination," in *London Times*, 16.12.1939.

Frýd, Norbert. *Lahvová pošta, aneb konec posledních sto let*, Prague, 1971.

Fuchs, František. "Die tschechish-jüdische Widerstandsbewegung in Theresienstadt," in *Theresienstädter Studien und Dokumente 1997*, ed. Miroslav Kárný, Raimund Kemper, and Margita Kárná, Prague, 1997.

Fučík, Julius. *Notes from the Gallows*, New York, 1948.

———. *Reportáž psaná na oprátce: První úplné kritické a komentované vydání*, ed. František Janáček et al., Prague, 1995.

Fučíková, Gusta. *Vzpomínky na Julia Fučíka*, Prague, 1961.

Gajan, Koloman. "Postoj T. G. Masaryka k židovství a sionismu za první republiky," in *Hilsnerova aféra a česká společnost 1899–1999*, ed. Miloš Pojár, Prague, 1999.

———. "T. G. Masaryk a Nahum Sokolov," in *Židovská ročenka 5763*, 2002–3.

Gajanová, Alena. *Dvojí tvář předmnichovského fašismu*, Prague, 1962.

Gebhart, Jan. "Někteří z mnohých, k činnosti Josefa Fischera, Karla Bondyho a Miloše Otto Bondyho v českém odboji za druhé světové války," in *Postavení a osudy židovského obyvatelstva v Čechách a na Moravě v letech 1939–1945: Sborník studií*, ed. Helena Krejčová and Jana Svobodová, Prague, 1998.

Gebhart, Jan, and Jan Kuklík. *Dramatické i všední dny Protektorátu*, Prague, 1996.

"Gedenkblatt für Dr. Paul Eppstein," reprint in *Jüdische Sozialarbeit*, Frankfurt, Jahrgng 4, no. 3–4, 9.18.1959.

Gelber, N. M. "Kavim leKidmat Toldoteha shel haZionut beBohemia uMoravia," in *Prag ve Yerushalaim: Essays in Memory of Leo Herrmann*, ed. Felix Weltsch, Jerusalem, 1954.

Gerlach, Wolfgang. "Document: Armin T. Wegner's Letter to German Chancellor Adolf Hitler, Berlin, Easter Monday, April 11, 1933," in *Holocaust and Genocide Studies* 8, no. 3, Winter 1994.

Gil (Lipshitz), J. *A History of the Jewish Infantry Brigade Group*, Tel Aviv, 1950.

Ginz, Peter, and Chava Pressburger. *The Road through Theresienstadt* (exhibition catalogue), Yad Vashem (Art Museum), 1984.

Gissing, Vera. *Pearls of Childhood*, London, 1988.

Gold, Hugo. *Die Juden und Judengemeinden Mährens in Vergangenheit und Gegenwart*, Brno, 1929.

Gold, Hugo, ed. Steinherz Festschrift, "Samuel Steinherz, zum 80 Geburtstage," in *Zeitschrift für die Geschichte der Juden in der Tschechoslowakei* 5, no. 2, Prague, 1938.

Goldmann, Nahum. *Memories: The Autobiography of Nahum Goldmann: Sixty Years of Jewish Life*, transl. Helen Sebba, London: Weidenfeld and Nicholson, 1969.

——. "Recollections of Czech Jewry," in *Review of the Society for the History of Czechoslovak Jews* 1, New York, 1987.

Goldstücker, Eduard. "Die Prager deutsche Literatur als historische Phenomenon," in *Weltfreunde: Konferenz über die Prager deutsche Literatur*, Prague, 1965.

——. *The Germans and the Jews*, Los Angeles, 1973.

——. "Jews between Czechs and Germans around 1848," in *The Czech National Revival: The Germans and the Jews*, Los Angeles, 1972.

——. "Prague German Literature: Its Socio-Historical Setting," in *The Czech National Revival*, Los Angeles, 1972.

Goldstücker, Eduard, František Kaufman, and Paul Reimann, eds. *Franz Kafka aus Prager Sicht*, Prague, 1963.

Golz-Godlust, Marie. *Der grosse Tag*, Stuttgart, 1988.

Goshen, Zeev. "Eichmann und die Nisko-Aktion in Oktober 1939: Eine Fallstudie zur NS-Judenpolitik in der letzten Etappe vor der 'Endlösung,'" in *vz* 29, 1981.

Gottlieb, František. "Julius Zeyer (1841–1901)," in *Židovská ročenka* 5730, 1970–71.

Gottwald, Klement. *Deset let*, Prague, 1947.

Gradowski, Salmen. *In Harts fun Gehinem: A Dokument fun Oyschwitser Sonderkommando*, Jerusalem, 1977.

Graus, František. "Prague 1389–1419–1422," in *Struktur und Geschichte, Vorträge und Vorschungen* 7, Singmaringen, 1971.

Green, Gerald. *The Artists of Terezín*, New York, 1985.

Grňa, Josef. *Sedm roků na domácí frontě*, Brno, 1968.

Grňa-Vlk, Josef. *Partyzánské historky*, Brno, 1946.

Grňová, Jana. *Svatobořický tábor*, Brno, 1948.

Grossmann, Kurt R. "Refugees to and from Czechoslovakia," in *The Jews of Czechoslovakia*, vol. 2, Philadelphia, 1971.

Guth, Otakar. "1918 (28.10) 1938," in KČŽ 57, 1938–39.

Haas, Leo. "Die Affäre der Theresientstädter Maler," in *Terezín, 1941–1945*, ed. František Ehrmann, Otto Heitlinger, and Rudolf Iltis, Prague, 1965.

Hahn, Fred. "The Jews among the Nations in Bohemia and Moravia," in *Religion and Nationalism in Eastern Europe and the Soviet Union*, Boulder, London, 1987.

Hájek, Hanuš. Letter to the editor, in *Svědectví* 18, no. 70–71, 1983.

Hájková, Alena. "Die sieben Tapferen," in *Theresienstadt in der "Endlösung der Judenfrage,"* ed. Miroslav Kárný, Vojtěch Blodig, and Margita Kárná, Prague, 1992.

———. "Příběh skupiny Otakara Weisla," in *Nisko 1939–1994*, ed. Ludmila Nesládková, Ostrava, 1995.

Hájková, Alena, and František Janáček. "Na okraj motáků: Vysvětlivky a komentáře," in Julius Fučík, *Reportáž psaná na oprátce: První úplné, kritické a komentované vydání*, Prague, 1995.

Harris, Jeremy D. "Broadcasting the Massacres: An Analysis of the BBC's Contemporary Coverage of the Holocaust," in YVS 25, 1996.

Hartmann, Moritz. *Gesammelte Werke*, vol. 1, Stuttgart, 1874.

Hasek, Jaroslav. *The Good Soldier Svejk*, transl. Cecil Parrott. London: Penguin Books, 1973.

Hauner, Milan. "Hodnoty a hodnocení v naší historiografii," in *150,000 slov* 4, no. 10 (1985).

Hauner, Milan, Radomír V. Luža, Theodor Procházka, Stanley B. Winters, and Jonathan Zorach, "Munich 1938 from the Czech Perspective," roundtable, in *East Central Europe* 8, nos. 1–2, 1981.

Havel, Václav. "The New Year in Prague," in *New York Review of Books* 38, no. 5, 7.3.1991.

Havránek, Jan. "The Development of Czech Nationalism," in *Austrian History Yearbook*, vol. 3, pt. 2, 1967.

———. "Fascism in Czechoslovakia," in *Native Fascism in the Successor States, 1918–1945*, ed. Peter F. Sugar, Santa Barbara CA, 1971.

Heiber, Helmut. "Zur Justitz im Dritten Reich: Der Fall Eliáš," in VZ 3, 1955.

Heinemann, John L. *Hitler's First Foreign Minister, Constantin Freiherr von Neurath: Diplomat and Statesman*, London, 1979.

Herben, Jan. "T. G. Masaryk über Juden und Antisemitismus," in *Masaryk und das Judentum*, ed. Ernst Rychnovský, Prague, 1931.

Heřman, Jan. "The Conflict between the Jewish and non-Jewish Population in Bohemia before the 1541 Banishment," in JB 6, no. 2, 1970.

———. "The Development of Bohemian and Moravian Jewry, 1918–1938," in *Papers in Jewish Demography, 1969*, ed. U. O. Schmelz, P. Glikson, and S. Della Pergola, Jerusalem, 1973.

———. "The Evolution of the Jewish Population in Bohemia and Moravia, 1754–1953," in *Papers in Jewish Demography, 1977*, Jerusalem, 1980.

Hermelink, Heinrich. *Kirche im Kampf: Dokumente des Widerstands und des Aufbaus der Evangelischen Kirche in Deutschland*, Tübingen, Stuttgart, 1950.

Heroes and Victims, Preface by Jan Masaryk, London: Czechoslovak Ministry of Foreign Affairs and Information Service, 1945.

Herrmann, Hugo. "Zur čechisch-jüdischen Frage," in *Selbstwehr*, 7.4.1911.

Herzl, Theodor. *The Diaries of Theodor Herzl*. Entry of August 30, 1899, ed. and. transl. Marvin Lowenthal, New York, 1956.

— —. "Die Jagd in Böhmen," originally printed in *Die Welt*, November 5, 1897, Czech translation in *Židovský kalendář*, 1938–39.

Heumos, Peter, and Peter Becher, eds. *Die Emigration aus der Tschechoslowakei nach Westeuropa und den Nahen Osten 1938–1945*, München, 1989.

——. *Drehscheibe Prague—Staging Point Prague: German Exiles 1933–1939*, München, 1989.

Hilberg, Raul. *The Destruction of European Jews: A Documented Narrative History*, Chicago, 1961.

——. "The Judenrat as a Conscious or Unconscious Tool," in *Patterns of Jewish Leadership in Nazi Europe, 1933–1945*, Proceedings of the Third Yad Vashem International Conference, April 1977, ed. Yisrael Gutman and Cynthia J. Haft, Jerusalem, 1979.

Hilsnerova aféra a česká společnost 1899–1999: Sborník přednášek na Univerzitě Karlově v Praze ve dnech 24.–26. listopadu 1999, ed. Miloš Pojar, Prague, 1999.

Himmler, Heinrich. *Geheimreden 1933 bis 1945 und andere Ansprachen*, ed. B. F. Smith and A. F. Peterson, Frankfurt, Wien, 1974.

"Himmler's Vermerk über seinen Besuch bei Mussolini," vz 4 (1956).

Hinsley, F. H. *British Intelligence in the Second World War*, vol. 1, London, 1979.

Hiršal, Josef. *Vínek vzpomínek*, Prague, 1992.

Hirschler, Gertrud. "The History of Agudath Israel," in *The Jews of Czechoslovakia*, vol. 2, Philadelphia, 1971.

Hitler, Adolf. *The Testament of Adolf Hitler: The Hitler-Bormann Documents, February–April 1945*, ed. Francois Genond, London, 1960.

Hoch, Charles. *The Political Parties in Czechoslovakia*, Czechoslovak Sources and Documents, no. 9, Prague, 1936.

Hoffmann, Stanley. *Decline or Renewal? France since the 1930s*, New York, 1974.

Homádka, J. L. "Křesťané a židé," published in *Křesťanská revue*, quoted in *Židovské zprávy*, 24.2.1939.

Hostovský, Egon. "The Czech-Jewish Movement," in *The Jews of Czechoslovakia*, vol. 2, Philadelphia, 1971.

——. "Participation in Modern Czech Literature," in *The Jews of Czechoslovakia*, vol. 1, Philadelphia, 1968.

——. *Letters from Exile*, transl. Ann Křtil, London, 1942.

——. *Vzpomínky, studie a dokumenty o jeho díle a osudu*, ed. Rudolf Sturm, Toronto, 1973.

Huták, B. *With Blood and Iron: The Lidice Story*, London, 1957.

Hyndráková, Anna, Helena Krejčová, and Jana Svobodová, eds., *Prominenti v ghettu Terezín 1942–1945: Dokumenty*, Prague, 1996.

Iggers, Wilma A. "The Flexible National Identities of Bohemian Jewry," in *East Central Europe* 7, pt. 1, 1980.

——. *The Jews of Bohemia and Moravia: A Historical Reader*, Detroit, 1992.

Iltis, I. "K osmdesátým sedmým narozeninám J. B. Foerstra," in VŽONP, 15.1.1947.

Iltis, Rudolf, ed. *Jewish Studies: Essays in Honor of the Very Reverend Dr. Gustav Sicher Chief Rabbi of Prague*, Prague, 1955.

In Memoriam Marie Schmolka, London, 1944, ed. Fay Grove. Reprint Tel Aviv, 1970.

"In Namen des Deutschen Volkes," in *Todesurteile des Volksgerichthofs*, Luchterhand, 1981.

Ivanov, Miroslav. *The Assassination of Reinhard Heydrich, May 27, 1942*, London, 1973.

Jablonický, Jozef. *Z ilegality do povstania, kapitoly z občianského odboja*, Bratislava, 1969.

Jabotinsky, Vladimir. "Tribute to T. G. Masaryk's 80th Birthday," in *Jewish Daily Bulletin*, 7.3.1930.

Jäckel, Eberhard. *Hitlers Weltanschauung*, Tübingen, 1969.

Jacobi, Gerhard. *Racial State: The German Nationalities Policy in the Protectorate of Bohemia-Moravia*, New York: Institute of Jewish Affairs, 1944.

Jacobi, Walter. *Golem, metlo Čechů: Rozklad českého nacionalizmu*, Prague, 1941.

——. *Země zaslíbená*, Prague, 1943.

Jahrbuch der Gesellschaft für die Geschichte der Juden in der Čechoslovakischen Republik, ed. Samuel Steinherz, 9 vols., Prague, 1929–38.

Jakobson, Roman. "The Language and Writings of the Czech Jews in the Přemyslid Age," in *The Cultural Almanac ROK*, Moravian Library, New York, 1957.

——. "Řeč a písemnictví českých Židů v době přemyslovské." Moravian Library, ROK, 1957; reprinted in *Židovská ročenka*, 1992–93.

Jakobson, Roman, and Morris Halle. "Language and Literature of Bohemian Jewry in Early Middle Ages," in *For Max Weinreich on his Seventieth Birthday: Studies in Jewish Languages, Literature and Society*, The Hague, 1955.

Janáček, František. *Dva směry v začiatkoch národného odboja: October 1938–June 1940*, Bratislava, 1962.

Janoušek, Oldřich, ed. *Z počátku odboje 1938–1941*, Prague, 1969.

Jászi, Oscar. *The Dissolution of the Habsburg Empire*, Chicago, 1964.

Jelínek, Zdeněk. "Richard Feder und das Theresienstädter Ghetto," in *Theresienstadt in der "Endlösung der Judenfrage,"* ed. Miroslav Kárný, Vojtěch Blodig, and Margita Kárná, Prague, 1992.

Jellinek, Fritz. *Die Kriese des Bürgers*, Zürich, 1936.

Jesenská, Milena. "Denní zprávy na posledních stránkách," in *Přítomnost* 15, 12.10.1938.

——. "Dobrá rada nad zlato", in *Přítomnost* 16, 8.3.1939.

——. "Jak tato doba si zahrála s našimi nervy," in *Přítomnost* 15, 29.12.1938.

——. "Nad naše síly," in *Přítomnost* 15, 10.10.1938.

——. "O umění zůstat stát," *Přítomnost* 16, 5.4.1939.

——. "Poslední dny Karla Čapka," in *Přítomnost* 16, 11.1.1939.

——. "Pověz kam utíkáš—povím ti, kdo jsi," in *Přítomnost* 15, 14.9.1938

——. "Proč nemluvíte mladí?" in *Přítomnost* 16, 25.1.1939.

——. "Statisíce hledají zemi nikoho," in *Přítomnost* 15, 20.7.1938.

Jewish Gold and Other Precious Metals, Precious Stones and Objects Made of Such Materials:

Situation in the Czech Lands in the Years 1939 to 1945, Report by a team of experts, Prague 2001.

Jirásková, Marie. "Stručná zpráva o trojí volbě (M. Jesenská, J. von Zedtwitz a J. Nachtmann v roce 1939 a v čase následujícím)," in *Literární Noviny*, no. 40, 5.10.1995.

Jirotka, Zdeněk. "Židovské listy v letech 1939–1944," unpublished dissertation, Faculty of Journalism, Charles University, Prague.

Josko, Anna. "The Slovak Resistance Movement," in *A History of the Czechoslovak Republic 1918–1948*, ed. Victor S. Mamatey and Radomír Luža, Princeton NJ, 1993.

Das jüdische Prag: Eine Sammelschrift, Prague, 1917, 2nd ed. Introduction by Robert Weltsch, Kronberg/TS, 1978.

Jungk, Peter Stephan. *Franz Werfel, Eine Lebensgeschichte*, Frankfurt, 1987.

Jurášek, Stanislav. *Předpisy o židovském majetku a další předpisy Židů se tykající*, Prague, 1940.

K. J., "The Jewish Question in Bohemia," in *Přítomnost*, no. 3, 3.2.1943.

Kadlec, Josef M. *Svatá země v československém odboji*, Prague, 1947.

Kafka, František. "Odešel František Langer," v ŽONP, 1.9.1965.

——. "Od zašlápnutých výhonků k mrtvým tvůrcům," in *Židovská ročenka* 5725, 1964–65.

Kafka, Franz. *Brief an den Vater*, München, 1960.

——. *Dearest Father: Stories and Other Writings*, transl. E. Kaiser and E. Wilkins, New York, 1954.

——. *The Diaries of Franz Kafka 1914–1923*. Entry of 2.12.1921, New York, 1965.

——. *Letters to Milena*, ed. Willi Haas, New York, 1953.

Kalendarium 1941, in *Hefte von Auschwitz* 2, 1959.

Kaplan, Karel. *Die politischen Prozesse in der Tschechoslowakei, 1948–1954*, München, 1986.

——. *Dva retribuční procesy: Komentované dokumenty 1946–1947*, Prague, 1994.

Karas, Joža. *Music in Terezín 1941–1945*, New York, 1985.

Karbusický, Vladimír. "Pavel Haas: Vier Lieder auf Worte der Chinesischen Poesie," in *Kontexte: Musica Judaica 1994*, ed. Vlasta Benetková, Vladimír Karbusický, Jitka Ludvová, and Marta Ottlová, Prague, 1995.

Kárný, Miroslav. "Die Judenfrage in der nazistischen Okupationspolitik," in *Historica* 21, Prague, 1982.

——. "Die Theresienstädter Herbsttransporte," in *Theresienstädter Studien und Dokumente 1997*, ed. Miroslav Kárný, Raimund Kemper, and Margita Kárná, Prague, 1997.

——. "Jakob Edelsteins letzte Briefe," in *Theresienstädter Studien und Dokumente 1997*, ed. Miroslav Kárný, Raimund Kemper, and Margita Kárná, Prague, 1997.

——. *"Konečné řešení": Genocida českých židů v německé protektorátní politice*, Prague, 1991.

——. *Tajemství a legendy Třetí říše*, Prague, 1983.

——. "Terezínské balíčky ve světle archívních dokumentů," in *Vlastivědný sborník Litoměřicko* 23, 1987.

——. "Vorgeschichte des Regierungsverordnung über die Rechtsstellung der Juden im öffentlichen Leben," in *Judaica Bohemiae* 30–31, 1996.

Kárný, Miroslav, and Ludvík Václavek. "Deník Otto Wolfa z let 1942–1943," in *Okresní archív v Olomouci*, 1987.

———. "Otto Wolfs Tagebuch 1942–1943," in *Germanistisches Jahrbuch* DDR-ČSSR, 1987–88.

Kárný, Miroslav, Vojtěch Blodig, and Margita Kárná, eds. *Theresienstadt in der "Endlösung der Judenfrage*," Prague, 1992.

Kárný, Miroslav, Jaroslava Milotová, and Dagmar Moravcová, eds. *Anatomie okupační politiky hitlerovského Německa v "Protektorátu Čechy a Morava*," Sborník k problematice dějin imperialismu, vol. 21, Prague, 1987.

Kárný, Miroslav, Jaroslava Milotová, and Margita Kárná, eds. *Deutsche Politik im "Protektorat Böhmen und Mähren" unter Reinhard Heydrich 1941–1942: Eine Dokumentation*, Berlin, 1997.

Kastner, Rudolf. Der Bericht des jüdischen Rettungskomitees aus Budapest 1942–1945, typescript, Geneva, 1946.

Kaufmannová, Heda. Memoir published in two parts in the *samizdat* issue *Historické Studie*, nos. 21 and 22, 21.6.1987 and 22.1.1988.

Kautman, František. "Kafka, Hašek, Weiner a Jesenská," in *Svědectví*, čtvrtletník pro politiku a kulturu, 69, 1983.

———. *Masaryk, Šalda, Patočka*, Prague, 1990.

Kaznelson, Siegmund. "Erinnerungen an gemeinsame Kampfjahre," in *Dichter, Denker, Helfer: Max Brod zum 50. Geburstag*, ed. Felix Weltsch, Moravská Ostrava, 1934.

Kelly, David. *The Czech Fascist Movement 1922–1942*, Columbia University Press, New York, 1995.

Kennan, George F. *From Prague after Munich: Diplomatic Papers 1938–1940*, Princeton NJ, 1968.

Kermish, Joseph. "The Activities of the Council for Aid to Jews "Żegota," in *Rescue Attempts during the Holocaust*, Proceedings of the Second Yad Vashem International Historical Conference, April 1974, ed. Yisrael Gutman and Efraim Zuroff, Jerusalem, 1977.

Kerner, Robert J., ed. *Czechoslovakia: Twenty Years of Independence*, Berkeley, Los Angeles, 1940.

Kestenberg-Gladstein, Ruth. "Čechen und Juden in altväterischer Zeit," in JB 4, no. 1, 1968.

———. "The Jews between Czechs and Germans in the Historic Lands, 1848–1918," in *The Jews of Czechoslovakia*, vol. 1, Philadelphia, 1968.

———. *Neuere Geschichte der Juden in den böhmischen Ländern*, Erster Teil: Das Zeitalter der Aufklärung, 1780–1830, Tübingen, 1969.

Kieval, Hillel J. *The Making of Czech Jewry: National Conflict and Jewish Society in Bohemia 1870–1918*, New York, Oxford, 1988.

Kisch, Egon Erwin. *Tales from Seven Ghettos*, London, 1948.

Kisch, Guido. *Der Lebensweg eines Rechtshistorikers: Erinnerungen*, Singmaringen, 1975.

———. *Die Prager Universität und die Juden, 1348–1848*, Moravská Ostrava, 1935; 2nd ed., Amsterdam, 1969.

———. *In Search of Freedom: A History of American Jews from Czechoslovakia*, London, 1949.

———. "Jewish Historiography in Bohemia, Moravia, Silesia," in *The Jews of Czechoslovakia*, vol. 1, Philadelphia, 1968.

Kladivová, Vlastimila. "K historii činnosti ilegální KSČ v Praze v letech 1939–1942," in *Acta Universitatis Carolinae Philosophica et Historica*, no. 1, Proti fašismu a válce, 1962.

Klapálek, Karel. *Ozvěny bojů—vzpomínky z druhé světové války*, Prague, 1966.

Klarsfeld, Serge. *Vichy-Auschwitz: Le role de Vichy dans la solution finale de la question juive en France, 1943–1944*, Paris, 1985.

Kleinbergcr, A. F. "The Didactics of Rabbi Loew of Prague," in *Scripta Hyerosolymitana* 13, Jerusalem, 1963.

Klinger, Ruth. *Zeugin und Zeit: Ein Lebensbericht*, Zürich, 1979.

Kocourek, Ludomír. "Das Schicksal der Juden in Sudetengau im Licht der erhaltenen Quellen," in *Theresienstädter Studien und Dokumente 1997*, ed. Miroslav Kárný, Raimund Kemper, and Margita Kárná, Prague, 1997.

Kohn, Hans. "Before 1918 in the Historic Lands," in *The Jews of Czechoslovakia*, vol. 3, Philadelphia, 1971.

———. "Stimmen," in *Der Jude*, 1923.

Kohn, Jindřich. *Asimilace a věky*, 2 vols., Prague, 1936.

K(ojan), J(an). "Z paměti židomila," in *Židovská ročenka* 5740, 1979–80.

Kokoškovi, Jaroslav, and Stanislav Kokoškovi. *Spor o Agenta A54*, Prague, 1994.

Kokoška, Stanislav. "Zwei unbekannte Berichte aus dem besetzten Prag über die Lage der jüdischen Bevölkerung des Protektorats," in *Theresienstädter Studien und Dokumente 1997*, ed. Miroslav Kárný, Raimund Kemper, and Margita Kárná, Prague, 1997.

Kolář, Martin. "Hussite Songs, Discovered and Reviewed by M. Kolář," in *Památky archeologické a místopisné* 9, 1873.

Kolb, Eberhard. *Bergen-Belsen: Geschichte des "Aufenthaltlagers" 1943–1945*, Hannover, 1962.

Koňák, Zdeněk. "Jiří Orten," in *Hlas revoluce*, no. 18, 2.9.1966.

Kopecký, Václav. "K otázce antisemitismu": Problémy našeho boje za svobodu a budování lidové demokratické republiky," in *Cesta k svobodě*, no. 2, London, September 1944.

Kopold, Bedřich. "Nejen utrpení také i odplata," in *Nisko 1939–1994*, ed. Ludmila Nesládková, Ostrava, 1995.

Korbel, Josef. *Twentieth Century Czechoslovakia: The Meaning of its History*, New York, 1977.

Kosmala, Beate. "Ungleiche Opfer in extremer Situation: Die Schwierigkeit der Solidarität in okkupierten Polen," in *Solidarität und Hilfe für Juden während der NS-Zeit*, Regionalstudien 1, ed. Wolfgang Benz and Julianne Wetzel, Berlin, 1996.

Král, Josef. *Parašutisté: Reportáže z okupace*, Liberec, 1967.

Král, Václav. *Otázky hospodářského a socialního vývoje v českých zemích v letech 1938–1945*, 3 vols., Prague, 1957–1959.

Král, Václav, ed., *Lesson from History: Documents Concerning Nazi Policies for Germanization and Extermination*, Prague, 1961.

Kraus, Erich. Observations on Prague Jewish leadership, 1939–45,"Cíle ŽNO a ŽRS" (The aims of ŽNO and ŽRS). Copy in author's possession.

Kraus, F. R. "But Lidice Is in Europe," in *Terezín, 1941–1945*, ed. František Ehrmann , Otto Heitlinger, and Rudolf Iltis, Prague, 1965.

Kraus, J. S. "Or-Tomid: Spolek českých židů pro pěstování bohoslužby jazykem českým a hebrejským," in KČŽ 4, 1884–85.

Kraus, Otta. "Dětský blok v rodinném táboře v Birkenau," in *Terezínské listy* 9 (1978).

Kraus, Otta, and Erich Kulka (Schön). *Továrna na smrt*, Prague, 1946.

Krejčí, František. "Assimilation und Zionismus vom ethischen Stadpunkt," *Selbstwehr*, 11.6.1909.

Krejčová, Helena. "Českožidovská asimilace," in Ctibor Rybár, *Židovská Praha*, Glosy k dějinám a kultuře, Prague, 1991.

———. "The Czech Lands at the Dawn of the New Age (Czech Anti-Semitism 1945–1948)," in *Anti-Semitism in Post Totalitarian Europe*, Prague, 1993.

———. "Kalendář českožidovský 1881–1938," in *Židovská ročenka* 5750 (1989–90).

Krejčová, Helena, Jana Svobodová, and Anna Hyndráková, eds., *Židé v protektorátu: Die Juden im Protektorat Böhmen und Mähren: Hlášení Židovské náboženské obce v roce 1942, dokumenty*, Prague, 1997.

Křen, Jan. *Bílá místa v našich dějinách*, Prague, 1990.

———. "Czech Historiography at a Turning Point," in *East European Politics and Societies* 6, no. 2, Spring 1992.

———. "O Kafkovi, židovské otázce a antisemitismu, také českém," in *Svědectví* 18, no. 69, 1983.

———. "Vojenský odboj na počátku okupace Československa 1938–1940," in *Historie a vojenství*, 1961.

Krížková, Marie Rut. "Básník smrti a lásky," in *Židovská ročenka* 5733, 1972–73.

Kroener, Bernhard R., Rolf-Dieter Müller, and Hans Umbreit. *Das Deutsche Reich und der Zweite Weltkrieg: Organisation und Mobilisierung des Deutschen Machtbereichs*, vol. 5, pt. 1, Stuttgart, 1988.

Kronbauer, R. I. "Alexander Brandeis a jeho přátelské styky s českými umělci výtvarnými," in KČŽ 22, 1902–3.

Kryl, Miroslav. "Die deportationen aus Theresienstadt nach der Osten im Spiegel des Tagebuchs Willy Mahlers," in *Theresienstädter Studien und Dokumente 1995*, ed. Miroslav Kárný, Raimund Kemper, and Margita Kárná, Prague, 1995.

———. "Fritz Ullmann und seine Hilfe für die Theresienstädter Haftlinge," in *Theresienstädter Studien und Dokumente 1997*, ed. Miroslav Kárný, Raimund Kemper, and Margita Kárná, Prague, 1997.

———. *Osud vězňů terezínského ghetta v letech 1941–1945*, Brno, 2000.

Kuděla, Jiří. "Pražští židovští knihtiskaři, knihkupci a antikváři v 17. až 19. století," in *Documenta Pragensia* 9, 1990.

Kukánová, Zlatuše. "Seznam osob popravených za prvního stanného práva ve dnech 28. září až do 28. listopadu 1941," in *Sborník historick* 18, Prague, 1985.

———. "Seznam žen popravených z rozhodnutí stanného soudu v Praze, ve dnech 30. května až 3. července 1942," in *Sborník historick* 23, Prague, 1990.

Kuklík, Jan. "Antifašistická kultura proti Mnichovu," in *Mnichov 1938*, Prague, 1988.

———. *K problematice vzniku národní fronty v domácím odboji: Vývoj odbojové organizace PVVZ na území Čech v letech 1939–1941*, Prague, 1978.

———. "Kontrapropaganda v ilegálním tisku v letech 1939–1941," in *Historie a vojenství*, no. 1, 2000.

———. "Petiční výbor "Věrni zůstaneme' v odbobí Mnichova a za druhé Republiky," in ČsČH 17, no. 5, 1969.

Kulka, Erich. "Jews in the Czechoslovak Armed Forces during World War II," in *The Jews of Czechoslovakia*, vol. 3, Philadelphia, 1981.

———. "Nisko a účast ostravských Židů v boji československých vojsk proti nacistickému Německu v druhé světové válce," in *Nisko 1939–1994*, ed. Ludmila Nesládková, Ostrava 1995.

Kulko, Otto D. "Hayehadut haTschechit be'pros haShoah" (Ghetto in an annihilation camp), in *Gesher* 2–3, September 1969.

———. "Leberur hamediniut hayehudit shel ha-S.D. beartzot hakvushot harishonot," in *Yalkut Moreshet*, no. 18, Tel Aviv, November 1974.

Kuna, Milan. "Ester—rezistentní hra o záchraně Židů s hudbou Karla Reinera (Terezín 1943–1944)," in *Hudební věda* 31, 1994.

Kusin, Vladimir V. *The Intellectual Origins of the Prague Spring: The Development of Reformist Ideas in Czechoslovakia, 1956–67*. Cambridge Russian, Soviet and Post-Soviet Studies 6. Cambridge: Cambridge University Press, 2002.

———. *Hudba na hranicích života*, Prague, 1990.

Kvaček, Robert. "The Rise and Fall of Democracy," in *Bohemia in History*, ed. Mikuláš Teich, Cambridge, 1998.

Kvaček, Robert, and Dušan Tomášek. *General Alois Eliáš: Jeden český osud*, Prague, 1996.

Kwiet, Konrad. "Problems of Jewish Resistance Historiography," in LBIYB 24, 1979.

La deportation des Hongrois de Slovaquie, Association Hongroise des Affaires Étrangères, Budapest, 1947.

Laborie, Pierre. "The Jewish Statutes in Vichy France and Public Opinion," YVS 22, 1992.

Lágus, Karel. "Židé v boji proti hitlerismu," VŽONP, 1.5.1965.

Lagus, Karel, and Josef Polák. *Město za mřížemi*, Prague, 1964.

Lambert, Robert F. "Dlužníci Václava Černého," in *Západ*, April 1984.

Landes, Zdeněk. "O antisemitismu u nás," in *Židovské zprávy*, 30.6.1926, 7.9.1926.

———. "Přítomnost svědčí" in *Židovské zprávy*, 24.2.1939.

Langer, František. *Byli a bylo*, Prague, 1963.

———. *My Brother Jiří*, New York, 1961.

———. "Za války," in *Vzpomínky českých divadelníků na německou okupaci a druhou světovou válku*, ed. František Černý, Prague, 1965.

Langer, Jiří. *Devět Bran aneb chasidů tajemství*, Prague, 1992.

———. *Me'at Tsori*, Tel Aviv, 1944.

Laqueur, Walter. *The Terrible Secret: Suppression of the Truth about Hitler's "Final Solution,"* Boston, Toronto, London, 1980.

Lederer (Leda), Eduard. "Memories of Masaryk," in *Thomas G. Masaryk and the Jews*, ed. Ernst Rychnovský, New York, 1941.

———. *Žid v dnešní společnosti*, Prague, 1902.

Lederer, Zdeněk. *Ghetto Theresienstadt*, London, 1953.

Lehár, Lubomír. "Gestapo a odbojová skupina PVVZ," in *Historie a vojenství*, nos. 6–7, 1968.

Leist, Claus. "Philipp Manes: A Theresienstadt Chronicle," in *Journal of Holocaust Education* 6, no. 2, Autumn 1997.

Levett, Gordon. *Shabbes Goy*, Tel Aviv, 1990.

Lewis, Bernard. "Jews and Judaism between Two Cultures. Palimpsests of Jewish History: Christian, Muslim and Secular Diaspora," in Papers from the Tenth World Congress of Jewish Studies, *Jewish Studies* 30, 1990.

Lexa, John G. "Anti-Jewish Laws and Regulations in the Protectorate of Bohemia and Moravia," in *The Jews of Czechoslovakia*, vol. 3, Philadelphia, 1984.

Lieben, Salomon Hugo. "Briefe von 1744–1748 über die Austreibung der Juden aus Prag," in *JGGJČR* 4, 1932.

Lieben, Salomon Hugo, ed. *Die jüdischen Denkmäler in der Tschechoslowakei*, Prague, 1934.

Liehm, Antonín J. "Egon Hostovský," in *Generace*, Prague, 1988.

Lion, J., and L. Lukas. *Das Prager Ghetto*, Prague, 1959.

Lockhart, R. H. B. *Comes the Reckoning*, London, 1947.

Lón, František, Zdeněk Filip, and Karel Sommer. "Príšpěvek k historickému boji komunistů olomouckého kraje za vytvoření národní fronty proti okupaci v letech 1939–1941," in Acta Universitatis Palackianae Olomucensis, *Historica* 1, 1960.

Loewenstein, Karl. *Minsk: Im Lager der deutschen Juden*, Bonn, 1961.

Ludvová, Jitka. "Viktor Ullmann (1898–1944)," in *Hudební věda* 16, 1979.

Lukeš, Igor. "Czech Partial Mobilization in May 1938," in *Journal for Contemporary History* 31, no. 4, 1996.

Lützow, Count Franz von. *Bohemia: An Historical Sketch*, London, 1939.

Luža, Radomír. "The Communist Party of Czechoslovakia and the Czech Resistance, 1939–1945," in *Slavic Review* 28, December 1969.

———. "The Czech Resistance Movement," in *A History of the Czechoslovak Republic 1918–1948*, ed. Victor S. Mamatey and Radomír Luža, Princeton NJ, 1973.

———. *The Transfer of the Sudeten Germans: A Study of Czech-German Relations, 1933–1962*, New York, London, 1964.

Macek, Josef. *The Hussite Movement in Bohemia*, Prague, 1958.

MacDonald, Callum. *The Killing of SS Obergruppenführer Reinhard Heydrich*, New York, 1989.

Machta, Antonín. *Pankrác-Terezín*, Prague, 1946.

Mackenzie, Compton. *Dr. Beneš*, London, 1946.

Maimann, Samuel. *Das Mährische Jerusalem*, Prostějov, Selbstverlag, 1937.

Mainus, František. *Totální nasazení*, Brno, 1970.

Makarová, Elena. "From Bauhaus to Terezín: Friedl Dicker-Brandeis and Her Pupils," in *Yad Vashem Catalogue*, Jerusalem, 1990.

———. "Die Akademie des Überlebens," in *Theresienstädter Studien und Dokumente 1998*, ed. Miroslav Kárný, Raimund Kemper, and Margita Kárná, Prague, 1998.

Makarová, Elena. Sergei Makarov, and Victor Kuperman, eds. *University over the Abyss: The Story behind 489 Lectures in KZ Theresienstadt 1942–1944*, Jerusalem, 2000.

Mamatey, Victor, and Luža Radomír, eds. *A History of the Czechoslovak Republic, 1918–1948*, Princeton NJ, 1973.

Manfred, George. "Refugees in Prague 1933–1938," in *The Jews of Czechoslovakia*, vol. 2, Philadelphia, 1971.

Marcus, Gerhart. "Vorwort eines der Initiatoren" in *Viktor Ullmann, Die Referate des*

Symposions anlässlich des 50. Todestags 14–16 Oktober 1994 und ergänzende Studien, ed. Hans-Günter Klein, Hamburg, 1996.

Marek, Jan. "Sonderlager," in *Židovská ročenka* 5741, 1981.

——. "Zápisky z boje," unpublished MS, Děčín, 1968.

Mareni, Oskar A. "The *Erbrichterei* and Its Children" (Jerusalem, 1987–88), original letter in German, Yad Vashem Archives, 07/7-1.

Margry, Karel. "Theresienstadt (1944–1945): The Nazi Propaganda Film Depicting the Concentration Camp as Paradise," *Historical Journal of Film* 12, no. 2, 1992.

Marrus, Michael. "Coming to Terms with Vichy," in *Holocaust and Genocide Studies* 9, no. 1, Spring 1995.

Martinec, Jan. "Doktor chudých," in *Židovská ročenka* 5739, 1978–79.

März, Paul D. "Haha'avara Hachekhit—hatzala be'sha'at tzara," in *Prag ve Yerushalaim*: Essays in Memory of Leo Herrmann, ed. Felix Weltsch, Jerusalem, 1954.

——. "Trumat yehudey tshekhoslovakia lebinyan haaretz," in *Gesher* 2–3, September 1969.

Masaryk, Jan. *Speaking to My Country*, London, 1944.

Masaryk, T. G. *Národnostní filosofie*, Prague, 1905.

——. *The Making of a State: Memoirs and Observations, 1914–1918*, New York, 1927.

Mastný, Vojtech. *Czechs under Nazi Rule: The Failure of National Resistance, 1939–42*, New York, 1971.

——. "Tradition, Continuity and Discontinuity in Recent Czechoslovak History," in *Die Tschechoslowakei 1945–1970*, Nikolaus Lobkowicz and Friedrich Prinz, München, Wien, 1978.

McCagg, William O., Jr. *A History of Habsburg Jews, 1670–1918*, Bloomington, 1989.

McGovern, Hugh Hamilton, trans. "May," in *Translation*, N. Braybrooke and E. Icing, London, 1947.

Meissner, Alfred. *Geschichte meines Lebens*, Wien, Teschen, 1884.

Memorandum of the Czechoslovak Government on the Reign of Terror in Bohemia and Moravia under the Regime of Reinhard Heydrich, London: Czechoslovak Ministry of Foreign Affairs, c. 1942.

Mendelsohn, Ezra. *The Jews in East Central Europe between the World Wars*, Bloomington, 1983.

Mendes-Flohr, Paul R., and Jehuda Reinharz, eds. *The Jew in the Modern World: A Documentary History*, New York, 1984.

Merell, Jan. "How They Suffered and Died: A Catholic Priest Testifies to the Suffering of the Jews in the Little Fortress of Terezín," in *Terezín, 1941–1945*, František Ehrmann, Otto Heitlinger, and Rudolf Iltis, Prague, 1965.

Meyer, André. "Peter Kiens Libretto zum Kaiser von Atlantis: Ein Text voller Anspielungen," in *Viktor Ullmann, Die Referate des Symposions anlässlich des 50. Todestags 14–16 Oktober 1994 und ergänzende Studien*, ed. Hans-Günter Klein, Hamburg, 1996.

Meyer, Peter, et al. "Czechoslovakia," in *The Jews in the Soviet Satellites*, Syracuse NY, 1953.

Meyhofer, Rita. "Berliner Juden und Theresienstadt," in *Theresienstädter Studien und*

Dokumente 1996, ed. Miroslav Kárný, Raimund Kemper, and Margita Kárná, Prague, 1996.

Michel, Henri. "Jewish Resistance and the European Resistance Movement," in YVS 7, 1968.

———. *La guerre de l'ombre:; La résistance en Europe*, Paris, 1970.

———. *The Shadow War: Resistance in Europe 1939–1945*, London, 1972.

Migdal, Ulrike, ed. *Und die Musik spielt dazu: Chansons und Satiren aus dem KZ Theresienstadt*, Munich, Zürich, 1986.

Milotová, Jaroslava. "Die Zentralstelle für jüdische Auswanderung in Prag: Genesis und Tätigkeit bis zum Anfang des Jahres 1940," in *Theresienstädter Studien und Dokumente 1997*, ed. Miroslav Kárný, Raimund Kemper, and Margita Kárná, Prague, 1997.

Míšková, Alena. "Von Schönerer zum Genozid?" in *Židé v Sudetech: Die Juden im Sudetenland*, Prague, 2000.

Moravec, František. *Master of Spies: The Memoirs of General František Moravec*, London, 1975.

Moreillon, Jacques. "Red Cross Knew in 1942 of Massacre of Jews but Kept Silent," in *Jerusalem Post*, 31.8.1988.

Morse, Arthur D. *While Six Million Died*, New York, 1968.

Moskowits, Moses. "The Jewish Situation in the Protectorate of Bohemia and Moravia," in *Jewish Social Studies* 4, January 1942.

Moulis, Miloslav. *Mládež proti okupantům*, Prague, 1966.

Müllerová, Blanka. "Hans Krása: Kapitoly ze života a díla skladatele," Ph.D. thesis, Prague, 1966.

Muneles, Otto. *Bibliografický přehled židovské Prahy*, Prague, 1956.

Muneles, Otto, and Jan Heřman, eds. *Prague Ghetto in the Renaissance Period*, Prague, 1965.

Münzer, Zdenka. "The Old-New Synagogue in Prague: Its Architectural History," in *The Jews of Czechoslovakia*, vol. 2, Philadelphia, 1971.

Namier, Lewis B. *The Case for Bohemia*, London, 1919.

———. *Diplomatic Prelude 1938–1939*, London, 1952.

Nazi Dokumente sprechen: Sborník konference konané v listopadu 1997 v Kroměříši, Kroměříš, 1998.

Neher, André. *Le puits de l'exil*, Paris, 1987.

Němec, Ludvík. "Solution of the Minorities Problem," in *A History of the Czechoslovak Republic 1918–1948*, Victor S. Mamatey and Radomír Luža, Princeton NJ, 1973.

Němec, Petr. "Das tschechische Volk und die nationalsozialistische Germanisierung des Raumes," in *Bohemia*, 1991.

Nepalová, Šárka. "Die jüdische Minderheit in Böhmen und Mähren in den Jahren 1945–1948—Restitutionsfälle," in *Theresienstädter Studien und Dokumente 1999*, ed. Miroslav Kárný, Raimund Kemper, and Margita Kárná, Prague, 1999.

Nesládková, Ludmila, ed. *Nisko 1939–1994: The Case of Nisko in the History of the "Final Solution of the Jewish Problem,"* Ostrava, 1995.

Nettl, Paul. "Music," in *The Jews of Czechoslovakia*, vol. 1, Philadelphia, 1968.

Neumannová, Zdenka. "Protižidovská propaganda," in *Šest let okupace Prahy*, Prague, 1946.

Neuschl, Robert. *Křesťanská sociologie*, vol. 11, Brno, 1898.

Nežárecký, Josef B. *Židé v minulosti a přítomnosti: Příspěvek k řešení palčivého problému*, Prague, 1919.

Nielsen, Frederic W. *Reminiszenzen 1934–1979: Ein Beitrag zur Gegenwartsbewaltigung*, Stuttgart, 1980.

Nižňanský, Eduard. *Židovská komunita na Slovensku medzi československou parlamentnou demokráciou a slovenským štátom v stredoeuropskom kontexte*, Prešov, 1999.

Novák, Arne. *Přehledné dějiny literatury české od nejstarších dob až do naše dny*, 4 vols., Olomouc, 1936–39.

Novotný, Karel. "O pamětech Beneše," in *České země a Československo v Evropě XIX. a XX. století: Sborník prací k 65. narozeninám prof. dr. Roberta Kvačka*, ed. Jindřich Dejmek and Josef Hamzal, Prague, 1997.

Novotný, Josef. "Činnost KSČ v letech 1938–1941," in *Odboj a revoluce* 4, no. 4, 1966.

Odboj a revoluce 1938–1945: Nástin dějin československého odboje, Prague, 1965.

Offer, Karel. *Translation*, Second Series, Neville Braybroke and Elizabeth King, London, 1947.

Oldřich Sládek, *Přicházeli z nebe*, Prague, 1993.

Olivová, Věra. *The Doomed Democracy: Czechoslovakia in a Disrupted Republic, 1914–1948*, London, 1972.

Olivová, Věra, and Robert Kvaček. *Dějiny Československa*, Prague, 1967.

Opat, Jaroslav. "Masarykův realismus a naše nová státnost," in *Masarykova idea Československé státnosti ve světle kritiky dějin*, Sborník přispěvků z konference konané ve dnech 24. a 25. září 1992 v aule obchodní akademie v Hodoníně, Prague, 1993.

Opočenský, Jan. *The Collapse of the Austro-Hungarian Monarchy and the Rise of the Czechoslovak State*, Prague, 1928.

———. "Jiří Orten—básník i člověk," in *Židovská ročenka* 5740, 1980.

———. "Zapomenutý básník," in *Židovská ročenka* 5742, 1981–82.

Otáhal, Milan. "Ferdinand Peroutka: Muž Přítomnosti," in *Svědectví* 18, no. 70–71 (1983).

Otáhalová, Libuše, and Milada Červínková, eds. *Dokumenty z historie československé politiky 1939–1943*, 2 vols., Prague, 1966.

Otruba, Gustav. "Der Anteil der Juden am Wirtschaftsleben der böhmischen Ländern seit dem Beginn der Industrialisierung," in *Die Juden in den böhmischen Ländern*, Vorträge der Tagung des Collegium Carolinum in Bad Wiessee vom 27.–29. November 1981, ed. Ferdinand Seibt, München, Wien, 1983.

Palacký, František. *Dějiny národu českého v Čechách a na Moravě*, vol. 1, Prague, 1968.

Pařík, Arno. "Hana Volavková on Jewish Art and Monuments in Bohemia and Moravia," in JB25, no. 1, 1989.

Pasák, Tomáš. "Aktivističtí novináři a postoj generala Eliáše v roce 1941," in ČsČH 15, no. 2, 1967.

———. "Český antisemitismus na počátku okupace," in *Věda a život*, Brno, March 1969.

———. "Činnost protektorátní representace na podzim roku 1939" in ČsČH 17, no. 4, 1969.

———. "Der tschechische Faschismus," in *Fascism and Europe: An International Symposium*, Prague, August 28–29, 1969.

———. "General Alois Eliáš a odboj," in *Slovo k historii* 2, no. 27, Prague: Melantrich, 1995.

———. *Judr. Emil Hácha 1938–1945*, Prague, 1997.

———. "K problematice české kolaborace a fašismu za druhé světove války," in *Příspěvky k dějinám fašismu v Československu a v Mad' arsku*, Bratislava, 1969.

Patočka, Jan. *Co jsou Češi?* Malý přehled fakt a pokus o vysvětlení, Prague, 1990.

———. *Was sind die Tschechen?* Prague, 1992.

Pauker, Arnold. "Some Notes on Resistance," in LBIYB 16, 1971.

Paul, David W. *The Cultural Limits of Revolutionary Politics: Change and Continuity in Socialist Czechoslovakia*, New York, 1979.

Pechová, Oliva. "Malířský odkaz Petra Kiena," in *Terezínské listy* 3, 1973.

Peduzzi, Lubomír. *Pavel Haas: Život a dílo skladatele*, Brno, 1993.

———. "Složeno v Terezíně," in *Hudební rozhledy* 6, 1968.

Pěkný, Tomáš. *Dějiny Židů v Čechách a na Moravě*, Prague, 1993.

Penížek, Josef. "Masaryk and the Jewish Czechs," in *T. G. Masaryk and the Jews*, ed. Ernst Rychnovský, transl. B. R. Epstein, New York, 1941.

Peroutka, Ferdinand. "Češi, Němci a židé," in *Přítomnost* 16, 22.2.1939.

Peschanski, Denis. "The Statutes on Jews October 3, 1940 and June 2, 1941," in YVS 22, 1992.

Petrášová, Markéta. "Collections of the Central Jewish Museum 1942–1945," in JB 24, 1988.

Pfaff, Ivan. "Německá kultura v českém exilu 1933–1958," in *Svědectví* 18, no. 70–71, 1983.

Pick, Joseph C. "The Economy," in *The Jews of Czechoslovakia*, vol. 1, Philadelphia, 1968.

Píša, A. M. *Ivan Olbracht*, Prague, 1982.

Pitter, Přemysl. *Unter dem Rad der Geschichte: Ein Leben mit den Geringsten*, Zürich, 1970.

Plaček, Max. *Double Signature: Portraits of Personalities from the Terezín Ghetto*. Yad Vashem, Jerusalem, 1994.

Podlešák, Jan. "Mučedník za židovství a křesťanství; Život, dílo a smrt Alfreda Fuchse," in *Židovská ročenka* 5751, 1990–91.

Pojár, Miloš. "Masarykova návštěva Palestiny v r. 1927," in *Hilsnerova aféra a česká společnost 1899–1999*, Prague, 1999.

———. "T. G. Masaryk's Relations with Jews," in *Judaica Bohemiae* 38, 2002.

Poláček, Karel. *Poslední dopisy Doře*, ed. Martin Jelinovicz, Toronto, 1984.

Polak, Irma. "The Zionist Women's Movement," in *The Jews of Czechoslovakia*, vol. 2, Philadelphia, 1971.

Polák, Erik. "Die Bedeutung der Zeitschriften im Leben der Theresienstädter Kinder und Jugend," in *Theresienstadt in der "Endlösung der Judenfrage,"* Miroslav Kárný, Vojtěch Blodig, and Margita Kárná, Prague, 1992.

Polavský, Arnošt. *V boj: Třebechovice pod Orebem*, Dědourek, 1946.

Popper, Josef. "Work for Refugees," in *In Memoriam Marie Schmolka*, London, 1944, reissued Tel Aviv, 1970.

Poznanski, Renee. "The Jews of France and the Statutes on Jews," YVS 22, 1992.

Prečan, Vilém, ed. *Charta 77, 1977–1989: Od morální k demokratické revoluci*, Prague, 1990.

Presser, Jacob. *Ashes in the Wind: The Destruction of Dutch Jewry*, London, 1965.

Přibyl, Lukáš. "Osud třetího protektorátního transportu do Niska," in *Terezínské studie a dokumenty 2000*, Miroslav Kárný and Eva Lorenzová, Prague, 2000.

Proces s vedením záškodnického spiknutí proti republice: Horáková a společníci, Prague, 1950.

Procházka, Theodor. "Munich 1938 from the Czech Perspective," in *East Central Europe*, ed. Stanley B. Winter, 1981.

———. "The Second Republic, 1938–1939," in *A History of the Czechoslovak Republic 1918–1948*, Victor S. Mamatey and Radomír Luža, Princeton NJ, 1973.

Pujmanová, Marie. "Zase na světle božím," in *Kritický měsíčník* 1, 1945.

Putík, Alexander. "The Origins and Symbols of the Prague Jewish Town," JB 30–31, 1994–95.

Rabinowicz, Aharon Moshe. "The Jewish Minority," in *The Jews of Czechoslovakia*, vol. 1, Philadelphia, 1968.

———. "The Jewish Party: A Struggle for National Recognition, Representation and Autonomy," in *The Jews of Czechoslovakia*, vol. 2, Philadelphia, 1971.

Rabinowicz, Oskar K. "Czechoslovak Zionism: Analecta to a History," in *The Jews of Czechoslovakia*, vol. 2, Philadelphia, 1971.

R(ameš), Karel, *Žaluji: Pankrácká kalvárie*, 3 vols., Prague, 1946.

Rašla, Anton. *Civilista v armádě: Spomienky na roky 1938–1945*, Bratislava, 1967.

Rataj, Jan. "Český antisemitismus v proměnách let 1918–1945," in *Židé v české a polské občanské společnosti: Sborník přednášek*, Jerzy Tomaszewski and Jaroslav Valenta, Prague, 1999.

———. *O autoritativní národní stát: Ideologické proměny české politiky v Druhé republice 1938–1939*, Prague, 1997.

Rauschning. *Gespräche mit Hitler*, New York, 1940.

Relink, Karel. *Nenažranski, ministr: Humanista, filistr*, Prague, 1927.

———. *Spása světa, ubozí pronásledovaní židé*, Prague, 1926.

Remington, Robin A., ed. *Winter in Prague: Documents on Czechoslovak Communism in Crisis*, Cambridge, London, 1969.

Reznitschenko, Y., ed. *Theresienstadt*, Tel Aviv, 1947.

Rhode, Gotthold. "The Protectorate of Bohemia and Moravia," in *A History of the Czechoslovak Republic 1918–1948*, Victor S. Mamatey and Radomír Luža, Princeton NJ, 1973.

Rich, Norman. *Hitler's War Aims: The Establishment of the New Order*, vol. 2, London, 1974.

Riegner, Gerhard M. "Die Beziehung des Roten Kreuzes zu Theresienstadt in der Endphase des Krieges," in *Theresienstädter Studien und Dokumente 1996*, ed. Miroslav Kárný, Raimund Kemper, and Margita Kárná, Prague, 1996.

———. *Ne jamais désesperer: Soixante années ou service du peuple juif et des droits de l'homme*, Paris, 1998.

Riff, Michael A. "Czech Anti-Semitism and the Jewish Response before 1914," in *Wiener Library Bulletin* 29, 1976.

Ripka, Hubert. *Munich: Before and After*, London, 1939.

Rokycana, Jaroslav. "Za Leonem Bondym," in KČŽ 46, 1924–25.

Rosen, Chanan. "Yahasey Yisrael-Tshekhoslovakia beTmurat haItim," in *Gesher* 2–3, ed. Shlomo Shafir, Jerusalem, 1959–60.

Rossel, Maurice. "Besuch im Ghetto," in *Theresienstädter Studien und Dokumente 1996*, ed. Miroslav Kárný, Raimund Kemper, and Margita Kárná, Prague, 1996.

Rothkirchen, Livia. "Brennende Fragen der Historiographie von Theresienstadt," in *Theresienstadt in der "Endlösung der Judenfrage,"* Miroslav Kárný, Vojtěch Blodig, and Margita Kárná, Prague, 1992.

———. "Czech and Slovak Wartime Leadership: Variants in Strategy and Tactics," in *Holocaust and History: The Known, the Unknown, the Disputed and the Reexamined*, Michael Berenbaum and J. Abraham Peck, Bloomington, 1998.

———. "The Czechoslovak Government-in-Exile: Jewish and Palestinian Aspects in the Light of Documents," in YVS 9, 1973.

———. "Czechoslovakia," in *The World Reacts to the Holocaust*, ed. David S. Wyman, Baltimore, 1996.

———. "Deep-Rooted Yet Alien: Some Aspects of the History of the Jews in Subcarpathian Ruthenia," in YVS 12, 1977.

———. "The Protectorate Government and the 'Jewish Question,' 1939–1941," in YVS 27, 1999.

———. "Die Repräsentanten der Theresienstädter Selbstverwaltung; Differenzierung der Ansichten," in *Theresienstädter Studien und Dokumente 1996*, ed. Miroslav Kárný, Raimund Kemper, and Margita Kárná, Prague, 1996.

———. "The Role of the Czech and Slovak Jewish Leadership in the Field of Rescue Work," in *Rescue Attempts during the Holocaust*, Proceedings of the Second Yad Vashem International Historical Conference, April 1974, Yisrael Gutman and Efraim Zuroff, Jerusalem, 1977.

———. "The Slovak Enigma: A Reassessment of the Halt to the Deportations," in *East Central Europe* 10, nos. 1–2, ed. Stanley B. Winters, 1983.

———. "Slovakia: II, 1918–1938," in *The Jews of Czechoslovakia*, vol. 2, Philadelphia, 1971.

———. "Židé v domácím odboji (1938–1942)," in *Židé v novodobých dějinách: Soubor přednášek na FF ÚK*, ed. Václav Veber, Prague, 1997.

———. "The Zionist Character of Ghetto Terezín," YVS 11, 1976.

———. "The Zionist Character of the Self-Government in Terezín," in YVS 11, 1976.

Rothkirchenová, Livie. "Exil a návrat: Historické analogie v českém a hebrejském písemnictví," in *Pocta 650. výročí založení Univerzity Karlovy v Praze: Sborník příspěvků přednesených zahraničními bohemisty na mezinárodním symposiu v Praze 20–26. srpna 1998*, vol. 2, Prague, 1998.

Rothschild, Joseph. *East Central Europe between the Two World Wars*, Seattle, 1974.

Rudé právo 1939–1945, Prague, 1971.

Rupnow, Dirk. "Ihr müst sein auch wenn Ihr nicht mehr seid": "The Jewish Central Museum in Prague and Historical memory in the Third Reich," in *Holocaust and Genocide Studies* 16, no. 1, Spring 2002.

Rychlík, Jan. *Češi a Slováci ve 20. století: Česko-slovenské vztahy 1914–1945*, Bratislava, 1997.

Rychnovský, Ernst, ed., *Thomas G. Masaryk and the Jews*, transl. B. R. Epstein, New York, 1941.

Rybár, Ctibor. *Židovská Praha: Glosy k dějinám a literatuře*, Prague, 1991.

Rychlík, Jan, Thomas D. Marzík, and Miroslav Bielik, eds. "R. W. Seton-Watson and His Relations with Czechs and Slovaks," in *Documents—Dokumenty 1906–1951*, vol. 1, Prague, 1995.

Rys, Jan. *Hilsneriáda a T.G.M. 1899–1939*, Prague: Weisner, 1939.

Šach, Jan. "Judr. Karel Bondy," in *Historie a vojenství*, no. 1, 1994.

Sadek, Vladimír. "From the Documents Related to the War-time Central Jewish Museum in Prague," JB 16, no. 1, special issue, 1980.

——. "Dr. Otto Muneles und sein wisentschaftliches Werk," in JB 3, 1967.

——. "Rabi Loew: Sa vie, héritage pédagogique et sa legend," in JB 15, 1979.

Safrian, Hans. *Die Eichmann-Männer*, Wien, Zürich, 1995.

Šalda, F. X. "Fašismus a kultura," in *Přítomnost*, 9.3.1933.

——. "Genius řecký a genius židovský," in *Šaldův zápisník* 3, 1931; *Šaldův zápisník* 8, April 1936.

——. "Požáry," in *Listy pro umění a kritiku* 3 (1935).

Šaloun, Ladislaus. "Das Denkmal des Hohen Rabbi Loew am Prager Neuen Rathause," interview in *Das jüdische Prag: Eine Sammelschrift*, Prague, 1917; 2nd ed. Kronberg, 1978.

Sayer, Derek. *The Coasts of Bohemia: A Czech History*, translated from Czech by Alena Sayer, Princeton NJ, 1998.

Scheinpflugová, Olga. *Český román*, Prague, 1946.

Schellenberg, Walter. *The Labyrinth: Memoirs of Walter Schellenberg*, New York, 1956.

——. *Memoiren*, Köln, 1956.

Schieder, Theodor, ed. *Dokumentation der Vertreibung der Deutschen Bevölkerung aus der Tschechoslowakei*, München, 1984.

Schimmerling, Hanuš. "Der Jüdische Jugend im Widerstand," in *Theresienstadt in der "Endlösung der Judenfrage,"* Miroslav Kárný, Vojtěch Blodig, and Margita Kárná, Prague, 1992.

Schlamm, Willy. "Proč zemřel Karel Čapek," in *Přítomnost* 16, 25.1.1939.

——. "Why Did Karel Čapek Die," in *Saturday Review of Literature*, January 1939.

Schmelz, U. O., P. Glikson, and S. Della Pergola, eds. *Papers in Jewish Demography, 1969*, Jerusalem, 1973.

Schmidt-Hartmann, Eva. "Die deutschsprachige jüdische Emigration aus der Tschechoslowakei nach Grossbritannien, 1938–1945," in *Die Juden in den böhmischen Landern*, ed. F. Seibt, München, Wien, 1983.

Schmiedt, Shlomo. "HeHalutz in Theresienstadt: Its Influence and Educational Activities," in YVS 7, 1968.

Schneider, Hansjorg, and Ludwig Hoffmann. *Exil in der Tschechoslowakei in Grossbritannien, Skandinavien und in Palestina*, vol. 5, Leipzig, 1980.

Schönfeld, Willy, ed. *Přeškolování: Malá nauka o povolání pro praksi*, Prague, 1940.

Schulz, Ingo. "Wege und Irrwege der Ullmann-Forschung," in *Viktor Ullmann, Die*

Referate des Symposions anlässlich des 50. Todestags 14–16 Oktober 1994 und ergänzende Studien, ed. Hans-Günter Klein, Hamburg, 1996.

Schulz, Ingo, ed. *Viktor Ullmann: 26 Kritiken über Musikalische Veranstaltungen in Theresienstadt*, mit einem Geleitwort von Thomas Mandl, Hamburg, 1993.

Schwertfeger, Ruth. *Women in Theresienstadt: Voices from a Concentration Camp*, Oxford, New York, Hamburg, 1989.

Sefer haShomer haTza'ir, vol. 1, Levi Dror and Yisrael Rosenzweig, Merhavia, 1956–59.

Segert, Stanislav. "The Unity of the New-Covenant—the Unity of Brethren: A Comparison of Two Religious Communities," in *Jewish Studies: Essays in Honor of the Very Reverend Dr. Gustav Sicher Chief Rabbi of Prague*, ed. Rudolf Iltis, Prague, 1955.

Seifert, Jaroslav. *Všechny krásy světa*, Prague, 1982.

——. "Zhasněte svělta" in *Přítomnost* 16, 1939.

Seifert, Jaroslav, and Stanislav Segert. *Píseň Písní*, translated from the 1937 Stuttgart Hebrew edition of *Shir HaShirim*, illustrations by Arnošt Paderlík, Prague, 1958, rev. ed. 1963.

Sicher, Efraim. "The Concept of Work in the Writings of Chief Rabbi Dr. Gustav Sicher," in *Shvut*, Studies in Russian and East European History and Culture, Tel Aviv University, 5, no. 21, 1997.

Sicher, Gustav. *Volte život: Sborník z prací a úvah Gustava Sichera*, Prague, 1975.

Sidor, Karol. *Slovenská politika na pódě pražského snemu 1918–1938*, Bratislava, 1943.

Šimečka, Milan. *Kruhorá Obrana*, Paris, 1985.

Šimka, A. *Národněosvobozenecký boj na Jihlavsku*, Brno, 1963.

Simon, Ernst. "Jewish Adult Education in Nazi Germany as Spiritual Resistance," in LBIYB 1, London, 1956.

Singer, Ludvík. "Naše cíle," in *Židovské zprávy*, 5.4.1918.

Singer, Oskar. *Herren der Welt*, with an introduction by Walter Tschuppik, Prague, 1935.

Skilling, Gordon. *Czechoslovakia's Interrupted Revolution*, Princeton NJ, 1976.

Skoumal, Aloys. "S Erikem A. Saudkem," in *Vzpomínky českých divadelníků na německou okupaci a druhou světovou válku*, ed. František Černý, Prague, 1965.

Skutil, Jan. "Kurt Konrád, spolutvůrce pokrokové kulturní politiky a literární kritiky na Moravě v letech 1918–1938," in *Vlastivědný věstník moravsk*, 41, 1989.

Sládek, Oldřich. *Přicházeli z nebe*, Prague, 1993.

Sládek, Oldřich, and Jaroslav Žižka, eds. *KSČ proti nacismu*, Prague, 1971.

Slánská, Josefa. *Report on My Husband*, London, 1969.

Slavický. Milan. "Gideon Klein—torzo života a díla," in *Hudební věda* 14, Prague, 1977.

Šnejdárek, A. "Tajné rozhovory Beneše s Německem," ČsČH 9, Prague, 1961.

Šormová, Eva. *Divadlo v Terezíně 1941–1945*, Ústí nad Labem, 1973.

Spaniel, Otakar. *Československá armáda druhého odboje*, Chicago, 1941.

Spěváček, J. *Rudolf II a jeho doba*, Prague, 1987.

Spilka, Josef, ed. *Chléb se dělá ze zlata*, Prague, 1946.

Spira, Emil. "K dějinám Židů v Čechách: Doba válek křižáckých a posledních Přemyslovců," in KČŽ 1900–1.

Staněk, Tomáš. *Odsun Němců z Československa 1945–1947*, Prague, 1991.

Stein, Augustín. *Maarche-Lev: Modlitby Israelitův*, Prague, 1884.

Steiner, Max. "The Rise and Fall of a Jewish Community in Bohemia," in *YIVO Annual* 12, 1958–59.

Steinberg, Lucien. "Le rôle des Juifs de Tchécoslovaquie dans la guerre antinazie," in *Le monde juif*, Janvier–Mars 1967.

Steinherz, Samuel. "Die Einwanderung der Juden in Böhmen," in *Die Juden in Prag: Bilder aus ihren tausendjährigen Geschichte*, Prague, 1927.

Stehlíkova, Eva. "Proč mi bývá smutno," in *VŽONP*, October 1981.

Stölzl, Christoph. *Kafka's böses Böhmen: Zur Sozialgeschichte eines Prager Juden*, München, 1975.

——. *Kafkovy zlé Čechy: k sociální historii pražského žida*, Praha, 1997.

Stránský, Hugo. "Rabbi Judah Loew of Prague and Jan Amos Comenius: Two Reformers in Education," in *Comenius*, ed. Vratislav Bušek, New York, 1972.

——. "The Religious Life in the Historic Lands," in *The Jews of Czechoslovakia*, vol. 1, Philadelphia, 1968.

Stříbrný, Jan. "Židovští vojenští duchovní v Československém vojsku na západě v letech 1939–1945," in *Postavení a osudy židovského obyvatelstva v Čechách a na Moravě v letech 1939–1945*, Helena Krejčová and Jana Svobodová, Prague, 1998

Sturm, Rudolf, ed. *Egon Hostovský: Vzpomínky, studie a dokumenty o jeho díle a osudu*, Toronto, 1973.

Švanda, Jaroslav. "Deset adres Mileny Jesenské," in *Svědectví* 20, no. 80 1987.

Svátek, Josef. "Pogromy v Holešově v letech 1774–1918," in *Židovská ročenka* 5740, 1920.

Svoboda, Emanuel. "Mikoláš Aleš u Alexandra Brandeise," in *KČŽ* 34, 1914–15.

Swet, Gershon. "Mitnadvim LeTzava HaTshekhi," in *Ha'aretz*, 9.11.1939.

——. "400 Local Czecho-Slovaks for France to Join Up," in *Palestine Post*, 3.11.1939.

Táborský, Edvard. "Beneš a náš osud," in *Svědectví* 23, nos. 89–90, 1990.

——. *Czechoslovak Democracy at Work*, London, 1945; Princeton NJ, 1973.

——. "Politics in Exile, 1939–1945," in *A History of the Czechoslovak Republic 1918–1948*, Victor S. Mamatey and Radomír Luža, Princeton NJ, 1973.

——. *Pravda zvítězila: Deník druhého zahraničního odboje*, Prague, 1947.

Tancsik, Pamela. "Viktor Ullmann: Leben und Werk," in *Kontexte: Musica Judaica 1994*, Bericht über die musikwissenschaftliche Konferenz Praha 25.–26.10.1994, ed. Vlasta Benetková, Vladimír Karbusický, Jitka Ludvová, and Marta Ottlová, Prague, 1995.

Tegen, Susan. " 'The Demonic Effect'; Veit Harlan's Use of Jewish Extras in Jud Süss, 1940," *Holocaust and Genocide Studies* 14, no.2, Fall 2000.

Teichová, Alice. "The Protectorate of Bohemia and Moravia (1939–1945): The Economic Dimension," in *Bohemia in History*, ed. Mikuláš Teich, Cambridge, 1998.

The Terezín Diary of Egon Redlich, ed. Saul S. Friedmann. Translated from Czech by Laurence Kutler, Kentucky, 1992.

Terezín Memorialbook, Prague, 1996.

Tesař, Jan. *Mnichovský komplex: Jeho příčeny a důsledky*, Český Těšín, 2000.

Testimony of Pater Dr. Miloš Bič, Pastor of the Church of Czech Brethren at Domažlice, in *Terezín, 1941–1945*, František Ehrmann, Otto Heitlinger, and Rudolf Iltis, Prague, 1965.

Teytz, Viktor. "Bohumil Bondy," in *KČŽ* 27, 1907–8.

——. "Rozmluva s prof. Masarykem," in *Rozvoj*, 9.9.1909.

Thein, Hanuš. *Žil jsem operou Národního divadla*, Prague, 1975.

Tigrid, Pavel. "Jací jsme když je zle," in *Svědectví* 12, 1973.

Toland, John. "Reasons for Naturalizing the Jews in Great Britain and Ireland," in *The Jew in the Modern World: A Documentary History*, Paul R. Mendes-Flohr and Jehuda Reinharz, New York, Oxford, 1984.

Tomášek, Dušan, and Robert Kvaček. *Causa Emil Hácha*, Prague, 1995.

Tomaszewski, Jerzy, and Jaroslav Valenta, eds. *Židé v české a polské občanské společnosti: Sborník přednášek*, Prague, 1999,

——. *Obžalována je vláda*, Prague, 1999.

Tomek, Václav Vladivoj. *Dějepis města Prahy*, 2 vols., Prague, 1855.

Träger, Josef. *Egon Hostovský: Vzpomínky, studie a dokumenty o jeho díle a osudu*, ed. Rudolf Sturm, Toronto, 1973.

Tramer, Hans. "Prague—City of Three Peoples," in LBIYB 9, 1964.

Troller, Norbert. *Theresienstadt: Hitler's Gift to the Jews*, Chapel Hill, 1992.

Trunk, Isaiah. "Discussion," *Imposed Jewish Governing Bodies under Nazi Rule*, YIVO Colloquium, December 2–5, 1967, New York, 1972.

Tvarůžek, Břetislav. "Okupace Čech a Moravy a vojenská správa (15. březen az 15. duben 1939)," in *Historie a vojenství* 41, no. 3, 1992.

Tyl, Otakar, and Tana Kulišová. *Terezín: Malá pevnost-Ghetto*, Prague, 1955.

Uhlíř, František. *Prague and Berlin, 1918–1938*, London, 1941.

Unger, Michal, ed. *The Last Ghetto: Life in the Łodý Ghetto 1940–1944*, Jerusalem, 1991.

Urzidil, Johannes. *There Goes Kafka*, trans. Harold A. Besilius, Detroit, 1968.

Utermöhle, Walter, and Herbert Schmerling. *Právní postavení židů v Protektorátu Čechy a Morava*, Prague, 1940.

Utitz, Emil. "The Central Ghetto Library in the Concentration Camp Terezín," in *Terezín, 1941–1945*, František Ehrmann, Otto Heitlinger, and Rudolf Iltis, Prague, 1965.

——. *Psychologie des Leben im Theresienstädter Konzentrationslager*, Vienna, 1948.

Václavek, Ludvík. "Der Dichter Petr Kien (1919–1944)," in *Acta Universitatis Palackianae Olomucensis*, Facultas Philosophica, Philologia 66, 1993.

——. "Literární tvorba Petra Kiena," in *Terezínské listy* 3, 1973.

——. "Terezínské básně Ilsy Weberové," in *Terezínské listy* 5, 1975.

Věrni jsme zůstali: Účastsociální demokracie v domácím a zahraničním odboji, Prague, 1947.

Veselý-Štainer, Karel. *Cestou národního odboje: Bojový vývoj domácího odbojového hnutí v letech 1938–1945*, Prague, 1947.

Vilímek, Ladislav. "Jihlavský rabín Dr. Grünfeld," in *Židé a Morava*, Kroměříž, 1998.

Vilímková, Milada. "Seven Hundred Years of the Old-New Synagogue," in JB 1, 1969.

Vohryzek, Lev. "Masaryk a Židé," in vŽONP, 28.2.1935.

Vohryzek, Viktor. "Epištoly k českým židům," in *Českožidovské listy*, 15.3.1900, reprinted in Vohryzek, *K židovské otázce*, Prague, 1923.

Volavková, Hana. "Alexander Brandeis a jeho přátelé," in *Židovská ročenka* 5722, 1961–62.

——. "The Jewish Museum of Prague," in *The Jews of Czechoslovakia*, vol. 3, Philadelphia, 1984.

——. "Výmluvný dokument," in *Židovská ročenka* 5721, 1960–61.

——. *Zmizelá Praha*, Prague, 1947.

——. *Das Schicksal des jüdischen Museums in Prag*, Prague, 1965.

Volavková, Hana, ed. *I Never Saw Another Butterfly: Children's Drawings and Poems*, *Terezín 1942–1944*, Prague, 1965.

——. *Jewish Monuments in Bohemia and Moravia*, 8 vols. Prague, 1952.

The Von Hassell Diaries 1938–1944: The Story of the Forces against Hitler inside Germany as Recorded by Ambassador Ulrich von Hassell, a Leader of the Movement, London, 1948.

Vondra, Václav. "Karel Poláček," in *Práce*, 19.10.1974.

Votavová, Marcela. "Bedřich Fritta: Nástin osobnosti a díla," in *Terezínské listy* 9, 1978.

Vrabec, Václav. "Petiční výbor "Věrni zůstaneme,'" in *Odboj a revoluce*, 1967.

Vrána, Karel. "The Ecumenical Sense of Culture in J. A. Comenius," in *Comenius*, ed. Vratislav Bušek, New York, 1972.

Vrkočová, Ludmila. "Hudba terezínského ghetta," *Jazzpetit* 8, Prague, 1981.

Vyskočil, Josef. "Die tschechisch-jüdische Bewegung," in JB 3, no. 1, 1967.

——. "Českožidovské hnutí," in *Dějiny a současnost*, no. 4, 1966.

Warriner, Doreen. "Document: Winter in Prague," in *Slavonic and East European Review* 62, no. 2, April 1984.

Weber, Ilse. *In deinen Mauern wohnt das Leid: Gedichte aus dem KZ Theresienstadt*, Gerlingen, 1991.

Wehle, Kurt. "The Jews of Bohemia and Moravia, 1945–1948," in *The Jews of Czechoslovakia: Historical Studies and Surveys*, vol. 2, Philadelphia, 1971.

Weinberg, Gerhard L. "Secret Hitler-Beneš Negotiations in 1936–1937," in *Journal of Central European Affairs* 19, January 1960.

Weiner, Gustav. "Die Zeit vor der offiziellen Freizeitgestaltung: November 1941 bis February 1942: Entstehung und Anfänge der Freizeitgestaltung Februar 1942 bis Februar 1943," in *Und die Musik spielt dazu*, ed. Ulrike Migdal, Munich, Zürich, 1986.

Weiner, Richard. "Neviditelné ghetto," in *Přítomnost* 3, 1926.

Weiss, Arnošt. "Musical Events in Terezín 1942," in *Terezín, 1941–1945*, ed. František Ehrmann, Otto Heitlinger, and Rudolf Iltis, Prague, 1965.

Weisskopf, Kurt. *The Agony of Czechoslovakia, '38–'68*, London, 1968.

Weltsch, Felix. "Masaryk and Zionism," in *Thomas G. Masaryk and the Jews*, ed. Ernst Rychnovský, New York, 1941.

Weltsch, Robert. *Max Brod and His Age*, Leo Baeck Memorial Lecture 13, New York, 1970.

Wheeler Bennett, John W. *Munich: Prologue to Tragedy*, New York, 1948.

Winters, Stanley B. "Munich 1938 from the Czech perspective," *East Central Europe* 8, nos. 1–2, 1981.

Wiskemann, Elizabeth. *Czechs and Germans: A Study of the Struggle in the Historic Provinces of Bohemia and Moravia*, London, New York, Toronto, 1938.

Wlaschek, Rudolf M. *Juden in Böhmen: Beiträge zur Geschichte des europäischen Judentums im 19. und 20. Jahrhundert*, München, 1990.

Yahil, Leni. *The Rescue of Danish Jewry: Test of Democracy*, Philadelphia, 1969.

Za svobodu českého a slovenského národa: Sborník dokumentů k dějinám KSČ v letech 1938–1945, Ústav dějin Komunistické strany Československa, Prague, 1956.

Žáček, Joseph F. "Czechoslovak Fascisms," in *Native Fascism in the Successor States 1918–1945*, ed. Peter F. Sugar, Santa Barbara CA, 1971.

Zdeněk, Landes. "Přítomnost svědčí," in *Židovské zprávy*, 24.2.1939.

Zehngut, J. *Dějiny židovstva ostravského*, Ostrava, 1952.

Zeman, V. "Bez židův a proti židům," in KČŽ 35, 1915–16.

Zeman, Zbyněk. *Nazi Propaganda*, London, 1964.

Zeman, Zbyněk A. B., and Antonín Klímek. *The Life of Edvard Beneš 1884–1948: Czechoslovakia in Peace and War*, Oxford, 1997.

Zerubavel, Gilead, ed. *Magen baSeter: Palestinian Underground Activities in World War II*, Jerusalem, 1952.

Zíbrt, Čeněk. *Ohlas obřadních písní velikonočních Haggadah*, Prague, 1928.

Židé a Morava, Sborník příspěvků přednesených na konferenci konané 12. listopadu 1997 v Kroměříži, ed. Petr Pálka, Kroměříž, 1998.

"Židé a strana národní jednoty," in *Přítomnost* 15, 7.12.1938.

Židovská otázka a její řešení: Zionistický výbor pro Čechy, 2nd ed., Prague, 1912.

Židovská ročenka 5742, 1981–82.

Zinner, Paul E. *Communist Strategy and Tactics in Czechoslovakia, 1918–1948*, London, Dunmow, 1963.

Zohn, Harry. "Participation in German Literature," in *The Jews of Czechoslovakia: Historical Studies and Surveys*, vol. 1, Philadelphia, 1968.

Zucker, Otto. "Theresienstädter Bericht, 1941–1943," introduction by Miroslav Kárný in *Theresienstädter Studien und Dokumente 1995*, ed. Miroslav Kárný, Raimund Kemper, and Margita Kárná, Prague, 1995.

Zwergbaum, Aharon. "Exile in Mauritius," in YVS 4, 1960.

Index

Adam, Robert, 388n10
Adler, Friedrich, 23
Adler, H. G., 136, 244–45, 275, 276, 278, 280, 385n43
Adler, Norbert, 27
Adler, Simon, 214
Agde camp, 163
Agrarian Party, 30, 54, 73, 74, 102
agriculture, 37–38
Agudath Israel, 378n48
Ahad Ha'am, 4, 5, 21, 312n24
Aktion Gitter, 99
Albright, William F., 3
Aleichem, Sholom, 272
Aleš, Mikuláš, 20
Alexandrovskij (Soviet ambassador), 88
Al S'fod, 277, 386n56
Ältestenrat (1943–45), 135, 257, 260, 376n15
Altneuschul, 1, 20, 101, 290, 337n17
Altneuschul (Herzl), 1
Alt-Prager Almanach (Nettl), 36
Alžběta, Polaková (Weissberger), 155
Amarant, Siegmund, 349n58
American Joint Distribution Committee (JDC), 53, 117, 253, 342n98
Amsterdam, 122
Ämtliches deutsches Ortsbuch, 104
Ančerl, Karel, 270
Ančerl, Karl, 281
Andrlová, Věra, 201
Andršt (Malina), 199
anti-Semitism: and assimilation, 84–85; in Communist era, 306; in Czech army, 172–73; in Czechoslovakia, 45–47, 50–52; to eliminate Jewish influence, 87–94; in First Republic, 298; at German University of Prague, 45, 46, 55;

literature, 16–17, 46, 57–58; and Munich Agreement, 96; nature of Czech, 303; Peroutka on, 92–93; post-war, 27–28, 184–85, 290–92, 295; in press, 28, 140, 332n111, 347n9, 357n70; in Protectorate, 99–103, 140, 143; raising awareness of, 216, 217; rise of, 16–18; toward refugees, 79
"An Appeal to the World," 65
Aragon, Louis, 209
"Arco, Arconauten." *See* Prager Kreis
Arijský boj, 102, 121
arm deal, 286, 388n10
Army Archives: rescue of, 198
Army Organization, 192, 193, 199, 203, 205
art, 272–73, 280
assimilation, 5, 13, 15–16, 21–22, 32–33, 42–44, 243, 297, 306–7. *See also* Czech-Jewish movement
Association for Cooperation with the Germans, 176
l'Association Internationale pour la Protection de l'Enfance, 77
Association of Catholics, 92
Association of Czech Writers, 66
Aubrechtová, Věra, 201, 366n91
Auschwitz, 122, 177, 206, 245–46, 262, 263, 264, 280, 300, 383n130
Auschwitz Protocol, 262
Aus der Tiefe rufe ich, Herr, su dir (Psalm 130), 277
Austria, 78, 224, 238–41, 243–45, 267, 268, 281
Austria-Hungary, 14
Austrian *Anschluss*, 60, 64, 76
Avinur, Asher (Feuerstein), 367n98
"Avowal of Belief" (Weber), 271
Avriel, Ehud, 286

Bachmann, Friedrich, 143
Bachrach, K., 187
Bacon, Yehuda, 280
Badeni language ordinances, 17
Baeck, Leo, 246, 259, 260, 263, 281, 282
Balak, 287
Baláz, Julius, 363n28
Bálek, Stanislav, 201
Balfour Declaration, 29, 284, 285
Bálkova, Věra, 201
Barber, Stephen, 372n3
Barbey, Frederic, 248
Barbusse, Henri, 209
Bar Kochba Association of Jewish Students, 4, 21, 22, 25
Barlas, Chaim, 112
Barou, Noah, 173, 178, 181
Barta, Drahomír, 201
Barth, Karl, 65
Barthová, Kamila, 157
Bass, Eduard, 334n151
Bassevi, Jacob, 9
Baštýř, Mořic, 15
Bauer, František, 200, 231
Bauer, Herta, 200, 231
Baum, Frantiáka, 199, 366n77
Baum, Jiří, 196, 200, 365n57
Baum, Josef, 199, 366n77
Baum, Oskar, 23
Bauman, Zygmunt, 305
Baumel, Dr., 326n148
Baumgarten, Margareta, 194
Bavier, Jean de, 254
BBC, 205, 261
Bechyně, Rudolf, 45
Beck, Josef, 326n148
Bednář, Kamil, 210
Beer-Konrád, Kurt, 151, 193–95, 204, 364n46, 369n118, 369n120
Beer-Konrád, Reiman, 369n120
Bělohlávek, Bedřich, 66
Benátky nad Jizerou, 106
Ben Avi, Itamar, 324n103
Ben Chorin, Yehuda (Brieger), 287

Benda, Julien, 94
Benda, Lucian, 85–86
Beneš, Eduard, xiii; abdication, 185; aid offered to, 356n48; aid to refugees, 54, 74; on anti-Semitism, 56; appointment of Syrový, 83; career of, 353n1; on channels of communication, 190; criticism of, 350n67; on Czech army in Palestine, 166; on Czechs in Protectorate and Palestine, 161; destruction of likenesses, 100–101; and Eliáš, 142, 147, 150, 158; exile, 71, 160, 168–69, 301; on Heydrich's assassination, 353n124; historical assessment of, 96–97, 185–86; on Hitler, 52, 64; influences on policy, 304; intelligence received by, 178–81; on minorities, 27, 28, 161, 170–75, 185, 284–85, 357n58, 358n74; and Munich crisis, 64–65; and nonaggression toward Germany, 74–75; pledge of loyalty, 327n11; policy on Jewish workers, 91; as president, 56; on resistance, 113, 144, 159, 182–83; return to Czechoslovakia, 185, 284; and World Jewish Congress, 149; on Zionism, 49
Beneš, K. J., 195
Beneš, Vincenc, 90
Ben-Gurion, David, 286, 287
Ben-Zvi, Yitzhak, 163, 355n19
Beran, Rudolf, 73, 86, 107, 141, 143, 192
Berdych, František, 151
Berdych, Václav, 369n121
Bergen-Belsen, 254
Berger, Jasha, 368n110
Bergl, Josef, 36
Bergmann, Dáša, 344n131, 351n98
Bergmann, Hugo, 20, 21, 27
Bergmann, Karel, 344n131
Bergmann, Quido, 125
Bergmann, Shmuel Hugo, 352n99
Bergmann, Zdenko, 154, 351n98
Bergmann family, 351n98, 352n99
Berman, Karel, 278, 282

Bernadotte, Folke, 380n75
Bernheim, Franz, 320n25
Best, Werner, 256
Bezruč, Petr, 24
Bible, 2–3
Bíček, František, 101
Biddle, Anthony J. Drexel, Jr., 178
Bílek, František, 1, 59, 311n5
Bílý, General, 369n120
Birkenau, 257–58, 260, 261, 280
"B-Juden," 116
Bláma, 110
Bloch, Felix, 245, 272, 384n28
blood libel, 17, 100
B'nai Brith Lodge, 36
Board of Deputies of British Jews, 172
Bohemia, 40, 51
Bohemia: anti-Semitism, 184–85; arrests,
    110; assimilation of Jews, 18–19; Cath-
    olic organizations, 14, 16; confiscation
    of Jewish property, 144–45; Czech-
    Jewish movement, 32; dejudaization
    campaign, 123; fascism, 45–46; during
    First Republic, 26; Germanization, 12,
    217; ghettos, 124; historical relics, 135;
    Jewish occupations, 37; Jewish-owned
    establishments, 338n40; Jewish popu-
    lation, 8–11, 36–38, 82, 174, 288,
    333n112; Jewish question, 207; Jewish
    rights, 29; Jewish status, 34–35, 297;
    national revival, 3, 4; Nazi policy in,
    104, 121; occupation, 284; Orthodox
    tradition, 20–21, 34; PVVZ members,
    363n36; refugees in, 75, 81; rescue
    from, 96, 221; during Second Repub-
    lic, 72; segregation of population, 108;
    Terezín inmates from, 268; transports
    to Terezín, 239; Zionism, 30, 85
Böhm, Joseph, 222–23
Böhme, Horst, 123
Böhmer. *See* Sudeten Germans
Böhmische Escompte Bank, 106
Boleslav, Mladá, 121
Bondy, Alexander, 154

Bondy, Bohumil, 15, 19
Bondy, Filip, 197
Bondy, Hilde (Bergmann), 154
Bondy, Jiří, 154
Bondy, Karel, 195–98, 200, 364n55
Bondy, Lazar Gottlieb, 19
Bondy, Leon, 19
Bondy, Max, 197–98
Bondy, Miloš Otto, 191
Bondy family, 351n98, 352n99
Bonn, Hanuš, 45, 58, 117, 118, 126, 211,
    371n159
Bořek-Dohalský, Zdeněk, 152, 200, 231,
    366n86, 375n70
Borovský, Karel Havlíček, 13
Bourdet, A., 337n24
boycotts, 60, 205
Brandeis, Alexander, 19–20, 59
Brandeis, Louis D., 4
Bratislava, 57, 175, 358n88
Bratislava Komenský University, 46
Braun, Major, 192
Brecht, Berthold, 66, 73
Bretholz, Berthold, 36
Březovský, Boněk, 210
Brihah, 286
British Mandatory Government of Pal-
    estine, 81
Brno, 19, 38, 55, 102, 120, 125, 221
Brodetsky, Selig, 173
Brod, Max, 6, 20, 23, 27, 30, 41, 47, 80
Brody, Heinrich (Hayyim), 20
Brody, I., 319n7
Brožík, Václav, 20
Brundibár, 257, 282, 381n100
Brunskill, S., 167
Buber, Martin, 5, 21, 22, 47
Budapest, 46
Budapest Relief and Rescue Committee,
    255
Budějovice, 284
Bukovina, 29–30
Burckhardt, Carl J., 248, 249, 251–52,
    303, 379nn68–69, 380n71

Burger, Anton, 244
"The Burned Book," 209
Butter, Oscar, 88
Bystřice labor camp, 133, 157

Café Arco, 44
Café Continental, 73
Café Esplanade, 102
Campion, Miss, 251
Čapek, J. B., 2, 66
Čapek, Karel: on anti-Semitism, 52, 90;
    death, 64, 95, 327n7, 335n159; defense
    of republic, 66; on intellectuals, 94;
    prayer, 68; and refugees, 73, 75; *White
    Plague*, 34, 196, 216
Carpatho-Russia, 174
Carr, Wilbur J., 68, 79, 88, 92, 99,
    328n32
Catholic organizations, 14, 16
Čechoslovak v Orientě, 163
Čech (parachutist), 365n71
Celan, Paul, 273
cemetery, Jewish, 102, 296
Central Council of National Jews from
    Czechoslovakia, 170
Central Federation of Jewish University
    Students, 45
Central Jewish Museum, 213–15
Central Leadership of Home Resistance
    (ÚVOD), 176, 193, 205. *See also* Home
    Resistance
Černý, Bohumil, 294
Černý, František, 226
Černý, Jiří, 227
Černý, Josef, 53
Černý, Tomáš, 15
Černý, Václav, 210, 294, 330n67
České Budějovice, 34, 46, 55, 106, 146
České listy (Kapper), 13
Českožidovské listy, 15
Český zápas, 292
Chad Gadja, 342n107
Chadt, Zdeněk, 157
Chamberlain, H. S., 58

Chamberlain, Neville, 60
Charles University, 35, 47, 52, 91–92,
    322n66
Charles VI, King, 10–11
Charter 77, 293
Cheb (Eger), 60, 80
Chelmno death camp, 125
Chenevière, Jacques, 248, 251
children, 133, 153, 221–22, 238, 240–41,
    271, 278–80, 282–83
Christian Church, 292–93
Christian Socialists, 73
Christian X, King of Denmark, 254
Churavý, Colonel (Vlk), 195, 199
Churchill, Winston, 180
Church of Czech Brethren, 221–22
Chvalkovský, František, 72, 87–89, 91,
    142, 301
Cila, Svatopluk, 225
Čipek family, 223
"Civil Resistance," 200
civil service, 102–5
Čižek, Professor, 199, 200
Clementis, Vlado, 287
clergy, 221
Cocteau, Jean, 209
Committee for the Assistance of Refugees,
    209
Committee of National Solidarity, 99, 103,
    107, 143, 144, 152, 336n5
Communists: aid to refugees, 53, 72, 80–
    81, 222; and Eliáš, 150–51; influence
    on Beneš, 304; intelligence on Protec-
    torate, 180; Jews under, 288–89, 291–
    93; on Munich Agreement, 327n10;
    occupation of Czechoslovakia, 158,
    284, 287, 288, 290–95, 305–7; as refu-
    gees, 331n88; on State Council, 172; at
    Terezín, 244, 279. *See also* Czech
    Communist Party (CCP)
Communists' Central Association to Aid
    Refugees, 53
Concise History of Czech Literature
    (Novák), 41–42

Constitutional Committee on the Law
Regarding the Residence of Aliens, 53
cotton industry, 12
Croatia, 249
Culbertson, Paul T., 250, 379n62
culture, 15, 19–20, 209–10, 241, 242,
244–45, 255, 265, 297–98, 306–7. *See
also* art; music; religion; theater;
writing
Čurda, Karel, 154
Czech, Ludwig, 38–39, 51, 324n111
Czech Academy of Science, Literature
and Arts, 14
Czech Communist Party (CCP), 31; on
Czech-Soviet treaty, 57; first illegal
Central Committee, 151; hostility
toward German Communist Party, 73–
74; intelligence and sabotage, 204–7;
Jewish membership, 96; resistance, 64,
189–90, 193–95; in Vršovice youth
group, 201, 202. *See also* Communists
Czech Government-in-Exile: Beneš's control of, 160; Eliáš's cooperation with,
142; goal, 301; and Home Resistance,
189, 304; and Palestine, 166, 182; on
Protectorate governments, 138; recognition of, 148, 150, 168–69, 172; rescue efforts, 182–84; on Slovakian
deportations, 177–78, 180; as source of
intelligence, 175, 177
Czech historiography, 293, 295
Czech-Jewish movement: and anti-
Semitism, 17–18, 28, 46, 58; and
assimilationists, 84–85, 243–44; and
Jewish population in Czechoslovakia,
82–83; on Jewish question, 86; literature, 41–45; and outbreak of war, 24;
purpose, 15–16; on refugees, 54–55;
strengthening, 32–33; and Zionism,
33, 49. *See also* assimilation
Czech-Jews, 92–93, 116, 356n48, 377n26
Czech language, 18–19, 23–24, 29, 31, 34,
43
Czech National Bank, 105

Czechopress, 163
Czechoslovak, 357n70
Czecho-Slovak Agreement of Pittsburgh
(1918), 51
Czechoslovak Army, 161–69, 172–73,
192, 220–21, 243, 300, 335n171,
355n29
Czechoslovak Constitution, 319n12
Czechoslovak Consulate in Jerusalem, 47
Czechoslovakia: citizenship, 73, 92; economic resources, 105–6; exports, 37,
88; Jewish population, 8–11, 29, 36–
38, 82–83, 288, 306–7, 333n112,
345n155, 354n11, 390n51; national
awakening, 12–15, 17; Nazi policy in,
104–7, 121–23, 140–41, 158–59, 217,
298–300; occupation by Communists,
158, 284, 287, 288, 290–95, 305–7;
policy on Israel, 286–90; population,
26, 285; refugees in, 72–82; reputation
as democracy, 305; resistance, 113–14;
support of Jewish state, 306; as transit
point for survivors, 286
Czechoslovakia My Fate (Drtina), 161
Czechoslovakian League against Anti-
Semitism, 58, 347n9, 372n3
Czechoslovak-Israel Friendship League,
288
Czecho-Slovak Ministry of Finance, 81
Czechoslovak National Bank, 72
Czechoslovak National Committee, 27,
142, 147–49, 162, 163, 169
Czechoslovak National Council, 181–82
Czechoslovak National Democratic Party.
See National Union
Czecho-Slovak Parliament, 93
Czechoslovak Populist Party, 30
Czechoslovak Press Bureau, 61
Czechoslovak Red Cross, 46
Czechoslovak Social Democratic Workers'
Party, 30, 32, 39
Czechoslovak-Soviet treaty of mutual
assistance, 46, 57
Czechoslovak Zionist Executive, 30

Czech Security Service, 219
Czech-Slovak Republic, 65
Czech Socialist Party, 30
Czech transfer, 81, 161–62
Czech United National Party, 88
Czech University, 52
Czestapo, 102

Daluege, Kurt, 156–57, 224
Danish Jews, 246, 254–56, 258, 263
Danish Red Cross, 254–55
David, Jožka, 181–82
Day of Czech National Independence,
    182
Defense Loan, 57
Defense Training Program, 57
Dějiny cionistického hnutí (Lichtwitz), 59
De Lacroix, 88
Demec, 192, 220
democracy: eclipse of, 94–97
Department G, 126–27, 130
deportations: and Final Solution, 123–24;
    first campaign, 110–13, 145–47, 222,
    299–300; Hácha on, 152; ICRC on,
    250–51; intelligence on, 177; JRC
    involvement in, 111, 123, 125–27, 302;
    legislation, 93; of political detainees,
    361n4; press on, 188, 362n10; PVVZ on,
    197; second government on, 159; from
    Terezín, 236, 238–39; to Terezín,
    124–28, 133–35, 158, 300
Deutsch, Aladar, 21
Deutsch, Egon, 244, 382n122
Deutschland über alles, 275
Devět bran (Kara), 59
Diamant, Ervin, 363n28
Dicker-Brandeis, Friedl, 280
Dieses Volk (Baeck), 282
Divišová, Alena, 368n110
Dlesk, Ladislav, 225
Dobkin, Eliahu, 112
Dobříš, 102
Dobrovský, Josef, 11
Dodal, Irene, 272

Dohalská, Anna, 200, 231
Donath, Oskar, 36, 42
Doron, Uriel. *See* Felix, Otto
Dostál, Karel, 89
Drang nach Osten policy, 60, 140–41
Drázda, František, 103
Drei Reden über das Judentum (Buber), 22
Dresdner Bank, 106
Drexler, Pavel, 102
Drtina, Prokop, 161, 185
Drucker, Leopold, 363n28
Drummond, Edouard, 16
Dryák, Václav, 225
Dulles, Allen Welsh, 254
Dunant, Paul, 246, 262–64
Dvořáček, Jan Amos, 293
Dvořák, Antonín, 3

"Eagle of Duke Wenceslas," 157
"East," 124, 127, 235–37, 238, 300. *See
    also* Auschwitz
Easterman, Alexander L., 178–79, 181,
    253
Echad mi Jodea, 342n107
economy, 37–41, 69, 184, 297, 299
Edelstein, Jacob: arrest and deportation,
    244, 261; on Czech transfer, 162; on
    deportations, 111–13, 125, 126;
    knowledge of Final Solution, 301;
    leadership, 116, 235, 237, 240; letter to
    Ullmann, 376n11; religion, 266; on
    rescue through work, 238; travel, 117,
    122
Edelstein, Mirjam, 260–61, 382n120
Eden, Anthony, 180
Edict of Tolerance (1782), 11
education, 38, 269–70, 279, 298
Ehrenfeld, Nathan, 20
Eichler, Benjamin, 289
Eichmann, Adolf: at Altneuschul, 101; on
    contact between Jewish communities,
    132; dejudaization of Poland, 110–13;
    on deportations, 127; establishment of
    Zentralstelle, 145; and inspection of

Terezín, 254–56, 262; interrogation of artists, 245; meeting with Heydrich, 123; reorganization of Terezín administration, 240; on Terezín, 234; on travel of Jewish leaders, 117; trial, 122

Einsatzgruppen, 123, 231

Eisenmann, Louis, 59

Eisner, F. L., 46

Eisner, Pavel: on aid to refugees, 208, 370n148; on assimilation, 307; correspondence with Fischl, 371n165; eulogy of Fischer, 43; on Foerster, 334n137; on Jewish identity, 23; on Jewish literature, 42; on Kafka in Prague, 6; on Orten, 211; works, 212

Elbert, Erwin, 246

elderly, 238–40, 267, 281

Eliáš, Alois, xiii; arrest and execution, 151–52, 205; and Beer-Konrád, 204; and Bondy, 196; and cooperation with Nazis, 138, 147–50, 299; evidence on, 349n47, 350n62; failure to resign, 150–51; historical assessment of, 158–59; on Jewish question, 339n48; objectives, 142–44; optimism, 107; as prime minister, 100, 141–43; and resistance, 369n122

Eliot, T. S., 213

Ellnerová, Helena, 201, 202, 367n96

Emerson, Sir Herbert, 78

emigration, 118–20, 122, 161–66, 220–21, 224, 302, 354n14. *See also* deportations; Zentralstelle für jüdische Auswanderung

Emig[ration]-direct, 53

"The Emperor of Atlantis or: Death Resigns," 274–75

Engel, Alfred, 30, 214

Eppstein, Paul, 240, 245, 252–53, 255–60, 377n22

Erben, Eva, 228–29

Etter, Philip, 251

Executive Committee of the Central Zionist Federation, 83

export industries, 37, 88

Faktor, Emil, 118

Falknov, 80

Familiants' Law (1727), 10–11

Fantlová-Reimová, Milada, 154

Farkas, Endre (Yona), 368n110

fascism, 45–47, 107, 143, 144, 150, 338n27

Faucher, General, 79–80

Feder, Richard, 135–36, 266, 281, 288, 389n25

Federation of Orthodox Jews from Czechoslovakia, 170

Feierabend, Ladislav, 142, 147

Feilchenfeld, Dr., 106

Feiwel, Berthold, 21

Felix, Otto, 286, 388n10

Feller, Pavel, 363n29

Ferrière, Suzanne, 251

Fest, Jindřich, 206

Feuchtwanger, Lion, 75

Feuerstein, Emil, 205

Feuerstein, Vojtěch (Fai), 202, 203, 367n98

Fiala, Jozef, 221

Fikejsová, Růžena, 365n57

Finale di Cantata Judaica, 278

Final Solution, 123, 127, 139, 141, 233, 249, 251–52, 260, 301, 304

Finger, Rudolf, 223

First Congress of the Czech Slavonic Working People, 16

First Republic (1918–38), 26, 298; agriculture, 37–38; assimilation, 32–33; economy, 37–41; treatment of Jews during, 161, 303

Firt, Julius, 40, 58, 209–10, 322n62, 332n110

Fischer, Fridrich, 363n29

Fischer, Josef, 66, 191, 195–96, 200, 361n8, 362n11, 364n52

Fischer, Karel, 15
Fischer, Karl, 267
Fischer, Milena (Balcarová), 196
Fischer, Otokar, 42–43, 64, 73, 211,
    322nn65–66, 322n70
Fischl, Karel, 27
Fischl, Viktor, 59, 177, 371n165
Fischof, Franz, 101
Fleischmann, Jan, 227
"Flight into the Book" (Hora), 209
Foerster, Josef Bohuslav, 91, 333n137
Foltýn, Leo, 244, 382n122
Formis, Rudolf, 74, 329n50
France: aid to refugees, 81; bitterness
    toward, 68, 74, 114–15; Czech Army
    in, 163–64, 168, 169; defeat of, 148;
    resistance, 139–40; treatment of
    Beneš, 168–69; treaty with, 56–57, 64
Francis I, King, 12
Frankensteinová-Volavková, Hana, 214
Frank, Jan, 193, 204, 364n46, 369n119
Frank, Karl Hermann: on Eliáš's procla-
    mation, 350n79; on exemptions, 148,
    149; and inspection of Terezín, 262;
    meeting with Heydrich, 123; memo on
    Czech problems, 104–5, 115; as minis-
    ter of state, 157–58; on resistance, 147,
    223, 260; as state secretary of Protecto-
    rate, 99; trial, 286
František Winternitz, Český žid-legionář,
    59
Františkovy Lázně, 80
Franz Kafka in Prague (Eisner), 6
Fr. Borový publishing house, 211
Freemason Lodge, 196
Freemasonry, 16
Frei, Dr., 363n29
Freizeitgestaltung, 238, 276, 281, 382n121
Freizügigkeitsgesetz, 12
French Association of Writers, 66
French-Tunisian agreement (1881), 98
Freund, Arnošt, 206
Freund, Eugen, 363n29
Freund, Heřmann, 207, 370n142

Frick, Wilhelm, 157
Frič, Vladimír, 47
Frída, Emil. *See* Vrchlický, Jaroslav
"Friday Circle," 40, 43
Friedl, Josef, 195, 199
Friedmann, Cecilie, 135
Friedmann, Desider, 246
Friedmann, Elie, 368n110
Friedmann, František, 33, 117, 130, 132–
    34, 162, 255
Friedmann, Richard Israel, 111–12, 122,
    125, 127, 130, 135, 301
Frischer, Arnošt (Ernst), 32, 173, 174,
    177–81, 358n78
Frischmann, 110
Fritta, Bedřich. *See* Taussig, Fritz
Frýd, Norbert, 121, 212, 371n169
Frýdek-Místek, 110–11
Fuchs, Alfred, 41, 221
Fuchs, František, 289, 291
Fuchs, Gerhard, 193–94, 222–23
Fuchs, Rudolf, 23–24
Fuchs, Valerie, 193–94
Fuchs, Walter, 349n54
Fuchsová, Hanka, 200
Fučík, Julius, 194, 197, 204, 364n46,
    369n124
Fučíková, Gusta, 198, 204
Funk, Emilie, 225
Fürth, Erich, 106
Fürth, Karel, 157
Fürth, Leopold, 157

Gach, Dr., 55
Gajda, Rudolf, 46, 73
Galicia, 29–30
Gall, Otto, 200, 231, 363n36, 366n87
Gartesier, Colonel, 250
Gebhardt, Professor, 252
Geneva, 131–32, 175, 358n88
Geneva Convention, 252, 253
German Communist Party, 73–74
Germanization: goal of, 104, 114, 217,
    297; intelligence on, 176; and Jewish

question, 145, 299; Namier on, 112; Peroutka on, 93; and refugees, 54–55; trigger of process, 10–12, 153

German language, 11–12, 18–19, 23–24, 29, 34, 82, 104, 161

German Military Authority, 107

German People's Court, 206

German Red Cross, 252–53

Germans: Beneš's on transfer, 170–71, 174, 185; in Czech army, 335n171; in Czechoslovakia, 12, 217; minority status, 50, 170–75, 185, 304, 358n74; nationalism, 208; political party, 30; at Terezín, 238–41, 243–45, 267, 268, 281, 377n26. *See also* Germany; Sudeten Germans

German Security Services, 143, 205, 300

German Social Democrats, 39, 75

German Socialist movement, 50–51

German University of Prague, 45, 46, 52, 55, 57

Germany: emigration to, 224; propaganda, 55–62, 71, 76, 87, 96, 101–2, 114, 121–23, 153, 190, 242–45, 254–56, 265–66; refugees from, 53–55, 78. *See also* Germans

Geschke, Hans Ullrich, 147, 349n47

Gestapo, 74, 80, 99–101, 103, 108, 111, 231, 234

"Ghetto Lullaby," 275

ghettos, 233–34. *See also* Terezín

Gide, André, 209

Ginz, Petr, 242

Girczik, Obersturmführer, 133

"Give! Build! Live!" campaign, 120–21

Glas, Egon, 361n4

Glaser, Anton, 21

Glaser, Kurt, 204, 369nn124–25

Goebbels, Joseph, 58, 77

Goering, Hermann, 123

"Goethe und Ghetto" (Ullmann), 265

Gold, Hugo, 36

Golden Bull of Charles IV of 1356, 99

Golding, Lewis, 209

Goldman, Rudolf, 223

Goldmann, Nahum, 55–56, 174, 181, 301

Goldschmid, Alfred, 244, 382n122

Goldschmidt, Joseph, 225

Goldstein, Angelo, 31, 32, 36, 53, 55, 60, 163, 165, 173, 358n75

Goldstücker, Eduard, 286, 289

Goltz, Hans, 225

Goltz-Goldlust, Marianne, 224–25

Gorazd, Bishop, 154

go-slow campaign, 205

Gottlieb, František, 292, 322n65

Gottwald, Klement, 65, 284, 285, 287, 327n10, 364n42

Gradowski, Salmen, 280

Gratzer, Hugo, 27

Grawitz, Dr., 252, 380n75

Great Britain: aid to refugees, 77, 79, 81–82, 99–100; bitterness toward, 67–68, 74, 114–15; Czech immigrants in, 169–70; and Czech transfer, 162; and Jewish army, 164, 166–68, 355n26; recognition of Czech Government-in-Exile, 148, 150, 169, 172; treatment of Beneš, 168–69; treaty with, 64

"The Greek and the Hebrew Genius" (Šalda), 5

Gregory, Hermann von, 87

Gregory, Karl Freiherr von, 123

Grossmann, Kurt, 80

Grünbaum, Heiman, 27

Grünberger, Abraham, 368n110

Grünberger, Julius, 246

Grünfeld, Arnold, 110

Grunthal, 202

Guggenheim, Paul, 251

Günther, Hans, 101–2, 110–11, 122–24, 145, 245, 337n19

Günther, Rolf, 256

Guri, Chaim, 287

Gutfreund, Otto, 326n148

Guth, Otakar, 24, 59

Guth, Rudolf, 326n148

Gutmann family, 37, 105

Haas, Hugo, 89
Haas, Leo, 245, 272, 384n28
Haas, Pavel, 89, 274, 276–78, 282, 333n128
Ha'avara Fund, 162
Hába, Alois, 278
Habsburg Empire, 9–10
Hácha, Emil: anti-Soviet statements, 150; cooperation with Nazis, 138, 176, 299; death, 158; on deportations, 152; on exemptions, 147–48; on Government-in-Exile, 350n67; on Jewish question, 87; mourning of Heydrich, 156; in Protectorate, 98–100; role in occupied Czechoslovakia, 143
Hachenburg, Hanuš, 268
HADEGA, 108
Haganah, 286, 287
Haggadah, 119
Hájek, Jiří, 293
Hájek, Miloš, 203, 224
Halas, František, 44, 66, 115, 199, 210
Halder, General, 97
Halifax, Lord, 100
Halifax, Viscount, 88–89
Hamšík, Lieutenant Colonel, 107
Hanák, Miloš, 176, 184, 207
Hartmann, Moritz, 13
Hartmann, Walter, 252, 259, 380n76
Hašek, Jaroslav, 41, 289
HaShomer HaTza'ir, 166, 188, 223
Hasidic movement, 44
Haskalah, 11
Hauner, Milan, 97
Haushofer, Albrecht, 74–75
Havel, Václav, 7, 293
Havelka, Jiří, 142
Hebrew Emigration Aid Society (HIAS), 53
Hebrew University in Jerusalem, 47
HeHalutz Center, 130, 202, 238, 342n103, 345n150, 368n109, 381n104
Heiber, Helmut, 151
Heidenkampf, Dr., 256
Heilbronn, Leo, 272

Heimstätte für Juden, 262
Heine, Heinrich, 3, 42
Heller, Jiří, 202
Hellerová, Vlasta, 226
Henlein, Konrad, 57, 60–61, 73, 143, 260
Hennigsen, Juel, 256
Henschel, Herr, 382n121
Hergeth, Armin, 229–30
Heřmánek, Karel, 224
Heřmánek, Václav, 224
Hermann Göring Werke, 106
Herren der Welt (Singer), 187, 216
Herrmann, Hugo, 22
Herrmann, Leo, 21, 162, 163, 166, 168
Herz, Alexander, 363n29
Herzl, Theodor, 1, 21, 22, 25, 33, 279
Heydekampf, 382n110
heydrichiáda, xiii, 155–56, 223–24, 303
Heydrich, Reinhard, xiii; assassination, 151, 153–56, 159, 178, 183, 206, 223; "attack" in Gleiwitz, 109–10; on Czech government, 158; on exemptions, 148, 159; on "final objective," 123–24; political program, 153; as Reichsprotektor, 123, 151, 152, 205, 222, 303; on Terezín, 234
HICEM, 53, 117
Hilarová, Dagmar, 247
Hilberg, Raul, 134
Hilf, Alois, 28
Hilsner, Leopold, 4, 17
The Hilsner Affair and TGM (Rys-Rozsévač), 100
Himmler, Heinrich, 123, 146, 243, 254, 261, 377n21, 380n71
Himmler-Musy negotiations, 246
Hindemith, Paul, 278
Hinsley, Cardinal, 177
Hiršal, Josef, 210, 341n88, 370n156
Hirsch, Fredy, 280
Hirsch, Isidor, 35
The History of the Jews in Bohemia, Moravia and Silesia 906–1620 (Bondy), 19
Hitler, Adolf: appeasement of, 64; on

assassination of Heydrich, 153; on Final Solution, 249, 301; goal in Czechoslovakia, 104, 140–41, 217, 298–99; meetings with Chvalkovský, 91; *Mein Kampf*, 216; nonaggression pact with Czechoslovakia, 75; personality, 364n56; in Prague, 98; rise to power, 50, 51; on self-determination, 60–64; Wegner's warning about, 229

Hlinka, Andrej, 51

Hoch, Rabbi Dr., 110

Hodža, Milan, 56, 60

Hofer, Hans, 268

Hoffmann, Kamil, 23–24

Hoffmann, Stanley, 138–39

Hohenlohe-Langenburg, Egon, 254, 380n85

Holešov synagogue, 337n14

Hollar, Master, 119

Holocaust: postwar ideas about, 292–93

Holzner, Lydia, 154

Holzner family, 351n98, 352n99

Home Resistance, xiii, 361n2; and Beneš, 171, 182–83; on deportations, 111; direction of, 189; German manipulation, 150, 301; and Government-in-Exile policy, 189, 304; and intelligence, 175, 180; on Jewish question, 207; participants, 187–88. *See also* Central Leadership of Home Resistance (ÚVOD)

Hoop, Augustin von, 371n156

Hora, Josef, 66, 209

Horák, Corporal, 50

Horáková-Králová, Milada, 199, 366n78

Horthy, Admiral, 298

Hostovský, Egon, 42, 44–45, 58, 95, 294, 323n81, 326n147

Hromádka, J. L., 65, 91

Hroznětín, 80

Huber, Max, 248, 251

Hübschmann, Antonín. *See* Fischer, Josef

Hungarians, 30, 34, 143, 159, 161, 185, 286, 354n12

Hungary: annexation of Subcarpathian Ruthenia, 97; cession of territory to, 77; deportations from, 250; effect on Czech policies, 56; ICRC in, 249, 254; Jewish entrepreneurship in, 19; leadership, 298; nationalism, 208; occupation, 132; refugees in, 191; rescue organizations, 189

Hussitism, 2–3, 9

Huxley, Aldous, 209

Hvass, Frants, 256, 258, 381n101

Ibn Yaqub, Ibrahim, 8

identity cards, 201, 367n95

Illnerová, Rokyta, 197

Ingr, Sergey, 168

intellectuals: aid to refugees, 208–9; and anti-Semitism, 89–91; and eclipse of democracy, 94, 96; in First Republic, 37–41, 298; intelligence on Protectorate, 180; and JRC activities, 117; Kafka on, 83; loyalty, 332n105; and propaganda, 87; resistance, 187, 216

intelligence, 175–86, 191, 203–8, 230

International Committee of the Red Cross (ICRC), xiv; draft appeal, 251; information received by, 248–50; inspection of Terezín, 134, 234, 243, 245, 246, 252, 254–59, 261–64; intervention at Terezín, 247, 251–54; knowledge of Final Solution, 249, 251–52, 260; position of, 247–48, 303; and rescue efforts, 182, 360n119. *See also* Czechoslovak Red Cross; Danish Red Cross; German Red Cross; Swedish Red Cross

Israel, 285–90. *See also* Palestine

Istanbul, 130–32, 175–76, 180, 184, 204, 255

Jablonec, 80

Jabotinsky, Vladimir, 5

Jahn, Kryštof, 229

Jahn, Ludmila, 229

Jahrbuch der Gesellschaft für die Geschichte der Juden in der Čechoslovakischen Republik, 36

Jakobovits, Tobias, 36, 214

Jaksch, Wenzel, 79, 358n74

Jakubec, Antonín, 86

Janáček, Leoš, 277

Janetschek, Theodor, 234

Jankovec, Wolfgang, 195

Janovice, 157

Janowitz, Leo, 235, 257–58, 381n105

Jáša, Václav, 55

Jászi, Oscar, 307

Jeiteles family, 13

Jelínek, Jaroslav, 95

Jerusalem, 6, 163

Jesenská, Milena: on anti-Semitism, 91; on Czech traitors, 197; death, 328n25; defense of republic, 66–68; leadership, 95–96; on Munich Agreement, 72; and refugees, 75, 77, 78, 80, 220, 335n165; tour of Sudeten area, 76

"Jew Hunting," 209

Jewish Agency for Palestine, 81, 173, 380n78

Jewish Army, 164, 166–68, 355n26

Jewish Colonization Association (ICA), 53

Jewish Committee for Aid to Refugees from Germany, 53

Jewish Council for Vocations, 38

Jewish Council of Elders, 130, 133, 136, 235, 237–40, 246. *See also* Jewish Religious Congregation of Prague (JRC)

Jewish historiography, 293–95

Jewish Museum, 35, 295, 296

Jewish National Council, 28

Jewish Party of Czechoslovakia, 28, 29, 31–32, 55–57, 81. *See also* National Jews from Czechoslovakia

Jewish property: confiscation, 105–10, 143–45, 176–77, 208, 236, 299, 304; and JRC, 129–30; restitution, 285, 295; value, 335n154

Jewish question: and anti-Semitism, 295; Beneš on, 161, 185, 284–85; Eliáš on, 339n48; and Germanization, 145, 299; Masaryk on, 184; and Nisko-Lublin plan, 146–47; participation in solution, 86–88, 94; postwar, 207–8; three periods in approach to, 218

Jewish Relief Committee, 72

Jewish Religious Community, 36, 277

Jewish Religious Congregation of Prague (JRC): abolition, 130; coercion by Nazis, 116–17, 120–21, 124, 134–36, 187, 300–301; collection of historically valuable material, 128–29, 135, 302; and deportations, 111, 123, 125–27, 302; handling of Jewish property, 129–30; knowledge of murder in Poland, 346n159; members, 122, 341n92; parcels to, 345n150; records, 341n91; security, 101; strategy, 301–2; travel, 117–18, 122; under Zentralstelle, 110. *See also* Jewish Council of Elders

Jewish Town Hall, 9, 28

Jews: aid to refugees, 222; categories, 334n149; communications between communities, 130–34; under Communists, 288–89, 291–93; community membership, 332n100; definition, 110, 143–44; exempted, 147–48, 159, 218, 302; in First Republic, 161, 303; identity, 20–25, 28, 185, 188–89, 268, 285; intelligence reports on victims, 181; life in Protectorate, 99–103, 114, 115, 140, 143; population in Czechoslovakia, 8–11, 29, 36–38, 82–83, 288, 306–7, 333n112, 345n155, 354n11, 390n51; relationship with Czechs, 1–2, 12–13, 15, 108, 289, 293, 306; resistance, 188–93, 201–2, 206–7, 214–15, 300–301; status, 34–37, 170–75, 217, 297–98, 304

Jews and Judaism in Nineteenth- and Twentieth-Century Czech Literature (Donath), 42

Jidishe Bühne troupe, 272
Jihlava district, 75
Jihlava synagogue, 101
Jílemnický, P., 66
Jirát, Vojtěch, 211
Jistebnický kancionál, 2
Jöckl, 228
John, Jaromir, 212
Joodse Raad, 122
Josefov, 1, 15
Joseph II, King, 11
Judaica Bohemiae, 291
Judaism, 3–7
Jüdenrate (Judenrat), 134, 136, 137, 238,
    302, 376n14. *See also* Jewish Council of
    Elders
"Judeo-Bolshevism," 46, 57
Der Jüdischer Frauenverein, 21
Jüdischer Volksverein, 21
Ein jüdisches Kind, 275
Jüdisches Nachrichtenblatt (JNBL),
    342n100
Jüdisches Nachrichtenblatt / Židovské listy,
    118–19
Jugl, Karel, 119, 342n107
Julie, Sedláková (Polák), 155
Julie, Soinarová (Bloch), 155
Junod, Marcel, 111, 248

Kadlec, Josef, 162–68
Kafka, Emil, 83–84, 117, 332n103
Kafka, Erich, 126
Kafka, František, 292
Kafka, Franz, 5–6, 20, 23, 28, 41, 67, 116,
    289, 318n82
Kafkas böses Böhmen (Stölzl), 295
Kahn, Franz, 30, 116, 130, 145, 146, 162,
    235, 255, 279
Kahn, Olga, 246
Kaiser von Atlantis, 275, 276, 282
Kalandra, Záviš, 44
Kalendář česko-židovský, 15, 44
Kalfus, Dr., 162
Kalla, Lt. Col., 168

Kallus (commissar of Pankrác prison), 223
Kaltenbrunner, Ernst, 242–43
Kamenetz Podolsk, 250
Kanner, Mikuláš, 363n28
Kantor, Dr., 106
Kapper, Siegfried, 13, 23
Kapper club, 58–59
Kapras, Jan, 92
Kara, Avigdor, 59
Karlovy Vary, 49, 80
Karlsbad Eight Point Program, 60
Kašpar, Karel, 373n16
Kastner, Rezsö, 132, 136, 246, 255, 263
Katowice region, 146
Katz, Leopold, 15, 311n9
Kaufmann, Gerhard S., 371n167
Kaufmann, Viktor, 196, 200, 361n8,
    364n56
Kaufmannová, Heda, 188, 361n8
Kautman, František, 6
Keitel, General, 97
Kelsen, Hans, 55, 57
Kennan, George, 49, 142, 158
Kertesz, Stephen, 176
Kestenberg, Ruth, 36
Kfar Masaryk, 166, 356n37
Kibbutz Beit Alpha, 48–49
Kien, Petr, 272–74
Kieval, Hillel J., 25
Kinský, Count, 348n20
Kinšperk synagogue, 80
Kisch, Alexander, 20
Kisch, Egon Erwin, 23, 40, 73
Kisch, Guido, 13, 36
Kladno mines, 105–6
Klang, Heinrich, 246
Klapka, Otakar, 149
Klatovy, 101, 102
Klausnitzer, Hauptsturmführer, 132, 255
Klaus Synagogue, 214
Klecanda, Ludvík, 86
Klein, Bohumil, 192–93
Klein, Gideon, 212, 267, 273, 276, 282
Klein, Robert, 40

Klemeš, Jaroslav, 226
Klíma, Ivan, xi
Kliment, Gustav, 183
Klineberger, 17
Klinger, Eugen, 220
Klumpar, 147
Koch, Walter, 51–52
Kochta, J., 198–99
Kodíček, Milan, 170
Kohn, Hans, 20
Kohn, Jindřich, 24, 32, 59
Kohn, Jiří, 207
Kohn, Moric, 363n28
Kohn, Pavel, 206
Kohout, Pavel, 289
Kokoschka, Oscar, 209
Kolár, Joseph Jiří, 210
Kolár, Martin, 311n9
Kolínský, 197
Komenský, Jan Amos (Comenius), 3, 5
Königliches Landestheater, 15
Kook, Chief Rabbi, 48
Kopecký, Jaromír, 134, 175, 249, 258, 359n88
Kopecký, Václav, 207–8, 287
Kopta, J., 66
Körbel, Gert, 256
Korbel, Josef, xi
Kořínek, Karel. *See* Eisner, Pavel
Košatová, Bauerová, 227
Košice program, 284
Kostka, Vilém, 210, 370n156
Kotlár, Václav, 223
Kozower, Philipp, 246
Kralice Bible, 2
Králíček family, 223
Králová, Eva, 202, 203
Kramář, F., 60
Krämer, Salo, 111, 129, 130, 345n149
Krämer Department, 129–30
Krása, Hans, 276
Kraus, Arnošt, 322n66
Kraus, Erich, 116–17, 130, 134, 136, 342n94

Kraus, Lev, 363n28
Kraus, Ota, 292
Kreibich, Karel, 172, 288
Krejcarová-Jesenská, Milena. *See* Jesenská, Milena
Krejčí (collaborationist government), 156
Krejčí, František, 22–23, 47
Krejčí, Jan, 86
Krejčí, Jaroslav, 152–53
Krejčí, Ludvík, 64
Křen, Jan, xii, 294, 295
Křesťanská revue, 332n109
Kripo, 156
Kristallnacht, 80
Krofta, Kamil, 74–75, 181
Krofta, Karel, 56
Kruh, Ernst, 367n95, 368n110
Krumey, Haupsturmführer, 246, 263
Krychtálek, 360n126
Kubiš (parachutist), 154
Kučera, František, 226
Kugel, Chaim, 32, 60, 163, 355n20, 355n30
Kundt, Ernst, 92
Kuratorium pro výchovu mládeže v Čchách a na Moravě, 153
Kvapil, J., 66
Kvapil, Jaroslav, 207
Kynšperk synagogue, 101
Kysela, Jiří, 201, 203, 366n91
Kyselová, Olga, 367n91

Labor Exchange, 120
Labor Office, 368n109
LaGuardia, Fiorello, 168
Landau, Moses Israel, 13–14
Landräte, 108
Langer, František, 20, 42–44, 66, 326n148
Langer, Herbert, 130
Langer, Jiří (Mordechai), 43–44, 59, 322n65, 323n75
Langerová, Eva, 202, 203
language, 17, 19, 31, 272, 298. *See also* Czech language; German language

Language Law, 31
Lány, E., 181
Laufer, Stefan, 363n29
law of free movement, 12
Law of Restitution (1946), 285
League of Friends of Jewish Palestine, 288
League of Nations, 31, 55
Lebenhart, Filip, 21
Lebensraumprogramm, 98
Lebowitz, Jani, 368n110
Lederer, Eduard, 17, 18, 32, 378n37
Lederer, Miloš, 202, 203, 367n97
Lederer, Pavel, 202, 367n97
Lederer, Viktor, 367n97
Lederer, Zdeněk, 240, 260
Lehner, Otto, 246, 262–63, 383n129
Leimer, Willy, 231
Lemberger (Limberský), 368n110
Leopold II, King, 12
Leopold, Singer, 157
Leo XIII, Pope, 16
Leshem, 368nn109
Lessing, Theodor, 74, 208–9, 329n49
Letenská-Čalounová (actress), 365n72
Letters from Exile (Hostovský), 323n81
Levett, Gordon, 287
Lewis, Bernard, 4
Lewit, Walter, 225
Lewit, Yvonne, 225
Ležáky, 156
Liberec, 80
Liblice, 289
Libuše, 114
Lichtheim, Richard, 379n69
Lichtwitz, Hans, 59
Lidice, 155–56
"The Lidice Sheep" (Weber), 271
Lidové noviny, 39, 40
Lieben, Salomon, 34
Lieben, Salomon Hugo, 28, 34, 36, 214
Lieben family, 278
Ligue International contre l'Anti-sémitisme, 58, 216

literature, 16–17, 46, 57–58, 209–12. *See also* writers; writing
"Little Entente," 56
Löb, Dr., 106
Locker-Lampson, Colonel, 77
Lockhart, Bruce, 170, 172, 177, 193
Lodý ghetto, 118, 124–25, 130, 345nn151–52
Loew, Judah ben Bezalel (the Maharal), 1, 2, 9, 102, 292
Loewenstein, Karl, 239, 377n20
London News Chronicle, 79
Lord Mayor's Fund, 79
Lorenz, Arnošt, 194, 222
Löwy, Moritz, 21
Lublin, 111, 146–47
Lubsky, 157
Lueger, Karl, 16
Lukáč, E. B., 66
Lukeš, Václav, 351n98
Lux, Stefan, 58
Luža, Radomír, 97

Maccabi, 21, 47, 191, 221, 363n28
Mácha, Karel Hynek, 3, 247
Machar, J. S., 22
Maclay, Sir Ronald, 79, 331n80
Magdeburg Barracks, 275
Maglione, Cardinal, 252
Maharal. *See* Loew, Judah ben Bezalel (the Maharal)
Mährisch Ostrau, 112–13
Maisl, Mordechai (1528–1601), 9
Majerová, M., 66
Majsky, Ivan, 80–81
The Making of Czech Jewry (Kieval), 25
Makovský, František, 242, 376n8, 381n102
Malcolm, Sir Neil, 53, 79–80
Malý, Josef, 226
Manes, Philip, 270
Mann, Heinrich, 73, 208
Mann, Thomas, 73, 208
Mareni, Zofia-Zosha, 109

Margulies, Emil, 32, 320n25
Mariánské Lázně, 80
Maria Theresa, Queen, 11
März, Paul, 30, 162, 163, 355n20, 355n30
Masaryk, Jan, 71, 162, 182, 184, 248–49, 284–87, 303
Masaryk, T. G.: aid to refugees, 54; on assimilation, 18; and Bar Kochba Association of Jewish Students, 21; and Ben Avi, 324n103; and Czech-Jewish relations, xii, 24, 318n88; on Czechs in Protectorate and Palestine, 161, 166; death, 60, 64, 327n11; Declaration of Independence, 26–27; destruction and removal of likenesses, 71, 100–101; German language usage, 12; on Hilsner trial, 17; on Jewish minority, 27; leadership, 298; legacy, xi; in Palestine, 48–49; philosophy, 4–5; and *Přítomnost*, 67; retirement, 56; review of *Mein Kampf*, 216; studies of, 41
Masaryk and the Jews (Rychnowský), 41
Masarykova, Alice, 48
Masaryk University, 92
Mašín, Colonel, 198
Mastníková, 199
Mastný, Vojtěch, 74, 364n44
Mathesius, B., 66
Maurer, 123
Mauthausen, 122, 206
Maximilian (1564–76), 9
Mayr-Harting, Robert, 50
Meijers, Edward Maurice, 246
Mein Kampf (Hitler), 98, 216, 364n56
Meissner, Alfred, 12, 38–39, 246
Melkman, Joseph, 122
Der Mensch und sein Tag (Adler), 275
Merell, Jan, 228
Meyers, Bishop, 177
Michel, Henry, 189
Michl, Max, 227
Mikulov, 35
Milič House, 221

Minařík, Dr., 86
Ministry of Church Affairs, 291
minority status, 27–28, 31, 50, 60, 170–75, 185, 298, 304, 306, 358n74
Minsk, 124, 125
mixed marriages, 21, 37, 49, 130, 133
Mizrachi Party, 32
Mladočeši, 17
Modernity and the Holocaust (Bauman), 305
Möhs, Ernst, 245, 256, 382n110
Moldovan, Lazar, 130–32
Moravec, Emanuel, 153, 156, 178, 183, 360n127
Moravec, František, 142, 175, 190, 220, 230
Moravec family, 154
Moravia: anti-Semitism, 185; arrests, 109, 110; Catholic organizations, 14, 16; confiscation of Jewish property in, 144–45; Czech-Jewish movement, 32, 33; dejudaization campaign, 123; deportations from, 128; fascism, 45–46; during First Republic, 26; Germanization, 12, 217; ghettos, 124; historical relics, 135; Jewish identity, 21; Jewish occupations, 37; Jewish-owned establishments, 338n40; Jewish population, 10–11, 37, 82, 174, 288, 333n112; Jewish rights, 29; Jewish status, 34–35, 297; language of Jews, 19; Nazi policy in, 104, 121; Orthodox tradition, 34; PVVZ members in, 363n36; rescue from, 96, 221; Terezín inmates from, 268; transports to Terezín, 239; Zionism, 30, 85
Moravian Holešov riots, 27
Moravská Ostrava, 29–31, 38, 55, 89, 111, 120, 146, 248, 340n67
Moreillon, Jacques, 249
Most, 80
Motzkin, Leo, 320n25
Müller, Dr., 86
Müllerová, Zdena, 365n68

Muneles, Otto, 214, 372n177
Munich Agreement, 63–66; and anti-
    Semitism, 96; bitterness over, 66–68;
    Communists on, 327n10; economic
    repercussions, 69; effect on Hostovský,
    44; effect on refugees in Czechoslo-
    vakia, 78–79, 81; international conse-
    quences, 97; Jewish response, 83; psy-
    chological effects, 71–72; and Supreme
    Council, 35
"Munichites," 300
Municipal Council of Prague, 72
Munk, Erich, 256
Münzer-Penížek, Josef, 40
Murmuelstein, Benjamin, 135, 240, 245,
    247, 252–53, 259, 260, 262, 263,
    382n118
Museum of Arts and Crafts, 19
music, 266–71, 274–78
Musy, Jean-Marie, 261, 378n48
Myslbek, Josef Václav, 20

Namier, Lewis M., 166, 172, 356n33
Namier, Louis, 112–13, 340n73
Narcissenfeld, Vojtěch, 368n110
Národní arijská kulturní jednota, 103
Národní listy, 14, 17, 40, 94
Národní osvobození, 72
Národní politika, 332n111
Naše vojsko, 358n70
Nashashibi, Ragheb Bey, 48
National Association of Cooperative
    Stores, 56
National Café, 86
National Coordinating Committee, 53–
    54, 80
Nationalists, 73
National Jewish Council, 27
National Jews from Czechoslovakia, 171–
    75. See also Jewish Party of
    Czechoslovakia
National Liberals, 17
National Movement of Working Youth,
    192, 205–6

National Socialist Czech Workers Party, 102
National Theater in Prague, 14, 89, 90, 95
National Union, 30, 64, 92
National Union of Czech Jews, 15, 17–18
Naujocks, Alfred, 329n50
Nazi Fascist Community, 46
Nazis: coercion, 116–17, 120–21, 124,
    134–37, 187, 300–301; cooperation
    with, 136–39, 147, 149–50, 152–53,
    176, 182–83, 299; and ghettoization,
    233–34; informants, 224, 226; policy
    in Czechoslovakia, 104–7, 121–23,
    140–41, 158–59, 217, 298–300; varia-
    tions in policy, 304
Nazism, 46–47, 50–52, 63, 74
Nazi-Soviet Non-Aggression Pact (1939),
    193
Nebeský, Josef, 149
Nebeský, Václav Bolemír, 13
Nečas, Jaromír, 55, 142
Nečásek (police commissioner), 146
Nejedlý, Zdeněk, 73, 201
Nepomuk, Johan, 20
Nerad, Antonín, 365n64
Neruda, Jan, 58
Nettl, Paul, 36, 277
Neubauer, Leo, 337n24
Neues Deutsches Theater, 15
Neumann, Angelo, 15
Neumann, Arnošt (Ephraim), 202, 203,
    224, 368nn101–2, 368n110
Neumann, Emil, 213
Neumann, Ervin, 58, 59
Neurath, Konstantin von, 99, 121–23,
    141, 143–46, 148, 217–18, 299
Neuschl, Robert, 16
Neuwirth, Dr., 126
Newton, 88–89
New York World's Fair, 168–69
Nezval, V., 66
Niehaus, L., 253, 259, 380n76
Nikolsburg (Mikulov) Yeshiva, 9
The Nine Gates to Chassidic Mysteries
    (Langer), 44

Nisko, 112–13, 146–47, 248, 301, 340n67
Nisou, 80
Nordau, Dr., 33
Notes from the Gallows, 197
Nováček, Antonín, 352n101
Nováček, Jiřina, 155
Nováček family, 154–55
Novák, Arne, 22, 41–42, 47
Novák, (journalist), 360n126
Novomeský, L., 66
NSDAP, 98, 100, 148
Nuremberg Laws, xiii, 46, 55–56, 102, 110, 143–44, 221, 243, 299, 339n48

Obrana národa (ON), 141, 147. *See also* Army Organization
Odložilík, Otakar, 10
Ohrensteinová, Berta (Rosenzweig), 116
Olbracht, Ivan, 3, 44, 66, 73
Old-New Synagogue. *See* Altneuschul
Oliner, Jente, 261
Olomouc, 100, 338n27
Olšovy Vraty concentration camps, 80
Olympic Games (1936), 57
open university, 269–70
Operation Albrecht I, 110, 147
Operation Anthropoid, 153–55, 183
Operation Musy, 261
Operation Nahshon, 288
Organization of Czechoslovaks in Palestine (OCP), 164–65
Orsenigo (Papal Nuncio), 252
ORT, 117
Orten, Jiří, 45, 58, 115–16, 118, 210–11, 341n88, 371n159
Orten, Ornest, 115
Orten, Ota, 116
Orten, Zdeněk, 116
Orthodox tradition, 20–21, 34
Österreicher, Erich, 255–56
Ostrava, 31, 101, 110–11

Palacký, František, 11–12
Palestine: Beneš on, 173–74; Czech

Army in, 161–68, 300; and Czech Government-in-Exile, 166, 182; emigration to, 161–66, 354n14; escape to, 221; letter to Jews in, 131–32; and solution to Jewish question, 185; Yishuv in, 47–50, 130, 165, 255. *See also* Israel
Palička, Josef, 223
Pankrác prison, 197, 304
parachutists, 153–55, 183, 199, 200, 365n71
Paris Peace Conference, 27
Parkus, František, 110
Pasák, Tomáš, 152, 294, 337n24, 339n48
Pascuala, F., 196
Pátková, Zdena, 199
Patočka, Jan, 97, 293, 361n140
Pavlát, Leo, 293, 296
Pažout, Milan, 224
Peace of Westphalia, 10
Peduzzi, Lubomír, 277–78
Peel Commission, 59
Penížek, Josef, 4
Peretz, I. L., 272
Peroutka, Ferdinand, 28, 67, 75, 84–86, 92–93, 332n110, 334n150, 334n152, 335n158, 347n9
Pešek, Josef, 195
Pétain, Philippe, 139
Petchek family, 72
Petiční výbor. *See* PVVZ
Petránková-Šimková, M., 203
Petrbok, J., 48
Petschek, Julius, 103
Petschek and Weinmann firm, 37
Petschek family, 104, 106, 220
Pfaff, Ivan, 294
Pfeiffer (parachutist), 365n71
Pick, Otto, 23
Picková, Jiřina, 196, 198, 200
Pika, Heliodor, 388n10
Pik, Mayor of Pilsen, 102
Pilar, André de, 251
Pilsen, 34, 55, 102, 109, 284

Pilsudski, Marshal, 298
Pinkas Synagogue, 295
Pinkhof, Menachem, 122
Píša, A. M., 334n139
Písně odsouzených, 59
Pitter, Přemysl, 221–22
Plaček, Max, 272–73
The Plague City (Kien), 273
Plamínková, Františka, 336n10
Plašil family, 223
Poalei-Zion Workers' Party, 32, 87, 170
poetry, 13. *See also* writing
pogroms, 102
Pojar, Miloš, 296
Poláček, Karel, 40, 78, 129, 136–37, 212,
    345n147
Polák (parachutist), 365n71
Polák, Ernst, 67
Polák, Eugen, 201, 367n93
Polák, Filip, 110
Polák, Hanuš, 201, 203, 367n93
Polák, Josef, 213, 214
Polák, Ladislav, 201–3, 369n113
Polák, Vladimír, 201
Polák family, 367n93
Poland, 77, 109–13, 189, 191, 220–21,
    250, 286, 298, 346n159
Polish Government-in-Exile, 180
Polish political party, 31–32
political-ideological struggle, 190–95
political parties, 30–31
Politické ústředí (PÚ), 147, 192, 193
Pollertová, Anna (Baum), 196, 198–200
Pollertová, Irena, 199, 366n76
Pollertová, Jaromir Herbert, 199,
    366n76
Popper, Joseph, 34, 36, 53
Pospíšil family, 223
postage stamps, 290
Postoloprty labor camp, 133
"Povstaň, povstaň," 2
Požáry, 47
Prager Kreis, 23, 67, 297–98
Prager Richtung im Zionismus, 22

Prager Tagblatt, 40, 41, 49, 51, 57
Prague: anti-Semitism, 27–28, 102;
    assembly point, 127–28; assimilation,
    33; B'nai Brith, 36; Christian conver-
    sions, 37; cooperation of Jewish groups
    in, 117; cultural center, 47; Czech-
    Jewish coexistence in, 1–2, 15; Easter
    night pogrom, 9, 314n9; final trans-
    ports of full Jews from, 130; Hitler in,
    98; Jewish community organizations,
    82–83; Jewish identity, 21–23; Jewish
    population, 8–11, 38, 345n155,
    390n51; Jewish status, 34, 297–98;
    Kafka on, 5–6; law of free movement,
    12; letters smuggled from, 130–32,
    346n159; liberation, 158; literature
    about, 3; Orthodox tradition in, 20;
    refugees in, 55, 73, 77–78; rescue
    from, 221; resistance, 113; segregation
    of population, 108; survival rate of
    deportees from, 345n152; textile
    industry, 19; Zionism, 30, 49
Prague Aubrecht press, 196
Prague Central Committee (CCP), 151,
    364n44. *See also* Czech Communist
    Party (CCP)
Prague Circle. *See* Prager Kreis
Prague Ghetto massacre, 59
Prague International Exhibition of Car-
    icature, 209
"The Prague Jew," 210
Prague L.G.B. iron firm, 19
Prague Parliament, 31, 32
Prague Secret Police, 154
Prague Spring, 96, 289, 290
Prague University, 14. *See also* Czech
    University; German University of
    Prague
Pravda vítězí, 196
Právo lidu, 332n109
Právo na domovinu (Weizmann), 59
"A Prayer for Tonight" (Čapek), 68
Přehledy, 203
Přerov, 100

press: anti-Semitism, 28, 140, 332n111, 347n9, 357n70; arrests, 147; boycott, 205; control of, 153; on deportations, 188, 362n10; illegal, 193–94; Jewish, 40–41, 334n151; on Jewish leadership, 389n35; post-Munich Agreement, 71–72; powerlessness, 95

Příbram, 102

Přítomnost, 67, 75, 77, 80, 322n70, 334n152, 347n9

Procházka, Theodor, 335n160

Prokes, Jaroslav, 36

Pro lid, 17

Prossnitz, Heinz, 261

Pro strach židů (Neruda), 58

Protectorate. *See* Reich Protectorate of Bohemia and Moravia

Protocols of the Elders of Zion, 16

prstýnkáři, 197

Pruchová, Vilemína, 226

pseudo-democracy, 284

Pujmanová, M., 66

Pujmanová, Marie, 72

PVVZ, 65, 66, 188, 191–93, 195–200, 231, 363nn35–36

quisling governments, 138–39

Qumran Scrolls, 2

rabbis, 35

Rábl, Rudolf, 73

Rada, Vlastimil, 212

Radost ze života, 153

Raffelstatten Toll Ordinances, 8

Rahm, Karl, 126, 259

Rašín, Alois, 88

Rašín, Ladislav, 65, 88, 91, 333n121

Rauschning, Hermann, 104

Ravensbrück, 264

razzias, 101, 222

Red Cross. *See* International Committee of the Red Cross (ICRC)

Redlich, Egon, 239, 244, 245, 269–71, 376n15

Reich Protectorate of Bohemia and Moravia: anti-Semitism, 99–103, 140, 143; and Czech transfer, 161–62; designation, 98, 299; German language in, 104; intelligence on, 177–78, 180; lack of aid network, 218; loss of authority, 145; mixed marriages, 133; origin, 140–43; population, 217, 345n155; rescue efforts, 183–84; resistance, 123–24; segregation of population, 108; state of emergency, 223–24, 227, 352n102

Reichsbank, 72, 108, 339n54

"Reich's Home for the Aged," 239. *See also* elderly

Reichsicherheitshauptamt (RSHA), 103–4, 145

Reicín, Bedřich, 230

Reiman, Milan, 151, 152, 204, 221, 369n122

Reiner, Karel, 118

Reiner, Karl, 275–76

Reiner, Maxim, 34, 332n103

Reisz, Julius, 31

Reitler, Julius, 15

religion, 36–37, 266, 267, 281

Relink, Karel, 46

Remarque, Erich Maria, 209–10

Renner, Karel, 201

Rennerová, Zdeňka, 201

rescue efforts, 130–32, 182–84, 189–91, 218–27, 303–5. *See also* resistance

resistance: beginning of organized, 192; Beneš on, 113, 144, 159, 182–83; collapse, 205; French, 139–40; of intellectuals, 187, 216; of Jews, 188–93, 201–2, 206–7, 214–15, 300–301; in Protectorate, 123–24; spiritual, 265, 268; weakness, 176. *See also* Home Resistance; rescue efforts

Ribbentrop, Joachim von, 74, 87, 89

Rice, Elmer, 109

Riegner, Gerhard, 178, 249, 251–52, 379n69

Riga, 124, 236
Řiháček, Petr, 226
Řiháček, Tomáš, 226
Ripka, Hubert, 303
Riva restaurant, 101
Rohling, August, 14, 16, 100
Rojko (ss Commander), 213
Rokycana, Jaroslav Polák, 119–20
Rolland, Romain, 204
Roosevelt, Franklin, 252
Rose, Maximilian, 176
Rosenberg, K., 337n24
Rosenfeld, 206
Rosenthal, Mark, 103
Rosenzweig-Moir, Josef, 115
Rossel, Maurice, 256, 257, 258, 259
Rothschild family, 105, 106
Rottová, Anka, 199–200
Roubitschek, Sophie, 21
Roudnice, 102
Rozvoj, 16, 18, 59, 84, 86
Rudé Právo, 193
Rudi, Thomas, 79
Rudolph II (1576–1612), 9
Rufeisen, Josef, 30, 163, 355n20, 355n30
Rumania, 56, 84–85, 249, 286, 332n109
Runciman, Lord Walter, 60
Rušánek, Maxmilian, 372n3
Russian Revolution, 28–29
Růžička, Rudolf, 35, 47
Růži ran (Skoumal), 212
Rychnowský, Ernst, 41
Ryšánek, Maxmilian, 216
Rys-Rozsévač, Jan, 100

Sabath, Adolf J., 4
Sabbateian Frankism, 11
sabotage, 204–8, 304
Sachs, Nelly, 273
Šachta, Šimon, 287
Sádlo, Jan, 226
Salaspils concentration camp, 376n10
Šalda, F. X., 5, 22, 46–47, 50, 60, 64, 73, 94, 209

Šalda Committee, 53
Šaloun, Ladislav, 1, 311n6
Salus, Hugo, 23
Salus, Miloš, 269
Samek, Ervin, 225
Sarid, 48
Saudek, Eric A., 211–12
Schächter, Rafael, 212, 267, 270–71, 278
Scharf, Jakub, 15
Schellenberg, Walter, 194–95
Schieszel, Karel, 90
Schlamm, Willy, 73
Schliesser, Karl, 246
Schmerling, Herbert, 338n40
Schmolka, Marie, 53–54, 78, 79, 80, 100, 117, 330n57, 336n10
Schmoranz, Zdeněk, 147
Schön, Vojtěch, 266
Schönberg, Arnold, 274
Schönbrunn [Svinov], 69
Schorsch, Gustav, 273
Schrámek, Marie, 225
Schul, Zikmund, 274, 276, 278
Schuster, Heinz, 130–33
Schutz polizei (Schupo), 156
Schwalb, Nathan, 130–31, 249, 381n104
Schwartz, Anna, 199
Schwartz, Leo, 205
Schwartz, Vincy, 199, 211
Schwartzbart, Ignacy, 178
Šebor, Miloš, 145, 146
Second Zionist Territorial Conference, 30
Šedivý, František, 226
Segert, Stanislav, 2
Seghers, Anna, 66, 73
Seidl, Siegfried, 156, 234
Seifert, Jaroslav, 3, 66, 335n160
Sekanina, Ivan, 73
Selbstwehr, 21, 41, 47
Sharett, Moshe (Shertok), 113, 162–63, 168, 182, 355n19
Sharett, Yehuda, 274
Shaw, G. B., 209

Shertok, Moshe. *See* Sharett, Moshe (Shertok)
Shick, Ota, 176
Shimoni, David, 277
Sicher, Gustav, 6, 35, 288, 292, 313n36
Sidor, Karel, 85
Siebenschein, Hugo, 148
Silberschein, Abraham, 249, 379n57
Silesia, 26, 34–35, 37, 82, 109
Silverman, Sydney S., 173, 178
SIMAN (Czechoslovak Liaison Officer Staff Captain), 167
Šimečka, Milan, 307
Šimek, Dr., 203
Simon, Ernst, 279
Simon, Jan, 213
Singer, Jiří, 89
Singer, Leo, 145–46
Singer, Ludvík, 25, 27, 31
Singer, Oscar, 118, 187, 216, 342n102, 361n1
Sipo, 156
Six-Day War, 290
SJC, 259
Škába, Hanuš, 201
Škoda munition works, 105
Skotnický, 250
Skoumal, Aloys, 212
Škroup, František, 20
Škroup, Ladislav, 317n65
Slánský, Rudolf, 306, 388n12. *See also* Slánský trials
Slánský trials, 152, 221, 286, 289, 294, 306, 388n12
Slavata, Jaroslav, 58
Slavík, Juraj, 177
Slavische Melodien (Kapper), 13
Slovakia: cooperation with Nazis, 139; emigration to, 224; exemptions, 159; during First Republic, 26; ICRC in, 249; independence, 97; and intelligence, 175, 177–78, 180; Jewish communities, 29; Jewish population, 174, 333n112; Jewish status, 34, 143; postwar attitude toward Jews, 303; postwar population, 285; refugees from, 85; rescue organizations, 189, 191, 303–4; right-wing demonstrations, 57. *See also* Slovaks
Slovak language, 31
Slovak National Uprising, 260
Slovaks, 26, 51, 62, 170–71, 183, 185. *See also* Slovakia
Slovo a svět (Fischer), 42–43
Small Fortress, 122, 234, 376n6. *See also* Terezín
Smetana, Oldřich, 41, 206, 226
Smutný, Jaromir, 138, 143–44, 160–61, 183, 185, 356n48
Social Democratic Party, 55
Social Democratic Party, 32, 170. *See also* National Jews from Czechoslovakia
Social Democratic Relief Committee, 53
Social Institute of the Jewish Religious Congregations of Prague, 54
Socialist refugee committee, 72
Society for the History of the Jews in the Czechoslovak Republic, 36
Sokol, 14, 57, 86, 188
Sokolow, Nahum, 27
solidarity, 216–18, 227–32, 304, 305
Sonata No. 7, 274, 385n38
Sonnenschein, Rabbi, 48
Soviet Union: aid to refugees, 80–81, 331n88; Beneš on, 183, 185–86; Eliáš on, 150–51; escapees in, 113; invasion of, 123, 150; liberation of Lodý, 345n152; liberation of Terezín, 247, 261, 263; policy on Israel, 288, 290; recognition of Czech Government-in-Exile, 172; treaty with, 46, 57, 64, 169; writers, 66. *See also* Communists
Spanish International Brigade, 190
Special Courts (*Sondergerichte*), 223–27
Spiegel, Käthe, 36
Spiegel, Ludwig, 51
Spier, Jo, 256, 258, 382n108
Spilberk Fortress, 101–2, 125
Spina, Franz, 50

Spitzer, Jiří, 205
Spitzy, Reinhard, 254
Společenský klub, 90, 333n133
Spolek českých akademiků-židů (Society
    of Czech-Jewish academics), 15
Squire, Leland Harrison, 249
Squire, Paul C., 249, 251
ss (Security Police): arrests in Protecto-
    rate, 101; concentration on, 103; on
    Czech-Jewish relations, 108; deporta-
    tion of Jews, 124–25, 128; headquar-
    ters, 103; at Lidice, 156; methods, 302;
    at Terezín, 234, 235, 242, 243, 245,
    255
Stahlecker, Walter, 104, 148
Štancl, Oldřich, 205–6
State Council (*Státní rada*), 169, 171–73,
    175
State Jewish Museum of Prague, 291. *See
    also* Jewish Museum
State Security police, 291, 292
Steffen, Albert, 276
Stein, Augustín, 15, 34
Stein, Karel, 213, 342n93
Stein, Walter, 223
Steinbach, Karel, 327n7
Steiner, Hanna, 53, 100, 117, 122, 127,
    336n10, 344n141
Steiner, Rudolf, 276
Steinherz, Samuel, 36, 45
Stern, Gustav, 40
Sternbuch brothers, 378n48
Steuer, 356n48
St. Germain-en-Laye treaty, 28
Stichová, Eva, 203
Štiplová, Božena, 351n98
Stölzl, Christopher, 295, 318n82
Stopford, Robert J., 77, 348n20
Stránský, Adolf, 15, 38–39, 92
Stránský, Hugo, 170
Stránský, Jan, 93
Stránský, Jaroslav, 39, 65, 92, 171,
    334n144
Strass, František, 245

Strass, Karel, 212, 384n28
Strasser, Gregor, 329n50
Strauss, Leo, 266, 268
Street Scene, 109
Streicher, Julius, 87, 140, 347n9
Stříbrný, Jiří, 46, 73
Stricker, Fráňa, 206
Stricker, Jiří, 206
Stricker, Robert, 245, 246
Stross, Otto, 86, 187–88
Der Stürmer, 87, 140, 347n9
St. Wenceslas Day, 113–14
St. Wenceslas statue, 156
Subcarpathian Ruthenia: anti-Semitism,
    46; during First Republic, 26; Hun-
    garian annexation of, 97; Jewish popu-
    lation, 82, 288, 320n15; Jewish rights,
    29; Jewish status, 34, 185; refugees
    from, 85, 332n112
Sudeten area, 60–65, 69, 78–81
Sudeten German Party (SDP), 46, 52, 56,
    57, 61, 63, 87, 93, 98
Sudeten Germans, 50, 51, 60, 63, 76,
    354n12. *See also* Germans
Šulc, František, 223
Supplement to the Law of the Organiza-
    tion of the Jewish Religious Commu-
    nity, 35–36
Supreme Council of the Federation of
    Jewish Religious Communities in
    Bohemia, Moravia, and Silesia, 34, 35,
    55, 57, 61, 87, 326n156
Svátek, J. J., 22
Svatobořice, 157
Svatopluk guards, 102, 338n27
Švenk, Karel, 267, 383n8
Svět proti Hitlerovi, 194, 222
Swedish Red Cross, 263
Switzerland, 175, 204, 246–48, 261–62
Sykes, Sir Mark, 48
synagogues, 80, 101
Synek, Otto, 193, 205, 364n46
Synek, Victor, 193, 364n46
Syrový, Jan, 76–77, 79–80, 83

Táborský, Edvard, 160, 185
Talich, Václav, 90
Der Talmudjude (Rohling), 14
Talmud Jude (Rohling), 16
Taub, Siegfried, 38, 51
Taube, Carlo S., 275
Taube, Erika, 275
Tausigová, Elsa, 226
Taussig, František, 364n46
Taussig, Fritz, 118, 193, 245, 272, 384n28
Taylor, Λ. J. P., 298
Taylor, Myron C., 252, 254, 380n78
Tchelet Lavan, 47
Terezín, xiv; administration, 235–40; aid
    to, 130–31, 182, 345n150, 378n35;
    bank, 236–37; Beneš on, 181; con-
    struction, 236–37; death toll, 240,
    377n23; deportations to, 124–28, 133–
    35, 158, 300; free time activities, 238,
    266–67, 274, 279; human solidarity,
    227–32; ICRC inspection and interven-
    tion, 134, 234, 243, 245–47, 251–59,
    261–64; JRC activities in, 135–36;
    legacy, 282; liberation, 247, 261, 263;
    living conditions, 227–28, 240, 242–
    43, 246–47, 266; population, 244, 246,
    281, 377n31; as propaganda, 242–45,
    254–56, 265–66; purpose, 233–34,
    302; relationships between inmates,
    241–42; rescue efforts, 182; Small For-
    tress, 122, 234, 376n6; transports from,
    236, 238–39, 245–46, 260–61
"Terezín March," 267
Tesař, Jan, 300
Teytz, Viktor, 24
Thadden, Eberhard von, 256, 258, 380n76
theater, 272
Theaterverein, 15
Thein, Hanuš, 90
Theresienstadt. *See* Terezín
Thierack, Otto, 151
Thon, Zdeněk, 58, 188
t'Hooft, Visser, 250
Three Addresses (Buber), 5

Thümmel, Paul, 177, 230–31
Tichá, Ludmila, 219, 344n143
Tigrid, Pavel, 335n158
Tilschová, A. M., 66
Titz, Karl, 55
Toland, John, 10
"To the Roots" (Fischer), 42
Tracts of Young Czechoslovakia, 58
Tradesmen's Party, 30
Träger, Josef, 212, 294
La trahison des clercs (Benda), 94
Trampem od Nilu až k Jordánu (Petrbok),
    48
Transcarpathian Ukraine, 185
Trautmannsdorf, Count, 74
Treuhandstelle, 129–30
The Trial (Kafka), 23
Tribuna, 28, 40
Tribuna tisková korespondence (Tri-Kor),
    216, 372n3
Trnava, 303
Trnka, Jiří, 213
Troller, Norbert, 272
Troutbeck, J. M., 140, 348n20
Tršovice, 157
Trunečka, Alois, 223
Trunk, Isaiah, 376n14
trusteeships, 106–8
Tschuppik, Walter, 220
Tuka, Vojtěch, 183
Türk-Neumann, Hede, 202, 224,
    368n101, 368n103, 368n110
Tvrdková, Olga, 201
Twentieth-Century Czechoslovakia
    (Korbel), xi
"2,000 Words to Workers, Farmers, Scien-
    tists, Artists and Everyone" (Vaculík),
    290

Uhlířské, 157
Ullmann, Fritz, 112, 237, 249, 257, 260–
    61
Ullmann, Viktor, 244–45, 265, 272, 274–
    78, 282, 383n8, 385n43

Umschulungslager, 111
Ungar, Otto, 245, 272, 384n28
Unger, Zikmund, 266
Union of Czech Jews, 170
Union of Czech Writers, 289
Union of Orthodox Rabbis of the United
    States and Canada, 378n48
Union of Progressive Students, 209
Unitas Fratrum, 2
United States, 84, 172
Unity of Bohemian Brethren. *See*
    Hussitism
Universal Christian Council for Life and
    Work, 379n63
Úřad lidové osvěty, 153
Urbánek, Zdeněk, 210, 229, 231–32,
    371n158
Urzidil, Johannes, 23, 318n83
Utermöhle, Walter, 338n40
Utitz, Emil, 269, 275, 281

Va'ad Hahazalah, 130–31
Vach, Vilém, 227
Václavek, Ludvík, 273
Vaculík, Ludvík, 290
Valčík (parachutist), 154
Vančura, Bohumil, 58, 216, 221, 347n9
Vančura, Vladislav, 66, 73, 210, 370n155
Vaněk ("Jindra"), 360n128
Vaněk, Zdeněk, 368n110
Van Tijn, Mrs., 122
Vašek, Anton, 177
Vatican, 177, 248, 249, 252, 380n78
Vboj, 147, 193
Velvet Revolution, 295–96, 306
Venkov, 84–86
Ve Pštrosce, house at 7, 198
Veritas, 21
Veselý-Štainer, Karel, 198
Věstník čsl. Ligy proti antisemitismu, 216,
    347n9, 372n3
Věstník židovské obce náboženské v Praze,
    83, 332n99
Vichy government, 139, 159

Vienna, 46, 146
*Vier Lieder auf Worte der chinesischen
    Poesie*, 278
Vítkovice, 109
Vítkovice Iron Works, 105, 106
Vlajka, 100, 102, 144, 176, 337n14
Vočadlo, Otakar, 67–68, 328n28
vocational reorientation program, 118
Vogel, Jaroslav, 89
Vogel, Jiří, 247
Voglová, Alena, 202, 369n115
Vohryzek, Lev, 18
Vohryzek, Viktor, 16–18, 23
Vojta, General, 369n120
Volavková, Hana, 211
Voňáčková, Dora, 129, 345n147
von Burgsdorff (Undersecretary of State),
    148, 229
Voska, 86
Vrba, Rudolf, 16
Vrchlický, Jaroslav, 1, 3
Vršovice youth group, 200–203, 223
Vsetín synagogue, 101

Wald, Arnošt, 259
Walpole, Hugh, 209
Wannsee Conference, 127, 233
Warner, Miss, 251
War of the Jews (Josephus), 2
Warriner, Doreen, 68
Wassermann, Jacob, 73
Weber, Ilse, 69–71, 109, 271, 329n36
Weck, René de, 249–50
Wegner, Armin, 229–30, 374n58
Weidmann, František, 101, 116, 118, 125,
    130, 235, 246
Weil, Jiří, 212, 292, 371n168
Weiner, Bedřich, 206
Weiner, Erich, 266
Weiner, Richard, 33, 40
Weinmann, Rudolph, 262, 263
Weinmann family, 72, 106
Weisel, Otakar, 207, 370n141
Weiss, Eugen, 272

Weiss, František, 363n28
Weiss, Josef, 206
Weiss, Milan, 207
Weisskopf, Franz Carl, 73
Weissmantl, O., 337n24
Weizmann, Chaim, 59, 182, 284–85
Weizsäcker, Ernst von, 350n62
Wells, H. G., 66, 209
Weltsch, Felix, 4, 20
Weltsch, Robert, 20
"We Remain Faithful," 65, 66, 192,
     327n11. *See also* PVVZ
Werfel, Franz, 23, 24, 65–66, 106
Werfel, Rudolf, 106
Werner, 360n126
Wertheimer, Jakob, 21
Wessely, Wolfgang, 14
The White Plague (Čapek), 34, 196, 216
Wilson, Orme, 74
Winter, Arnošt, 40
Winter, Gustav, 39–40
Winter, Lev, 38–39
Winton, Nicholas, 82
Wirth, Zdeněk, 214
Wir tote klagn an, 280
Wise, Stephen G., 140, 174, 181
Wise Engelbert (John), 212
Wisliceny, Dieter, 132, 255
Witt, Zikmund, 40
Wolf, Bertold, 219–20
Wolf, Cantor Bertold, 128
Wolf, Felicitas-Lici, 128, 219, 345n144
Wolf, Kurt, 220, 344n142
Wolf, Otto, 128, 219, 220, 344n142,
     345n144
Wolf, Rosalia, 128, 219, 345n144
Wolf, Václav, 206
Wolmar, Wolfram von, 123
Woodward, Kerry, 275
Work Detail, 235–36
Worker's Academy, 192
World Conference on Faith and Order,
     379n63
World Council of Churches, 250, 379n63

World Jewish Congress, 65, 149, 172, 174,
     253, 301, 328n17
Woskin-Nahartabi, Moses, 214
writers, 41–45, 90, 208–13
writing, 265, 269–71, 273

"Ye Who Are God's Warriors," 311n9
Yiddish language, 272
Yugoslavia, 56, 191

Zak, Emil, 58
Žalud, Josef, 15
Zápotocký, Otakar, 225
Za svobodu, 195–96
Žatec airfield, 287
Zdařil, Jaroslav, 219, 344n143
Zedtwitz, Joachim von, 220
*Zeitschrift für Geschichte der Juden in der
     Tschechoslowakei* (Gold), 36
Zelenka, František, 212–14, 272, 371n167
Zelmanovits, Leo, 170, 173
Zeman, Kamil. *See* Olbracht, Ivan
Ženíšek, František, 20
Zenkl, Petr, 72
Zentralmuseum, 128–29
Zentralstelle für jüdische Auswanderung,
     103–4, 110, 117, 120, 126, 127, 145,
     299, 341n91
Zeyer, Julius, 3
Zibrín, 192, 220, 363n29
Zíbrt, Čeněk, 59
Židé a my (Slavata), 58
Židovská otázka (Klecanda), 86
Židovské zprávy, 25, 41
Žid v dnešní společnosti (Lederer), 18
Židvstvo (Eisner), 46
Ziegler, O., 107
Zionist Federation of Czechoslovakia, 59,
     288
Zionists: Beneš on, 285; on Czech Army,
     163–66; and Czech-Jews, 33, 49, 116;
     and deportations, 113; in Home Resis-
     tance, 188, 189; in Jewish Council of
     Elders, 235; and Jewish Party, 32; and

Jewish population in Czechoslovakia, 82–83; and Jewish question, 86–87; Masaryk on, 4–5; organizations, 21, 85; in postwar Czechoslovakia, 27–30; support of, 47–49; at Terezín, 243, 281; during war, 24–25

Živnostenská Banka, 14

Zlé noci (Simon), 213

Zohn, Harry, 23

zprávy z domova, 192

Zucker, Alois, 15, 19

Zucker, Franz, 246

Zucker, Otto, 376n11; to Auschwitz, 245; on construction of Terezín, 237, 376n12; on Czech transfer, 162; death, 260; on deportations, 125–27, 239; fund, 120–21; leadership, 116, 235; on living conditions at Terezín, 240; on minority rights, 60; musical composition dedicated to, 277; "reply" to Kastner, 256; and Ullmann, 274

Zuckermann, Dr., 206

Zweig, Arnold, 75